From "Radical Extremism" to "Balanced Copyright"

From "Radical Extremism" to "Balanced Copyright"

Canadian Copyright and the Digital Agenda

edited by Michael Geist

Published in 2010 by

Irwin Law
14 Duncan Street
Suite 206
Toronto, Ontario
M5H 3G8

www.irwinlaw.com

ISBN: 978-1-55221-204-2

e-BOOK ISBN: 978-1-55221-206-6

Canada Cataloguing in Publication available from Library and Archives Canada

We acknowledge the assistance of the OMDC Book Fund, an initiative of Ontario Media Development Corporation.

The publisher acknowledges the financial support of the Government of Canada through the Book Publishing Industry Development Program (BPIDP) for its publishing activities.

Printed and bound in Canada.

1 2 3 4 5 14 13 12 11 10

Contents

Introduction

Michael Geist

Copyright has long been viewed as one of the government's most difficult and least rewarding policy issues. It attracts passionate views from a wide range of stakeholders, including creators, consumers, businesses, and educators and it is the source of significant political pressure from the United States. Opinions are so polarized that legislative reform is seemingly always the last resort, arriving only after months of delays.

The latest chapter in the Canadian copyright saga unfolded in June 2010 as Industry Minister Tony Clement and Canadian Heritage James Moore tabled copyright reform legislation billed as providing both balance and a much-needed modernization of the law. The introduction marked the culmination of months of public discussion and internal government debate.

Since the failure of Bill C-61—the Conservative government's first attempt at copyright reform in 2008 that died on the order paper months after introduction—the government had worked to craft legislation that might satisfy external pressures while garnering favourable reviews at home. In 2009, Clement and Moore held a national copyright consultation that generated considerable praise for its openness and broad participation. In fact, with over 8,000 submissions, roundtable meetings with ministers, and two public town halls, the consultation was lauded as the most successful public policy consultation in Canada in recent memory.

Emboldened by the consultation's success and the evident interest in the issue, Clement and Moore promised new legislation by the summer of

2010 and lived up to this commitment with Bill C-32, tabled in the House of Commons on 2 June 2010.

From the moment of its introduction, it was readily apparent that the bill would be the target of unprecedented scrutiny and public debate. Virtually every copyright stakeholder group wasted little time in posting their quick analysis, often welcoming the introduction of the bill, but reserving judgment on the fine print. Those groups were joined by the tens of thousands of Canadians who over the prior two years had joined Facebook groups, raised copyright concerns with their elected representatives, or participated in the copyright consultation.

The government also mobilized with a media campaign characterizing the bill as "balanced copyright." Clement and Moore actively engaged with the public, responding to dozens of comments posted on Twitter and assuring the public that they were open to potential amendments. Balance became the watchword of the legislation, as even Canadian Recording Industry Association adopted it by providing financial backing for a website called Balanced Copyright for Canada.

The claims of balance were based largely on efforts to find compromise positions on some of the most contentious copyright issues. Bill C-32 included sector-specific reforms with something for almost everyone: new rights for performers and photographers, a new exception for Canadian broadcasters, new liability for BitTorrent search services, as well as the legalization of common consumer activities such as recording television shows and transferring songs from a CD to an iPod. In fact, there was even a "YouTube" user-generated content remix exception that granted Canadians the right to create remixed work for non-commercial purposes under certain circumstances.

There were a number of areas where the government worked toward a genuine compromise. These included reform to Canada's fair dealing provision, which establishes when copyrighted works may be used without permission. The government rejected both pleas for no changes as well as arguments for a flexible fair dealing that would have opened the door to courts adding exceptions to the current fair dealing categories of research, private study, news reporting, criticism, and review. Instead, it identified some specific new exceptions that assist creators (parody and satire), educators (education exception, education Internet exception), and consumers (time shifting, format shifting, backup copies).

The Internet provider liability provisions similarly represented a compromise, as the government retained a "notice-and-notice" system that requires providers to forward allegations of infringement to subscribers.

The system is costly for the providers, but has proven successful in discouraging infringement.

It also compromised on the statutory damages rules that create the risk of multi-million dollar liability for cases of non-commercial infringement. The new rules reduced non-commercial liability to a range of $100 to $5,000, a figure that is not insignificant, but well below the $20,000 per infringement cap currently found in the law.

Critics of the bill argued that these attempts at balance were ultimately undermined by the anti-circumvention provisions found in Bill C-32. Those provisions — widely referred to as the digital lock rules — adopted a foundational principle that anytime a digital lock is used, it trumps virtually all other rights. The digital lock rules quickly became the primary focus of public debate, with criticism from all opposition parties and dozens of public interest and education groups.

That criticism soon led to the other watchword of Bill C-32. The government opened with the balanced copyright moniker, but Moore escalated the rhetoric weeks later by telling an intellectual property conference "the only people who are opposed to this legislation are really two groups of radical extremists." The media seized on the radical extremist comment as well as Moore's contention that critics "pretend to be for copyright reform," and were "babyish" who "try to find technical, nonsensical, fear-mongering reasons to oppose copyright reform." He urged supporters of Bill C-32 to confront the critics "every step of the way" until they are defeated.

Moore's call for confrontation predictably left many groups disappointed that an issue of such importance — copyright law reform is widely viewed as an integral part of a digital economy strategy — had quickly degenerated into name calling rather than substantive debate and discussion about how Canada could update its copyright law in a manner that meets the public interest, complies with international treaties, and addresses legitimate consumer and creator expectations.

This book represents an effort by some of Canada's leading copyright experts to shift away from the sloganeering about balance and the name calling of "radical extremists" toward an informed analysis of Bill C-32 and the future development of Canadian copyright law. Responding to the need for non-partisan, expert analysis of Bill C-32, an exceptional group of Canadian scholars have come together to assess Canada's plans for copyright reform.

This is the second such initiative, following on the successful 2005 book, *In the Public Interest: The Future of Canadian Copyright Law*, which responded to the introduction of Bill C-60. It brought together the majority of Canadian academics researching and writing about intellectual property with representatives from ten universities stretching from Dalhousie on the east coast to the University of British Columbia on the west. *In the Public Interest* covered a wide range of issues related to copyright reform and though Bill C-60 died on the order paper months after the book was published, it has continued to serve as a useful volume on Canadian copyright law issues.

This book followed much the same approach. All contributors from the first book were invited to participate once again. In addition, new intellectual property scholars were identified and given the opportunity to contribute. Once the dust settled, there were twenty articles on copyright written by independent scholars from coast to coast. The diversity of contributors provides a rich view of Bill C-32 and Canadian copyright law more generally, tackling the history of Canadian copyright, technology issues, the link between copyright and creativity, as well as education and access issues.

While I am honoured to have again served as editor (and contribute my own work on the flexibility in implementing the anti-circumvention provisions in the World Intellectual Property Organization's Internet treaties), it should be noted that each contributor was given complete freedom to address whatever element of copyright reform they saw fit. There was no editorial attempt to prescribe a particular outcome or perspective. Rather, this book endeavoured to bring together as many non-partisan Canadian copyright scholars and experts as possible and gave each the latitude to provide their unique perspective and analysis.

Contributions are grouped into five parts. Part one features six articles that establish the context for Bill C-32. While the last book examined contextual issues such as political rhetoric, this book includes several articles that provide a historical context for Canadian copyright reform. The emergence of Canadian copyright history as a fertile area for scholarly research is a recent and welcome development, since it enables us to better situate the latest round of reforms with the historical context.

Part two contains six articles on the intersection between copyright and technology. Several articles focus on anti-circumvention legislation and digital locks, while others touch on rights management information and intermediary liability.

The creator perspective on copyright reform can be found in the four articles in part three on creativity. Each article touches on a different issue including transformative works, moral rights, user generated content, and the Montreal independent music scene's view of copyright.

Parts four and five delve into education and access issues. Professors Margaret Ann Wilkinson and Sam Trosow discuss the increasingly contentious issues raised by educational licencing and the reform proposals in Bill C-32, while the access chapter includes important contributions on copyright reform and fact-based works and the copyright restrictions on public sector information.

CONTEXT

Sara Bannerman provides the first of several articles that examine current Canadian copyright reform through a historical lens. Bannerman notes that virtually from the moment of confederation, Canada has grappled with contentious copyright reform issues. Reform efforts have invariably come as a response to international pressures, with the United Kingdom exerting significant influence over the early attempts to craft a genuine made-in-Canada copyright law. Bannerman also places the spotlight on the challenges Canada has faced with international copyright treaties, with attitudes that have ranged from outright rejection to strong support.

In light of the international pressures and inconsistent responses to international treaties, Bannerman argues that Canadian copyright reform has historically been characterized by three elements that can be seen in the current round of reforms: slow progress, a minimalist approach, and made-in-Canada approaches that endeavour to respond to domestic Canadian demands and meet the technical requirements of international treaties.

While Bannerman places Canadian copyright reform into historical perspective, Blayne Haggart provides a regional governance analysis in his article by assessing the respective copyright law approaches in Canada, the United States, and Mexico. Notwithstanding a concerted effort to integrate the North American economy through regional trade agreements, Haggart observes that each country continues to possess distinct copyright regimes.

Using a historical institutionalist approach, Haggart concludes that US-style copyright laws are not a foregone conclusion for Canada and Mexico. Rather, current governance structures provide each country with considerable latitude in establishing country-specific, autonomous copyright laws. In fact, Haggart notes that it is the very presence of NAFTA — which guarantees Canada and Mexico access to the US market — that limits the U.S.'s ability to exert significant trade pressures on both countries.

Myra Tawfik also provides historical context in her article. Tawfik delves deeper into the historical purposes behind copyright law, particularly the importance of enlightenment and education. While most historical analysis has emphasized the importance of publishers (in early copyright laws) and authors (in the 20th century), Tawfik notes that it is education and public access that has consistently influenced copyright norms. Indeed, while publishers are often viewed as the "winners" in the early copyright laws, publisher rights faced significant limitations with the law ensuring rights of access that established important limits on copyrights.

Interestingly, Tawfik observes that prioritizing knowledge dissemination was a foundational objective in both the United Kingdom and France. Although France is often associated with author rights, French parliamentarians grappled with concerns that creator rights might interfere with the public interest in learning and education. Having identified the importance of education within the copyright construct, Tawfik then travels back to the 1830s in Lower Canada, where the same priorities and concerns manifested themselves. Given this historical context, Tawfik is sharply critical of Bill C-32's digital lock provisions, concluding that the bill has "in one simple but sweeping legislative device, entirely forsaken the educative function that has been an essential feature of the law from its inception."

Meera Nair offers a third historical piece, one focused specifically on the history and controversies associated with fair dealing within Canadian copyright law. Nair notes the long history behind fair dealing and the reasonableness of its evolution (particularly in light of the 2004 Supreme Court of Canada decision in *CCH Canadian v. Law Society of Upper Canada*).

Nair is critical of both sides of the fair dealing debate, suggesting that critics have consistently undermined fair dealing by seeking to substitute a core element of copyright law with licencing, while lamenting that the education community — an obvious beneficiary of a balanced fair dealing provision — has generally been too timid in exercising its rights. With Bill C-32 setting the stage for another policy battle over the scope of fair dealing, Nair expresses the view that it is at a crossroads, with the very real possibility that it could ultimately become little more than a historical artifact.

Abraham Drassinower's article uses a different lens to examine current Canadian copyright law and reform — the 2007 Supreme Court of Canada decision *Euro-Excellence Inc. v. Kraft Canada Inc.* The Euro-Excellence case may have focused on the interplay between parallel imports and intellectual property law, but Drassinower demonstrates why it offers important insights into the "balance" in copyright law and the differences between copyright, patents, and trademarks.

The article features an exhaustive analysis of Justice Michel Bastrache's opinion in the Euro-Excellence decision, leading to a better understanding of the limits of copyright law in protecting the work of authors. Applied to Bill C-32's anti-circumvention rules, Drassinower offers a stinging conclusion that by "denying the field of permissible use, anti-circumvention denies copyright itself."

While Drassinower considers a single case in his article, Mistrale Goudreau focuses more broadly on the role of the courts in interpreting copyright law. The sole French-language article in this volume, Goudreau also reaches back into history to note the integral role that courts have played in defining concepts such as fair dealing and originality. She is more critical of Canadian legislative reforms, suggesting that they have often placed courts in the difficult position of being forced to make sense of the law. Goudreau expresses concern that the same may hold true for Bill C-32, noting that it leaves important issues open to interpretation.

TECHNOLOGY

Carys Craig opens the series of articles on the intersection between copyright and technology with an examination of the impact of digital locks on fair dealing. Craig welcomes the inclusion of fair dealing reform within Bill C-32, noting that an expansion of fair dealing consistent with the Supreme Court of Canada's CCH decision is long overdue and was notably absent from both Bills C-60 and C-61. However, Craig demonstrates why the expansion does not go far enough, concluding that they are "insufficient to ensure the breadth of applicability that the copyright balance demands."

Craig uses the absence of a specific exception for parody within the current law to shine the spotlight on why fair dealing reform is desperately needed. She is generally supportive of the new fair dealing provisions in Bill C-32, but believes that critics have overstated their breadth. In Craig's view, copyright policy would be better served with an open-ended fair use provision. While she believes the Bill C-32 fair dealing provisions could be improved, she reserves her harshest criticism for the impact of the bill's anti-circumvention provisions on fair dealing, concluding that they undermine the social goals of the copyright system and hold the potential to eviscerate fair dealing in the digital age. In order to address these faults, Craig identifies a wide range of potential reforms to the Bill C-32 provisions.

My substantive contribution to this collection focuses on the legal requirements to comply with the World Intellectual Property Organization's

Internet treaties. The government has identified ratification of the WIPO Internet treaties as one of Bill C-32's chief goals, leading to a robust debate on the degree of flexibility contained in those treaties to comply with the digital lock requirements. My article examines the issue from four perspectives: the plain language of the statutory requirements, the legislative history behind the inclusion of anti-circumvention provisions within the treaty, state practice in implementing those requirements, and scholarly analysis of the treaty obligations.

The article confirms that the WIPO Internet treaties offer considerable flexibility in implementation. The legislative history is particularly noteworthy since the record makes it readily apparent that the intent of the negotiating parties was to provide flexibility as the basis for consensus. Countries were free to implement stricter anti-circumvention provisions, but consensus was reached by leaving the specific implementation to individual countries.

Ian Kerr follows with a remarkable article on digital locks and their broader impact on society and ethics. Drawing from a long history of locks, Kerr identifies a crucial concern with policy and business approaches that rely on the use of digital locks, namely the use of technology to shift social defaults that undermine individual freedoms.

Given their power, Kerr expresses concern that the impact of digital locks will be felt far beyond the copyright realm. Rather, he fears that it will impede moral development by "programming people to do the right thing" and in the process remove their ability to make moral choices grounded in ethics and the law. Illustrated through a series of powerful anecdotes, Kerr demonstrates how technology can effectively usurp the role of individual choice and by "automating virtue" would impair our ability to make the morally right choice.

While Bill C-32's digital rights management provisions have garnered the lion share of attention, Mark Perry focuses his analysis on rights management information, the less-discussed and typically less controversial aspect of WIPO Internet treaty implementation. Perry explains that RMI is used for more than just encrypting information about works, since modern RMI systems often also capture considerable information about the user, including viewing or listening habits.

Perry criticizes Bill C-32's RMI provisions on the grounds that they adopt a minimalist approach and miss the opportunity to implement a more forward-looking vision of RMI. He identifies four features that should be included in the RMI legislative package, including transparency (ensuring the RMI information is fully readable by all users), balance (RMI should identify the portions of the work not subject to copyright), privacy (users should know what information about them is collected), and freshness (data should be kept updated).

David Lametti's article proceeds from an interesting premise. He argues that Bill C-32, particularly the digital lock provisions, is fundamentally flawed and at odds with the longstanding principles of balance in copyright. Assuming the bill becomes law, however, Lametti explores how it might be saved, relying on "virtue ethics" as the basis for hope that all actors, including copyright owners and users, will exercise ethical decision-making to avoid the more problematic elements of the bill.

Lametti examines the ethical approach to copying across several forms of media, including music, movies, and books. His analysis demonstrates that the ethical approach is invariably context specific and far less reflective of the right/wrong paradigm that often dominates copyright debates. Instead, he identifies instances where copying clearly should be permitted on ethical grounds (even if the law states otherwise) as well as instances where permitted copying is still deserving of compensation or prior permission. Although reliance on virtue ethics might sound unlikely in the current environment, Lametti notes that copyright has always relied on informal norms and notions of fairness to address competing claims.

Greg Hagen's article rounds out the technology section with an assessment of Bill C-32's attempt to "modernize" Internet service provider liability. After considering the current state of Canadian law with respect to Internet intermediaries — including recent Supreme Court of Canada jurisprudence — Hagen provides a detailed examination of the bill's provisions.

Hagen identifies the major policy battlegrounds, including the scope of coverage (all Internet intermediaries, ISPs, information location tool providers) and the preferred response to allegations of infringement. He notes that that Bill C-32 rejects the so-called "graduated response" approach that has been adopted in a handful of countries around the world, but also declines to embrace emerging proposals to encourage the availability and dissemination of copyrighted content while compensating copyright owners through a system of levies or compulsory licences.

CREATIVITY

Graham Reynolds opens the creativity section with a look at transformative works. Reynolds acknowledges that transforming existing expression is not new, but maintains that technology has democratized the practice by giving anyone with a computer and Internet access the ability to create, distribute, and access transformative works. He notes that Canadian copyright law has failed to keep pace with this new power of creativity, leaving an emerging generation of creators at legal odds with existing copyright owners.

Reynolds argues that transformative works should not be treated as acts of infringement under the Copyright Act. While supportive of several measures in Bill C-32, particularly the inclusion of parody and satire within fair dealing and the introduction of a right to create non-commercial user-generated content, he expresses concern that the digital lock provisions may undo many of the benefits for creators who would face liability in their efforts to access digitally-locked works. Reynolds also calls for the expansion of fair dealing by including a right to engage in transformative use of copyright-protected expression.

Tina Piper's contribution is based on a lengthy study into the Montreal independent music scene. The music industry has been divided on Bill C-32, with some offering strong support for the bill, while others lamenting the emphasis on digital locks ahead of levy-based compensation schemes.

Piper's work delves into the copyright culture among musicians and discovers that copyright is rarely a major focus. Rather, she finds that many musicians and labels pay scant attention to copyright policy developments and are skeptical of the emphasis on copyright policy as a key mechanism to encourage the creation of new music. In fact, many are supportive of sharing and strategies that provide free access to their music, identifying increased performance revenues and band profile as clear benefits. Interestingly, Piper found far greater interest in federal and provincial grant programs such as FACTOR, which were lauded as providing real revenues to Canadian artists.

Daniel Gervais focuses on two issues at the intersection between copyright and creativity: music file sharing and user generated content. His article, which is an addendum to his contribution to *In the Public Interest*, argues in favour of legalized file sharing as part of a broader new compensation system. Gervais sketches out a proposed framework for full legalization, including a new levy and the active participation of Internet service providers in collecting new revenues.

Gervais also offers a helpful analysis of Bill C-32's user generated content provision, supporting the government's vision of facilitating this form of creativity, but identifying potential concerns that will ultimately fall to the courts to interpret. A particular challenge will be the need to navigate between commercial and non-commercial uses given the potential for non-commercial uses to attract wide audiences and generate commercial benefits.

Mira Sundara Rajan, a leading expert on moral rights, continues her examination of the issue by criticizing the absence of serious moral rights reform in Bill C-32. Sundara Rajan focuses on moral rights for performances, a relatively new right that is included in the WIPO Internet treaties. She describes the reforms in the bill as a "welcome improvement" for performers, but argues that more could be done.

Indeed, Sundara Rajan envisions Canada as a potential moral rights leader by adopting stronger moral rights for both performers and authors. While acknowledging that Bill C-32 meets the minimum international requirements, she suggests that experience to date reveals that the minimalist approach has done little to benefit creators. In its place, she maintains that comprehensive moral rights reforms are needed to better position creators when negotiating rights with industrial interests.

EDUCATION

Margaret Ann Wilkinson provides the first of two articles on copyright and education. Wilkinson navigates the complex and confusing labyrinth of educational licencing in light of both Bill C-32 and recent education copyright tariff proposals. The role of the Copyright Board of Canada is discussed as Wilkinson endeavours to break down the various rights holders and competing sources of royalty demands.

While the Copyright Board tariff proposals will play out for the next few years, Wilkinson contextualizes those proposals in light of the potential changes found in Bill C-32. Wilkinson expresses support for the inclusion of "education" within the fair dealing categories, arguing that it should be given wide ambit in light of recent Supreme Court of Canada jurisprudence. Moreover, Wilkinson assesses the impact of the provisions targeted at libraries, museums, and archives, noting that several longstanding concerns remain unaddressed.

Sam Trosow continues the assessment of Bill C-32's impact on Canadian education, with a detailed analysis of the practical application of fair dealing reform. Trosow criticizes the conservative, risk-averse approach adopted by many Canadian educational institutions, noting that the Supreme Court of Canada's CCH decision appears to provide far broader latitude to exercise fair dealing rights than is presently used by those institutions.

Trosow is generally supportive of Bill C-32's educational provisions, but remains skeptical about their application in practice. Having noted the prioritization of limiting risk, he is ultimately unsure if they will have their desired effect.

ACCESS

The final section of the volume includes two contributions related to access. Teresa Scassa examines the impact of copyright reform on fact-based works. While many copyright observers will be familiar with the principle that copyright law protects expression rather than facts, Scassa notes the proliferation of fact-based works in databases, maps, videos, photographs, and other sources. Rather than addressing their growing commercial importance, Bill C-32 remains silent. In fact, Scassa expresses concern that the digital lock provisions within the bill could impede access to these works.

Scassa posits that the challenge associated with fact-based works may stem from the distinction between facts and information. Unlike facts, which do not enjoy copyright protection, information may be protected by copyright. Scassa argues the "challenge of the information society is to recognize the extent to which facts are constantly being transformed into information, to recognize the difficulties in separating the information from the underlying fact, and to decide what to do about recognizing, protecting and rewarding the authorship of information where warranted."

Closely associated with fact-based works is the burgeoning interest in public-sector information, including government geographical information, weather data, reports, and studies. Elizabeth Judge provides a comparative analysis on the use and reuse of public-sector information, noting that many other countries have moved far ahead of Canada in offering their data in open formats accompanied by open licences.

Judge identifies several alternatives to moving toward open data, including government-backed initiatives and the adoption of open licences such as a Crown Commons licence modeled on the Creative Commons licence. She notes that crown copyright remains an impediment to access to Canadian public sector information, but concludes that open licensing offers a mechanism to overcome that barrier without the need for statutory reform.

ACKNOWLEDGMENTS

Bringing a peer-reviewed book of this size to publication frequently requires several years of work. Thanks to the remarkable efforts of Irwin Law, the contributors to this volume, and a special group of research assistants, that time frame shrank to several months.

Thanks are due first and foremost to the contributors. Each was asked to set aside their previously established summer research plans to focus on this project by submitting articles within weeks of the introduction of Bill C-32. Following peer and citation reviews, each was again asked to set aside other work to bring the final product to fruition. Despite these exceptionally tight timelines, each contributor embraced this project with great enthusiasm and professionalism.

Once the initial articles were delivered, two additional sets of contributors emerged. First, thanks to the international panel of peer reviewers who not only provided helpful advice that improved the quality of each article, but did so within strict timelines to ensure that the project remained on schedule. Second, thanks to the first rate group of student editors, including Andre Garber, Rachel Gold, Joel Kom, Frances Munn, Jonathan O'Hara, Keith Rose, Peter Waldkirch, and Paul Willetts, who provided exceptional citation and fact checking reviews. Their work was particularly valuable given the decision to again use the University of Ottawa's Law and Technology Journal citation guide, which adopts an open access model to legal citation.

Thanks also goes to Jeffrey Miller at Irwin Law, whose support for the project never wavered. Despite a busy summer publication schedule, Jeff agreed to take on this book on short notice with a commitment to ensuring that the book would be available under an open licence and ready for public consumption by early fall.

Thanks as well to the Social Sciences and Humanities Research Council of Canada and the Canada Research Chair program as this book benefited from their financial support.

Thanks also to my colleagues and family for their support throughout this project. It is a privilege to work together with such an inspiring group of engaging colleagues at the University of Ottawa. The technology law group is the rarest of academic teams — world class scholars, energetic colleagues, and valued friends.

My wife Allison did not write a single word in this book, yet there should be no doubt that it would not have been possible without her encouragement and support. She is the foundation of our family and her energy, wisdom and love make everything seem possible.

In the introduction to *In the Public Interest*, I noted that Jordan, Ethan, and Gabrielle, my three fantastic children, were too young to concern themselves with copyright, yet they would ultimately bear the brunt of today's copyright policy choices. Five years later, they are all still relatively young, but now far more seized with copyright issues. From homework projects involving mashups to the music and video on their beloved iPods, they represent a new generation for whom the Internet and technology is an integral part of their lives and for whom copyright law can facilitate even greater opportunities if we get the policy balance right.

Michael Geist
Ottawa, ON
September 2010

PART ONE

Context

CHAPTER ONE

Copyright:

Characteristics of Canadian Reform

Sara Bannerman

Canadian copyright has been called "the most contentious, the most controversial subject that has ever been before the Parliament of Canada," occasioning "more friction in the parliament of Canada ... than any other subject."[1] That statement, though made in 1923, is still true today as Canada embarks on its third attempt in five years to revise Canadian copyright law. Tensions arise not only out of the conflicting demands of Canadian copyright stakeholders; they also arise out of the various international pressures on Canadian copyright policy and efforts to meet those demands while tailoring Canadian copyright to domestic circumstances. The attempt, under Bill C-32, to bring Canada into conformity with the World Intellectual Property Organization (WIPO)'s 1996 Internet treaties is an effort to navigate these tensions — occasioning as much friction and controversy as its predecessors.

The current copyright reform initiative can be viewed in light of a number of trends that have characterized Canadian copyright reform since the time that Canada's first copyright Act was put in place in 1868. Most importantly, Canadian copyright has always taken place in the context of the push and pull of international pressures. Domestic and international demands often conflict, and there is often significant resistance within Canada to demands for reform coming from outside the country. While

1 *Debates of the Senate, Second Session — Fourteenth Parliament,* 1923 (13-14 Geo. V), at 568–69.

in the early days of Canadian copyright such conflict resulted in rebellion against Imperial and international copyright norms, this type of conflict has been replaced by a slow and relatively obliging tendency in reform, generally involving unhurried progress, minimalist adhesion to international treaties, and carving out made-in-Canada approaches. Although there have been instances where Canada has stepped into the role of a leader on international copyright, that position has been quickly abandoned and leadership left to stronger powers. In general, made-in-Canada approaches result in innovative policy solutions on narrow issues alongside a general acquiescence to the visions of copyright forged in international institutions and larger countries.

Since Canadian Confederation in 1867, there have been four major successful copyright reforms. Canada's first *Copyright Act* of 1868 underwent major revisions in 1875, 1924, 1985, and 1997. Canada passed its first post-Confederation copyright Act in 1868, basing the Canadian Act on the American model.[2] In 1875, provisions were added to the Act intended to encourage British copyright holders to print and publish (or reprint or republish) their works in Canada.[3] In 1924, Canada put a new Act into effect, adopting more directly the British legislative model and the wording of the British *Copyright Act*.[4] The *Copyright Act* of 1924 has remained the basis for Canadian copyright and has undergone several revisions, most significantly in 1985 and 1997.[5] Bill C-32 represents the third attempt to initiate a fifth major reform to Canadian copyright, following previous attempts in 2005 and 2008.

Seen in light of past trends, Bill C-32 includes some made-in-Canada solutions on narrow issues but, on broader issues, abandons made-in-Canada solutions in favour of a more American maximalist approach. In important regards it abandons the tendency, adopted in past reforms, to maintain Canadian policy flexibility by adhering on a minimalist basis to international treaties.

---

2 *An Act Respecting Copyrights*, S.C. 1868 (31 Vict.), c. 54 [*Canada Copyright Act 1868*].

3 *An Act Respecting Copyrights*, S.C. 1875 (38 Vict.), c. 88 [*Canada Copyright Act 1875*].

4 *An Act to Amend and Consolidate the Law Relating to Copyright*, S.C. 1921 (11–12 Geo. V), c. 24 [*Canada Copyright Act 1921*]; and *An Act to Amend the Copyright Act*, S.C. 1923, (13–14 Geo. V), c. 10 [*Canada Copyright Act 1923*].

5 *Copyright Act*, R.S.C. 1985, c. C-42, http://laws.justice.gc.ca/eng/C-42/index.html [*Canada Copyright Act 1985*]; and *An Act to Amend the Copyright Act*, R.S.C. 1997, c. 24, www.wipo.int/clea/en/text_html.jsp?lang=EN&id=624 [*Canada Copyright Act 1997*].

A. INTERNATIONAL PRESSURE

Canadian copyright holders form, with their international counterparts, an epistemic community that exerts significant international and domestic influence, and that acts as a driver of copyright reform internationally. This epistemic community of copyright holders has been highly influential, especially among governments who view copyright, creators, and the creative industries, as important drivers of economic growth, national culture, and national pride, and as important symbols of civilization and modernity. Copyright reform responds to an internationalized agenda that enrols domestic governments and international institutions, and that is inscribed in legal statutes and in international texts and treaties.

In the nineteenth and early twentieth century, the British Imperial government was enrolled in an international effort on behalf of copyright owners to maintain and expand markets for British books throughout the British Empire, as well as in efforts to create a legal regime that covered the whole British Empire. In the twentieth century, international institutions and networks have been enrolled in efforts to create an international copyright regime that spans the globe. Such efforts have been driven by the efforts of copyright exporters to protect and expand foreign markets. Though the *Berne Convention* has remained the foundation stone of international copyright, the two WIPO Internet Treaties — the *WIPO Copyright Treaty* (WCT) and the *WIPO Performances and Phonograms Treaty* (WPPT) — as well as the World Trade Organization's *Agreement on Trade-Related Aspects of Intellectual Property* (TRIPs Agreement), and various trade and plurilateral agreements are now the main vehicles for the internationalization and expansion of copyright and the protection of foreign markets by copyright exporters today.

Following Canadian confederation in 1867, Canada's first copyright Act, enacted in 1868, was instituted in relative freedom from international pressures.[6] It was modelled on earlier legislation of the Province of Canada and Lower Canada, and was based on the American model of copyright. The American model, in turn, derived a number of features from the British model, such as the requirements to register the work and deposit copies with specific institutions.[7] The Canadian *Copyright Act* also differed from the British model in several key ways that mirrored the American

---

6 *Canada Copyright Act 1868*.

7 *An Act for the Protection of Copy Rights*, S.Prov.C. 1832 (2 Will. IV), c. 53 [*Canada Copyright Act 1832*] and *An Act for the Protection of Copy Rights in this Province*, S.L.C. 1841 (4 & 5 Vict.), c. 61 [*Canada Copyright Act 1841*]; see also W.L. Hayhurst, "Intellectual

approach to copyright, in that it required a copyright notice to appear on most types of works[8] and emulated the American term of protection (twenty-eight years with a possible extension of fourteen years, whereas Britain provided a term of the life of the author plus seven years, or forty-two years from the date of first publication, whichever was longer).[9] The emulation of American law was voluntary and reciprocal; American law would also follow the Canadian law of 1868 in 1891, when it added domestic manufacture provisions.[10]

After 1868, reform to Canadian copyright took place under imperial and international pressure. Initially, this came primarily from the British Imperial government, acting on behalf of British copyright owners to ensure that Canadian copyright provisions did not interfere with British authors and publishers' ability to capitalize on the Canadian market. The Imperial government worked to ensure that Canadian copyright was compatible with Imperial law and that Canadian policies did not interfere with British efforts to establish a copyright treaty with the Americans—a key to establishing British publishing houses in the United States.[11]

Canada's rebellious reaction to imperial pressures was first evidenced in 1872, when Canadian Parliament unanimously passed a copyright Act that provided for the compulsory licensing of British books.[12] This was a

---

Property Laws in Canada: The British Tradition, the American Influence, and the French Factor" (1996) 10 IPJ 281 [*Hayhurst*].

8 *Canada Copyright Act 1868*; and *An Act to Amend Several Acts Respecting Copy Rights*, § 5, 4 Stat. 436 (1831), www.copyrighthistory.org/cgi-bin/kleioc/0010/exec/ausgabe/%22us_1831%22 [*US Copyright Act 1831*].

9 *Canada Copyright Act 1868*; *An Act to Amend the Law of Copyright, 1842* (U.K.), 5 & 6 Vict., c. 45, www.copyrighthistory.org/cgi-bin/kleioc/0010/exec/ausgabe/%22uk_1842%22 [*UK Copyright Act 1842*], s. 3; and *US Copyright Act 1831*, §§ 1 & 2. See also *Hayhurst*.

10 The 1868 act required that works be "printed and published" in Canada to be eligible for Canadian copyright protection: *Canada Copyright Act 1868*. The United States did not include such a provision in their copyright act of 1831, but introduced their "manufacturing clause", which required books to be "printed from type set within the limits of the United States, or from plates made therefrom, or from negatives, or drawings on stone made within the limits of the United States, or from transfers made therefrom," in 1891. *An Act to Amend Title Sixty, Chapter Three, of the Revised Statutes of the United States, Relating to Copyrights*, § 4956, 26 Stat. 1106 (1891), www.copyrighthistory.org/cgi-bin/kleioc/0010/exec/ausgabe/%22us_1891a%22 [*US Copyright Act 1891*].

11 Great Britain, *Correspondence with the United States Respecting Copyright Convention, Part 1: 1881–1884*. (London: n.p., n.d.) See also Catherine Seville, *The Internationalisation of Copyright Law: Books, Buccaneers and the Black Flag in the Nineteenth Century* (Cambridge: Cambridge University Press, 2006) [*Seville*].

12 *Seville* at 103.

made-in-Canada solution intended to meet specifically Canadian needs. The Canadian government wanted to encourage a domestic printing and publishing industry that could viably compete with American printers and publishers to serve the Canadian market. The compulsory licensing provisions were intended to put Canadian printers and publishers on an equal footing with the Americans who, in 1872, did not yet recognize international copyright. American printers and publishers were therefore able to reprint British works without permission of the copyright holder and export them to Canada by paying a 12.5 percent tariff. The Act of 1872 would have allowed Canadian printers to reprint British works in Canada as well, upon license from the Governor General for a fee of 12.5 percent that would go to the British copyright holder.[13] The Act, however, was refused royal assent by the Imperial government.[14] A number of reasons were given. Alongside concerns about the practicality of the proposal and its fairness to British copyright holders, the British did not want Canadian reprints circulating in Canada that would be cheaper than those sold in Britain.[15] In addition, the British were apprehensive that the Canadian proposal might affect British international copyright interests; British officials were interested in establishing a bilateral copyright agreement with the United States and were worried that the United States would not be willing to establish a treaty recognizing British copyright "whilst every publisher in Montreal can reprint [British works] on payment of a moderate percentage without the author's leave, and can smuggle them into the United States."[16] An Anglo-American copyright arrangement was not reached until almost twenty years later in 1891.[17]

---

13 *Ibid.*

14 "Earl of Dufferin to Early of Kimberly, 9 August 1872" in Great Britain, *Copyright (Colonies): Copies of Extracts from Correspondence between the Colonial Office and any of the Colonial Governments on the Subject of Copyright* (London: n.p., 1875).

15 These concerns had been expressed in "Board of Trade to Colonial Office, 27 July 1869" in Canada, House of Commons, *Colonial Copyright: Return to an address of the Honourable the House of Commons* (29 July 1872).

16 *Ibid.*; see also *Seville* at 90-94.

17 In 1891 the United States passed a new copyright act, providing another front on which Canada could attempt to assert its copyright independence. The 1891 Act, called the "Chace Act" after American Senator Jonathan Chace who introduced the bill, extended copyright protection, under specific conditions, to citizens of certain other countries. The countries to which this would apply were to be declared by Presidential proclamation. Countries eligible for such a proclamation included those who granted copyright to American citizens on substantially the same basis as its own citizens, and countries "party to an international agreement which provides for reciprocity in the grant of copyright, by the terms of which agreement the United

It was in this context that Canada's 1875 *Copyright Act* was passed by the Canadian Parliament and sanctioned by the Imperial Parliament.[18] The 1875 *Copyright Act* continued to emulate, like the Canadian *Copyright Act* of 1868, the American model, but it did not include the compulsory licensing system. It granted Canadian copyright to works first or simultaneously printed or published in Canada (or reprinted or republished in Canada), subject to the same set of formalities (domestic printing, registration and deposit) as had been in place under the 1868 Act, and banned importation of foreign reprints of such works. In prohibiting the import of foreign reprints of British works copyrighted in Canada, the Act put in place a compromise solution that did not go so far as the compulsory licensing provisions of the 1872 Act in encouraging domestic printing, but did provide some incentive for British publishers to republish their work in Canada. Under the 1875 Act, only by obtaining Canadian copyright protection via printing and publishing (or reprinting and republishing) in Canada could British publishers gain exclusive access to the Canadian market by excluding foreign reprints.[19] This was a made-in-Canada solution tailored to fit within imperial constraints.

Following this compromise, the revolutionary approach to Canadian copyright reappeared in 1889. A second attempt to institute a compulsory licensing system was made in that year, when Canadian Parliament again passed a copyright Act containing compulsory licensing provisions.[20] By 1886, Imperial control had been transferred, in part, onto international agreements. The *Berne Convention for the Protection of Literary and Artistic Works* had been put in place in 1886, and Canada had been signed on to the convention by the Imperial government.[21] Although Prime Minister Macdonald and his government had, behind closed doors, agreed to sign the *Berne Convention* under the British signature in 1886, by 1889 domestic interest groups had voiced their objection to implementation

---

States of America may at its pleasure become a party to such agreement." *US Copyright Act 1891* at 1110.

18 *Canada Copyright Act 1875*.

19 *Ibid.* See also Gordon Roper, "Mark Twain and His Canadian Publishers," (1966) 5 *Papers of the Bibliographical Society of Canada*, at 40–41.

20 *An Act to Amend "The Copyright Act," Chapter sixty-two of the Revised Statutes*, S.C. 1889 (52 Vict.), c. 29.

21 *Actes de la troisième conférence international pour la protection des oeuvres littéraires et artistiques réunie à berne du 6 au 9 septembre 1886*, (Berne: Conseil Fédérale Suisse, 1886) (ftp://ftp.wipo.int/pub/library/ebooks/Internationalconferences-recordsproceedings/BerneConference1886).

of the treaty.[22] The *Berne Convention* was seen as being inappropriate for the North American situation, disallowing the types of domestic printing and compulsory licensing provisions that would have put Canadian printers and publishers on par with their American counterparts who did not yet recognize international copyright — measures seen as important drivers of development in the Canadian printing and publishing industries. Canada's 1889 copyright Act, which contained such provisions and therefore constituted a rebellion against of British copyright norms and a rejection of the norms of the recently-instituted *Berne Convention*, was unanimously passed in Canadian Parliament along with a request that the *Berne Convention* be denounced on Canada's behalf.[23] The Act of 1889, however, like the Act of 1873 before it, was prevented from coming into force by the Imperial government, and Canada's request to denounce the convention was rejected.[24] Canada's revolutionary approach to copyright had failed, and British control over Canadian law was retained.

The United States did not recognize international copyright until 1891, and did not join the *Berne Convention* until over a century later in 1989, preferring a made-at-home model of copyright. American requirements of registration and domestic manufacture, which were seen as protecting the American printing and publishing industry, were disallowed for parties to the *Berne Convention*.[25] The *Berne Convention*, however, remained in

---

22 Sir R. Herbert to Sir J. Pincefort (12 June 1886), *Switzerland No. 2: Further Correspondence Respecting the Formation of an International Copyright Union* (C. 4606) (London: 1886), Ottawa, Library and Archives Canada (RG7 G21 Vol. 115 File 206 Part 2b); John Lowe, Memorandum (9 February 1889), Ottawa, Library and Archives Canada (RG13 A-2 Vol. 2361 File 1912-1424 Part 4); "The Copyright Bill" *The Globe Toronto* (16 May 1888) 8; "Notes" *The Globe Toronto* (18 May 1888) 3; "Copyright Law as Before" *The Globe Toronto* (18 May 1888); John Lowe to Fred Daldy (13 June 1888), Ottawa, Library and Archives Canada (RG17 A16 Vol. 1655); Richard T. Lancefield, *Notes on Copyright Domestic and International* (Hamilton: Canadian Literary Bureau, 1896).

23 Great Britain. *Report of the Departmental Representatives Appointed to Consider the Canadian Copyright Act of 1889* (E 1701) (London:n.p., 1892) in Prime Minister Abbott fonds (MG26 C), Vol. 5 File: Copyright; see also Lord Stanley of Preston to Lord Knutsford (16 and 17 August 1889) in Great Britain, *Correspondence on the Subject of the Law of Copyright in Canada* (C. 7783) (London: George Edward Eyre and William Spotiswoode, 1893), Ottawa, Library and Archives Canada (RG13 A-2 Vol. 2361 File 1912-1494 Part II).

24 Lord Knutsford to Lord Stanley of Preston (25 March 1890), *Correspondence on the Subject of the Law of Copyright in Canada* (C. 7783) (London: George Edward Eyre and William Spotiswoode, 1893), Ottawa, Library and Archives Canada (RG13 A-2 Vol. 2361 File 1912-1494 Part II).

25 Interpretations of the principle of no formalities was still unclear in 1897, with various countries taking different positions on the issue. Bureau International de

force in Canada, providing, along with Imperial control, a further set of restrictions on Canadian law that prevented Canada from following more closely the American model of copyright. Efforts to incorporate provisions that would meet specifically Canadian needs, especially in the context of Canada's close proximity to the United States and their variant approach to copyright, were restricted by Imperial and international controls.

Imperial control continued to be exerted on Canada's 1921 *Copyright Act* through an arrangement made eleven years earlier, under which British colonies agreed to adopt British copyright provisions in exchange for continued copyright recognition throughout the British Empire.[26] This arrangement saw Canada copy, word for word, the British *Copyright Act* into Canadian law in what is often referred to as Canada's "first sovereign" copyright law, which came into force in 1924.[27]

Although earlier Canadian copyright was based on American and British copyright models, beginning in the 1930s, Canadian copyright legislation began to incorporate some elements of the European authors' rights tradition. In 1931 Canada became the first copyright country to incorporate moral rights in its legislation.[28] Canada's move in 1931 was the result of an effort to conform to the moral rights provisions of the newly revised *Berne Convention*.

Canada's next major copyright reform did not take place until 1985. The 1985 reform took place again in a period of relative independence from international pressures. The United States had still not yet formally adhered to the *Berne Convention* and, in 1984, withdrew from the United Nations Economic, Scientific, and Cultural Organization (UNESCO), home

---

l'Union, *Actes de la conférence réunie à Paris du 15 avril au 4 mai 1896*, (Berne: Bureau International de l'Union, 1897) at 161. However, the principle was solidified in 1908. Sam Ricketson and Jane Ginsburg, *International Copyright and Neighbouring Rights: The Berne Convention and Beyond*, 2d ed. (London: Oxford University Press, 2006) at 96.

26 Great Britain, *Minutes of Proceeding of the Imperial Copyright Conference, 1910*, Ottawa, Library and Archives Canada (Microfilm reels B-2392 to B-2393).

27 The Canadian act was, in almost all sections, copied from British legislation, with a few differences regarding registration and compulsory licensing, as well as some minor variations with regard to compulsory licensing of gramophone recordings intended to make Canadian law reflective of American legislation. *Canada Copyright Act 1921; Canada Copyright Act 1923; An Act to Amend and Consolidate the Law Relating to Copyright, 1911* (U.K.), 1&2 Geo. V, c. 46.

28 *An Act to Amend the Copyright Act*, S.C. (21-22 Geo. V), c. 8 (assented to 11 June 1931) [*Canada Copyright Act 1931*]; see also Ysolde Gendreau, "Surfacing: the Canadian intellectual property identity," in Ysolde Gendreau, ed,. *An Emerging Intellectual Property Paradigm: Perspectives from Canada* (Cheltenham, UK: Edward Elgar, 2008) 295 at 298 [Gendreau].

to the *Universal Copyright Convention*. The country was in the process of moving towards adhesion to the *Berne Convention* and towards the inclusion of intellectual property measures under the *General Agreement on Tariffs and Trade* (*GATT*). During the time that Canada's 1985 revision took place, however, the United States was sidelined in international copyright policy-making, with no role in the *Berne Convention* and a reduced role in UNESCO's *Universal Copyright Convention*.[29] Absent American pressure, Canada's 1985 reforms extended Canadian copyright but did not see Canada implement the 1971 revision of the *Berne Convention*. Canadian copyright was extended to include computer programs, to strengthen moral rights, and to institute copyright collectives.[30]

Revisions to Canadian copyright that followed responded more directly to international agreements. Canada implemented the 1971 revision of the *Berne Convention* in 1993 in order to comply with the *North American Free Trade Agreement* (NAFTA), which, at American insistence, had made compliance with the 1971 revision a requirement—a measure probably aimed at Canada, the only party to NAFTA not yet in compliance.[31] Canada also added a rental right for computer programs and protection for compilations of data and other material (copyright in databases) as a result of its NAFTA obligations.[32] Further amendments were made to the *Copyright Act* in 1994 under the *World Trade Organization Agreement Implementation Act* in response to the *TRIPs Agreement*. These extended the rights under the *Copyright Act* to all WTO member countries, and expanded performers' rights.[33]

Canada's 1997 reform, seen as a Phase II that completed the Phase I of reform which had occurred in 1985, brought Canada into compliance with the 1961 *Rome Convention for the Protection of Performers, Producers of Phonograms and Broadcasting Organizations* by granting rights in public performances and broadcasts for performers and producers of sound recordings.[34] It also instituted the private copying levy; exceptions for non-

---

29 Orrin G. Hatch, "Better Late than Never: Implementation of the 1886 Berne Convention" (1989) 22 Cornell International Law Journal 171 at 178.

30 *Canada Copyright Act 1985*.

31 *North American Free Trade Agreement Implementation Act*, S.C. 1993, c. 44, s. 52-80, http://laws.justice.gc.ca/en/N-23.8/index.html [*Canada NAFTA Implementation Act 1993*]; also see Sunny Handa, "A Review of Canada's International Copyright Obligations," 42 *McGill Law Journal* (September, 1997), 976 [Handa]. The NAFTA also required compliance with the substantive provisions of the *Geneva Phonograms Convention*.

32 See Handa.

33 Canada, *World Trade Organization Implementation Act*, SC 1994, c. 47 (www.canlii.org/en/ca/laws/stat/sc-1994-c-47/latest/sc-1994-c-47.html).

34 *Canada Copyright Act 1997*.

profit educational institutions, libraries, archives, museums, broadcasters and persons with perceptual disabilities; statutory damages, and wide injunctions.[35] Following the Phase II reform, Canada acceded formally to the most recent (1971) revision of the *Berne Convention* on 26 March 1998.[36]

The current round of reform takes place in the context of domestic and international pressure, most significantly from the United States, to ratify the WIPO Internet Treaties and to increase copyright enforcement. Canada has been repeatedly placed on the United States Trade Representative's Special 301 Priority Watch List and is often cited as a copyright backwater by American industry groups.[37] The first effort of the Conservative government to reform copyright was, according to Haggart, an effort to demonstrate that the Conservative government was more friendly to the United States than had been the previous Liberal government; direction came from the Prime Minister's Office to satisfy US demands.[38]

Canada's early efforts to follow the American model of copyright in some respects were a result largely of pressure to compete on a level playing field with the United States. Whereas early American influence took place through lobbying, diplomacy, modeling and competition, Canada's recent efforts at reform respond to demands that are now also backed by the WTO dispute settlement mechanism and possible US trade sanctions under the Special 301 process. At the same time, there remains room — as in the past — for Canadian policy innovation. While international, as well as domestic, pressure is a relatively constant feature of Canadian copyright reform, Canada's responses to this pressure have ranged between rebellion and compliance. Bill C-32, like C-60 before it, bows to international demands by going above and beyond the minimum requirements of the WIPO Internet treaties.

---

35 *Ibid.*; Canada, Department of Industry Canada and Department of Canadian Heritage, *A Framework for Copyright Reform* (Ottawa: Department of Industry Canada and Department of Canadian Heritage, 2001) 4–5, http://strategis.ic.gc.ca/pics/rp/framework.pdf [*A Framework for Copyright Reform*]

36 Handa at 969; World Intellectual Property Organization, *Berne Notification 193: Accession by Canada to the Paris Act (1971)* (26 March 1998) (www.wipo.int/treaties/en/notifications/berne/treaty_berne_193.html).

37 United States Trade Representative, 2010 Special 301 Report, 30 April 2010, www.ustr.gov/webfm_send/1906

38 Blayne Haggart, "North American Digital Copyright, Regional Governance and the Persistence of Variation," Paper presented at the Annual Conference of the Canadian Political Science Association, Montreal, 1–3 June 2010 at 10 (www.cpsa-acsp.ca/papers-2010/Haggart.pdf).

B. RESISTANCE TO INTERNATIONAL NORMS

Bill C-32, like its 2005 and 2008 predecessors, is intended to "bring Canada in line with international standards" by implementing the WIPO Internet treaties.[39] Although the implementation of international copyright agreements is often portrayed as an uncontentious technical step—as a matter of keeping up with technology and progress—the implementation of international copyright treaties has, in Canada, historically been highly contentious and problematic. Canada, as a result, has adhered in fits and starts to the various texts of international copyright treaties, first refusing to adhere, then adhering with great fanfare. Canada's slowness in implementing the treaties, now 14 years old, reflects traditional tensions between transnational groups of rights holders and Canadian consumers and users.

Beginning with the copyright rebellion of 1889, Canada maintained its opposition to the *Berne Convention* until 1910. Canada's fourth Prime Minister, John Thompson, took the view that the benefits that Canadian copyright holders received under the *Berne Convention* did not equal the harm caused to Canadian printing and publishing industry:

> the condition of the publishing interest in Canada was made worse by the Berne Convention . . . . The monopoly which was, in former years, complained of in regard to British copyright holders is now to be complained of, not only as regards British copyright holders, but as to the same class in all countries included in the Berne Copyright Union. Canada is made a close market for their benefit, and the single compensation given by the convention for a market of five millions of reading people is the possible benefit to the Canadian author . . . [who has been described as] "belonging rather to the future than to the present."[40]

The terms of the *Berne Convention*, Thompson felt, largely favoured densely populated and highly urbanized countries such as those in Europe, but that such terms were unsuited to relatively less developed countries like Canada:

> The Berne Convention had in view considerations of society which are widely different from those prevailing in Canada. In Europe the reading population in the various countries is comparatively dense;—in

---

39 Canada, Industry Canada and Canadian Heritage, *Press Release: Government of Canada Introduces Proposals to Modernize the Copyright Act*, 2 June 2010, http://strategis.ic.gc.ca/eic/site/crp-prda.nsf/eng/h_rp01149.html

40 John Thompson to Governor General in Council, 1892, 7 in Library and Archives Canada, RG13 A-2 Vol. 85 File 892-217.

> Canada, a population considerably less than that of London is dispersed over an area nearly as large as that of Europe. In the cities of Europe, especially in Great Britain, the reading public is largely supplied from the libraries, while, in Canada, as a general rule, he who reads must buy. In European countries the reading class forms but a fraction of the whole population, while in Canada it comprises nearly the whole population.[41]

However, views changed after the turn of the century. At an Imperial Copyright Conference in 1910 Canada was the strongest voice among the colonies arguing for colonial copyright sovereignty. At the conference, the British colonies agreed in principle to implement the *Berne Convention* in exchange for copyright sovereignty — the ability to repeal Imperial copyright law in the dominions and to enact domestic copyright laws without interference from the Imperial government, as long as these were "substantially identical" to Imperial copyright legislation.[42] In cases where a self-governing dominion failed to enact legislation that was "substantially similar", they could expect to lose copyright recognition throughout the British Empire and internationally.[43]

Fourteen years later, according to the agreement made in 1910, Canada put in place its own "sovereign" copyright Act, copied word-for-word from the British Act, and adhered to the *Berne Convention* in 1924 with great fanfare.[44] Canadian newspapers trumpeted Canada's entry into the *Berne Convention*; the headline in The *Globe* read: "Copyright Troubles Finally Adjusted: Canada at last adheres with other Nations to the Berne Convention."[45]

Despite the fanfare, Canada later refused to implement the next revision of the *Berne Convention* in 1948. Canada's delegate to the revision conference in 1948 made the distinction between countries who were net copyright importers and net copyright exporters: "Canada is a nation that *consumes* literary and artistic works,» noted the Canadian delegate.[46] This

41 *Ibid.*

42 Great Britain. *Minutes of Proceeding of the Imperial Copyright Conference, 1910*, 207 — Resolution 2c. Imperial copyright laws were in place and governed copyright in Canada alongside domestic Canadian legislation until 1924.

43 *Ibid.* — Resolution 2d.

44 See note 27, above.

45 "Copyright Troubles Finally Adjusted: Canada at last adheres with other Nations to the Berne Convention," *The Globe*, 18 March 1924, 2.

46 Author's translation; emphasis added. *Documents de la conférence réunie à Bruxelles du 5 au 26 juin 1948*, 204–5 (ftp://ftp.wipo.int/pub/library/ebooks/Internationalconferences-recordsproceedings/BruxellesConference1948)

overt identification of Canada as a copyright consumer — one which had not been as much highlighted in the 1920s when Canada was new to the *Berne Convention* — would remain at the centre of Canadian copyright policy throughout the 1950s, '60s, and '70s.

The revisions to the *Berne Convention* made in 1948 would have made necessary a number of changes to Canadian copyright law that the government was unwilling to make. The Royal Commission on Patents, Copyright, Trade Marks and Industrial Designs (the Ilsley Commission) reported that implementing the 1948 revision of the *Berne Convention* would entail the following changes to Canadian copyright: first, Canada would have been required to grant more extensive performance rights to authors; second, Canada would have been obliged to give authors a right to authorize retransmission of their works such as by a satellite or cable retransmission of a broadcast; and finally, Canada would have been obliged to submit unsettled disputes with other union members to the International Court of Justice. As well, Canada would have become tied to a term of copyright (already in place since 1924) that lasted for the life of the author plus fifty years. The Commission recommended against all of these changes on the argument that they would reduce Canada's ability to legislate freely,[47] that Canada's term of protection should emulate that of the United States rather than retain the term of life plus fifty years, as required under the Brussels revision,[48] and that Canada ought not to "submit itself to the interpretation of the Convention by any authority other than its own Parliament."[49] Ratification of the 1948 version of the *Berne Convention* was due 1 July 1951.[50] Although work towards a redrafting of the *Copyright Act* had begun prior to June 1949,[51] no new copyright Act was passed in Canadian Parliament. Canada would never ratify the 1948 Act of the *Berne Convention*.

Canada also refused to sign or implement the 1967 revision of the *Berne Convention*. While many countries refused to ratify that revision, Canada had its own reasons.[52] The Secretary of State for External Affairs, in the

---

47 Canada, Royal Commission on Patents, Copyright, Trade-marks and Industrial Designs, *Report on Copyright*. (Ottawa: Supply and Services Canada, 1957) 13.

48 *Ibid.*, 19–23.

49 *Ibid.*, 15.

50 *Berne Convention for the Protection of Literary and Artistic Works*, Brussels Act of 26 June 1948, Art. 28 (www.oup.com/uk/booksites/content/9780198259466/15550020).

51 C. Stein, Under-Secretary of State to the Under-Secretary of State for External Affairs, 9 June 1949. RG103 Vol. 4 File 5-3-2-2.

52 The revision of 1967, once signed, did not receive a sufficient number of ratifications to come into force. This was due to controversy over special provisions put in place for developing countries under the revision.

days leading up to the conference, questioned whether Canada's commitment to the *Berne Convention* was in the national interest:

> Successive revisions of the Berne Convention have progressively extended the monopoly rights of copyright holders. The current revisions suggested for the Stockholm conference are intended to extend these rights still further. Unfortunately, this raises the question of the cost in relation to the value of present copyright legislation as a device for encouraging creativity in Canada before the Economic Council's report is available. An important consideration in the study of this matter is the fact that as much as 90% of the total cost (about $8 million) of copyright to the public in Canada is accounted for by the protection given foreign works. In turn, compensation to Canadian authors by way of payments from overseas to Canada is minimal. That raises the fundamental question of whether protection of the kind Canada is committed to by adhering to the Berne Union is in the national interest.[53]

It was therefore recommended to Cabinet that Canada should refrain from supporting any proposed revision to the *Berne Convention* that would reduce the government's flexibility of action.[54] Canada did not sign the revised *Berne Convention* of 1967.[55]

Canada, again, did not sign the revised text of the *Berne Convention* of 1971.[56] Canada's position again was that it did not support the revisions as a whole because they were seen as involving a commitment to higher levels of intellectual property rights.[57] The Canadian delegation was instructed not to sign the revised treaties.[58] This position was consistent

---

53 Secretary of State for External Affairs, Memorandum for Consideration by the Cabinet Committee on Economic and Fiscal Policy, 8 June 1967. Library and Archives Canada, RG19 Vol 5167 File 8510-C785-1 Pt 1.

54 *Ibid.*

55 *Records of the Intellectual Property Conference of Stockholm June 11 to July 14, 1967.* Geneva: World Intellectual Property Organization, 1971, 1282, 1319 (ftp://ftp.wipo.int/pub/library/ebooks/Internationalconferences-recordsproceedings/StockholmConferenceRecords1967)

56 *Records of the Conference for Revision of the Universal Copyright Convention, Unesco House, Paris, 5 to 24 July 1971* (Paris: UNESCO, 1973) (ftp://ftp.wipo.int/pub/library/ebooks/Internationalconferences-recordsproceedings/ParisConference1971RevisionOfTheBerneConvention-en).

57 *Memorandum to the Cabinet*, 29 June 1971, Cabinet document 700-71, Library and Archives Canada, RG19 Vol 5574 File 8510-C785-1, Pt 2.

58 *Ibid.*, and in RG25 Vol 10904 File 55-19-4-BERNE pt 6-1; Record of Cabinet Decision, Cabinet Committee on External Policy and Defence, 29 June 1971, Library and Archives Canada, RG25 Vol. 10904 File 55-19-4-BERNE pt 6-1.

with the recent report of the *Economic Council of Canada*, which had recommended that Canada not adopt higher levels of copyright protection and was therefore viewed as precluding accession to the revised treaties.[59] It continued to be viewed as questionable whether Canada should accede to the 1948 revision of the *Berne Convention*.[60] Canada would not accede to the 1971 revision of the *Berne Convention* until the 1990s, when it did so in order to conform to the *North American Free Trade Agreement*.[61]

Canada's lengthy refusal to adopt the provisions of 1971 was based on views outlined in a number of domestic reports and policy studies. In 1977 Andrew A. Keyes and Claude Brunet prepared a report titled *Copyright in Canada: Proposals for a Revision of the Law*. Following an examination of the available options with regard to the *Berne Convention*, including accession, withdrawal, and maintaining the status quo, the authors came to the conclusion that:

> the fully developed nations, largely exporters of copyright material, have a stronger voice in international copyright conventions, and a tendency has existed over the past half century for developing countries, including Canada, to accept too readily proffered solutions in copyright matters that do not reflect their economic positions.[62]

Further, they argued that "succeeding revisions of [the *Berne Convention*] or, indeed, that of the *Universal Copyright Convention*, do not meet Canadian needs, at least at this stage in Canada's growth."[63] As such, they concluded that Canada should "remain at the present level of international participation in respect of the *Berne Convention* and the *Universal Copyright Convention*."[64]

By 1984, prevailing views within the government had once again begun to change. The Department of Consumer and Corporate Affairs and the Department of Communications jointly prepared the paper *From Guten-*

---

59 *Paris Revision Conference of the Universal Copyright Convention and the Berne Copyright Convention, Paris, July 5-24, 1971: Report of the Canadian Delegation*, 24. Library and Archives Canada, RG25 Vol. 10904 File 55-19-4-BERNE pt 6-2.

60 *Ibid.*

61 *Canada NAFTA Implementation Act 1993* s. 52-80; also see Handa at 976.

62 Andrew A. Keyes and Claude Brunet, *Copyright in Canada: Proposals for a Revision of the Law* (Ottawa: Consumer and Corporate Affairs Canada, 1977) 234.

63 *Ibid.*

64 *Ibid.* at 236. Keyes affirmed this view again in 1993, arguing that "Canada . . . as a net importer would only increase its trade deficit by assuming further commitments." Andrew A. Keyes, "What is Canada's International Copyright Policy?" 7 IPJ (1993) 299 at 302.

berg to Telidon: A White Paper on Copyright, issued as part of a public consultation on copyright reform. The paper did not address the topic of possible accession to the 1971 revision of the *Berne Convention* in any extended discussion, but took the position that:

> Since Canadian creators receive national treatment protection in [countries that are Canada's major trading partners and who belong to one or both of the major copyright conventions], they benefit from Canada's participation in these conventions. The government intends that Canada's international obligations be met in the spirit as well as in the letter of the law.[65]

At the same time, the government observed that a number of flexibilities were available to Canada as a result of Canada's not being bound by the later text.[66]

Following the 1984 report *From Gutenberg to Telidon* under the Liberal government, the Conservatives came to power. In January 1985 the Conservatives referred the question of copyright, along with the 1984 report, to the Standing Committee on Communications and Culture. An all-party subcommittee, following ten months of hearings held in Ottawa, Toronto, and Montreal and the examination of over 300 written briefs, tabled a new report in 1985 called *A Charter of Rights for Creators*.[67] Copyright reform was seen in *A Charter of Rights for Creators* as being important to encouraging what some hoped would be "a new era of Canadian cultural production."[68] In contrast to the 1977 Keyes-Brunet report, the subcommittee placed the creator as the primary and foremost interest in copyright law: "because of the special contribution creators make to Canadian society, they must be fairly rewarded."[69] Such a reward would demonstrate that the Sub-Committee recognized "how much value [Canada] attaches to the contribution of creators to the national life. The *Copyright Act* is seen as a very significant symbol of the country's scale of values and a sig-

---

65 Canada. Department of Communications and Department of Consumer and Corporate Affairs, *From Gutenberg to Telidon: A White Paper on Copyright: Proposals for the Revision of the Canadian Copyright Act* (Ottawa: Department of Consumer and Corporate Affairs and Department of Communications, 1984) at 4.

66 *Ibid.* See in particular the discussion of a retransmission right in Appendix I.

67 Canada, House of Commons, Sub-Committee on the Revision of Copyright, *A Charter of Rights for Creators: A Report of the Sub-Committee on the Revision of Copyright, Standing Committee on Communications and Culture* (Ottawa: Queen's Printer, 1985) xii.

68 *Ibid.* at 5. The subommittee noted such optimism must be dampened by realism.

69 *Ibid.* at xii.

nal to creators of their social merit or worth."[70] The resulting 1985 revision of the *Copyright Act* did not see Canada adhere to the 1971 revision of the *Berne Convention*.[71] It did, however, set the tone for further revisions in the 1990s that would bring Canada into conformity with the *Berne Convention* and other international copyright treaties.

Canada signed the WIPO Internet treaties in 1996 and has, in the time since, repeatedly stated its intention to implement the treaties.[72] Implementation requires parties to grant copyright holders 'making-available rights'—the exclusive right to make their work available, for example on the Internet; to provide legal remedies against the circumvention of technological protection measures, and to provide legal remedies against the removal or alteration of rights management information or the distribution of works whose rights management information have been removed.[73]

Canada's future adherence to the WIPO Internet treaties is often portrayed as an uncontentious technical step—as a matter of keeping up with progress.[74] However, the implementation of those treaties, like the implementation of past international copyright treaties, has been, in Canada, highly contentious and has spawned widespread criticism, controversy, and Internet activism. The implementation of WIPO Internet treaty provisions with regard to technological protection measures has been a prime issue of contention in Canada. The first effort to do so, in 2005 under Bill C-60, was viewed as a made-in-Canada approach to implementation. Under Bill C-60, an infringement would only occur if the purpose of the circumvention was to infringe copyright; and no limitations were placed on the manufacture or sale of circumvention devices.[75]

---

70 *Ibid.* at 4

71 *Canada Copyright Act 1985*.

72 *A Framework for Copyright Reform*, 6; Canada, Industry Canada and Canadian Heritage, *Press Release: Government of Canada Introduces Bill to Amend the Copyright Act*, 20 June 2005 (www.ic.gc.ca/eic/site/ic1.nsf/eng/02279.html); Canada, Industry Canada and Canadian Heritage, *Press Release: Government of Canada Proposes Update to Copyright Law: Balanced Approach to Truly Benefit Canadians*, 12 June 2008 (www.ic.gc.ca/eic/site/ic1.nsf/eng/04204.html); Canada, Industry Canada and Canadian Heritage, *Press Release: Government of Canada Introduces Proposals to Modernize the Copyright Act*, 2 June 2010 (http://strategis.ic.gc.ca/eic/site/crp-prda.nsf/eng/h_rp01149.html)

73 *WIPO Copyright Treaty*, 20 December 1996 (www.wipo.int/treaties/en/ip/wct/index.html); *WIPO Performances and Phonograms Treaty*, 20 December 1996 (www.wipo.int/treaties/en/ip/wppt/index.html).

74 *WIPO Copyright Treaty*, *ibid.*; *WIPO Performances and Phonograms Treaty*, *ibid.*

75 Bill C-60, *An Act to Amend the Copyright Act*, 1st Sess., 38th Parl., 2005 (as read on First Reading 20 June 2005), www2.parl.gc.ca/HousePublications/Publication.aspx?DocId=4580265&Mode=1&Language=E [Bill C-60]; Michael Geist, "Anti-Circum-

The next effort in 2008, although heralded as a "made in Canada bill,"[76] stepped away from this made-in-Canada approach. Bill C-61 was viewed as adopting a solution that stood closer to the American approach — a "Canadian *DMCA*" (the American *Digital Millennium Copyright Act*) — by its critics.[77] Bill C-61 would have made circumvention illegal regardless of whether the circumvention was for infringing purposes, and would have prohibited the manufacture, import, and provision of circumvention devices.[78] Bill C-32 would also place a ban on the manufacture, import, distribution, sale, rental, or provision of circumvention devices, like C-61, does not include a general exception for circumvention for non-infringing purposes.[79] Such provisions remain highly controversial and place consumers and users at risk of infringement for a wide variety of things, such as circumventing to gather a clip from a DVD for classroom use, to transfer a CD track to an MP3 player, or to transfer ebook content from an old device to a new one. In light of such controversy, and in light of Canada's history with international copyright, any expectation that Canadian copyright revision should proceed smoothly or quickly belies Canada's history with international copyright agreements generally.

C. A SLOW AND MINIMALIST APPROACH

Because Canadian copyright reform is often bogged down by conflicting domestic and international demands, Canadian copyright reform often involves three elements: slow progress, a minimalist approach to conformity with international treaties, and carving out made-in-Canada approaches that attempt to respond to domestic Canadian demands while meeting the technical requirements of international treaties.

---

vention Legislation and Competition Policy: Defining a Canadian Way?" in Michael Geist, ed., *In the Public Interest: The Future of Canadian Copyright Law* (Toronto: Irwin Law, 2005) 211–50.

76 Industry Canada and Canadian Heritage, "Government of Canada Proposes Update to Copyright Law: Balanced Approach to Truly Benefit Canadians," 12 June 2008 (http://www.ic.gc.ca/eic/site/ic1.nsf/eng/04204.html).

77 Cory Doctrow, *Canadian DMCA is worse than the American one*, 12 June 2008, http://boingboing.net/2008/06/12/canadian-dmca-is-wor.html.

78 Bill C-61, *An Act to Amend the Copyright Act*, 2d Sess., 39th Parl., 2008 (as read on First Reading 12 June 2008), www2.parl.gc.ca/HousePublications/Publication.aspx?Docid=3570473&file=4 [Bill C-61]

79 Bill C-32, *An Act to Amend the Copyright Act*, 3d Sess., 40th Parl., 2010 (as read on First Reading 2 June 2010), www2.parl.gc.ca/HousePublications/Publication.aspx?DocId=4580265&Mode=1&Language=E [*Bill C-32*], s. 47.

At the time of writing, it has been fourteen years since the *WIPO Internet Treaties* were signed. Compared to past experience, fourteen years is not a long time for Canadian implementation of an international copyright treaty. Canada was signed on to the original *Berne Convention* under the British in 1886. However, it took Canada thirty-eight years to implement the agreement. It therefore wasn't until 1924 that Canada implemented what by then was the 1908 revision of the *Berne Convention*, doing so under the imperative of conformity with the British approach.[80]

Canada's early copyright followed the British model rather than taking a minimalist approach; although a term of the life of the author plus fifty years was not required under the *Berne Convention* until 1948, Canada adopted that term in 1924. Following that, it took Canada a relatively short three years to implement the 1928 revision of the *Berne Convention*, which it did in 1931, granting moral rights and broadcast rights in copyright works.[81]

It took ten years for Canada to ratify the *Universal Copyright Convention* (UCC), which it did in 1962.[82] Indecision over whether or how to change Canadian law in order to implement the convention contributed to the long wait. After ten years spent considering a possible copyright overhaul, Canada decided, in keeping with a truly minimalist approach, that no change to the actual law was necessary in order to meet the standards of the UCC, which was ratified without legislative change.[83]

Canadian implementation of the 1971 (current) revision of the *Berne Convention* in 1993 in order to conform with NAFTA took twenty-two years.[84] Canada then formally acceded to the convention in 1998 — twenty-seven years after the agreement was put in place — making the few chan-

---

80 *Canada Copyright Act 1923;* Note du Conseil fédéral addressée à tous les États membres de l'Union pour la protection des œuvres littéraires et artistiques (29 January 1924), Ottawa, Library and Archives Canada (RG25 G-1 Vol. 1260 File 218 Part I).

81 *Canada Copyright Act 1931.*

82 Telegram messages 9 and 10 May 1962 from UNESCODEL Paris; Department of External Affairs Press Release (10 May 1962), Ottawa, Library and Archives Canada (RG103 Vol. 6 File 5-3-5-2 Part 2). See also RG103 Vol 5 File 5-3-5-2 Vol 1 Part 2

83 Noel Dorion, Secretary of State, Memorandum to Cabinet (22 February 1961), Ottawa, Library and Archives Canada (RG103 Vol. 6 File 5-3-5-2); Memorandum signed by W.A. Kennett (26 May 1961), Ottawa, Library and Archives Canada (RG19 Vol. 5167 File 8510-C785-1 Pt 1). See also *Debates of the House of Commons, Fourth Session — Twenty-Fourth Parliament 9–10 Elizabeth II, 1960–61*, Vol. VI, 1960–61 (Ottawa: Roger Duhamel, 1961) at 5677; and *Debates of the House of Commons, Fifth Session — Twenty-Fourth Parliament 10–11 Elizabeth II, 1962*, Vol. III, 1962 (Ottawa: Roger Duhamel, 1962) at 3023, and generally RG103 Vol. 6 File 5-3-5-2.

84 *Canada NAFTA Implementation Act 1993*, ss. 52–80.

ges to the *Copyright Act* required under the agreement.[85] Implementation of the *TRIPs Agreement* also involved making the several specific changes to Canadian law required under the agreement.

Implementation of international copyright treaties takes place, in general, more quickly if either no reform to domestic law is required or if the changes required are relatively uncontroversial. If however, the changes required are controversial, or if a significant overhaul of the *Copyright Act* is contemplated — as in the current case of contemplated copyright reform — implementation in Canada can take much longer. Canada's generally minimalist approach to the implementation of international copyright treaties, adopted in the 1960s and seemingly abandoned under Bill C-32, reflects Canada's position as a net copyright importer — a consumer of foreign works — preserves policy flexibility, and can, as Gendreau notes, allow Canada to reserve further revisions as bargaining chips for use in future international negotiations.[86]

D. CANADIAN POLICY INNOVATIONS

Conflicting domestic and international demands have led not only to slow progress and a minimalist approach in implementing international treaties; it has also led to a number of made-in-Canada approaches to copyright intended to meet domestic needs while satisfying international requirements. A general acquiescence to international demands is often accompanied by innovative policy solutions on narrow issues. At times, made-in-Canada solutions present challenges as to whether the new solution is in compliance with international treaty obligations. In some cases, the result is a useful made-in-Canada approach. In other cases, Canadian policy innovations are never used in practice. This pattern is true not only for Canada, but also for less powerful countries generally.

The Canadian copyright reforms of the 1870s resulted in innovative publishing requirements that encouraged domestic printing without going so far as to deny copyright to foreigners as was the practice at the time in the United States. Reforms to Canadian copyright in 1900 built on the innovations of the 1970s; whereas the 1875 *Copyright Act* had allowed a publisher who had obtained a license from the copyright owner to publish a British work in Canada to exclude the import of foreign reprints from

85 World Intellectual Property Organization, *Berne Notification 193: Accession by Canada to the Paris Act (1971)*, (March 26, 1998).

86 Gendreau at 307.

the United States, the 1900 Act would also allow the licensee to apply to the Minister for an order that would prohibit imports of the same work from England, thus reserving the Canadian market entirely for the licensee.[87] These were Canadian policy innovations that were relatively successful in meeting Canadian concerns while setting out an approach that satisfied the British while also taking into account Canada's place next to the United States.

The establishment of the Canadian Copyright Board in 1936 as the Copyright Appeal Board is often seen as a Canadian contribution to the structure of international copyright.[88] The creation of the Board resulted from two Canadian Royal Commissions in the 1930s, held to investigate the activities of the Canadian Performing Right Society in Canada. The first was chaired by Mr. Justice Ewing and reported in 1932, following private meetings in Alberta between the parties involved. The second, chaired by Judge James Parker, held sittings in Toronto, Montreal, Ottawa, Halifax, Moncton, Winnipeg, and Regina, and reported in 1935. While the Ewing Commission recommended certain changes to the way that broadcast license fees were calculated, the Parker Commission went further to recommend the creation of an independent body to examine the fees charged.[89] This presented a question as to whether such a body might contravene rights guaranteed under the *Berne Convention* by regulating performance rights; the Commission concluded that such regulation was permissible.[90] Amendments to the Canadian *Copyright Act* in 1936 created the Copyright Appeal Board, now known as the Copyright Board of Canada.[91]

Canada's made-at-home solution to the dilemma of uncontrolled private copying of audio recordings was, in 1997, to legalize the copying of

---

87 *Canada Copyright Act 1875*, ss. 11 and 15; Canada, *An Act to Amend the Copyright Act*, S.C. 1900 (63–64 Vict.), c. 25; see also Eli MacLaren, "'Against all Invasion': The Archival Story of Kipling, Copyright, and the Macmillan Expansion into Canada, 1900–1920" 40 Journal of Canadian Studies (2006) 139 at 144.

88 *Gendreau* at 96 and 304.

89 Canada, Commission to Investigate whether or not the Canadian Performing Right Society Limited is complying with the terms and conditions of the *Copyright Amendment Act, 1931*, in relation to certain radio broadcasting stations in Alberta, *Report* (N.p.: n.d., 1932.); Canada, Royal Commission Appointed to Investigate the Activities of the Canadian Performing Rights Society, and Similar Societies, *Report* (Toronto: n.p., 1935).

90 Canada, Royal Commission Appointed to Investigate the Activities of the Canadian Performing Rights Society, and Similar Societies, *Report* (Toronto: n.p., 1935) 49.

91 *An Act to Amend the Copyright Amendment Act, 1931*, S.C. 1936 (1 Ed. VIII), c. 28 (assented to 23 June 1936), ss. 10A, B, & C.

audio recordings of musical works onto an audio recording medium for the private use of the person making the copy, while also instituting a remuneration mechanism to compensate eligible authors, performers, and makers of sound recordings by collecting a levy on blank audio recording media.[92] The proceeds of this levy are distributed to both Canadian and foreign composers, but only to Canadian performers and sound recording makers and foreign performers and sound recording makers from countries that provide reciprocal rights.[93] While this solution has provided millions of dollars in remuneration to some copyright and neighbouring rights holders, it has also been controversial and may not comply with Canada's international treaty obligations under the *Rome Convention*, nor the WIPO *Performers and Phonograms Treaty* (WPPT), should Canada, as expected, move to ratify that treaty.[94] Bill C-32 proposes no change to the private copying regime and, if passed unchanged in this respect, may not comply with the WPPT.[95] Canadian innovations occasionally butt up against international treaties and sometimes require innovative legal arguments as to their compliance therewith.

Canada has also created a number of made-in-Canada policy solutions designed to simultaneously meet domestic and international demands that, for one reason or another, can be considered failures. Canada's first efforts to conform to international treaty obligations while custom-building domestic policies to Canadian demands took began during the drafting of Canada's 1924 *Copyright Act*.[96] That Act varied slightly from the text of the British *Copyright Act*; Canadian legislators went to great lengths to include, inside the otherwise British text, certain compulsory licensing provisions and a voluntary registration system. The compulsory licensing provisions were implemented in retaliation for American domestic printing requirements (the manufacturing clause) and, in order to conform to the *Berne Convention*, were severely narrowed so as not to apply to British subjects (other than Canadian citizens) or to countries adhering to the 1908 revision of the *Berne Convention* and additional protocol.[97] These provisions were intended to allow Canadians to obtain a government license

92 *Canada Copyright Act 1997* at Part VIII.

93 Andrew F. Christie, John Davidson, and Fiona Rotstein, "Canada's Private Copying Levy — Does it Comply with Canada's International Treaty Obligations?" (2006) 20 IPJ 111 (http://papers.ssrn.com/sol3/papers.cfm?abstract_id=980845).

94 *Ibid.*

95 Bill C-32; *Ibid.*

96 *Canada Copyright Act 1921*; *Canada Copyright Act 1923*.

97 *Canada Copyright Act 1923*, s.2.

to republish American books if these were not printed in Canada. This provision might be seen either as unnecessary or as a failure, as it was rarely, if ever, used.[98]

The domestic demands of smaller net copyright importers often conflict with international efforts to bolster rights holders' demands in ways that make workable compromise difficult. Efforts to create compulsory licensing systems or other special provisions in the interests of developing or intermediate countries have, in many cases, resulted in narrow and complex solutions that fail to be used. For example, the 1971 Appendix to the *Berne Convention*, instituted for the benefit of developing countries, has also had little practical effect.[99] Ricketson and Ginsburg write:

> It is hard to point to any obvious benefits that have flowed directly to developing countries from the adoption of the Appendix. Indeed, only a handful of developing countries have availed themselves of its provisions in the time since its adoption. Furthermore, of those countries that have made the necessary declarations, very few actually seem to have implemented such licensing schemes in their domestic laws.[100]

The current copyright bill also proposes a number of made-in-Canada solutions.[101] First, it would institute a notice-and-notice system requiring internet service providers to forward notice of claimed infringement to the Internet user in order to avoid paying statutory damages.[102] The notice-and-notice system was created by Canadian internet service providers and has been in use by them for some time. It acts as an alternative to the American notice-and-takedown system, which requires internet service providers to remove allegedly infringing content on notification of an alleged infringement under certain procedures. The American system has been criticized for requiring the takedown of content without sufficient oversight, leading to potential abuse. Second, the current copyright bill provides a set of made-in-Canada provisions for the benefit of people

---

98 Canada, Royal Commission on Patents, Copyright, Trade Marks and Industrial Designs, *Report on Copyright*. (Ottawa: Supply and Services Canada, 1957) at 31.

99 *Berne Convention for the Protection of Literary and Artistic Works. Paris Act of July 24, 1971, as Amended on September 28, 1979*, (Geneva: World Intellectual Property Organization, 1979) at Appendix (www.wipo.int/treaties/en/ip/berne/trtdocs_wo001.html)

100 Sam Ricketson and Jane Ginsburg, *International Copyright and Neighbouring Rights: The Berne Convention and Beyond*, 2d ed. (London: Oxford University Press, 2006) 957.

101 *Bill C-32*.

102 *Ibid.*, s.47.

with print disabilities.[103] These provisions are intended to allow, on certain conditions, non-profit organizations working for the benefit of persons with print disabilities, to make special-format copies of works and to share those special-format copies with similar organizations in other countries. They respond to efforts internationally to allow greater international circulation of works for the benefit of the visually impaired. The approach set forward in the current copyright bill has been trumpeted as being forward-thinking, and criticized for placing too many limitations and conditions on organizations attempting to work for the benefit of the print disabled.[104] Third, C-32 creates an exception for user-generated content, also known as "the YouTube exception," to allow individuals to create "mash-ups" using existing works and to post these online, on various conditions, including that the use of the new work is non-commercial, and that there is no substantial adverse effect on the exploitation of the existing work.[105]

It remains to be seen whether Canada's latest copyright innovations will meet with success domestically, and whether they will be taken up as examples for other countries to follow. Canada's notice-and-notice regime, while practicable and well-used, may be ill-timed to act as a model for other countries, many of whom have already adopted the American notice-and-takedown approach. The proposed provisions for the benefit of the print disabled may, on the other hand, be well timed. However, if critics are correct, they may prove narrow, burdensome, and bureaucratic, consigning them to the same failure that has met various other approaches intended to meet the needs of Canadian interests, developing countries, and other special cases. The "YouTube exception" is narrower than exceptions provided under fair use, and this narrowness may restrict its attractiveness as model. Gendreau notes that, generally, made-in-Canada approaches have not met with the success that would see them set precedents for other countries to follow:

> Even when it has been the first to introduce certain schemes, whether it be moral rights in copyright countries, an administrative tribunal

---

103 *Ibid.*, s.36.

104 Vincent Doré, *Bill C-32: Improving Global Access to Copyrighted Material for the Print Disabled*, www.iposgoode.ca/2010/06/bill-c-32-improving-global-access-to-copyrighted-material-for-the-print-disabled; Knowledge Ecology International, *KEI critical of Canada's Bill C-32 provisions on export of accessible works for persons with disabilities*, http://keionline.org/node/866.

105 Bill C-32, s. 22.

> to oversee the setting of copyright royalties, or compulsory licenses for the exportation of patented drugs to developing countries, these measures have not been recognised as trail-blazing breakthroughs that were meant to be followed by other countries.[106]

The made-in-Canada solutions under C-32 may not be intended to act as a model for other countries to follow. This may make Canada's international negotiating position less favourable. For example, had Canada's notice-and-notice regime been legislated earlier, Canada might be in a stronger position now to press for the preservation of flexibility for such solutions under international agreements, such as the *Anti-Counterfeiting Trade Agreement* (ACTA), which is currently under negotiation. Policy solutions that have widespread appeal and that have been adopted by many countries are more likely to be incorporated and made room for in international agreements, whereas unique solutions that are not taken up elsewhere can be left to butt up against international obligations.

E. CANADIAN LEADERSHIP

Canada has often historically been situated as a *potential* leader in international copyright, but has generally ceded this leadership to stronger powers. Canada's copyright rebellion of 1889 failed after being put down by the British who feared that Canada's withdrawal from the *Berne Convention* might break up the Berne international copyright system. British officials saw Canada as a leader among British colonies and feared that if Canada were to withdraw from the *Berne Convention*, other colonies and countries might follow Canada's lead. A British committee studying the matter wrote that "the lead given to Canada would not improbably be followed by other colonies, and thus the whole system of Imperial copyright would be broken up."[107] Canada's rebellion was put down and the *Berne Convention* held together.

In the early twentieth century, Canada was the lead colony in the British Empire and the colony with the most radical stance on copyright issues. In 1910 Canada led efforts at the Imperial Copyright Conference for significant change in the Imperial copyright system; Canada's loud protests against Imperial copyright law and insistence on copyright autonomy

---

106 Gendreau at 296.

107 Great Britain. *Report of the Departmental Representatives Appointed to Consider the Canadian Copyright Act of 1889* (E 1701), London: n.p., 1892, Ottawa, Library and Archives Canada (Prime Minister Abbott fonds (MG26 C), Vol. 5 File: Copyright) 19.

led to eventual copyright "sovereignty" for British colonies. At the same time, the copyright sovereignty won by Canada was a relative sovereignty tempered by obligations that had been transposed onto the international copyright system.

In the 1960s and '70s, Canada attempted to take leadership to create a coalition of intermediate countries who were not considered to be "developing" but who were net copyright importers. After discussions with several other countries in 1969, Canadian delegates reported that:

> There is strong evidence that support for Canada's position is available from certain other countries if it is properly explored and developed. There appears to be every possibility that Canada for the first time can play a leading role in shaping the course of international copyright by fostering and leading a block of countries with interests similar to Canada. To a large extent we could conceivably control a certain balance of power, given active participation.[108]

However, this initiative failed for a number of reasons: the lack of support found amongst other countries; hesitancy of various government officials to support such a stand; the clash between visions of an activist Canada and the more traditional vision of Canada as a good international citizen aligned with major powers; and fears that such a stance would affect Canada's relations with countries like the United States, the United Kingdom and France. Perhaps what was missing more than anything was a firm high-level policy on Canada's position in international copyright; Canadian delegates, returning from international meetings, repeated the hope that a more in-depth examination of Canada's position would soon become available, and the need for such an undertaking.[109]

Canada is one amongst a large majority of countries in the world that are net copyright importers. Canadian expertise in copyright; the country's bilingualism and bijuralism that place Canada between the major traditions of copyright and *droit d'auteur*, the country's long history of commitment to copyright multilateralism; Canada's position as a significant economy that is nevertheless a copyright importer; and Canada's

---

108 *Report of the Canadian Delegation: Meetings of the Intergovernmental Copyright Committee of the Universal Copyright Convention and the Permanent Committee of the Berne Union, Paris, December 15-19, 1969*, Ottawa, Library and Archives Canada (RG19 Vol 5168 File 8510-6785-3 pt 4).

109 *Ibid.* See also, *Memorandum to the Minister: Report of the Canadian Delegation at the Washington Meeting, September 29–October 3, 1969*, 10 October 1969, 2 and 4, Ottawa, Library and Archives Canada (RG19 Vol 5574 File 8510-C785-1 Part 2).

proximity to the United States all place Canada in a position of potential leadership in international copyright. However, tensions among domestic and international demands often prevent a leadership position from being realized.

If Canada is to lead in the sense of proffering workable made-in-Canada solutions to problems in international copyright, three problems must be overcome: first, the tendency to take a very slow approach to implementing international copyright norms. This is because this slow approach, while allowing Canada to benefit from the experiences of other countries, prevents Canada's solutions from setting a timely example for others to follow. Second, Canada must avoid instituting solutions that are so narrow, burdensome, and bureaucratic that they are not used by those they are intended to benefit. Third, firm high-level policy direction has been historically difficult to ascertain on matters of copyright. Such direction — consistent with the historical emphases on copyright independence, safeguarding the interests of Canadian consumers and creators, finding innovative solutions to meet the needs of both consumers and creators, and support for international copyright and copyright multilateralism — is necessary if Canada is to leverage its position on international copyright and create made-in-Canada solutions to problems in international copyright.

F. CONCLUSION

David Vaver predicts that, in the new millennium, "there will be no *Canadian* copyright law."[110] Due to the pressure of international agreements, he argues that Canadian copyright law will come to look more and more like the laws of other countries. Since 1842, Canada's law has operated under international and imperial pressures to conform to norms that left little room for variance. At the same time, space has been made for distinct, if minor, Canadian variations that sometimes comply with and sometimes challenge international copyright norms.

Bill C-32 responds to the same pressures, domestic and international, that have historically characterized Canadian copyright reform. Canada's past responses to this pressure have ranged from rebellion to compliance. Bill C-32, to a greater extent than its predecessor in Bill C-60, bows to international demands and goes beyond the minimum requirements of the WIPO Internet treaties. Bill C-32 thus abandons the trend, adopted in

110 David Vaver, "Copyright in Canada: The New Millennium," (1997) 12 IPJ 117 at 120.

past reforms, of maintaining Canadian policy flexibility and adhering on a minimalist basis to international treaties.

Canadian copyright has traditionally focussed on copyright independence, safeguarding the interests of Canadian consumers as well as Canadian creators, finding innovative solutions to meet the needs of both consumers and creators, and support for international copyright and copyright multilateralism. The made-in-Canada elements of C-32 are relatively narrow compared to previous bills that asserted a made-in-Canada stance on the broader issue of anti-circumvention. Bill C-32, while including innovative solutions for the benefit of specific interests such as the print disabled, internet service providers, and mash-up video creators, departs from the tradition of maintaining maximum independence and safeguarding consumer interests on the issue of anti-circumvention measures.

Although Canada has historically been situated as a *potential* leader in international copyright, leadership has generally been ceded to stronger powers; under C-32, Canada would repeat this trend. The previous Bill C-60 was trumpeted as a "made-in-Canada" copyright bill. Bill C-32, on the central issue of anti-circumvention, would drop this vision of Canadian independence and innovation, instead following an American-led maximalist implementation of the WIPO Internet treaties.

CHAPTER TWO

North American Digital Copyright, Regional Governance, and the Potential for Variation

Blayne Haggart

In 1994, Canada, the United States, and Mexico implemented the North American Free Trade Agreement (NAFTA), which was designed to provide a framework for the governance of a North American economy. One of the most significant parts of the agreement was Chapter 17, which dealt with intellectual property (IP) and was designed to bring Mexican IP law in line with that of the United States (Canadian IP law was already substantially similar to that of the US). Referring to the copyright sections of Chapter 17, Acheson and Maule describe the treaty as a step in the continuing harmonization of North American copyright law, itself embedded in a process of global harmonization spearheaded by the 1995 Agreement on the Trade-Related Aspects of Intellectual Property (TRIPs) at the World Trade Organization (WTO).[1]

Even given the NAFTA's effect on Mexico, and the tighter incorporation of Mexico and Canada into the economic orbit of the regional and global hegemon, the three countries continue to possess distinctive copyright regimes. This is all the stranger as the United States has placed IP and copyright policy at the heart of its international economic agenda since the mid-1980s.[2] Instead, somewhat ironically, the structure of the NAFTA has

---

1 Keith Acheson & Christopher J. Maule, "Copyright, Contract, the Cultural Industries, and NAFTA" in Emile G. McAnany & Kenton T. Wilkinson, eds. *Mass Media and Free Trade: NAFTA and the Cultural Industries* (Austin: University of Texas Press, 1996) 351.

2 See the 1995 *Agreement on Trade-Related Aspects of Intellectual Property* (TRIPs), which paved the way for the creation of the World Trade Organization, Chapter 17

allowed Canada and Mexico some leeway to pursue independent copyright policies, within a global copyright regime shaped largely by the United States. Over fifteen years after the NAFTA was concluded, domestic factors continue to be at least as significant as US-based pressures for harmonization in the making of copyright policy.

The complex nature of the North American governance of copyright policy can be seen in the processes that have shaped the three countries' attempts to implement two 1996 US-backed treaties, the World Intellectual Property Organization (WIPO) *Copyright Treaty* (WCT) and *Performances and Phonograms Treaty* (WPPT), jointly known as the WIPO Internet treaties. The most controversial part of the treaties requires legal protection for technological protection measures (TPMs), or digital locks applied to digital products like MP3s, ebooks, and movies, and the devices that read them.

The three countries, however, have taken dramatically different paths in their attempts to implement this part of the Internet Treaties. The United States adopted a strong, "maximalist" approach to the legal protection of TPMs, outlawing the trade in devices that can circumvent TPMs, while Canada and Mexico have yet to implement their commitments, almost fouteen years after the treaties were concluded. In Canada's case, successive governments have proposed different approaches to TPMs; the current Conservative government appears set on following the US "maximalist" approach, while the previous Liberal government advocated a "minimalist" approach that would have made it a crime to break a digital lock only if it were done for purposes of infringing the underlying copyright. In Mexico, full implementation of the treaties is likely several years away, though its domestic situation seems to favour the adoption of a US-style approach.

While these events seem to indicate a convergence on a "North American" view of TPMs, from a governance perspective this headline view obscures a messier reality: that decisions regarding how to implement the WIPO Internet treaties continue to be made by domestic governments and are shaped by interests, foreign and domestic, working through domestic institutions. Consequently, whether the countries move toward increasing

---

of the 1994 North American Free Trade Agreement, Chapter 17 of the 2005 United States–Australia Free Trade Agreement, Article 14 of the 1985 United States–Israel Free Trade Agreement, and Article 4 of the 2001 United States–Jordan Free Trade Agreement. Other examples are available at www.ustr.gov/trade-agreements/free-trade-agreements.

similarity or persistent differences is an open question, dependent on the dynamics in play within the three countries. Furthermore, the NAFTA, North America's "external constitution,"[3] which provides a baseline for copyright law in the three countries, contains both the potential to promote and hinder this harmonization.

Using an historical institutionalist approach, which emphasizes historical contingency and institutional persistence, this paper uses the implementation of the legal protection of TPMs to demonstrate the subtle regional dynamics and dominant domestic politics that have shaped the three countries' responses to these treaties. It argues that while the United States government and US copyright industries are influential in shaping the copyright policies of its neighbours, the triumph of US-style copyright law in Canada and Mexico depends more on the domestic configuration of institutions and interests than on regional dynamics. Most importantly from a democratic-governance perspective, US-style copyright law in Canada and Mexico is not a foregone conclusion. The particular nature of North American regional and copyright governance, described below, provides the three federal governments with a significant degree of leeway in setting autonomous copyright policies.

Understanding how North American copyright policymaking functions requires understanding the interplay of domestic and regional institutions. In Canada, this question has a particular urgency given the recent introduction of Bill C-32, *The Copyright Modernization Act*. In addition to the public-policy issues raised by the bill, ably discussed elsewhere in this volume, there lies the larger question of how much ability Canada has to chart its own path on copyright reform in a way that responds to Canadians' needs and desires.

This paper is divided into four sections. The first provides a brief overview of historical institutionalism, particularly as a way to think about regional governance, while the second provides a very brief overview of copyright, the requirements of the Internet treaties, and the specific way in which the three North American countries have (or have not) implemented the treaties. The third section analyzes the implementation process and policy dynamics in the three countries. The paper then offers some overall comments and conclusions in the context of Bill C-32.

---

3 Stephen Clarkson, "Canada's Secret Constitution: NAFTA, WTO and the End of Sovereignty?" (Ottawa: Canadian Centre for Policy Alternatives, 2002) (www.policyalternatives.ca/sites/default/files/uploads/publications/National_Office_Pubs/clarkson_constitution.pdf).

A. HISTORICAL INSTITUTIONALISM

The shadow of Europe looms large over theories of how regions work. The two main "grand theories" of regional integration, neofunctionalism and intergovernmentalism, were developed to explain and legitimize Western Europe's postwar attempts at integration, including the European Union.[4] However, these theories do not translate well to North America, whose regional governance remains "undertheorized."[5] Their focus on strong supranational institutions as a driver of regional integration, for example, is not very helpful to understanding a continent characterized by a regional/global hegemon and weak supranational institutions.

In contrast, a mid-range approach like historical institutionalism (HI) offers a useful way to study North America because it does not privilege any particular configuration of institutions; nor does it assume that supranational institutions are necessarily positive forces for integration. In HI, institutions are seen as semi-persistent "constraints or rules that induce stability in human interaction"[6] and structure individuals' and groups' interactions with each other and with broader social forces. Actors pursue strategic self-interests, which are partly shaped by the institutional "rules of the game," and encounter institutions both as constraints on action and as rules that can be modified by the actors.[7] Change in HI is not driven wholly from on high (structuralism) or below (individualism/atomism), but emerges through the interaction of both within an institutional structure whose rules and procedures structure these changes.

---

4 Thomas Diez & Antje Wiener, "Introducing the Mosaic of Integration Theory" in *European Integration Theory* (Oxford: Oxford University Press, 2004) 1 at 13–14. For an overview of the regionalism literature, including neofunctionalism and intergovernmentalism, see Young Jong Choi & James A. Caporaso, "Comparative Regional Integration" in Walter Carlsnaes, Thomas Risse, & Beth A, Simmons, eds., *Handbook of International Relations*. 3d ed. (London: Sage, 2005) 480.

5 Laura Spitz, "The Evolving Architecture of North American Integration, 80 University of Colorado Law Review (May, 15 2009) 735 at 735 (http://ssrn.com/abstract=1405397).

6 T.R. Voss, "Institutions" in N. J. Smelser and P. B. Baltes, eds., *International Encyclopedia of the Social & Behavioral Sciences* (Amsterdam and New York: Elsevier Science, 2001) 7561 at 7561.

7 One way to think of this is by introducing time into one's analysis, as in Archer's "morphogenic" analytic approach. In the initial time period, actors confront institutions as pre-existing rules. In the second period, however, actors can work to modify these rules, so that the rules have been changed in the third period. The choice of time periods is made for analytical purposes: in actuality, actors continually make and remake institutions (Margaret S. Archer, *Realist Social Theory: The Morphogenetic Approach* (Cambridge: Cambridge University Press, 1995)).

One test of a theory's usefulness is where it directs the researcher's eye. HI emphasizes institutional persistence, and particularly the concept of "path dependence," which refers to the claim that the initial establishment of an institution is highly sensitive to historical contingency, in which small, early events can have large future consequences.[8] Once established, institutions structure future actions, resulting not so much in institutional stasis, but, rather, "constrained innovation"[9] and institutional persistence: "preceding steps in a particular direction induce further movement in the same direction."[10] Understanding what leads to path dependence or divergence from a path requires paying attention to "who is invested in particular arrangements, exactly how that investment is sustained over time, and perhaps those who are not invested in the institutions are kept out," and what might impair this form of reproduction and lead to change.[11]

An HI approach starts with the relevant institutions and asks how they structure and constitute actors. It also requires identifying the underlying processes that support these institutions, including the various paradigms and public sentiments that support or undermine them, and the frames and programs that are deployed by interested actors in order to promote their perspective. Attention must be paid to the (potentially conflicting) logics of competing and complementary institutions, as well as to changes in these institutional supports over time, either as the result of exogenous or endogenous shocks. HI also requires the identification of the relevant actors, their interests, resources and strategies employed.

Such an approach is particularly useful when considering how policies develop in a region like North America, in which domestic institutions retain official decision-making power within a continental market governed by the NAFTA.

---

8 Ira Katznelson, "Periodization and Preferences: Reflections on Purposive Action in Comparative Historical Social Science" in James Mahoney & Dietrich Rueschemeyer, eds., *Comparative Historical Analysis in the Social Sciences* (Cambridge: Cambridge University Press, 2003) 270 at 291; Paul Pierson & Theda Skocpol, "Historical Institutionalism in Contemporary Political Science" in Ira Katznelson & Helen Milner, eds., *Political Science: The State of the Discipline* (New York: Norton, 2002) 693 at 699 (http://gking.harvard.edu/ArticleS/PieSk002.pdf).

9 John L. Campbell, *Institutional Change and Globalization* (Princeton: Princeton University Press, 2004).

10 Paul Pierson, "Increasing Returns, Path Dependence, and the Study of Politics" (2000) 94 The American Political Science Review 251 at 251–52.

11 Kathleen Thelen, "Historical Institutionalism in Comparative Politics" (1999) 2 Annual Review of Political Science 369 at 391.

B. NORTH AMERICAN REGIONAL INSTITUTIONS AND ACTORS

North America is characterized by a significant economic imbalance between the regional/global hegemon, the United States, and its neighbours, whose economic well-being depends to a large degree on access to the US market. In 2008, the United States was the destination for 78% of Canada's exports and the source of 52% of its imports. Similarly, Mexico sent 80% of its exports to the United States and received 49% of its imports there. In contrast, the United States sent only 20% of its exports to Canada and 12% to Mexico, and received only 16% and 10% of its imports from Canada and Mexico, respectively.[12] This imbalance and dependence has long caused policymakers in Canada and Mexico, at the very least, to pay attention to their neighbour's concerns.

As Sell, Drahos and Braithwaite and others have documented,[13] the United States has pursued strong international copyright reform that favours its copyright industries since the mid-1980s. Since that time, US governments have depended mainly on trade agreements to convince other countries to adopt US-style copyright and IP regimes, specifically, offering market access (or threatening economic sanctions) in exchange for stronger IP protection. The TRIPs Agreement, for example, was the price demanded by the United States for the World Trade Organization, and a deal on agriculture desired by developing countries.[14] What is true internationally is also true in North America. The United States, working for and with its content industries, has been the most insistent actor for copyright reform in Canada and Mexico. In the negotiations that led to the NAFTA, it was the party that was most interested in IP issues, and in the debate over the implementation of the WIPO Internet treaties, it has been the most insistent voice in favour of their (US-style) implementation.

---

12 World Trade Organization Statistics Database, Trade Profiles, http://stat.wto.org/CountryProfile/WSDBCountryPFView.aspx?Language=E&Country=CA,MX,US.

13 Susan K. Sell, *Private Power, Public Law: The Globalization of Intellectual Property Rights* (Cambridge: Cambridge University Press, 2003); Peter Drahos with John Braithwaite, *Information Feudalism: Who Owns the Knowledge Economy?* (London: Earthscan Publications Ltd., 2002).

14 Sell, above note 13 at 37; Drahos with Braithwaite, above note 13 at 11. Though, as Sell remarks, developing countries asked for, and received, the phase-out of the *Multi-fibre Agreement*, which protected US textile interests, in return. Thumm provides more background on the fears and desires of developing and developed countries with respect to the negotiation of the TRIPs (Nikolaus Thumm, *Intellectual Property Rights: National Systems and Harmonisation in Europe* (New York: Physica-Verlag, 2000) at 63–64).

Institutionally, the NAFTA has had two main effects on North American copyright policies. First, it reoriented Mexican copyright law. The United States used the promise of enhanced market access to exact concessions on copyright, primarily from Mexico. Prior to the NAFTA, and the subsequent 1997 overhaul of Mexico's *Ley Federal del Derecho de Autor*, Mexican copyright law (or *derechos de autor*, literally authors' rights) and the domestic institutions supporting it had been mainly concerned with protecting authors' moral rights in their works. As part of the overall NAFTA deal, itself rooted in the neoliberal model that replaced Mexico's discredited import-substitution-industrialization model,[15] Mexico agreed to US demands that it restructure its copyright regime to emphasize copyright as an economic right available to publishers, distributors and other middlemen — including foreign companies — rather than just a primarily moral right available to authors. It therefore expanded the number, type and focus of Mexican groups with a stake in the copyright debate. Post-NAFTA, Mexican copyright law is now more focused on the contractual aspects of copyright than it was before.[16]

Second, the NAFTA has, somewhat ironically, constrained the ability of the United States to influence economic and copyright policy in its neighbours. It cannot be modified easily: the NAFTA does not contain any mechanisms to allow for routine updating of or changes to the NAFTA. This lack is particularly important when dealing with an issue like copyright, where technological change often leads to pressure for change in copyright law. As a result, NAFTA's copyright provisions are quite brittle: they lock in a certain level copyright protection that will come under increasing pressure with the normal passage of time and technological change. Any change must therefore come via a channel other than the NAFTA itself.

As well, by ensuring Canada and Mexico of a certain level of guaranteed access to its market, the United States has effectively limited its ability to link copyright reform to market access. Far from being a force for convergence, the NAFTA is, at least potentially, a force for continued policy divergence.

The overall effect of the NAFTA is therefore indeterminate. Altering the focus of Mexican copyright does influence the future direction of Mexican

---

15 Stephanie R. Golob, "Beyond the Policy Frontier: Canada, Mexico and the Ideological Origins of NAFTA" (2003) 55 World Politics 361. For an overview of how the NAFTA changed Mexican IP and copyright law, see Maryse Robert, Negotiating NAFTA: Explaining the Outcome in Culture, Textiles, Autos, and Pharmaceuticals (Toronto: University of Toronto Press, 2001).

16 Robert, above note 15 at 53.

copyright-policy debates. This change, however, came at the price of a reduced ability of the United States to influence directly Mexican (and Canadian) copyright policy: with the NAFTA and secure market access in place, the United States could no longer use the carrot of increased market access or the stick of reduced access to convince Mexico or Canada to change its laws. Instead, the US government (a regional actor in this sense) has had to resort to other means of influence, such as deploying (not inconsequential) diplomatic pressure via its embassies, its content industries (such as Hollywood and the music industry, themselves global players with interests in Canada and Mexico), and through the Special 301 process, an annual, though largely toothless, review of other countries' IP policies.

As for other actors, there is little or no evidence of regional civil-society groups and little cross-border cooperation beyond information-sharing. Indeed, Mexico's nascent copyright civil-society groups have stronger links to Spain and the rest of Latin and South America than they do with groups in the US or Canada.[17]

North American copyright governance, therefore, is characterized by a brittle regional framework that is not easily modified. While the regional hegemon, the United States, may be interested in copyright reform in Canada and Mexico, in the absence of strong regional institutions and with no mechanism to make regional law, pressure to reform copyright law must run through domestic institutions, which can be expected to have a determinative effect on the copyright debate in the three countries. This is, indeed, the case.

C. THE 1996 WIPO INTERNET TREATIES AND TECHNOLOGICAL PROTECTION MEASURES

On December 20, 1996, Canada, Mexico, and the United States joined over sixty other countries in adopting the Internet treaties. The treaties were a US-driven response[18] to the challenges posed to copyright policy in a

---

17 For example, the first academic book on copyright and "free culture" was a co-production involving the Spanish Embassy in Mexico's *Centro Cultural de España:* Alberto López Cuenca & Eduardo Ramírez Pedrajo, eds., *Propiedad Intelectual, Nuevas Tecnologías y Libre Acceso a La Cultura* (Puebla: Universidad de las Américas Puebla/Centro Cultural de España México, 2009) (www.ccemx.org/img_act_x_tipo/propiedadint.pdf).

18 Pamela Samuelson, "The US Digital Agenda at the World Intellectual Property Organization" (1997), http://people.ischool.berkeley.edu/~pam/courses/cyberlaw97/docs/wipo.pdf.

digital age: how to enforce copyright law given technology (personal computers and the Internet) that allowed individuals to reproduce and distribute, easily and inexpensively, anything that could be converted into zeroes and ones.

One of the responses, covered in the treaty, concerned extending legal protections to digital locks, or TPMs. TPMs control the access and use of the work that it has locked down. For example, someone can place a TPM on a .pdf file that requires the user to input a password before the work can be copied or altered. Or a TPM on a song or a movie can limit the number of times it is played, on what machines it can be played, or how many times (if at all) it can be copied.

As these examples show, while TPMs can limit copy making (which copyright also does), their uses can also extend toward attempts at market control (e.g., making some works useable only on some machines) and interfering with existing user rights under copyright (among other issues).[19] For example, every copyright law allows copying for academic purposes. However, a password-protected .pdf that prevents an academic from copying a paragraph from that document is a (small) restriction on her legal rights. These digital locks can have similar effects when placed on works already in the public domain, restricting the legal right of users to copy these works.[20]

From the copyright owner's perspective, TPMs have a significant drawback—they can be broken, often quite easily. TPMs on their own cannot fully lock down digital content. In response, copyright owners have sought to make it illegal to break TPMs. Such legal protection presents a difficult policy issue: how to ensure that such protection does not interfere

---

19 See, e.g., Jeremy de Beer, "Constitutional Jurisdiction Over Paracopyright Laws" in Michael Geist, ed., *In the Public Interest: The Future of Canadian Copyright Law* (Toronto: Irwin Law, 2005) 89 (www.irwinlaw.com/content/assets/content-commons/120/Two_01_deBeer.pdf); Jeremy de Beer, "Copyright and Innovation in the Networked Information Economy" *Social Science Research Network* (May 26, 2009) (http://ssrn.com/abstract=1410158); Pamela Samuelson, "DRM {and, Or, Versus} the Law" (2003) 46 Communications of the ACM 41; Ian R. Kerr, Alana Maurushat, & Christian S. Tacit, "Technical Protection Measures: Tilting at Copyright's Windmill" (2002-2003) 34 Ottawa Law Review 6 (www.commonlaw.uottawa.ca/index.php?option=com_docman&task=doc_download&gid=232); Jessica Litman, *Digital Copyright* (Amherst: Prometheus Books, 2006); and Tarleton Gillespie, *Wired Shut: Copyright and the Shape of Digital Culture* (Cambridge: MIT Press, 2007).

20 Copyright is a right limited in time: after a certain amount of time (generally speaking, life of the author plus 50 years in Canada; life plus 70 years in the United States and life plus 100 years in Mexico), a work is said to enter into the "public domain" and be freely copiable by anyone without permission or payment.

with users' right to break locks when the locks have nothing to do with copyright or to exercise their rights under copyright law.

During the negotiations that led to the Internet treaties, the United States, backed by its content industries, pushed for a ban on the sale of all devices that could circumvent digital locks, a maximalist position that would have provided strong protection to copyright owners' works, but with the major negative effect of making it impossible for non-hackers to access the tools needed to exercise their legal and legitimate rights.[21] This position has the potential to render impotent the user-creator-owner balances that have been negotiated into copyright law over centuries. TPMs protected too strongly allow those who control the locks to set the conditions of use, potentially far and beyond those allowed by copyright law. At its worst, legal protection of TPMs has the potential to effectively privatize copyright law by placing it in the hands of those who control the digital locks.

However, as the result of objections by developing countries and US consumer-electronics industries (who make their living by providing access to copyrighted works), the final wording required only that signatories

> provide adequate legal protection and effective legal remedies against the circumvention of effective technological measures that are used by authors in connection with the exercise of their rights under this Treaty or the Berne Convention and that restrict acts, in respect of their works, which are not authorized by the authors concerned or permitted by law.[22]

A minimalist interpretation of these provisions would make it a crime to break a digital lock only if it is done for the purpose, or with the effect of, violating an underlying copyright. While there is some controversy over this language, particularly the meaning of "adequate" and "effective,"[23] the treaties provide countries with significant leeway in interpreting how

21 Samuelson, above note 18.

22 WIPO *Copyright Treaty*, Art. 11. The WIPO *Performances and Phonograms Treaty* (Art. 18) uses the same language with respect to performers and phonograms producers.

23 See, e.g., Sam Ricketson & Jane C. Ginsburg, *International Copyright and Neighbouring Rights: The Berne Convention and Beyond*, 2d ed., vol. 2 (Oxford: Oxford University Press, 2006); and Myra Tawfik, "International Copyright Law: W[h]ither User Rights?" in Michael Geist, ed., *In the Public Interest: The Future of Canadian Copyright Law* (Toronto: Irwin Law, 2005) 66 at 80 (www.irwinlaw.com/content/assets/content-commons/120/One_03_Tawfik.pdf).

strong protection should be, and seems to limit it only to copyright, and is not meant to be an expansive right.[24]

1) Country Choices

a) The United States

The three North American countries have implemented the treaties in different ways. In 1998, the United States passed the *Digital Millennium Copyright Act* (DMCA), a maximalist interpretation of the treaties. Section 1201 of the DMCA, subject to certain limitations, protects a TPM that restricts access and use in the service of a copyright owners' rights. What makes the DMCA a maximalist interpretation of the WIPO Internet treaties is that it forbids people to "manufacture, import, offer to the public, provide, or otherwise traffic in any technology, product, service, device, component, or part thereof," that would allow individuals to circumvent TPMs designed to control access or limits copying of a work, if the following criteria are met:

- The device is primarily designed for this purpose,
- It has only limited commercially significant otherwise, or
- It is marketed as such a circumvention device.[25]

Despite provisions to allow for circumvention in limited cases, including the exercise of fair-use rights and non-copyright-related matters, this ban, and a triennial "rule-making" process that allows for the expansion of this list, prohibiting trade in the tools needed for most people to exercise these rights makes it difficult for users to exercise their rights under the law. Since the passage of the DMCA, the US government and US content industries have aggressively sought the implementation of DMCA-type rules by other countries, including Canada and Mexico.

b) Canada

In Canada and Mexico, the situation is more complicated. Canada, following public hearings and studies in 2001 and 2002, has attempted to implement the treaties three times. In 2005, a minority Liberal government

---

24 That said, proponents of US-style TPM protection argue that strong protection is needed in order for the law to "adequately" and "effectively" protect copyright owners' rights.

25 *Digital Millennium Copyright Act*, 17 USC. §§ 1201(a)(2) and 1201(a)(3)(B) (2000) (www.law.cornell.edu/uscode/html/uscode17/usc_sec_17_00001201----000-.html).

proposed a "minimalist" bill, C-60,[26] that would have made it illegal to break a TPM only for the purposes of infringing the underlying copyright; trade in circumvention devices was ignored.[27] The bill died on the order paper when the January 2006 election was called. In December 2007, the current minority Conservative government attempted to introduce a bill that would have largely copied the TPM provisions of the US DMCA. However, its introduction to Parliament was delayed for six months by an unexpected public-grassroots outcry during a particularly sensitive period in which the minority Conservative government could not be sure that it could control the House of Commons;[28] the delay was enough to make the eventual bill, C-61, *An Act to Amend the Copyright Act* (which kept the controversial US-style TPM protections), a second victim of an election call, in September 2008. In the summer of 2009, the government held public hearings into copyright reform, in which most Canadians voiced strong opposition to DMCA-style TPM protection. In June 2010, the government introduced Bill C-32, *The Copyright Modernization Act*, which included several new consumer-friendly amendments, but with TPM provisions that essentially duplicated Bill C-61 and the DMCA.[29] As of July 2010, it had passed First Reading, with committee hearings planned for fall 2010.

c) Mexico

Mexico, as part of a comprehensive reform of its copyright law instigated by its NAFTA obligations, provided limited legal protection for TPMs in 1997, but only for those protecting computer software. In language similar to that which would be drafted into the 1998 US DMCA, Article 112 of the *Ley Federal del Derecho de Autor* (LFDA) prohibits "the importation, manufacture, distribution and use of equipment or the services intended to eliminate the technical protection of computer programs, of transmissions across the spectrum of electromagnetic and telecommunications networks and programs' electronic elements," while Article 231(V) imposes criminal sanctions on the importation, sale, lease of any program

26 Bill C-60, *An Act to Amend the Copyright Act*, 1st Sess., 38th Parl., 2005 (as read at first reading by the House of Commons 20 June 2005).

27 Sam N.K. Banks and Andrew Kitching, "Bill C-60: *An Act to Amend the Copyright Act*" (Legislative Summary, 20 September 2005), (www2.parl.gc.ca/Sites/LOP/LegislativeSummaries/Bills_ls.asp?lang=e&source=library_prb&Parl=38&Ses=1&ls=C60).

28 Blayne Haggart, *North American Digital Copyright, Regional Governance and the Potential for Variation* (PhD dissertation, Carleton University) [forthcoming].

29 See Michael Geist, "The Case for Flexibility in Implementing the WIPO Internet Treaties: An Examination of the Anti-Circumvention Requirements" in this volume.

or performance of any act that would have as its purpose the deactivation of the protective electronic controls of computer software. Violation of these articles is punishable by imprisonment of three to ten years and a fine of 2,000 to 20,000 times the minimum daily wage. Furthermore, while the LFDA does not define circumvention, a non-paper presented at WIPO by the *Instituto Nacional del Derecho De Autor* (INDAUTOR), Mexico's copyright authority, suggests that currently circumvention would only become a legal issue if an underlying copyright or author's rights had been infringed.[30] A 2003 copyright-reform bill was silent on TPMs and WIPO treaty implementation generally.

D. EXPLAINING IMPLEMENTATION

1) United States

US implementation of the Internet treaties can be explained almost completely without reference to international or regional factors. US copyright policymaking is a pragmatist's game, involving tradeoffs among various interest groups that have a seat at the table. As Litman documents extensively, copyright-law reform has since the early 1900s involved inter-industry negotiations overseen by a state that acts an arbiter, ratifying the consensus reached by the players at the table.[31] As a result, copyright law reflects the interests and relative strength (economic and political) of those who have been invited to the table, although legislation is crafted in such a way as to offer narrow exceptions to win the support of the various groups involved. Generally speaking, this process is friendly to the status quo: already-established groups have the advantage over upstarts, and specific interests (i.e., industries) generally outclass the overall "public interest," and every invited guest does better than the wallflowers.

In US copyright policy, the content industries—particularly the motion picture and music industries—currently deploy the most politically influential lobbyists, a fact reflected in the general bias of US copyright industry and in the DMCA itself. As two economists critical of copyright argue, Congress has been "bought and paid for" by a content industry,[32]

30 Mexico, Instituto Nacional del Derecho De Autor, *Internet & Technology Provisions: Questions for Discussion*, (Mexico City: Instituto Nacional del Derecho De Autor, 2008) (On file with the author).

31 Litman, above note 19.

32 Michele Boldrin and David K. Levine, *Against Intellectual Monopoly* (Cambridge: Cambridge University Press, 2008) (http://levine.sscnet.ucla.edu/general/intellectual/against.htm).

that has, for example, received (in a separate 1998 bill[33]) retroactive term-of-protection extensions. Article 1, Section 8, Clause 8 of the US Constitution requires that copyright (and IP generally) "promote the Progress of Science and useful Arts, by securing for limited Times to Authors and Inventors the exclusive Right to their respective Writings and Discoveries." A retroactive extension of rights to cover already-created works cannot possibly induce future innovation, meaning that this bill cannot be characterized as anything but pure rent-seeking by the content industries, which own the vast majority of copyrights.

The process that led to the DMCA conformed to this historical pattern of inter-industry bargaining overseen by a generally copyright-friendly congress. In Litman's definitive account of the political process that led to the DMCA, she describes what ended up being a "hodgepodge,"[34] reflecting competing views expressed by the various Congressional committees (which often hold divergent views on what the law should do) and the stakeholders these committee represented.

Generally speaking, however, the TPM provisions were of the maximalist kind desired by the content industries. Groups critical of legal protection of TPMs — research libraries, the consumer-electronics industry and a group of academics and lawyers concerned with "fair use" issues[35] — each received limited exceptions, including a "Rule-making process" that would require the Librarian of Congress to review the legislation every three years in order to determine whether further exemptions should be added to this list.[36] However, the blanket ban on the manufacture and traffic in circumvention devices has been criticized for effectively making it impossible for those lacking the technological savvy to build programs to break digital locks (i.e., most people) to exercise their rights under the *Copyright Act*.[37]

---

33 *Sonny Bono Copyright Term Extension Act of 1998*, Pub.L. 105-298 (http://frwebgate.access.gpo.gov/cgi-bin/getdoc.cgi?dbname=105_cong_public_laws&docid=f:publ298.105.pdf).

34 Litman, above note 19 at 143.

35 Fair use refers to the user rights in copyright law that allow for the making of copies for an open-ended list of activities deemed to be in the public interest.

36 The DMCA overall represented a compromise between the content industries, which wanted legal protection for TPMs and the powerful telecommunications lobby, which wanted (and received) protection from liability for the infringing acts of its customers (above note 33).

37 For an overview of the effects of this section of the DMCA, see Electronic Frontier Foundation (EFF), *Unintended Consequences: Twelve Years Under the DMCA* (March 2010) (www.eff.org/wp/unintended-consequences-under-dmca).

In the end, the TPM language of the DMCA was almost exclusively a function of the domestic US political process. Specifically, the open language of the Internet treaties, while much more permissive than that originally sought by the United States (that language was eventually incorporated into the DMCA), both avoided constraining the US policy-making process in any way while allowing the United States to continue, in good faith, to promote its maximalist approach to copyright (i.e., the DMCA) to other countries as *the* legitimate way that the Internet treaties should be implemented.

2) Canada

Of the three countries, Canadian copyright policies are the most complex, involving a somewhat unique bureaucratic setup, a weak "domestic" lobby for copyright reform, anti-American sentiments and, since the early 2000s, the politicization of what traditionally been seen as a technical, commercial (and politically neutral) law. Taken together, these factors explain both why after 10 years the treaties have still not been implemented and why two maximalist copyrights bills and one minimalist bill have been tabled, but not passed, to date.

Canada's domestic copyright-policymaking institutions[38] are biased toward compromise. Unusually, copyright is the joint responsibility of two departments, the Department of Industry and the Department of Canadian Heritage, each with conflicting, and sometimes diametrically opposed mandates.[39] Generally speaking, performers, writers and other creators — and, most importantly, industry groups like the Canadian Recording Industry Association (CRIA) — see Heritage Canada as their voice,[40] while Industry Canada tends to represent technology industries, consumers, business and investors, from the point of view of wishing to increase Canadian productivity and innovation. On the issue of TPMs,

---

38 This chapter's focus on lawmaking by necessity puts to one side the other ministries and quasi-governmental agencies, which also affect actual policy.

39 Doern & Sharaput remark that the linkage between trade and IP has given the Canadian Department of Foreign Affairs and International Trade an important — they say central — role in the making of IP policy, including copyright (G. Bruce Doern & Markus Sharaput, *Canadian Intellectual Property: The Politics of Innovating Institutions and Interests* (Toronto: University of Toronto Press, 2000). Outside of a trade-negotiation context, however, Foreign Affairs' role is limited and Canadian Heritage and Industry continue to have the official lead on the file.

40 *Ibid.*

then, Heritage Canada's stakeholders favour a maximalist implementation of Canada's WIPO obligations, while Industry Canada's favour a minimalist approach.[41] The vigour with which each bureaucracy defends its mandate often interferes with the timely pursuit of reform, even when their respective ministers are ostensibly in agreement about what should be done.[42]

This tendency to balance largely explains the 2005 bill. As Doyle documents thoroughly, the bill reflected the strenuous lobbying by CRIA of the Department of Canadian Heritage and its then-Minister, Sheila Copps.[43] However, despite Copps' clout in the Liberal party as a senior minister, the strength of the eventual bill's TPM regulations were mitigated by concerns from the civil servants in both the departments of Heritage and Industry about the soundness of the US DMCA approach.[44]

The other truth that must be considered is that, when faced with departments with opposing mandates, political power must be used to break the deadlock. This became clear in the run-up to the eventual introduction, in June 2008, of the minority Conservative government's Bill C-61. Specifically, it demonstrated the often-ignored, but central role of the Prime Minister's Office and the Privy Council Office as the final arbiter of what proposals get introduced to Parliament.

The Conservative government's decision to follow the US DMCA model on TPM protection was political. The PMO's insistence on passing a law the US government would like came over the objections of then-Industry Minister Maxime Bernier, and went against the bureaucratic consensus, circa 2005, described by Doyle (2006). As Michele Austin, then-Industry Minister Maxime Bernier's (2006–2007) chief of staff, recounted in an interview with the author:

> The Prime Minister's Office's position was, move quickly, satisfy the United States and both of our positions were, politically speaking, "Listen, there have been mistakes made in the DMCA, there are a list of exceptions that have been created by court, can we not have DMCA

41 There are exceptions to this rule. In the recent debate, the Entertainment Software Association of Canada, representing video-game manufacturers, has justified its support for DMCA-style legal protection for TPMs in terms of promoting innovation and employment in the Canadian video-game industry.

42 Haggart, above note 28.

43 Copps was Heritage Minister from 1997 to 2003; her Liberal successors continued to support her position.

44 Simon Doyle, *Prey to Thievery* (Ottawa: Simon Doyle, 2006) at 81–82 (www.lulu.com/product/file-download/prey-to-thievery/566014).

> lite?" And they said: 'We don't care what you do, as long as the US is satisfied.'[45]

US pressure on Canada to implement the WIPO Internet treaties predates the Conservative government. For several years, Canada has faced "considerable" American pressure to ratify the treaties quickly with legislation modeled on the US DMCA.[46] It has been mentioned by successive US Ambassadors to Canada and Canada continues to be mentioned on the US Special 301 Watch List (and the higher-level "Priority Watch List" in 2009) of countries with IP laws it deems inadequate. While these actions amount to no more (or no less) than attempts at moral suasion, possible reasons for the PMO's position include a desire to demonstrate that the new Conservative government was more US-friendly than its Liberal predecessor and, more proximately, US insistence in August 2007, within the context of the Security and Prosperity Partnership of North America (SPP), that it would not discuss border-related impediments to Canadian access to the US market if Canada did not move on the copyright file.[47]

In August 2007, Bernier was shuffled to Foreign Affairs and replaced by Jim Prentice, who began to make plans to introduce a copyright bill that would include DMCA-style TPM provisions. While the government had planned to introduce the bill in December 2007, its eventual introduction was delayed until June 2008 for several reasons, including an unexpected burst of grassroots opposition to the bill, instigated by a Facebook group, Fair Copyright for Canada,[48] started by University of Ottawa law professor Michael Geist, combined with Cabinet-level concerns with the bill. Appealing both to policy arguments and emotion, opponents denounced this (as-yet unseen) "born in the USA" copyright bill (thus appealing to a current of anti-Americanism that is rarely hard to find in Canadian political discourse) and calling for public hearings to determine what a balanced "made in Canada" bill should look like. Blindsided by this opposition, and unsure at the time of the strength of the government in the House of Commons, the government decided to postpone the bill for six months. While the resulting bill largely reflected the DMCA position on TPMs, public op-

45 Haggart, above note 28.

46 Myra J. Tawfik, "International Copyright Law: W[h]ither User Rights?" above note 23 at 79.

47 Michael Geist, "How the US Got its Canadian Copyright Bill" *Toronto Star* (June 16, 2008) (www.thestar.com/sciencetech/article/443867).

48 www.facebook.com/group.php?gid=6315846683.

position had been sufficient to delay the bill long enough to make it a victim of the government's September 2008 election call.

The public opposition, however, has had a lasting effect, turning what had previously been an arcane, technical issue into a topic for popular political debate. More concretely, in the summer of 2009, the Conservative government reversed its opposition to public consultations and held a series of cross-country consultations on copyright reform, at which public opposition to DMCA-style TPM protection ran strong. However, it was not enough to override the continued Conservative government's insistence on a maximalist approach to TPM protection. In June 2010, the Conservative government introduced Bill C-32, *The Copyright Modernization Act*. While it contained several new and novel user rights — rights that quite possibly would not have been included had it not been for the protests of the previous two years — it followed Bill C-61's lead on TPM protection. This suggests the effectiveness of "Facebook activism" is dependent on the context in which it occurs. In December 2007 it was unclear how strong the opposition parties, particularly the Liberals, were. Facing a particularly contentious vote on whether to continue Canada's military involvement in the Afghan war in the winter 2008 session, the Conservative government, facing unexpected public opposition, decided that discretion was the better part of valour and delayed the introduction of the bill.

This delay, however, was purely tactical, a matter of working on the bill's communications strategy rather than reconsidering the substance of bill itself. That Bill C-32 contains the same TPM provisions, as well as user rights that would be overridden by digital locks,[49] suggests very strongly that the Conservative government is fully committed to DMCA-like TPM provisions, seeing the issue largely in the context of Canada-US relations, and that it takes public opposition to these provisions as a communications problem to be managed rather than as a policy issue to be reconsidered.

While this current government has decided to follow the US lead on TPM protection, the larger point concerns Canadian political autonomy. That successive Liberal and Conservative governments adopted diametrically opposed approaches to TPMs demonstrates that US-style protection of TPMs in Canada is not a foregone conclusion. The decision to "make the Americans happy" was but one of several possible policy choices and is based on a specific perception of the issue, with which reasonable people

---

49 See, for example, Carys Craig, "Locking Out Lawful Users: Fair Dealing and Anti-Circumvention in Bill C-32" in this volume.

can take issue. Canadian governments retain the ability to implement a "made-in-Canada" copyright policy, should they so desire.

3) Mexico

On the surface, the explanation for why Mexico has yet to extend TPM protection in any form to non-software digital works is quite straightforward, involving a relative lack of interest in the issue from the main groups involved in the making of Mexican copyright policy. Creators (represented in Mexico by *sociedades de gestión colectivas* (collection management societies)), the copyright industries, the US government (whose interests are aligned with the US-based copyright industries), and Mexican copyright authorities have been, until recently, much more concerned with traditional large-scale, commercial unauthorized copying of CDs, DVDs and books, which remains endemic in Mexico. Broadband Internet penetration rates in Mexico remain low compared with its northern neighbours, meaning that unauthorized online digital copying has been treated as a secondary issue.

For Mexico, the most significant recent development in copyright policy was the 1997 modernization of its copyright law. As already mentioned, these changes to the *Ley Federal del Derecho de Autor* moved Mexican copyright policy away from being primarily a moral right exercised by authors to being a commercial right exercised by copyright owners. Directly related to TPMs, the 1997 changes included a limited form of legal protection for TPMs, but only for those protecting computer software. This was done in the context of the NAFTA negotiations and was the result of US pressure concerning the software industry, which the US saw as a pressing issue.[50] This finding is unsurprising, given traditional US policy to link market access with IP reform.

Domestic ideas, institutions and actors remain central to understanding the development of Mexican copyright law. Although the next major changes to the law occurred in 2003, despite continuous demands from the US government and industries,[51] new rules for TPMs were not a part of these reforms. The 2003 reforms were undertaken to address the concerns of domestic groups (i.e., the *sociedades de gestión colectivas*). This indicates that, despite the 1997 reforms, which effectively gave greater standing

50 Luis Schmidt, "The New Digital Agenda" *Copyright World* (February 23, 2009) 17.

51 US, United States Trade Representative, *Special 301 Report*, www.keionline.org/ustr/special301; International Intellectual Property Alliance, "Country Report: Mexico," www.iipa.com/countryreports.html.

to foreign copyright owners, traditional domestic interests continued to shape Mexican copyright policy. More generally, it also reflects both the extent to which the treaties were seen by US-based industries and the US government as a secondary issue to physical piracy and the reality that the United States lacked the ability to dictate the pace of reforms, absent a compelling carrot and stick.

There are indications that within the next five years (i.e., by 2015), as Mexican broadband penetration increases and as digital-copyright issues become more important to Mexican copyright interests, Mexico will implement the treaties. The institutional, political and ideational factors — domestic and international — influencing the development of Mexican copyright, make conditions favourable for the adoption of US-style rules regarding TPMs.

The 1997 NAFTA-mandated changes have in practice been reinforced by traditional Mexican views of copyright as an author's right that should be maximized and that downplays users' rights. This traditional approach has, in effect, merged with the economic view of copyright, specifically one that advocates maximizing the economic rights of copyright and neighbouring rights[52] owners. In this sense, it is debatable the extent to which the 1997 changes were imposed on Mexican authorities, as opposed to being welcomed. For example, INDAUTOR sees its role primarily as protecting and maximizing authors' and owners' rights, which fits well with drives to implement the WIPO Internet treaties along US-desired lines. In 2007, for example, the type of people working at INDAUTOR began to change, following the hiring of a lawyer comfortable with the industry side of copyright as the head of INDAUTOR, and the subsequent hiring of staff with a similar background. This suggests a new comfort level with US views on TPMs and copyright generally; INDAUTOR has also indicated a desire to implement the Internet treaties.[53]

Both domestic and "foreign" copyright actors have also been active. With the blessing of INDAUTOR and the *Instituto Mexicano de la Propiedad Industrial* (IMPI) (which enforces the commercial aspects of Mexico's copyright law), the main stakeholders in Mexican copyright policymaking, the *sociedades de gestión colectivas* and the copyright industries in late 2009 have joined forces in the *Coalición por el Acceso Legal a la Cultura* (Coali-

52 Neighbouring rights are those rights given for those activities indirectly related to the creative process, such as to producers of phonograms.

53 Haggart, above note 28.

tion for the Legal Access to Culture),[54] with the goal of reaching common positions on issues of mutual concern. This alliance is significant given that historically Mexican copyright law has been treated, as in the United States, as a technical, apolitical matter best left to negotiations among the various parties, overseen by the government. Such a coalition indicates a high degree of consensus on copyright reform going forward. While the groups involved see TPM implementation as a secondary issue (more important for them is implementing rules governing the liability of Internet Service Providers for copyright violations carried out by their customers[55]), the fact that these groups have called for the Internet treaties' full implementation, combined with their pursuit of maximalist copyright policies, further suggests a sympathy with US-style TPM rules.

With no other major groups opposed to strong TPM protection in Mexico, potential public interest represents a wild card. Presently, copyright is not a pressing public issue, since inexpensive bootlegged works are freely available everywhere, and only about 9.8% of Mexican households had broadband Internet access in 2008.[56] However, if awareness grows, digital copyright in general could easily become politicized, as it has in Canada. Already, some Mexican academics are trying to draw attention to the perils of maximalist copyright for access to information and culture. For example, in June 2009, the first Mexican academic book dealing with these issues was published;[57] and in March 2010, the *Centro Cultureal de España México* hosted a three-day workshop, "*Comunidades, cultural libre y propiedad intellectual*" (communities, free culture and intellectual property) as part of the 2010 *Festival de México*, an annual arts and culture festival held in Mexico City.

Some Mexican politicians also seem increasingly to be paying greater attention to copyright as an innovation and economic, rather than purely cultural, issue. In October 2008, the president of the Senate *Comisión de Ciencia y Tecnología*, Francisco Castellón Fonsecal (from the left-leaning

---

54 "Reconocen a Coalición por el Acceso Legal a la Cultura," Publimetro (4 May 2010), www.publimetro.com.mx/entretener/reconocen-a-coalicion-por-el-acceso-legal-a-la-cultura/njed!o3v9wEhzv5jB9sEASORj3A.

55 In fact, one of the main reasons for the coalition seems to be to form a counterweight to the economically and politically powerful telecommunications industry in the upcoming battle over ISP liability.

56 Organization for Economic Cooperation and Development, "2a. Households with broadband access (2004–2008)," *OECD Broadband Portal* (10 June 2010) (www.oecd.org/dataoecd/20/59/39574039.xls).

57 López Cuenca & Ramírez Pedrajo, above note 17.

Partido de la Revolución Democrática, or PRD), argued to consider regulating copyright for its cultural and economic effects, since it has the potential to generate as much or more revenues than industrial property (i.e., patents),[58] and in March 2010, he criticized negotiations over the Anti-Counterfeiting Trade Agreement (ACTA), which was (at the time of writing of this chapter) being negotiated in secret among a host of developed countries, for its potential effects on individual freedoms.[59] However, whether copyright will become sufficiently politicized to affect traditional inter-industry negotiation processes remain unclear.

E. ANALYSIS AND CONCLUSION

One of historical institutionalism's strengths is that it reminds one to focus on how all interested actors interact within all relevant institutions, be they international, regional or domestic. In a subject area like copyright, where analyses usually focus on domestic laws or international treaties, its sensitivity to how these "levels" interact with the added "level" of the region, is particularly helpful.

An examination of these three mini-case studies through this lens of historical institutionalism demonstrates the extent to which the Canadian, US and Mexican decisions to implement (or not) the Internet treaties, and the manner of implementation, have been shaped primarily by domestic, not regional, politics. It has failed to observe any strong regional institutional or regional-actor influences. To the extent that any clearly North American dynamic is at work, it involves

a) the NAFTA as a restraint on the US ability to refuse its neighbours access to its markets if its policy proposals are not adopted;
b) the US and its industries as significant actors in the making of Canadian and Mexican public policy; and
c) the degree to which the NAFTA reshaped the Mexican copyright landscape, giving voice to actors that otherwise would not have been as important, and potentially affecting the course of future legislative reform.

---

58 Senado de la República, *B-0564 Seminario: "Derecho De Autor En El Entorno Digital"* (1 November 2008), (http://comunicacion.senado.gob.mx/index.php?option=com_content&task=view&id=7856&Itemid=163).

59 Francisco J. Castellón Fonseca, News Release, "Piden Comparecencia De Titulares De Economía, PGR e IMPI Para Que Expliquen Contenido De ACTA" (4 March 2010), http://www.prd.senado.gob.mx/cs/informacion.php?id_sistema_informacion=4713.

In short, North American copyright regimes continue to be shaped significantly by domestic politics. Domestically, each country is characterized by a unique constellation of interest groups, as well as the institutional frameworks in which they operate.

One interesting point that emerges from this analysis is the extent to which the copyright debate in the United States is relatively self-contained, while the debates in Mexico and Canada are affected by US-based actors promoting US-derived solutions. Not only are the two countries responding to initiatives from a US-influenced treaty, but actors in both countries also couch their arguments for and against TPM protection in terms of the US DMCA. This state of affairs reinforces the extent to which copyright policy in Mexico and Canada is driven—though not dictated by—the United States.

Despite this lack of regional governance, both the Canadian and Mexican governments have shown signs of adopting US-style TPM protections. The pressure for this adoption, however, can only be understood in terms of their respective domestic debates, and masks the potential in all three countries to adopt autonomous copyright policies. In Mexico, meanwhile, the bias in favour of TPMs is the result not just of a NAFTA-instigated rewriting of Mexican copyright law, but of the long-held view of copyright (or *derechos de autor*) as something to be maximized, not balanced. The concept of user rights is underdeveloped in Mexico, and the Mexican-based groups interested in copyright are strongly in favour of maximizing protection in general; there is no reason why this support would not extend to TPMs. And while civil-society involvement in the Canadian debate complicates (although likely not fatally) the government's ability to implement DMCA-style TPM protection, this opposition is almost completely absent in Mexico.

In Canada, the different approaches seen in the Liberal and Conservative bills suggests strongly that the importance of US influence—the United States and its industries being the main advocates for DMCA-type law—is in the eye of the beholder. Put another way, the identity of the Prime Minister, and their perception of the various political imperatives of the copyright debate, matter.

With respect to Bill C-32, the relative autonomy of domestic institutional copyright frameworks suggests that, despite the NAFTA and despite the economic asymmetry between the United States and Canada, there is nothing stopping the Canadian government from implementing a copyright regime that satisfies its WIPO obligations (should it choose to do so—signing a treaty does not oblige a country to implement it) without signing off on DMCA-type rules for TPMs. In fact, successive Liberal and Conservative governments have consistently defied US wishes in their proposals addressing ISP liability: the Liberals' Bill C-60,[60] and both the Conservatives' Bill C-61[61] and C-32[62] advocated a "notice-and-notice" system, in contrast to the DMCA's "notice-and-takedown" regime.[63] While the reasons for this difference are beyond the scope of this paper,[64] the fact of this difference between Canadian proposed policy and US policy suggests, taken together with the differences between the Liberal and Conservative approaches to TPM protection, strongly suggests that the Canadian government largely controls its own copyright future.

The emergence of a North American copyright regime is highly dependent on domestic factors, and that, to a significant extent, each North American government remains master of its own copyright policy. The governments of Canada and Mexico may choose to follow the US lead, and they may do so in response to US pressure (as in the Canadian Conservative case) or in response to a mix of US influence and domestic interest-group preference (as in the case of Mexico). Neither case, however, takes away from the crucial point, from the perspective of those who value democratic decision-making: Convergence is a choice; it is not preordained.

---

60 Bill C-60, *An Act to Amend the Copyright Act*, 1st Sess., 38th Parl., 2005 (as read at first reading by the House of Commons 20 June 2005), proposed sections 40.1–40.3.

61 Bill C-61, *An Act to Amend the Copyright Act*, 2nd Sess., 39th Parl., 2008 (as read at first reading by the House of Commons 20 June 2008), proposed sections 41.25–41.27.

62 Bill C-32, *An Act to Amend the Copyright Act*, 3rd Sess., 40th Parl., 2010 (as read at first reading by the House of Commons 20 June 2005), proposed sections 41–25-41.27.

63 *Digital Millennium Copyright Act*, above note 25. In the former, Internet service providers are exempted from liability if, upon receiving a notice of infringement from a copyright owner, they pass the notice on to the accused client in a prescribed way. In the latter, upon reception of a notice of infringement, ISPs must remove the content from their network or face potential liability.

64 They are discussed at length in the author's forthcoming dissertation.

CHAPTER THREE

History in the Balance:

Copyright and Access to Knowledge

Myra Tawfik

A. INTRODUCTION

Copyright law is generally understood to encompass within its policy embrace the interests of three constituent groups: users, creators and copyright industries.[1] Each of these groups has found enough support in the history of copyright law to argue that its interests should predominate within the legal framework. As interested parties, their advocacy position is to be expected. The role of Parliament is different however. It is the legislature's responsibility to be dispassionate, to mediate between these often competing interests in order to craft appropriate legislation in the name of the greater good. And by "appropriate," I mean balanced in setting the appropriate parameters between adequate protection and adequate access.

The idea of "balance" within copyright law is not a new concept nor is it the creation of "radical extremists"[2] or "pro-user zealots."[3] Rather, as the

---

1 In this paper, I will refer to authors and creators interchangeably. I will also speak of publishers, content providers and industry to designate the same constituent group. The term copyright holder will be used to designate both creators and content providers.

2 Minister of Canadian Heritage and Official Languages, James Moore, in a speech to the Chamber of Commerce IP Council on June 22, 2010. See CBC, "Copyright Debate Turns Ugly," online: www.cbc.ca/technology/story/2010/06/23/copyright-heritage-minister-moore.html.

3 Sarmite Bulte, former Chair of the Standing Committee on Canadian Heritage. See www.robhyndman.com/2006/01/12/controversy-over-bulte-comments-at-all-candidates-debate.

history of copyright law demonstrates, the entire legislative system required a balancing between the various interests in order to achieve its primary policy objective: that of fostering an environment for the generation, dissemination and acquisition of knowledge. The focus was not on pitting creators against industry or industry against users as we are wont to do in this modern era. Rather, the law reflected a tripartite, integrated system that encouraged creators to generate knowledge, industry to disseminate it and users to acquire it and, hopefully, reshape it into new knowledge. As such, the genesis of copyright law, including the earliest Canadian experience, has much to teach modern copyright policy-makers about establishing the appropriate normative policy framework. This is especially so in relation to the latest attempt at copyright reform, *An Act to amend the Copyright Act* (Bill C-32), introduced on 2 June 2010.[4]

Part 1 of this paper will discuss the nature and purpose of copyright law by canvassing the early experiences of the UK, France, the US and Canada. Part 2 will turn to review of Bill C-32 in light of the policy lessons gleaned from history.

B. PART 1: THE NATURE AND PURPOSE OF COPYRIGHT LAW: LESSONS FROM HISTORY

The first copyright statute originated 300 years ago in England in the form of the Statute of Anne or *An Act for the Encouragement of Learning by Vesting the Copies of Printed Books in the Authors or Purchasers of such Copies, during the Times therein mentioned*.[5] Although its very title sets out its underlying purpose, tracing its contours has posed somewhat of a challenge to scholars.

The traditional view of the law was that it was designed primarily with publishers in mind — in other words, that it sought, first and foremost, to meet the needs of the book trade.[6] However, in the last decades of the twentieth century, scholars began to place more emphasis on situating

---

4 59 Eliz. II, 2010. Text of Bill available at www2.parl.gc.ca/content/hoc/Bills/403/Government/C-32/C-32_1/C-32_1.PDF.

5 8 Anne c. C19 (1709/11710).

6 A. Birrell, *Seven Lectures on the Law and History of Copyright in Books* (London: Cassell, 1899). L.R. Patterson, *Copyright in Historical Perspective* (Nashville: Vanderbilt University Press, 1968). See also in this regard the work of book historian J. Feather Publishing, *Piracy and Politics: An Historical Study of Copyright in Britain* (London: Mansell, 1994); J. Feather "The Book Trade in Politics: The Making of the *Copyright Act 1710*" (1980) 8 Publishing History 19; J. Feather "The Commerce of Letters: The Study of the 19th c. Book Trade" (1984) 17 Eighteenth-Century Studies 405.

the author within the copyright paradigm as one of, if not the principal beneficiary of the legislation. [7]

The new millennium has seen yet another shift in focus. This time the spotlight is on the public interest in access to knowledge and learning both at the local and the international levels.[8] Scholars have begun retracing the historical record to study the extent to which early policy-makers were concerned about "user rights' or more broadly, the public interest in the circulation of knowledge.[9] I would suggest that this most recent revisiting of the past is a direct reaction to the global trend towards increased copyright controls.[10] This does not mean, however, that in pursuing a particular agenda there isn't truth to be found within the pages of history.

As I see it, the evolution of the historical scholarship has been a progressive panning out to capture more within the lens of inquiry.[11] This has

---

7 See in this respect the work of M. Rose, *Authors and Owners: The Invention of Copyright* (Cambridge, Harvard University Press, 1993); B. Sherman & L. Bently *The Making of Intellectual Property Law* (Cambridge: Cambridge University Press, 1999); J. Feather "Publishers and Politicians: The Remaking of Copyright Law in Britain 1775–1842 Part II: The Rights of Authors" (1989) 25 Publishing History 45; J. Feather "From Rights in Copies to Copyright: The Recognition of Authors' Rights in English Law and Practice in the Sixteenth and Seventeenth Centuries" (1992) 10 Cardozo Arts & Ent L.J. 455.

8 See, for example, R. Okediji "The International Copyright System: Limitations, Exceptions and Public Interest Considerations for Developing Countries" Issue Paper 15 UNCTAD-ICTSD (2005) (http://ictsd.net/downloads/2008/12/okediji_copyright_2005.pdf); U. Suthersanen "Education, IPRs and Fundamental Freedoms: The Right to Knowledge" (2005) at www.iprsonline.org/unctadictsd/docs/Suthersanen_A2K.pdf; P.K. Yu, "A Tale of Two Development Agendas" (2009) 35 Ohio Northern U. L.R. 466. See as well the Access to Knowledge movement at www.a2knetwork.org.

9 For example, R. Deazley, *The Origin of the Right to Copy: Charting the Movement of Copyright Law in Eighteenth Century Britain (1695–1775)* (Oxford: Hart Publishing, 2004); E. Alexander, *Copyright Law and the Public Interest in the Nineteenth Century* (London: Hart Publishing, 2010); T. Ochoa & M. Rose, "The Anti-Monopoly Origins of the Patent and Copyright Clause" (2002) 84 J. Patent & TM Office Soc'y 909; L.R. Patterson & C. Joyce "Copyright in 1791: An Essay Concerning the Founders' View of the Copyright Power to Congress in Article I, Section 8, Clause 8 of the US Constitution" (2003) 52 Emory L.J. 909; C. Dallon, "The Problem with Congress and Copyright Law: Forgetting the Past and Ignoring the Public Interest" (2004) 44 Santa Clara L.R. 365; M.J. Madison, "Beyond Creativity: Copyright as Knowledge Law" (forthcoming 2010, Vanderbilt Journal of Entertainment and Technology Law).

10 For example, much of the recent American scholarship on the intent behind the Constitutional Clause arose out of the *Eldred v. Ashcroft* litigation (537 U.S. 186, U.S. Supreme Court 2003) relating to the constitutionality of extending the term of US copyright law. See Ochoa & Rose and Patterson & Joyce above note 9.

11 Ironically, the Internet that is often characterized as the bane of the music and film industries has been a boon for legal historians who are now able to engage online

manifested itself in greater scrutiny of the involvement of all the key players in the copyright paradigm as well as an enlargement of the scope of investigation to consider broad socio-political and cultural contexts. In so doing, we are moving closer to a more genuine and complete understanding of the nature and purpose of the law.

1) Copyright Laws reflect Enlightenment Values on Education and Learning

It is highly significant that copyright laws originated during the Enlightenment.[12] Although copyright scholars have discussed the role that Enlightenment ideas played in establishing the rights of authors within the legal construct,[13] the influence of another key pillar of Enlightenment thinking has been left largely unexplored. Enlightened societies placed an enormous value on knowledge and learning as both necessary for individual human fulfillment and for socio-economic and cultural development. I would suggest that this aspect played a more significant role in both the emergence of the law and in its substance than we have generally acknowledged. As Mark Rose points out "... the establishment of the author as the owner and the establishment of the rights of the public at large were both Enlightenment products, embedded in Enlightenment modes of thought."[14]

---

with the primary historical texts and sources. One excellent example can be found at *Primary Sources on Copyright (1450–1900)* www.copyrighthistory.org. A joint project between the University of Cambridge, UK, and Bournemouth University, UK, the website provides free public access to multi-jurisdictional primary sources. Access to learning has never been more robust thanks to the advent of the Internet and its immense potential for global education should be celebrated.

12 Roughly 18th century Europe and characterized by an emphasis on individual freedoms, democratic values and political emancipation grounded in rational inquiry and critical thought. On the Enlightenment in Europe see, for example, Porter, below note 17; T. Munck, The *Enlightenment: A Comparative Social History 1721–1794* (London: Arnold Publishers, 2000); J. Van Horne Melton, *The Rise of the Public in Enlightenment Europe* (Cambridge: Cambridge University Press, 2001). For the US and Lower Canada see, for example, H.F. May, *The Enlightenment in America* (NY: Oxford University Press, 1976); M. Trudel, *L'Influence de Voltaire au Canada*, vol. I (Montreal, Fides, 1945); F. Ouellet, *Lower Canada 1791–1840: Social Change and Nationalism* (Toronto: McLelland and Stewart, 1980); Y. Lamonde, *Histoire Sociale des idées au Quebec* (Montreal: Fides, 2000).

13 See for example, M. Woodmansee & P. Jaszi, eds., *Copyright and the Construction of Authorship: Textual Appropriation in Law and Literature* (Durham: Duke University Press, 1994); D. Saunders, *Authorship and Copyright* (London: Routledge, 1992).

14 M. Rose "Nine-Tenths of the Law: The English Copyright Debates and the Rhetoric

Enlightened societies were especially mindful of encouraging the creation and diffusion of "useful knowledge"—a term that frequently appears in the writings of the time. In fact, one need only reflect on the Preamble of the Statute of Anne itself that refers to the "encouragement of learned men to compose and write useful books" to recognize that the term "useful" had a central meaning at the time. Useful knowledge was didactic, scientific, practical, utilitarian, and inured to the benefit of society at large.[15] The more educated and learned the population, the more civilized and economically advanced the society.

Coupled with the need to encourage learned individuals to generate useful knowledge lay the public interest in diffusing or disseminating that knowledge. The culture of knowledge characteristic of this period manifested itself in the emergence of a multitude of agencies through which useful knowledge could be widely disseminated. We find, during the long eighteenth century and into the nineteenth, a proliferation of learned societies and scientific associations.[16] Other important vehicles to promote the dissemination of knowledge included the establishment of circulating libraries and eventually the public library system. Similarly, energies were directed towards the establishment of institutions of higher learning such as Universities and cultural and scientific institutions such as museums. This was also a period marked by heightened attention to developing affordable systems of public education—especially elementary education. A society could not continue to grow, develop and flourish without providing for the means to educate successive generations and this was particularly true in developing societies like the United States and British North

---

of the Public Domain" (2003) 36 Law and Contemporary Problems 76 at 76. See also in this regard C. Hesse, "The Rise of Intellectual Property 700BC–AD2000: An Idea in the Balance" (2002) Deadalus (Spring) 26.

15 On "useful knowledge" see J. Gascoigne, *Joseph Banks and the English Enlightenment: Useful Knowledge and Polite Culture* (Cambridge: Cambridge University Press, 2003); J. Burns, "From 'Polite Learning' to 'Useful Knowledge' 1750–1850" (1986) 36 History Today 21.

16 Examples include the august Royal Society of London established in 1660 and the American Philosophical Society founded by Benjamin Franklin in 1745. The first such society to be formed in Canada was the Literary and Historical Society of Quebec founded in 1824. According to *History of the Book in Canad*a vol. 1 (Toronto: University of Toronto Press, 2004) at 176: ". . . these first societies (for men only) focused on debate, discussion and essay reading in the period prior to 1840. They often provided public cultural amenities such as lecture series and *conversazioni*, and sometimes they attempted to establish library collections." See also J.E. McClellan III, "Learned Societies" in Alan Charles Kors, ed., *Oxford Encyclopedia of the Enlightenment* (New York: Oxford University Press, 2002) 4, vol. 4, at 43–47.

America where poverty and illiteracy were the greatest barriers to socio-economic development.

It was, however, print technology that provided the most important vehicle for the mass dissemination of knowledge. As Roy Porter has suggested: "Central to enlightened modernizing were the glittering prospects of progress conveyed through print."[17] The printed book as the material repository of knowledge was the ideal medium for the diffusion of ideas. It could be easily multiplied, was highly portable, and could circulate widely. What was needed was a regulatory scheme to encourage book production so as to effect the broad policy objective of encouraging learning. It is therefore within this framework that copyright law must be cast. Copyright law should be understood as the "law of the book." Its focus was on encouraging book production and distribution within circumscribed limits so as to ensure that useful knowledge would not only be generated but that it would also be widely disseminated.

2) Copyright Law in the Developed and Developing Worlds of the Eighteenth and Nineteenth Centuries

It is instructive to look back at the historical record of the UK and France who were, in the eighteenth and nineteenth centuries, highly developed societies with sophisticated publishing industries as well as a growing professional authorial class. These jurisdictions were also book-exporting nations and yet, in step with the ideals of the time, they nevertheless remained mindful of the role copyright law played in the advancement of education and learning.

Although publishers were the most vocal lobbyists for copyright legislation, the Statute of Anne was not exactly what they had wished for. [18] The legislation gave them exclusive rights only for a limited time and the House of Lords forever dashed any claim to perpetual rights in 1774.[19] Further, although authors do figure in the Statute of Anne and its later iterations and judicial interpretations, their interests did not predominate for reasons that author and lexicographer Samuel Johnson explained in 1773:

> There seems . . . to be in authors . . . a right, as it were, of creation which should from its nature be perpetual; but the consent of na-

17 R. Porter, *Enlightenment* (London: Penguin Books, 2000) at 13–14.

18 R. Deazley, *On the Origins of the Right to Copy: Charting the Movement of Copyright Law in Eighteenth-Century Britain (1695–1775)* (Oxford: Hart Publishing, 2004).

19 *Donaldson v. Beckett* (1774), 98 Eng. Rep. 257.

> tions is against it; and indeed reason and the interests of learning are against it; for were it to be perpetual, no book however useful, could be universally diffused amongst mankind should the proprietor take it into his head to restrain circulation . . . . For the general good of the world, therefore, whatever valuable work has once been created by an author, and issued out by him, should be understood as no longer in his power, but as belonging to the publick; at the same time, the author is entitled to an adequate reward. This he should have by an exclusive right to his work for a considerable number of years.[20]

The overall construction of the legislation ensured that users could access the latest knowledge and ideas. The law achieved this by protecting the interests of authors and publishers, certainly. But it also set parameters or limits to the monopoly. It did so through a number of devices. These included registration requirements and other formalities, a limited term of protection, a free library book deposit for the benefit of University libraries and a complaint process for usurious book pricing. In fact, the Statute of Anne can be understood as anti-monopolistic in nature and designed to enable access to education and learning.[21]

As Ronan Deazley concludes:

> A statutory phenomenon, copyright was fundamentally concerned with the reading public, with the encouragement and spread of education, and with the continued production of useful books. In allocating the right to exclusively publish a given literary work, the eighteenth century parliamentarians were not concerned primarily with the rights of the individual, but acted in the furtherance of these much broader social goals. The pre-eminence of the common good as the organizing principle upon which to found a system of copyright regulation is revealed. This element of the public interest, overlooked or perhaps ignored in other historical tales of the origin of copyright, once lay at its very core.[22]

---

20 *Boswell's Life of Johnson*, vol. 2 at 220 — entry dated 1773.

21 Deazley, above note 18; M. Rose above note 14; L.R. Patterson & C. Joyce above note 9; T. Ochoa & M. Rose above note 9. See as well D.W.K. Kong, "The Historical Law and Economics of the First Copyright Act" (2006) 2 Erasmus Law and Economics Review 35.

22 Deazley, above note 18 at 226.

The same considerations were at play in post-revolutionary France when it passed its first Act in 1793 — the *Décret de la Convention Nationale du dix-neuf juillet 1793 relatif aux droits de propriété des Auteurs d'écrits en tout genre, des Compositeurs de musique, des Peintres et des Dessinateurs*.

Even though France is considered a strong "author-centric" jurisdiction, there is evidence to suggest that early French policy-makers were equally concerned with encouraging the diffusion of knowledge. Indeed, French parliamentarians debated the extent to which creators' rights ought to interfere with the public interest in education and learning. As Anne Latournerie notes: "*En France également, même si on s'est longtemps focalisé sur la défense des droits d'auteur, la propriété publique est la règle, dans l'esprit des législateurs révolutionnaires, et le droit d'auteur est l'exception.*"[23]

Significantly, the copyright file was given to the Committee on Public Instruction whose mandate was to establish a system of public education for the country.[24] This would suggest that early French legislators understood copyright law and the advancement of formal education as intimately connected. Thus, the French legislation included similar limits on the copyright monopoly as the Statute of Anne including a fixed term of protection, registration and other formal requirements and a library deposit for the benefit of the National Library. As Jane Ginsburg suggests ". . . without denying the presence of a strong authors' rights current in the revolutionary laws . . . revolutionary legislators generally resolved that public-versus-private tension by casting copyright primarily as an aid to the advancement of public instruction."[25]

It is important to understand as well that the discourse was no different at the international level. At the inception of the *Berne Convention for the Protection of Literary and Artistic Works* in 1886, the Chair of the Berne Convention Drafting Committee, Swiss politician Numa Droz remarked:

> Consideration also has to be given to the fact that limitations on absolute protection are dictated, rightly in my opinion, by the public interest. The ever-growing need for mass instruction could never be

---

23 A. Latournerie, "Droits d'auteur, droits du public: une approche historique" (2004) 22 L'Economie Politique 21–33 at 22. See too J. Ginsburg ""A Tale of Two Copyrights: Literary Property in Revolutionary France and America" (1990) 64 Tul. L. Rev 991.

24 D.S. Muzzey, "State, Church and School in France I: The Foundations of the Public School System in France" (1911) 19 The School Review 178; C. Hesse, "Enlightenment Epistemology and the Laws of Authorship in Revolutionary France, 1777–1793" (1990) 30 Representations 109. See also Ginsburg, above note 23.

25 Ginsburg above note 23 at 1014.

met if there were no reservation of certain reproduction facilities, which at the same time should not degenerate into abuses.[26]

Thus, the *Berne Convention* and its later revisions as well as agreements like the WIPO Internet Treaties,[27] which Bill C-32 is designed to implement, contain "reservations of certain reproduction facilities" in the name of public instruction and learning, among other public interest considerations. None of these treaties vest absolute control over the copyright work in any one of the three constituent groups within their contemplation.[28]

Nowhere is the link between copyright and the dissemination of knowledge more apparent than in the history of the developing country that was nineteenth century America. Article 1, Section 8, Clause 8 of the US Constitution empowers Congress "to promote the progress of science and useful arts by securing for a limited times to authors and inventors the exclusive right to their writings and discoveries." At the time, the term "progress' would have signified "diffusion"[29] and the term "science" would have been used in its broad sense as "knowledge."[30] Thus, Congress' mandate was to promote the diffusion of knowledge by giving exclusive rights to authors for the limited time necessary to achieve that overarching policy goal. Confirming this public policy orientation of the Constitutional clause, George Washington observed: ". . . there is nothing which can better deserve your patronage than the promotion of science and literature. Knowledge is, in every country, the surest basis of public happiness."[31]

To add further gloss to the intent behind the Constitutional clause, the original recommendation regarding copyright was part of a larger list of proposals for Congressional powers. The various suggestions, most of which were lost in the final Constitution, are most telling in identifying the overall context within which copyright law was situated. Among

---

26 M. Ficsor, *The Law of Copyright and the Internet: The 1996 WIPO Treaties — Their Interpretation and Implementation* (Oxford: Oxford University Press, 2002) at 258.

27 WIPO *Copyright Treaty* (WCT) 36 ILM 65 (1996) and WIPO *Performers and Phonograms Treaty* 36 ILM 76 (1996) [WIPO Internet Treaties].

28 See M.J. Tawfik, "International Copyright Law: W[h]ither User Rights?" in M. Geist ed., *In the Public Interest: The Future of Canadian Copyright Law* (Toronto: Irwin Law, 2005).

29 Malla Pollack, "What is Congress Supposed to Promote? Defining 'Progress' in Article 1, Section 8, Clause 8 of the US Constitution or Introducing the Progress Clause" (2002) 80 Nebraska L. Rev. 754.

30 From the Latin "*scientia*" meaning knowledge. See M. Madison, above note 9.

31 Speech to both Houses of Congress delivered on 8 January 1790. See J. Sparks, ed., *The Writings of George Washington*, vol. XII (Boston: American Stationers' Company, 1837) at 9.

twenty enumerated items, following appear in direct succession or closely together:

- To secure to literary authors their copy rights for a limited time
- To establish a University
- To encourage by proper premiums and provisions, the advancement of useful knowledge and discoveries

...

- To establish seminaries for the promotion of literature and the arts and sciences

...

- To grant patents for useful inventions
- To secure to Authors exclusive rights for a certain time . . .[32]

One clearly grasps the extent to which it was deemed to be Congress' responsibility to provide for vehicles through which citizens could access knowledge and learning including through the mechanism of a copyright law.

The first US Act, modeled on the Statute of Anne, was similarly entitled *An Act for the Encouragement of Learning by securing the copies of Maps, Charts and Books to the authors and proprietors of such copies, during the times therein mentioned.*[33] It reflected the same balance of rights or exclusive entitlements coupled with similar limitations such as a fixed term, a mandatory book deposit and compliance with registration and other formalities. In addition, the US Act limited eligibility for protection to American citizens or permanent residents thereby enabling the free circulation of the works of foreign authors. In nineteenth century America, copyright law was understood as an agent to advance the country's socio-political goals by rejecting any restrictions on book circulation that would inhibit the ability of Americans to access the latest knowledge and ideas. As Meredith McGill notes:

> [t]he notion that an individual author had a natural right to his printed text . . . was fundamentally incompatible with the political philosophy that associated the depersonalization of print with a kind of selfless publicity, the exercise of civic virtue. Perpetual private ownership and control over printed texts was unacceptable in

---

32 D. Oliar, "The (Constitutional) Convention on IP: A New Reading" (2009) 57 UCLA L.R. 421 at 437–38.

33 1 Statutes at Large 124 (1790). The one difference related to the use of the term "securing" in the US Act as opposed to "vesting" in the Statute of Anne. The US decision in *Wheaton v. Peters*, 33 U.S. 591 (1834), held that the change in term was of no consequence.

> a culture that regarded the free circulation of texts as the sign and guarantor of liberty.[34]

British copyright laws impeded timely and affordable access to the latest knowledge. As a result, US copyright law disregarded the interests of British authors and publishers and allowed for the wide circulation of unauthorized cheap American reprints of British works. Indeed, as scholars like McGill have demonstrated, the "culture of reprinting" characteristic of this period was an essential element of US economic and cultural development.[35] So inextricably tied were copyright law, the free flow of ideas and knowledge and America's political ideology that one nineteenth century US Senator expressed it thus: "The multiplication of cheap editions of useful books, brought within the reaches of all classes, serves to promote that general diffusion of knowledge and intelligence, on which depends so essentially the preservation and support of our free institutions."[36]

It is truly ironic that it was this liberal policy regarding access to knowledge that has enabled the US to become, today, the strongest advocate for access controls.

3) The Emergence of Copyright Law in Canada

The first Canadian copyright statute, *An Act for the protection of Copy Rights/ Acte pour protéger la proprieté litteraire* was passed in Lower Canada in 1832

---

34 M. McGill, *American Literature and the Culture of Reprinting 1834–1853* (Philadelphia: University of Pennsylvania Press, 2003) at 48. McGill argues further at 82: "Foreign authors' disenfranchisement under American law was not inconsistent but integral to many Americans' understanding of the nature and scope of domestic copyright protection."

35 In addition to McGill, see also Z. Khan, *The Democratization of Invention: Patents and Copyrights in American Economic Development (1790–1920)* (Cambridge: Cambridge University Press, 2005); R.A. Gross, "Building a National Literature: The United States 1800-1890" in S. Eliot & J. Rose, eds., *A Companion to the History of the Book* (Oxford: Wiley-Blackwell, 2007); and C. Dallon above note 9.

36 Khan, above note 35 at 225. This 19th century copyright policy of allowing cheap British reprints to circulate freely in the US market had deleterious consequences on Canada during the latter half of the century. See in this regard, G. Parker, *The Beginnings of the Book Trade in Canada* (Toronto: University of Toronto Press, 1985); P.E. Moyse, "Canadian Colonial Copyright: The Colony Strikes Back" in Y. Gendreau, *An Emerging Intellectual Property Paradigm: Perspectives from Canada* (Cheltenham: Edward Elgar, 2008); M. Nair, "The *Copyright Act 1889*: A Canadian Declaration of Independence" (2009) 90 The Canadian Historical Review 1; S. Bannerman, *Canada and the Berne Convention 1886– 1971* (forthcoming, UBC Press).

and was derived from US law.[37] This first Lower Canadian Act was replicated in the *Copyright Act* of the Province of Canada in 1841,[38] which was, in turn, adopted by the Dominion of Canada in 1868.[39]

A study of the documents surrounding the enactment of this statute offers insight into what first motivated policy-makers to bring copyright law to Lower Canada. Not surprisingly, Enlightenment ideas about education and learning were as much a part of Lower Canadian values as anywhere else and, as we will see, played a very prominent role in the decision to enact a copyright law. Indeed, in the first decades of the 19th century Lower Canada saw a proliferation of the same agencies for the diffusion of knowledge that were to be found in the UK, Europe and the United States. These included the establishment of learned societies whose benefits were seen to extend beyond individual edification to the betterment of society as a whole. As one anonymous commentator stated in reference to the establishment of the Literary and Historical Society of Quebec in 1824, "[t]he number and importance of the Institutions or Societies, in any country, afford a very sure criterion, whereby we may judge of the progress it is making in civilization, and of its remoteness from barbarism." [40] This was also a period marked by an increase in the availability and variety of print material — newspapers, pamphlets and books — published domestically as well as imported from abroad signaling a thirst for knowledge on the part of a growing readership.[41]

However, one of the most significant preoccupations of those early decades remained the problem of devising an affordable State-run public education system. It was this particular legislative portfolio that led directly to the enactment of the first Canadian *Copyright Act*.

The difficulties in bringing public education, especially elementary education, to nineteenth century Lower Canada have been well-documented.[42]

---

37 2 Will IV c. 53. It was copied from the US Act of 1831, 4 Stat. 436 (1831).

38 4 & 5 Vict c. 61.

39 31 Vict c. 54.

40 *Canadian Magazine and Literary Repository*, Volume 2, No. 8, February 1824 (Montreal: N. Mower) at 111. Other notable civic initiatives of the period designed to encourage learning included, among others, the founding of McGill College in 1821.

41 See Trudel, Ouellet, & Lamonde, above note 12. See also G. Gallichan, *Livre et Politique au Bas-Canada 1791–1849* (Sillery: Les Editions du Septentrion, 1991).

42 See J.J. Jolois, *Joseph-Francois Perrault (1753–1844)et les Origines de l'Enseignement Laïque au Bas-Canada* (Montreal: Presses de l'Université de Montreal, 1969); J.D. Wilson, F.M. Stamp, & L-P. Audet, *Canadian Education: A History* (Scarborough: Prentice-Hall, 1970); B. Curtis, "Tocqueville and Lower Canadian Educational Networks" (2006) 7 Encounters on Education 113.

In 1800, the House of Assembly first debated the need to provide for a system of free public education for the colony and in 1801, the first *Education Act* was passed.[43] This Act did not achieve the desired results and the ensuing decades were marked by a series of failed legislative initiatives. Breakthroughs began in the late 1820s and the early 1830s as more schools were established. This led to a greater need for a stable supply of affordable schoolbooks. As a result, Lower Canadian teachers began to write or compile their own teaching manuals and schoolbooks. Preferring these to British or American imports and wanting to print multiple copies for use in their schools, they quickly discovered that the cost of printing their manuscripts was well beyond their means. Consequently, they began to petition the House of Assembly asking that it either assume the cost of printing or grant a sum of money to defray the costs.

In the fall of 1831, the House of Assembly was seized of two petitions from schoolteachers that it referred to the Standing Committee on Education and Schools ("the Committee"). [44] One of the petitions came from Joseph Lancaster, the British education pioneer who had recently settled in Montreal, in which he sought an "Act to secure the Copyright of any of his Publications respecting Education."[45] Lancaster had become familiar with copyright law and its advantages while residing in the United States.[46] The other petition was from William Morris, Master of the British and Canadian School at Quebec whose plea to the Committee was as follows:

> I lay before the Committee a Manuscript Book containing a treatise on Arithmetic and practical Geometry. I have adopted in my School,

---

43 *An Act For the Establishment of Free Schools and the Advancement of Learning in This Province*, 41 Geo III, c. 17.

44 Journals of the House of Assembly of Lower Canada, 2 Will. IV, at 49 and 102.

45 2 Will. IV, 23 November 1831, at 49. Lancaster arrived in Montreal in 1829 but his monitorial school system was already well-known in Lower Canadian educational and political circles as his system had been officially adopted by the Lower Canadian legislature in 1815. William Morris, the other petitioner, was the head of the British and Canadian School at Quebec, a Lancasterian school. On Lancaster's influence on Lower Canadian education see B. Curtis, "Joseph Lancaster in Montreal (*bis*): Monitorial Schooling and Politics in a Colonial Context" (2005) 17 Historical Studies in Education 1.

46 Lancaster first arrived in 1818 and secured a US copyright in 1820 for his publication *Letters on National Subjects Auxiliary to Universal Education and Scientific Knowledge*. Although Lancaster had published teaching manuals and other books on his pedagogical method prior to his arrival in the US, he did not secure copyright in his native England. On Joseph Lancaster, see D. Salmon, *Joseph Lancaster* (London: Longmans, Green & Co, 1904).

> as much as I could, the system contained in my Book; the want of printed Copies has prevented me from making use of it altogether. I am of opinion that if my work was printed and put into practice, children could learn all the rules that it contains in one year. I have not dared to get it printed. . .I believe the work would cost about 81 pounds for 1000 which would make about 2 shillings per Copy, for the printing solely, which added to the binding, would make it too dear to expect an extensive sale.[47]

The Committee recommended that Morris be given an allowance of 50 pounds as an aid to publication. It also stipulated that one thousand copies should be produced and sold at the affordable price of 2 shillings each. Finally, it concluded its report on Morris' petition with the hope that: "this very valuable Book may be improved and translated in French for the use of the Elementary Schools throughout the Province."[48]

The Committee went further, however. Its deliberations led it to the following conclusion:

> The necessity of such Books, and the little encouragement existing at present for time, talents and capital employed in this way, as well as the special application of Mr. Lancaster for a Copyright induced your Committee to recommend the introduction of a Bill securing Copyright.[49]

Unfortunately, a detailed analysis of the Committee's copyright recommendation is beyond the scope of this paper but, for our purposes, it is enough to highlight the clear underlying rationale that led to the law's introduction. Firstly, it is telling that, just as in France, a committee established to deal with public instruction was seen as the appropriate body to address matters pertaining to copyright law. Further, the Committee's recommendation was a direct response to the problem of providing for an affordable and adequate supply of schoolbooks. The barrier that existed at the time was the high cost of printing. The belief was that copyright law would reduce the cost of printing by encouraging publishers to take advantage of economies of scale secured by exclusive printing rights for a fixed duration. However, the Committee's response to Morris' petition is not limited to the concern over facilitating book production in and of itself. In its estima-

47 First Report of the Standing Committee on Education and Schools, 23 January 1832, 2 Will. IV, Appendix I.i. at 10.

48 *Ibid.* at 2–3.

49 *Ibid.*

tion, schoolbooks and other books were to be affordable, printed in sufficient numbers to ensure wide distribution and, ideally, accessible in both French and English. Thus, it expressly established both the maximum cost per volume and the minimum print run as conditions of the grant to Morris; conditions that were designed specifically to ensure that the general population would have access to this useful book. In recommending the enactment of a copyright law to address similar concerns, the Committee would have been thinking along the same policy lines, believing that copyright would result in greater public accessibility to useful works.

It is worth stressing that although he was one of the most prominent Quebec publishers of his time, John Neilson, who chaired the Committee, had never expressed an interest in copyright law in his capacity as publisher. Rather, Neilson is remembered for, among other things, his championing of the cause of education.[50] Further, although the legislation originated out of petitions from authors, these petitioners were not asking specifically to be rewarded for their intellectual exertions. Rather, they petitioned as teachers seeking to provide their students with access to the teaching tools they had developed.

4) Copyright History: Remembering Copyright's Educative Function

In undertaking this brief historical survey, I am not suggesting that time has stood still and that we ought to be considering copyright revisions in light of nineteenth century law. Obviously we have moved well beyond the particular legislative agenda that so exercised Lower Canadian policy-makers in 1832. Nor am I intending to suggest that the substantive provisions of these early statutes should be the models for contemporary legislative drafting. There is no question that modern copyright legislation looks very different from the Statute of Anne or its early North American progeny. Rather, understanding the historical origins of the law reminds us of the way in which copyright policy was conceived — a conception that is as relevant today as it was then.

Unfortunately, contemporary copyright discourse often places too high a premium on rewarding "creativity" at the expense of other equally important interests such as those of users. The mistaken assumption is that copyright law is a vehicle for the protection of authors and industry but,

---

50 On John Neilson, see *Dictionary of Canadian Biography*, vol. VII, online at www.biographi.ca.

as we have seen, copyright law has never been about that dimension alone. Nor, frankly, should it be.

History teaches us that copyright law emerged out of Enlightenment ideas about the benefits of learning and the diffusion of knowledge. Viewed in this light, it is clear that authors and publishers were never intended to be the primary beneficiaries of the legislative scheme. Rather, they were the means by which a greater public interest purpose could be achieved. As Michael Madison aptly captures it: "Copyright began as knowledge law, and knowledge law it should remain." [51]

The recent pronouncements by the Supreme Court of Canada are a clear affirmation that this conception of the law remains very much a part of the contemporary legal framework. In the Court's estimation:

> The *Copyright Act* is usually presented as a balance between promoting the public interest in the encouragement and dissemination of works of the arts and intellect and obtaining a just reward for the creator . . . . The proper balance . . . lies not only in recognizing the creator's rights but in giving due weight to their limited nature.[52]

The Supreme Court's conceptualization of "fair dealing" also reflects a similar appreciation:

> The fair dealing exception, like other exceptions in the *Copyright Act*, is a user's right. In order to maintain the proper balance between the rights of a copyright owner and users' interests, it must not be interpreted restrictively. As Professor Vaver . . . has explained . . . : "User rights are not just loopholes. Both owner rights and user rights should therefore be given the fair and balanced reading that befits remedial legislation."[53]

Indeed, all the key players, authors, publishers and users were and remain integral parts of a larger public interest whole. They each play a role in the development and dissemination of knowledge and learning and the law must be triangulated so as to ensure that, together, they achieve this goal. For creators, this means offering exclusive rights in order to encourage them not only to create but also to make their works public. On the industry side this goal manifests itself in offering excusive rights to en-

51 Madison, above note 9 at 12.

52 *Theberge v. Galerie d'Art du Petit Champlain*, [2002] 2 S.C.R. 336 at paras. 30–31, online at: http://csc.lexum.umontreal.ca/en/2002/2002scc34/2002scc34.pdf.

53 *CCH Canadian Ltd v. Law Society of Upper Canada*, 2004 SCC 13, [2004] 1 S.C.R. 339 at para. 48, online at: http://csc.lexum.umontreal.ca/en/2004/2004scc13/2004scc13.pdf.

courage investment in production and distribution. On the user side this means setting limits to the exclusive rights of copyright holders to ensure reasonable access and use of copyright content in order to acquire, share, transform and advance knowledge. The idea has always been about properly calibrating the law to ensure its overall purpose — a purpose that transcends any one group's exclusive interests.

C. PART 2: ASSESSING BILL C-32 IN SAFEGUARDING ACCESS TO KNOWLEDGE AND LEARNING

Bill C-32 provides for a number of legislative reforms to bolster the rights of each key constituent in the copyright equation. [54] Importantly, it offers a number of safeguards and enhancements for users of copyright works. One of the more salient features is the addition of "education" as an enumerated category within the fair dealing provision but there are a number of initiatives within the Bill that provide allowances for educational, personal or other public interest uses. [55] All of the proposed measures are designed to ensure that users can access and engage with copyright works outside of the direct control and oversight of the copyright holder.

Not surprisingly, these proposals have elicited criticism from certain creator and industry groups. For example, Canadian copyright licensing body, Access Copyright, argues that these provisions undermine the copyright holder's entitlement to compensation.

> [Bill C-32] . . . introduces new exceptions and greatly expands existing ones. These changes undercut the existing rights and abilities of content owners to monetize their works. New exceptions, which create a sudden increase in uncompensated uses of works, will result in significant lost sales and millions of dollars in revenue losses to

---

54 The official website is entitled *Balanced Copyright* at www.balancedcopyright.gc.ca. Press releases speak of a "fair, balanced and common-sense approach." See for example, "Government of Canada Introduces Proposals to Modernize the *Copyright Act*" at http://www.ic.gc.ca/eic/site/crp-prda.nsf/eng/h_rp01149.html.

55 Proposed sections 29–30 and their respective subsections. For a summary of these initiatives see the Government of Canada Fact Sheets "What the New *Copyright Modernization Act* Means for Consumers" and "What the New *Copyright Modernization Act* Means for Teachers and Students" at www.ic.gc.ca/eic/site/crp-prda.nsf/eng/h_rp01157.html.

> Canadian content owners from collective licences alone. Canadian content owners rely on these important sources of income.[56]

But we have seen that copyright law is not designed for the sole purpose of providing revenue streams for copyright holders. The goal of encouraging learning is equally essential and can only be achieved by providing limitations and exceptions to the copyright holder's rights. There are and always will be legitimate uses of a work that the copyright holder will not, as a matter of policy, be able to monetize. Bill C-32 is giving due recognition to a normative feature of the law that is centuries old.

When all is said and done, however, critics of the educational provisions may be agitating unnecessarily. The recognition and enhancement of user rights in Bill C-32 may well be nothing but smoke and mirrors when considered in light of the provisions relating to "technological protection measures" (TPMs).[57] The Bill makes it an infringement of copyright to circumvent TPMs that are designed to control access to and infringements of the work.[58] Bill C-32 does not discriminate between tampering with TPMs for infringing or non-infringing purposes and leaves it entirely to the discretion of the copyright holder to decide whether and how to use these controls. Further, it provides copyright holders with a wide range of remedies.[59]

---

56 Access Copyright, "Improving Canada's Digital Advantage" at http://de-en.gc.ca/wp-content/themes/clf3/upload/2266/Access%20Copyright%20Digital%20Advantage%20Submission%20%28final%29.pdf. See also the statement of ANEL (the Quebec French-language book publishing lobby), "Le project de loi sur le droit d'auteur C-32 constitue une atteinte sans précédent aux droits des créateurs" at www.anel.qc.ca/PDFAutoG/1_20100630133222.pdf.

57 David Fewer of the Canadian Internet Policy and Public Interest Clinic (CIPPIC) aptly describes the bill as "Jekyll and Hide" in its approach. See www.cippic.ca/uploads/Media_Release--Copyright_Bill_C-32--7June10.pdf.

58 The proposed definition of "technological protection measure"

> . . . means any effective technology, device or component that, in the ordinary course of its operation,
>
> (*a*) controls access to a work, to a performer's performance fixed in a sound recording or to a sound recording and whose use is authorized by the copyright owner; or
>
> (*b*) restricts the doing — with respect to a work, to a performer's performance fixed in a sound recording or to a sound recording — of any act referred to in section 3, 15 or 18 and any act for which remuneration is payable under section 19. [s. 41]

It is to be noted that the TPM provisions apply to both copyright holders and performers in respect of their performances.

59 See proposed s. 41.1(2). The bill does restrict the availability of certain remedies. See ss. 41.2, 41.1(3)), and 41.19.

It is true that Bill C-32 does provide for certain allowable exceptions. Importantly, circumventing TPMs to permit individuals with perceptual disabilities to enjoy copyright works is expressly deemed non-contravening.[60] However, the other limitations are all targeted towards narrowly circumscribed activities by specific users such as for law enforcement and national security, computer program interoperability, encryption research, personal information privacy, network or computer security, ephemeral reproductions by broadcasters or for receiving radio signals.[61] Nowhere does the Bill permit circumvention for fair dealing or any similar legitimate use. By providing such unregulated discretion on copyright holders to use digital locks, Bill C-32 entirely disregards the educative mission that is a foundational aspect of the law; one that requires that all users have the ability to use copyright works for purposes deemed reasonable and in the public interest.

To reflect back on Samuel Johnson's observation, copyright law must guard against the possibility that a "proprietor" will take it into his or her head to restrain the circulation of books and the knowledge they contain. Are we so convinced that copyright holders are that much more generous now than they were in eighteenth century England that this fear is no longer justified — that it is no longer the role of the State to guard against the risk of denial of access?[62] Are contemporary circumstances that different that we can justify disregarding the legacy of our earliest Canadian policy-makers who understood the law's purpose as one of dismantling, rather than erecting, barriers to knowledge and learning?

Do the WIPO Internet Treaties require such an absolutist approach to TPMs? Opinion remains divided on this question[63] but if the lessons from

---

60 Section 41.16.

61 See ss. 41.11–41.18.

62 The proponents of the "Access to Knowledge" movement at the international level have highlighted the harms of overprotection on access and use of copyright material. This is as much a modern concern as it was an historic one. See for example the sources cited in note 8 and more generally the Consumer Project on Technology at www.cptech.org/a2k/ and Consumers International at http://a2knetwork.org/about.

63 The argument raised to defend the absolutist position such as that adopted in Bill C-32 is that there is no meaningful way of protecting the legitimate interests of the copyright holder if there are allowances for fair dealing uses in that once a TPM is circumvented copyright content can be circulated with impunity. The commentary is divided on whether this fear is sufficient to justify such a displacement of basic copyright principles and on the correct interpretation of the WIPO Internet Treaties. On these issues see the differing opinions compiled by G. D'Agostino, "A Sampling of

the past offer any guidance then Canada should be aligning itself with those who take the position that our international treaty obligations can be met by limiting liability for circumvention to infringing uses.[64]

In defending the position taken in respect of TPMs, federal government representatives have dismissed concerns about the reach of their proposals.[65] Firstly, they claim that the provisions will not lead to an increased use of digital locks because their use is so unpopular. They argue that these measures will only be used routinely by those industries that are hardest hit by unauthorized copying. The Government seems to be placing inordinate faith on the fact that as digital delivery of content becomes the norm, copyright holders, especially big industry, will act with generosity (or at the very least with generous self-interest) in the way they manage their use of digital locks so as not to unduly "restrain circulation" of copyright works. It is also relying on the fact that individuals will protest their use so as to cause copyright holders to hesitate in the face of a resistant customer base. The Government expressly acknowledges that "[t]he success of TPMs depends on market forces. Creators may decide whether or not to use a TPM, and consumers can then decide whether or not to buy the product."[66] In this way, policy-makers are gambling that public pressure will compel copyright holders to use TPMs sparingly. However, to leave such important policy issues to be decided outside of the reach of the legislature is, in my estimation, a clear abdication of Governmental responsibility over defining the appropriate contours of the law.

Secondly, Government officials claim that abuses by copyright holders can be remedied by regulation — in effect recognizing the potential for

---

Commentary on Technological Protection measures" at www.iposgoode.ca/2010/06/bill-c-32-a-sampling-of-commentary-on-technological-protection-measures.

64 See for example: C. Craig, "Digital Locks and the Fate of Fair Dealing in Canada: In Pursuit of Prescriptive Parallelism" (2010) 13 The Journal of World Intellectual Property 503; B. Fizgerald & N. Suzor, "Getting the Balance Right: A Submission to the House of Representatives Standing Committee on Legal and Constitutional Affairs — Inquiry into technological protection measures (TPM) exceptions" (2005) available at http://nic.suzor.com/_media/publications/qut_gettingthebalanceright.pdf; E. Dellit & C Kendall, "Technological Protection Measures and Fair Dealing: Maintaining the Balance between Copyright Protection and the Right to Access Information" (2003) Digital Technology Law Journal 1.

65 Technical Briefing on the *Copyright Modernization Act*, teleconference hosted by Heritage Canada and Industry Canada on 2 June 2010. See as well Industry Canada, *Copyright Modernization Questions and Answers*, http://www.ic.gc.ca/eic/site/crp-prda.nsf/eng/h_rp01153.html#amend.

66 Industry Canada, *Copyright Modernization Questions and Answers*, *ibid.*

abuse. It is true that Bill C-32 allows the Governor in Council to make regulations if, in particular cases, a TPM "would unduly restrict competition in the aftermarket sector."[67] Further the Governor in Council may exclude the application of the anti-circumvention prohibitions in specific circumstances taking into account factors such as whether the TPM "could adversely affect" a number of enumerated activities including criticism, review, parody, teaching, scholarship or research.[68] However, relegating these concerns to regulation by the Governor in Council reinforces the entire orientation of the Bill, which appears geared towards providing the copyright holder with near-absolute discretionary control over the work through the use of digital locks.

Only time will tell if the Government is correct in its gambit should the Bill pass in its current form. In the meantime, I make no apologies for my cynicism. It seems to me that more than one copyright holder might well take it into his or her head to restrain circulation through the indiscriminate use of digital locks and that public opposition will not be sufficient to temper the generous bounty the Bill has provided. Further, by refusing to expressly recognize allowances for the legitimate exercise of user rights in TPM controlled works, Bill C-32 has, in one simple but sweeping legislative device, entirely forsaken the educative function that has been an essential feature of the law from its inception. Remaining faithful to the policy lessons of the past would have required a more measured — indeed, a more balanced — response.

---

67 Section 41.21 (1).

68 Section 41.21 (2).

CHAPTER FOUR

Fair Dealing at a Crossroads

Meera Nair*

A. INTRODUCTION

Shortly before his death Harold Innis wrote: "Law is apt to become anything 'boldly asserted and plausibly maintained.'"[1] Applying these words to the present environment suggests that copyright is mere moments away from becoming a means of absolute control. While those familiar with the law are cognizant of copyright's structure of limited rights, lay people see copyright as all-encompassing and act accordingly. Music downloading notwithstanding, perception is that copyrighted material cannot lawfully be used without permission. Judging by the proposed changes to the *Copyright Act*, perception is becoming nine-tenths of the law.

The future cost of treating copyrighted material as absolute property is difficult to assess. *Cost* must reflect the sum total of different manifestations; what will be the effect upon creativity in the arts, innovation in media, development in research, success in education, and the use of our bedrock democratic principle of freedom of expression? Intellectual effort

* I thank Michael Geist for his guidance, and librarians Mark Bodnar, Carla Graebner, and Sylvia Roberts, for their invaluable assistance. The comments of an anonymous reviewer were also very much appreciated. This work was funded, in part, by a grant from the Social Sciences and Humanities Research Council of Canada, provided through the Department of Economics at Simon Fraser University.

1 Harold Innis, *Changing Concepts of Time* (Lanham: Rowman & Littlefield Publishers, Inc., 2004) at 52.

is collaborative; implicitly, or explicitly, each new work draws in artifacts from other works. The means by which this time-honoured process of creativity achieves legitimacy in the system of copyright is through the limits upon control as prescribed by law. Copyright is not, nor has it ever been, a grant of absolute control.

Historical exploration is often used to probe the uncertainty of the relationship between control and creativity. Researchers in humanities, law, economics, and communication have drawn correlations between the flourishing of the arts and letters to periods of little, or no, protection of intellectual work. Common to the ancient civilizations, with attention upon the Greek, Chinese, Islamic, Jewish and Christian traditions, there was "a striking absence of any notion of human ownership of ideas or their expressions."[2] Eighteenth century France, in its day the epitome of culture, did not place authors at the centre of domestic copyright law.[3] In a rare empirical study, the creative output of 646 European music composers born between 1650 and 1849 was studied to the conclusion that it remains unproven as to whether stronger copyright laws made an appreciable difference in income levels, and thus the creative output, of composers.[4] Closer to our own time, popular music as it developed in mid-twentieth century America owes its genesis to unauthorized samplings from the blues tradition which itself had freely taken from West African antecedents.[5] And, throughout the twentieth century, the means by which creative effort reached mainstream audiences was inversely linked to copyright protection — from the player piano on, new media technology thrived in the spaces uncontrolled by copyright law.[6]

Those who are inclined to the position that stronger copyright protection is necessary to further creative effort, may be interested in the thoughts of a respected and influential figure within the American justice system. Judge Richard Posner of the United States Court of Appeals for the Seventh Circuit turns to one of our native sons on this matter:

---

2 Carla Hesse, "The rise of intellectual property, 700B.C.–A.D.2000: an idea in balance." (2002) 131(2) *Daedalus: Proceedings of the American Academy of Arts and Sciences*, 26 at 27.

3 Jane Ginsburg, "A Tale of Two Copyrights: Literary Property in Revolutionary France and America" in Brad Sherman & Alain Strowel, eds., *Of Authors and Origins: Essays on Copyright Law* (Oxford: Clarendon Press, 1994) at 144.

4 F.M. Scherer, *Quarter Notes and Bank Notes: The Economics of Music Composition in the Eighteenth and Nineteenth Centuries* (Princeton: Princeton University Press, 2004) at 194–96.

5 Siva Vaidhyanathan, *Copyrights and Copywrongs: The Rise of Intellectual Property and How It Threatens Creativity* (New York: New York University Press, 2001) at 14–15 and 117–48.

6 Lawrence Lessig, *The Future of Ideas* (New York: Vintage Books, 2002) at 107–10; see also Jessica Litman, *Digital Copyright* (Amherst: Promethus Books, 2001) at 173–74.

> The pervasiveness of borrowing in literature is captured in Northrop Frye's dictum that "poetry can only be made out of other poems; novels out of other novels." Frye had some tart words about copyright. He notes the challenge to the assumptions underlying the copyright law posed by "a literature which includes Chaucer, much of whose poetry is translated or paraphrased from others, Shakespeare, whose plays sometimes follow their sources almost verbatim; and Milton, who asked for nothing better than to steal as much as possible out of the Bible."[7]

While history alone cannot offer proof, it lends itself to persuasion. Throughout copyright's 300 year existence the law has operated as a system of limited rights.[8] Canada risks its creative and innovative potential if the limitations are diluted to such an extent as to render them useless.

It may be argued that copyright's limits are intact; that its structural design remains unaltered. The idea/expression dichotomy means that while creative expressions are protected, their underlying ideas are open to all; the inadmissibility of facts and data for copyright protection implies that the basic building blocks of knowledge are equally available; and the limited term of copyright ensures that copyrighted works themselves eventually become available for unfettered use.[9] And, depending on jurisdiction, measures like fair dealing permit some productive uses of copyrighted work.[10] It is this element that is essential for copyright to meet its

---

7 Northrop Frye, *Anatomy of Criticism: Four Essays* (Princeton: Princeton University Press, 1957) at 95–104, quoted by William M. Landes & Richard A. Posner, *The Economic Structure of Intellectual Property Law* (Cambridge: Belknap Press, 2003) at 59–60.

8 The birth of modern copyright law is usually ascribed to the *Statue of Anne* (1710); see Litman, above note 6 at 15.

9 With respect to the presumed benefit of dividing protection between ideas and expression, Rosemary Coombe writes that "the imagery of commerce is a rich source for expressive activity. In consumer cultures, most pictures, texts, motifs [etc.] are governed, if not controlled by regimes of intellectual property." See Rosemary Coombe, *The Cultural Life of Intellectual Properties: Authorship, Appropriation, and the Law* (Durham: Duke University Press, 1998) at 6. And the copyright term most commonly used throughout the world, lifetime of the creator plus fifty years, is far beyond that of the original statute which provided protection for fourteen years, renewable for another fourteen; see Benjamin Kaplan, *An Unhurried View of Copyright* (New York: Columbia University Press, 1967) at 7.

10 In Canada, individuals may engage in unauthorized reproduction of copyrighted material for the purposes of private study, research, criticism, review and news reporting, under certain conditions, including citation; see *Copyright Act*, R.S.C. 1985, c. C-42, http://laws.justice.gc.ca/en/C-42, ss. 29–29.2. Left unarticulated within the statute, but of importance in practice, is that the dealing must be fair. Guidance in the determination of

implicit mandate to foster creativity;[11] exceptions are the only means by which copyrighted material may be legitimately utilized, without authorization, *during* the term of protection.

Proponents of Bill C-32 will no doubt point to the proposed expansion of fair dealing—including categories for parody, satire and education—as evidence of recognition of the importance that copyright's reach be limited.[12] Indeed, this could be a productive step forward. Unauthorized use of copyrighted material for parody and satire does not yet have official sanction in Canada. Further detracting from the viability of these creative forms is a Federal Court decision in 1997 which held that parody could not be sheltered under the fair dealing allowance of criticism.[13] This decision elicited concern but continues to be influential.[14] Explicitly recog-

---

fairness was provided by the Supreme Court of Canada in 2004, see *CCH Canadian*, below note 21.

11 Canadian copyright law draws, in part, from common law antecedents. Notably, both British and American laws have articulated purposes to copyright. British law is derived from the *Statute of Anne* (1710), the title of which begins with "An Act for the Encouragement of Learning. . ." (http://avalon.law.yale.edu/18th_century/anne_1710.asp). American development of copyright law takes its mandate from their constitution. Article 1, Section 1, Clause 8 begins as "To promote the progress of science and the useful arts. . ." (http://avalon.law.yale.edu/18th_century/art1.asp#1sec8). In contrast, Canadian law has no explicitly written purpose.

12 Bill C-32, *An Act to Amend the Copyright Act*, 3d Sess., 40th Parl., 2010, at s. 29.

13 A representation of Bibendum, the Michelin Man, as a figure of oppression provoked this declaration from Teitlebaum J.: "I am not prepared to read in parody as a form of criticism and thus create a new exception." See *Compagnie Générale des Établissements Michelin-Michelin & Cie v. National Automobile, Aerospace, Transportation and General Workers Union of Canada (CAW-Canada)*, [1997] 2 F.C.306, www.canlii.org/en/ca/fct/doc/1996/1996canlii3920/1996canlii3920.html [*Michelin*] at para 68.

14 In *Michelin* the property rights of the plaintiff were disproportionately enjoyed over the defendant's right of freedom of expression; see *Michelin, ibid.* at para. 85–114. Jane Bailey comments that "the *Michelin* conclusion that users must justify their expression *vis-à-vis* the copyright owner's intended use of the 'property' mistakenly places the property cart before the constitutional horse." See Jane Bailey, "Deflating the Michelin Man," in Michael Geist, ed., *In the Public Interest: The Future of Canadian Copyright Law* (Toronto: Irwin Law, 2005) 125 at 141–42. Curious too was the imposition of an added code of conduct upon fair dealing: "even if parody were to be read in as criticism, the Defendants would have to adhere to the bundle of limitations that go with criticism, including the need to treat the copyright in a fair manner. The Defendants held the 'Bibendum' up to ridicule." See *Michelin*, above note 13 at para. 75. Michael Rushton comments that with this interpretation, fair dealing was reduced "to an obligation to use the materials in an impartial way." See Michael Ruston, "Copyright and freedom of expression: an economic analysis," in Ruth Towse, ed., *Copyright in the Cultural Industries* (Cheltenham: Edward Elgar, 2002) 51 at 58. In light of subsequent jurisprudence Emir Aly Crowne-Mohammed determines that parody's fortunes should have changed: "Lower courts should not feel constrained

nizing parody and satire as eligible forms of fair dealing opens a door to greater creative latitude in Canada. The merit of which may enjoy broader support than most copyright-related issues.[15] But such cooperation may be for naught; Bill C-32 also stipulates strict observance of technology protection measures (TPMs) even when a use is fair dealing.[16]

Allied to a diminishment of fair dealing through TPMs is an existing trend where the legitimate ambit of fair dealing has been encroached upon within educational institutions. Although fair dealing's predisposition to educational activities, via the purposes of private study, research, criticism, and review, should have set the exception on firm ground in the education community, this has not been the case.[17] Bill C-32's proposed inclusion of "education" as a permissible category of fair dealing drew immediate condemnation.[18] The depth of the misunderstanding of copyright,

---

by *Michelin*, which can no longer survive in light of the clear and unanimous guidance provided by the Supreme Court in *CCH*." See Emir Aly Crowne-Mohammed, "Parody as fair dealing: a guide for lawyers and judges in Canada," (2009) Journal of Intellectual Property Law & Practice 4(7) 468 at 471. Yet in November 2008 a parodied version of the *Vancouver Sun* newspaper was denied the defense of fair dealing by citing *Michelin*, see *Canwest v. Horizon*, 2008 BCSC 1609, www.canlii.org/en/bc/bcsc/doc/2008/2008bcsc1609/2008bcsc1609.html at para. 14

15 Access Copyright, a nonprofit copyright collective representing authors and publishers, signalled support for an exception for parody during last year's public consultation on copyright; see Access Copyright, www.ic.gc.ca/eic/site/008.nsf/eng/02603.html.

16 Bill C-32, above note 12 at s. 41. Interestingly enough, the US Librarian of Congress recently relaxed some of their prohibitions upon circumventing technological protection measures. Included was a measure that directly benefits educational uses of copyrighted materials, the extraction of clips from movies encrypted on DVDs, for the purposes of criticism and review, circumscribed by a requirement of good faith. This expands a previous allowance offered only to film and media studies professors; now all college and university professors, together with film and media studies' students, have permission. Creation of documentary films and noncommercial videos are also sheltered. See *Statement of the Librarian of Congress Relating to Section 1201 Rulemaking* at www.copyright.gov/1201/2010/Librarian-of-Congress-1201-Statement.html.

17 See below section B, "Seeds of Doubt."

18 Bill C-32 was unveiled on 2 June 2010; the next day Access Copyright announced: "On behalf of creators and publishers Access Copyright is deeply concerned by the extension of fair dealing to cover education and the introduction of numerous other exceptions in the *Copyright Act* which undermine the ability of creators and publishers to get paid for the use of their works" (www.marketwire.com/press-release/Access-Copyright-Is-Deeply-Concerned-Governments-Lack-Support-Remuneration-Creators-1270887.htm). On 8 June 2008, the response from the Writers Union of Canada came: "This new 'fair dealing' for the purpose of education is a wholesale expropriation of writers' rights and opens the door for the education sector to copy freely from books and other copyright material without paying writers."; see http://writersunion.ca/av_pr060810.asp.

the belief that it is meant to operate as an instrument of absolute control, is illustrated by David Lewis Stein: "But to writers, this 'fair dealing' feels like expropriation of property. It feels like the government saying, 'We are going to let people occupy rooms in your house and they won't have to pay any rent.'"[19]

The inclusion of education merely acknowledges that some of the existing copying carried out in educational institutions is legitimate fair dealing and should not be subjected to systems of permission or payment. The benefit of the inclusion is the clarity fair dealing brings to an otherwise unwieldy law. Students, teachers and educational staff are caught in a web of institutional exceptions granted to "Educational Institutions", "Libraries, Archives and Museums", and, "Libraries, Archives and Museums in Educational Institutions."[20] Simplifying the application of exceptions would facilitate observance of the law. This does not mean avoiding deliberate thought, quite the contrary. It is precisely because fair dealing does not sanction mass copying that any decision to copy requires careful consideration. While this may sound daunting, the Supreme Court of Canada has already provided cogent, and accessible, instruction.

In 2004, via *CCH Canadian v. Law Society of Upper Canada*, the nuance of fair dealing was made evident; our high court explained that each claim of fair dealing must stand on its own merits and must be examined holistically.[21] Briefly, a library which had reproduced single copies of reported decisions, case summaries, and other material pertinent to legal research, at the request of patrons, was deemed to have engaged in fair dealing and thus not guilty of copyright infringement. This issue was examined from first principles by considering what the intention of the system of copyright is, and, how does fair dealing fit within the system?[22]

Fair dealing is an imprecise doctrine; it permits some unauthorized reproduction of copyrighted material for certain purposes and under certain conditions. Its lack of explicit instruction is often seen as an impediment

---

19 David Lewis Stein, "New copyright legislation is bad news for Canadian writers," *TheStar.Com*, 14 July 2010, www.thestar.com/opinion/editorialopinion/article/835450--new-copyright-legislation-is-bad-news-for-canadian-writers.

20 See *Copyright Act*, above note 10 at ss. 29.4–30, 30.1–30.3, and 30.4

21 *CCH Canadian Ltd. v. Law Society of Upper Canada*, [2004] 1.S.C.R 339, 2004 SCC 13, www.canlii.org/en/ca/scc/doc/2004/2004scc13/2004scc13.html at paras. 47–73 [*CCH Canadian* cited to S.C.R.].

22 "In order to maintain the proper balance between the rights of a copyright owner and users' interests, [fair dealing] must not be interpreted restrictively . . . . As an integral part of the scheme of copyright law, the s. 29 fair dealing exception is always available." *Ibid.* at paras. 48–49.

to its use. Through the ruling as a whole, Canadians were offered with precision what ought to be self-evident: fair dealing's merit lies in its fluidity. Fair dealing is necessarily as indeterminate as the creative process it supports. To navigate the indeterminacy, decisions of fair dealing should include inquiry from a number of perspectives: the purpose of the dealing, the character of the dealing, the amount of the dealing, alternatives for the dealing, the nature of the work, and the effect of the dealing on the work.[23]

The story of *CCH Canadian* is well documented and noted for bringing attention to the vital role fair dealing plays in the pursuit of creativity.[24] Unfortunately, the guidance articulated through *CCH Canadian* was quickly set aside in the public eye and creators were seen to be under siege by copyright exceptions run wild.[25] This theme did not abate; it found new voice throughout last year's public consultation on copyright. In the face of proposals to give more flexibility to fair dealing, a prominent submission took great care to emphasize the instability of such an idea,[26] despite compelling evidence to the contrary.[27] Perhaps the greatest risk to a meaningful fair dealing provision in Canada lies in the continued insistence that fair dealing is only necessary when the market cannot meet Canadians' need for access to copyrighted work.[28]

To the casual onlooker it appears inevitable that fair dealing must give way. Yet there is nothing inevitable about such a step — fair dealing's precarious footing is a consequence of multiple events occurring within the last six years. This paper presents that history through the dialogue that has surrounded the exception. Worth repeating is the axiom that intel-

---

23 *Ibid.* at paras. 53–60. The framework of exploration was set against a critical point, the library had a clearly articulated policy on reproduction of materials, which illustrated that its own practices were compliant with fair dealing; *Ibid.* at paras. 61–63.

24 To name just a few: Teresa Scassa, "Recalibrating Copyright Law? A Comment on the Supreme Court of Canada's Decision in *CCH Canadian Limited et al. v. Law Society of Upper Canada*" (2004) 3(2) C.J.L.T. 89, http://cjlt.dal.ca/vol3_no2/pdfarticles/scassa.pdf; Carys Craig, "The Changing Face of Fair Dealing in Canadian Copyright Law," in Michael Geist, ed., *In the Public Interest: The Future of Canadian Copyright Law* (Toronto: Irwin Law, 2005) 437; Michael Geist, *Our Own Creative Land: Cultural Monopoly and the Trouble with Copyright* (Toronto: University of Toronto Hart House Lecture Committee, 2006); Laura J. Murray & Samuel E. Trosow, *Canadian Copyright — A Citizen's Guide* (Toronto: Between the Lines, 2007); and Giuseppna D'Agostino, "Healing Fair Dealing — A Comparative Analysis of Canada's Fair Dealing to U.K. Fair Dealing and U.S. Fair Use" (2008) 53(2) McGill L.J. 309 (http://lawjournal.mcgill.ca/documents/dAgostino.pdf).

25 See below section B. "Seeds of Doubt."

26 See below section C. "Fair Use or Not Fair Use."

27 See below section D. "Fair Use — Restoring the Reputation."

28 See below section E. "Market Expansion and Market Failure."

lectual effort requires collaboration. If future intellectual effort can only proceed via authorized collaboration, what impact will this have upon Canada's wellbeing?[29]

B. SEEDS OF DOUBT

To better understand fair dealing as it stands now, one must be aware of its prior journey. Fair dealing entered Canadian law in 1921 and saw some interesting moments in the twentieth century;[30] however, for the purposes here, the journey begins in March 2004 with ruling of *CCH Canadian*. This carefully chosen starting point needs explanation; it marks a change of perspective on the part of the Ministry of Canadian Heritage with respect to the role played by exceptions to copyright. In 2002, the Director General had said:

> We have recognized exceptions with regard to fair dealing and educational use, and these exceptions have been accepted by rights holders, as a general rule. Of course they don't like them, and we understand that. Nevertheless, copyright is about balancing interests between rights holders and users.[31]

29 Bearing in mind that common law copyright is depicted as an instrument which encourages creativity, by assigning limited property rights to the creators of intellectual works. The assumption is that the subsequent proliferation of creative effort benefits society as a whole. Yet doubts of the efficacy of copyright were raised early in its development. The extent of differing opinions was such that, in 1876, it became an object of study by the British Government: see *Royal Commission on Laws and Regulations Relating to Home, Colonial and Foreign Copyrights: Report, Minutes of Evidence, Appendix* (London: Eyre and Spottiswoode, 1878). Skepticism continued into the twentieth century under no less a voice than Arnold Plant: see Arnold Plant, "The Economic Aspects of Copyright in Books." (1934) 1(2) *Economica* 167 <http://www.jstor.org/stable/2548748>. For more recent criticism of the rationale of intellectual property see David Vaver, "Intellectual Property: The State of the Art." in David Vaver, ed., *Intellectual Property Rights: Critical Concepts in Law* (London: Routledge, 2006) vol.1; see also David K. Levine & Michele Boldrin, *Against Intellectual Monopoly* (New York: Cambridge University Press, 2008). And this year, writing for the Conference Board of Canada, Ruth Corbin observes "Stronger rights are not necessarily more effective in achieving desirable economic outcomes. The pursuit of effective rights rather than stronger rights is more likely to achieve consensus among diverse groups of stakeholders."; see Ruth Corbin, *Intellectual Property in the 21st Century* (Ottawa: The Conference Board of Canada, 2010) at 81 (www.conferenceboard.ca/temp/32eb4957-d647-4389-8953-fdf29fad937c/10-186_IPRreport_WEB.pdf).

30 Craig, above note 24 at 440-446; see also D'Agostino, above note 24 at 329-333.

31 Canada, Standing Committee on Canadian Heritage, *Evidence*, 37th Parl., 1st sess., (11 June 2002), www2.parl.gc.ca/HousePublications/Publication.aspx?DocId=525054&Language=E&Mode=1&Parl=37&Ses=1.

Whereas three weeks after *CCH Canadian* that same director had adopted a new position:

> The objective, of course, is to again find the right balance in terms of the overall public interest . . . . It's only when the market doesn't work, when it's impossible for rights holders to apply their licensing abilities, that we talk about an exception approach, again with a view to meeting the overall public interest.[32]

Intentionally or otherwise, the impression cast was that fair dealing operates solely in response to market failure.

At that time, copyright policy in Canada was under review. Both the Canadian Heritage and Industry Ministries were involved, with committee meetings conducted through the Ministry of Canadian Heritage. Throughout the proceedings, staff and committee members openly described themselves as supporting creators' rights.[33] This perspective was capitalized upon by rights holders' representatives who invoked *CCH Canadian* as signaling open season upon Canadian creators. Although the decision explained in detail that multiple lines of inquiry are needed, and that each situation must be judged on its own merits, rights holders' representatives omitted reference to that guidance and instead warned that fair dealing posed great unfairness to their clientele:

> . . . you are of course aware that the Supreme Court of Canada, in its ruling on the *Law Society of Upper Canada vs. Thompson Canada Limited*, considerably broadened the concept, or scope, of exceptions by establishing these exceptions—which were previously considered privileges—as users' rights.[34]

> . . . The Supreme Court has decided that under the existing fair dealing exemption, lawyers can copy legal writings and others can provide a reproduction and distribution service for them without the consent of the copyright owner.[35]

---

32 Canada, Standing Committee on Canadian Heritage, *Evidence*, 37th Parl., 3d sess. (25 March 2004), www2.parl.gc.ca/HousePublications/Publication.aspx?DocId=1268317&Language=E&Mode=1&Parl=37&Ses=3.

33 Remarks of a Member of Parliament: "I want to declare up front a bias: I'm on the side of the creators." Canada, Standing Committee on Canadian Heritage, *Evidence*, 37th Parl., 3d sess. (27 April 2004), www2.parl.gc.ca/HousePublications/Publication.aspx?DocId=1329168&Language=E&Mode=1&Parl=37&Ses=3.

34 *Ibid.*

35 *Ibid.*

> . . . I do implore you that you as legislators should not be looking at how the court has interpreted the law we now have. Please give us the law we need.[36]
>
> . . . Since the Supreme Court came down with its ruling on the *CCH* case, many of us have been wondering what the impact of the court's expanded definition of fair dealing will be . . . The court has clearly taken some broad policy positions on copyright issues, but this government should not hesitate to seize back the momentum in defining that policy.[37]
>
> . . . The most recent Supreme Court judgment on copyright—and it has been discussed a great deal—exacerbated this imbalance, by allowing a generous interpretation of exceptions for users, and by making simple exceptions into rights for users, rights that are to be incorporated broadly and liberally.[38]

It appeared that creators were no longer safe in Canada. A Member of Parliament said:

> . . . I too have heard about the court ruling, and as a consumer of creative works, I was somewhat shocked to see that we are being taken further and further away from the concept of the creator. . . . I think this sends out the wrong message to people. Now, people think that works are free of charge, that they can download compact discs from the Internet, that there is no charge with on-line downloading, and the same applies to written works.[39]

With creators' rights perceived as threatened, the environment was not conducive to a request from a representative of the Council of Ministers of Education Canada (CMEC) for permission to use publicly available material obtained from the Internet free of charge in Canadian classrooms.[40]

---

36 Canada, Standing Committee on Canadian Heritage, *Evidence*, 37th Parl., 3d sess. (28 April 2004), www2.parl.gc.ca/HousePublications/Publication.aspx?DocId=1336967&Language=E&Mode=1&Parl=37&Ses=3.

37 Canada, Standing Committee on Canadian Heritage, *Evidence*, 37th Parl., 3d sess. (29 April 2004), www2.parl.gc.ca/HousePublications/Publication.aspx?DocId=1339917&Language=E&Mode=1&Parl=37&Ses=3.

38 *Ibid.*

39 *Ibid.*

40 "We are proposing an amendment to permit the educational use of publicly available Internet materials, one that is intended to address educational needs and ultimately clarify and enhance respect for copyright ownership on the Internet": Standing Committee on Canadian Heritage (27 April 2004), above note 33.

CMEC's position was a curious one from the outset; "publicly available" should absolve any teacher or student from charges of infringement. If a copyright holder posts material on the Internet, without invoking any form of technological protection, he or she has implicitly given consent to use of the material. With consent, there is no infringement. And if a copyright holder was to argue against implicit consent, fair dealing should be given due consideration.[41] CMEC could have relied upon *CCH Canadian* to reassure rights' holders of the subtlety of fair dealing, that it is not a blanket invitation for copying en masse. Yet as Laura Murray observed soon after:

> Instead of invoking *CCH v. Law Society* to bolster a claim about fair dealing, [the CMEC representative] left that to . . . a coalition of Québec copyright collectives, who used the case as a warning to the government not to grant any exceptions, because the courts would defend and perhaps even broaden them.[42]

In the years following *CCH Canadian*, Canadian education institutional representatives remained disquietly silent on the decision, focusing their efforts instead on a continuing plea for an educational exemption for use of publicly available material from the Internet. It was not until 2008 that a body representing academic practitioners showed enthusiasm for fair dealing and *CCH Canadian*:

> Fair Dealing is the right, within limits, to reproduce a substantial amount of a copyrighted work without permission from, or payment to, the copyright owner. Its purpose is to facilitate creativity and free expression by ensuring reasonable access to existing knowledge while at the same time protecting the interests of copyright owners. . . . [It is important] that universities and colleges codify robust fair dealing practices in institutional policy. Such guidelines are necessary because the *Copyright Act* does not contain a simple formula that sets out exactly what may or may not be copied without permission or payment.[43]

---

41 Sam Trosow provides a four-part series explicitly refuting a need for this exemption; see Sam Trosow, "Educational Use of the Internet Amendment: Is it Necessary?" (31 January 2008), http://samtrosow.ca/content/view/27/43.

42 Laura J. Murray, "Protecting Ourselves to Death: Canada, Copyright, and the Internet" *First Monday* (4 October 2004), (http://firstmonday.org/htbin/cgiwrap/bin/ojs/index.php/fm/article/view/1179/1099).

43 "Fair Dealing," in CAUT, *Intellectual Property Advisory*, December 2008, No. 3 at 1, (www.caut.ca/uploads/IP-Advisory3-en.pdf).

In their advisory document the Canadian Association of University Teachers (CAUT) gave the details of *CCH Canadian* together with an explanation of the step-by-step evaluation conducted by the Supreme Court. The case's relevance to university research and teaching was identified, as was the urgency that universities in Canada take steps to preserve the free and open exchange of information as is necessary to advance knowledge: "This can be achieved by molding existing practices of sharing to fit within the fair dealing parameters set out by the Supreme Court of Canada in the *CCH* decision."[44]

The reference to "existing practices" is critical as *CCH Canadian* contained a warning: "It may be relevant to consider the custom or practice in a particular trade or industry to determine whether or not the character of the dealing is fair."[45] Meaning, the element of fairness is contingent on what is considered customary behavior within the group affected. Academic endeavor is predicated upon the tradition of sharing. Fortunately, as educational uses of copyrighted material, particularly at the university level, routinely involve private study, research, criticism and review, and, the citation necessary for a legitimate claim of fair dealing is the backbone of academic practice, universities occupy a strong position with respect to lawful observance of fair dealing. What is missing is an articulated stance, together with widespread understanding, that utilization of copyrighted material is in accordance with the principles of fair dealing.[46]

But it does not appear that Canadian universities have placed a priority upon codifying robust fair dealing practices. A study that examined policies addressing the inclusion of copyrighted material in original research found a noted absence of influence from *CCH Canadian*.[47] Although not exhaustive (the data set is a cross-section of Canadian universities), the study illustrates that fair dealing is not well understood. Some institutions have diminished the role of fair dealing, favouring instead a system of permission (and potential payment) for inclusion of material that would legitimately sit as fair dealing. Despite five years of incubation, *CCH Canadian* has not, to any appreciable degree, taken root in the Canadian university landscape.

The limited presence of fair dealing at Canadian universities was reflected in last year's public consultation. Scholarly associations, library

---

44 *Ibid.* at 4–5.

45 *CCH Canadian*, above note 21 at para. 55.

46 *Ibid.* at paras. 61–63.

47 Meera Nair, *From Fair Dealing to Fair Duty — the Necessary Margins of Canadian Copyright Law* (Ph.D. Dissertation, Simon Fraser University, 2009) at 148–88. [unpublished].

communities, individual academic practitioners, students, and citizens submitted thoughtful arguments to protect and expand fair dealing.[48] However, official engagement from universities themselves was modest; only six written submissions appear on the consultation website.[49] This is regrettable; fair dealing's reputational capital could have been enhanced with lasting attention from the executive branch of Canadian universities. In the face of a campaign which at best seeks to constrain fair dealing, and at worst to discredit it entirely, the reticence of universities may prove to be a missed opportunity.

C. FAIR USE OR NOT FAIR USE — THAT BECAME THE QUESTION

At the end of the consultation period, a joint submission appeared, titled *Why Canada Should Not Adopt Fair Use*.[50] Prepared by a leading Canadian law firm, and endorsed by over forty copyright representative organizations, the thrust of the argument aims at negating requests that fair dealing be amended to operate with greater flexibility. The submission of the Canadian Internet Policy and Public Interest Clinic (CIPPIC) is used as illustration of the desire to expand fair dealing. As CIPPIC writes,

> the current law denies the defense to any dealing that does not fit within an enumerated category, no matter how fair. Amending the

48 All written submissions are publicly available at the consultation website, www.ic.gc.ca/eic/site/008.nsf/eng/home. It is beyond the confines of this paper to credit all those who engaged with consultation; with regret the author has limited recognition to the following: Canadian Association of Music Libraries, Archives and Documentation Centres, www.ic.gc.ca/eic/site/008.nsf/eng/02935.html; Canadian Federation for Humanities and Social Sciences, www.ic.gc.ca/eic/site/008.nsf/eng/02006.html; Ian D. Allen, www.ic.gc.ca/eic/site/008.nsf/fra/01785.html; David Gilbert, www.ic.gc.ca/eic/site/008.nsf/eng/02491.html; Sara M. Grimes, www.ic.gc.ca/eic/site/008.nsf/eng/02722.html; Darryl Moore, www.ic.gc.ca/eic/site/008.nsf/eng/02015.html; Duncan Murdoch, www.ic.gc.ca/eic/site/008.nsf/fra/01331.html;. And it must be emphasized that Canadians engaged with all the challenges inherent to copyright; a noteworthy submission is that of violin maker, Gerard Ivan Samija, www.ic.gc.ca/eic/site/008.nsf/eng/02253.html.

49 Athabasca University, www.ic.gc.ca/eic/site/008.nsf/eng/02825.html; Concordia University, www.ic.gc.ca/eic/site/008.nsf/eng/02473.html; Queen's University, www.ic.gc.ca/eic/site/008.nsf/eng/02378.html; Trinity Western University, www.ic.gc.ca/eic/site/008.nsf/eng/02565.html; University of Alberta, www.ic.gc.ca/eic/site/008.nsf/eng/02651.html; University of Saskatchewan, www.ic.gc.ca/eic/site/008.nsf/eng/02858.html.

50 Access Copyright *et. al.*, *Why Canada Should Not Adopt Fair Use: A Joint Submission to the Copyright Consultation*, www.ic.gc.ca/eic/site/008.nsf/eng/02524.html.

provision to read, "... fair dealing for purposes including," rather than "... for the purposes of," would accommodate those practices.[51]

The framework offered in *CCH Canadian* resembles that prescribed in the fair use provisions of the United States; provisions which are predicated upon the language of "for purposes such as."[52] American law stipulates that judgments of fair use must be made by considering four factors:

(1) the purpose and character of the use, including whether such use is of a commercial nature or is for non-profit educational purposes;
(2) the nature of the copyrighted work;
(3) the amount and substantiality of the portion used in relation to the copyrighted work as a whole; and
(4) the effect of the use upon the potential market for or value of the copyrighted work.[53]

By removing the specificity of purpose within fair dealing, and following the guidance provided in *CCH Canadian*, Canadian fair dealing will, in terms of the letter of the law, be closely aligned to the United States' implementation of fair use. The joint submission gives a list of objections to fair use:

1) the Canadian government had already rejected such consideration;
2) it would reduce revenue to Canadian creative industries;
3) it will place Canada in a precarious position with respect to international rules concerning exceptions; and
4) it will introduce greater uncertainty at a time when "most stakeholders are calling for greater certainty and clarity in Canadian copyright law."[54]

For each objection raised, a nuanced explanation or rebuttal exists. Carys Craig explains the previous deliberations by the government; fair dealing was considered a success by comparing the relatively low rates of litigation in Canada to the litigious atmosphere surrounding fair use in the United States. "It would have been more appropriate to regard the rarity of fair dealing in Canadian courts as indicative of its impotence rather

---

51 Canadian Internet Policy and Public Interest Clinic, www.ic.gc.ca/eic/site/008.nsf/fra/02666.html, emphasis omitted.

52 USC 17, U.S.C. § 107 (2000 & Supp. IV 2004), www.law.cornell.edu/uscode/html/uscode17/usc_sec_17_00000107----000-.html.

53 *Ibid.*

54 Access Copyright *et. al.*, above note 50.

than its success: the predictable result of a restrictive defense, ill-equipped to ameliorate the position of users or restrain the demands of owners."[55] The claim of reduced revenues to Canadian creative industries is a disingenuous one — as if simply making fair dealing's current list of purposes illustrative is sufficient for any use to be a lawful exception. Fulfilling the category of use is merely the first step; the multiple levels of inquiry as presented in *CCH Canadian* must still be addressed. If fair dealing remains stringently closed, it is not the current creative industries that will feel the most pain.

The value of an illustrative set of purposes is that it permits uses, which may have the hallmarks of fair dealing, the possibility of being considered so. This not only promotes future creativity, it also protects existing creative practices. A submission on behalf of appropriation artists highlights the inter-dependency of creative works:

> Today many artists and creators use, reproduce, appropriate and incorporate materials found within popular culture and society. These raw materials reflect and embrace the world around us: snippets of film and TV, radio spots, advertisements, news headlines, bits of text, characters, fragments of song . . . and so on. Artists use this source material just as artists have used raw material for thousands of years. . . . The practice of appropriation is a fundamental part of many creative cultural activities. . . . Artists who use appropriation in their practice, rely on Canada's fair dealing exception to create. Fair dealing is a narrow right, at times too narrow to support this work . . . Creators should enjoy the support of the law, and not have to work under conditions of uncertainty and fear.[56]

The artists' invocation of the theme of certainty lies in opposition to that of the joint submission. In the hands of the latter "certainty and clarity" can only be achieved by strictly curtailing fair dealing. In and of itself this is true — setting rules that limit creative behaviour will achieve certainty, albeit with an undesirable effect. As new media have historically developed in spaces outside the strictures of copyright, this point was emphasized by a coalition of telecommunications, broadcasting, retail, Internet, technology, research and security organizations. In the eyes of Bell, Google, Rogers Communication Inc., Telus, the Canadian Wireless and Telecommunications Association, and others, fair dealing should be expanded and

55 Craig, above note 24 at 441.

56 Appropriation Art Coalition, www.ic.gc.ca/eic/site/008.nsf/eng/02734.html.

protected from the deleterious effects of technological protection measures.[57] To do otherwise risks "harming emerging Canadian industries and exposing Canadian businesses and consumers to unnecessary and costly litigation."[58]

The coalition also makes an interesting comment with respect to international requirements:

> Given that it has now been over a decade since the WIPO treaties were finalized, Canada actually finds itself in a somewhat unique position among developed nations. Canada is able to learn from the steps taken by other nations to meet their own 1996 WIPO treaty obligations, and to do so in a much more mature online environment. Similar to other nations, Canada should take advantage of the considerable flexibility the WIPO treaties provide to meet our obligations.[59]

The joint submission refrains from consideration of the flexibility available within the WIPO treaties. Attention is drawn instead to the experiences of Australia, United Kingdom, New Zealand, and the European Union; each considered and rejected adopting fair use or expanding fair dealing. Some common elements were cited in the reasons for rejection: fear of uncertainty, disruption of licensing models, and concerns over compliance with international regulations.[60] From the language employed, it would seem that international regulations are only about the rights of the copyright holder. Whereas the Preamble of the WIPO Copyright Treaty includes: "The Contracting Parties . . . [recognize] the need to maintain a balance between the rights of authors and the larger public interest, par-

---

57 Business Coalition for Balanced Copyright, www.ic.gc.ca/eic/site/008.nsf/eng/02534.html.

58 *Ibid.*

59 *Ibid.* This same sentiment was expressed by Bruce Lehman, the principal architect of the United States' *Digital Millennium Copyright Act* (1998), at a conference titled *Musical Myopia, Digital Dystopia: New Media and Copyright Reform*, held at McGill University in March 2007, "Canada has the benefit of the soon-to-be decade of experience of the U.S. . . . in some areas our policies have not worked out too well . . . Attempts at copyright control have not been successful; at least with regards to music" (at 12:58). Video coverage available at: http://video.google.com/videoplay?docid=4162208056624446466&hl=en#; Michael Geist, a panelist at the same conference, writes that "In a later afternoon discussion, Lehman went further, urging Canada to think outside the box on future copyright reform. While emphasizing the need to adhere to international copyright law (i.e., Berne), he suggested that Canada was well placed to experiment with new approaches." Michael Geist, "*DMCA* Architect Acknowledges Need For A New Approach" (23 March 2007), www.michaelgeist.ca/content/view/1826/125.

60 Access Copyright *et. al.*, above note 50.

ticularly education, research and access to information, as reflected in the Berne Convention."[61]

The *Berne Convention for the Protection of Literary and Artistic Works* (1886) was the first international agreement on minimal standards of copyright protection.[62] From its infancy on, the negotiation of the standards included awareness that the grant of copyright must be limited, and, member states must be permitted some latitude as to how exceptions to copyright were implemented in domestic law.[63] A proposal to formally introduce the allowance of exceptions came forward during the 1967 Stockholm negotiations; after much discussion the following was accepted as Article 9(2):

> It shall be a matter for legislation in the countries of the Union to permit the reproduction of such works in certain special cases, provided that such reproduction does not conflict with the normal exploitation of the work and does not unreasonably prejudice the legitimate interests of the author.[64]

This has come to be known as the Berne three-step test: (1) the exception must be for a specific circumstance; (2) it must not conflict within the realm of exchange that is usually associated to the work; and (3) must not unreasonably detract from the author's wellbeing. The joint submission questions the adherence of United States to the *Berne Convention*: "Many authorities have reviewed the fair use system for compliance with the three-step test and have expressed the opinion that it is non-compliant."[65] A specific complaint is issued via the words of a respected scholar Sam Ricketson: "The real problem, however, is with a provision that is framed in such a general and open-ended way."[66]

This selective invocation of Ricketson's work does not illustrate the context in which he makes that statement. In the work cited, a study prepared for WIPO Standing Committee on Copyright and Related Rights in 2003, Ricketson examines different styles of limitations. He contrasts an open-ended provision which is guided by leading principles, with a closed-list

---

61 *WIPO Copyright Treaty*, World Intellectual Property Organization, 20 December 1996, <http://www.wipo.int/treaties/en/ip/wct/trtdocs_wo033.html#preamble>.

62 *Berne Convention for the Protection of Literary and Artistic Works*, 9 September 1886, with subsequent revision, <http://www.wipo.int/treaties/en/ip/berne/trtdocs_wo001.html>.

63 Sam Ricketson. *The Berne Convention for the Protection of Literary and Artistic Works: 1886-1986* (London: Centre for Commercial Law Studies, Queen Mary College, 1987) at 477.

64 *Ibid.* at 481.

65 Access Copyright *et. al.*, above note 50.

66 Sam Ricketson quoted in Access Copyright *et. al.*, above note 50.

provision. Illustrating the endpoints are Section 107 of the US *Copyright Act* (1976) and Article 5 of the EC Information Society Directive, with the Australian *Copyright Act* (1968) serving as a midpoint position.[67]

Ricketson sees some merit to American fair use: "There is the obvious advantage of flexibility here: it enables new kinds of uses to be considered as they arise, without having to anticipate them legislatively."[68] He then states that the indeterminate language surrounding the purpose of use may not comply with the first of the Berne three step tests, "although it is always possible that, in any given case, [the purposes] will find support under other provisions of Berne, such as Articles 10 and 10*bis*."[69] Similarly, Ricketson has praise and concern with the EC's Article 5: "The advantage of the extensive listing is that each exception and limitation is relatively self-contained and can be considered on its own terms. It is still possible that some of these might still fail the separate requirements of the three-step test."[70] The Australian Act is flavoured by both approaches, containing many specifically delineated exceptions and "several broader provisions (those concerned with fair dealings of works) that reflect the more open-ended U.S. fair use formula, although these are still kept within relatively limited confines as to purpose."[71]

Returning to the present concern of shaping fair dealing in more flexible terms, it remains that the United States has been party to the *Berne Convention* for more than twenty years, with its illustrative set of fair use purposes.[72] The joint submission presents the view that the United States escapes international scrutiny by virtue of the fact that it is the United States;[73] if so, this is a rather damning indictment of the usefulness of

---

67 Sam Ricketson, *WIPO Study on Limitations and Exceptions of Copyright and Related Rights in the Digital Environment* (Geneva: WIPO, 2003) at 67 (www.wipo.int/edocs/mdocs/copyright/en/sccr_9/sccr_9_7.pdf).

68 *Ibid.* at 68.

69 *Ibid.* at 69. Articles 10 and 10*bis* of Berne offer a range of exceptions that member states can draw upon; See *Berne Convention*, above note 62.

70 Ricketson, above note 67 at 72.

71 *Ibid.* at 73. Illustrative of such a "broader provision" is the Australian fair dealing exception for study and research; see Myra Tawfik, "International Copyright Law and 'Fair Dealing' as a 'User Right'" (April–June 2005) *UNESCO Copyright Bulletin*, http://unesdoc.unesco.org/images/0014/001400/140025e.pdf at 12–14. With reference to a more comprehensive work of Ricketson's that expressly focused upon Australian copyright law, Tawfik notes there is only a "very fine line," between Ricketson's deemed status of Australian compliance and American non-compliance; *Ibid.* at 14.

72 The *Berne Convention* entered into force for the United States on 1 March 1989, see www.wipo.int/treaties/en/ShowResults.jsp?lang=en&treaty_id=15.

73 Access Copyright *et. al.*, above note 50 at n.70.

our prevailing world trade body. A more reassuring indication of the value of international trade governance comes from another respected scholar, Pamela Samuelson:

> The true mission of TRIPs is not to raise levels of intellectual property protection to ever higher and higher planes, as some right holders might wish, but to encourage countries to adopt intellectual property policies that promote their national interests in a way that will promote free trade and sustainable innovation on an international scale.[74]

For most of its existence the United States permitted itself a flexible regime of fair use and has also been the site of extensive developments in creativity and new media.[75] To prove the correlation is not possible, but to ignore the element of correlation is unwise. In any case, the joint submission refrains from counterfactual reflection and instead concentrates on portraying fair use as dysfunctional: "Many other U.S. scholars have also concluded that there are significant problems with the fair use model."[76] There is a degree of truth to this statement, but it invites closer scrutiny. The real question is *why* fair use has its challenges in the context of American events. If fair use has proven problematic in the United States, this does not negate the possibility that flexible fair dealing will be successful in Canada. Success or failure will be dependent on Canadian circumstances.

D. FAIR USE — RESTORING THE REPUTATION

The doctrine of fair use with its four factor analysis has attracted considerable scholarly attention. During the public consultation a key work was identified by the Canadian Copyright Institute:

> It is instructive that for every one case on fair use decided in the courts in the US, there have been approximately 2.4 academic articles written on the subject (Barton Beebe, An Empirical Study of U.S. Fair

74 Pamela Samuelson quoted in Tawfik, above note 73 at 9. The *Trade Related Aspects of Intellectual Property Agreement* (TRIPs) established 15 April 1994 sets as its foundation the standards set by the *Berne Convention*, see Sam Ricketson and Jane Ginsburg, *International Copyright and Neighboring Rights — The Berne Convention and Beyond*, Volume 1 2d ed., (Oxford: Oxford University Press, 2005) at 157-158.

75 Lessig and Litman, above note 6.

76 Access Copyright *et. al.*, above note 50.

> Use Opinions, 1978–2005, 156 U. Pa. L. Rev). This level of academic interest does not suggest a clear and predictable law.[77]

This limited reference to Barton Beebe's work is curious, given that the institute describes its purpose as "to encourage a better understanding of copyright law on the part of its members and the public, and to engage in and to foster research and reform in copyright law.[78] Beebe's work is a landmark empirical study of American fair use case law.[79] He begins by identifying a flaw in the existing scholarship:

> Yet, remarkably, we continue to lack any systematic, comprehensive account of our fair use case law. Instead, like the "great men" approach to history, we pursue a "leading cases" (or "usual suspects") approach to fair use. This anecdotal method, one essentially of connoisseurship, derives conventional wisdom about our case law from a limited aristocracy of hand-picked opinions appearing primarily in the U.S. Reports — or in the student casebooks. Whether these opinions have any influence on or are representative of the true state of our fair use doctrine as it is practiced in the courts remains an open, and strangely unasked, question.[80]

Beebe answers this question with a content analysis of a data set consisting of all reported American opinions which drew, in a substantive way, upon fair use's four factor analysis. The 306 opinions studied span the effective date of the 1976 codification of fair use through to January 2005. Beebe's complete methodology is rigorous and fully disclosed;[81] the criteria by which cases are assembled are broader than that of a preceding study of fair use cases.[82]

---

77 Canadian Copyright Institute, www.ic.gc.ca/eic/site/008.nsf/eng/02553.html.

78 *Ibid.*

79 Barton Beebe, "An Empirical Study of U.S. Copyright Fair Use Opinions: 1978–2005." (2008) 156(3) U. Pa. L. Rev. 549 (www.bartonbeebe.com/documents/Beebe%20-%20Empirical%20Study%20of%20FU%20Opinions.pdf).

80 *Ibid.* at 552.

81 *Ibid.* at 623.

82 A previous cross-sectional study is found in David Nimmer, ""Fairest of Them All" and Other Fairy Tales of Fair Use" (2003) 66 (1,2) Law & Contemp. Probs. 263 (www.law.duke.edu/shell/cite.pl?66+Law+&+Contemp.+Probs.+263+(WinterSpring+2003)). Nimmer studied sixty fair use opinions and concludes that courts first decide on the outcome for fair or unfair use, and then position the four factors to support that outcome. Beebe conducts a logistic regression upon Nimmer's data set and indicates that "the only significant factor outcome was the second, going to the nature of the plaintiff's work, and the coefficient was *negative*" (emphasis in original). See Beebe, above note 79, n.12. Nimmer's

Beebe examines the manner in which the four factor analysis entered American law, and identifies the late 1980s as the timeframe when American courts began a trajectory of mechanical application of the four factors.[83] In the years following "judges rarely explicitly considered factors beyond the four listed in section 107 and, with the exception of the second factor, rarely failed to consider fewer than all four factors."[84] While the mechanistic approach within American courts did not make for good law, it lent itself to systematic study. Beebe presents extensive summary statistics where distributions of the 306 opinions are described along multiple dimensions: time, venue (district or circuit court), posture (preliminary injunction, summary judgment, or bench trial opinion), and the nature of the copyrighted work at issue (print media dominated the case law).[85] The perception that fair use decisions are inherently unstable, and prone to reversal, is not borne out by the evidence. The rate of reversal at the circuit court level is closely in line with the overall circuit court reversal rates, and at the district court level the numbers are similarly uninteresting.[86]

Beebe's analysis of the win rates presents a high degree of favour to the plaintiffs, but he suggests an explanation:

> Some defendants who are otherwise committed to defending against a copyright infringement claim on grounds such as copyrightability or substantial similarity may find it relatively inexpensive also to plead a fair use defense, even when the defense may be frivolous or at least very weak in light of the facts. Because conscientious judges will dutifully consider each of the four factors, as section 107 instructs them to do, even when the outcome of the fair use test is obvious, opinions addressing even essentially extraneous fair use defenses

---

own assessment of his methodology illustrates its subjectivity; see Nimmer at 267, n.27. The joint submission makes repeated reference to Nimmer's study: i.e., "Even if Canada was able to import all facets of the U.S. system intact, scholars such as Nimmer suggest that no clear direction would be ascertainable from the U.S. example, with the statutory fair use factors providing no correlation whatsoever with the prospects of success in any given case." See Access Copyright *et. al.*, above note 50.

83 The starting point roughly corresponds to the US Supreme Court's 1985 ruling in *Harper & Row, Publishers, Inc. v. Nation Enterprises*, 471 U.S. 539 (1985), www.law.cornell.edu/copyright/cases/471_US_539.htm. Beebe, above note 79 at 562.

84 *Ibid.* at 563–64. The Supreme Court of Canada expressly instructs that fair dealing's multifaceted inquiry should not be held rigidly, not all questions may apply all the time and there may be questions that are not reflected in the framework; see *CCH Canadian*, above note 21 at paras. 53–60.

85 Beebe, above note 79 at 564–81.

86 *Ibid.* at 574–75.

> will have come within those sampled for this study. This would drive down overall fair use win rates.[87]

To resolve the problem of a frivolous fair use plea, Beebe offers a reasonable quantitative determination; that the strength or weakness of the claim of fair use would be reflected in the proportion of words in the opinion. With a frivolous claim, judges would be likely to expediently dismiss the effort. By excluding forty-two opinions which devoted less than 10 percent of the opinion to fair use, the defendant win rate of the remaining opinions rises.[88]

Beebe employs regression and correlation analyses to investigate both the interaction between the four factors of judgment, and, what sub-factors may have implications for each individual factor decision. The analyses are complex and should be examined first hand; for this paper Beebe's findings on the first and fourth factors are of note. These factors draw consideration to questions of commerciality; the first factor examines the defendant's use of the work, and the fourth factor considers the effect on the plaintiff's market. Beebe shows that these two factors received a high degree of attention and were almost evenly weighted in deliberations.[89] This supports the view that American decisions of fair use have placed undue emphasis on commercial consideration.[90] But Beebe does not stop here; he questions why judges had this inclination.

Beebe's answer relies on multiple dimensions of inquiry. He begins with a prevailing concern of fair use; that judges tend to make a decision, and then adjust the four factor analysis to support the decision.[91] Beebe refers to this practice as stampeding, and agrees with its existence in two cases decided by the United States' Supreme Court:

> In *Sony*, the district court found that three (or perhaps four) factors favored fair use, while the Ninth Circuit found that all four factors disfavored fair use. At the Supreme Court, the five-justice majority

87 *Ibid.* at 580.

88 *Ibid.* at 580-81.

89 *Ibid.* at 582-86.

90 William Patry, *The Fair Use Privilege in Copyright Law*, 2d ed. (Washington DC: The Bureau of National Affairs, Inc., 1995) at 419–32. See also Margaret Jane Radin, "Incomplete Commodification in the Computerized World" in Niva Elkin-Koren & Neil Weinstock Netanel, eds., *The Commodification of Information* (The Hague: Kluwer Law International, 2002) at 10.

91 David Nimmer (above note 82) writes that "the four factors fail to drive the analysis, but rather serve as convenient pegs on which to hang antecedent conclusions." Quoted in Beebe, above note 79 at 589.

> then found that all four factors favored fair use, while the four dissenters found that all four factors disfavored fair use. *Harper & Row* stampeded back and forth in essentially the same way.[92]

Yet after examining the fair use case law as whole, the evidence does not support the conclusion that factor outcomes are always distorted one way or the other.[93] And through his analysis of fair use cases which reached the United States' Supreme Court, Beebe uncovers the reasons for the overt emphasis upon commerciality which explains "why our fair use doctrine has to some extent run off the rails of section 107."[94]

The prominence of commerciality, through the first and fourth factors, was set in the 1984 *Sony* decision, even though that action was inconsistent with the statutory language of the law.[95] Although the United States' Supreme Court sought to correct its mistakes, with some success in 1994,[96] lower courts continued to place undue emphasis upon commerciality:

> Overall, despite the language of section 107, the commerciality inquiry and the *Sony* presumption in particular remain exceptionally tenacious memes in the fair use case law. No doubt this reflects in part their high fitness for a litigation environment pervaded with commercial expression. But it is also a consequence of the Supreme Court's repeated attempts to maintain appearances by reconstruing what it should simply have rescinded and replaced.[97]

If the instability of fair use, to the degree that it exists, has its foundations in the mishandling of the commerciality elements by an obdurate high court, Canadian fear of fair use should lessen. The framework provided

---

92 Beebe, above note 79 at 589–90. Footnotes omitted.

93 *Ibid.* at 591–93

94 *Ibid.* at 596.

95 *Sony Corp. of Am. v. Universal City Studios, Inc.*, 464 U.S. 417 (1984), www.law.cornell.edu/copyright/cases/464_US_417.htm; see Beebe, above note 79 at 598–99. With respect to the ruminations on commerciality as found in *Sony*, William Patry makes an intriguing observation: "Most basic is the seldom-noted fact that since the use before the Court was noncommercial, the statement is pure dictum. It was made in passing, without any explanation of what such a presumption might mean or how it was to be applied." See Patry, above note 90 at 430.

96 Beebe, above note 79 at 600–1 with respect to *Campbell v. Acuff-Rose Music, Inc.*, 510 U.S. 569 (1994). In *Campbell*, fair use is famously described as a providing "breathing space within the confines of copyright" necessary to accommodate the need of, "simultaneously [protecting] copyrighted material and [allowing] others to build upon it" (at para. 575).

97 Beebe, above note 79 at 602.

through *CCH Canadian* expressly places the element of commerciality as dependent upon context. With respect to the purpose of the dealing:

> Courts should attempt to make an objective assessment of the user/defendant's real purpose or motive in using the copyrighted work. . . . Moreover, as the Court of Appeal explained, some dealings, even if for an allowable purpose, may be more or less fair than others; research done for commercial purposes may not be as fair as research done for charitable purposes.[98]

The language, "may not be," makes evident that further investigation is needed before proceeding to conclusion. In terms of considering the effect on the market, "Although the effect of the dealing on the market of the copyright owner is an important factor, it is neither the only factor nor the most important factor that a court must consider in deciding if the dealing is fair."[99] And to further safeguard against any tendency to elevate the element of commerciality, the Supreme Court went one degree further with:

> The availability of a licence is not relevant to deciding whether a dealing has been fair. As discussed, fair dealing is an integral part of the scheme of copyright law in Canada. Any act falling within the fair dealing exception will not infringe copyright. If a copyright owner were allowed to license people to use its work and then point to a person's decision not to obtain a licence as proof that his or her dealings were not fair, this would extend the scope of the owner's monopoly over the use of his or her work in a manner that would not be consistent with the *Copyright Act*'s balance between owner's rights and user's interests.[100]

These safeguards ought to please Canadian copyright holders. If we must draw conclusions about the American experience of fair use, their lack of holistic examination has been to the detriment of some copyright holders. While intuitively it might be expected that emphasis upon commerciality would forever bias the final outcome, this proved to be false, and, ironically, in some hands the converse became a constructed truth:

> A finding that the defendant's use was for a commercial purpose (which was made in 64.4% of the opinions) did not significantly influence the outcome of the fair use test in favor of an overall finding of

98 *CCH Canadian*, above note 21 at para. 54.

99 *Ibid.* at para. 59.

100 *Ibid.* at para. 70.

> no fair use. Rather, it was a finding that the defendant's use was for a *noncommercial* purpose (which was made in 15.4% of the opinions) that strongly influenced the outcome of the test in favor of an overall finding of fair use.[101]

Fortunately, Canadian courts would be hard-pressed to follow the *non sequitur* reasoning that if commerciality disallows fair use, then noncommerciality implies fair use. By the guidance expressed through *CCH Canadian*, nothing is presumptive; an evaluation of fair dealing must include multiple points of inquiry, with the added reminder that even the framework provided may require adjustment depending on the situation.[102]

Beebe's overall conclusion is encouraging; his view is that Americans can trust that a population of judges over time will systematically present the way forward to better practice of the fair use doctrine:

> It appears that for all of their fractiousness, judges applying fair use doctrine have done just that. Where the nonleading cases declined to follow the leading cases, they repeatedly—and systematically—did so in ways that expanded the scope of the fair use defense. To be sure, the data reveal many popular practices that impair the doctrine: courts tend to apply the factors mechanically and they sometimes make opportunistic uses of the conflicting precedent available to them. These are systematic failures that require intervention. Nevertheless, as a whole, the mass of nonleading cases has shown itself to be altogether worthy of being followed.[103]

With respect to adding flexibility to fair dealing, whether it is under the name of fair use or any other, Canada is well-positioned to circumvent the growing pain experienced by the United States. A greater difficulty in moving forward with a flexible regime of fair dealing is the continued insistence that fair dealing should be subservient to market transactions of copyrighted material.

---

101 Beebe, above note 79 at 602 (emphasis in original). These results draw from a logistic regression model of "the outcome of the fair use test as a function of (1) a variety of factual findings made by judges in the 297 dispositive opinions, and (2) whether the opinion was written by a district or circuit court of the Second or the Ninth Circuits. The results of this model . . . correctly classified 85.1% of the 297 opinion outcomes," *Ibid.* at 594.

102 *CCH Canadian*, above note 21 at para. 60.

103 Beebe, above note 79 at 622.

E. MARKET EXPANSION AND MARKET FAILURE

At the outset of this paper, it was claimed that a sequence of events came together to destabilize both the value of fair dealing and the guidance offered through *CCH Canadian*. Three such events have been elaborated upon: (1) the immediate reaction to *CCH Canadian* was hostile and given a platform within the government; (2) the delayed and modest engagement by Canadian educational bodies with fair dealing; and (3) a deliberate effort to paint a flexible regime of fair dealing as unstable. A fourth element exists, although it cannot be contained as a finite event. It is an ongoing campaign to expand collective management of copyright and promote licensing, particularly through digital operations.

In this regard, the activities of Access Copyright are germane. While much of their submission is the same as that of the joint submission described earlier, Access Copyright goes further and explicitly invokes the market failure perspective of fair dealing and other exceptions. In their view, exceptions are only required when "there is a demonstrated public policy need for access to copyright protected materials and the market has not met or is unable to meet that demand."[104] Again, Canadians are well served by previous research. Extensive literature exists concerning the challenges wrought by the nature of exceptions within a market framework.[105] What Canadians may find interesting is that our experiences are mimicking a theoretical exercise proposed in the United States when Americans were contemplating the intersection of digital works and worldwide networks within the ambit of copyright. Technology presented the vision of effortless communication between copyright holders and the buying market. The seeming ease of pecuniary exchange played well to arguments for reducing or eliminating fair use.[106]

Implicitly supporting the impetus provided by technology was a seminal paper in 1981 by Wendy Gordon, arguing that "the presence or absence of the indicia of market failure provides a previously missing rationale for predicting the outcome of fair use cases."[107] However, twenty years later,

---

104 See Access Copyright, above note 15.

105 With focus on the discipline of Law and Economics, see Ruth Towse, Christian Handke & Paul Stepan, "The Economics of Copyright Law: A Stocktake on the Literature." (2008) Review of Economic Research on Copyright Issues 5(1) 1, http://ssrn.com/abstract=1227762.

106 Ben Depoorter & Francesco Parisi, "Fair Use and Copyright Protection: A Price Theory Explanation." (2002) Int'l Rev. L. & Econ. 21, 453 at 454, http://ssrn.com/abstract=259298.

107 Wendy J. Gordon, "Fair Use as Market Failure: A Structural and Economic Analysis of the "Betamax" Case and its Predecessors." (1982) 82(8) Colum. L. Rev. 1600 at 1605, http://www.jstor.org/stable/1122296.

Gordon revised some aspects of her original position.[108] With others, Gordon credits the work of Lydia Loren who draws attention to the reality that market failure exists in two dimensions:

> The market failure theory of fair use asserts that the right of fair use should exist only when a failure in the market exists. The fact that one type of market failure may have been cured through the implementation of a permission system by the copyright holder does not preclude, however, the presence of a different kind of market failure. If copyright is to remain true to its constitutionally mandated goal, courts must be willing to recognize the most important kind of market failure relevant to fair use: the inability to internalize the external benefits of certain kinds of use. This holds especially true for non-transformative uses in the context of research, scholarship and teaching.[109]

"Inability to internalize external benefits," may need some explanation. Externalities are unintended consequences; they may be negative, such as pollution, or positive as in this case where one work fosters future works. Speaking abstractly, in any market transaction the cost of both negative and positive externalities ought to be reflected in the pricing of the item of exchange. In the context of copyright, the positive outcome propagated by a work implies a higher value of a work. Assuming that the effects of a work could be quantified, its impact is set upon an indeterminate number of variables — the degree and frequency to which the original work contributes to future works. To compensate, the ensuing price will likely be too high for current markets to absorb the work to full efficiency. This will lead to an under-consumption of that work, which in turn means a subsequent loss of positive social benefit, and is equally a market failure.[110]

---

108 Wendy J. Gordon, "Excuse and Justification in the Law of Fair Use: Commodification and Market Perspectives" in Niva Elkin-Koren & Neil Weinstock Netanel, eds., *The Commodification of Information* (The Hague: Kluwer Law International, 2002) 149–92 at 152.

109 Lydia Pallas Loren, "Redefining The Market Failure Approach To Fair Use In An Era Of Copyright Permission Systems." (1997) 5 J. Intel. Prop. L., 1 at 57–58 (http://legacy.lclark.edu/~loren/articles/fairuse.htm).

110 Michael Heller brings this into more conventional language, albeit through the unconventional word: underuse. *Underuse* is not a generally recognized word, whereas *overuse* is common parlance. Heller focuses on the problem that lack of productive use of resources is an inefficiency society cannot afford. "When we lack a term to describe a social condition, it is because the condition does not exist in most people's minds . . . It is unsurprising that we have overlooked the hidden costs of fragmented ownership."

While this category of market failure can be mitigated through fair use or fair dealing, it relies on a wider understanding of the creative process. Ben Depoorter and Francesco Parisi write: "This solution obviously begs the question of why the producers of the original work should bear the entire cost of the subsidy, rather than spreading its cost across a broader group of individuals."[111] The answer is straightforward; the producers of an original work are *not* bearing the cost of the subsidy, in fact they are re-paying the costs of their own past debts. Their creative effort is predicated upon previous generations of creative activity. Such a debt cannot be paid to the past; it can only be discharged in the future.

Regrettably, Gordon's initial theoretical rationale was effectively followed in the United States, as shown by the emphasis upon commerciality. What Canadians must take note of was the inclination by American courts to see systems of licensing as sufficient to deny fair use.[112] A point that was pressed during the copyright consultations; the General Counsel for Access Copyright made a concerted effort to override fair dealing when licenses are available:

> There's one solution in our *Copyright Act* for other types of exceptions which I think is one that we could continue to use, and those are exceptions that I like to call smart exceptions. They're exceptions that exist in the *Copyright Act* to ensure that access is provided so that the user, where there is an access need in a very specific situation where there is a justified reason that access should be provided such as in the education sector, that there is an exception in place. But that exception gets trumped when the work becomes commercially available or when a license is available.[113]

Given that it was the overt emphasis upon commerciality of the fair use deliberations which lead to its troubles in the United States, it would imprudent for Canada to take this step.

See Michael Heller, *The Gridlock Economy: How Too Much Ownership Wrecks Markets, Stops Innovation, and Costs Lives* (New York: Basic Books, 2008) at 23.

111 Depoorter and Parisi, above note 106 at 457.

112 *Ibid.* at 456; see also Loren, above, note 109 at 32048. Again, the Supreme Court of Canada has expressly refuted the proposition that licensing on its own can deny fair dealing: see above note 100.

113 See remarks made at the Gatineau Roundtable discussion, 29 July 2009, www.ic.gc.ca/eic/site/008.nsf/eng/h_04028.html.

F. CONCLUSION

In terms of Bill C-32, the issue of fair dealing seems a modest one. Debate will focus upon whether or not individuals may circumvent a technological protection measure for non-infringing purposes such as fair dealing. This is a poor compromise as it still requires that Canadians must break into a work to exercise a legitimate right. The submission of David Gilbert returns to mind: "If digital locks are necessary then so are digital locksmiths."[114] And yet, this scenario is the most hopeful outcome.

The greater challenge rests on encouraging Canadians to continue using fair dealing. To whatever extent fair dealing exists on paper, legal text alone cannot keep fair dealing as a meaningful component within the system of copyright. If the measure is not actively used, its merit is lost. This paper has traced the diminishment of fair dealing over the last six years — from the high point of endorsement by the Supreme Court of Canada in 2004 to its ongoing denigration.[115] The relentless, albeit misplaced, criticism discourages use of fair dealing.

If, in practical terms, fair dealing is consigned to obscurity, future Canadians may not notice. That will be a pity; that a once viable means to foster Canadian talent and creativity was blunted through innuendo and misdirection. In that scenario, Canadian creative effort will be confined to derivative work for which the input copyright permission is easily obtained through direct-click business models. This is not tragic, but it

---

114 Gilbert, above note 48.

115 Access Copyright solicited active participation from its affiliates during the consultation process, by some rather inflammatory language. For instance, a newsletter sent out under the title of "Copyright Debate Takes Aim at Your Livelihood," spoke of, "individuals who do not agree you should get fair compensation for digital and other reproductions of your works" (private email received by the author). After the consultations closed, Access Copyright continued to emphasize the great risk of expanding fair dealing, "Adding 'such as' [to fair dealing] can be *so* detrimental to existing business models that over 50 Canadian organizations, including Access Copyright, who represent hundreds of thousands of creators and publishers from <u>across</u> the country joined forces to submit a paper during the Copyright consultations that warned against expanding fair dealing" (emphasis in original). See Access Copyright, *Copyright Reform Bill This Spring?* at www.accesscopyright.ca/default.aspx?id=314. And the collective ensured that the Federal Government continued to hear their concerns during meetings this past spring, even though, as the Access Copyright General Counsel observed, copyright was not the theme of those meetings: see Canada, Standing Committee of Canadian Heritage, *Evidence*, 40th Parl., 3d sess. (20 April 2010), www2.parl.gc.ca/HousePublications/Publication.aspx?DocId=4447614&Language=E&Mode=1&Parl=40&Ses=3.

will not place Canada in any position of strength in a world influenced by knowledge economies.

Chad Gaffield, President of the Social Sciences and Humanities Research Council of Canada, has alerted the government to the possibility that Canada will be left as a digital colony, and, indicated that such a possibility can be avoided:

> Canada has key advantages. Thanks to broadband penetration, talented Canadians are not just seeking information, they're using it and reusing it. They are interacting with it and with others. They are seeking to manipulate and comment on it, to rework it, and to create new content. Indeed, the world is beginning to recognize a distinctly Canadian way of understanding communication and the importance of communication technologies. Let me conclude by emphasizing that we must admit that despite promising signs and the reality of our potential, Canadians are not taking full advantage of the digital opportunities, whether on our campuses, in our businesses, in our communities, or anywhere. We can and must do more. But on the path to creating the future we want, we must first cross the threshold of the imaginable.[116]

Crossing the threshold of the imaginable requires a dispassionate analysis of the role played by copyright in creative effort. Anxiety over financial returns to creators is understandable; to suggest that effectively absolute copyright protection is the only way forward is not. However, as that course of action plays well to the current population of rights holders, it is a more appetizing political decision. But good politics is not the same as good policy. And limiting Canadian policy to such narrow terms is a disservice to the many Canadians who engaged with the intricacies of copyright during last year's public consultation. While the consultation illustrated the polarity of opinion, pitting those who ask for expansive copyright against those who oppose copyright in any sense, it also encouraged Canadians to better educate themselves about the issues at hand. Many did just that and showed a credible understanding of the give and take represented within the system of copyright.[117]

---

116 Canada, Standing Committee of Canadian Heritage, *Evidence*, 40th Parl., 3d sess. (27 October 2009), www2.parl.gc.ca/HousePublications/Publication.aspx?DocId=4181231&Language=E&Mode=1&Parl=40&Ses=2.

117 This interest could be further encouraged, a task well suited to postsecondary education. Our school system consciously fosters the practices necessary for legitimate operation of fair dealing. Children begin their educational lives with lessons in sharing; as they move

The importance of the exception cannot be overstated; not merely because of the access it can facilitate but because of what it is: the only component within the system of copyright that actively supports creativity itself. Fair dealing addresses the creative needs required prior to completion of a work, and serves as a counterbalance to the distribution rights that control the work after completion. Enough has been written to assure rights holders that fair dealing is not a thinly disguised vehicle for wholesale expropriation. A recent court decision gives added credence through practice.[118] It now falls to the government to move this issue forward. Bill C-32 positions fair dealing at a crossroads: in one direction fair dealing receives encouragement and is actively practiced by Canadians; in another fair dealing settles quietly into the pages of law books and only historians will remember that Canada had an opportunity to introduce a more vibrant atmosphere for creative activity.

---

forward the importance of doing their own work is impressed upon them; in the realm of high school students are taught the formalities of citation; and through postsecondary education they prepare themselves for professional engagement with copyrighted materials. *At that stage*, explaining the concept of fair dealing as a principle of law is appropriate. Teaching Canadians students how to operate legitimately with copyright is not only an ethical obligation, but leaves them better positioned in a world which places weight upon information commodities.

118 On 23 July 2010 the Federal Court of Appeal (FCA) released their decision concerning tariffs on photocopied material for use in elementary and secondary schools; see *Alberta Education v. Access Copyright*, 2010 FCA 198, www.canlii.org/en/ca/fca/doc/2010/2010fca198/2010fca198.html. The FCA conducted a multifaceted inquiry (as instructed by *CCH Canadian*) set upon existing fair dealing categories of private study, research, criticism and review, and ruled that the majority of photocopying taking place in schools remain subject to pecuniary compensation (at paras. 36–48). This decision is significant; it recognizes that educational activity can be represented through the existing fair dealing categories and simultaneously reinforces that a category by itself does not automatically confer legitimacy upon a claim of fair dealing.

CHAPTER FIVE

The Art of Selling Chocolate:

Remarks on Copyright's Domain

Abraham Drassinower*

A. INTRODUCTION

On 27 July 2007, the Supreme Court of Canada released a significant decision dealing with copyright and parallel imports, *Euro-Excellence Inc. v. Kraft Canada Inc.*[1] The decision is truly extraordinary. It offers an opportunity to study systematically the interaction of several copyright issues: including the rights (or lack thereof) of exclusive licensees as plaintiffs in

---

* Earlier versions of this paper were presented at the University of Ottawa Faculty of Law Torys LLP Technology Law Speaker Series; Torys LLP Intellectual Property CLE Program; ALAI Canada (Montreal) Speaker Series; ALAI Canada (Toronto) Speaker Series; and the University of Toronto Faculty of Law "Legal Conceptions of Reputation" Colloquium. I want to thank participants in those workshops for their comments, including Jane Bailey, Mario Bouchard, Jennifer Chandler, Jeremy DeBeer, Ysolde Gendreau, Vincent de Grandpré, Elizabeth Judge, Ian Kerr, Howard Knopf, Andrea Rush, Andrew Shaughnessy, Barry Sookman, Simon Stern, Sam Trosow, Peter Wells, and Peter Wilcox. I also want to thank Bruce Chapman, Yoav Mazeh, Laura Murray, Andrea Slane, and Arnold Weinrib for discussions during the composition of the paper, Ariel Katz and two anonymous reviewers for helpful comments on an earlier draft, and Diana Lee for her research assistance. It goes without saying that the responsibility is all mine. The Social Sciences and Humanities Research Council of Canada and the Centre for Innovation Law and Policy at the University of Toronto Faculty of Law provided support during the completion of the paper.

1 2007 SCC 37, http://csc.lexum.umontreal.ca/en/2007/2007scc37/2007scc37.html [*Euro-Excellence*].

parallel import situations, the distinction between exclusive licensees and assignees, the nature of works of authorship, the characteristics of copyright infringement, the status of copyrightable works when used as trademarked logos, the limits (if any) of concurrent copyright and trade-mark protection, and even the distinction between trade-mark, copyright, and patent as autonomous yet related legal regimes.

If that were not enough, the decision has yet another attraction. It regales us not with one or two, but with nothing less than four different judgments. In addition to the reasons for judgment by Justice Rothstein (writing for himself, Binnie and Deschamps JJ), we have a dissent by Justice Abella (writing for herself and McLachlin CJC), a set of concurring reasons by Justice Fish, and yet another set of reasons by Justice Bastarache (writing for himself, LeBel and Charron JJ), concurring in result, but developing a markedly distinct aspect of the case, and in fact dissenting from the reasons offered by Justice Rothstein to reach the very same result. The effect of these overlapping yet distinct and concurring judgments, which both partially agree and partially disagree with each other in multiple respects, is that, aside from the relatively easy statement that the defendant parallel importer won the case, it is difficult to identify with clarity or conviction what the law of parallel imports of copyrighted works is in Canada. One would be forgiven for jesting that *Euro-Excellence* is a law professor's dream.

I suspect that one would also be forgiven for failing to engage directly in the immediate controversies that the case dramatizes through its judgments, and for choosing instead to emphasize certain aspects of the case with a view to plumbing its contribution to an ongoing juridical conversation in Canada about the nature and scope of copyright protection—that is, a conversation about how to define and how to limit copyright. This conversation is certainly worthy of our attention, all the more so when the recurrent agitations of copyright reform threaten both to distract us from, and to compel us toward, the exigencies and serenities of clear thinking.

The most salient recent moments in that conversation are the well-known Supreme Court of Canada decisions in *Théberge v. Galerie d'Art du Petit Champlain inc.*[2] and *CCH Canadian Ltd. v. Law Society of Upper Canada*.[3] I want in what follows to frame *Euro-Excellence* as another iteration

2 *Théberge v. Galerie d'Art du Petit Champlain inc.*, 2002 SCC 34, http://csc.lexum.umontreal.ca/en/2002/2002scc34/2002scc34.html [*Théberge*].

3 *CCH Canadian Ltd. v. Law Society of Upper Canada*, 2004 SCC 13, http://csc.lexum.umontreal.ca/en/2004/2004scc13/2004scc13.html, [2004] 1 S.C.R. 339 [*CCH*].

of issues treated in those landmark decisions. More specifically, I want to frame *Euro-Excellence* in light of (a) the evolving roles in Supreme Court of Canada copyright jurisprudence of the concepts of "balance," "reproduction," and "user rights" in the copyright system, and (b) the distinctions between copyright, patent and trade-mark as legal regimes.

It will become clear in the course of my discussion that, of the four *Euro-Excellence* judgments, Justice Bastarache's is by far the best suited to that purpose. I will first review very briefly the facts and procedural history of the case, as well as the basic contours of each of the judgments in *Euro-Excellence*. On that basis, I will move on to an analysis of Justice Bastarache's judgment. My aim is less to offer a detailed exegesis of the judgment than to tease out the ways in which the concept of copyright's own specific domain interacts with that of copyright's purpose, and to speculate about the implications that this interaction holds for our understanding of copyright subject-matter and copyright infringement.

Boldly put, my purpose is to thread through a copyright sensibility that conceives of the domain of copyright as a domain of authorship, and of authorship as an act of communication. This is a sensibility far more sympathetic to education, parody and satire than to efforts to lock up digitally the contributions of authorship — a sensibility that, by its very nature, refuses to impart juridical reality to the persistent metaphor that works of authorship are but intangible chattels, presumptively subject to unencumbered ownership.[4]

---

4 For the proposed widening of fair dealing in Canada so as to include education, parody and satire, see Bill C-32, *An Act to amend the Copyright Act*, 3d Sess., 40th Parl., 2010, cls. 21–22 (first reading 2 June 2010), www2.parl.gc.ca/HousePublications/Publication.aspx?Docid=4580265&file=4. For proposed provisions prohibiting circumvention of technological protection measures ("digital locks") in Canada, see Bill C-32, cl. 47. For once proposed anti-circumvention provisions, including provisions for allowable circumvention for non-infringing purposes, see Bill C-60, *An Act to amend the Copyright Act*, 1st Sess., 38th Parl., 2004–2005, cl. 27 (first reading 20 June 2005), www2.parl.gc.ca/HousePublications/Publication.aspx?Docid=2334015&file=4 (e.g., the owner of copyright in a work is entitled to remedies against a person who "for the purpose of an act that is an infringement of the copyright" in the work circumvents without the consent of the copyright owner a technological protection measure protecting the work). On the historical construction of authors as owners in copyright law, see Mark Rose, *Authors and Owners: The Invention of Copyright* (Cambridge, MA: Harvard University Press, 1993). On works of authorship as communicative acts, see Immanuel Kant, "On the Wrongfulness of Unauthorized Publication of Books," in Mary J. Gregor trans. & ed., *Practical Philosophy* (Cambridge: Cambridge University Press, 1996) at 23.

In the context of copyright reform, this sensibility conflicts with anti-circumvention regimes, particularly when proposed, as in Bill C-32, in the absence of provisions for allowable circumvention for non-infringing purposes. In my view, digital locks manifest an aspiration to enable copyright holders to exclude others from any and all uses of locked up content. From this perspective, anti-circumvention regimes implement the proposition that copyright holders are, or should be, entitled to exclude others from any and all uses of locked up content. Where (a) digital locks grant a copyright holder unencumbered control, and (b) circumventing digital locks is unlawful, then (c) lawful copying can take place only at the copyright holder's pleasure.[5] This is radically at odds with the fundamentals of copyright. Copyright law is not a prohibition on copying but, on the contrary, a highly elaborate juridical effort to distinguish between permissible and impermissible copying. The idea/expression dichotomy, for example, is but an assertion that, as a copyright law matter, ideas, even if original, are free as the air to common use. Similarly, fair dealing is but an affirmation of the category of permissible use as constitutive of copyright law. While there can be no doubt that copyright is a prohibition on certain kinds of copying, nor can there be any doubt that the proposition that all copying gives rise to liability is incompatible with copyright law. A copyright holder's unencumbered control of any and all uses of a work is foreign to copyright. To the extent that anti-circumvention regimes grant or seek to grant copyright holders such control, they are at odds with the very logic that structures copyright law as an institutionalized distinction between permissible and impermissible use. In denying the field of permissible use, anti-circumvention denies copyright itself.

To be sure, a world in which permissible use flourishes untrammeled to the point of denying the field of impermissible use is also — and per-

---

5 Of course, no digital lock is perfect. For example, it is hard to imagine how a digital lock could prevent someone from memorizing and then transcribing for purposes of criticism and review a poem to which he or she has had access. My point, however, is not that digital locks are perfect. My point is that certain unauthorized uses of copyrighted works are best regarded, not as the outcome of imperfections in the technology of digital locks, but rather as "user rights" integral to copyright law. The fact that digital locks are imperfect is not an argument to tolerate them. There is after all no reason to assume that the uses that current technologies cannot prevent coincide with those that copyright law puts beyond the reach of the copyright holder's control. "User rights" are not some kind of collateral benefit flowing from imperfections in the technology of control. Rather, they are best grasped as juridical limits that the law of copyright would impose on technological protection measures. In short, the aspiration to control any and all uses of locked-up content is inconsistent with copyright law.

haps more obviously — incompatible with the structure of copyright law. This is indeed the dystopian vision that copyright holders fear, and it is indeed the vision that catalyzes digital locks and anti-circumvention regimes. Whether anti-circumvention regimes, even those that include provisions for allowable circumvention for non-infringing purposes, can be rendered compatible with the fundamentals of copyright is thus an unavoidable and difficult question. What seems more than clear, however, is that an anti-circumvention regime devoid of such provisions is intolerable. By eliminating, or seeking to eliminate, the category of unauthorized yet permissible use from the copyright landscape, it would operate like an encysted foreign body undermining copyright law from the inside out.

In *CCH*, the Supreme Court of Canada famously held that so-called copyright "exceptions" are rather "user rights" as constitutive of copyright law as "author rights." The decision corroborates what the fundamentals of copyright have taught all along. Copyright deprived of legitimate unauthorized use is, literally, use-less copyright. The reflection that follows seeks to render certain aspects of *Euro Excellence*, the most recent of the Supreme Court of Canada's copyright decisions as a deepening and continuation of the copyright sensibility animating *CCH*.

B. *EURO-EXCELLENCE INC. v. KRAFT CANADA INC.*

Plaintiff Kraft Canada Inc. is the exclusive Canadian distributor of Côte d'Or and Toblerone chocolate bars. Kraft Canada Inc. sued defendant Euro-Excellence Inc. for copyright infringement arising from unauthorized importation for purposes of sale and distribution of copyrighted works (i.e., the Côte d'Or and Toblerone logos) appearing on the wrappers in which the chocolate bars were sold and distributed by Euro-Excellence Inc. in Canada. Basically, the fact giving rise to the action is that Euro-Excellence Inc. imported into Canada for purposes of sale chocolate bars legally acquired elsewhere. The issue is whether that importation—more specifically, the importation of the copyrighted logos on the chocolate wrappers—is wrongful pursuant to Section 27(2)(e) of the *Copyright Act*.[6]

---

6 *Copyright Act*, R.S.C. 1985, c. C-42, http://laws.justice.gc.ca/en/C-42/39253.html [*Copyright Act*]. Section 27(2) provides that:

> It is an infringement of copyright for any person to
>
> (a) sell or rent out,
>
> (b) distribute to such an extent as to affect prejudicially the owner of the copyright,
>
> (c) by way of trade distribute, expose or offer for sale or rental, or exhibit in public,
>
> (d) possess for the purpose of doing anything referred to in paragraphs (a) to (c), or

The trial judge and the Federal Court of Appeal both held in the plaintiff's favour.[7] The Supreme Court of Canada reversed that finding in a 7:2 decision. The decision, as noted above, is composed of four distinct judgments.

The judgments are organized around two basic issues:

1) whether an exclusive licensee can succeed in an action against a parallel importer. That is, does the *Copyright Act* extend protection to exclusive licensees against parallel importation? This is the exclusive licence issue.
2) whether the sale or distribution of consumer goods to which copyrighted works are affixed as trade-marked logos is an infringing sale or distribution of the copyrighted works themselves within the meaning of the parallel import provisions of the *Copyright Act*. That is, is the copyrighted work being "sold" or "distributed" when it is printed on the wrapper of a consumer product? This is the sale issue.

Justice Rothstein focuses on the exclusive licence issue. He finds that "The Canadian *Copyright Act* does not extend protection against parallel importation to exclusive licensees."[8] Thus, plaintiff Kraft Canada Inc. cannot win the case because it is a mere licensee—albeit an exclusive licensee—and not an assignee. As to the sale issue, Justice Rothstein finds that there is nothing in

---

(e) *import into Canada for the purpose of doing anything referred to in paragraphs (a) to (c),*

a copy of a work, sound recording or fixation of a performer's performance or of a communication signal that the person knows or should have known infringes copyright or would infringe copyright if it had been made in Canada by the person who made it [emphasis added].

7 For discussion of *Euro-Excellence* published prior to the Supreme Court of Canada decision, see Teresa Scassa, "Using Copyright Law to Prevent Parallel Importation: A Comment on *Kraft Canada Inc. v. Euro-Excellence Inc.*," (2006) 85 Can. Bar. Rev. 409–28 (www.commonlaw.uottawa.ca/index.php?option=com_docman&task=doc_download&gid=934); Robert J. Tomkowicz, "Copyrighting Chocolate: *Kraft Canada Inc. v. Euro-Excellence*," (2007) 20:3 Intellectual Property Journal 399–426 [Tomkowicz, "Copyrighting Chocolate"]. For commentary on the Supreme Court of Canada decision, see Leah M. Howie, "Using Copyright Law to Stop Grey-Marketed Candy" (2008) 21 Intellectual Property Journal 245; Pierre-Emmanuel Moyse, "*Kraft Canada c. Euro-Excellence*: l'insoutenable légèreté du droit" (2008) 53 McGill L.J. 741 (http://lawjournal.mcgill.ca/documents/Moyse.pdf); David Nimmer, "Copyright Law and the Restoration of Beauty" (2009) 47 Osgoode Hall L.J. 553 (http://ohlj.ca/english/documents/4-47_3_Nimmer_FINAL.pdf); Arthur Renaud, "The Elephant Parades the Circus Ring: Grey Goods versus Copyright — No Clear Winner . . . Yet" (2007–2008) 39 Ottawa L. Rev. 281; David Vaver, "Chocolate, Copyright, Confusion: Intellectual Property and the Supreme Court of Canada" (2008) 1 Osgoode Hall Rev. L. Pol'y. 5 (http://ohrlp.ca/images/articles/Volume1/d%20vaver%202008%201%20ohrlp%205.pdf).

8 *Euro-Excellence*, above note 1 at para. 50.

the *Copyright Act* to negate the proposition that a copyrighted work is being sold when it is printed on the wrapper of a consumer product.[9]

Justice Fish concurs with Justice Rothstein in regard to the exclusive license issue. He indicates, however, that it is not clear that plaintiff Kraft Canada Inc. would have won had it been an assignee. On the contrary, he expresses "grave doubt whether the law governing the protection of intellectual property rights in Canada can be transformed in this way into an instrument of trade control not contemplated by the *Copyright Act*."[10]

In her dissent, Justice Abella finds that the *Copyright Act* does extend protection against parallel importation to exclusive licensees. She also finds, moreover, that the *Copyright Act* provides no basis for a restrictive definition of "sale." "When a product is sold," she writes, "title to its wrapper is also transferred to the purchaser."[11] Thus, there is no basis to exclude the sale of copyrighted works printed on wrappers from the legitimate domain of copyright law.

Justice Bastarache's judgment focuses not on the exclusive licence issue but on the sale issue. His question is whether the works were sold or distributed within the meaning of Section 27(2)(e) of the Act. Justice Bastarache's answer is a resounding "No." He held that, irrespective of the distinction between an exclusive licence and an assignment, Euro-Excellence Inc. imports did not fall within the scope of the provision. In Justice Bastarache's view, the provision governs the parallel importation of copyrighted works *as such*, not as merely ancillary or incidental attachments to the distribution and sale of other consumer goods. In short, Justice Bastarache found that Euro-Excellence Inc. imported and sold *chocolate bars* but not *copyrighted works* in Canada.

The first sentence of his judgment, formulated as a rhetorical question, tells the whole story: "Can a chocolate bar be copyrighted because of protected works appearing on its wrapper?" Since it is uncontroversial that there neither is nor can be copyright protection for chocolate bars, it is trivially true that there can be no copyright liability for the parallel importation of chocolate bars. Of course, no one had argued that the chocolate bars were as such subject to copyright protection. But Justice Bastarache's point is that

> if a work of skill and judgment (such as a logo) is attached to some other consumer good (such as a chocolate bar), the economic gains associated with the sale of the consumer good must not be mistakenly

9 *Ibid.* at paras. 4, 5 and 8.

10 *Ibid.* above note 1 at para. 56.

11 *Ibid.* at para. 110.

> viewed as the legitimate economic interests of the copyright holder of the logo that are protected by the law of copyright.[12]

The incidental attachment of the logos to the chocolate bars does not magically transform the plaintiff's commercial interests in chocolate sales into interests actionable as a matter of copyright law. The point is not that Kraft Canada Inc. was a mere exclusive licensee. Rather, the point is that Euro-Excellence Inc. was not selling copyrighted works. Euro-Excellence Inc. would not have been liable for copyright infringement even if the parent companies had assigned the relevant copyrights to Kraft Canada Inc.[13]

C. JUSTICE BASTARACHE'S JUDGMENT

Justice Bastarache's reasons for finding that no sale of copyrighted works had taken place are complex but may be summarized for discussion purposes into two basic moments or stages. The first deals with the purpose of the *Copyright Act*. The second provides—in light of that purpose—an interpretation of section 27(2)(e) of the *Act* that excludes merely incidental uses of copyrighted works from the web of liability for parallel importation of copyrighted works. The result is that, as we just noted, no liability for parallel importation arises on the facts of the case.

The first stage in Justice Bastarache's judgment—the stage dealing with the purpose of the *Act*—can be further divided into four sub-stages. I will call these stages the *Théberge* step, the *CCH* step, the *SOCAN* step,[14]

---

12 *Ibid.* at para. 85.

13 This is why Bastarache J stated that he need not deal with the licensing issue. Nonetheless, he did add that he agreed with Abella J that the *Copyright Act* extends protection against parallel imports to exclusive licensees. *See Euro-Excellence*, above note 1 at para. 75. As an aside, it is apt to point out here that, in spite of the fragmentation of the Court in *Euro-Excellence*, it seems likely that the Court would find unanimously that section 27(2)(e) provides protection against parallel imports where the plaintiff is an assignee of the copyright and the defendant imports, not copies of works attached incidentally to some consumer good, but rather copies of works themselves (e.g., copies of films). For remarks suggesting a different interpretation of section 27(2)(e), see Ariel Katz, "*Euro Excellence v. Kraft*," University of Toronto Faculty of Law Blog, 2 August 2007, at http://utorontolaw.typepad.com/faculty_blog/2007/08/euro-excellence.html.

14 *Society of Composers, Authors and Music Publishers of Canada v. Canadian Assn. of Internet Providers*, 2004 SCC 45, http://csc.lexum.umontreal.ca/en/2004/2004scc45/2004scc45.html, [2004] 2 S.C.R. 427 [*SOCAN*].

and the *Kirkbi* step,[15] referring in that way to each of the recent Supreme Court of Canada cases on which Justice Bastarache relies.

1) *Théberge*

Justice Bastarache extracts three related concepts from *Théberge*: (a) the concept of "balance," and with it the concepts of (b) the "limited nature" of the creator's rights, and thus of (c) the "legitimate interests" of the copyright holder. The basic point is that because the *Copyright Act* is a "balance" between authors and users, creators and public, we must understand the rights of authors as "limited." To put it otherwise, the rights of authors must be understood in relation to other rights and/or interests that are equally constitutive of the copyright system. The "limited nature" of the rights of authors is thus a corollary of the proposition that copyright is not only about authors; it is also about users. By the same token, the fact that the rights of authors are "limited" entails that the *Copyright Act* protects not all or any interests of authors but only their "legitimate economic interests"—that is, only those economic interests that are consistent with the "balance" at the heart of copyright.[16]

The well-known passage from *Théberge* on which Justice Bastarache relies reads as follows:

> The *Copyright Act* is usually presented as a balance between promoting the public interest in the encouragement and dissemination of works of the arts and intellect and obtaining a just reward for the creator . . . . The proper balance among these and other public policy objectives lies not only in recognizing the creator's rights but in giving due weight to their limited nature.[17]

---

15 *Kirkbi AG v. Ritvik Holdings Inc.*, 2005 SCC 65, http://csc.lexum.umontreal.ca/en/2005/2005scc65/2005scc65.html [*Kirkbi*].

16 *Euro-Excellence*, above note 1 at para. 76. In *Théberge* (above note 2), the plaintiff complained that a process used by the defendant to lift the ink that was used in printing a paper poster and transferring it onto a canvas infringed his copyright. The phrase "legitimate economic interest" appears at para. 38:

> My colleague, Gonthier J, takes the position that if the image were transferred from one piece of paper to a different piece of paper with no other "change", there is a new "fixation" and that would be "reproduction." But in what way has the *legitimate economic interest* of the copyright holder been infringed? The process began with a single poster and ended with a single poster. The image "fixed" in ink is the subject-matter of the *intellectual* property and it was not reproduced. It was transferred from one display to another [emphasis added].

17 *Théberge*, above note 2 at paras. 30–31.

The imperative to give "due *weight* to their [i.e., the creator's rights] limited nature" (emphasis added) captures the immanent connection between the concepts of "balance" and "limited nature" that is now part and parcel of Canadian copyright law. The rights of authors are limited because, in accordance with the balanced nature of copyright protection, they must share the copyright stage with the rights of users.

2) *CCH*

Justice Bastarache presents *CCH* as an elaboration of the concept of the "limited nature" of the rights of the copyright holder. He tells us that *CCH* recognized and elaborated on this "limited nature" in two ways: (a) in its definition of originality, and (b) in its treatment of fair dealing.[18]

a) Originality

CCH accomplished a transition from the sweat of the brow to the skill and judgment standard of originality.[19] The proposition that skill and judgment, and not sweat of the brow, is the originality standard implies two important observations underlined in Justice Bastarache's judgment.

The first is that originality is not about "*all* types of labour."[20] It is only about labour involving skill and judgment. More precisely, it is only about labour involving a *specific* type of skill and judgment. Not any and all types of skill and judgment will do.

To appreciate the nature of the shift, consider, for example, the classic sweat of the brow authority, *Walter v. Lane*.[21] In *Walter*, the House of Lords

---

18 *Euro-Excellence*, above note 1 at para. 77.

19 To speak of a transition is to imply that, prior to *CCH*, the originality standard was unambiguously a sweat of the brow standard. But that is not necessarily accurate. It suffices for present purposes to note, however, that *CCH* certainly resolved any extant ambiguities against the sweat of the brow standard, and in favour of the skill and judgment standard. On the struggle between originality standards, see Abraham Drassinower, "Sweat of the Brow, Creativity and Authorship: On Originality in Canadian Copyright Law," (2003–2004) 1:1–2 University of Ottawa Law and Technology Journal 105–123, http://www.uoltjca/articles/vol1.1-2/2003-2004.1.1-2.uoltj.Drassinower.105-123.pdf [Drassinower, "On Originality"].

20 *Euro-Excellence*, above note 1 at para. 78.

21 *Walter v. Lane*, [1900] A.C. 539 (H.L.) [*Walter*]. Strictly speaking, of course, use of the phrase "sweat of the brow" to refer to *Walter* is anachronistic. The phrase describes a school of thought with respect to the originality requirement, but the word "original" did not find its way into the English *Copyright Act* until 1911, eleven years after *Walter*. Still, in the pre-1911 jurisprudence, including *Walter*, the debate about copyrightability took place through inquiry into the meaning of the word "author."

held that the labour invested in the purely mechanical verbatim transcription of a public speech gave rise to copyright protection. Therefore, the unauthorized reproduction of the verbatim report by the defendant gave rise to copyright liability. The reproduction in fact amounted to an unauthorized transfer of value from plaintiff to defendant. Lord Halsbury held that to prevent the "grievous injustice" involved in such misappropriation of another's effort is in fact the purpose of the *Copyright Act*.[22]

On the basis of the skill and judgment standard, however, unauthorized transfers of value, even if resulting from a deliberate act of the defendant's, do not *as such* sound in copyright. Not any or all value will do. Thus, for example, the labour invested in the production of garden variety, alphabetically arranged phone directories is not subject to copyright protection.[23] Only the products of authorship—defined as skill and judgment—will do. In other words, once the sweat of the brow standard is discarded, the sense of grievous injustice associated with unauthorized transfers of value by way of reproduction is no longer the central organizing principle of copyright law.[24] Copyright law is not an unfair competition

---

See Robert Howell and Ysolde Gendreau, "Qualitative Standards for Protection of Literary and Artistic Property," in Canadian Comparative Law Association, *Contemporary Law 1994* (Cowansville, QC: Les Éditions Yvon Blais, 1994) 518 at 521–22 and 542–45.

22 See *Walter*, above note 21 at 545:

> I should very much regret it if I were compelled to come to the conclusion that the state of the law permitted one man to make profit and to appropriate to himself the labour, skill, and capital of another. And it is not denied that in this case the defendant seeks to appropriate to himself what has been produced through the skill, labour, and capital of others. In the view I take of this case I think the law is strong enough to restrain what to my mind would be a grievous injustice. The law which I think restrains it is to be found in the *Copyright Act*, and the Act confers what it calls copyright — which means the right to multiply copies — which it confers on the author of books first published in this country.

23 See, e.g., *Feist Publications v. Rural Telephone*, 499 U.S. 340 (1991), http://supreme.justia.com/us/499/340/case.html [*Feist*]; *Tele-Direct (Publications) Inc. v. American Business Information Inc.*, [1998] 2 F.C. 22 (C.A.), http://reports.fja.gc.ca/eng/1997/1998fc21425.html/1998fc21425.html.html; *CCH*, above note 3.

24 See for example, *Feist*, above note 23 at para. 9:

> It may seem unfair that much of the fruit of the compiler's labor may be used by others without compensation. As Justice Brennan has correctly observed, however, this is not "some unforeseen byproduct of a statutory scheme." . . .]It is, rather, the "essence of copyright," . . . and a constitutional requirement. The primary objective of copyright is not to reward the labor of authors, but "[t]o promote the Progress of Science and useful Arts." . . . To this end, copyright assures authors the right to their original expression, but encourages others to build

regime. The mischief that the *Copyright Act* targets is not the misappropriation of another's *labour*, but the misappropriation of another's *authorship*. Copyright is less about the protection of value than about the protection of a specific value—the value of authorship.[25]

The second observation contained in the affirmation of skill and judgment as the originality standard can be formulated as follows. In *CCH*, the Court affirmed the skill and judgment standard as a fair yet workable standard, occupying a space between the British "sweat of the brow" standard, on the one hand, and the American creativity standard, on the other.[26] The Court articulated its own skill and judgment standard in terms of the copyright balance between authors and users, creators and public. In the Court's eyes, whereas the sweat of the brow standard is too authored-centered, the creativity standard is too public-centered.

In this vein, the Court rejected the American creativity standard on the grounds that it amounts to a novelty requirement, more suitable for patent law than for copyright law, requiring too much from authors in exchange for copyright protection.[27] While it is at least doubtful that the Court's construal of the American creativity standard is correct,[28] what matters about the Court's discussion is that it demonstrates that the Court's deployment of the idea of "balance" permeates not only the scope of copyright protection but also its subject matter. While the creativity

---

> freely upon the ideas and information conveyed by a work . . . . This principle, known as the idea/expression or fact/expression dichotomy, applies to all works of authorship. As applied to a factual compilation, assuming the absence of original written expression, only the compiler's selection and arrangement may be protected; the raw facts may be copied at will. The result is neither unfair nor unfortunate. It is the means by which copyright advances the progress of science and art.

25 This was, in fact, the position adopted by Lord Robertson in his dissent in *Walter*. Though by no means unaware of the skills of the stenographer, Lord Robertson says of the verbatim reports in issue in the case that it is hard to see "how, in the widest sense of the term 'author', we are in *the region of authorship*" (emphasis added). See *Walter*, above note 21 at 561. For discussion, see Drassinower, "On Originality," above note 19.

26 *CCH*, above note 3 at para. 24.

27 *CCH*, above note 3 at para. 24: "A creativity standard implies that something must be novel or non-obvious—concepts more properly associated with patent law than copyright law."

28 See *Feist*, above note 23 at para. 10: "Originality does not signify novelty . . . ." For comment, see, for example, Daniel Gervais and Elizabeth F. Judge, *Intellectual Property: The Law in Canada* (Toronto: Thomson Carswell, 2005), at 21–25 [Gervais and Judge, *Intellectual Property*].

standard (as construed by the *CCH* Court) may well be suitable to the balance sought in patent law, it is nonetheless unsuitable to the balance at stake in copyright law. In *CCH*, that is, the Court rejects the creativity standard because it is extraneous to the copyright balance, although the very same standard may be suitable for the patent balance. In the Court's hands, the proposition that copyright is not about creativity turns out to be an affirmation of the distinction between copyright and patent. To put it otherwise, the division between copyright and patent, originality and novelty, is part and parcel of the Court's understanding of the "limited nature" of the rights at issue in copyright.

Note that the two aspects of the Court's definition of originality (on the one hand the distinction between originality and sweat of the brow, and on the other the distinction between originality and creativity) can be grasped as a single moment, involving an elaboration of the specificity of copyright *vis-à-vis* an unfair competition or misappropriation of value regime, on the one hand, and a patent regime, on the other. The question of the limits of copyright is also a question about the specificity of copyright. Justice Bastarache's analysis of *CCH* thus brings into relief the observation that, with respect to the originality requirement, the twin concepts of "balance" and "limits" deployed in *Théberge* bring in their wake issues not only of copyright scope (i.e., limits) but also of copyright subject matter (i.e., the specificity of copyright *vis-à-vis* other legal regimes).

b) Fair Dealing

CCH redefined fair dealing as a user right. It established that, as a user right, and not as a mere exception to copyright infringement, fair dealing ought to be given large and liberal interpretation.[29]

The defence of fair dealing specifies situations in which the defendant's unauthorized act of substantial reproduction does not give rise to copyright liability. Justice Bastarache points out that the formulation of fair dealing as a user right entails the proposition that substantial reproduction is not wrongful, *per se*, as a matter of copyright law. The point is not only that not all unauthorized reproductions amount to infringement. Rather, the point is that unauthorized reproductions pursuant to fair dealing are to be viewed, not as wrongs to be excused, but as exercises of user rights integral to copyright law.

If the originality requirement restricts entry into the world of copyright by defining the specific nature of copyright subject matter, the defence of

29 *CCH*, above note 3 at paras. 48 and 51.

fair dealing affirms that copyright subject matter is itself protected only in a "limited" way. In other words, fair dealing comes to limit the scope of copyright subject matter by providing that the protection of skill and judgment must not itself be extended beyond its proper limits. Just because something is original, it does not follow that this something is protected against any and all unauthorized reproduction. On the contrary, users, too, have rights, and fair dealing is indeed an instance of such rights.

It is on the basis of this combined operation of originality and fair dealing that Justice Bastarache held that we must be careful to understand that the "legitimate economic interests" protected under copyright are limited in two senses — at the level of subject matter by way of originality and at the level of scope by way of fair dealing. He stated that

> . . . sometimes a substantial reproduction of a copyrighted work will not be an infringement, because copyright protection is limited to protection of legitimate economic interests which are the result of an exercise of skill and judgment, *and* that protection must not be extended beyond its proper limits.[30]

In Justice Bastarache's hands, then, the *Théberge* balance emerges as a twofold limitation on authorial entitlement. Viewed as a single conceptual stroke, this twofold limitation is a way of saying that not substantial reproduction but impingement upon "legitimate economic interest" is what defines copyright infringement. Copyright, one might say, is not about copying *simpliciter*. It is not the category of "reproduction," but rather that of "legitimate economic interest" that presides over the analysis of copyright infringement.

The upshot of Justice Bastarache's analysis of *CCH* is that, in addition to fair dealing as a mode of limiting the scope of authorial right, there are *other limits*, also flowing from the purpose of copyright as a balance, to be imposed on that scope. This is how Justice Bastarache puts it:

> The *CCH* decision thus confirms that in order to protect the essential balance which lies at the heart of copyright law, care must be taken to ensure that copyright protection is not allowed to extend beyond the legitimate interests of a copyright holder. Copyright will not be granted to works which are not the result of an exercise of skill and judgment, which is the special kind of labour for which copyright is the appropriate protection. Similarly, once copyright is granted in a

30 *Euro-Excellence*, above note 1 at para. 79 (emphasis added).

> given work, the protection that it provides must not be extended beyond its natural limits, and must take proper account of user rights *such as* the right to deal fairly with a copyrighted work.[31]

The phrase is worth repeating: "user rights *such as* the right to deal fairly with a copyrighted work." Fair dealing is an instance of a higher order category of user rights. The key to *CCH* is not so much that fair dealing ought to be given large and liberal interpretation, but rather that reproduction is not *per se* wrongful, and that, therefore, there are and must be other instances of user rights, instances that do not meet the requirements of the fair dealing defence. In short, fair dealing is not the only way to make non-infringing reproductions. This articulation of the category of non-infringing reproduction or non-infringing use is the fundamental teaching of *CCH*.[32]

c) *SOCAN*

The twin ideas of "balance" and "limits" that animate *Théberge*, then, find further elaboration in *CCH*. Specifically, as we just noted, *CCH* brings into relief the proposition that not all reproduction is wrongful. In this conceptual sequence, *SOCAN* now comes to confirm the view that the purposive interpretation of the *Act* dislodges the primacy of "reproduction" as an organizing principle of copyright law. Justice Bastarache wrote:

> This Court's recent decision in *Society of Composers, Authors and Music Publishers of Canada v. Canadian Assn. of Internet Providers* . . . confirms this purposive interpretation of the Act. In that case, Binnie J wrote, at para. 116: "'Caching' is dictated by the need to deliver faster and more economic service, and should not, *when undertaken only for such technical reasons*, attract copyright liability" (emphasis added). While 'caching' is certainly an instance of substantial reproduction, it is a technical process only; as such it does not consist in an attempt to appropriate the legitimate economic interests of the copyright holder, and therefore does not constitute infringement.[33]

Once again, not "reproduction" but "legitimate economic interest" grounds the category of infringement. The reproductions involved in *SOCAN* did

---

31 *Ibid.* at para. 80 (emphasis added).

32 See Abraham Drassinower, "Taking User Rights Seriously," in Michael Geist, ed., *In The Public Interest: The Future of Canadian Copyright Law* (Toronto: Irwin Law, 2005), at 462 [Drassinower, "User Rights].

33 *Euro-Excellence*, above note 1 at para. 81.

not give rise to liability even though they would not have met the fair dealing criteria. *SOCAN* provides an example of a limitation on the rights of the copyright holder which (a) reminds us that reproduction *per se* does not give rise to liability, and (b) reminds us that fair dealing is but an instance of a higher order category of user rights, of which the "caching" involved in *SOCAN* is yet another example.

d) *Kirkbi*

Justice Bastarache now connects the foregoing discussion of the central concepts of "balance," "limits," "reproduction," and "user rights" to the question of the proper divisions between patent, trade-mark, and copyright. That is, the role of *Kirkbi* in the unfolding logic of Justice Bastarache's judgment is to grasp the question of the limits of copyright as a determination of the specificity of copyright vis-à-vis trade-mark and patent. The upshot of this move is the proposition that, because copyright operates in its own "domain,"[34] it should not be used to achieve through the "backdoor" what trade-mark (and/or patent) cannot do. "Merely incidental" uses of copyrighted works ought not to masquerade as infringements of copyright to achieve through copyright what cannot be achieved through trade-mark. To do otherwise is to run contrary to copyright's own balance.[35] Thus the concept of "limits" now reverberates at a third level: (a) subject matter, as in the originality analysis in *CCH*; (b) scope, as in the fair dealing analysis in *CCH* and in the analysis of "caching" in *SOCAN*; and (c) domain, as in the analysis in *Kirkbi* of the proper relation or distinction between copyright, trade-mark and patent.

In *Kirkbi*, the argument from the category of domain operates to preclude the use of trade-mark to achieve what cannot be achieved through patent. The expiry of the patent over the Lego blocks gave rise to an attempt on the part of the patentee to perpetuate the monopoly by claiming

---

34 *Ibid.* at para. 95: "copyright's intended domain."

35 *Ibid.* at para. 88:

> This interpretation of s. 27(2) respects copyright's insistence that only *legitimate* economic interests receive copyright protection. To allow s. 27(2) to protect all interests of manufacturers and distributors of consumer goods would upset the copyright balance. Far from ensuring a "just reward" for creators of copyrighted works, it would allow a copyright to be leveraged far beyond the use intended by Parliament, allowing rights to be artificially enlarged into protection over consumer goods. This undue expansion of copyright would certainly be a failure to give heed to Binnie J's insistence, at para. 31 of *Théberge*, that the law give due weight to the limited nature of the rights of a copyright holder.

a trade-mark over the shape of the blocks. The Supreme Court held against such an attempt to extend the monopoly, on the grounds that the doctrine of functionality—whether under the *Trade-Marks Act* or as a matter of passing off at common law—precluded the operation of the shape of the blocks as a trade-mark.[36]

The central proposition that trade-mark cannot be used to achieve "backdoor" patent protection was formulated in *Kirkbi* at a high level of generality. Thus, Justice LeBel wrote not specifically of the patent/trade-mark relation but generally of the importance of "basic and necessary distinctions between different forms of intellectual property and their legal and economic functions."[37] Justice Bastarache now leverages this proposition to find in *Kirkbi* a pronouncement not only about the relation between trade-mark and patent but also about the relation between copyright and trade-mark. He writes:

> This focus on the fundamental natures and purposes of different sorts of intellectual property protections and the necessary divisions between them suggests that each form of protection relies on some core normative notion which must ground the economic interests claimed.[38]

He calls this normative notion "a principled fulcrum on which we may undertake copyright's balance."[39]

What, precisely, *is* this "principled fulcrum"?

There can be no doubt that this question gives us ample reason to pause. The concept of "balance" has an irreducibly central position in Supreme Court of Canada copyright jurisprudence. Since Justice Binnie iterated the concept in *Théberge* in March 2002, the Supreme Court has decided four copyright cases,[40] in each of which, albeit in varying ways, "balance" has played an unmistakable role. The concept has, in fact, provided both the vocabulary and the underlying grammar through which the Court approaches the formulation of the purpose of copyright law, and therefore the interpretation of the *Copyright Act*.

---

36 *Kirkbi*, above note 15.

37 *Ibid.* at para. 37.

38 *Euro-Excellence*, above note 1 at para. 82.

39 *Ibid.* at para. 84.

40 *CCH*, above note 3; *SOCAN*, above note 14; *Robertson v. Thomson Corp.*, [2006] 2 S.C.R. 363, 2006 SCC 43 (http://scc.lexum.umontreal.ca/en/2006/2006scc43/2006scc43.html); and *Euro-Excellence*, above note 1.

In such a context, Justice Bastarache's assertion that the balance is inoperable in the absence of a "principled fulcrum" that animates it cannot help but attract our attention. What is it about the maturing constellations of meanings surrounding the well-settled copyright balance that Justice Bastarache seeks to bring into relief through his reliance on *Kirkbi*?

In my view, the role of *Kirkbi* in Justice Bastarache's judgment is to make explicit a dimension of the copyright balance that was not explicitly treated in *CCH*. Recall for a moment that it was on the basis of "balance" that the Court in *CCH* rejected the "sweat of the brow" and creativity standards. Both "sweat of the brow" and creativity were said to be off-side the true copyright balance. Whereas the "sweat of the brow" standard is said to be too low, and therefore too author-centered, favouring authors at the expense of users, the creativity standard is said to be too high, and therefore too public-centered, favouring users at the expense of authors. Note, however, that, notwithstanding the Court's insistence, there is absolutely nothing in the idea of balance *per se* that can, in any way, guide the determination as to which standard to adopt.

Consider, for example, that in *Théberge*, Justice Binnie reminds us that the concept of balance has been integral to copyright jurisprudence since time immemorial. "This is not new," Justice Binnie writes of the copyright balance, citing a 1769 English case as evidence of the longevity of the concept of balance.[41] When *CCH* was decided, we had as a copyright jurisdiction held the idea of balance together with the "sweat of the brow" originality standard for quite some time. That is, the proposition that the idea of balance is *per se* sufficient to give up the "sweat of the brow" standard is remarkably vacuous. Similar observations can be made about the creativity standard. While the *CCH* Court rejected creativity in the name of balance, the United States has been deploying creativity as the originality standard, precisely in the name of its own version of the copyright balance, since at least the *Feist* decision in 1990, if not longer. Again, then, it seems radically insufficient merely to assert without more ado that the creativity standard ought to be rejected in the name of balance. Simply put, something other than the bare idea of "balance" must be at work here.

What is missing here (or rather, to be more precise, what was not explicitly articulated in *CCH*) is the apparently trivial proposition that the copyright balance is not just any which balance but specifically a balance between authors and users in respect of works of authorship. That is, when we speak about balancing in copyright we are talking not just about "bal-

41 *Théberge*, above note 2 at para. 30.

ancing" in the abstract but about balancing in a specific domain, about balancing in the domain of authorship.[42] We need to think not just about balancing but about what it is in particular that is on the balance. Justice Bastarache's basic point in discussing *Kirkbi* is that, once we do that, it becomes clear that that not all values can get on the balance. The legitimate economic interests of authors *as authors* can get on the balance, but not all or any interests or values generated by their labour.

This is of course already familiar from *CCH*. *CCH* teaches that not all or any kind of labour counts. In *Euro-Excellence*, Justice Bastarache is doing little more than asking us to take this seriously. He is asking us to see the category of skill and judgment not as the result of the balancing process, but rather as a prior determination, independent of that balancing, that specifies what kind of values get on the balance to begin with. The skill and judgment specific to authorship is thus the "principled fulcrum," the "core normative notion" that defines copyright's domain and orients copyright's balance.

It is the distinction between copyright and other intellectual property regimes that renders the copyright balance intelligible as a balance involving authors rather than inventors, and, as in *Euro-Excellence*, authors rather than trade-mark owners. It is this aspect of *CCH* that Justice Bastarache brings into relief through his reliance on *Kirkbi*. He reminds us, as it were, of what we already knew from *CCH*: namely, that the question of the limits of copyright is also a question about the specificity of copyright.[43]

Once this principled fulcrum is in place, we can readily understand the basic thrust of Justice Bastarache's judgment. Euro-Excellence Inc. is accused of selling works. More precisely, the action against Euro-Excellence Inc. cannot succeed in the absence of a showing that Euro-Excellence Inc. was involved in the sale of copyrighted works. On Justice Bastarache's construal, Euro-Excellence Inc. was not involved in any such sale. To be sure, Euro-Excellence Inc. was involved in the sale of chocolate bars to which the copyrighted works were affixed as trade-marks. But this means only that there was a "close association" between the transactions in ques-

---

42 See Abraham Drassinower, "Canadian Originality: Remarks on a Judgment in Search of an Author," in Ysolde Gendreau, ed., *An Emerging Intellectual Property Paradigm: Perspectives from Canada* (London: Edward Elgar Publishers, 2009) at 139.

43 On the specificity of copyright, see Abraham Drassinower, "Authorship as Public Address: On the Specificity of Copyright *vis-à-vis* Patent and Trade-Mark," 2008:1 Michigan State Law Review 199–232 [Drassinower, "Authorship as Public Address"].

tion (i.e., the sale of chocolate bars) and the artistic works in issue.[44] We should not confuse this "close association" of the works to the transaction with the quite different proposition that it is the works that are sold in the transaction. The benefits to be derived from the sale of a chocolate to which an artistic work is affixed as a logo do not fall within the "legitimate economic interests" of a copyright holder *as copyright holder*. The role of the copyrighted logos is "merely incidental" to the sale of chocolate bars. In short, the category of domain functions as an imperative to (a) specify the interests proper to copyright as a legal regime, and to (b) distinguish those interests from other (extraneous) interests in situations of "close association." The concept of "merely incidental" is nothing but a way to operationalize that distinction.

Note that this does not mean that, in Justice Bastarache's view, the logos play no role in the transaction. On the contrary, they most certainly do.[45] What Justice Bastarache is telling us is that the logos do not play a role in the transaction *as works of authorship*. To be sure, they function as trade-marks: as indications of source differentiating chocolate bars provided by Kraft Canada Inc. from chocolate bars provided by others in the marketplace. But that is precisely the point: the logos are not functioning as works of authorship in the chocolate transaction, and so they do not, in their role as trade-marks, get into the copyright balance to begin with.

---

44 *Euro-Excellence*, above note 1 at para. 85:

> Section 27(2) of the Act is meant to prohibit secondary infringement resulting from the wrongful appropriation of the gains of another's skill and judgment by way of the acts enumerated in paras. *(a)* to *(c)*. Conversely, other economic interests — although they may seem to be *closely associated* with the interests legitimately protected as emanating from that skill and judgment — are not protected. [emphasis added]

45 *Ibid.* at para. 104:

> Similarly, I do not mean to suggest that logos play no role whatsoever in the sale of chocolate bars. So I think it is therefore useful to stress, once again, that in the s. 27(2) analysis the logos must be viewed strictly through the copyright lens *as works*. The analysis does not speak to the possibility — indeed, the certainty — that the logos, as trade-marks, can play a large role in the sale of the chocolate bars and are of great value to KCI [Kraft Canada Inc.]. It is not disputed that part of the reason that a consumer buys a Côte d'Or bar or a Toblerone bar is because of the reputation and goodwill associated with each brand. But that is not a consideration which is relevant under the *Copyright Act*. It cannot be reasonably maintained that anyone buys a Côte d'Or or Toblerone because of the logos as works of art.

Their identity as works of authorship is merely incidental to the transaction of which they are, or may be, an integral aspect only as trade-marks.

In essence, Justice Bastarache is asking us to distinguish between patterns of ink and works of authorship as a matter of copyright law. The insight is that a pattern of ink can assume different legal meanings, on the one hand as an indicator of source in the marketplace, and on the other as a work of authorship. The point is that the function of the pattern of ink as an indicator of source should not be conflated with the identity of that very same pattern of ink as a work of authorship. Thus, the bare fact that a certain pattern of ink is printed on a chocolate bar wrapper is not sufficient reason for the legal finding that, as a copyright law matter, the sale of the chocolate bar and its wrapper amounts to the sale of a copy of a work of authorship.[46] On the contrary, the thought that the pattern of ink is one and the same thing in both instances, as trade-mark and as work of authorship, is an illusion for which Justice Bastarache's judgment in *Euro-Excellence* is the required therapy.

D. PATTERNS OF INK AND WORKS OF AUTHORSHIP

This distinction between patterns of ink and works of authorship may at first sight seem foreign, but it is in fact thoroughly familiar to copyright lawyers. The defence of independent creation and the defence of fair dealing, for example, both affirm the proposition that the mere physical identity of patterns of ink in the plaintiff's and the defendant's respective works need not give rise to copyright liability. Assume for a moment that a lay audience were to be shown two identical sheets of paper with identical text on them. It is reasonable to expect that, when asked whether

46 This distinction between patterns of ink and works of authorship is Bastarache J's answer to Abella J's statement in *Euro-Excellence*, above note 1 at para. 110, that "When a product is sold, title to its wrapper is also transferred to the purchaser." Abella J also adds in this context that "The Act is indifferent as to whether the sale of the wrapper is important to the consumer." This last statement strikes me as perfunctory. Where work "A" deals fairly with work "B," a substantial part of work "B" is also printed in every copy of work "A." At the time of sale, title to the sheet of paper on which both works are printed, as well as to the ink on that sheet of paper, is transferred to the purchaser of a copy of work "A." But it does not necessarily follow that a copy of work "B" has been either bought or sold. Moreover, since — to give but one example — "[i]t may be relevant to consider the custom or practice in a particular trade or industry to determine whether or not the character of the dealing is fair" (*CCH*, above note 3 at para. 55), it seems inaccurate to assume without more ado that the Act is indifferent as to whether the use of a work is important to its intended audience.

the sheets are copies of each other, most members of that audience would reply affirmatively. If we were to ask the very same question to a group of copyright lawyers, however, we would likely get an answer along the following lines: "Well, it depends. There is certainly substantial similarity, or even identity, but it does not follow that we have an instance of copying. In order to show copying we would have to inquire whether there is a causal connection between these two sheets — that is, whether there was actual copying involved or whether, on the contrary, what we have before us is an instance of independent creation." The copyright lawyer is well aware that mere identity does not in and of itself give rise to liability.[47] The copyright liability inquiry is more complex than a mere ascertaining of substantial similarity or identity between patterns of ink on sheets of paper.

The complexity is even greater in the case of the defence of fair dealing. As is well known, the defence operates to preclude liability even where there is a finding of substantial similarity (or identity) *and* causal connection. If the defence of independent creation warns us away from inferring liability from mere identity, the defence of fair dealing warns us away from inferring liability even from identity *coupled with actual copying*. Thus, strictly speaking, a finding of "reproduction" (i.e., substantial similarity coupled with actual copying) is not in and of itself sufficient to warrant the inference that liability obtains. The defence of fair dealing thus confirms that the copyright liability inquiry is far more complex than the ascertaining of physical similarity, even where such similarity is the result of copying.

In this light, Justice Bastarache's judgment in *Euro-Excellence* covers strikingly familiar territory. The heart of the judgment is an insistence upon the fundamental importance of the distinction between patterns of ink and works of authorship for the analysis of infringement pursuant to section 27(2). It is because of that distinction that the sale of chocolate bars in wrappers carrying patterns of ink physically identical to certain works of authorship need not amount to the sale of those works of authorship themselves.

---

47 On establishing infringement and the role of independent creation, see *Francis Day & Hunter Ltd., and another v. Bron (trading as Delmar Publishing Co.) and another* [1963] 1 Ch. 587 (C.A.) at 627 (per Diplock LJ):

> Even complete identity of the two works may not be conclusive evidence of copying, for it may be proved that it was impossible for the author of the alleged infringing work to have had access to the copyright work. And, once the impossible (*viz.*, copying) has been eliminated, that which remains (*viz.*, coincidence [i.e., independent creation]) however improbable, is the truth; I quote inaccurately, but not unconsciously, from Sherlock Holmes.

The analogy with fair dealing is instructive. Dealing fairly with a work of authorship for the purposes of criticism, for example, is not within the legitimate interests of the copyright holder. In the same vein, Justice Bastarache's point is that precluding parallel importation of consumer goods to which copyrighted works are incidentally affixed as trade-marked logos is not within the legitimate economic interests of the copyright holder. Both situations involve unauthorized yet non-infringing uses of copyrighted works (or, to be fastidiously precise, of patterns of ink identical to copyrighted works). By the same token, both situations illustrate that the concept of legitimate economic interest belongs on a higher normative plane than that of mere use. Not all unauthorized uses of copyrighted works are within the copyright holder's exclusive rights.

The analogy can be developed further still. The defence of fair dealing operates through a legal test that assists in the determination of whether the substantial reproduction giving rise to the fair dealing inquiry is an infringing one. These are the fair dealing factors formulated in *CCH*:

a) the purpose of the dealing,
b) the character of the dealing,
c) the amount of the dealing,
d) alternatives to the dealing,
e) the nature of the plaintiff's work, and
f) the effect of the dealing on the market of the work.[48]

Similarly, Justice Bastarache offers a legal test to assist in the determination whether a given use of a copyrighted work pursuant to Section 27(2) is an infringing one. Parallel importation or sale of a copyrighted work merely incidental to the parallel importation or sale of a consumer good is not parallel importation or sale of the work as such. The factors to be examined in making the determination whether the work is merely incidental to the consumer good are

a) the nature of the product,
b) the nature of the protected work, and
c) the relationship of the work to the product.[49]

Justice Bastarache explains that "[i]f a reasonable consumer undertaking a commercial transaction does not think that the copyrighted work

48 *CCH*, above note 3 at paras. 53–60.

49 *Euro-Excellence*, above note 1 at para. 94.

is what she is buying or dealing with, it is likely that the work is merely incidental to the consumer good."[50]

The bare statement of this test is, I think, sufficient to allay concerns that Justice Bastarache's interpretation of section 27(2) is untenable because it is inconsistent with section 64 of the *Copyright Act*. Justice Rothstein formulates the objection as follows:

> Section 64 of the *Copyright Act* . . . addresses the very issue that is fundamental to my colleague's approach: can a work of art appearing on a label and receiving trade-mark protection also be the subject of copyright protection? Parliament concluded that works can receive concurrent copyright and trade-mark protection.[51]

Nothing in Justice Bastarache's judgment, however, is inconsistent with the proposition that, to repeat Justice Rothstein's words, "works can receive concurrent copyright and trade-mark protection." Justice Bastarache nowhere states that there can be no concurrent protection. In fact, he specifically states that such concurrent protection exists.[52] What his judgment affirms is that copyright liability pursuant to Section 27(2) does not arise automatically from the mere use of particular patterns of ink in association with a consumer good. The question whether such use gives rise to copyright liability is to be answered through the application of the merely incidental test. Where the application of the test yields the conclusion that the use of the copyrighted work in question is more than merely incidental, copyright liability arises. The use in issue would in that instance sound in copyright as well as trade-mark law (if indeed the conditions for trade-mark infringement are present, of course!). Concurrent protection would indeed obtain.

The difference between Justice Rothstein and Justice Bastarache is not about concurrent protection. It is about the interpretation of Section 27(2). Assume, for example, that the logos in issue in *Euro-Excellence* were no longer subject to copyright protection because the person who auth-

---

50 *Ibid.* at para. 94. Recalling a remark of Binnie J.'s at the hearing, we might say that, on the facts of *Euro-Excellence*, it is not as if the reasonable consumer keeps the wrapper and throws away the chocolate!

51 *Ibid.* at para. 9. Abella J makes a similar claim at para. 110.

52 *Ibid.* at para. 87: "While it certainly true that one work can be the subject of both copyright and trade-mark protection (see s. 64(3)(b) of the Act), it is equally certain that different forms of intellectual property protect different types of economic interests."

ored them has been dead for longer than 50 years.[53] In that case, the parallel importation of the chocolate bars would not give rise to any copyright liability, regardless of concurrent protection issues pertinent to Section 64 of the *Copyright Act*. To state the obvious, the fact that Section 64 extends concurrent copyright protection to logos used as trade-marks does not mean that Section 64 grants copyright where none exists to begin with. Although copyright and trade-mark protection may be concurrent, the copyright inquiry is radically independent from the trade-mark inquiry.

Justice Bastarache's position is that the use of the logos in *Euro-Excellence* does not sound as a copyright matter pursuant to Section 27(2). He would reach that conclusion even if the logos were unregistered under the *Trade-Marks Act*, and even if the use of the logos could not under any circumstance sustain a passing-off action at common law. As it happens, of course, it is unlikely that the plaintiff Kraft Canada Inc. could sustain, on the facts as we know them, either a trade-mark infringement or a passing-off action against the defendant Euro-Excellence Inc. But the point here is that the trade-mark aspect of the case is on the facts as irrelevant to Justice Bastarache's analysis of Section 27(2) as it would be were this a case where the copyright had expired. Justice Bastarache's judgment is about liability under the *Copyright Act*. Properly construed, his reasoning is *not* that no copyright liability arises because the logos are being used as trade-marks. His reasoning is that no copyright liability arises because the use of the logos by Euro-Excellence Inc. does not fall within the meaning of Section 27(2). Strictly speaking, Justice Bastarache's judgment has nothing to do with concurrent protection.

Distilled to its essence, the heart of Justice Bastarache's judgment is rather the distinction between patterns of ink and works of authorship. It is on the basis of this distinction that Justice Bastarache can examine the sale of chocolate bars and conclude that no copyright liability arises. Simply put, his point is that the mere presence of shapes of ink (albeit identical to the works of authorship in issue) printed on the chocolate bar wrappers cannot in and of itself ground liability. The transaction whereby title to the wrapper is transferred to a purchaser is not, by that token alone, a sale of a "copy of a work" within the meaning of Section 27(2).

---

53 Section 6 of the *Copyright Act*, above note 6, provides that "[t]he term for which copyright shall subsist shall, except as otherwise expressly provided by this Act, be the life of the author, the remainder of the calendar year in which the author dies, and a period of fifty years following the end of that calendar year."

It is tempting to object that Justice Bastarache's reliance on *CCH* and *SOCAN* is suspect in that the (so-called) "exceptions" to infringement formulated in each of those cases tracked a provision in the statute — namely, the fair dealing provision in *CCH*[54] and the common carrier exception in *SOCAN*[55] — exempting the defendants from liability. In *Euro-Excellence*, by contrast, we can find no provision in the *Act* stating that "merely incidental" uses of copyrighted works are to be exempted from liability pursuant to Section 27(2).

Two important observations are worth underlining in this respect. The first is that neither in *CCH* nor in *SOCAN* were the provisions in question interpreted in the absence of pivotal references to the purpose of the *Copyright Act* as a balance between authors and users. In *CCH*, it was attentiveness to the purpose of the *Act* that in fact led the Court to alter significantly what many would have regarded as the accepted interpretation of fair dealing as a mere exception to be narrowly construed,[56] an interpretation that more than certainly would have fallen short of affirming the legality of the reproductions in issue in *CCH*. Similarly, in *SOCAN*, it was attentiveness to the purpose of the *Act* that led the Court to reject the Court of Appeal's narrow interpretation of the common carrier exception,[57] an interpretation that would have fallen short of affirming the legality of "caching." Thus, Justice Bastarache's reliance on the purpose of the *Act* to interpret Section 27(2) is by no means surprising.

More importantly — and this is the second observation worth underlining here — the demand that there be an additional provision exempting certain otherwise infringing acts from liability under Section 27(2) mis-

---

54 *Ibid.* at s. 29.

55 *Ibid.* at s. 2.4(1)(b).

56 *CCH*, above note 3 at para 48: "The fair dealing exception, like other exceptions in the *Copyright Act*, is a user's right. In order to maintain the proper balance between the rights of a copyright owner and users' interests, it must not be interpreted restrictively."

57 *SOCAN*, above note 14 at para. 115:

> In the Board's view, the means "necessary" under s. 2.4(1)(b) were means that were content neutral and were necessary to maximize the economy and cost-effectiveness of the Internet "conduit." That interpretation, it seems to me, best promotes "the public interest in the encouragement and dissemination of works of the arts and intellect" (*Théberge*, above, at para. 30) without depriving copyright owners of their legitimate entitlement. The creation of a "cache" copy, after all, is a serendipitous consequence of improvements in Internet technology, is content neutral, and in light of s. 2.4(1)(b) of the Act ought not to have any *legal* bearing on the communication between the content provider and the end user.

construes what one might call the jurisprudential location of Section 27(2) in the structure of the *Act*. The demand for an exempting provision seems to rely on the view that just as the fair dealing provision in Section 29, for example, narrows the reach of the right of reproduction granted under Section 3(1), so must an exempting provision narrow the reach of Section 27(2), if Justice Bastarache's interpretation is to have any semblance of a statutory basis. But this view rests on the assumption that Section 27(2) is akin to Section 3(1), a provision granting rights to be limited elsewhere. In *CCH*, the Supreme Court warned that, procedurally, fair dealing as a defence should not obscure the integral role of fair dealing as a user right in the overall structure of the copyright system.[58] It seems only natural to heed the parallel warning to steer away from concluding that any and all limitations imposed on authorial right require some kind of exempting provision. Especially in the case of Section 27(2), which grants the copyright holder under specific conditions rights additional to those already granted under the core copyright definition in Section 3(1),[59] it seems odd to await yet another limiting provision before allowing oneself to get on in earnest with the task of interpreting the words of the provision itself (i.e. Section 27(2)) — as does Justice Bastarache in *Euro-Excellence* — in light of the scheme and purpose of the *Act*, in particular, in light of the balance of authors and users and the specificity of copyright's own domain.

Justice Bastarache's interpretation of Section 27(2) in fact affirms a fundamental distinction familiar in copyright law — a distinction between mere physical identities and infringing copies — from a standpoint able to integrate recent and seminal Supreme Court of Canada decisions affirming the centrality of the concepts of "balance," "limits," and "user rights" in Canadian copyright. Of course, this is not to say that Justice Bastarache's judgment does not bring difficulties of its own in its wake. But it *is* to say that the view that the judgment lacks statutory and/or jurisprudential basis is either exaggerated or misplaced. The judgment is neither more nor less lacking in statutory and/or jurisprudential basis than anything else that the Supreme Court of Canada has done with copyright law at least since *Théberge*. On the contrary, among its virtues is having focused the issues in *Euro-Excellence* through a prism that advances the ongoing conversation about copyright and its limits (re)initiated in *Théberge*.

---

58 *CCH*, above note 3 at para. 48.

59 *Copyright Act*, above note 6, s. 3(1): "For the purposes of this Act, 'copyright', in relation to a work, means the sole right to produce or reproduce the work or any substantial part thereof . . . ."

E. CONCLUSIONS

What does remain unresolved and undeveloped in the judgment is the extent to which the conceptual structure deployed by Justice Bastarache in the interpretation of Section 27(2) would exert pressure on the interpretation of Section 3(1). Two examples will suffice to illustrate.

The first example I have in mind is a variation on the facts of *Euro-Excellence*. Assume for a moment that Euro-Excellence Inc. acquired in Europe not the wrapped chocolate bars but only the chocolate bars themselves, so that Euro-Excellence Inc. would have had to manufacture the wrappers. Assume also that Euro-Excellence Inc. goes ahead and manufactures the wrappers without authorization from the holder of the copyright in the relevant logos. Presumably no trade-mark issue would arise on these facts, as Euro-Excellence would still be offering genuine Kraft chocolate bars to the public. The resolution of the copyright issues, however, is not immediately self-evident, at least not from Justice Bastarache's perspective.

On the one hand, if—as Justice Bastarache appears to insist[60]—the "merely incidental" analysis is to be restricted to Section 27(2), there can be no doubt that Euro-Excellence is on these facts liable for copyright infringement, specifically, for the unauthorized reproduction on the chocolate bar wrappers of the copyrighted works. On the other hand, however, recall that Justice Bastarache found no liability on the actual facts of the case on the grounds that the "legitimate interests" of the copyright holder do not encompass the sale of chocolate bars in wrappers on which certain patterns of ink (i.e., the copyrighted works in issue) happen to appear merely incidentally. Such sales are not sales of copies of the work within the meaning of Section 27(2). But if chocolate bar sales involving merely incidental ink-patterns do not fall within the "legitimate interests" of the copyright holder, there seems to be no reason to conclude that the reproduction of such ink-patterns *solely for the purpose of being used merely incidentally* in the sale of chocolate bars does fall within such interests.

Indeed, the basic thrust of Justice Bastarache's focus on the specific authorship interests of the copyright holder would suggest that no liability would arise on those facts. Just as chocolate bar sales are not truly sales of copyrighted works appearing on wrappers merely incidentally, so reproductions of copyrighted works for the sole purpose of appearing merely incidentally on chocolate bar wrappers are not truly reproductions of the copyrighted works *as works*. There is as little reason to believe that these

60 *Euro-Excellence*, above note 1 at para. 95.

reproductions for merely incidental use would engage the specific authorship interests of the copyright holder as there is reason to believe that chocolate bar sales do. This conclusion is possible, however, only once it is admitted that the purpose of the reproductions is relevant to the interpretation of the scope of the core exclusive right of reproduction granted to the copyright holder in Section 3(1) of the *Copyright Act*.

Evidence that such a line of thought is by no means foreign to copyright jurisprudence can be gleaned from the second example I have in mind and which I offer by way of conclusion. Assume that a patentee has submitted to the Patent Office as part of her patent specification certain diagrams disclosing her invention. Also assume that these diagrams are copyrightable, and that, because it is a reproduction of those diagrams "in any material form,"[61] the construction of the invention they disclose infringes the copyright in the diagrams. Thus, *prima facie*, it would seem that both during and after the expiration of the patent, the patentee has a cause of action in copyright against unauthorized construction of the invention disclosed in her drawings. Where this option is pursued after the expiration of the patent, the copyright would have the effect of providing a "backdoor" extension of the patentee's monopoly.

Courts have handled this difficulty by appeal to a concept of "deemed abandonment" of the relevant copyrights in patent drawings.[62] The concept of deemed abandonment, however, seems less than accurate. The point is not so much that the patentee has a right—albeit deemed abandoned or licensed by implication[63]—to rely on her copyright in the patent diagrams, but rather that her copyright does not from the very outset

---

61 The phrase "in any material form" appears in the core definition of "copyright" in s. 3(1) of the Act (see *Copyright Act*, above note 6). On the move from two-dimensional form (e.g., a drawing) to three-dimensional form (e.g., a doll or model) as copyright infringement, see *King Features Syndicate Inc. v. O. & M. Kleeman Ltd.*, [1941] A.C. 417 (H.L.).

62 See *Catnic Components Ltd. v. Hill & Smith Ltd.*, [1978] F.S.R. 405 (Ch.); *Burnaby Machine & Mill Equipment Ltd. v. Berglund Industrial Supply Co.* (1984), 81 C.P.R. (2d) 251 (F.C.T.D.); *Rucker Co. v. Gavel's Vulcanizing Ltd.* (1985), 7 C.P.R. (3d) 294 (F.C.T.D.). For discussion, see Gervais and Judge, *Intellectual Property*, above note 28 at 597–600; Tomkowicz, "Copyrighting Chocolate," above note 7 at 423–25. See also Robert J. Tomkowicz and Elizabeth F. Judge, "The Right of Exclusive Access: Misusing Copyright to Expand the Patent Monopoly" (2006) 19:2 Intellectual Property Journal 351–91 (http://papers.ssrn.com/sol3/papers.cfm?abstract_id=819109).

63 Gervais and Judge, *Intellectual Property*, above note 28 at 599, suggesting an implied licence solution.

encompass what we might regard as non-authorial uses of the diagrams.[64] Thus, while reproduction of the diagrams as posters (or perhaps even as three-dimensional models) would be actionable, reproduction of the diagrams as working inventions would fall outside the legitimate domain of the copyright, not because the patentee has abandoned or licensed the latter reproduction, but because it was not within the purview of her right to begin with.[65]

In short, the point is that, construed from an authorship-specific standpoint attentive to copyright's own domain, the core exclusive right of reproduction granted in Section 3(1) of the *Copyright Act* is less an absolute right to reproduce physical patterns in any and all contexts than a far more richly textured right to reproduce works as works.[66] Only the legitimate interests of authors as authors are protected under the *Copyright Act*.

---

64 Compare Tomkowicz, "Copyrighting Chocolate," above note 7 at 424, suggesting a "limited judicial doctrine of copyright misuse" rooted in the purpose of the *Copyright Act*.

65 *Euro-Excellence*, above note 1 at para. 103 (Bastarache J):

> The above does not imply that the Côte d'Or or Toblerone logos are not copyrightable works. Quite the opposite: the logos have been properly registered and there is no reason to dispute the trial judge's conclusions that the logos meet the Act's originality threshold and are therefore copyrightable works. KCI [Kraft Canada Inc.], as holder of those copyrights in Canada, would surely succeed in an action for copyright infringement against a defendant who produced and distributed posters of the logos, for example. However, it is necessary to ensure that this legitimate copyright protection is not illegitimately leveraged into a protection for a market in consumer goods.

66 On the concept of "works as works," see Drassinower, "Authorship as Public Address," above note 43 (analyzing works of authorship as communicative acts).

CHAPTER SIX

Réforme du droit d'auteur et interprétation judiciaire

Mistrale Goudreau

ABSTRACT

For many years Canada has pursued a broad copyright reform process. Several proposals to amend the *Copyright Act* have been brought before Parliament, some of which have resulted in important legislative modifications while other bills have died on the Order Paper. These legislative efforts received wide public attention but may have obscured the fact that the courts have greatly contributed to the design of the Canadian copyright regime. Key legislative concepts such as the criteria of "originality", the "substantial part" test, and the "fair dealing" exception have relied on caselaw for their definition. On the other hand, legislative reforms have been ad hoc, with very detailed and narrow provisions. Because of this approach to drafting, the courts have been presented with difficult statutory interpretation challenges and to some extent have adopted unconventional solutions. Bill C-32, if enacted, will also involve issues of interpretation which will require the courts' productive intervention.

La *Loi sur le droit d'auteur* du Canada, sanctionnée en 1921[1] et mise en vigueur en 1924, a plus d'une fois été qualifiée de dépassée, désuète, d'où l'affirmation répétée à outrance du besoin de moderniser la législation.

---

1 *Loi sur le droit d'auteur*, S.R.C 1985, ch. C-30, http://laws.justice.gc.ca/fr/C-42/ [la *Loi*].

Pourtant la question de cette modernisation de la loi n'a cessé d'être étudiée par l'État canadien et un nombre impressionnant d'études et de rapports ont été au fil des ans classés sur les rayons[2]. En 1988, la Phase I de la réforme fut finalement adoptée[3]. En 1997, on réussit à faire passer le cap à la Phase II[4]. Si on fait abstraction de certaines modifications législatives restreintes, il faut convenir que depuis, le processus de réforme stagne. Certes, le gouvernement s'est engagé dans un vaste processus de consultation, notamment en 2001[5] et en 2009[6], a établi un cadre de révision de la *Loi sur le droit d'auteur*[7], puis un programme de réforme continu, classant les enjeux en catégories pour lesquelles on prévoyait des interventions législatives à court, moyen et long termes[8], abandonnant, ce faisant, toute numérotation des phases de réforme. Mais les deux projets de loi déposés à la Chambre des communes, l'un en 2005, l'autre en 2008, devant adapter

---

2 Les rapports les plus importants sont : *Rapport de la Commission Ilsley*, Commission royale sur les brevets, le droit d'auteur, les marques de commerce et le dessin industriel, Ottawa, 1957; AA. Keyes & C. Brunet, *Le droit d'auteur au Canada. Propositions en vue d'une révision de la loi*, Ministère des approvisionnements et services Canada, 1977; *Livre blanc sur le droit d'auteur, De Gutenberg à Télidon*, Ministère des approvisionnements et services Canada, 1984; En 1985 un sous-comité de la Chambre des communes produisit son propre rapport : *Une charte des droits des créateurs et créatrices, Rapport du sous-comité sur la révision du droit d'auteur*, Comité permanent des communications et de la culture, Chambre des communes, octobre 1985, auquel le gouvernement fournit une réponse : *Réponse du gouvernement au rapport du sous-comité sur la révision de la Loi sur le droit d'auteur* (1986).

3 *Loi modifiant la Loi sur le droit d'auteur et apportant des modifications connexes et corrélatives*, L.C. 1988, c. 15, traitant des programmes d'ordinateur, des dessins industriels, du droit moral, des sociétés de gestion et de la Commission du droit d'auteur.

4 *Loi modifiant la Loi sur le droit d'auteur*, L.C. 1997, c. 24, traitant notamment des droits voisins, du régime de la copie privée et créant une série d'exceptions aux droits des titulaires de droit d'auteur. Voir sur cette phase II notre commentaire « Et si nous discutions de rédaction législative... Commentaire sur la Loi de 1997 modifiant la *Loi sur le droit d'auteur* », (1998) 11 *Cahiers de propriété intellectuelle* 7.

5 Direction de la politique de la propriété intellectuelle, Industrie Canada, et la Direction de la politique du droit d'auteur, Patrimoine canadien, *Document de consultation sur les questions de droit d'auteur à l'ère numérique*, le 22 juin 2001, www.ic.gc.ca/eic/site/crp-prda.nsf/fra/h_rp01102.html.

6 Pour un compte rendu, voir le site de Industrie Canada : www.ic.gc.ca/eic/site/008.nsf/fra/accueil.

7 Industrie Canada et Patrimoine canadien, *Cadre de révision du droit d'auteur*, Ottawa, Industrie Canada et Patrimoine canadien, 2001, www.ic.gc.ca/eic/site/crp-prda.nsf/fra/rp01101.html.

8 Industrie Canada, *Stimuler la culture et l'innovation: Rapport sur les dispositions et l'application de la Loi sur le droit d'auteur*, (Loi sur le droit d'auteur — Rapport sur l'article 92), Industrie Canada, Octobre 2002, http://strategis.ic.gc.ca/eic/site/crp-prda.nsf/fra/rp00863.html.

la loi à l'environnement numérique, sont morts au feuilleton[9] et on peut s'interroger sur les chances de survie du dernier rejeton, le projet de loi C-32 introduit à la Chambre des communes le 2 juin 2010[10].

Dans ce contexte bouillonnant de consultation et d'activités parlementaires, on se serait attendu à ce que les tribunaux aient peu à dire en matière de droit d'auteur, la retenue judiciaire étant de mise lorsque l'action législative est imminente. Au contraire, les juges au cours des dernières années, ont rendu des décisions majeures et dans les faits, le régime canadien du droit d'auteur tient autant à l'intervention judiciaire qu'à l'activité législative. Pourtant, la plus grande attention a été apportée par les médias aux projets de réforme législative alors qu'en comparaison, les apports des tribunaux ont été moins mis en lumière. Le présent commentaire veut analyser l'interaction entre réforme législative et construction judiciaire, en montrant l'importance de l'apport des tribunaux au droit d'auteur canadien et en soulignant combien le dernier projet de loi à l'étude, le projet de loi C-32, laisse aussi une large place à l'activité créatrice des juges.

Pour faire cette démonstration, nous procéderons en exposant les particularités de la *Loi* qui suscitent l'interprétation judiciaire. En second lieu, nous analyserons le projet de loi C-32 et identifieront certains secteurs où les tribunaux auront probablement à intervenir pour clarifier l'état du droit si le projet de loi C-32 est adopté.

Voyons la première question : pourquoi les tribunaux ont-ils été si sollicités dans l'interprétation des lois sur le droit d'auteur ? La raison est d'abord historique. Les lois sur le droit d'auteur sont tirées de textes législatifs réputés pour leur caractère obscur et complexe; déjà en 1878 le rapport des commissaires anglais[11] décrivait les lois applicables, notamment celle de

---

9 *Loi modifiant la Loi sur le droit d'auteur*, Chambre des communes du Canada, projet de loi C-60, Première session, trente-huitième législature, 53–54 Elizabeth II, 2004–2005, première lecture le 20 juin 2005, www2.parl.gc.ca/HousePublications/Publication.aspx?pub=bill&doc=c-60&parl=38&ses=1&language=E&File=14 (mort au feuilleton); *Loi modifiant la Loi sur le droit d'auteur*, Chambre des communes du Canada, projet de loi C-61, Deuxième session, trente-neuvième législature, 56–57 Elizabeth II, 2007–2008, première lecture le 12 juin 2008, www2.parl.gc.ca/House-Publications/Publication.aspx?Docid=3570473&file=4 (mort au feuilleton).

10 *Loi modifiant la Loi sur le droit d'auteur*, Chambre des communes du Canada, projet de loi C-32, Troisième session, quarantième législature, 59 Elizabeth II, 2010, première lecture le 2 juin 2010, www2.parl.gc.ca/HousePublications/Publication.aspx?Docid=4580265&file=4.

11 *Royal Commissioners' Report* , 1878, Primary Sources on Copyright (1450–1900), eds L. Bently & M. Kretschmer, www.copyrighthistory.org.

1842[12], comme « wholly destitute of any sort of arrangement, incomplete, often obscure and even when it is intelligible upon long study, it is in many parts so ill expressed that no one who does not give such study to it can expect to understand it. »[13] La loi canadienne[14] a hérité des structures de la loi anglaise de 1911 et mérite à bien des niveaux des commentaires semblables. Le gouvernement l'a reconnu, insérant dans son programme de réforme à long terme la « clarification et simplification de la *Loi* »[15]. Notre propos portera donc en premier lieu sur une étude de l'économie de la *Loi sur le droit d'auteur*.

A. L'ÉCONOMIE DE LA *LOI SUR LE DROIT D'AUTEUR* SUSCITE L'INTERPRÉTATION JUDICIAIRE

Deux caractéristiques de la loi canadienne en font un cas spécial d'interprétation : c'est une loi qui ébauche à certains égards une armature sommaire laissant au judiciaire le fardeau de fabriquer les pièces maîtresses de la structure, alors qu'à d'autres égards, elle tombe dans le pointillisme exagéré, forçant une interprétation peu orthodoxe de ses dispositions.

Passons en revue ces deux aspects.

1) L'armature sommaire de la *Loi sur le droit d'auteur*

Voyons une définition succincte du droit d'auteur canadien proposée par l'Office de la propriété intellectuelle du Canada : « Dans sa plus simple expression, le « droit d'auteur » signifie le « droit de reproduire ». En règle générale, le droit d'auteur désigne le droit exclusif de produire ou de reproduire une œuvre (ou une partie importante de cette œuvre) sous une forme quelconque. » [16] « Le droit d'auteur s'applique à toutes les œuvres originales de nature littéraire, dramatique, musicale et artistique. »[17]

---

12 *Copyright Law Amendment Act*, 1842, 5 & 6 Vict., c. 45, *Primary Sources on Copyright (1450–1900)*, eds L. Bently & M. Kretschmer, www.copyrighthistory.org [*Copyright Act 1842*].

13 Un autre estime que la *Loi* de 1842 serait « a notorious and flagrant example of bad drafting », F.P. Notes, (1900) 16 L.Q.R. 1, p. 6.

14 *Supra* note 1.

15 *Supra* note 8, p. 51.

16 Office de la propriété intellectuelle du Canada, *Le guide des droits d'auteur*, Gatineau (Québec) (2008), www.ic.gc.ca/eic/site/cipointernet-internetopic.nsf/vwapj/2010guidedroitsdauteur-2010guidecopyrights-fra.pdf/$file/2010guidedroitsdauteur-2010guidecopyrights-fra.pdf, à la page 3.

17 *Ibid.*, p. 4.

« Qu'est-ce que vous ne pouvez pas protéger par droit d'auteur?

- les titres et les courtes combinaisons de mots;
- les idées : le droit d'auteur porte uniquement sur l'expression fixe (p. ex. texte, enregistrement, dessin, etc.) d'une idée et non sur l'idée elle-même; . . .
- les données factuelles : les faits, les idées et les nouvelles font partie du domaine public. Autrement dit, ils appartiennent à tout le monde et personne ne peut détenir un droit d'auteur sur ces objets; cependant, la disposition, l'adaptation et la traduction des données factuelles peuvent être protégées par droit d'auteur. Par exemple, dans le cas d'un article de magazine rapportant des faits, la façon dont l'information est formulée peut être protégée par le droit d'auteur mais pas les faits qui sont relatés. »[18]

Ce simple énoncé suit dans les grandes lignes la terminologie de la loi[19] et déjà soulève de graves questions d'interprétation. Qu'est-ce ce qu'une œuvre, ou une de nature littéraire, ou une œuvre originale, ou une partie importante d'une œuvre, ou une reproduction sous une forme matérielle quelconque, ou encore en quoi réside la distinction entre l'idée et son expression ? Ces questions ont toutes fait l'objet de nombreuses décisions judiciaires, dont plusieurs de la Cour suprême, dans les deux dernières décennies[20].

---

18 *Ibid.*, p.4.

19 Voir les articles 3 et 5 de la *Loi:*

> 3. (1) Le droit d'auteur sur l'œuvre comporte le droit exclusif de produire ou reproduire la totalité ou une partie importante de l'œuvre, sous une forme matérielle quelconque. . . .
>
> 5. (1) Sous réserve des autres dispositions de la présente loi, le droit d'auteur existe au Canada, pendant la durée mentionnée ci-après, sur toute œuvre littéraire, dramatique, musicale ou artistique originale. . .

20 Voir notamment *Apple Computer, Inc. c. Mackintosh Computers Ltd.*,http://csc.lexum.umontreal.ca/en/1990/1990scr2-209/1990scr2-209.html, [1990] 2 R.C.S. 209 [*Apple Computer, Inc. c. Mackintosh Computers Ltd.*]; *Euro-Excellence Inc. c. Kraft Canada Inc.*, 2007 CSC 37, http://csc.lexum.umontreal.ca/en/2007/2007scc37/2007scc37.html, [2007] 3 R.C.S. 21 [*Euro-Excellence Inc. c. Kraft Canada Inc.*]; *Théberge c. Galerie d'Art du Petit Champlain inc.*, 2002 CSC 34, http://csc.lexum.umontreal.ca/en/2002/2002scc34/2002scc34.html, [2002] 2 R.C.S. 336 [*Théberge c. Galerie d'Art du Petit Champlain inc.*]; *CCH Canadienne Ltée c. Barreau du Haut-Canada*, 2004 CSC 13, http://csc.lexum.umontreal.ca/fr/2004/2004csc13/2004csc13.html, [2004] 1 R.C.S. 339 [*CCH Canadienne Ltée c. Barreau du Haut-Canada*]; *Desputeaux c. Éditions Chouette (1987) inc.*, 2003 CSC 17, http://csc.lexum.umontreal.ca/en/2003/2003scc17/2003scc17.html, [2003] 1 R.C.S. 178; *Robertson c. Thomson Corp.*,

En fait, le législateur emploie souvent dans la loi de concepts fondamentaux flous, dont le sens doit être dégagé par la jurisprudence. Le fait est très connu et a été commenté à moult reprises. Moins connue est la raison de l'incorporation de ces notions. En certains cas, la vérité est simple : ces concepts ont été initialement le fruit de décisions jurisprudentielles et ont été par la suite enchâssés dans la loi. La construction est donc judiciaire. Examinons quelques exemples : la notion d'originalité, le concept de « partie importante », la notion d'utilisation équitable.

a) La notion d'originalité

Sans doute la condition d'originalité, nommée la « pierre angulaire du droit d'auteur »[21], est la plus illustrative des ambiguïtés persistantes des lois anglaises et canadiennes[22]. Cette exigence est devenue applicable aux œuvres littéraires, musicales, artistiques et dramatiques de par la loi anglaise de 1911[23].

Les lois antérieures formaient un tableau disparate[24] et celles relatives à la propriété littéraire ne mentionnaient pas l'exigence d'originalité. Le *Sta-*

2006 CSC 43, http://csc.lexum.umontreal.ca/fr/2006/2006csc43/2006csc43.html, [2006] 2 R.C.S. 363[*Robertson c. Thomson Corp.*]; *Boutin c. Distributions C.L.B. Inc.*, [1994] 2 R.C.S. 7 http://csc.lexum.umontreal.ca/fr/1994/1994rcs2-7/1994rcs2-7.html.

21 *Robertson c. Thomson Corp.*, *supra* note 20, au par. 35.

22 Sur les raisons de l'ambiguïté du concept, voir Abraham Drassinower, « Sweat of the Brow, Creativity, and Authorship: On Originality in Canadian Copyright Law », (2003-2004) 1 U.O.L.T.J. 105, www.uoltj.ca/articles/vol1.1-2/2003-2004.1.1-2.uoltj.Drassinower.105-123.pdf, et sur son évolution, Carys J. Craig, « The Evolution of Originality in Canadian Copyright Law: Authorship, Reward and the Public Interest », (2005) 2.2 U.O.L.T.J. 425, www.uoltj.ca/articles/vol2.2/2005.2.2.uoltj.Craig.425-445.pdf.

23 Article 1 du *Copyright Act 1911*, (1911) 1 & 2 Geo. V, c. 46, repris à l'article 4 de la Loi canadienne de 1921, *supra* note 1.

24 Voir notamment *An Act for the Encouragement of Learning, by Vesting the Copies of Printed Books in the Authors or Purchasers of such Copies, During the Times therein mentioned*, 1710, 8 Anne, c.19 (*Primary Sources on Copyright (1450–1900)*, eds L. Bently & M. Kretschmer, www.copyrighthistory.org) [*Statute of Anne*]; *Engraving Copyright Act 1735*, 8 Geo II, c. 13 (*Primary Sources on Copyright (1450–1900)*, eds L. Bently & M. Kretschmer, www.copyrighthistory.org) [*Copyright Act 1735*]; *Engraving Copyright Act 1767*, 7 Geo III, c. 38 (*Primary Sources on Copyright (1450–1900)*, eds L. Bently & M. Kretschmer, www.copyrighthistory.org) [*Engraving Copyright Act 1767*]; *Models and Busts Act 1798*, 38 Geo.III, c.71 (*Primary Sources on Copyright (1450–1900)*, eds L. Bently & M. Kretschmer, www.copyrighthistory.org) [*Models and Busts Act 1798*]; *Copyright Act 1814*, 54 Geo III, c. 156 (*Primary Sources on Copyright (1450–1900)*, eds L. Bently & M. Kretschmer, www.copyrighthistory.org) [*Copyright Act 1814*]; *Dramatic Literary Property Act 1833*, 3 & 4 Wm IV, c. 15 (*Primary Sources on Copyright (1450–1900)*, eds L. Bently & M. Kretschmer, www.copyrighthistory.org); *Publication of Lectures Act*

tute of Anne accordait une protection à « any book »[25], l'expression « book » n'étant pas définie. La *Loi* de 1814 visait, elle, les « books » mais aussi les « maps and prints »[26]. En 1842, la *Loi* précisait que « in the construction of this act, the word « book » shall be construed to mean and include every Volume, Part or Division of a Volume, Pamphlet, Sheet of Letter-press, Sheet of Music, Map, Chart, or Plan separately published »[27]. Aucune loi n'exigeait expressément un apport spécial de l'auteur.

Seules les lois plus axées sur les arts plastiques visaient des œuvres ayant un élément de créativité. La loi sur les gravures de 1735[28], dans son préambule, faisait mention des personnes qui « have by their own genious, industry, pains, and expence, invented and engraved or worked » et celle des modèles et bustes de 1798[29] des personnes qui « have by their own genious, industry, pains, and expence, improved and brought the art of making new models . . . ». On emploie des mots tels que « invent », « from his own work and invention »[30], ou « new model »[31], alors qu'une telle terminologie est absente dans les lois sur la propriété littéraire.

Pourtant, même en l'absence de mention dans ces textes législatifs antérieurs à 1911, les tribunaux anglais avaient déduit du concept d'auteur cette notion d'originalité[32]. Certes il n'y avait pas unanimité : ainsi tous ne

---

1835, 5 & 6 Wm IV, c 65 (*Primary Sources on Copyright (1450–1900)*, eds L. Bently & M. Kretschmer, www.copyrighthistory.org); *Copyright Act 1842*, *supra* note 12.

25 *Supra* note 24, a. I.

26 *Copyright Act 1814*, *supra* note 24, a. II.

27 *Copyright Act 1842*, *supra* note 12, a. II.

28 *Copyright Act 1735*, *supra* note 24. Au Canada, la première loi sur le droit d'auteur fera l'amalgame des lois de propriété littéraire et propriété artistique en protégeant « toute personne . . . qui sera ou seront les auteurs de quelques livre ou livres, carte, plan ou œuvre de musique . . . ou qui inventera, dessinera, gravera à l'eau forte, ou au burin, ou qui fera graver à l'eau forte ou au burin, ou faire d'après son propre dessein, aucune estampe ou gravure » *Acte pour protéger la propriété littéraire*, (1832) 2 Will. IV, c. 5, a. I. Un effort créatif n'était mentionné que dans la partie de la disposition visant les arts plastiques. Un libellé semblable est utilisé dans les lois subséquentes: voir *An Act for the protection of Copy Rights in this Province*, (1841) 4-5 Vict., c. 61, a. I; *An Act respecting Copyrights*, (1868) 31 Vict., c. 54, a. 3; *Copyright Act*, (1875) 38 Vict., c. 88, a. 4. Ces deux dernières lois n'ont exigé une condition d'originalité que pour les « painting, drawing, statuary/statue, sculpture or photograph ».

29 *Models and Busts Act 1798*, *supra* note 24.

30 *Copyright Act 1735*, *supra* note 24, a. I.

31 *Models and Busts Act 1798*, *supra* note 24, a. I et II.

32 Voir l'analyse de Nigel P. Gravells, « Authorship and Originality: the Persistent Influence of *Walter v Lane* », (2007) Intellectual Property Quarterly 267, p. 268. Au même effet, *Sawkins v Hyperion Records Ltd*, [2005] EWCA Civ 565, www.bailii.org/ew/cases/EWCA/Civ/2005/565.html, au para. 33. Le copyright de common law aurait aussi exigé

s'entendaient pas pour en faire une exigence pour la protection de la *Loi* de 1842[33], mais la notion était clairement connue des tribunaux. Certains[34] voient dans la décision *Matthewson v Stockdale* de 1806[35] le germe de la notion, le tribunal reconnaissant au demandeur un « copyright in that particular work, which has cost him considerable expense and labour ». Dans *Dicks v Yates*[36], en 1881, la Division de la Chancellerie estime qu'il est établi en droit « that to be the subject of copyright the matter must be original, it must be a composition of the author, something which has grown up in his mind ». De même manière, la Chambre des Lords apporte cette précision à l'égard des compilations en 1894 :

> « The real truth is, that although it is not to be disputed that there may be copyright in a compilation or abstract involving independent labour, yet when you come to such a subject-matter as that with which we are dealing, it ought to be clearly established that, looking at theses tables as a whole, there has been a substantial appropriation by the one party of the independent labour of the other, before any proceeding on the ground of copyright can be justified. . . It appears to me the only part to the work which can be said to indicate any considerable amount of independent labour, and be entitled to be regarded as an original work. I refer to the part on pages 63, 65, 67 and 69 containing the information with regard to excursions. »[37]

Pourtant lorsque le concept fut introduit dans le projet de loi en 1911, une proposition fut faite à la Chambre des communes de le retirer[38], au motif que son incorporation au texte législatif pourrait conduire à exclure de la

---

une originalité de l'oeuvre : *Drone on Copyright* (1879), (*Primary Sources on Copyright (1450–1900)*, eds L. Bently & M. Kretschmer, www.copyrighthistory.org), p. 110.

33 Voir les motifs des juges Halsbury, Davey et Brampton dans la décision *Walter v. Lane*, [1900] AC 539 et la discussion de Nigel P. Gravells, *supra* note 32, p. 271.

34 *Telstra Corporation Limited v Desktop Marketing Systems Pty Ltd*, [2001] FCA 612, www.austlii.edu.au/au/cases/cth/federal_ct/2001/612.html, au para. 55, inf. sur le fond *Telstra Corporation Limited v Phone Directories Company Pty Ltd*, [2010] FCA 44, www.austlii.edu.au/au/cases/cth/FCA/2010/44.html.

35 (1806), 12 Ves Jun 270 (Ch.); 33 ER 103.

36 (1881), 18 Ch.D. 76, p. 92.

37 *Leslie v. Young & Sons*, [1894] A.C. 335 (H.L.), p. 341–342 [*Leslie v. Young & Sons*]. La même année, la High Court de l'Ontario reconnut un droit d'auteur dans des formulaires, indiquant que « the purely commercial or business character of the composition or compilation does not oust the right to protection if time, labour, and experience have been devoted to its production » *Church v. Linton* (1894), 25 O.R. 131 (Ont. H.C.), p. 135.

38 HC Deb 28 July 1911 vol 28 cc1911-45 http://hansard.millbanksystems.com/commons/1911/jul/28/clause-1-copyright#S5CV0028P0_19110728_HOC_138; E.J.

protection les traductions et les gravures. Malgré les interventions de ses opposants, l'expression fut adoptée, mais cet épisode montre bien que les parlementaires étaient conscients de son caractère ambigu.

b) La notion de « partie importante » d'une œuvre

De même, le concept de violation par appropriation d'une « partie importante » d'une œuvre (« substantial part ») est en grande partie d'origine jurisprudentielle [39]. Les premières lois anglaises sur la propriété littéraire visaient simplement le « sole right and liberty of printing such Book » ou exigeaient que le contrefacteur se dessaisisse des « sheets being part of such Book or Books » [40]. Par contraste, la loi sur les gravures de 1735[41] protégeait les images « in the whole or in part, by varying, adding to, or diminishing from the main design », tout comme celle sur les moules et bustes de 1798[42], bien que cette précision n'ait pas été apportée aux cas de vente ou importation des moules et bustes[43]. Craignant une interprétation restrictive de leurs droits, les libraires tentèrent de faire élargir le libellé de la loi de 1710. Jane Gainsburg explique :

> « The booksellers themselves seem to have appreciated the potential consequences of the absence from the *Statute of Anne* of "or any parts thereof" language. They petitioned parliament in 1735 for amendments extending the prohibition to unauthorised publication "in parcels at different times and in different publications", apparently in response to the growing practice of magazine serialisation. This

---

Macgillivray, *The Copyright Act, 1911, Annotated*, London, Stevens And Sons, Limited, 1912, www.archive.org/details/copyrightact1911oogrearich, p. 3.

39 Evan James Macgillivray, *A Treatise upon the Law of Copyright*, John Murray (publ.), London, 1902, www.archive.org/details/treatiseuponlawooomacgrich, p. 99 [*Macgillivray* (1902)].

40 Ainsi le *Statute of Anne*, *supra* note 24, énonçait: « [the] Author of any Book or Books already composed and not printed and published [. . .] shall have the sole liberty of printing and reprinting such Book and Books. . . Then such offender or offenders shall forfeit such Book or Books and all and every sheet or sheets being part of such Book or Books. . . That then he and they so making default in not delivering the said printed Copies as aforesaid shall forfeit besides the value of the said printed Copies the sum of five pounds for every Copy not so delivered ».

41 *Copyright Act 1735*, *supra* note 24.

42 *Models and Busts Act 1798*, *supra* note 24.

43 C'est ainsi que Lord Ellenborough dans l'affaire *Gahagan v. Cooper*, (1811) 3 Camp. 111 arriva à la conclusion que la prohibition de manufacture s'étendait à la copie modifiée, mais que la prohibition de vente ou d'importation ne visait que les copies exactes, commentant : « [t]he statute seems to have been framed with a view to defeat its own object ».

bill having failed, the booksellers petitioned two years later, also unsuccessfully, for a three-year embargo on unauthorised translations and abridgements. [On the 1735 and 1737 bills, see generally, Ronan Deazley, *On the Origin of the Right to Copy: Charting the Movement of Copyright Law in Eighteenth-Century Britain (1695–1775)* (Oxford 1994), pp. 94–108.] The legislative record thus seems to favour narrow construction of the scope of the reproduction right in books. »[44]

En 1842, le législateur anglais précisa finalement qu'un livre inclut « every volume, part or division of a volume »[45], sans expliquer quelle proportion devait être reprise pour constituer une violation du droit conféré. Une lecture stricte de la loi aurait pu mener à la conclusion que le droit conféré inclut le droit exclusif de faire une copie de n'importe quelle partie du livre. Mais comme l'explique Evan James Macgillivray[46], animés par la maxime *de minimis non curat praetor*, les tribunaux conclurent que la violation ne se produisait que si on prenait une partie importante du livre. Dès 1829, on décidait que l'appropriation d'une partie non significative ne donnait pas un droit d'action[47]. En 1894, la Chambre des Lords jugeait qu'il fallait « a substantial appropriation by one party of the independant labour of the other » pour donner ouverture à une action en violation de droit d'auteur[48].

c) La notion d'utilisation équitable

Les tribunaux décideront aussi qu'un usage juste, équitable, d'une œuvre à des fins comme la critique, la recherche et la dissémination des connaissances ne donne pas un droit d'action[49]. Ce sera la naissance de la notion d'utilisation équitable. Ainsi en 1802, dans l'affaire *Cary v. Kearsley*[50], Lord

---

44 Jane C. Ginsburg, « "Une chose publique"? The Author's Domain and the Public Domain in Early British, French and US Copyright Law », (2006) 65(3) Cambridge Law Journal 636, p. 647

45 *Copyright Act 1842*, *supra* note 12, a. II. La première loi canadienne donnait le droit d'imprimer, ré-imprimer, publier et vendre « tel livre ou livres, carte, plan ou oeuvre de musique, estampe, figue en talle douce ou gravure, soit le tout ou partie d'iceux » : *Acte pour protéger la propriété littéraire*, *supra* note 28, a. I.

46 *Macgillivray* (1902), *supra* note 39, p. 97-99, citant plusieurs décisions, dont *Sweet v. Benning*, (1855) 16 C. B. 459, 139 Eng. Rep. 838 (Common Pleas); *Chatterton v. Cave*, (1875) LR (10 CP) 572; *Leslie v. Young & Sons*, *supra* note 37.

47 *Baily v. Taylor*, (1829) 1 R & M 73, 48 E.R. 118 (Rolls CT).

48 *Leslie v. Young & Sons*, *supra* note 37, p. 341.

49 Hugh Laddie et al., *The Modern Law of Copyright and Designs*, (London: Butterworths, 2000) p. 146, §3.133.

50 *Cary v. Kearsley* (1802), 4 Esp. 168, 170 Eng. Rep. 679 (K.B.).

Ellenborough affirma : « a man may fairly adopt part of the work of another... for the promotion of science and the benefit of the public . . . ». La reproduction de parties pour des fins de critique fut elle aussi acceptée relativement rapidement[51] .

Par contre, la notion d'utilisation équitable a eu au début peu de succès auprès des parlementaires. Les efforts de Thomas Noon Talfourd pour faire accepter l'exception pour « the publication of any extracts fairly and bona fide made from any Book for the purpose of criticism, observation or argument, or to any translation into another language, or abridgment fairly made of any book » dans la *Loi* de 1842 se sont soldés par un échec[52]. Ce ne sera que dans la loi anglaise de 1911[53], et celle de 1921[54] au Canada que l'exception sera intégrée. Ce seront les tribunaux qui détermineront les critères applicables pour évaluer le caractère équitable d'une utilisation, l'affaire *CCH Canadienne Ltée c. Barreau du Haut-Canada*[55] étant la décision la plus marquante au Canada.

Ces trois exemples montrent bien que les tribunaux ont grandement influencé le régime canadien du droit d'auteur en lui fournissant plusieurs notions clés, lesquelles furent incorporées dans la loi anglaise de 1911 et dans la loi canadienne de 1921. Mais là ne s'arrêtent pas les particularités des lois sur le droit d'auteur.

À compter de 1911, la forme des textes législatifs commence à changer. S'agissant de faire une synthèse des différentes lois s'appliquant aux différents types de productions (littéraires, dramatiques, musicales et artistiques), la loi de 1911 certes essaie d'établir un régime commun, mais malgré tout, entre dans de multiples détails et prévoit des exceptions en fonction des particularités de chaque discipline. Ce souci du détail, de la

---

51 *Whittingham v. Wooler* (1817) 2 Swanst. 428, 36 Eng. Rep. 679; *Bell v. Whitehead* (1839), 8 LJ Ch. 141; voir l'analyse de ces décisions dans Melissa De Zwart, « A Historical Analysis of the Birth of Fair dealing and Fair Use: Lessons for the Digital Age », 2007 (no. 1) Intellectual Property Quarterly 60, p. 80 et suivantes et une étude plus poussée de la jurisprudence dans William Patry, *The Fair Use Privilege in Copyright Law*, (Washington: The Bureau of National Affairs, 1985) p. 3–18.

52 Catherine Seville, *Literary Copyright Reform in Early Victorian England : the Framing of the 1842 Copyright Act*, (Cambridge : Cambridge University Press, 1999) [C. Seville], p. 240.

53 *Supra* note 23, article 2.

54 *Supra* note 1, article 17(2)a).

55 *Supra* note 20. Sur l'analyse de la décision, voir entre autres Daniel J. Gervais, « Canadian Copyright Law Post-*CCH* », (2004) 18 Intellectual Property Journal 131; Teresa Scassa, « Recalibrating Copyright Law?: A Comment on the Supreme Court of Canada's Decision in *CCH Canadian Limited et al. v. Law Society of Upper Canada* », (2004) 3 Canadian journal of Law and Technology 89.

législation au cas par cas, va non seulement persister mais s'accentuer avec les années. Macgillivray explique le début du phénomène :

> Taking it as a whole, the *Copyright Act*, 1911, is a valuable measure in the interests of literature and art. It may be said that the Government has made too many concessions, both to the socialistic demands of the members of the Labour Party, who believe that there should be no copyright, and to the demands of the makers of mechanical instruments, who appealed to the Government to save a great industry from possible bankruptcy. It was obvious, however, after the first few days in Committee, that it had become a question of passing the Bill with these concessions or abandoning it altogether.[56]

Le texte de loi de 1911 est aussi rédigé avec l'idée de ratifier les versions plus récentes de la *Convention de Berne*[57] et la loi canadienne de 1921 est forgée sur le modèle de la loi anglaise[58]. La loi canadienne sera plus tard modifiée pour accéder aux versions de 1931 et de 1971 de la *Convention de Berne*[59]. Cette convention internationale et d'autres auxquelles le Canada a adhéré ont donc eu un impact certain sur le libellé de ces lois[60], ce qui explique aussi la longueur du texte législatif. C'est bien la deuxième caractéristique de la loi canadienne, cette abondance de dispositions, souvent très détaillées, qui crée des problèmes particuliers d'interprétation. Voyons ce second aspect.

---

56 Macgillivray (1912), *supra* note 38, p. vi.

57 *Ibid.* Le titre officiel est la *Convention de Berne pour la protection des oeuvres littéraires et artistiques* du 9 septembre 1886, complétée à Paris le 4 mai 1896, révisée à Berlin le 13 novembre 1908, complétée à Berne le 20 mars 1914 et révisée à Rome le 2 juin 1928, à Bruxelles le 26 juin 1948, à Stockholm le 14 juillet 1967 et à Paris le 24 juillet 1971 et modifiée le 28 septembre 1979,www.wipo.int/treaties/fr/ip/berne/trtdocs_wo001.html#P19_188.

58 John S. McKeown, *Fox Canadian Law of Copyright and Industrial Designs*, 3 ed., (Scarborough : Carswell, 2000) p. 38.

59 M. Goudreau, *International Encyclopaedia of Laws: Intellectual Property — Canada*, (Alphen aan den Rijn (Pays-Bas) : Kluwer Law International, 2009) p. 26, §19.

60 En certains cas on reproduira quasi verbatim le texte international. Ainsi les définitions de l'article 2 de la canadienne sont inspirées de l'article 2 de la *Convention de Berne*. La disposition sur le droit moral (l'ancien a. 12(7)) introduite au Canada en 1931 (*Loi modifiant la Loi sur le droit d'auteur*, (1931) 21-22 Geo.V, c. 8, a. 5) était largement copiée de l'article 6(bis) de la *Convention* de *Berne*, *supra* note 57.

2) Un texte de loi embrouillé

Alors que, comme nous l'avons vu, la *Loi* consacre quelques grands principes, (protection réservée à l'œuvre originale, interdiction en principe de reprendre une partie importante, exception en cas d'utilisation équitable), elle renferme aussi des dispositions pointues, farcies de conditions et de termes eux-mêmes définis par la loi. Évidemment, il y aura superposition de dispositions, recoupement, chevauchement, ce qui, en interprétation des lois, cause des problèmes particuliers. Les tribunaux sont habituellement réfractaires à voir la même situation de faits visée par deux dispositions de la même loi. Le législateur n'étant pas censé parler pour ne rien dire[61], le juge tentera normalement de trouver une application propre à chaque disposition.

En matière de droit d'auteur, la règle d'interprétation sera souvent délaissée. Prenons deux exemples : l'article 2 qui introduit bon nombre de définitions et l'article 3(1) qui traite des droits exclusifs de l'auteur.

L'article 5 prévoit que le droit d'auteur existe au Canada à certaines conditions sur toute œuvre littéraire, dramatique, musicale ou artistique originale. Les notions d'œuvre littéraire, d'œuvre musicale, d'œuvre dramatique et d'œuvre artistique sont, elles, définies à l'article 2. Mais voilà que l'article rajoute que « toute œuvre littéraire, dramatique, musicale ou artistique originale » « s'entend de toute production originale du domaine littéraire, scientifique ou artistique quels qu'en soient le mode ou la forme d'expression, tels les compilations, livres, brochures et autres écrits, les conférences, les œuvres dramatiques ou dramatico-musicales, les œuvres musicales, les traductions, les illustrations, les croquis et les ouvrages plastiques relatifs à la géographie, à la topographie, à l'architecture ou aux sciences. »[62] Les plaideurs ont tenté de donner un sens à cette dernière définition en prétendant qu'une œuvre est protégée par la *Loi* pour autant qu'elle se qualifie soit selon les définitions particulières, soit en vertu de la définition générale. L'argument fut refusé par les cours[63], l'une d'elle sou-

61 P.-A. Côté, *Interprétation des lois*, 4e éd., (Montréal : Éditions Thémis, 2009) p. 318, § 1047–1050.

62 La définition est semblable à celle de l'article 2 de la *Convention de Berne*, *supra* note 57.

63 *Cuisenaire v. South West Imports Ltd.*, 54 C.P.R. 1, [1968] 1 Ex. C.R. 493 (C. Échiq.), [*Cuisenaire v. South West Imports Ltd.*], conf. *Cuisenaire v. South West Imports Ltd.*, [1969] R.C.S. 208, http://csc.lexum.umontreal.ca/en/1968/1969scr0-208/1969scr0-208.html; *Réseau de Télévision CTV Ltée c. Canada*, [1993] 2 C.F. 115 (C.A.F.), http://reports.fja.gc.ca/fra/1993/1993cfa0399.html/1993cfa0399.html.html .

lignant que la définition générale n'a pas vraiment élargi la portée de la *Loi*[64].

L'article 3 est un autre exemple de redondance. Au paragraphe (1), l'auteur est protégé contre la reproduction d'une partie importante d'une oeuvre sous une forme matérielle quelconque. Ce paragraphe doit-il être distingué de l'alinéa 3(1)(a) qui donne un droit sur les traductions ou de l'alinéa 3(1)d) qui concerne la confection d'un support, à l'aide duquel l'œuvre peut être reproduite, représentée ou exécutée mécaniquement; ou de l'alinéa 3(1)(c) qui traite de la transformation d'un roman en œuvre dramatique, par voie de représentation publique ou autrement; ou encore de l'alinéa 3(1)(e) qui envisage l'adaptation cinématographique ? Ne pourrait-on pas dire que tous ces actes sont des reproductions sous une forme matérielle quelconque ? Confrontée à la question, la Cour suprême considèrera que les circuits de la microplaquette électronique incorporant un programme informatique sont une reproduction, mais laissera en suspens la question de savoir s'ils sont aussi une traduction et la confection d'un moyen de reproduire l'œuvre[65].

En fait, souvent un même geste se trouve visé par plusieurs dispositions et les juges passeront en revue chaque droit exclusif pour évaluer s'il y a violation. Ainsi l'entreprise de câblodistribution qui transmet des signaux de télévision aux abonnés, de nos jours, fait une télécommunication au public des œuvres (al. 3(1)(f)), mais avait aussi été considérée comme faisant une représentation publique des œuvres et autorisant une représentation publique de ces œuvres[66], forçant le législateur à préciser que telle n'était pas le cas[67].

La règle est donc de considérer chaque droit exclusif de l'auteur comme un droit légal distinct. Un usager peut être tenu de payer séparément pour deux ou plusieurs droits. Ainsi les entreprises de télécommunications sans fil qui vendent des sonneries de téléphone cellulaire aux propriétaires de téléphones devront payer pour la reproduction des sonneries et aussi pour l'acte accessoire de télécommunication de la sonnerie choisie à l'abonné[68].

---

64 *Cuisenaire v. South West Imports Ltd.*, *supra* note 63.

65 *Apple Computer, inc. c. Mackintosh Computers ltd.*, *supra* note 20.

66 *Assoc. Canadienne de Télévision par Câble c. Canada*, [1993] 2 C.F. 138 (C.A.F), http://reports.fja.gc.ca/fra/1993/1993cfa0403.html/1993cfa0403.html.html .

67 Voir l'article 2.3 de la *Loi*, *supra* note 1.

68 *Assoc. canadienne des télécommunications sans fil c. Société canadienne des auteurs, compositeurs et éditeurs de musique* (C.A.F.), 2008 CAF 6, http://reports.fja.gc.ca/fra/2008/2008caf6/2008caf6.html, [2008] 3 R.C.F. 539 [*A.C.T.S.F. v. SOCAN*]. Les tribunaux suivent ici le raisonnement de la Cour suprême dans l'affaire *Bishop v.*

Au niveau des exceptions, le dédoublement se produit aussi. L'exemple le plus frappant a été fourni par la décision de la Cour suprême dans l'affaire *CCH Canadienne Ltée c. Barreau du Haut-Canada*[69]. La Bibliothèque du Barreau offre un service de photocopie sur demande à ses membres. La Cour estime qu'en l'espèce, la reproduction des œuvres et l'envoi des copies par fax par le Barreau, dans le cadre du service de photocopie, sont couverts par l'exception d'utilisation équitable pour fin de recherche, quand bien même une autre exception plus pointue y serait éventuellement applicable[70].

La Cour déclare :

> 48 Avant d'examiner la portée de l'exception au titre de l'utilisation équitable que prévoit la *Loi sur le droit d'auteur*, il importe de clarifier

---

Stevens, [1990] 2 R.C.S. 467, http://scc.lexum.umontreal.ca/en/1990/1990scr2-467/1990scr2-467.html . Pourtant en général, les contrats de licence de droit d'auteur définissent l'usage permis, sans nécessairement préciser quel droit exclusif de l'auteur est impliqué. Voir Daniel J. Gervais, « Canadian Copyright Law Post-*CCH* », (2004) 18 I.P.J. 131, p. 147. En traitant, dans l'analyse des contrats de licence, les droits exclusifs des auteurs comme de droits légaux distincts, les tribunaux s'écartent des règles d'interprétation usuelles en matières contractuelles. Normalement un contrat oblige non seulement à ce qui est exprimé, mais aussi à « tout ce qui en découle d'après sa nature, et suivant les usages, l'équité ou la loi » (article 1434 du Code civil du Québec, www2.publicationsduquebec.gouv.qc.ca/dynamicSearch/telecharge.php?type=2&file=/CCQ/CCQ.html). Domat explique : « toutes ces suites des conventions sont comme des pactes tacites et sous-entendus, qui en font partie; car les contractants consentent à tout ce qui est essentiel à leurs engagements. » (Jean Domat, *Oeuvres complètes*, nouvelle édition revue et corrigée par Joseph Remy (Paris : Alex-Gobelet, 1835), p. 134. Pareillement, la Common Law estime que des obligations implicites peuvent être reconnues lorsque « necessary to give efficacy to the contract » : *G. Ford Homes Ltd. v. Draft Masonry (York) Co. Ltd.* (1983), 43 O.R. (2d) 401, 1 D.L.R. (4th) 262 (C.A. Ont.); *Zeitler v. Zeitler Estate*, 2010 BCCA 216, www.courts.gov.bc.ca/jdb-txt/CA/10/02/2010BCCA0216.htm. Ce genre d'argument ne sera, ni plaidé, ni retenu dans l'analyse de la *Loi sur le droit d'auteur*, puisque « le droit de reproduire une œuvre musicale et le droit de la communiquer au public par télécommunication constituent des droits légaux distincts [et] force est alors de constater que le tarif 24 [qui porte sur la communication au public par télécommunication] prévoit une rémunération pour un droit qui n'est pas visé par les ententes portant sur les droits de reproduction. » Voir *A.C.T.S.F. v. SOCAN*, aux para. 13–15.

69 *Supra* note 20.

70 Il s'agit de l'article 30.2, qui est entré en vigueur après que les audiences en première instance dans l'affaire *CCH* eurent lieu. La Cour d'appel décide d'examiner les nouvelles dispositions, soulignant que « les parties cherchent maintenant à se faire aider pour l'avenir, et non pas à obtenir des réparations pour leurs comportements antérieurs » : *CCH Canadienne Ltée c. Barreau du Haut-Canada*, http://decisions.fca-caf.gc.ca/fr/2002/2002caf187/2002caf187.html, [2002] 4 C.F. 213 (C.A.F.), para. 136. La Cour suprême fera de même, voir *supra* note 20, aux para. 83-84.

> certaines considérations générales relatives aux exceptions à la violation du droit d'auteur. Sur le plan procédural, le défendeur doit prouver que son utilisation de l'œuvre était équitable; cependant, il est peut-être plus juste de considérer cette exception comme une partie intégrante de la *Loi sur le droit d'auteur* plutôt que comme un simple moyen de défense. Un acte visé par l'exception relative à l'utilisation équitable ne viole pas le droit d'auteur. À l'instar des autres exceptions que prévoit la *Loi sur le droit d'auteur*, cette exception correspond à un droit des utilisateurs. Pour maintenir un juste équilibre entre les droits des titulaires du droit d'auteur et les intérêts des utilisateurs, il ne faut pas l'interpréter restrictivement. Comme le professeur Vaver, [David Vaver, *Copyright Law*, Toronto : Irwin Law, 2000] l'a expliqué, à la p. 171, [traduction] « [l]es droits des utilisateurs ne sont pas de simples échappatoires. Les droits du titulaire et ceux de l'utilisateur doivent donc recevoir l'interprétation juste et équilibrée que commande une mesure législative visant à remédier à un état de fait. »
>
> 49 À titre de partie intégrante du régime de droit d'auteur, l'exception relative à l'utilisation équitable créée par l'art. 29 peut toujours être invoquée. Ainsi, une bibliothèque peut toujours tenter d'établir que son utilisation d'une œuvre protégée est équitable suivant l'art. 29 de la *Loi sur le droit d'auteur*. C'est seulement dans le cas où elle n'est pas en mesure de prouver l'application de cette exception qu'il lui faut s'en remettre à celle que prévoit l'art. 30.2 au bénéfice des bibliothèques. . . .

Bref l'exception générale ne cède pas le pas devant l'exception particulière. Les différentes autres exceptions sont toutes des alternatives, mêmes si redondantes.

Dans la même affaire, la Cour va aussi décider que le Barreau n'a pas autorisé la violation du droit d'auteur en mettant des photocopieuses libre-service ainsi que des exemplaires des œuvres à la disposition des usagers de la bibliothèque, rendant en bien des cas inutile l'exception de l'article 30.3(1), qui vise les reproductions au moyen d'une machine à reprographier libre-service.

Qu'en est-il maintenant du projet de loi C-32 ?

B. LES CARACTÉRISTIQUES DU PROJET DE LOI C-32 ET LA PLACE QU'IL LAISSE À L'ARBITRAGE DES JUGES

Au point de vue de la structure, le projet de loi C-32 s'inscrit parfaitement dans la tradition des lois antérieures. On crée des règles particulières pour certains secteurs ou activités définis. On maintient, ou élargit, ou même renforce certains des apports jurisprudentiels, par exemple en traitant de la non-responsabilité des fournisseurs de services réseau neutres et en élargissant la notion d'utilisation équitable. On enligne le libellé de la loi canadienne sur les textes internationaux.

1) Les règles particulières

On introduit une série d'exceptions qui, par contre, ne peuvent en général pas être appliquées aux œuvres protégées par des serrures numériques[71]. Voyons les principales exceptions. D'abord on instaure une exemption pour l'utilisateur qui crée un contenu non commercial[72]. L'exception demeure toutefois floue dans la mesure où il faut démontrer que l'utilisation de la nouvelle œuvre ou l'autorisation de la diffuser n'a aucun effet négatif important, pécuniaire ou autre, sur l'exploitation de l'œuvre originale.

On permet aussi la reproduction dans plusieurs circonstances de la vie quotidienne. La personne physique peut reproduire à des fins privées toute œuvre si elle a obtenu la copie originale de façon licite[73], sauf pour les œuvres musicales que le consommateur reproduit sur un support audio, qui demeurent assujetties au régime compensatoire assorti d'une exception pour copie privée régi par les articles 79 et suivants de la *Loi*. La personne physique pourra aussi reproduire une seule fois une émission radiodiffusée dans le but de regarder l'œuvre en différé à des fins privées, à condition que le signal soit reçu de façon licite[74].

Une personne propriétaire d'une copie d'un programme d'ordinateur ou détentrice d'une licence peut aussi se faire des copies de sauvegarde. Des exceptions sont également applicables pour la reproduction d'un programme d'ordinateur à des fins d'interopérabilité, de chiffrement, de recherche et de correction de problèmes de sécurité[75].

On modifie aussi le régime applicable aux enregistrements éphémères faits par les radiodiffuseurs[76]. Présentement, l'exception ne s'applique pas aux cas où le radiodiffuseur peut obtenir une licence d'une société de ges-

---

71 Voir les articles 29.22, 29.23, 29.24 et 30.04 que les articles 22 et 27 du projet de loi C-32, *supra* note 10 proposent d'intégrer dans la *Loi*.

72 Article 22 du projet de *loi C-32*, *supra* note 10, introduisant l'article 29.21.

73 Article 22 du projet de *loi C-32*, *supra* note 10, introduisant l'article 29.22.

74 Article 22 du projet de *loi C-32*, *supra* note 10, introduisant l'article 29.23.

75 Article 31 du projet de *loi C-32*, *supra* note 10, introduisant l'article 30.6.

76 Article 34 du projet de *loi C-32*, *supra* note 10.

tion[77]. Le projet de loi fait disparaître cette condition et, de ce fait, élimine l'obligation actuelle des radiodiffuseurs de payer des redevances. Cet avantage ne s'applique pas aux autres entreprises commerciales qui reproduisent et de façon accessoire diffusent des œuvres comme les entreprises de téléphone cellulaire qui enregistrent des sonneries pour les distribuer à leurs abonnés et qui doivent payer des redevances conformément à deux tarifs[78].

On le voit, les exceptions sont conçues pour des circonstances précises sans portée générale et leur traitement ne semble pas répondre à une logique certaine. Parfois certaines exceptions tombent si des copies sont disponibles sur le marché[79], d'autres si une licence peut être obtenue d'une société de gestion[80]. Certaines exceptions s'accompagnent de redevances pour copie privée, d'autres non[81]. Et un bon nombre des exceptions sont inutilisables si l'œuvre est protégée par une serrure numérique : à quoi bon une exception qui dépend du bon vouloir du titulaire du droit d'auteur, qui peut mettre le verrou à son choix ?

Or, en parallèle à ces dispositions, on maintient le recours à des notions générales, en renforçant ou élargissant le recours aux tribunaux.

2) Le renforcement des apports jurisprudentiels

a) La responsabilité des fournisseurs de services réseau

Déjà on le sait, la Cour suprême avait exempté de responsabilité le fournisseur de services Internet (autre qu'un fournisseur de contenu) sur la base de l'al. 2.4(1)b), même celui qui crée une « antémémoire » pour des raisons purement techniques[82]. La Cour avait toutefois laissé la porte ouverte à une responsabilité pour avoir omis de « retirer » un contenu illicite après

---

77 Article 30.9 de la *Loi*, *supra* note 1.

78 *A.C.T.S.F. v. SOCAN*, *supra* note 68.

79 Comparez l'exception proposée par l'article 22 (introduisant l'article 29.23) avec les exceptions pour les établissements d'enseignement proposées par l'article 27 du projet de loi C-32, *supra* note 10.

80 Comparez le régime pour les établissements d'enseignement (article 30.02(4) introduit par l'article 25 du projet de loi et l'article 30.3 de la *Loi*) avec le nouveau régime pour les entreprises de radiodiffusion (article 34 du projet de *loi C-32*, *supra* note 10).

81 Voir l'al. 29.22 (3) introduit par l'article 22 du projet de *loi C-32*, *supra* note 10.

82 *Société canadienne des auteurs, compositeurs et éditeurs de musique c. Assoc. canadienne des fournisseurs Internet*, 2004 CSC 45, http://csc.lexum.umontreal.ca/fr/2004/2004csc45/2004csc45.html , [2004] 2 R.C.S. 427, [*SOCAN v. Assoc. canadienne des fournisseurs Internet*]. Le projet de loi crée aussi une exception concernant la mise en antémémoire : voir les al. 31.1(3) à (6), introduits par l'article 35 du projet de loi C-32, *supra* note 10.

avoir été avisé de sa présence, ce qui équivaudrait à une « autorisation » en vertu de l'article 3(1). Le projet maintient le principe de la non-responsabilité du fournisseur de service neutre[83]. La question sera de déterminer ce que sont les activités neutres d'un fournisseur de service. De plus, le projet de loi impose des obligations en cas de réception d'un avis de prétendue violation : c'est l'instauration du système de « notice and notice »[84]. Également, le projet de loi crée à l'article 27 (2.3) et (2.4), un nouveau cas de violation du droit d'auteur lorsqu'un fournisseur de service sait ou devrait savoir que son service est principalement destiné à faciliter l'accomplissement d'actes qui constituent une violation du droit d'auteur. Les facteurs pour déterminer la violation sont énumérés dans la loi et toutes ces dispositions laissent une large marge d'appréciation au tribunal.

b) L'utilisation équitable.

L'article 21 du projet de loi élargit la notion d'utilisation équitable d'une œuvre en la rendant applicable aux activités à des fins d'éducation, de parodie ou de satire, mettant fin à la jurisprudence restrictive qui avait refusé d'appliquer l'exception aux parodies[85]. La notion pourra donc être utilisée pour compléter les exceptions particulières applicables aux établissements d'enseignement, suivant la démarche établie par la Cour suprême dans l'affaire *CCH Canadienne Ltée c. Barreau du Haut-Canada*[86]. Et c'est bien là que l'on reconnaît la structure particulière de la loi canadienne qui permet aux tribunaux, en marge des dispositions détaillées, de continuer à reconnaître aux usagers un droit à l'utilisation équitable des œuvres. En certains cas, comme par le passé, les tribunaux pourraient valider certaines pratiques en imposant des conditions moins lourdes que celles prévues dans le texte législatif. Prenons un exemple : l'article 30 permet la publication d'extraits d'œuvres littéraires dans un recueil qui est composé principalement de matières non protégées, qui est préparé pour être utilisé exclusivement dans les établissements d'enseignement et qui est désigné

---

83 Article 31.1 introduit par l'article 35 du projet de loi C-32, *supra* note 10.

84 Article 41.25 introduit par l'article 47 du projet de loi C-32, *supra* note 10.

85 *Compagnie Générale des Établissements Michelin-Michelin & Cie v. National Automobile, Aerospace, Transportation and General Workers Union of Canada (CAW-Canada)*, [1997] 2 C.F. 306 (C.F. 1ière inst.) http://reports.fja.gc.ca/eng/1996/1997fc19917.html/1997fc19917.html.html ; *Rôtisseries St-Hubert Ltée c. Syndicat des travailleurs(euses) de la Rôtisserie St-Hubert de Drummondville (C.S.N.)*, [1987] R.J.Q. 443; (1986), 17 C.P.R. (3d) 461 (C.S.); *Canwest v. Horizon*, 2008 BCSC 1609, www.courts.gov.bc.ca/jdb-txt/SC/08/16/2008BCSC1609.htm.

86 *CCH Canadienne Ltée c. Barreau du Haut-Canada*, *supra* note 20.

comme tel dans le titre et dans les annonces faites par l'éditeur. On doit de plus indiquer la source de l'emprunt de même que le nom de l'auteur et on ne peut pas faire, en cinq ans, plus de deux emprunts au même auteur. Un tribunal pourrait décider qu'une utilisation équitable pour fins d'éducation permet de faire plus de deux emprunts au même auteur au cours des cinq dernières années, façonnant une exception plus large que celle offerte par le texte de loi.

Est-ce que l'utilisation équitable pourrait exempter de façon générale l'institution d'enseignement qui reproduit des portions d'œuvres pour ses élèves ? Le 23 juillet 2010, la Cour d'appel fédérale[87] approuvait la décision de la Commission du droit d'auteur[88], selon laquelle tend à être inéquitable la reproduction d'extraits d'œuvres faites à l'initiative de l'enseignant pour ses classes ou à la demande de l'étudiant qui a reçu de son professeur instruction de lire. Le motif déterminant de ces décisions semble avoir été qu'en la circonstance, la fin réelle ou principale de la reproduction est l'enseignement ou l'étude « non privée » [89]. Il faudrait donc voir si l'élargissement de l'exception « aux fins d'éducation » changerait l'interprétation judiciaire du caractère équitable des reproductions aux bénéfices des élèves[90].

---

87 *Alberta (Education) v. Access Copyright* [English], 2010 FCA 198, http://decisions.fca-caf.gc.ca/en/2010/2010fca198/2010fca198.html, [*Alberta (Education) v. Access Copyright*].

88 *Décision Tarif des redevances à percevoir par Access copyright pour la Reproduction par reprographie, au Canada, d'oeuvres de son répertoire (Établissements d'enseignement — 2005-2009)*, [2009] C.B.C. No. 6 www.cb-cda.gc.ca/decisions/2009/Access-Copyright-2005-2009-Schools.pdf, [*Décision Établissements d'enseignement* — 2005–2009]

89 Voir les para. 98 de la *Décision Établissements d'enseignement* — 2005-2009, *supra* note 88 et para. 46 du jugement *Alberta (Education) v. Access Copyright*, *supra* note 87.

90 Il est vrai que la Cour d'appel fédérale déclare au para. 21 que : « this amendment serves only to create additional allowable purposes; it does not affect the fairness analysis. As the parties agree that the dealing in this case was for an allowable purpose, the proposed amendments to the Act do not affect the outcome of this case and no more will be said about Bill C-32. » *Ibid*. Néanmoins, il nous semble que la commission et la cour ont trop insisté sur le but véritable de la reproduction (soit l'enseignement ou l'étude « non privée ») dans leur analyse du caractère inéquitable des reproductions, pour qu'on puisse nier l'impact possible du projet de loi C-32. Une utilisation à des fins d'enseignement ne peut être *ipso facto* considérée déraisonnable si on permet, de par la loi, les utilisations équitables à des fins d'éducation.

3) Une harmonisation avec les textes internationaux

Le projet de loi vise à transposer en droit interne les dispositions du *Traité de l'OMPI sur le droit d'auteur* (le « *Traité de l'ODA* »)[91] et du *Traité de l'OMPI sur les interprétations et exécutions et les phonogrammes* (le « *Traité de l'OIEP* »)[92].

En fait, il s'agit essentiellement de compléter le régime de protection des droits patrimoniaux des artistes interprètes ou exécutants et des producteurs de phonogrammes[93] et d'ajouter nommément à la liste des droits exclusifs le droit de distribution[94] et le droit de mise à disposition[95]. Le projet de loi C-32 propose aussi de prohiber le contournement des mesures techniques de protection[96], suivant l'article 11 du *Traité de l'ODA* et l'article 18 du *Traité de l'OIEP*, avec une série d'exceptions très limitées. Enfin le projet de loi, comme le *Traité de l'OIEP*, accorde à l'artiste interprète ou exécutant des droits moraux[97].

Il est à noter qu'à l'égard des deux nouveaux droits, le projet de loi rejoint en partie la jurisprudence. L'affaire *Socan* avait déjà établi que la communication via Internet était une télécommunication[98]. En ce qui concerne le droit de distribution, le projet de loi adopte un principe d'épuisement des droits à l'échelle internationale. En pratique, les titulaires ne conservent à ce titre que le contrôle du premier transfert de la propriété de l'objet tangible qui contient l'œuvre. Le nouveau droit de distribution est donc bien limité.

En pratique, les titulaires ont peut-être encore un droit sur les transactions futures, par le jeu des dispositions sur les violations à des étapes ultérieures. En effet dans l'affaire *Euro-Excellence Inc. c. Kraft Canada Inc.*[99], cinq juges sur neuf avaient estimé que les articles 2.7, 13(7) et 27 (2) de la *Loi* permettraient à un licencié exclusif (donc détenteur d'un intérêt) de

91 *Traité relatif aux droits d'auteur de l'Organisation mondiale de la propriété intellectuelle* (OMPI), 20 déc. 1996, www.wipo.int/treaties/fr/ip/wct/trtdocs_wo033.html, 36 I.L.M. 65.

92 *Traité de L'Organisation mondiale de la propriété intellectuelle sur les interprétations et exécutions et les phonogrammes*, 20 déc. 1996, www.wipo.int/treaties/fr/ip/wppt/trtdocs_wo034.html, 36 I.L.M. 76.

93 Voir les articles 8 et suivants du projet de *loi C-32*, *supra* note 10.

94 Voir l'article 4 du projet de loi *C-32*, *supra* note 10, ajoutant l'al. 3(1)j) à la *Loi*.

95 Voir l'article 3 du projet de loi *C-32*, *supra* note 10, ajoutant l'al. 1.1 à l'article 2.4 de la *Loi*.

96 Voir l'article 47 du projet de loi *C-32*, *supra* note 10.

97 Voir l'article 10 du projet de loi *C-32*, *supra* note 10.

98 *SOCAN v. Assoc. canadienne des fournisseurs Internet*, *supra* note 82, au par. 42.

99 *Supra* note 20.

poursuivre un importateur qui vendrait des exemplaires dans le marché réservé au licencié. Ces dispositions ne sont pas modifiées par le projet de loi[100] et on peut présumer que les opinions émises dans la décision *Euro-Excellence* sont encore valables. Un quasi droit de distribution existerait donc sous le couvert des recours contre les « violations à des étapes ultérieures ».

En résumé, le projet de loi C-32 instaure de nouvelles règles, notamment à l'égard des exceptions, des droits voisins et du contournement des mesures de protection techniques. En même temps, il maintient ou élargit plusieurs des solutions dégagées par les tribunaux et en cela, confirme le rôle crucial que doit jouer la jurisprudence dans le régime canadien du droit d'auteur.

C. CONCLUSION

Dans ce bref commentaire, nous avons voulu montrer le poids considérable de la jurisprudence dans l'élaboration du droit d'auteur au Canada. Plusieurs des concepts clés sont d'origine jurisprudentielle et leur contenu laissé à l'arbitrage des juges. Leur intégration au texte de loi fut souvent d'abord rejetée par les parlementaires, puis acceptée lorsque la jurisprudence fut suffisamment développée pour en montrer la sagesse[101].

Le projet de loi C-32, et la *Loi sur le droit d'auteur* dans son entier, restent chargés de dispositions particulières — et quelquefois redondantes-, modèles de législation au cas par cas. Ces dispositions sont parfois difficiles à harmoniser avec les principes fondamentaux de la *Loi*, fondés sur des concepts larges laissés à l'appréciation des tribunaux et cet ordre des choses demande des efforts particuliers au niveau de l'interprétation de la *Loi sur le droit d'auteur*. Un survol de l'histoire des législations de droit d'auteur nous amène à penser que c'est peut-être à dessein que le législateur procède ainsi, choisissant de reprendre ou de laisser se développer les solutions jurisprudentielles, tout en posant des règles précises pour certaines situations déterminées qui préoccupent davantage l'opinion publique du moment. On connaît déjà en matière constitutionnelle la métaphore du dialogue entre le législateur et les tribunaux qui censurent les

---

100 On ajoute simplement l'al. 2.1 pour préciser que la production d'un exemplaire couvert par une exception au Canada ne peut mener à une violation à des étapes ultérieures.

101 Voir notamment l'analyse de C. Seville, *supra* note 52, p. 247.

textes sur le fondement des chartes[102]. Peut-être assiste-t-on en matière de droit d'auteur à une autre sorte de dialogue entre les pouvoirs législatif et judiciaire, le législatif sollicitant l'aide des tribunaux dans l'élaboration des règles de droit. Le projet de loi C-32, qui, à bien des égards, laisse des questions en suspens, ou encore introduit des nouvelles règles qui feront appel à la sagesse des tribunaux, nous semble, lui aussi, faire appel à une forme d'échange entre ces pouvoirs de l'État. Il faudra bien sûr attendre de connaître le sort du projet de loi C-32 avant de dire qu'il fait partie du dialogue.

102 P. W. Hogg et A. A. Bushell, « The *Charter* Dialogue between Courts and Legislatures (Or Perhaps the *Charter of Rights* Isn't such a Bad Thing After All) », (1997) 35 Osgoode Hall Law Journal 75.

PART TWO

Technology

CHAPTER SEVEN

Locking Out Lawful Users:

Fair Dealing and Anti-Circumvention in Bill C-32

Carys Craig

A. INTRODUCTION

Fair dealing and other exceptions to copyright owners' rights perform a vital role in the copyright system: they permit substantial uses of copyright-protected works, which would otherwise be infringing, in order to ensure that copyright does not defeat its own ends. By creating the necessary "breathing space"[1] in the copyright system, the fair dealing defence acknowledges the collaborative and interactive nature of cultural practices, recognizing that copyright-protected works can be used, copied, transformed, and shared in ways that actually further — as opposed to undermine — the purposes of the copyright system.[2] If copyright is to be justified as a means to encourage the creation and exchange of intellectual

1 In the famous US Supreme Court decision of *Campbell v. Acuff-Rose Music, Inc.*, 510 U.S. 569, www.law.cornell.edu/copyright/cases/510_US_569.htm, 114 S. Ct. 1164 (1994) at 579 [*Campbell* cited to U.S.], Justice Souter referred to the "fair use doctrine's guarantee of breathing space within the confines of copyright." The need for breathing space flows from "the need simultaneously to protect copyrighted material and to allow others to build upon it": (*ibid.* at 575).

2 In this sense, the concept of fair dealing embraces the dilemma that pervades all aspects of copyright policy-making: the need to minimally restrict the general dissemination and use of cultural products, and maximally promote both knowledge production and the distribution of authorized copies of protected works. See Economic Council of Canada, *Report on Intellectual and Industrial Property* (Ottawa: Public Works and Government Services Canada, 1971) at 31–35.

works to the benefit of authors and society as a whole, then a suitable fair dealing defence is an essential part of that justification.

Unfortunately, the fair dealing defence in Canada has always lacked the strength that this role requires of it. For many years, the restrictive contours of the defence as framed in the *Copyright Act*, combined with a judicial tendency to reject the defence out of hand, ensured that fair dealing was rarely invoked, and seldom applied. The fate of fair dealing seemed to improve with the now famous case of *CCH Canadian Ltd. v. Law Society of Upper Canada* [*CCH*],[3] in which the Supreme Court of Canada acknowledged the importance of the defence in striking the necessary balance between owners' rights and users' interests. In the copyright reform process that has unfolded since that ruling, I hoped (as did many others) to see an expansion in the statutory formulation of fair dealing to allow it to better perform this vital role.[4] Of the three most recent attempts at copyright reform in Canada,[5] only the latest, Bill C-32, includes any significant improvement to the fair dealing provisions of the *Copyright Act*.[6] These potential improvements do not go far enough, in my view, but there is a larger problem looming than the definitional boundaries of fair dealing: the proposed protection of technological protection measures [TPMs] or "digital locks" threatens to undermine the significance of fair dealing and other exceptions by making them ineffectual in the face of technical controls.

In what follows, I will briefly outline the nature and role of fair dealing in Canadian copyright policy post-*CCH*, and then I will examine the potential impact of the proposed fair dealing and anti-circumvention

---

3 2004 SCC 13, www.canlii.org/ca/cas/scc/2004/2004scc13.html, [2004] 1 S.C.R. 339 [*CCH* cited to S.C.R.].

4 See Carys Craig, "The Changing Face of Fair Dealing in Canadian Copyright Law: A Proposal for Legislative Reform" in M. Geist, ed., *In the Public Interest: The Future of Canadian Copyright Law*, (Toronto: Irwin Law, 2005), at 437–61, www.irwinlaw.com/pages/content-commons/the-changing-face-of-fair-dealing-in-canadian-copyright-law--a-proposal-for-legislative-reform---carys-craig ["Changing Face of Fair Dealing"]. See also, Laura J. Murray & Samuel E. Trosow, Canadian Copyright Law: A Citizen's Guide (Toronto: Between the Lines, 2007).

5 Bill C-60, *An Act to Amend the Copyright Act*, first reading 20 June 2005, www.parl.gc.ca/PDF/38/1/parlbus/chambus/house/bills/government/C-60_1.PDF; Bill C-61, *An Act to Amend the Copyright Act*, first reading 12 June 2008, www2.parl.gc.ca/housepublications/publication.aspx?docid=3570473&language=e&mode=1&File=14; Bill C-32, *An Act to Amend the Copyright Act*, first reading 2 June 2010, www2.parl.gc.ca/HousePublications/Publication.aspx?Docid=4580265&file=4.

6 *Copyright Act*, R.S.C. 1985, c. C-42, http://laws.justice.gc.ca/en/C-42 [*Copyright Act*].

provisions of Bill C-32. I will suggest that the minimal expansion of fair dealing to cover "new" purposes, as well as the addition of a few new user exceptions, while welcome, is insufficient to ensure the breadth of applicability that the copyright balance demands; but more importantly, I will argue, the extensive protection of TPMs without any regard for lawful uses of copyright material has the potential to effectively eviscerate fair dealing in the digital age. Acts permitted in relation to owned content can be prevented by the use of TPMs, and rendered unlawful by proposed anti-circumvention provisions. To extend legal protection to TPMs in a manner that fails to guard the contours of fair dealing and user rights from technological encroachment is to undermine the social goals of the copyright system, and to relinquish the policy balancing act performed in their name.

The following section offers an introduction to the fair dealing defence and the role that it plays in maintaining Canada's "copyright balance." Part C considers the drawbacks of the existing fair dealing provisions in Canada's *Copyright Act* while Part D goes on to canvass the proposed additions to fair dealing and other user exceptions found in Bill C-32. Part E tackles the problematic interaction of copyright exceptions and TPMs that control access to, and the uses that can be made of, protected content. The new anti-circumvention prohibitions found in Bill C-32 and their relation to the fair dealing and user exception provisions will be explored in Part F. Finally, in Part G, I will suggest possible ways in which Bill C-32 could be revised in order to safeguard user rights and maintain an appropriate balance in Canada's copyright system going forward.

B. THE ROLE OF FAIR DEALING IN CANADA'S COPYRIGHT SYSTEM

Fundamentally, copyright policy assumes that the restriction of the public's use of works through the creation of private rights can further the public's interest in the widespread creation and distribution of works. The limits to these private rights, defined by fair dealing and other exceptions—and circumscribed by the boundaries of the public domain—are therefore essential to ensure that the copyright system does not defeat its own ends.

In recent years, the Supreme Court of Canada has articulated the purposes of Canadian copyright law, and has acknowledged the inherent tensions that these purposes present, as well as the vital role that fair dealing and the public domain must play in alleviating them. In *Théberge v. Galerie D'Art du Petit Champlain Inc.*,[7] the Supreme Court identified copyright's purpose as "a balance between promoting the public interest in the encouragement and dissemination of works of the arts and intellect and obtaining a just reward for the creator." The Court went on to explain that "[t]he proper balance among these and other public policy objectives lies not only in recognizing the creator's rights but in giving due weight to their limited nature."[8]

The *Théberge* decision represented a crucial moment in Canadian copyright policy, cementing a vision of copyright as a system intended not only to protect the rights of authors and their assignees, but also (and equally) to further the wider public interest. In describing how the metaphorical balance might be struck, it brought into the equation and attributed "due weight" to the limits of the rights that the system protects. Regarded in this way, the boundaries and limitations of the copyright interest are not external to copyright policy—they are a central part of how the system works.

The significance of this insight became clear with the Supreme Court's ruling in *CCH*:

> [T]he fair dealing exception, like other exceptions in the Copyright Act, is a user's right. In order to maintain the proper balance between the rights of a copyright owner and users' interests, it must not be interpreted restrictively. As Professor Vaver has explained, "User rights are not just loopholes. Both owner rights and user rights should therefore be given the fair and balanced reading that befits remedial legislation."[9]

In the name of balance, the Court generously interpreted the fair dealing provisions in order "to ensure that users' rights are not unduly constrained."[10] Against the backdrop of copyright's public purpose, fair dealing was recognized to be central—not exceptional—to the system. Chief Justice McLachlin wrote: "the fair dealing exception is perhaps more properly understood as an integral part of the *Copyright Act* than simply a defence. Any act falling within the fair dealing exception will not be an infringement of copyright."[11] Put otherwise, fair dealing does not merely

---

7 2002 SCC 34, www.canlii.org/ca/cas/scc/2002/2002scc34.html, [2002] 2 S.C.R. 336, (2002), 210 D.L.R. (4th) 385 [*Théberge* cited to S.C.R.].

8 *Ibid.* at paras. 30–31, Binnie J.

9 *CCH*, above note 3 at para. 48.

10 *Ibid.* at para. 51. The Court allowed the defendant Library to claim a "research" purpose in the provision of copying services to its patrons.

11 *Ibid.* at para. 48.

excuse infringement, but rather *defines* it; the owner's rights end where the user's rights begin. Following the *CCH* decision, it should be clear that, rather than a marginal exception to the norms of Canadian copyright law, the fair dealing defence is an instantiation of the public-author balance; one that is necessary to support the normative claims so often made on behalf of the system. Drassinower explains: "the defence of fair dealing . . . is to be understood and deployed not negatively, as a mere exception, but rather positively, as a user right integral to copyright law."[12]

It is also important to underscore, at this juncture, the potential significance of the term "users' rights" employed by the Supreme Court. Much has been made of this terminology and the equality it brings to the balancing of authorial and public claims.[13] For the purposes of my argument, however, its importance lies primarily in the positive nature of a "user right," in contrast to the negative nature of mere defences, justifications, exemptions or even privileges. A basic Hohfeldian analysis[14] reveals that, when conceptualized as a privilege, fair dealing establishes only the liberty or freedom to act: the owner has no right to prevent the privileged activity, and the user owes no duty to refrain from the activity. But conceptualized as a right, fair dealing establishes a corresponding *duty* on behalf of the owner to honour the user's right: in this analysis, the user has a *positive* claim-right against the copyright owner to be permitted to deal fairly with the work. Where fair dealing is recognized as a "user right," it can be argued that copyright owners have a correlative *obligation* to permit users' fair dealings with their works.

C. THE INADEQUACY OF THE EXISTING FAIR DEALING PROVISIONS

The existing fair dealing defence permits fair dealings with copyright protected works for the purposes of research or private study, criticism or review, or news reporting.[15] Acts undertaken for these purposes that would *prima facie* constitute infringement are nonetheless lawful if found to be

---

12 Abraham Drassinower, "Taking User Rights Seriously," in M. Geist, ed., *In the Public Interest: The Future of Canadian Copyright Law* (Toronto: Irwin Law, 2005), 462–79, www.irwinlaw.com/pages/content-commons/taking-user-rights-seriously---abraham-drassinower at 467.

13 Craig, "Changing Face of Fair Dealing," above note 4 at 454–55.

14 See W.N. Hohfeld, *Fundamental Legal Conceptions as Applied in Judicial Reasoning* (New Haven, CT: Yale University Press, 1946).

15 *Copyright Act*, above note 6, ss. 29-29.2.

fair, and if—in the case of criticism, review or news reporting—there is sufficient acknowledgement of the source and author of the protected work. As such, Canada's fair dealing provisions do not provide a general, open-ended defence for any dealing that can be regarded as "fair"; the fairness of a particular dealing is relevant to infringement proceedings only if it was undertaken for at least one of these specified purposes.[16] In addition, where the dealing is for any purpose other than research or private study, the defence can succeed only if there has been sufficient acknowledgement of the source of the copied work.[17] There are therefore three hurdles to be met by a defendant who claims to have dealt fairly with a work: first, the purpose must be one of those listed in the Act; second, the dealing must be fair; and finally, sufficient acknowledgement must have been given where required by the Act. Failure to overcome any one of these hurdles causes the defence to fail.

This triple-tiered approach stands in contrast to the American equivalent of "fair use." Under the US law, the purposes listed in the provision are not exhaustive,[18] and failure to acknowledge source is not a bar to the defence. The US fair use provision is open-ended, and the overarching consideration for the courts is one of fairness; fairness is to be determined with reference to a non-exclusive list of relevant factors such as the purpose and character of the use, the nature of the protected work, the amount of the work that has been used, and the likely consequence of this use upon the market for the original.[19]

---

16 *CCH Canadian Ltd.* v. *Law Society of Upper Canada*, 2002 FCA 187, www.canlii.org/en/ca/fca/doc/2002/2002fca187/2002fca187.html, [2002] 4 F.C. 213, (2002), 212 D.L.R. (4th) 385 at para. 127 [*CCH (FCA)* cited to F.C.]. Linden J. explained the significance of the closed list of purposes in the Act: "If the purpose of the dealing is not one that is expressly mentioned in the Act, this Court is powerless to apply the fair dealing exemptions."

17 Both ss. 29.1 and 29.2 of the *Copyright Act*, above note 6, contain the caveat: ." . . if the following are mentioned: the source: and if given in the source, the name of the author, in the case of a work, performer, in the case of a performer's performance, maker, in the case of a sound recording, or broadcaster, in the case of a communication signal."

18 17 U.S.C. § 107 (1976), www.copyright.gov/title17/92chap1.html#107 provides: "The fair use of a copyright work . . . , for purposes *such as* criticism, comment, news reporting, teaching . . . , scholarship, or research, is not an infringement of copyright" [emphasis added].

19 *Ibid.*: "In determining whether the use made of a work in any particular case is a fair use the factors to be considered shall include: 1) the purpose and character of the use, including whether such use is of a commercial nature or is for nonprofit educational purposes; 2) the nature of the copyrighted work; 3) the amount and the

The significance of this difference becomes apparent when one considers, for example, the case of parody. Under the US fair use model, parodies of protected works will typically enjoy the protection of the fair use defence because they represent precisely the kind of "transformative," creative use that copyright is designed to foster.[20] In Canada, the position is far less clear. In *Cie Générale des Établissement Michelin-Michelin & Cie. v. C.A.W. — Canada*,[21] it was held that the defendants' parody of a corporate logo could not be included within the category of "criticism."[22] Justice Teitelbaum observed that, in contrast to the US position, the exceptions to acts of copyright infringement are "exhaustively listed as a closed set," and inferred from this that "[t]hey should be restrictively interpreted as exceptions." Parody was thought to require an explicit new exception because it did not expressly appear in the closed set of permitted purposes.[23] However, from a copyright policy perspective, the transformative value of parody and the power that it wields as a means of social critique make a strong case for its inclusion in the fair dealing defence.[24] The precarious situation of parody in Canadian copyright law — particularly compared to the room accorded to such uses in the US regime — thus exemplifies the shortcomings of a closed-purpose approach, and underscores the general

---

substantiality of the portion used in relation to the copyrighted work as a whole; and 4) the effect of the use upon the potential market for or value of the copyrighted work."

20 In *Campbell*, above note 1 at 577, the court explained that fair use "permits and requires courts to avoid rigid application of the copyright statute when, on occasion, it would stifle the very creativity which that law is designed to foster."

21 [1997] 2 F.C. 306, www.canlii.org/en/ca/fct/doc/1996/1996canlii3920/1996canlii3920.html, (1997), 71 C.P.R. (3d) 348 (F.C.T.D.) [*Michelin* cited to F.C.].

22 *Ibid.* at para. 66: "[P]arody does not exist as a facet of 'criticism,' an exception to infringement in Canadian copyright law. I do accept that parody in a generic sense can be a form of criticism; however, it is not 'criticism' for the purposes of the *Copyright Act* as an exception under the fair dealing heading."

23 *Ibid.* at para. 63. "[E]xceptions to copyright infringement should be strictly interpreted. I am not prepared to read in parody as a form of criticism and thus create a new exception." The defendants' position also suffered at the third hurdle of the fair dealing inquiry: the additional requirement that the source be mentioned. The implicit acknowledgement of source or allusion to the original that is characteristic of parody was held to be insufficient mention for the purposes of the Act (*ibid.* at paras. 68–69). Also, the Court held that the parody was unfair because it held the plaintiff's work up to ridicule (*ibid.* at para. 70).

24 As explained by Justice Souter in *Campbell*, above note 1 at 579: "[T]he goal of copyright, to promote science and the arts, is generally furthered by the creation of transformative works. Such works thus lie at the heart of the fair use doctrine's guarantee of breathing space within the confines of copyright."

inadequacy of Canada's current fair dealing defence to advance the public purposes of copyright.

While the exclusion of parody in *Michelin* was determined by a narrow interpretation of enumerated purposes, the Supreme Court has now opined that these purposes "should not be given restrictive interpretation."[25] The large and liberal reading of purposes advocated by the Court in *CCH* could permit, one would think, the inclusion of parody within the category of "criticism."[26] Whether Canadian courts will agree with this assessment, however, remains to be seen. The British Columbia Supreme Court was recently presented with an opportunity to consider the inclusion of parody as a fair dealing purpose post-*CCH*, but it simply ruled, citing Justice Teitelbaum in *Michelin*, that "parody is not an exception to copyright infringement under the *Copyright Act*, and therefore does not constitute a defence."[27] It is also notable that, in *Michelin*, the defence would have failed even if the use had been held to be for a permitted purpose because the treatment of the plaintiff's work was considered unfair,[28] and the implicit acknowledgement of source, insufficient.[29] As such, even if future courts see fit to bring parodies within the fair dealing purposes on the basis of *CCH*, the three hurdle test presents other grounds upon which parodists could be prevented from successfully claiming the defence.

There are many examples of activities that may benefit from the fair use doctrine in America, but fail to squeeze within the tight confines of statutory fair dealing: educational and classroom uses may be excluded if they do not fit the definition of "private study or research";[30] both time- and space-shifting content may be excluded if they do not fit the defin-

---

25 *CCH*, above note 3 at para. 54.

26 See for example Giuseppina D'Agostino, "Healing Fair Dealing: A Comparative Analysis of Canadian Fair Dealing to U.K. Fair Dealing and U.S. Fair Use" (2008) 53(2) McGill L.J. 309, http://lawjournal.mcgill.ca/documents/dAgostino.pdf at 359: "In light of *CCH*'s liberal interpretation of the enumerated grounds, it may be argued that 'criticism' could now encompass parody."

27 *Canwest Mediaworks Publications Inc. v. Horizon Publications Ltd.*, 2008 BCSC 1609 at para. 14.

28 *Michelin*, above note 21, at paras. 68-69.

29 *Ibid.* at para. 70. I have written more extensively about the shortcomings of the *Michelin* ruling elsewhere. See Craig, "Putting the Community in Communication: Dissolving the Conflict between Freedom of Expression and Copyright" (2006) 56(1) U.T.L.J. 75, www.jstor.org/pss/4491681.

30 *Boudreau* v. *Lin* (1997), 150 D.L.R. (4th) 324, http://www.canlii.org/en/on/onsc/doc/1997/1997canlii12369/1997canlii12369.html, (1997), 75 C.P.R. (3d) 1 (Ont. S.C.) at 335 [*Boudreau* cited to D.L.R.]: "The material was distributed to all the members of the class of students. This does not qualify as 'private study.'"

itions of "private study" or "review";[31] transformative practices such as the creation of "fan fiction" or "machinima," appropriation art or digital sampling may be excluded if they fail to fit the definition of "criticism or review";[32] and so on. The fundamental problem is that, no matter how large and liberal the interpretation of a defendant's purposes, not all fair dealings will be subsumable into the specified purposes: there is a limit to how far a "users' rights" approach can stretch the finite meanings of words like "research," "private study," "criticism," "review" and "news reporting." The power to achieve the appropriate balance between owners' and users' rights is therefore beyond the reach of Canada's courts. Rather than struggling to fit users within restrictive categories, the central concern of any fair dealing inquiry should be "to see . . . whether the new work merely 'supersede[s] the objects' of the original creation . . . or instead adds something new, with a further purpose or different character, altering the first with new expression, meaning, or message."[33] Copyright law, with the help of fair dealing, should aim to encourage the creation of new expressions, meanings and messages, even if this sometimes means permitting the use of protected expression.[34]

D. NEW EXCEPTIONS IN BILL C-32

On 2 June 2010, the Canadian government released its much anticipated copyright reform bill, Bill C-32, accompanied by claims that this legislation offers "a fair, balanced, and common-sense approach, respecting both the rights of creators and the interests of consumers in a modern

---

31 See *Tom Hopkins International Inc.* v. *Wall & Redekop Realty Ltd.* (1984), 5 W.W.R. 555, www.canlii.org/en/bc/bcsc/doc/1984/1984canlii519/1984canlii519.html, (1984),1 C.P.R. (3d) 348 at 352–53 (B.C.S.C.): "as interesting as the time-shifting concept may be, this does not seem to be a realistic exception to the clear language contained in our legislation." See also Craig, above note 4 at 457-58.

32 See for example Rebecca Tushnet, "Payment in Credit: Copyright Law and Subcultural Creativity" (2007) 70 Law & Contemp. Prob. 135; Graham Reynolds "All the Game's a Stage: Machinima and Copyright in Canada" (forthcoming 2010) Journal of World Intellectual Property.

33 Justice Souter in *Campbell*, above note 1 at 579.

34 As Justice Binnie wrote in *Théberge*, above note 7 at para. 32: "[E]xcessive control by holders of copyrights and other forms of intellectual property may unduly limit the ability of the public domain to incorporate and embellish creative innovation in the long-term interests of society as a whole, or create practical obstacles to proper utilization. This is reflected in the exceptions to copyright infringement enumerated in ss. 29 to 32.2, which seek to protect the public domain in traditional ways such as fair dealing."

marketplace."[35] In particular, with respect to users and consumers, it was claimed that the bill would "legitimiz[e] Canadians' everyday activities."[36] The bill is said to achieve this through the inclusion of several new exceptions from which users may benefit. Perhaps most notably, additional purposes have been added to the fair dealing defence, which may address several of the concerns raised above. Section 29 of the Act is to be expanded to include "fair dealing for the purpose of research, private study, education, parody or satire."[37]

The inclusion of parody and satire as enumerated fair dealing purposes will overcome many of the doubts and concerns that have persisted as a result of the *Michelin* ruling even after the *CCH* case. Indeed, the fact that the categories in section 29 are not subject to an acknowledgement requirement (in contrast to dealings for the purpose of criticism) further secures the position of parody as a potentially permitted use. Moreover, by including "satire" specifically, the bill has wisely avoided the artificial and problematic distinction between parody and satire that has arisen in the US context.[38] This distinction (between parodic works that specifically target the original and satirical works that use protected material to comment on other facets of society) is difficult for even literary theorists to maintain or apply.[39] It is also difficult to justify from a policy perspective; excluding satire from the realm of fair use silences a powerful and socially valuable form of critical expression for which permission is unlikely to

---

35 Balanced Copyright, News Release, *Government of Canada Introduces Proposals to Modernize the Copyright Act*, 2 June 2010, www.ic.gc.ca/eic/site/crp-prda.nsf/eng/h_rp01149.html.

36 Balanced Copyright, *Copyright Modernization Act — Backgrounder*, www.ic.gc.ca/eic/site/crp-prda.nsf/eng/h_rp01151.html.

37 Bill C-32, above note 5, s. 21.

38 This distinction emerged from the *Campbell* decision in which Justice Souter wrote: "Parody needs to mimic an original to make its point, and so has some claim to use the creation of its victim's (or collective victims') imagination, whereas satire can stand on its own two feet and so requires justification for the very act of borrowing" (above note 1, at 580–581). The Ninth Circuit, in particular, has maintained a strict distinction between parody and satire, such that the classification of a work can determine the availability of a fair use defence. See for example *Dr. Seuss Enters. v. Penguin Books USA*, 109 F.3d 1394 (9th Cir. 1997).

39 Compare E. Gredley and S. Maniatis, "Parody: A Fatal Attraction? Part 1: The Nature of Parody and its Treatment in Copyright" [1997] 7 EIPR 339 at 343: "Basing a legal theory on the distinction between [parody and satire] may, however, lead the courts into the need to devise near impossible distinctions between satiric parodies and parodic satires."

be granted by the copyright owner.[40] The explicit inclusion of both parody and satire within section 29 is therefore a welcome amendment to the Act, and one that advances the goals of copyright law by making space for transformative downstream uses of protected material.

The addition of "education" as a free-standing purpose is also potentially significant to the extent that it overcomes the possible limitations that may have been found to inhere in the definition of "private study." While the latter category left open contentious questions about the applicability of fair dealing to copies made for study purposes in the context of *classes* of students,[41] the inclusion of "education" as a permitted purpose would undermine the validity of such tenuous but crucial distinctions. Copies made for educational or instructional purposes will be able to clear the first hurdle of the fair dealing inquiry, and the application of the defence will turn, then, on the fairness of the use that is made in light of all the relevant circumstances.[42]

Also welcome is the creation of a new exception, for "non-commercial user-generated content."[43] Sometimes referred to as "the YouTube exception," this would permit the use of legitimately acquired material in the creation of new works, as well as their use and dissemination, provided that the user's purposes are not commercial in nature, the source is mentioned where reasonable, and the new work has no "substantial adverse effect" on the exploitation of the original. The government's fact sheet offers as examples "making a home video of a friend or family member dancing to a popular song and posting it online, or creating a 'mash-up' of video clips."[44] In our digital environment, facilitated by new technologies and their accessibility, the transformative use of cultural content—mixing, mashing, (re)making and disseminating—is increasingly fundamental to the processes of cultural engagement and democratic participation. The creation of this exception goes some distance towards acknowledging and making space for this new reality. Of course, the user's rights in this

---

40 See Nicolas Suzor "Where the Bloody Hell does Parody Fit in Australian Copyright Law?" (2008) 13 Media & Arts Law Review 218, 238–43. See also Daniel Austin Green "Gulliver's Trials: A Modest Proposal to Excuse and Justify Satire" (2006) 11 Chapman Law Review 283.

41 See for example, *Boudreau*, above note 29.

42 *CCH*, above note 3 at para. 53: The factors to consider include: the purpose of the dealing, the character of the dealing, the amount of the dealing, alternatives to the dealing, the nature of the work, and the effect of the dealing on the work.

43 C-32, above note 5, s. 29.21.

44 Balanced Copyright, *What the New Copyright Modernization Act Means for Consumers*, www.ic.gc.ca/eic/site/crp-prda.nsf/eng/rp01186.html [Balanced Copyright].

instance remain subject to the commercial (and attribution) interests of the owner of the original content, such that the owner's rights essentially take priority. Nonetheless, this is an important addition to the exceptions offered by the Act, both from a practical perspective (legalizing common, non-commercial creative practices), and from a policy perspective (limiting owners' legal claims where the full enforcement of their rights would unduly restrain creative play and upset the copyright balance).

I also raised, in the preceding section, concerns about legal limits on common space-shifting and format-shifting practices. The new bill addresses these concerns to a significant extent, creating exceptions for "reproduction for private purposes"[45] and for "fixing signals and recording programs for later listening or viewing."[46] A new exception is also added for the making of "backup copies" of a lawfully owned or licensed copy of a protected work.[47] Each of these sections is subject to a fairly extensive list of limitations, however, which are said "[t]o ensure that the legitimate interests of rights-holders are respected."[48] Thus, for example, a person recording a program for later viewing can benefit from the exception only if "the individual keeps the recording no longer than is reasonably necessary in order to listen to or view the program at a more convenient time."[49] A person reproducing a work for private purposes can benefit from an exception only if that copy or reproduction is destroyed before giving away or selling the original.[50] Perhaps most importantly, however, all three defences are unavailable where the user has circumvented a technological protection measure in order to perform the permitted action.

I will return to consider more fully the interaction of exceptions and TPM protection in the following section. Before I do so, however, it seems important to identify what are, in my view, the shortcomings of the revisions to the fair dealing provisions and consumer exceptions even in their own right. For one thing, the additions to section 29 do not give much, if anything, more than that to which users would be entitled under the existing provisions. Educational uses are readily assumable within the category of "research or private study," particularly when these terms are given a suitably liberal reading. Parody and satire can be easily brought

45 C-32, above note 5, s. 29.22.

46 *Ibid.*, s. 29.23.

47 *Ibid.*, s. 29.24.

48 Balanced Copyright, above note 44.

49 C-32, above note 5, s. 29.23(d).

50 *Ibid.*, s. 29.22(4). A similar condition exists for reproductions made for back-up purposes: s. 29.24(3).

within the category of "criticism," broadly interpreted. The explicit inclusion of these purposes is certainly preferable to relying upon an appropriate interpretation of existing categories by the courts, but it is properly understood as an affirmation of the state of current fair dealing doctrine post-*CCH*, and not the creation of "new" exceptions as some would have it portrayed.

Exceptions for user-generated content, back-up copies, copies for personal use and for later listening and viewing can more properly be characterized as "new," excluded as they likely are from the limited fair dealing purposes. However, from a common sense user perspective, it seems reasonably obvious that such activities should not have been regarded as infringing in the first instance; they are "socially beneficial and cause little prejudice to right holders' ability to exploit their works."[51] Few people unfamiliar with copyright law would have imagined that they were breaking the law when they shot or shared a home video of their toddler dancing to a Beyoncé hit, or recorded a TV show to watch when the kids were in bed. Under a US fair use model, many of these uses could be presumed (or have been held)[52] to fall within the fair use defence, highlighting the inherent flexibility and trans-temporality of the American approach. What we have in Bill C-32 is a piecemeal expansion of the narrowly constructed exceptions that already exist in the *Copyright Act*; what we need instead is a broad, principled and purposive approach to user rights that is capable of evolving and expanding to embrace new and common practices as they arise.

I have argued elsewhere that the only way for Canada to ensure that socially beneficial uses are not excluded is to adopt an open-ended fair dealing provision based upon the US fair use model. In the words of Britain's Whitford Committee: "Any sort of work is likely to be of public interest, and the freedom to comment, criticize, to discuss and to debate, ought not, in principle, to be restricted to particular forms ('criticism or review' or 'reporting current events')."[53] A flexible fair use model permits courts to ad-

---

51 Industry Canada, *Supporting Culture and Innovation: Report on the Provisions and Operation of the Copyright Act* (Ottawa: Intellectual Property Policy Directorate, 2002), http://strategis.ic.gc.ca/epic/internet/incrp-prda.nsf/en/rp00873e.html#B2_8 at B.2.8.

52 *Sony Corporation v. Universal City Studios*, 464 U.S. 417, www.law.cornell.edu/copyright/cases/464_US_417.htm, 104 S. Ct. 774 (1984): A majority of the court supported the District Court's holding that the recording of television programs for later viewing was typically a fair use, thus permitting the ruling that the Betamax video recorder was capable of substantial non-infringing uses.

53 Sir John Whitford, *Copyright and Designs Law: Report of the Committee to Consider the Law on Copyright and Designs*, (London: HMSO, 1977), cmnd. 6732 at para. 676 [*Whitford Report*].

dress challenges posed by new technologies and unforeseen developments in a principled manner, guided by the policy concerns underlying the law. A purpose-specific model guarantees that Parliament is always playing catch-up, with socially beneficial uses stifled along the way. As Murray and Trosow explain, "[a]ugmenting the list of categories might be part of a clarification of fair dealing. But adding categories alone would be unlikely to create laws flexible enough to address the range of appropriate and fair uses . . ."[54]

The fair dealing provisions should be revised to expressly include the purposes enumerated in the Act and those proposed in Bill C-32 as *examples* of the kind of uses that may be considered fair, but without restricting the defence to those purposes exclusively. It should also provide a non-exhaustive list of factors to be considered in determining the fairness of a use, incorporating the factors set out by the Court of Appeal and endorsed by the Supreme Court in *CCH*.[55] The current acknowledgement requirement should either be removed or relegated to a consideration in fairness determinations; there is no place for such mechanical rules in a flexible fair use model.[56] Finally, in order to ensure adequate space for parody, satire and other transformative uses that could be regarded as prejudicial to the honour or reputation of the original author, fair dealing should be available as a defence to both economic and moral rights infringement claims.

The goal should be to achieve, through statutory revision, a fair dealing defence that is capable of principled application, guided by the purposes that underlie the copyright system, and responsive to the ever changing

---

54 Murray & Trosow, above note 4 at 204.

55 *CCH (FCA)*, above note 16 at paras. 150-60; *CCH*, above note 3 at paras. 53-60 (endorsing Linden J's factors).

56 Murray & Trosow, above note 4 at 204, have proposed the following revision along the same lines:

> 29 (1) Fair dealing for purposes such as research, private study, [education, parody, satire] criticism, review or news reporting does not infringe copyright.
>
> (2) In determining whether the use made in any particular case is fair dealing, the factors to be considered shall include—
>
> (a) the purpose of the dealing,
> (b) the character of the dealing,
> (c) the amount of the dealing,
> (d) the nature of the work or other subject matter,
> (e) available alternatives to the dealing,
> (f) the effect of the dealing on the work or other subject matter,
> (g) the extent to which attribution was made where reasonable in the circumstances.

nature of cultural creativity and exchange in the (post)modern, digital environment. Even with the proposed improvements to fair dealing and other user exceptions found in Bill C-32, defences in the Copyright Act would remain "statutorily restrictive and not easily capable of a remedial, flexible, or evolutionary interpretation."[57] The more numerous and specific the exceptions are, the less conducive they are to broad interpretation.[58] The limited purposes and specific exemptions approach to user rights, which is perpetuated in Bill C-32, reflects a vision of fair dealing as an exceptional derogation from general principles, antithetical to the normative presupposition of the copyright system: namely, that the author should have exclusive control over the use of her work. This vision is at odds with the goal of Canadian copyright—to achieve a balance between promoting the public interest and obtaining a just reward for the creator. The words of Mr. Justice Laddie, spoken with reference to British copyright law, should resonate with Canadians contemplating Bill C-32:

> Rigidity is the rule. It is as if every tiny exception to the grasp of copyright monopoly has had to be fought hard for, prized out of the unwilling hand of the legislature and, once, conceded, defined precisely and confined within high and immutable walls . . . . [T]he drafting of the legislation bears all the hallmarks of a complacent certainty that wider copyright protection is morally and economically justified. But is it?[59]

E. THE INTERACTION OF USER RIGHTS AND ANTI-CIRCUMVENTION

While policy-makers tinker with the fair dealing and user exception provisions in the Act, however, these exceptions are undercut by technological

---

57 Howard Knopf, "Limits on the Nature and Scope of Copyright" in Gordon F. Henderson, ed., *Copyright and Confidential Information Law of Canada* (Scarborough: Carswell, 1994), at 257.

58 Justice McLachlin (as she then was) once stated: "an implied exception . . . is all the more unlikely . . . in light of the detailed and explicit exception's in [the Act] providing for matters as diverse as private study, research or critical review, educational use, disclosure of information pursuant to various Federal Acts, and performance of musical works without motive or gain at an agricultural fair." *Bishop v. Stevens*, [1990] 2 S.C.R. 467, www.lexum.umontreal.ca/csc-scc/en/pub/1990/vol2/texte/1990scr2_0467.txt at paras. 478–79.

59 Justice Laddie, "Copyright: Over-Strength, Over-Regulated, Over-Rated" (1996) 18(5) European Intellectual Property Review 253 at 259.

capabilities. Acts permitted in relation to owned content — users' rights to research, study, criticize, transform, even read and listen — can be prevented by the use of technical controls. The overarching problem associated with the widespread use of TPMs in the distribution of digital content is simple enough to state: TPMs do not — and generally cannot — distinguish between lawful and unlawful uses and users. There is no necessary (and, typically, no practical) correlation between the limits imposed on would-be users by TPMs and the rights granted to copyright owners under the law.

The effect of a TPM is thus to prevent the kinds of activities that are recognized, within the realm of copyright policy, to be deserving of protection from private owner interests, and to be central to the balance that copyright must strike. Simply put, TPMs deny users the ability to exercise their rights and thereby tip the balance away from users and the public interest. It may be argued that a TPM-free version of a protected work will typically be available for anyone who wishes to deal fairly with it, but it is not satisfactory to restrict fair dealings to technologically inferior versions of copyright works.[60] Beneficiaries of copyright exceptions, like right holders, should be able to enjoy the opportunities presented by digital technologies, and should be free to engage with cultural resources in the technological environment in which they are situated.

I have argued elsewhere that copyright reform for the digital age should aim to achieve "prescriptive parallelism" to the greatest extent possible;[61] that is to say, "the traditional copyright balance of rights and exceptions should be preserved in the digital environment."[62] The availability and protection of TPMs should not, therefore, alter the copyright balance with respect to the enjoyment of exceptions and limitations.[63] Unfortunately, the anti-circumvention provisions found in Bill C-32 make no attempt to achieve prescriptive parallelism or to maintain the traditional copyright balance, instead sacrificing user rights and privileges to the ultimate power of technical control.

---

60 Stefan Bechtold, "Digital Rights Management in the United States and Europe" (2004) 52 American Journal of Comparative Law 323 at 363.

61 Carys Craig, "Digital Locks and the Fate of Fair Dealing: In Pursuit of 'Prescriptive Parallelism'" (2010) 13:4 *Journal of World Intellectual Property* 503, www3.interscience.wiley.com/journal/117991912/home; earlier draft available at http://ssrn.com/abstract=1599610 ["Digital Locks"].

62 Jerome H. Reichman, Graeme B. Dinwoodie & Pamela Samuelson, "A Reverse Notice and Takedown Regime to Enable Public Interest Uses of Technically Protected Copyrighted Works" (2007) 22 Berkeley Technology Law Journal 981 at 1042.

63 *Ibid.* at 1041–42.

Bill C-32 essentially mirrors the stringent anti-circumvention provisions found in the much derided US *Digital Millenium Copyright Act* [DMCA], [64] and repeats the mistakes that were made in the last attempt at copyright reform in Bill C-61. It contains thirteen complex sections with innumerable subsections prescribing the broad protection of TPMs and setting out narrow limits thereto. Notably, the protection afforded to TPMs includes not only TPMs that restrict protected uses of underlying works but also extends to pure access-control TPMs.[65] While circumvention liability is limited to the circumvention of access controls, this fact should offer little comfort to would-be fair users. Proponents of Bill C-32 have placed much significance on this technical distinction, arguing that, because there is no blanket prohibition against circumventing copy-control protection measures, the bill would not permit TPMs to trump fair dealing activities.[66] In practice, however, a protected access-control TPM operates as a "virtual lock" that excludes outsiders from the digital content,[67] and thereby prevents them from lawfully accessing the protected work—a necessary precondition to dealing fairly with it. The bill crosses another important line by prohibiting, in addition to circumvention activities and services, devices or technologies that permit the circumvention of access- or use-control TPMs.[68] These broad prohibitions would deny fair users who are permitted to circumvent copy-control measures the means by which to do so. In sum, the combined effect of the access-control circumvention prohibition and the circumvention service and device prohibitions is the practical restriction of otherwise lawful fair use activities in relation to TPM-protected content.

---

64 *Digital Millennium Copyright Act*, 17 U.S.C. §1201, ss. (a)–(b) (1998), www.copyright.gov/legislation/dmca.pdf [DMCA].

65 A "Technological protection measure" is defined as "any effective technology, device or component that, in the ordinary course of its operation controls access to a work . . . or restricts the doing . . . of any [infringing] acts." See Bill C-32, above 5, s. 41. Notably, the new user exceptions for format and time shifting or backup copies are subject to a non-circumvention proviso that covers any TPM within this broad definition.

66 See for example James Gannon, "Top 5 Myths About the New Copyright Bill and Digital Locks," http://jamesgannon.ca/2010/06/03/top-5-myths-about-the-new-copyright-bill-and-digital-locks/.

67 Ian R. Kerr, A. Maurushat, & C.S. Tacit, "Technical Protection Measures: Tilting at Copyright's Windmill" (2002–2003) 34(1) Ottawa L. Rev. 7 at 19–20.

68 Whether a particular technology would be caught by this prohibition was to be determined in light of its primary purpose (s. 41.1(c)(i)), commercial significance (s. 41.1(c)(ii)) or the manner in which it is marketed (s. 41.1(c)(iii)).

Bill C-32 sets out specific exceptions to circumvention liability—as well as numerous exceptions to these exceptions—relating to law enforcement or national security,[69] computer program interoperability,[70] encryption research,[71] the collection/communication of personal information,[72] the security of computer systems/networks,[73] persons with perceptual disabilities,[74] ephemeral recordings by broadcast undertakings,[75] and radio apparatus.[76] Thus, for example, a person circumventing a TPM for the purpose of encryption research would escape liability only if: it would not have been practical to carry out the research without circumventing the TPM; s/he lawfully obtained the protected work; s/he informed the copyright owner who applied the TPM (presumably, that s/he would be circumventing the TPM for research purposes); *and* s/he did nothing in relation to the underlying work that would constitute an infringement of copyright.[77] The criticism leveled by Jessica Litman against the exceptions to circumvention liability in the DMCA applies with full force to Bill C-32: these exceptions are "cast in prose so crabbed and so encumbered with conditions as to be of little use to anyone who doesn't have a copyright lawyer around to explain which hoops to jump through."[78]

The bill establishes the power for the Governor in Council to make additional regulations creating further specific exceptions where technological measures "would unduly restrict competition in the aftermarket sector in which the technological protection measure is used."[79] In the only implicit acknowledgement of fair dealing practices to be found in these provisions, section 41.21(2)(a) envisages the possibility of further regulations restricting liability for acts of circumvention (but, notably, not for liability relating to circumvention services or technologies) to be made in consideration of an open list of factors, including: whether the prohibition against acts of circumvention could adversely affect authorized uses; whether it would adversely affect criticism, review, news reporting, commentary, parody, satire, teaching, scholarship or research that could be

69 Bill C-32, above note 5, s. 41.11.

70 *Ibid.*, s. 41.12.

71 *Ibid.*, s. 41.13.

72 *Ibid.*, s. 41.14.

73 *Ibid.*, s. 41.15.

74 *Ibid.*, s. 41.16.

75 *Ibid.*, s. 41.17.

76 *Ibid.*, s. 41.18.

77 *Ibid.*, s. 41.13.

78 Jessica Litman, *Digital Copyright*, (New York, NY: Prometheus Books, 2001) at 31.

79 C-32, above note 5, s. 41.2(1).

made or done in respect of the work; whether the circumvention could adversely affect the market for the underlying work; and the work's commercial availability. An interesting provision contemplates the possibility of a positive claim against copyright owners, empowering the Governor in Council to make regulations that would actually require owners to provide access to a protected work to persons entitled to benefit from any limitations established under section 41.21(2)(a).[80]

Overall, Bill C-32 fails to reflect the lessons readily drawn from the experiences of the United States and Europe: it seeks to establish broad anti-circumvention rights covering devices and services, access- and use-control measures, and to do so without tying these rights to copyright infringement; it sets out numerous complex exceptions with no general "fair circumvention" exception; it neglects even to offer lip-service to the preservation of fair dealing rights comparable to statements found in Article 6(4) of the EU Directive[81] or section 1201(c) of the DMCA;[82] it offloads the responsibility for carving out any more exceptions on the Governor in Council, without making clear on what basis such exceptions would be regulated, on whose request, and subject to what evidentiary burden; and it establishes no positive obligations for content providers, leaving any such obligations to be created through regulation, and only in respect of any new exceptions made under this regulatory power.

It is also significant that many of the "new" user exceptions that were included in the bill — which were much lauded as exemplifying the government's commitment to a fair balance between owners and users — are made subject to non-circumvention provisos. Thus, reproduction for private purposes is permitted only if "the individual, in order to make the reproduction, did not circumvent . . . a technological protection measure."[83] Similar restrictions apply to recordings made for later listening and viewing,[84] and to the making of backup copies.[85] As Graham Reynolds explains:

---

80 *Ibid.*, s. 41.21(2)(b).

81 Directive 2001/29/EC on the Harmonisation of Certain Aspects of Copyright and Related Rights in the Information Society, Article 6(4), 2001 O.J. (L 167) 10, http://eur-lex.europa.eu/LexUriServ/LexUriServ.do?uri=OJ:L:2001:167:0010:0019:EN:PDF [Copyright Directive].

82 §1201(c)(1) DMCA, above note 64, explicitly states that, "[n]othing in this section shall affect rights, remedies, limitations, or defenses to copyright infringement, including fair use, in this title."

83 Bill C-32, above note 5, s. 29.22(1)(c).

84 *Ibid.*, s. 29.23(1)(b).

85 *Ibid.*, s. 29.24(1)(c).

> This approach to protecting TPMs undermines the balance between copyright owners and other parties that Bill C-32 purports to achieve. If the bill is passed in its current form, users, consumers, follow-on creators, and future innovators can effectively be prevented from exercising their rights — both those that existed before Bill C-32 and those introduced by it — through the application of a digital lock.[86]

This limitation on the application of the new user exceptions will render them redundant in the face of TPMs, thereby privileging owners' use of technical controls over the public policy goals that the exceptions are ostensibly designed to serve. If fair dealing is "an integral part of the *Copyright Act*,"[87] then it should not be "unduly constrained"[88] by the use of TPMs. Permitted uses are not infringements of copyright, but in fact further the purposes of the copyright system; anti-circumvention laws that essentially prohibit permitted uses extend the scope of owners' rights at the expense of users and the public interest, and thereby frustrate copyright's goals. The existing anti-circumvention provisions in Bill C-32 do not meet the demands of prescriptive parallelism because they fail to protect the role of fair dealing and copyright exceptions that the Supreme Court has recognized as central to the purposes of Canada's copyright system.

F. WHAT CAN BE DONE TO ENSURE BALANCE AND PROTECT USER RIGHTS?

If the *Copyright Modernization Act* is going to maintain an appropriate balance between owners and users in the digital environment, then the protection afforded to TPMs must be as carefully circumscribed as the copyright interest itself. The anti-circumvention provisions must be redrafted to ensure minimal disruption of the existing copyright balance. The simplest solution would be to rewind to the approach taken in Bill C-60, where TPM protections closely aligned with the existing rights of copyright owners, essentially reinforcing copyright proper by limiting unlawful circumvention to acts undertaken for purposes of copyright infringement.[89] The prohibition against circumvention should be restricted

---

86 Graham Reynolds, "How Balanced is Bill C-32?" *The Mark* (9 June 2010), http://www.themarknews.com/articles/1667-how-balanced-is-bill-c-32.

87 *CCH*, above note 3 at para. 48.

88 *Ibid.* at para. 51.

89 Bill C-60, above note 5, s. 34.02.

to circumvention "for the purpose of an act that is an infringement of copyright."[90]

Consistent with this approach, protection should be afforded only to use-control TPMs; copyright does not grant to owners exclusive control over access to protected works, and anti-circumvention provisions ought not to do so indirectly.[91] This could be achieved by defining technical measures in terms of their ability to inhibit or prevent infringing acts, as was done in Bill C-60, and ideally with the explicit exclusion of measures that control access to works for non-infringing purposes, as seen in the New Zealand legislation.[92]

Furthermore, the anti-circumvention provisions should not include service or device prohibitions. While such prohibitions may be the easiest way to prevent circumvention activities, circumvention services and technologies must be available to those who wish to access and use protected works in non-infringing ways. In *CCH*, the Supreme Court denied the plaintiff copyright owners the easiest route towards preventing a widespread, potentially infringing activity because the result would have been to shift the copyright balance too far in favour of owners' rights, and to interfere with "the proper use of copyrighted works for the good of society as a whole."[93] The same reasoning ought to warn us away from the enactment of circumvention service and device prohibitions as a shortcut to restrict circumvention activities. Where a distributor of circumvention services or technologies ought to be liable for subsequent infringement by third parties, that person will incur liability for "authorizing infringement" under existing copyright norms.[94]

---

90 *Ibid.*

91 See Craig, "Digital Locks" above note 61 at 8-10 [cited to SSRN].

92 See New Zealand's *Copyright Act* 1994 No. 143 (as amended by the *Copyright (New Technologies) Amendment Act 2008* (NZ), www.legislation.govt.nz/act/public/1994/0143/latest/DLM345634.html. Section 226 includes in its definition of TPM the following clarification: (b) for the avoidance of doubt, [TPM] does not include a process, treatment, mechanism, device, or system to the extent that, in the normal course of operation, it only controls any access to a work for non-infringing purposes (for example, it does not include a process, treatment, mechanism, device, or system to the extent that it controls geographic market segmentation by preventing the playback in New Zealand of a non-infringing copy of a work).

93 *CCH*, above note 3 at para. 41, refusing to find that the provision of photocopies by the Great Library amounted to authorizing infringement..

94 The *Copyright Act* makes it unlawful to authorize an infringing act: ss. 3, 27(1). The Supreme Court explained in *Society of Composers, Authors and Music Publishers of Canada v. Canadian Association of Internet Providers*, 2004 SCC 45, www.canlii.org/en/ca/scc/doc/2004/2004scc45/2004scc45.html, [2004] 2 S.C.R. 427, (2004), 240 D.L.R.

If circumvention services are to be prohibited, however, then this prohibition should be expressly limited to cases where the service provider "knows or has reason to believe that the service will, or is likely to, be used to infringe copyright in a TPM work."[95] If device prohibitions remain in the bill, they should similarly be restricted to cases where the manufacturer, importer or distributor knows that the device "will, or is likely to, be used to infringe copyright in a TPM work."[96] An exception must then be carved out to allow for the provision of circumvention devices to persons lawfully offering circumvention services to facilitate lawful uses. New Zealand, for example, has established a system whereby people wishing to carry out permitted acts in relation to TPM-protected works can seek assistance from a "qualified person" who can lawfully provide circumvention services and can lawfully be supplied with circumvention devices.[97]

Finally, any anti-circumvention provisions in Canada should operate "without prejudice" to the exceptions contained in the *Copyright Act*. Tying circumvention liability to copyright infringement would go a large way to achieving this goal by implicitly permitting the circumvention of TPMs for the purposes of fair dealing and other lawful acts. However, it would be preferable to see an explicit statement that circumvention is not prohibited when undertaken for lawful purposes including fair dealings. New Zealand's amended Copyright Act, for example, expressly states that anti-circumvention rights "do not prevent or restrict the exercise of a permitted act."[98] Similarly, the recently released Indian Copyright (Amendment) Bill, 2010, states that nothing in its anti-circumvention provision "shall prevent any person from doing anything referred to therein for a purpose not expressly prohibited by this Act."[99] And needless to say, the new user excep-

---

(4th) 193, at para. 127 [cited to S.C.R.]: "The knowledge that someone might be using neutral technology to violate copyright (as with the photocopier in the *CCH* case) is not necessarily sufficient to constitute authorization, which requires a demonstration that the defendant did '(g)ive approval to; sanction, permit; favour, encourage' the infringing conduct"; (citing *CCH*, above note 16, para. 38).

95 *Cf.* New Zealand's *Copyright Act* 1994 No 143, s. 226A(2), www.legislation.govt.nz/act/public/1994/0143/latest/DLM1705876.html.

96 *Cf. Ibid.*, s. 226C(1), www.legislation.govt.nz/act/public/1994/0143/latest/DLM1705882.html .

97 *Ibid.*, ss. 226D and 226E, www.legislation.govt.nz/act/public/1994/0143/latest/DLM1705887.html.

98 *Ibid.*, s. 226D, http://www.legislation.govt.nz/act/public/1994/0143/latest/DLM1705887.html#DLM1705887.

99 Indian Copyright (Amendment) Bill, 2010, s. 65A(2)(a), http://prsindia.org/uploads/media/Copyright%20Act/Copyright%20Bill%202010.pdf. The provision contains a proviso requiring that "any person facilitating circumvention by another person of

tion provisions dealing with copies made for private, time-shifting, and backup purposes should be amended to ensure that these activities do not constitute copyright infringement notwithstanding the circumvention of any digital locks undertaken for the purpose of such permitted acts.

In order to ensure that fair dealings and other permitted acts are not only lawful on the books but also possible in practice, a revised bill should establish positive obligations for right holders to facilitate fair and lawful dealings with TPM-protected works.[100] This could take the form of a basic requirement in the Act—similar to that found in the German law[101]—that owners make available the means by which lawful acts may be carried out in relation to TPM-protected works. Ideally, this would involve more than a bald statement of obligation, but would in fact include some mechanism by which users could vindicate their rights.[102] Various efforts to establish such mechanisms have already been made in other jurisdictions, most notably in Europe where member states are to "take appropriate measures to ensure that right holders make available to the beneficiary of an exception or limitation . . . the means of benefiting from that exception or limitation."[103]

---

a technological measure for such a purpose shall maintain a complete record of such other person including his name, address and all relevant particulars necessary to identify him and the purpose for which he has been facilitated."

100 *Cf.* Kerr *et al.*, above note 67 at 78, where they propose a possible "access-to-works right" that could impose upon copyright owners a "positive obligation to provide access-to-a-work when persons or institutions fall within an exception or limitation set out in the *Copyright Act.*"

101 Section 95b(1) of the German Copyright Act (Urheberrechtsgesetz, UrhG), added by the Law for the Regulation of Copyright in the Information Society 2003, requires rightholders to provide necessary means for users to benefit from recognized exemptions. See Wencke Baesler, "Technological Protection Measures in the United States, the European Union and Germany— How Much Fair Use Do We Need in the 'Digital World'?" (2003) 8 Virginia Journal of Law & Technology 13, www.vjolt.net/vol8/issue3/v8i3_a13-Baesler.pdf, at 20-22.

102 Reichman, above note 62 at 1045, and his co-authors argue that if the principle of prescriptive parallelism is to be respected in the face of TPM protections, "users need a mechanism by which to vindicate their rights and to secure the certainty required to engage in creative activity privileged under traditional copyright principles" . The authors suggest a "reverse notice-and-takedown" regime which operates on a similar premise: "users would be able to give copyright owners notice of their desire to make public interest uses of technically protected copyrighted works, and right holders would have the responsibility to take down the TPMs or otherwise enable these lawful uses" (*ibid.* at 985).

103 Copyright Directive, above note 81. I have canvassed in more detail the various approaches taken by different European States elsewhere. See Craig, "Digital Locks" above note 61.

Canada could, for example, empower a "locked out" fair user to initiate a legal action, to instigate formal arbitration or mediation proceedings, or to follow a new administrative procedure by which a request or complaint could be lodged. It would be preferable, however, to establish a route that is less onerous and costly, and therefore less likely to prove prohibitive. This may require the identification of an intermediary body or bodies to facilitate fair dealings and permitted acts by providing TPM-free copies, circumvention services or "digital keys" on request.[104] This role could be performed by existing institutions (public libraries, archives, educational institutions or the Copyright Board), for instance, or by a new administrative body, housed at CIPO, and created for specifically for the task.[105] With an appropriate declaration of lawful purpose, user identification and/or traceable copies or keys, the appropriate intermediary or "qualified person" could ensure that fair dealing practices are both practical and possible, while allowing a copyright owner to protect his or her copyright interest in the work.[106]

The development of an adequate lawful use infrastructure is, admittedly, a complicated and potentially resource-heavy proposition. It is also difficult to conceive of a lawful use mechanism that does not have a chilling effect on fair dealing practices by increasing user transaction cost and inhibiting spontaneous uses. Some effort must be made, however, to maintain user rights in the face of digital locks and so to safeguard the copyright balance. At the very least, then, users seeking to make lawful use of protected works and the third parties who assist them should be

---

104 I have discussed the various forms that such an intermediary could take, and the manner in which its role could be performed in more detail elsewhere. See Craig, *ibid*. For some important proposals in this regard, see for example Daniel L. Burk & Julie E. Cohen, "Fair Use Infrastructure for Rights Management Systems" (2001) 15 Harvard Journal of Law and Technology 41; Paul Ganley, "Digital Copyright and the New Creative Dynamics" (2004) 12(3) International Journal of Literature of Law & Information Technology 282–332; Reichman *et al*, above note 62.

105 France established an entirely new administrative body, the Autorité de regulation des measures techniques de protection, or ARMTP, which is empowered to hear claims brought by consumers, the beneficiaries of exceptions, and can order rightholders to take necessary steps to allow the exception to be exercised and impose financial penalties for failure to comply. See Jane Winn and Nicolas Jondet, "A 'New Deal' for End Users? Lessons from a French Innovation in the Regulation of Interoperability" (2009) 51(2) William & Mary Law Review 547, http://wmlawreview.org/files/Winn-Jondet_final.pdf.

106 It should be noted that a system that requires users to identify themselves and their intended activities in order to benefit from exceptions inevitably raises privacy concerns that would have to be overcome (Burk and Cohen, above note 104 at 63–65).

shielded from liability; preferably, owners seeking to benefit from technical controls should be obligated by law to make available the means necessary for such users to carry out lawful acts; ideally, users will have an affordable and accessible mechanism through which they can enforce their rights to make lawful uses of protected works.

In our networked society, our culture is digitized; our information, news, research and educational resources and entertainment all come to us in digital packets. Increasingly, the way in which consumers access, use and consume digital content *is* the way in which we, as citizens, explore, experience and engage with our cultural environment. When it comes to technical and legal controls over intellectual works, the ability of the public to actively and meaningfully participate in our culture is at stake.

G. CONCLUSION

Bill C-32, it is claimed, "is a fair, balanced, and common-sense approach, respecting both the rights of creators and the interests of consumers in a modern marketplace."[107] Unfortunately for consumers, users and the Canadian public in general, the pervasive reference to "balance" in this latest round of copyright reform is little more than empty rhetoric. It is true, certainly, that Bill C-32 contains several new (or at least newly confirmed) exceptions and defences for users dealing with protected works. There is, most notably, the welcome (and long overdue) addition of "education, parody or satire" to the list of purposes that can fall within the protective scope of the fair dealing defence, as well as a new defence for "non-commercial user-generated content." These provisions, however, replicate the existing approach to copyright exceptions in Canada's *Copyright Act*, adding more categories of potentially permitted uses that are restrictive, piecemeal, and "not easily capable of a remedial, flexible or evolutionary application."[108] Indeed, the need to expressly include these specific exceptions speaks more to the shortcomings of the Canadian approach to fair dealing (in contrast to US fair use) than it does to the pursuit of a genuine balance between owners and users in the copyright reform process.

Bill C-32 also includes welcome user exceptions for private acts of format- and time-shifting, and making backup copies of lawfully acquired content, with the stated intention of "legitimizing Canadians everyday activities."[109]

107 Balanced Copyright, News Release, above note 35.

108 Knopf, above note 57.

109 Balanced Copyright, Backgrounder, above note 36.

While these exceptions are extremely sensible, and once again long overdue, they are also framed in restrictive language and subject to several provisos, reinforcing the sense that "every tiny exception to the grasp of copyright monopoly has had to be . . . prized out of . . . unwilling hand[s]."[110] The existence of these multiple, technically drafted provisos should also raise concerns about the accessibility of the new bill. In an age where copyright affects everyday users carrying out everyday activities, everyone should be able to know and understand the rules by which he or she is expected to abide. Broad, principled rules are far more conducive to general understanding and respect than are narrow, dense and overly legalistic ones.[111]

The most significant shortcoming of Bill C-32 with respect to user rights, however, is the consistent prioritization of TPM protection over copyright exceptions. Put another way, this amounts to the prioritization of private ordering over public policy. New user exceptions in the bill are explicitly unavailable where the would-be beneficiary of an exception has circumvented a TPM in order to carry out a permitted act. The fair dealing and user-generated non-commercial content defences do not fare much better even in the absence of an explicit circumvention carve-out. Where TPMs prevent access to a work, would-be beneficiaries of these defences are effectively locked out; circumvention of a TPM in such cases will give rise to liability under the anti-circumvention provisions notwithstanding the user's lawful intended purpose. Where a work is protected by a copy-control TPM, users may be unable to carry out fair dealings or use the work in the creation of a new one; without access to circumvention services or devices, they will be unable to benefit from the exceptions to which they are entitled.

The anti-circumvention rights established in Bill C-32 are unduly expansive, while the complexity and rigidity of the many narrowly framed exceptions again suggests nothing more than a grudging willingness to make minimal carve-outs from far-reaching prohibitions. Anti-circumvention rights create the potential for zones of exclusion far greater than

---

110 Laddie, above note 59.

111 *Cp.* Samuel Trosow, "Why Copyright Fair Dealing Needs Flexibility" (12 March 2010) *Lawyers Weekly*, Volume 29, No. 41: "Parliament should avoid over-drafting technical rules with labyrinth exceptions and complex conditions and counter-exceptions. The law should be broadly understandable. As the roles of users and creators converge, Canadians will want to consistently engage in fair copyright practices. But respect for the law is eroded by the long cryptic passages that dwell on technical details and contain rules, exceptions, conditions and counter exceptions . . . . It is encouraged by adopting understandable principles that can be applied in practice."

traditional copyright affords. The bill does not tie circumvention liability to copyright infringement in any way, and it does not contain any general exception for circumventions carried out for the purpose of non-infringing acts, not to mention establishing a mechanism for ensuring that such acts are possible in practice. In this way, Bill C-32 fails to reflect the centrality of fair dealing and other exceptions in copyright law, treating them as marginal elements of the existing system that can be reduced or eliminated to better protect owner interests in the digital environment. In doing so, it threatens to significantly upset the copyright balance established in Canada and articulated by our Supreme Court.

Of course, Parliament is not constitutionally bound to follow the conclusions of the Supreme Court or to pursue the goals of the copyright system as defined by the Court—but one might expect that Parliament would be duly influenced by the reasoning of the highest court of the land, and would share its commitment to achieving a balanced copyright system.[112] As Geist explains, "[b]y sending a clear message about its support for a fair copyright balance [in *Théberge*], the Supreme Court has indirectly provided the most important submission on the current digital copyright reform consultations."[113] Fair dealing and the limits of the copyright interest are central to the balance articulated by the Court, but Bill C-32 does not reflect this balance in any meaningful way: to take it seriously would be to embrace the goal of prescriptive parallelism, and to ensure that fair and lawful dealings are permitted, encouraged and actively facilitated in the digital age.

---

112 Laura Murray, "Bill C-60 and Copyright in Canada: Opportunities Lost and Found" (2005) 30(4) Canadian Journal of Communication 649 at 652.

113 Michael Geist, "Key Case Restores Copyright Balance" *The Globe and Mail*, 18 April 2002, B16, www.michaelgeist.ca/content/view/181/77; cited in Kerr *et al.*, above note 67 at 41.

CHAPTER EIGHT

The Case for Flexibility in Implementing the WIPO Internet Treaties:

An Examination of the Anti-Circumvention Requirements

Michael Geist*

The introduction of Bill C-32,[1] the third attempt at Canadian copyright reform in five years,[2] was greeted with generally positive reviews, as many groups and individuals welcomed the good faith attempt to broker a compromise on many contentious copyright issues.[3] While copyright watchers have long recognized that any bill is guaranteed to generate some dis-

* My thanks to Keith Rose for his exceptional research assistance, Peter Waldkirch for his helpful citation review, and Jeremy deBeer and the article's peer reviewer for their comments and suggestions. This article benefited from financial support from the Social Sciences and Humanities Research Council of Canada and the Canada Research Chair program. Any errors or omissions remain the sole responsibility of the author.

1 Bill C-32, *An Act to amend the Copyright Act*, 3d Sess., 40th Parl., 2010, www2.parl.gc.ca/content/hoc/Bills/403/Government/C-32/C-32_1/C-32_1.PDF (First Reading: 2 June 2010).

2 The other two copyright bills were Bill C-60 [Bill C-60, *An Act to amend the Copyright Act*, 1st Sess., 38th Parl., 2005, www2.parl.gc.ca/content/hoc/Bills/381/Government/C-60/C-60_1/C-60_1.PDF (First Reading: 20 June 2005)] introduced by the Liberal government in June 2005, and Bill C-61 [Bill C-61, *An Act to amend the Copyright Act*, 2d Sess., 39th Parl., 2008, www2.parl.gc.ca/content/hoc/Bills/392/Government/C-61/C-61_1/C-61_1.PDF (First Reading: 12 June 2008)], introduced by the Conservative government in June 2008. Both died on the order paper.

3 See, e.g., Canadian Association of Research Libraries, News Release/Communiquée, "CARL Commends Government on Copyright Bill" (7 June 2010), www.carl-abrc.ca/new/pdf/carl_c-32_media_release_june2010.pdf. See also Retail Council of Canada, News Release/Communiquée, "Retail Council of Canada welcomes introduction of Copyright Modernization Act" (3 June 2010), www.retailcouncil.org/mediacentre/newsreleases/current/pr20100603.asp.

agreement — the copyright reform balancing act invariably means that no stakeholder views the law as perfect — Bill C-32 does a better job than its predecessors of addressing difficult issues such as fair dealing, intermediary liability, and statutory damages.

Much of the support for Bill C-32 came with one major caveat, however. The dominant focus of discussion upon introduction of the bill and for weeks thereafter was on the anti-circumvention provisions, which provide legal protection for technological protection measures (TPMs) such as copy controls on CDs, region coding on DVDs, and access controls on electronic books. Commonly referred to as the "digital lock" provisions, these rules were one of the few issues that the government left largely unchanged from Bill C-61, the failed copyright reform bill that died on the order paper in 2008.

While there has been considerable discussion on the need for anti-circumvention legislation, most of the debate has been focused on either the policy or political issues raised by the provisions. From a policy perspective, critics argue that Canadians would be better served by protection from digital locks rather than legal protection for them.[4] Supporters of the rules, including government ministers, have sought to assuage public concern by noting that some business sectors have abandoned the use of digital locks in consumer products.[5]

At a political level, all the Canadian opposition parties chose to focus their reaction to Bill C-32 by placing the spotlight on the potential harm caused by the anti-circumvention provisions. For example, Liberal MP and Industry critic Marc Garneau noted "the bill seems to be missing an exception that would allow people to break digital locks if it was for private, non-commercial use."[6] Meanwhile, NDP MP and Digital Affairs critic

---

4 See, e.g., Ian Kerr, "If Left to Their Own Devices . . . How DRM and Anti-Circumvention Laws Can Be Used to Hack Privacy" in Michael Geist, ed. *In the Public Interest: The Future of Canadian Copyright Law* (Toronto: Irwin Law, 2005) 167.

5 For example the government's Frequently Asked Questions (FAQ) list for Bill C-32, under the heading "Why does this bill favour strong protections for TPMs?" states: "There are some business models that rely on digital locks to protect their investments. These industries need to have the protection of the law. However, in other markets, in light of consumer demands, some businesses have chosen not to use TPMs. Creators may decide whether to use a TPM, and consumers can then decide whether to buy the product. . . . The success of TPMs depends on market forces." See Canada, Industry Canada, "Questions and Answers" (22 June 2010) www.ic.gc.ca/eic/site/crp-prda.nsf/eng/h_rp01153.html.

6 Peter Nowak, "Copyright bill would ban breaking digital locks" *CBC News* (3 June 2010), www.cbc.ca/technology/story/2010/06/02/copyright-bill-clement-montreal.html.

Charlie Angus, a former professional musician and perhaps the most active Member of Parliament on copyright issues, lamented "the only rights you will get under this bill are those that US-based entertainment concerns decide you get. If the technological protections override those rights, then you have no rights."[7]

The politics behind C-32's digital lock rules were not limited to domestic considerations. There was little doubt that the approach was designed with the United States in mind. As Blayne Haggart discusses in his chapter,[8] the US has been a vocal critic of Canadian copyright law for over a decade, leading some within the government to effectively establish a litmus test for the bill based on the assurance of US approval.[9] With that in mind, the anti-circumvention provisions in Bill C-32 are even more restrictive than the US approach found in the Digital Millennium Copyright Act and were therefore guaranteed of obtaining the desired support.[10]

Yet beyond the policy and politics, lies an important legal question that has been hotly debated within certain copyright law circles. That question is whether the Canadian anti-circumvention approach is necessitated not by policy or politics, but rather by international law. The anti-circumvention provisions represent Canada's attempt to implement the World Intellectual Property Organization's *Copyright Treaty* (WCT)[11] and *Performances*

---

7 See Blayne Haggart, "North American Digital Copyright, Regional Governance, and the Persistence of Variation" in this volume.

8 *Ibid.*

9 "The United States urges Canada to enact legislation in the near term to update its copyright laws and address the challenge of Internet piracy. Canada should fully implement the WIPO Internet Treaties, which Canada signed in 1997. Canada's weak enforcement of intellectual property rights is also of concern, and the United States continues to encourage Canada to improve its IPR enforcement system to provide for deterrent sentences and stronger enforcement powers." See U.S., Office of the United States Trade Representative, *2010 Special 301 Report* (30 April 2010), www.ustr.gov/webfm_send/1906 at 25. See also "Canada among top five on US piracy watch list" *Financial Post* (19 May 2010), www.financialpost.com/story.html?id=3047997; Paul Koring, "Canada placed on copyright blacklist" *The Globe and Mail* (30 April 2009), www.theglobeandmail.com/news/technology/download-decade/article1127052.ece.

10 *Digital Millennium Copyright Act*, Pub. L. No. 105-304, 112 Stat. 2860 (1998), http://frwebgate.access.gpo.gov/cgi-bin/getdoc.cgi?dbname=105_cong_public_laws&docid=f:publ304.105.pdf (codified at 17 U.S.C. (1998)) [*DMCA* cited to U.S.C.].

11 *WIPO Copyright Treaty*, 20 December 1996, WIPO Publication No. 226, (1997) 36 I.L.M. 65, www.wipo.int/export/sites/www/treaties/en/ip/wct/pdf/trtdocs_wo033.pdf (entered into force 6 March 2002) [*WCT*].

and Phonograms Treaty (WPPT)[12] — collectively referred to as the WIPO Internet treaties — which codify new legal obligations to provide "adequate legal protection and effective legal remedies against the circumvention of effective technological measures."[13]

As discussed below, these fourteen words have generated dozens of scholarly articles and other commentaries on the nature of the legal obligations they entail. For supporters of the US approach, the anti-circumvention provisions in Bill C-32 merely reflect the treaty requirements, which, in their view, provide only limited flexibility for implementation into domestic law. To critics, the WIPO Internet treaties are flexible instruments that offer countries far more latitude. While signatories may be free to exceed the treaty requirements, the legal question faced by Canadian policy makers and politicians is: What is the minimum required by the treaty to ensure full compliance?

This article makes the case for a flexible implementation that provides new legal protections for TPMs but preserves the viability of limitations and exceptions — affirmed in Canada by the Supreme Court as "user rights" — in the digital environment.[14] It argues that such an approach, which is perhaps best achieved by providing that circumvention is permitted for lawful purposes, is fully compliant with a country's obligations under the WIPO Internet treaties. Moreover, it argues that restrictions on the trafficking, distribution or marketing of circumvention tools or devices, while found in the DMCA (and now Bill C-32), is not a treaty requirement.

The case for WIPO Internet treaty implementation flexibility comes in four parts. The first part reviews the plain language of the anti-circumvention provisions and some of the efforts to interpret the resulting legal obligations.

The second part examines the legislative history behind the inclusion of anti-circumvention provisions in the WIPO Internet treaties. The record reveals considerable discomfort among many country delegations with the initial anti-circumvention proposals. This led to the rejection of the US DMCA-style approach that specifically included restrictions on traf-

---

12 *WIPO Performances and Phonograms Treaty*, 20 December 1996, WIPO Publication No. 227, (1997) 36 I.L.M. 76, www.wipo.int/export/sites/www/treaties/en/ip/wppt/pdf/trtdocs_wo034.pdf (entered into force 20 May 2002) [*WPPT*].

13 *WCT*, above note 11, art. 11; *WPPT*, above note 12, art. 18.

14 *CCH Canadian Ltd. v. Law Society of Upper Canada*, 2004 SCC 13, http://scc.lexum.umontreal.ca/en/2004/2004scc13/2004scc13.html, [2004] 1 S.C.R. 339 [*CCH* cited to LexUM/S.C.R.].

ficking in circumvention tools in favour of a more flexible approach that did not prescribe any specific legal measures.

The third part surveys state practice in implementing the WIPO Internet treaties. This includes a review of countries that have ratified the treaties as well as several countries preparing to do so. The review confirms that most countries have recognized the flexibility in the treaties by including exceptions, mandatory unlocking provisions, and other mechanisms to retain the copyright balance.

The fourth part canvasses some of the scholarly and legal analysis of the treaty obligations. Although there have been a few outspoken skeptics that dismiss the possibility of flexible implementation, there is a large body of published, peer-reviewed scholarly analysis from around the world that confirms that the WIPO Internet treaties offer considerable flexibility in implementation.

A. PART 1—THE PLAIN LANGUAGE OBLIGATIONS

Canada has faced mounting pressure in recent years over the state of its copyright law, with lobby groups and the US government pointing to its failure to ratify the WIPO Internet treaties as demonstrative of a legal system badly in need of updating.[15] Since their creation in 1996, the twin treaties have had a transformative impact on the scope of copyright law, creating what some experts have referred to as "super-copyright"[16] or "para-copyright."[17] Both treaties feature a broad range of provisions targeting digital copyright issues; however, the most controversial provisions mandate the establishment within ratifying states' national law of anti-circumvention provisions that provide "adequate legal protection and effective legal measures" against the circumvention of effective technological protection measures.[18]

The promise of TPMs have long been touted by movie, music, and software industry associations as providing important protections for their products, by using technology to prevent unauthorized access or use. Despite the support for TPMs, many advocates have acknowledged that all TPMs can be defeated. For example, in 2000, the Secure Digital Music In-

15 See 2010 *Special 301 Report*, above note 9 at 25.

16 Canada, Industry Canada, *Technological Measures Circumvention Provisions* by Mark S. Hayes (Ottawa: Davies, Ward & Beck, 2000), www.ic.gc.ca/eic/site/ippd-dppi.nsf/eng/ip01145.html at 5 [*Hayes*].

17 Dan L. Burk, "Anti-circumvention Misuse" (2002–2003) 50 UCLA L. Rev. 1095 at 1096.

18 *WCT*, above note 11, art. 11; *WPPT*, above note 12, art. 18.

itiative launched a public challenge to encourage the public to test whether it could crack SDMI, then-viewed as unbreakable technological protection.[19] A team of security researchers cracked SDMI with relative ease, confirming the technology community's view that no system is foolproof.[20]

Given the flawed protection provided by TPMs, supporters of technological protections have lobbied for additional legal protections to support them. Although characterized as copyright protection, this layer of legal protection does not address the copying or use of copyrighted work. Instead, it focuses on the protection of the TPM itself, which in turn attempts to ensure that the content distributor, not necessarily the creator or copyright owner, controls how the underlying content is accessed and used.

Both the WCT and WPPT contain anti-circumvention provision requirements. Article 11 of the WCT provides that:

> Contracting Parties shall provide adequate legal protection and effective legal remedies against the circumvention of effective technological measures that are used by authors in connection with the exercise of their rights under this Treaty or the Berne Convention and that restrict acts, in respect of their works, which are not authorized by the authors concerned or permitted by law.[21]

Similarly, Article 18 of the WPPT provides that:

> Contracting Parties shall provide adequate legal protection and effective legal remedies against the circumvention of effective technological measures that are used by performers or producers of phonograms in connection with the exercise of their rights under this Treaty and that restrict acts, in respect of their performances or phonograms, which

---

19 Janelle Brown, "Crack SDMI? No thanks!" *Salon* (14 September 2000), www.salon.com/technology/log/2000/09/14/hack_sdmi/index.html.

20 Scott A. Craver *et al.*, "Reading Between the Lines: Lessons from the SDMI Challenge" (Paper presented to the 10th USENIX Security Symposium, Washington, D.C., 15 August 2001), www.usenix.org/events/sec01/craver.pdf. The "cracking" of the SDMI protection led soon thereafter to litigation with the Recording Industry Association of America, after the RIAA threatened the researchers with liability if they publicly disclosed their analysis. See Scarlet Pruitt, "Silenced Professor Sues SDMI, RIAA" *PCWorld* (6 June 2001), www.pcworld.com/article/52006/silenced_professor_sues_sdmi_riaa.html. The case was ultimately dismissed due to lack of standing, after the RIAA denied they had threatened any legal action. See Electronic Frontier Foundation, Media Release, "Security Researchers Drop Scientific Censorship Case" (6 February 2002), http://w2.eff.org/IP/DMCA/Felten_v_RIAA/20020206_eff_felten_pr.html.

21 *WCT*, above note 11, art. 11.

> are not authorized by the performers or the producers of phonograms concerned or permitted by law.[22]

Article 31 of the Vienna Convention on the Law of Treaties provides that treaties "shall be interpreted in good faith in accordance with the ordinary meaning to be given to the terms of the treaty in their context and in the light of its object and purpose." Interpretation shall take into account subsequent agreements and practices, as well as relevant rules of international law, along with the context of the treaty. Special meanings shall be given to terms "if it is established that the parties so intended."[23]

The interpretation of several key words and phrases within the WIPO Internet treaties' anti-circumvention provisions play an important role in determining their scope and coverage once implemented into national law.

First, the treaties do not provide definitions for the words "adequate" and "effective" with respect to legal protections. Since all TPMs can be circumvented, the provision points to the fact that perfection is not required nor does a minimum global standard exist. Instead, any national legislation will be measured against an adequacy criterion such that the legal protections must provide some measure of protection that a reasonable person would perceive as evidencing effectiveness.

The meaning of "effective technological measures" has also generated some discussion among legal experts.[24] Given the imperfections of TPMs, it is clear that the provision does not afford protections merely for the most effective, technologically advanced TPMs. Conversely, a rights holder may not simply describe any technological control as a TPM and expect to benefit from legal protection. Protections that are plainly ineffective would be unlikely to merit legal protection.[25]

"Circumvention" is also subject to interpretation. Activities such as a brute force decryption of a TPM or hacking a closed system would obviously be covered by such a provision, though criminal provisions in

---

22 *WPPT*, above note 12, art. 18.

23 *Vienna Convention on the Law of Treaties*, 23 May 1969, 1155 U.N.T.S. 331 (entered into force on 27 January 1980, accession by Canada 14 October 1970), art. 31.

24 See, e.g., Ian R. Kerr, Alana Marushat & Christian S. Tacit, "Technological Protection Measures: Tilting at Copyright's Windmills" (2002-2003) 34 Ottawa L. Rev. 7 http://papers.ssrn.com/sol3/papers.cfm?abstract_id=793504 at 34-35 [*Kerr*].; see also Jacques de Werra, "The Legal System of Technological Protection Measures under the WIPO Treaties, the *Digital Millennium Copyright Act*, the European Union Directives and other National Laws (Japan, Australia)" (Paper presented to the ALAI Congress, June 2001) [unpublished], www.alai-usa.org/2001_conference/Reports/dewerra.doc at 10.

25 *Kerr*, *ibid*. at 35.

many jurisdictions, including Canada, could similarly be applied to incidents that are otherwise described as computer crime.[26] Circumvention could be interpreted to extend to more mundane activities, however, including posting passwords or registration numbers on the Internet.[27]

The latter half of the provision has also generated conflicting interpretations. As Professor Ian Kerr notes in his comprehensive study of TPMs:

> A literal interpretation of the requirements that TPMs must be "used by authors in connection with the exercise of their rights under this Treaty or the Berne Convention" and "restrict acts, in respect of their works, which are not authorized by the authors concerned or permitted by law" *suggests that TPMs must restrict acts that are protected by copyright law in order to qualify for legal protection* pursuant to article 11 of the WCT. According to this interpretation, article 11 of the WCT does not require states to prohibit the circumvention of a TPM in order to benefit from one of the exceptions to copyright (such as, for example, fair dealing in Canada). This suggests that only circumventions resulting in copyright infringement will be subject to article 11.[28]

Kerr acknowledges, however, that others have interpreted the clause differently, focusing instead on the latter phrase "restrict acts, in respect of their works, which are not authorized by the authors concerned or permitted by law". The alternate interpretation posits that this provision seeks to protect rights holders against the circumvention of TPMs which limit access, effectively creating a *sui generis* right of access control.[29]

Taken together, the WIPO Internet treaty language is remarkable for its brevity, leaving commentators to debate over the meaning of words that all would acknowledge are open to interpretation. Given the brief, open-ended language employed in the treaties, an examination of the legislative history that led to the adoption of the WIPO Internet treaties is needed to shed light on the intentions of the countries that negotiated them.

B. PART 2—THE WIPO INTERNET TREATY LEGISLATIVE HISTORY

The initial work behind the WIPO Internet treaties began in 1989 with the first session of the Committee of Experts developing model provisions

26 *Criminal Code*, R.S.C. 1985, c. C-46, ss. 342.1, 430(1).
27 *Kerr*, above note 24 at 24.
28 *Ibid.* at 24 [emphasis added].
29 *Ibid.* at 47.

for legislation in the field of copyright.[30] The interplay between law and technology — which later would come in the form of anti-circumvention legislation — did not start in earnest until the Fourth Session of the Committee of Experts in December 1994.[31] The issue did take hold, however, and over the next two years, several committee sessions followed by a WIPO Diplomatic Conference in December 1996 led to the agreement on the treaties.[32] This twenty-four-month period features a rich legislative history that provides considerable insight into the intentions of the parties in reaching consensus.[33]

1) Preparatory Meetings

The WIPO Internet treaties do not include any specific reference to access controls or to circumvention devices. Yet Dr. Mihály Ficsor, who served as the secretary to the Diplomatic Conference for the treaties and has emerged as the most vocal proponent of an inflexible implementation, has suggested that the preparatory negotiations reflected a complete consensus that the treaty must prohibit circumvention of access controls generally, and that the prohibition must extend to trafficking in devices.[34] However, the record of the meetings of the Committee of Experts cast doubt on these claims.

---

30 WIPO, *Report of the First Session of the Committee of Experts on Model Provisions for Legislation in the Field of Copyright*, (Geneva, 20 February to 3 March 1989) WIPO doc. CE/MPC/1/3, www.wipo.int/mdocsarchives/CE_MPC_I_1989/CE_MPC_I_3_E.pdf.

31 WIPO, *Report of the Fourth Session of the Committee of Experts on a Possible Protocol to the Berne Convention*, (Geneva, 5 to 9 December 1994) WIPO doc. BCP/CE/IV/3 [*BCP/CE/IV/3*].

32 WIPO, *Final Act of the Diplomatic Conference on Certain Copyright and Neighboring Rights Questions*, (Geneva, 2 to 20 December 1996) WIPO doc. CRNR/DC/98, www.wipo.int/edocs/mdocs/diplconf/en/crnr_dc/crnr_dc_98.pdf.

33 Article 32 of the Vienna Convention on the Law of Treaties [above, note 23] provides that supplemental information, "including the preparatory work of the treaty and the circumstances of its conclusion," may be used to clarify the meaning if the application of Article 31 "leaves the meaning ambiguous or obscure" or "leads to a result which is manifestly absurd or unreasonable."

34 Mihály Ficsor, "Only once more — and then Marry Christmas and Happy New Year to everybody, including Professor Geist and his devoted followers: the 1996 WIPO Diplomatic Conference, the WIPO Treaties and the balance of interests" *Barry Sookman* (23 December 2009), www.barrysookman.com/2009/12/23/only-once-more-and-then-marry-christmas-and-happy-new-year-to-everybody-including-professor-geist-and-his-devoted-followers-the-1996-wipo-diplomatic-conference-the-wipo-treaties-and-the-balanc.

a) Fourth Session

Meaningful debate about the inclusion of provisions relating to TPMs began at the Fourth Session of the Committee of Experts in December 1994. The US delegation stated that, in view of the ease with which digital works could be copied, rights holders were increasingly seeking to protect their works through the use of encryption and copy protection systems. In their view, it would be necessary to establish some norms to protect against the circumvention of such schemes.[35] The subject of TPMs was not on the work program for the meeting, but the Chairman proposed to defer debate on other matters in order to consider the issue.

At that point, no specific language was tabled. The US delegation indicated that it was considering a provision that would target trafficking in goods or services with the primary purpose or effect of circumventing technical security measures related to copyright.[36] There was explicit discussion about the importance of ensuring that the protection of TPMs did not conflict with lawful uses of protected works. Some delegations and representatives of non-governmental organizations attending as observers insisted that it would be necessary to impose limits and exceptions on the application of any new protections to allow for such lawful use.[37]

The Chairman's summary of the debate notes that there were unresolved issues in defining the appropriate scope of protection and linkages to other areas of law. However, the best approach seemed to be to tie the protection to the scope of copyright law. Foreshadowing the final outcome, he explicitly noted that one possibility would be simply to declare the act of circumvention itself unlawful, and to leave it to each Contracting Party to determine how best to implement that requirement.[38]

b) Fifth Session

At the fifth session in September 1995, there were still no explicit proposals to cover the circumvention of TPMs on the table but the US delegation stressed that, in its view, it was becoming urgent to define an aggressive schedule that would culminate in a full Diplomatic Conference in the second half of 1996.[39]

---

35 *BCP/CE/IV/3*, above note 31 at para. 13

36 *Ibid.* at para. 88.

37 *Ibid.* at para. 92.

38 *Ibid.* at para. 96.

39 WIPO, *Report of the Fifth Session of the Committee of Experts on a Possible Protocol to the Berne Convention*, (Geneva, 4 to 8 and 12 September 1995) WIPO doc. BCP/CE/

Other delegations expressed some reservations about the issue. For example, the Korean delegation emphasized that it only supported the protection of TPMs "provided that such measures did not prevent normal exploitation of the protected subject-matter."[40] The European Commission delegation pointed to Article 7(1)(c) of its computer programs directive as a model. This provision applied to distribution or possession for *commercial purposes*, and only where the device had the *sole intended purpose* of facilitating the unauthorized removal or circumvention of a TPM protecting a computer program.[41] Moreover, non-governmental organizations had their own concerns, with the Japan Electronic Industry Development Association stressing the importance of protecting exceptions for fair use and "safeguards for innocent infringers."[42]

c) Sixth Session

The first concrete proposals were presented at the sixth session in February 1996 with draft language presented by the US, Argentina, and Brazil. The US proposal did not target the act of circumvention, but rather focused on trafficking in circumvention devices or the provision of services. The specific text provided:

> Contracting Parties shall make it unlawful to import, manufacture or distribute any device, product or component incorporated into a device or product, or offer or perform any service, the primary purpose or effect of which is to avoid, bypass, remove, deactivate, or otherwise circumvent without authority, any process, treatment, mechanism or system which prevents or inhibits the unauthorized exercise of any of the rights under the Berne Convention or this Protocol.[43]

The Argentine and Brazilian proposals were broader in scope, applying to both the act of circumvention and trafficking in circumvention devices. However, both proposals were limited to copy controls, with no reference

---

V/9-INR/CR/IV/8, www.wipo.int/mdocsarchives/INR_CE_IV_1995/BCP_CE_V_9_INR_CE_IV_8_E.pdf at para. 20.

40 *Ibid.* at para. 25.

41 *Ibid.* at para. 319.

42 *Ibid.* at para. 339.

43 WIPO, *Proposals Submitted by the United States of America*, (Geneva, 1–9 February 1996) WIPO doc. BCP/CE/VI/8, www.wipo.int/mdocsarchives/BCP_CE_VI_1996/BCP_CE_VI_8_E.pdf, art. 7.

to access controls.[44] Notwithstanding claims that all proposals envisioned including access controls, no control that applied only after a work had been lawfully distributed to, or received by, a consumer would be covered under the Argentine or Brazilian proposals. For example, neither region coding nor the general Content Scrambling System (CSS) applied to DVDs would seem to fit the criteria for protection since neither inhibits copying[45] or communication to the public.

No delegation spoke in favour of a broader protection for access controls.[46] A number of delegations expressed concerns about the scope of the three proposals, however. For example, the Korean delegation supported mandatory exceptions with obligations imposed on rights-holders to serve the public interest.[47] The Danish delegation argued for a declaration of principle only, with more flexibility for Contracting Parties to implement measures as they saw fit.[48] Other countries were even less supportive: Thailand opposed including *any* protection for TPMs;[49] China thought the idea required further study, and was also not prepared to support inclusion of any measures at that time.[50]

Given the differing views, the Chairman's summary of the debate reflects the lack of consensus:

> There had been many suggestions concerning which technical measures should be covered, and it would be necessary to consider further the test of whether the devices should be designed for the given pur-

---

44 The Argentine and Brazilian proposals refer to encryption schemes intended to limit communication of signals to the public, but not to general access controls. See WIPO, *Comparative Table of Proposals and Comments Received by the International Bureau*, (Geneva, 1 to 9 February 1996) WIPO doc. BCP/CE/VI/12, www.wipo.int/mdocsarchives/BCP_CE_VI_1996/BCP_CE_VI_12_E.pdf.

45 CSS is not a copy-protection scheme. It is a pure access control, in that its sole function is to require an authorized key in order to decode the content for playback. A direct copy of the encoded bitstream on a DVD can easily be made without decoding the contents. No circumvention of the protection system occurs. The resulting copy will be entirely functional on authorized DVD players.

46 The delegation of Norway refers to preventing "illegal access" without defining what that means. However it also states that further elaboration is required. See WIPO, *Report of the Sixth Session of the Committee of Experts on a Possible Protocol to the Berne Convention*, (Geneva, 1 to 9 February 1996) WIPO doc. BCP/CE/V/9-INR/CR/VI/17-INR/CE/V/14 , www.wipo.int/mdocsarchives/BCP_CE_VI_1996/BCP_CE_VI_16_INR_CE_V_14_E.pdf at para. 207.

47 *Ibid.* at para. 200.

48 *Ibid.* at para. 202.

49 *Ibid.* at para. 206.

50 *Ibid.* at para. 208.

> pose, or, have it as their sole or primary purpose. Also the acts covered by the relevant provisions, such as importation, manufacturing, distribution or even use for defeating purposes, should be elaborated further, as should links to other legislation.[51]

Despite the lack of consensus on this particular issue, the sixth session concluded with a recommendation that a Diplomatic Conference be held in December 1996 with the aim of concluding the treaties.[52]

d) Seventh Session

The seventh and final preparatory session in May 1996 saw the introduction of yet another proposal (from the European Union) along with several explicit rejections from country delegations of any anti-circumvention provisions. The European Union proposal bore a striking resemblance to the US version, focusing solely on the trafficking of circumvention devices or provision of services, not on acts of circumvention.[53] The primary difference between the US and European proposals was that the E.U. version added a knowledge requirement.[54] Moreover, the European proposal required that the TPM be *designed* to prevent or inhibit infringement of a treaty right, rather than merely having that effect.

The debate that followed saw considerable disenchantment with all the proposals. The Canadian delegation explicitly stated that it was unable to support *any* of the proposals, due to on-going domestic studies, and noted serious concerns about the impact on lawful uses.[55] Other expressions of concern included:

- The delegation of Singapore felt the proposal went too far: it would interfere with legitimate uses; would harm industry; and would create

---

51 *Ibid.* at para. 236.

52 *Ibid.* at para. 275.

53 WIPO, *Proposals of the European Community and its Member States*, (Geneva, 22 to 24 May 1996) WIPO doc. BCP/CE/VII/1-INR/CE/VI/1, www.wipo.int/mdocsarchives/BCP_CE_VII_1_INR_CE_VI/BCP_CE_VII_1-INR_CE_VI_1_E.PDF.

54 Unlike the Basic Proposal, where the knowledge requirement was applied to the (intended) use of the device or service, the European proposal's knowledge requirement was aimed at the device's purpose. In practical terms, this would seem to frame the question in terms of the intent of the designer, rather than the intent of the user.

55 WIPO, *Report of the Seventh Session of the Committee of Experts on a Possible Protocol to the Berne Convention*, (Geneva, 22 to 24 May 1996) WIPO doc. BCP/CE/VII/4-INR/CE/VI/4 at para. 26 [*BCP/CE/VII/4*]. Only the Spanish version of this document is available online: www.wipo.int/mdocsarchives/BCP_CE_VII_INR_CE_VI/BCP_CE_VII_4_INR_CE_VI_4_S.pdf.

a barrier to innovation.[56] Furthermore, the proposal was so broad that it would capture both licit and illicit uses.[57]

- The delegation of Thailand thought the proposal was too vague, and would lead to confusion.[58] Further, the delegation stated that the proposals went too far, and compared them to past efforts to ban video recorders.[59]
- The Korean delegation again stressed its concerns about the harms to the public interest that could result from the protection of TPMs.[60] The delegation also thought the proposal would inappropriately impose liability on manufacturers of lawful products for the illicit acts of others.[61]
- The Chinese delegation thought the whole issue might not fit within the sphere of copyright.[62]
- The Ghanaian delegation felt that protection of TPMs could be oppressive to developing nations, and suggested the whole subject should be "reconsidered."[63]
- The Brazilian delegation stated that the grounds for protecting TPMs needed further clarification.[64]
- The Moroccan delegation simply noted that it was not fully in agreement with the European proposal.[65]
- The delegation from South Africa was concerned about the ambiguity of the language, and raised questions about the allocation of liability.[66]
- The Nigerian delegation, on behalf of the African Group, also expressed concerns about the vagueness of the language. The delegation went on to stress that the subject needed to be considered in terms of its impact on access to knowledge and economic and social development. The delegation asked that the committee reassess the question from the perspective of developing nations, and suggested that while some nations might wish to impose such prohibitions in their domestic codes, this might not be practical for developing nations.[67]

---

56 *Ibid.* at para. 14.
57 *Ibid.* at para. 42.
58 *Ibid.* at para. 15.
59 *Ibid.* at para. 41.
60 *Ibid.* at para. 19.
61 *Ibid.* at para. 40.
62 *Ibid.* at para. 21.
63 *Ibid.* at para. 22.
64 *Ibid.* at para. 25.
65 *Ibid.* at para. 30.
66 *Ibid.* at para. 32.
67 *Ibid.* at para. 34.

- The delegation from Guinea supported the Nigerian delegations' remarks.[68]
- The Egyptian delegation joined with those delegations seeking additional clarification.[69]

Given these comments, the final meeting of the Committee of Experts ended with no formal conclusions or recommendations about provisions for the protection of TPMs.[70]

2) Diplomatic Conference

The Diplomatic Conference in December 1996, which ultimately resulted in the conclusion of the WIPO Internet treaties, featured debate in both the Main Committee and within the Plenary on the anti-circumvention provisions. The starting point for the Diplomatic Conference was the US-backed "Basic Proposal" that provided:

> (1) Contracting Parties shall make unlawful the importation, manufacture or distribution of protection-defeating devices, or the offer or performance of any service having the same effect, by any person knowing or having reasonable grounds to know that the device or service will be used for, or in the course of, the exercise of rights provided under this Treaty that is not authorized by the rightholder or the law.
>
> (2) Contracting Parties shall provide for appropriate and effective remedies against the unlawful acts referred to in paragraph (1).

Dr. Ficsor's account of the Diplomatic Conference claims:

> The reports of Main Committee I and the Plenary of the Diplomatic Conference did not contain any statement or reference to any intention of any delegation to narrow the scope of the protection of TPMs from what was proposed previously.[71]

Yet the WIPO record—as well as that chronicled by other observers[72]—paint a much different picture. The very first statement about the

68 *Ibid.* at para. 35.

69 *Ibid.* at para. 36.

70 *Ibid.* at para. 107.

71 Mihály Ficsor, "Legends and reality about the 1996 WIPO Treaties in the light of certain comments on Bill C-32" *Barry Sookman* (17 June 2010), www.barrysookman.com/2010/06/17/legends-and-reality-about-the-1996-wipo-treaties-in-the-light-of-certain-comments-on-bill-c-32/.

72 Pamela Samuelson, "The US Digital Agenda at WIPO" (1996–1997) 37 Va. J. Int'l L. 369 [*Samuelson*].

draft articles protection of Technological Measures in the Summary Minutes, Main Committee I, is the demand by the Ghanaian delegation for the article to be dropped entirely, or at least substantially reduced in scope (the substantive impact of the proposal to replace the "primary purpose" standard with a "sole purpose" standard would be to exclude all multi-purpose devices from the scope of the provision).[73]

This was followed by a succession of critical comments from country delegations. The Canadian delegation insisted that draft wording was not acceptable, and that the provision should not "create problems for producers and sellers of equipment which might have a significant non-infringing use but which could also be used to defeat copyright protection."[74] In order for devices with significant non-infringing uses to be protected, the scope of protection of the Basic Proposal would need to be reduced.

The Korean delegation proposed changes aimed at ensuring that circumvention for the purposes of exercising an exception to exclusive rights remained not just lawful, but practically possible.[75] The South African delegation stated that the language of the Basic Proposal created "a danger that no provision could be adopted relating to technological measures."[76] It offered an alternate proposal, which ultimately became the basis for the language adopted unanimously that dropped any reference to devices and services, instead targeting only the *act* of circumvention. The delegations of Nigeria, Senegal and Côte d'Ivoire supported the positions of Ghana and South Africa, which clearly call for a reduction in scope of the provision, or in the alternative, its removal.[77]

Singapore called for reducing the "primary purpose" standard to a "sole purpose" standard, stressing "the need to ensure that bona fide legitimate manufacturers and users of general-purpose equipment would not be exposed to liability for the possible use of such devices for illegitimate purposes."[78]

Several countries called for narrowing the scope of the provisions. For example, Jamaica noted that "in the view of her Delegation, the formulation 'any of the rights covered by the rights under the Treaty' was too

---

73 WIPO, *Diplomatic Conference on Certain Copyright and Neighboring Rights Questions: Summary Minutes, Main Committee I*, (Geneva, 2 to 20 December 1996) WIPO doc. CRNR/DC/102, www.wipo.int/edocs/mdocs/diplconf/en/crnr_dc/crnr_dc_102.pdf at para. 517 [*Main Committee I*].

74 *Ibid.* at para. 523.

75 *Ibid.* at para. 518.

76 *Ibid.* at para. 519.

77 *Ibid.* at paras. 521, 522 and 533

78 *Ibid.* at para. 526.

broad and unprecise and its proposed amendment would not contravene the basic intention of the Article."[79] The Australian delegation sought to modify the provision to "confine its operations to clear cases of intended use for copyright breaches."[80] The Norwegian delegation "agreed with those who had proposed narrowing the scope of those provisions, for the main reason that such provisions should not prevent legitimate use of works, for example, private and educational uses, and use of works which had fallen into the public domain."[81] The German delegation also "joined those Delegations which had considered that the scope of the provisions in question should be narrowed."[82]

Contrary to Dr. Ficsor's contention,[83] of the nineteen delegations to speak in the debate in Main Committee I, thirteen of them spoke explicitly in favour of some amendment that would reduce the scope of the protection of technological measures, relative to the Basic Proposal. Three others contemplated some form of clarification to avoid over-application that would interfere with legitimate uses. Only three delegations — the US, Columbia, and Dr. Ficsor's native Hungary — were substantially satisfied with the scope of the proposal.

Opposition to the proposal was not limited to the Main Committee. The records of the Plenary also include critical comments. The Israeli delegation stated "concerning the proposals regarding technological measures . . . the language in the Basic Proposals was overly broad . . . ."[84] Indonesia thought the proposals needed more study,[85] Singapore thought that the Basic Proposal wording interfered with *bona fide* uses of technology,[86] and India warned that "fair use should not be allowed to be whittled away by the new treaties, diluting the applicability of all the limitations and exceptions contemplated by Article 9(2) of the Berne Convention."[87] Korea again expressed concern with the provisions, stating:

---

79 *Ibid.* at para. 531.

80 *Ibid.* at para. 536.

81 *Ibid.* at para. 537.

82 *Ibid.* at para. 539.

83 Above note 71.

84 WIPO, *Diplomatic Conference on Certain Copyright and Neighboring Rights Questions: Provisional Summary Minutes, Plenary*, (Geneva, December 2 to 20, 1996) WIPO doc. CRNR/DC/101, www.wipo.int/edocs/mdocs/diplconf/en/crnr_dc/crnr_dc_101.pdf at para. 388.

85 *Ibid.* at para. 390.

86 *Ibid.* at para. 408.

87 *Ibid.* at para. 437.

> the new treaties should respect the following principles: . . . technological measures such as copy-protection devices could be useful, but should not be over-employed to prohibit manufacture, importation or distribution of protection-defeating devices used within the permitted range of limitations on rights or in respect of non-copyrightable or public-domain materials.[88]

The record indicates that there were *no* unqualified endorsements of the Basic Proposal's provisions on Technological Measures in the Summary Minutes of the Plenary. Given the opposition at the Diplomatic Conference and in the months leading up to it at the Committee of Experts, it should come as no surprise that the Basic Proposal — the only document that required prohibitions against trafficking in circumvention devices — did not achieve consensus support.

US law professor Pam Samuelson chronicles what followed given the rising opposition to the Basic Proposal in her 1997 law review article, *The US Digital Agenda at the World Intellectual Property Organization:*

> Facing the prospect of little support for the Chairman's watered-down version of the US White Paper proposal, the US delegation was in the uncomfortable position of trying to find a national delegation willing to introduce a compromise provision brokered by US industry groups that would simply require states to have adequate and effective legal protection against circumvention technologies and services. In the end, such a delegation was found, and the final treaty embodied this sort of provision in article 11.[89]

The compromise position was to adopt the far more ambiguous "to provide adequate legal protection and effective legal remedies" standard. Not only does this language not explicitly require a ban on the distribution or manufacture of circumvention devices, it does not specifically target both access and copy controls. In fact, the record makes it readily apparent that the intent of the negotiating parties was to provide flexibility to avoid such an outcome. Countries were free to implement stricter anti-circumvention provisions consistent with the Basic Proposal (as the US ultimately did), but consensus was reached on the basis of leaving the specific implementation to individual countries with far more flexible mandatory requirements.

88 *Ibid.* at para. 425.

89 *Samuelson*, above note 72 at 414.

C. PART 3—STATE PRACTICE OF WIPO INTERNET TREATY IMPLEMENTATION

As noted above, according to the Vienna Convention on the Law of Treaties, state implementation is a factor in considering how to interpret treaty provisions. In view of the broad range of interpretations open to the anti-circumvention provisions in the WIPO Internet treaties,[90] it should come as little surprise to find that there is wide divergence among ratifying countries in the way they have implemented their anti-circumvention obligations into national law. Although a comprehensive review of the implementing legislation of the countries that have ratified the WIPO Internet treaties is beyond the scope of this article, a spectrum of approaches is presented below.[91]

1) Canada

Canada has introduced legislation designed to implement the WIPO Internet treaties on three occasions. The latter two attempts—Bill C-61[92] and Bill C-32[93]—mirror the US DMCA approach discussed below. The anti-circumvention provisions in Bill C-60, which was introduced by the Liberal government in 2005, differs in important ways from the more recent bills.[94] The Bill C-60 approach, which presumably reflected an internal government view that a flexible implementation of the anti-circumvention provisions was consistent with the WIPO Internet treaties, established the general prohibition on circumventing a technological measure:

> **34.02** (1) An owner of copyright in a work, a performer's performance fixed in a sound recording or a sound recording and a holder

---

90 See part four, below.

91 For a compendium of national implementing legislation, see WIPO, *Survey on Implementation Provisions of the WCT and WPPT*, (2003) WIPO doc. SCCR/9/6, www.wipo.int/edocs/mdocs/copyright/en/sccr_9/sccr_9_6.pdf.

92 *C-61*, above note 2.

93 *C-32*, above note 1.

94 While there are some differences between Bills C-61 and C-32 and the DMCA, the core anti-circumvention provisions are very similar, as both feature broad prohibitions on circumvention of copy and access controls, a limited series of exceptions, as well as provisions targeting circumvention devices. Differences between the proposed Canadian approach and the US statute include the identification of new exceptions, which includes a triennial review in the US, and the inclusion of exceptions in the US for "jailbreaking" cellphones and circumventing controls on DVDs for several purposes.

> of moral rights in respect of a work or such a performer's performance are, subject to this Act, entitled to all remedies by way of injunction, damages, accounts, delivery up and otherwise that are or may be conferred by law for the infringement of a right against a person who, without the consent of the copyright owner or moral rights holder, circumvents, removes or in any way renders ineffective a technological measure protecting any material form of the work, the performer's performance or the sound recording for the purpose of an act that is an infringement of the copyright in it or the moral rights in respect of it or for the purpose of making a copy referred to in subsection 80(1).[95]

This provision accomplished several things. First, it established who is entitled to exercise the new right against anti-circumvention, namely all copyright holders including owners and performers. Second, it granted those copyright holders the full scope of potential remedies, including injunctions and damages, in the event of infringement. Third, and most important, it rendered it an infringement to break a technological measure for the purpose of an act that constitutes copyright infringement. This provision did not make circumvention of a technological measure an infringement per se; an infringement would only occur where the purpose of the circumvention is to infringe copyright.[96] This limitation suggests that circumvention for the purposes of fair dealing would have been lawful under Canadian law. Moreover, this provision only targeted the act of circumvention; Bill C-60 did not establish legal limitations on circumvention tools or devices.

2) United States

As one of the primary supporters of the WIPO Internet treaties, the US was one of the first to attempt to implement the obligations into national law. Several implementing bills were tabled before the US Congress. Then Senator (later Attorney General) John Ashcroft introduced the *Digital Copyright Clarification and Technology Education Act of 1997*.[97] Rick Boucher (D-VA9) and Tom Campbell (R-CA15) introduced parallel legislation in the

---

95 C-60, above note 2, cl. 27.

96 A notable exception is that circumvention for the purposes of making a private copy, i.e., breaking anti-copying technology on music CD to make a private copy.

97 U.S., Bill S. 1146, *Digital Copyright Clarification and Technology Education Act of 1997*, 105th Cong., 1997, http://frwebgate.access.gpo.gov/cgi-bin/getdoc.cgi?dbname=105_cong_bills&docid=f:s1146is.txt.pdf [*Ashcroft*].

House of Representatives as the *Digital Era Copyright Enhancement Act of 1997*.[98] Neither bill included provisions on anti-circumvention devices. For example, the Ashcroft bill's anti-circumvention provision stated:

> CIRCUMVENTION CONDUCT — No person, for the purpose of facilitating or engaging in an act of infringement, shall engage in conduct so as knowingly to remove, deactivate or otherwise circumvent the application or operation of any effective technological measure used by a copyright owner to preclude or limit reproduction of a work or a portion thereof. *As used in this subsection, the term 'conduct' does not include manufacturing, importing or distributing a device or a computer program.*[99]

The Ashcroft bill also specifically excluded the application of a TPM to a fair use analysis.[100]

The Ashcroft and Boucher bills were abandoned, however, after legislation that ultimately led to the DMCA gained Congressional momentum. Representative Howard Coble introduced what would later become the DMCA with the *WIPO Treaties Implementation Act*.[101] The Coble bill sparked immediate concern from experts throughout the US. For example, a public letter signed by over 50 law professors noted that the US approach went far beyond what was required by the WIPO Internet treaties, with the authors calling specific attention to the changes that had occurred at the Diplomatic Conference and the rejection of provisions targeting circumvention devices:

> Had the December 1996 WIPO Diplomatic Conference adopted the original draft language on "Obligations concerning Technological Measures" in the final treaties, the analysis might well be different: That language would have called on treaty states to "make unlawful the importation, manufacture or distribution of protection defeating devices. . . ." In deleting this language and substituting the current formulation, however, the Diplomatic Conference conclusively rejected the proposition that the duty to provide protection and remedies

98 U.S., Bill H.R. 3048, *Digital Era Copyright Enhancement Act*, 105th Cong., 1997, http://frwebgate.access.gpo.gov/cgi-bin/getdoc.cgi?dbname=105_cong_bills&docid=f:h3048ih.txt.pdf.

99 *Ashcroft*, above note 97, s. 301 [emphasis added].

100 *Ibid.*, s. 202.

101 U.S., Bill H.R. 2281, *WIPO Copyright Treaties Implementation Act*, 105th Cong., 1997, http://frwebgate.access.gpo.gov/cgi-bin/getdoc.cgi?dbname=105_cong_bills&docid=f:h2281ih.txt.pdf.

> against "circumvention" must take the form of general prohibitions on devices. Nevertheless, the bills now pending take exactly this approach, and their broad prohibitory language poses a very real risk that good and useful technologies (such as encryption) will be outlawed.[102]

During hearings on the bills, US government officials acknowledged that the implementing legislation went beyond WIPO Internet treaty requirements. The US's chief policy spokesperson and proponent of the DMCA, Assistant Secretary of Commerce and Commissioner of Patents and Trademarks, Bruce A. Lehman, admitted during his congressional testimony that the provisions went beyond the requirements of the treaties.[103] Lehman stated that the administration's aim was not confined to changing US law. Rather, it hoped that the US model would be used to convince others to implement the WIPO Internet treaties:

> Approval of the legislation and ratification of the Treaties would go a long way to convincing other nations, particularly developing countries, to accede to the Treaties, which are of significant benefit to US copyright interests.[104]

That approach remains in place today, with the US the lead proponent of the Anti-Counterfeiting Trade Agreement, which includes anti-circumvention

---

102 Letter from Digital Future Coalition to The Honorable Howard Coble, Chairman, Subcommittee on Courts and Intellectual Property (16 September 1997), www.dfc.org/dfc1/Archives/wipo/profltr.html.

103 In response to the question "Could we meet those requirements by adopting a conduct oriented approach as opposed to a device oriented approach?" from Rep. Rick Boucher, Mr. Lehman's response was "In my personal view . . . the answer is yes. But in my personal view also that [*sic*] the value of the treaties would be reduced enormously, and we would be opening ourselves up to universal piracy of American products all over this planet." See U.S., *WIPO Copyright Treaties Implementation Act and Online Copyright Liability Limitation Act: Hearing on H.R. 2281 and H.R. 2280 Before the Subcommittee on Courts and Intellectual Property Committee on the Judiciary U.S. House of Representatives*, 105th Cong. (16 September 1997) at 62 (Bruce Lehman), cited in Bill D. Herman & Oscar H. Gandy, Jr., "Catch 1201: A Legislative History and Content Analysis of the DMCA Exemption Proceedings" (2006) 24 Cardozo Arts & Ent. L.J. 121, www.cardozoaelj.net/issues/06/Herman.pdf at 134. Years later, Lehman admitted that the DMCA approach had been a policy failure. See Bruce Lehman, Address (Musical Myopia, Digital Dystopia: New Media and Copyright Reform, Centre for Intellectual Property Policy, McGill University, 23 March 2007) [unpublished], video at www.archive.org/details/bongboing.mcgill at 20:30.

104 U.S., *Statement of Bruce A. Lehman Assistant Secretary of Commerce and Commissioner of Patents and Trademarks Before the Subcommittee on Courts and Intellectual Property Committee on the Judiciary U.S. House of Representatives,*105th Cong. (1998), http://judiciary.house.gov/legacy/41167.htm.

provisions designed to narrow the flexibility found in the WIPO Internet treaties and provide a model for other countries to follow.[105]

Marybeth Peters, the US Registrar of Copyrights, also appeared before the Congressional committees and specifically addressed whether the US proposal went beyond the treaty requirements by including provisions targeting circumvention devices. While supportive of their inclusion, Peters admitted that the treaty was flexible, with the decision left to implementing countries:

> Some have urged that the legislation not address the provision of products or services, but focus solely on acts of circumvention. They state that the treaties do not require such coverage, and argue that devices themselves are neutral, and can be used for either legitimate or illegitimate purposes.
>
> It is true that the treaties do not specifically refer to the provision of products or services, but merely require adequate protection and effective remedies against circumvention. As discussed above, however, the treaty language gives leeway to member countries to determine what protection is appropriate, with the question being whether it is adequate and effective.[106]

Peters similarly acknowledged that the treaties did not require anti-circumvention provisions targeting access to works:

> In this area too, the treaties do not specifically require protection for access controls in themselves. Again, the determination to be made by Congress is how best to ensure adequate and effective protection for technological measures used by copyright owners to prevent infringement.[107]

Notwithstanding the public concern and scope for greater flexibility in implementation, the US ratification of the WIPO Internet treaties was incorporated into the DMCA.[108] The US anti-circumvention provision includes the following:

---

105 Michael Geist, "US Caves on Anti-Circumvention Rules in ACTA" *Michael Geist* (19 July 2010), www.michaelgeist.ca/content/view/5210/125.

106 U.S., *Statement of Marybeth Peters Register of Copyrights Before the House Subcommittee on Courts and Intellectual Property on h.r. 2180 and h.r. 2281,*105th Cong. (1997), http://judiciary.house.gov/legacy/4012.htm.

107 *Ibid.*

108 See, e.g., U.S., Copyright Office, *Summary: The Digital Millennium Copyright Act of 1998* (December 1998), www.copyright.gov/legislation/dmca.pdf.

§ 1201. Circumvention of copyright protection systems

(a) Violations Regarding Circumvention of Technological Measures.—

(A) No person shall circumvent a technological measure that effectively controls access to a work protected under this title . . .

(2) No person shall manufacture, import, offer to the public, provide, or otherwise traffic in any technology, product, service, device, component, or part thereof, that—

(A) is primarily designed or produced for the purpose of circumventing a technological measure that effectively controls access to a work protected under this title;

(B) has only limited commercially significant purpose or use other than to circumvent a technological measure that effectively controls access to a work protected under this title; or

(C) is marketed by that person or another acting in concert with that person with that person's knowledge for use in circumventing a technological measure that effectively controls access to a work protected under this title.

(3) As used in this subsection—

(A) to "circumvent a technological measure" means to descramble a scrambled work, to decrypt an encrypted work, or otherwise to avoid, bypass, remove, deactivate, or impair a technological measure, without the authority of the copyright owner; and

(B) a technological measure "effectively controls access to a work" if the measure, in the ordinary course of its operation, requires the application of information, or a process or a treatment, with the authority of the copyright owner, to gain access to the work.

(b) Additional Violations

(1) No person shall manufacture, import, offer to the public, provide, or otherwise traffic in any technology, product, service, device, component, or part thereof, that —

(A) is primarily designed or produced for the purpose of circumventing protection afforded by a technological measure that effectively protects a right of a copyright owner under this title in a work or a portion thereof;

(B) has only limited commercially significant purpose or use other than to circumvent protection afforded by a technological measure that effectively protects a right of a copyright owner under this title in a work or a portion thereof; or

(C) is marketed by that person or another acting in concert with that person with that person's knowledge for use in circumventing protection afforded by a technological measure that effectively protects a right of a copyright owner under this title in a work or a portion thereof.[109]

In addition to the above-noted provisions, the DMCA contains a series of exceptions designed to preserve certain copyright rights. These include limited exceptions for non-profit libraries,[110] law enforcement,[111] reverse engineering,[112] encryption research,[113] security testing,[114] and privacy.[115] Moreover, the statute features a provision mandating a regular consultation on whether the DMCA provisions are likely to impair non-infringing uses of works.[116] The Librarian of Congress, together with the Registrar of Copyrights, are asked to consider a series of factors and to establish exceptions where needed.[117] While the additional exceptions have been extended in recent years to include unlocking and "jailbreaking" cellphones as well as circumventing TPMs on DVDs for a series of limited purposes,[118] none of the exceptions extend to the provisions on devices, including new technologies, products, services, devices, and components that are used for purposes related to circumvention.

3) Australia

Australia's implementation of the WIPO Internet treaties occurred in two phases — first within the *Digital Agenda Act* in 2000,[119] which amended the *Copyright Act* of 1968,[120] and second as part of the *US — Australia Free Trade*

---

109 *DMCA*, above note 10 §§1201(a)(1)-(2), (b)(1).

110 *Ibid.* §1201(d).

111 *Ibid.* §1201(e).

112 *Ibid.* §1201(f).

113 *Ibid.* §1201(g).

114 *Ibid.* §1201(j).

115 *Ibid.* §1201(i).

116 *Ibid.* §1201(a)(1)(C).

117 *Ibid.* §1201(a)(1)(C)(i)-(v).

118 U.S., *Exemption to Prohibition on Circumvention of Copyright Protection Systems for Access Control Technologies*, 75 Fed. Reg. 43825 (2010) (to be codified at 37 C.F.R. Part 201), www.copyright.gov/fedreg/2010/75fr43825.pdf.

119 *Digital Agenda Act 2000* (Cth.), www.austlii.edu.au/au/legis/cth/consol_act/caaa2000294.

120 *Copyright Act 1968* (Cth.), www.austlii.edu.au/au/legis/cth/consol_act/ca1968133.

Agreement (AUSFTA) which was concluded in 2004.[121]

The first set of reforms focused on the distribution of circumventing devices rather than the act of circumvention or the individuals who use circumvention technologies. It prohibited supplying circumvention devices and services whose purpose is to circumvent effective technological protection measures.[122] It is noteworthy that the law did not prohibit use of a circumventing device, only its distribution. A circumventing device was defined as "a device (including a computer program) having only a limited commercially significant purpose or use, or no such purpose or use, other than the circumvention, or facilitating the circumvention, of an effective technological protection measure."[123]

The Act contained an exception that permitted circumvention devices and services to be supplied in several circumstances. These included:

> (a) to a person authorised in writing by a body administering an educational institution to make reproductions and communications under the statutory licence in Part VB of the Act;
> (b) for the purpose of making reproductions and communications under that statutory licence;
> (c) of material which is not readily available in a form which is not protected by a technological protection measure.[124]

The High Court of Australia examined the first Australian implementation in *Sony v. Stevens*, a case that focused on circumvention devices.[125] Chief Justice Gleeson specifically discussed the requirements of the WIPO Internet treaties. After noting that the Australian reforms "were intended to ensure that Australia provided adequate legal protection and effective legal remedies to comply with 'the technological measures obligations' in two treaties negotiated in 1996 in the World Intellectual Property Organization," he concluded "it will be apparent that the provision is expressed in broad terms, leaving considerable scope to individual States in deciding on the manner of implementation."[126]

---

121 *Australia-United States Free Trade Agreement*, Australia and United States, 18 May 2004, www.dfat.gov.au/trade/negotiations/us_fta/final-text/ [*AUSTFA*].

122 *Digital Agenda Act*, above note 119, sch. 1, ss. 98-100.

123 *Ibid.*, sch. 1, ss. 4-5.

124 *Ibid.*

125 *Stevens v Kabushiki Kaisha Sony Computer Entertainment*, [2005] HCA 58; (2005) 221 ALR 448; (2005) 79 ALJR 1850 (6 October 2005), www.austlii.edu.au/au/cases/cth/HCA/2005/58.html.

126 *Ibid.* at para 12-13.

While Australia believed its initial implementation was consistent with the WIPO Internet treaties,[127] it amended the rules under US pressure.[128] The AUSFTA, a comprehensive free trade agreement, specifically mandated that Australia incorporate additional anti-circumvention provisions into its national law.[129] Article 17.4.7(a) required Australia to change its law by providing for a ban on both the distribution and use of devices for circumventing TPMs.[130] In addition, Article 17.4.7(b) required Australia to adopt a definition of a TPM that controls access to a protected work, or protects any copyright.[131]

4) European Union

The European Union approach to WIPO Internet treaty implementation is found in Directive 200½9/EC, better known as the European Copyright Directive (EUCD).[132] The directive entered into force in June 2001 and granted member states 18 months to implement its provisions within their national law.[133] The European Union formally ratified the WIPO Internet treaties in December 2009.[134]

---

127 "Importantly, the reforms in the bill are consistent with new international standards to improve copyright protection in the online environment adopted in the 1996 World Intellectual Property Organisation (WIPO) Copyright Treaty and WIPO Performances and Phonograms Treaty. Australia was an active participant in the Diplomatic Conference in December 1996 that agreed to the WIPO treaties, and the enactment of this bill will be a major step towards aligning our copyright laws with the obligations imposed by the treaties." Australia, Commonwealth, House of Representatives, *Parliamentary Debates* (2 September 1999), www.aph.gov.au/hansard/reps/dailys/dr020999.pdf at 9749 (Mr. Daryl Williams).

128 For an account of the process, including the involvement of the US Trade Representative in directing the implementation of the agreement, see Robert Burrell and Kimberlee Weatherall, "Exporting Controversy? Reactions to the Copyright Provisions of the US-Australia Free Trade Agreement: Lessons for US Trade Policy" 2008 Journal of Law Technology and Policy 259, http://papers.ssrn.com/sol3/papers.cfm?abstract_id=1010833.

129 *Copyright Act*, above note 120.

130 *AUSTFA*, above note 121, art. 23.4(1).

131 *Ibid.*, art. 17.4.7(a).

132 *Directive 2001/29/EC of the European Parliament and of the Council of 22 May 2001 on the harmonisation of certain aspects of copyright and related rights in the information society* (EU), O.J.L. 167/10, http://eur-lex.europa.eu/LexUriServ/LexUriServ.do?uri=OJ:L:2001:167:0010:0019:EN:PDF [*EUCD*]. For a critical analysis of the EUCD, see B. Hugenholtz, "Why the Copyright Directive is Unimportant and Possibly Invalid," 11 E.I.P.R. 501.

133 *Ibid.*, art 13.1.

134 European Commission, Press Release, IP/09/1916, "European Commission welcomes ratification of the WIPO Copyright Treaties" (14 December 2009), http://europa.eu/rapid/pressReleasesAction.do?reference=IP/09/1916.

Article 6 of the EUCD contains anti-circumvention provisions similar to those found in the DMCA. Article 6.1 requires that member states provide "adequate legal protection" against the deliberate circumvention of technological measures.[135] This applies regardless of whether such an act infringed any copyright, though a user must know or have reasonable grounds to know they are causing such circumvention. Article 6.2 focuses on circumvention devices, defining any device or service as one that is marketed or primarily designed to circumvent technical measures, or has only limited other commercial purpose.[136] The article bans the manufacture, importation, distribution, sale, rental or advertisement of circumvention devices or services. Moreover, possession of such devices for commercial purposes is also prohibited and recital 49 of the EUCD grants member states the right to further ban private possession of circumvention devices.[137]

The EUCD does contain one crucial article that seeks to address the issue of copyright balance. Article 6.4 provides that:

> Notwithstanding the legal protection provided for in paragraph 1, in the absence of voluntary measures taken by rightholders, including agreements between rightholders and other parties concerned, Member States shall take appropriate measures to ensure that rightholders make available to the beneficiary of an exception or limitation provided for in national law. . .the means of benefiting from that exception or limitation, to the extent necessary to benefit from that exception or limitation and where that beneficiary has legal access to the protected work or subject-matter concerned.[138]

The EUCD lists several exceptions that are mandatory. These include exceptions in relation to photocopying, copy and archiving activities by educational facilities, broadcaster ephemeral recordings, non-commercial broadcasts, teaching and research, use by disabled individuals, and public safety.[139] Moreover, member states are also permitted to take measures to preserve private copying rights.[140]

---

135 *EUCD*, above note 132, art. 6.1.

136 *Ibid.*, art. 6.2.

137 *Ibid.*, rct. 49.

138 *Ibid.*, art. 6.4.

139 Urs Gasser and Michael Girsberger, "Transposing the Copyright Directive: Legal Protection of Technological Measures in EU-Member States: A Genie Stuck in the Bottle?" (2004) Berkman Publication Series No. 2004-10, http://cyber.law.harvard.edu/media/files/eucd.pdf at 10.

140 *Ibid.* at 11.

Implementation of the EUCD varies considerably between member states. For example, in Germany paragraph 95a(2) of the *Copyright Act* limits the coverage of anti-circumvention protection solely to works that are subject to copyright protection. Accordingly, where TPMs are applied to non-copyrightable works, including in non-copyright cases and works in the public domain, the anti-circumvention protection does not apply.[141]

Denmark's implementation includes an explanatory text that indicates that only TPMs used to prevent copying are protected. Accordingly, if a TPM seeks to expand protection beyond mere copyright protection it does not enjoy legal protection. For example, encoding DVDs with regional coding would presumably not enjoy protection, an interpretation confirmed by the Danish Ministry of Culture which has opined that it would not be unlawful to circumvent DVD regional encoding for lawfully acquired DVDs, nor to circumvent a TPM if the sole purpose is to use a lawfully acquired work.[142]

Italy has moved the furthest toward applying the EUCD's Article 6.4 to private copying. Its legislation includes the right to make one copy for personal use notwithstanding a TPM, provided that the work is lawfully acquired and the single copy does not prejudice the interests of the rights holder.[143] Other member states have sought to provide users with a positive right of access. For example, Greece provides such a right with the condition that failure to obtain the right leads first to mediation, followed by a legal right of action.[144] Both Austria and the Netherlands have legislation that assumes access for non-infringing material—Austria has said it is "monitoring" the situation, while the Netherlands has included the ability for the Justice Minister to issue decrees on the matter.[145]

The EU experience to date illustrates the significant flexibility in implementing the WIPO Internet treaties. Although on the surface the EUCD appears similar to the DMCA, at the member state level it is clear that many countries have sought to closely link anti-circumvention legislation with traditional copyright infringement. Moreover, the EUCD's openness to the establishment of TPM exceptions to protect user exceptions represents an important potential compromise designed to preserve the copyright balance.

---

141 *Ibid.* at 13.

142 *Ibid.* at 14.

143 *Ibid.* at 23.

144 *Ibid.* at 21.

145 *Ibid.* at 22–23.

5) Japan

Japan's copyright law includes several different approaches from that found in the DMCA. First, circumvention only applies to copy controls, not access controls, since access is not traditionally a right under copyright law.[146] Second, the situations where the direct circumvention of copy control technologies is prohibited are very limited. Circumvention of copy controls is prohibited only when a business does so in response to a request from the public.[147] Circumvention of copy controls are permitted for all other statutory exceptions and for any access control.[148] Third, there are no criminal remedies in Japanese law for trafficking in tools to circumvent access controls.[149]

6) Switzerland

Switzerland formally enacted legislation to ratify the WIPO Internet treaties in 2008. Much like Bill C-60 in Canada and the New Zealand implementation discussed below, the Swiss law links circumvention to actual copyright infringement. Article 39a(4) includes a full exception for circumvention of TPMs for legal purposes, providing "the prohibition of circumvention can not be applied to People who are primarily circumventing for the purpose of a legal use."[150] This broad approach, which effectively preserves all exceptions in the digital environment, provides further evidence that linking circumvention to actual copyright infringement meets

---

146 The definition of "technological protection measure" in Article 2(1)(xx) of Japan's Copyright Law includes only those measures that restrict infringing acts. See generally "Copyright Law of Japan", trans. by Yukifusa Oyama, (2009) Copyright Research and Information Center, www.cric.or.jp/cric_e/clj/clj.html [*JCL*]. See also Japan, Office of Multimedia Copyright, Copyright Division, Agency for Cultural Affairs, "On the Law to Partially Amend the Copyright Law (Part 1)" by Takao Koshida (1999), www.cric.or.jp/cric_e/cuj/cuj.html at sec. III(2).

147 *JCL*, above note 146, art. 120*bis*.

148 See e.g. June M. Besek, "Anti-Circumvention Laws and Copyright: A Report from the Kernochan Center for Law, Media and the Arts" (2003–2004) 27 Colum. J.L. & Arts 385 at 435.

149 *Ibid.*

150 *Loi fédérale sur le droit d'auteur et les droits voisins*, R.S. 231.1 (1 July 2008), www.admin.ch/ch/f/rs/2/231.1.fr.pdf art. 39a(4) [*LDA*]. See also Rentch & Partner, "The Revision of the Swiss Copyright Act," www.copyright.ch/?sub_id=83&leng=1 ("Article 39a paragraph 3 E-URG provides for a prohibition of all preparatory acts aiming at the avoidance of technical protective measures, and Article 39a paragraph 4 E-URG merely permits the avoidance of such protective appliances in cases where they serve utilization purposes permitted by law.").

the adequacy standard required in the WIPO Internet treaties.[151] Moreover, the Swiss law also established a monitoring agency charged with tracking the use of TPMs and the potential misuse of such technologies.[152]

7) Developing Countries

The majority of countries that have ratified the WIPO Internet treaties are not developed countries such as the US, Australia, and EU, but rather developing countries from around the world.[153] Although the many smaller developing countries are not presently significant copyright importing or exporting countries, their ratifications were needed to obtain the minimum number of country ratifications in order for the treaties to take effect.

In 2003, WIPO released a comprehensive review of national implementing legislation.[154] Contrary to some expectations, WIPO's review demonstrated that many countries had ratified the WIPO Internet treaties without even including anti-circumvention provisions in their national laws. These countries include Argentina, Chile, Kazakhstan, Kyrgyzstan, the Philippines, Saint Lucia, and Senegal.[155] It may be possible that some of these countries have allowed for the WIPO Internet treaties to take direct effect within their countries and that they have therefore effectively incorporated the general WCT and WPPT's anti-circumvention provisions.

8) Non-parties

There are countries, such as New Zealand, which have not formally signed on to the WIPO Internet Treaties, yet are working towards compliance with them.[156] New Zealand's implementation of anti-circumvention meas-

---

151 Switzerland became a contracting party to the WIPO Internet treaties on July 1, 2008. See Swiss Federal Institute of Intellectual Property, News, "Ratification of two World Intellectual Property Organization (WIPO) treaties" (21 April 2008), https://www.ige.ch/en/legal-info/news/news-details/news/ratifikation-von-zwei-abkommen-der-weltorganisation-fuer-geistiges-eigentum-wipo-1/161/next/14.html.

152 *LDA*, above note 150, art. 39b.

153 See *WIPO Copyright Treaty*, Contracting Parties, www.wipo.int/treaties/en/ip/wct.

154 Above note 91.

155 *Ibid.*

156 See N.Z., Ministry of Commerce, "Digital Copyright Bill — Questions & Answers" (21 December 2006), www.beehive.govt.nz/node/28179, Q1 ("[The Copyright (New Technologies and Performers' Rights) Amendment Bill] incorporates many aspects of two treaties negotiated by the members of the World Intellectual Property Organisation (WIPO): the WIPO Copyright Treaty and the WIPO Performers and Phonograms Treaty."). See also Copyright Council of New Zealand, "International

ures came in the *Copyright (New Technologies) Amendment Act (2008)*.[157] The bill includes several unique characteristics. First, it expressly retains the right to circumvent a TPM for legal purposes identified in its copyright law. This provision is very similar to the Canadian Bill C-60 discussed earlier and supports the belief that there is sufficient flexibility in the WIPO Internet treaties to preserve existing national exceptions.

Second, the law recognizes that legalizing circumvention may mean little for many people who lack the technological savvy to do so. To remedy that inequity, the statute grants "qualified circumventers" the right to circumvent on behalf of users eligible to circumvent. The relevant provision states:

> (1) Nothing in this Act prevents any person from using a TPM circumvention device to exercise a permitted act under Part 3.
>
> (2) The user of a TPM work who wishes to exercise a permitted act under Part 3 but cannot practically do so because of a TPM may do either or both of the following:
>
> (a) apply to the copyright owner or the exclusive licensee for assistance enabling the user to exercise the permitted act:
>
> (b) engage a qualified person (see section 226D(3)) to exercise the permitted act on the user's behalf using a TPM circumvention device, but only if the copyright owner or the exclusive licensee has refused the user's request for assistance or has failed to respond to it within a reasonable time.

Other countries have also recently introduced anti-circumvention legislation into long-awaited copyright reform bills. For example, India's bill, which the government says will allow it to implement the WIPO Internet treaties, includes anti-circumvention provisions that preserve the right to circumvent for any legal purpose.[158] The provision states:

Copyright," www.copyright.org.nz/international.php ("New Zealand is not party to the WIPO Treaties, but is closer to compliance now that the Copyright (New Technologies) Amendment Act 2008 has come into force.").

157 *Copyright (New Technologies) Amendment Act 2008* (N.Z.) 2008/27, www.legislation.govt.nz/act/public/2008/0027/latest/096be8ed803869e1.pdf.

158 Government of India, Press Information Bureau, Press Release, "Amendment to the Copyright Act, 1957" (24 December 2009), www.pib.nic.in/release/release.asp?relid=56443 ("Amendments are being made to bring the Act in conformity with the World Intellectual Property Organisation (WIPO) Internet Treaties, namely WIPO Copyright Treaty (WCT) and WIPO Performances and Phonograms Treaty (WPPT) which have set the international standards in these spheres.").

65A. Protection of Technological Measures

(1) Any person who circumvents an effective technological measure applied for the purpose of protecting any of the rights conferred by this Act, with the intention of infringing such rights, shall be punishable with imprisonment which may extend to two years and shall also be liable to fine.

(2) Nothing in sub-section (1) shall prevent any person from:

(*a*) doing anything referred to therein for a purpose not expressly prohibited by this Act:

Provided that any person facilitating circumvention by another person of a technological measure for such a purpose shall maintain a complete record of such other person including his name, address and all relevant particulars necessary to identify him and the purpose for which he has been facilitated.[159]

Brazil's recently introduced proposal goes even further, permitting circumvention for fair dealing and public domain purposes, and establishing equivalent penalties for hindering or preventing the users from exercising their fair dealing rights.[160]

D. PART 4 — SCHOLARLY ANALYSIS OF WIPO INTERNET TREATY IMPLEMENTATION

In the nearly fourteen years since agreement was reached on the WIPO Internet treaties, there have been dozens of scholarly articles and analyses about the implications of the anti-circumvention provisions. This part provides a partial review of the scholarly perspective of the issue, noting scholars from around the world have concluded that there is considerable flexibility in the implementation of the anti-circumvention provisions that do not necessitate the inclusion of provisions barring the distribution of circumvention tools nor unduly limit adding exceptions to the anti-circumvention rules.

Dr. Ficsor is the unquestioned leader of those arguing for an inflexible implementation, complete with limited exceptions and strong anti-device provisions. He has written a text on the treaties as well as the WIPO Guide

---

159 Bill No. XXIV of 2010, *The Copyright (Amendment) Bill 2010*, http://copyright.gov.in/Documents/CopyrightAmendmentBill2010.pdf, cl. 36.

160 Brazil, *Consulta Pública Para Modernização da Lei de Direito Autoral: Lei Consolidada* [Public Consultation For Modernization of Copyright Law: Consolidated Law] (2010), www.cultura.gov.br/consultadireitoautoral/lei-961098-consolidada, art 107.

to its implementation.[161] Ficsor is unequivocal in claiming that "adequate" legal protections necessitate broad protections that bear a striking similarity to the Basic Proposal that failed to find consensus support at the 1996 Diplomatic Conference. He argues:

> Contracting Parties may only fulfil their obligations under Article 11 if they provide protection and remedies:
>
> - against preparatory acts (manufacture, importation and distribution of tools and offering of services);
> - against circumvention of access controls and copy controls (and any other control of exercise of rights);
> - against dual- or multi-use devices which are "primarily designed" for circumvention, have only limited commercial use other than circumvention, or are marketed for use for circumvention; and
> - against individual components of such a device.[162]

Professor Silke von Lewinski and Dr. Jörg Reinbothe, co-authors of another text on international copyright law and members of the European Union delegation at the 1996 Diplomatic Conference, are the most notable supporters of the Ficsor position. They argue:

> By its nature, Article 11 WCT provides for minimum protection, which Contracting Parties are free to go beyond in their domestic law. The question arises, whether this minimum protection only covers acts of circumvention. It seems that limiting the protection to such acts would not correspond to the objective of the provision. . . . Accordingly, the obligation to provide for "adequate protection" under Article 11 WCT would seem to require that rightsholders enjoy protection also against preparatory acts on top of protection against the acts of circumvention themselves.[163]

While the commentary from Ficsor and von Lewinksi are frequently cited as evidence for the requirement to implement the WIPO Internet

---

161 He also serves as a consultant to the International Intellectual Property Alliance (IIPA), a private sector coalition of seven US trade associations that include the Motion Picture Association of America, the Recording Industry Association of America, and the Business Software Alliance. See International Intellectual Property Alliance, Biography, "Dr. Mihály Ficsor", www.iipa.com/html/Bio_Mihaly_Ficsor.html.

162 Mihály Ficsor, *The Law of Copyright and the Internet* (Oxford: Oxford University Press, 2002) at 562.

163 Jörg Reinbothe and Silke von Lewinski. *The WIPO Treaties 1996: The WIPO Copyright Treaty and The WIPO Performances and Phonograms Treaty: Commentary and Legal Analysis* (London: Butterworths, 2002) at 142.

treaties with devices and limited exceptions, a broader examination of the global scholarly analysis indicate many experts disagree.[164]

In fact, WIPO has acknowledged the flexibility in the language. In a 2002 survey on intellectual property issues and the Internet, it noted "[t]he treaty language is general enough to allow significant flexibility to national governments in determining the details of appropriate implementation."[165] Consistent with both the legislative history and state practice, commentary from around the world has coalesced around the notion that the WIPO Internet treaties feature considerable flexibility in their implementation.

1) Canada

Mark Hayes, a prominent copyright lawyer in Toronto, was one of the first to opine on the WIPO requirements from a Canadian perspective. Retained by Industry Canada, Hayes delivered an 18-page memorandum on the implementation issues in 2000. Hayes concluded that access controls were beyond the requirement of treaties, noting:

> In order to constitute "adequate legal protection" under the WCT and WPPT, one does not have to go so far as to provide a right to prevent the circumvention of effective technological measures protecting access to a work. Nevertheless, in order for the right granted to be truly adequate, some measure of prohibition or limitation of certain devices may be necessary.[166]

The Hayes memorandum recommended implementing a new right to prevent circumvention, but argued against extending the right to access controls.

---

164 Note that this review should not be regarded as an exhaustive review of all WIPO Internet treaty implementation analysis, since such a review is beyond the scope of this paper. It is presented as evidence that independent expert analysis is at best split on the issue of the formal implementation requirements in the treaty and that there are many scholars who have concluded that domestic rules that preserve rights of access and omit provisions on circumvention devices can still be regarded as compliant with the obligations found in the treaties.

165 WIPO, *Intellectual Property on the Internet: A Survey of Issues*, (2002) WIPO doc. WIPO/INT/02, www.wipo.int/export/sites/www/copyright/en/ecommerce/pdf/survey.pdf at 35.

166 Canada, Industry Canada, *Memorandum Concerning the Implementation in Canada of Articles 11 and 18 of the WIPO Treaties Regarding the Unauthorized Circumvention of Technological Measures Used in Connection with the Exercise of a Copyright Right* by Mark S. Hayes (Ottawa: Ogilvy Renault, 2000), http://strategis.ic.gc.ca/epic/internet/inippd-dppi.nsf/vwapj/ogilvyrenault_e.pdf/$FILE/ogilvyrenault_e.pdf [*Hayes*].

Two years later, Professor Ian Kerr of the University of Ottawa was retained by the Department of Canadian Heritage to conduct a detailed study into the TPM issue. The Kerr study featured an exhaustive review of anti-circumvention legislation, warning against the potential effects of such rules. After recommending against implementation, Kerr offered several alternatives should the government proceed with WIPO Internet treaty ratification. Much like Hayes, Kerr focused on concerns associated with access:

> . . . any newly introduced access-control right must be counter-balanced by a newly introduced access-to-a-work right. Under this approach, copyright owners would have a positive obligation to provide access-to-a-work when persons or institutions fall within an exception or limitation set out in the *Copyright Act*. Such an obligation might entail the positive obligation to allow access-to-works in the public domain, or to provide unfettered access-to works to educational institutions and other organizations that are currently exempted from a number of the provisions in the *Copyright Act*.[167]

Selena Kim provided another Canadian perspective on WIPO Internet treaty implementation in an article published in the *Intellectual Property Journal*. Kim also concluded that there was considerable flexibility in treaty implementation, arguing that "prohibiting either the act of circumvention or the manufacture, import and distribution of circumvention devices would suffice to satisfy the terms of Article 11."[168]

2) United States

Given the controversy associated with the DMCA from its inception, there has been a great deal of scholarly discussion on the relationship between the US statute and the WIPO Internet treaties. Columbia law professor Jane Ginsburg, a strong supporter of the treaties, has acknowledged their limits with respect to including circumventions for non-infringing acts:

> Not all acts of circumvention are violations of article 11; member States incur no obligation to prohibit circumventions that allow the user to exploit a public domain work or to engage in an act authorized by the right holder, or, more importantly, that allow the user

167 *Kerr*, above note 24 at 78.

168 Selena Kim, "The Reinforcement of International Copyright for the Digital Age" (2002) 16 I.P.J. 93 at 118.

to engage in a non-infringing act, such as accessing a work in the public domain, or copying for the purposes endorsed by articles 10 and 10*bis*.[169]

In a 2004 report prepared for WIPO, US intellectual property expert Jeffrey Cunard emphasized the "substantial leeway" found in the treaties for implementation. The Cunard report on digital rights management stated:

> The two Articles give substantial leeway to the Contracting Parties in determining how to implement these obligations. So long as the legal protection is "adequate" and the legal remedies "effective," the obligations will be met. They do not have to be air-tight and prevent every single type of act of circumvention. In particular, the texts do not bar Contracting Parties from crafting appropriate exceptions and limitations to the legal protections and remedies, so long as those carve-outs do not undermine the protections envisioned by the Contracting Parties for "effective technological measures.[170]

Other scholars have reached similar conclusion on the flexibility of the treaties. Professor Timothy K. Armstrong, writing in the *Harvard Journal of Law and Technology*, noted "[a] statutory prohibition on circumventing DRM that hinders fair use goes well beyond the requirements of the WCT."[171]

Following an assessment of the treaty legislative history, lawyer and former law professor Brian Esler emphasized the flexibility within the treaties and the requirements for balance in concluding that the DMCA went beyond the requirements (and the spirit) of the WIPO Internet treaties:

> The word "adequate" here is important. Especially in the context of the defeated US and EU proposals, the WIPO treaties must be read to eschew strict liability for TPM circumvention and instead to contemplate a flexible, cautious and balanced approach. Such a reading is further bedrocked by the Agreed Statement to Article 10 in the 1996

---

169 Jane Ginsburg, "Legal Protection of Technological Measures Protecting Works of Authorship: International Obligations and US Experience" (2005) 29 Colum. J.L. & Arts 13 at 19.

170 WIPO, *Current Developments in the Field of Digital Rights Management*, prepared by Jeffrey P. Cunard, Debevoise and Plimpton, Washington, D.C. ,for World Intellectual Property Organization Standing Committee on Copyright and Related Rights Tenth Session, 2003, WIPO doc. SCCR/10/2, www.wipo.int/documents/en/meetings/2003/sccr/doc/sccr_10_2_rev.doc.

171 Timothy K. Armstrong, "Digital Rights Management and the Process of Fair Use" (2006) 20:1 Harv. J.L. & Tech. 49 at 67.

> WIPO Copyright Treaty, which recognized that technology and TPM may require "new exceptions and limitations" to copyright and its related rights. The US response not only goes will beyond the words or spirit of the WIPO Treaties, but indeed seems to have been largely unnecessary in light of existing law.[172]

Bentley Olive reached the same conclusion in a 2000 analysis of the DMCA, concluding that the US treaty went beyond the treaty requirements:

> The prohibition on certain circumvention devices is not required by the WIPO Treaties. . . . Because of the general requirements of the treaties, new section 1201's prohibition on the act of circumvention would seem to provide sufficient legal protection and remedies to satisfy the treaties. However, Congress went beyond the requirements of the treaties, and included prohibitions on certain circumvention devices.[173]

3) Europe

The European scholarly analysis exhibits a similar divergence from the Ficsor and von Lewinski position. Thomas Vinje, a leading intellectual property expert in Brussels, was among the first to assess the implications of the WIPO Internet treaties, providing a positive assessment in *European Intellectual Property Review* on the flexible language on the basis that it did not cover circumvention devices:

> This provision has the great advantage of applying to the act of circumvention, rather than to the manufacture or distribution of the device used to engage in the circumvention. This focus on acts facilitating infringement follows the tradition of copyright law, and avoids the problems inherent in any provision focusing instead on devices. In particular, it avoids threatening legitimate dual-use technology, diminution of the public domain and evisceration of copyright exceptions. By assuring that the sphere of application of the circumvention provision corresponds to that of copyright infringement, the Copyright Treaty preserves the delicate copyright balance.[174]

172 Brian W. Esler, "Protecting the Protection: A Trans-Atlantic Analysis of the Emerging Right to Technological Self-help" (2003) 43 IDEA 553 at 570.

173 Bentley J. Olive, "Anti-Circumvention and Copyright Management Information: Analysis of New Chapter 12 of the Copyright Act" (2000) 1 & 2 N.C. J.L. & Tech. 19 at 29.

174 Thomas C. Vinje, "The New WIPO Copyright Treaty: A Happy Result in Geneva" (1997) 5 E.I.P.R. 230 at 235.

Several years later, Pierre Sirinelli, a well-known French law professor warned the 2001 ALAI conference about the potential for overprotection in the implementation of the WIPO Internet treaties:

> . . . [t]aken together, a structure combining technological and legal protections in three strata — law, technology in aid of law, law in aid of technology — can lead to over protection. This can occur in two ways :
>
> First, by creating a sort of new right : the right of « access » becomes the queen of copyright prerogatives. An example suffices to demonstrate the proposition. A legitimate user who first pays for access to a work may not keep a copy if the work's conditional availability was reinforced by an anti-copy control. The difference with a book buyer is striking. While the book buyer may engage in unlimited re-readings, the lawful online user will have to pay for each new use.
>
> Second, the locking-up of the work combined with a prohibition on circumvention will prevent the doing of acts which lawmakers have nonetheless intended to be exempted from copyright's exclusive rights.[175]

Sirinelli acknowledged the "vagueness of the WIPO treaties" in canvassing the broad range of approaches found in countries that had implemented the treaties.

Other scholars from across Europe have examined specific aspects of WIPO Internet treaty implementation. German professor Stephan Bechtold concluded in 2004 that "Article 11 WCT only prohibits the actual act of circumventing. It does not target preparatory activities such as the production of circumvention devices."[176] Maja Bogataj wrote in the *Slovenian Law Review* that "[t]echnical measures that would prevent acts allowed to copyrighted works by copyright holders or the law would also not be protected."[177] In Norway, Thomas Rieber-Mohn of the University of Oslo reasoned that "technological measures restricting acts that either are authorised by the rightholder or permitted by law need not be protected."[178]

---

175 Pierre Sirinelli, "The Scope of the Prohibition on Circumvention of Technological Measures: Exceptions" trans. by Jane C. Ginsburg (General Report presented to the ALAI Congress, June 2001) [unpublished], www.alai-usa.org/2001_conference/Reports/GenRep_id2_en.doc at 5.

176 Stephan Bechtold, "Digital Rights Management in the United States and Europe" (2004) 52 Am. J. Comp. L. 323 at 332 n. 38.

177 Maja Bogataj,"Legal Protection of Technological Protection Measures Under the WIPO Treaties, European Directives and Slovenian Law" (2004) 1 Slovenian L. Rev. 27 at 32.

178 Thomas Rieber-Mohn, "Harmonising Anti-Circumvention Protection with Copyright Law: The Evolution from WCT to the Norwegian Anti-Circumvention Provi-

Kamiel Koelman, formerly with the Institute for Information Law at the University of Amsterdam concluded:

> Here the scope of the protection of the technological measure seems to coincide with the scope of copyright. Only against circumvention of a technological measure which restricts an act not permitted by law must protection be provided. Thus no legal remedies need be available when circumvention enables an act allowed on the basis of the limitations of copyright law.[179]

Taken together, it is apparent that many European scholars differ from the Ficsor and von Lewinski conclusions with regard to how the WIPO Internet treaties should be implemented into national law.

4) Rest of the World

Scholars from other parts of the world have also contributed their analyses on the implications of the WIPO Internet treaties. Professor Stephen Coronoes of the Queensland University of Technology in Australia concluded "strictly construed, the Internet Treaties do not require restrictions on devices and technology which might be used to perform the circumvention."[180] Mia Garlick, currently an advisor to the Australian government, argued in 2004 that a ban on the distribution of circumvention devices and access circumvention such as those found in the US DMCA go beyond the requirements of the WIPO Internet treaties:

> what constitutes "adequate and effective legal remedies" as required by the Articles is open to different interpretations. Section 1201 has adopted a wholesale ban of trafficking in circumvention devices and services and on access circumvention. In addition, both civil and criminal prosecutions are available. These measures do not necessarily constitute adequate legal protection and effective legal remedies, but arguably go beyond what is necessary to satisfy the wordings of the Articles for two reasons.[181]

---

sions" (2006) 37 International Review of Intellectual Property and Competition Law 182 at 184.

179 Kamiel J. Koelman, "A Hard Nut to Crack: The Protection of Technological Measures" (2000) 22 E.I.P.R. 272 at 272.

180 Dale Clapperton and Stephen Corones. "Locking In Customers, Locking Out Competitors: Anti-Circumvention Laws in Australia and their Effect on Competition in High Technology Markets" (2006) 30 Melb. U. L. Rev. 657 at 663–64.

181 Mia K. Garlick, "Locking up the bridge on the digital divide — a consideration of the global impact of the US anti-circumvention measures for the participation of

Richard Li-dar Wang, a law professor at the National Chiao Tung University in Taiwan, canvassed the implementation approaches in five countries in 2006 and concluded that inclusion of provisions targeting trafficking in circumvention devices was not required:

> Two more points about the scope of protection should be mentioned. First, article 11 is literally focused on circumvention acts; it does not refer to device-trafficking activities. In the negotiating process, the draft provision was abandoned because its main thrust — anti-trafficking — was not approved by most member states. As a result, the ratified article 11 does not require contracting parties to establish anti-trafficking regulations.[182]

Meanwhile, Dr. Marlize Conroy, who completed her doctorate on TPMs at the University of South Africa, commented in the flexibility in the treaty in her analysis in the *South African Mercantile Law Journal*:

> It is generally accepted that the technological protection measures referred to in art 11 include access and copy control. It also prohibits only the act of circumvention - it is silent about, for example, trafficking in devices used for circumventing purposes. Article 11 is flexible and leaves it to contracting parties to determine the scope of its implementation and to provide for exceptions to the prohibition.[183]

Moreover, her doctorate concluded that it was in South Africa's "best interest to the [*sic*] implement the provisions of Article 11 in such a manner that it still allows users access to and legitimate use of works protected by copyright."[184]

---

developing countries in the digital economy." (2004) 20:4 Santa Clara Computer & High Tech. L.J. 941 at s. III.D.

182 Richard Li-Dar Wang, "DMCA Anti-Circumvention Provisions in a Different Light: Perspectives from Transnational Observations of Five Jurisdictions" (2006) 34 A.I.P.L.A.Q.J. 217 at 228.

183 Marlize Conroy, "Access to Works Protected by Copyright: Right or Privilege?" (2006) 18 South African Mercantile Law Journal 413 at 416.

184 Marlize Conroy, *A Comparative Study of Technological Protection Measures in Copyright Law* (LL.D. Thesis, University of South Africa School of Law, 2006) [unpublished], http://uir.unisa.ac.za/bitstream/10500/2217/1/thesis.pdf, Summary.

E. CONCLUSION

When the Canadian government held a national consultation on copyright reform in 2009, the issue of anti-circumvention legislation figured prominently in thousands of responses. Many Canadians opposed any protection for TPMs,[185] others sought rules linking circumvention to actual copyright infringement,[186] and some supported DMCA-style rules.[187] My own submission supported anti-circumvention rules that prohibit circumvention for the purposes of copyright infringement.[188]

While debate on the ideal approach to Canadian anti-circumvention rules is important, the goal of this article is more modest. Rather than identifying the specific form of implementation, it merely seeks to make the case that there is considerable flexibility in how countries may implement the anti-circumvention provisions found in the WIPO Internet treaties in order to be fully compliant with their treaty obligations. While some have argued that nothing short of full protection against preparatory acts, copy controls, and access controls is required, an analysis of the plain language of the treaty, its legislative history, state practice, and scholarly analysis conclusively demonstrates that the very intention of the treaty drafters was to provide flexibility in implementation.

The interpretation of several key words and phrases within the WIPO Internet treaties' anti-circumvention provisions play an important role in determining the scope and coverage of anti-circumvention legislation once implemented into national law. The WIPO Internet treaty language is intentionally vague, leaving countries with considerable flexibility in their interpretation.

The WIPO Internet treaty legislative history, which occurred over a 24-month period from December 1994 to December 1996, demonstrates

---

185 David Allsebrook, "Copyright Consultations Submission" (2009) 2 Osgoode Hall Review of Law and Policy 108, http://ohrlp.ca/images/articles/Volume3/david%20allsebrook%2C%20copyright%20consultations%20submission%20%282009%29%202%20osgoode%20hall%20rev.l.pol%5C%27y.%20108.pdf.

186 Michael Geist, "Copyright Consultations Submission" (2009) 2 Osgoode Hall Review of Law and Policy 59, http://ohrlp.ca/images/articles/Volume3/michael%20geist%2C%20copyright%20consultations%20submission%20%282009%29%202%20osgoode%20hall%20rev.l.pol%5C%27y.%2059..pdf.

187 Barry Sookman, "Copyright Consultations Submission" (2009) 2 Osgoode Hall Review of Law and Policy 73, http://ohrlp.ca/images/articles/Volume3/barry%20sookman%2C%20copyright%20consultations%20submission%20%282009%29%202%20osgoode%20hall%20rev.l.pol%5C%27y%2073..pdf.

188 *Geist*, above note 186, at 64.

genuine discomfort and even opposition to anti-circumvention provisions. The Committee of Experts discussed the provisions over four sessions and was unable to achieve consensus. The WIPO Diplomatic Conference experienced even greater opposition, with the Basic Proposal that would have specifically targeted trafficking in circumvention devices being shelved after failing to garner the requisite support.

Instead, the record makes it readily apparent that the intent of the negotiating parties was to provide flexibility as the basis for consensus. Countries were free to implement stricter anti-circumvention provisions consistent with the Basic Proposal, but consensus was reached by leaving the specific implementation to individual countries.

The support for flexibility in implementation has since been reflected in state practice. The DMCA may be the best-known implementation of the WIPO Internet treaties, but it can hardly be considered the only model. Countries such as New Zealand and Switzerland have linked circumvention to actual copyright infringement, European countries have introduced a wide range of exceptions, Japan has rejected provisions prohibiting circumvention of access controls, and Canada has previously proposed legislation without reference to circumvention devices. Moreover, countries are still grappling with finding the right balance: India recently introduced anti-circumvention legislation that links circumvention to copyright infringement and Brazil proposed penalties to rights holders who use TPMs to restrict lawful access to works.

The broad array of implementation strategies is consistent with scholarly analysis of WIPO Internet treaty obligations. There are well-known scholars who advocate for US-style implementation, however, the majority of scholars around the world have concluded that the treaties offer far more flexibility and that the US approach extends well beyond the treaty requirements.

As Bill C-32 winds its way through the legislative process, stakeholders from across the spectrum will provide their views on whether or how the anti-circumvention provisions should be amended. While there will be many claims about the efficacy of TPMs, the desirability of anti-circumvention rules, and the impact of the copyright balance, the record conclusively demonstrates that Canada has the right under the WIPO Internet treaties to enact rules that link circumvention to actual copyright infringement and to reject the inclusion of comprehensive restrictions on the trafficking of circumvention devices.

CHAPTER NINE

Digital Locks and the Automation of Virtue

Ian Kerr*

"And what is good, Phaedrus,
And what is not good —
Need we ask anyone to tell us these things?"[1]

A. INTRODUCTION

Of all the "lock and key" narratives in the western cannon,[2] I think my favorite is the legend of the Gordian knot. Midas, the son of King Gordius,

* This chapter derives from two keynote addresses delivered in 2006 at New York University and the Banff Centre. I would like to thank Helen Nissenbaum, Michael Zimmer and Greg Hagen for those very special invitations. Thanks also to Niva Elkin-Koren and Abraham Drassinower for sharing their memorable insights following those lectures and to Dan Hunter, old bean, for making me promise to one day put the NYU keynote into writing (yes, I am slow to deliver). My work has — then and now — enjoyed tremendous support from the Social Sciences and Humanities Research Council and the Canada Research Chairs program and I am grateful for their generous contributions. Thanks also to jennifer barrigar, Michael Geist, David Matheson, Jason Millar, and the anonymous peer reviewers for their invaluable comments on an earlier draft. Special thanks to Golsa Ghamari, Sinziana Gutiu, and Kristen Thomasen for their brilliance, and for the high quality of research assistance that they so regularly and reliably provide. Saving the best for last, my extreme gratitude goes out on this one to Katie Szilagyi — engineer, law student *par excellence* and proud owner of these fine footnotes — for grace under pressure, her tireless enthusiasm, her ability to find anything under the sun, her insatiable intellectual curiosity, and her deep-seated disposition for *arête* . . . which she has not only cultivated for herself but, through collaboration, inspires in others.

1 Robert Pirsig, *Zen and the Art of Motorcycle Maintenance: An Inquiry into Values* (New York: Bantam, 1974) (epigraph).

2 For example, in the tale of Ali Baba and the Forty Thieves, the treasure chamber remained locked and inaccessible until the key — in this case the code words "Open

intricately tied the famous knot. It was initially fabricated as a physical lock. Woven in unfathomable complexity, the knot fastened his father's famous ox-cart[3] to a wooden post. As the Greek historian Plutarch described it, Midas tethered the ox-cart, "fastened to its yoke by the bark of the cornel-tree . . . the fastenings so elaborately intertwined and coiled upon one another that their ends were hidden."[4] Secured by the knot, Midas intended the cart to remain locked within the palace compound of the former kings of Phrygia at Gordium as an enduring legacy of his family's rule. However, due to a prophecy of the oracle of Telmissus, the knot became known not so much for what it prevented as for what it would one day permit. Indeed, the multitudes that sought to disentangle it over the years never intended to steal the cart. Rather, they hoped to fulfill the oracle's prophecy that, "was believed by all the barbarians, that the fates that decreed that the man who untied the knot was destined to become ruler of the whole world."[5]

Perhaps because of this rather strange divination, the Gordian knot became known in the region as a seemingly intractable puzzle, an intel-

---

Sesame!"—was uttered aloud. See Katie Daynes and Paddy Mounter, *Ali Baba and The Forty Thieves* (London: Usborne Publishing, 2007). In a famed fairy tale, heroine Rapunzel is locked in her tower with no way of entry, mandated to release her long hair as the golden stair/access key whenever the evil enchantress demands. When the enchantress discovers Rapunzel has been allowing a male suitor to also climb upon her hair, it is cut off—removing the key to the tower. Jacob Grimm, Wilhelm Grimm & Dorothée Duntze, *Rapunzel*, trans by. Anthea Bell (New York: North-South Books, 2007). The Lion, The Witch and the Wardrobe, one of C.S. Lewis' most famous stories from "The Chronicles of Narnia" series, uses a wardrobe as the gateway to the magical land of Narnia. The children are transported to Narnia, forgetting their real home in the process. They remain locked in Narnia until a lamppost triggers their memories. Their memories are the key to unlocking the wardrobe, enabling them to arrive back home. See C.S. Lewis, *The Lion, The Witch and The Wardrobe* (London: Geoffrey Bles, 1950).

3 Midas and his father, Gordius, appeared in town on the fabled ox-cart at a particularly auspicious time. An oracle had foretold that the new king would be brought to the Phrygians upon an ordinary ox-cart and that the appearance of an eagle would signify future greatness. Gordius was proclaimed king, ending the civil war in the region, and beginning the Phrygian dynasty. See Graham Anderson, *Folktale as a Source of Graeco-Roman Fiction: The Origin of Popular Narrative* (Lewiston, NY: Edwin Meller Press, 2007) at 53. For the significance of the Gordian knot, see Lynn E. Roller, "Midas and the Gordian Knot" (1984) 3:2 Classical Antiquity at 256–71. For discussion of the legend of Midas more generally, see Lynn E. Roller, "The Legend of Midas" (1983) 2:2 Classical Antiquity at 299–313.

4 Plutarch, *The Age of Alexander: Nine Greek Lives By Plutarch*, trans. by Ian Scott-Kilvert (Harmondsworth: Penguin Books, 1973) at 271.

5 *Ibid.*

lectual lock requiring an intellectual key. According to the legend, numerous puzzlers visited the palace with the hope of unlocking the mystery of the knot and winning the kingdom. Many tried and failed over the years. Finally, in one version of the legend, Alexander the Great discovered a solution during his visit to the palace; he swiftly drew his sword, slicing through the knot rather than untying it by hand.

For the most part, history has declared Alexander the hero of the prophecy. His defiant, brute force solution of hacking the knot with his sword has become a metaphor not only for resolving difficult problems by unanticipated means, but "with a single dramatic stroke."[6] Having abstracted the problem as one of freeing the ox-cart from the post rather seeing it merely as a problem of manually untying the knotted cord, the Alexandrian solution is a quintessential example of the gestalt shift,[7] and of the idea that true problem solving often requires violating established conventions. The Alexandrian solution also reminds us that anything that can be built can be un-built, anything that can be locked, unlocked.

This chapter is about digital locks. Like the Gordian knot, digital locks are, in part, designed as a restraint on the use of property. Only, these newer technical protection measures (TPMs) employ cryptographic rather than physical entanglements with the aim of precluding people from using digital works in ways that the copyright owner does not wish. Digital locks can be wrapped around music, movies, books, newspapers and other digital content to prevent or limit access to those works, or to control the number of copies made. They can also be woven into the code of electronic devices such as computers, e-book readers, phones and other media players to restrict customers from using competitors' applications and products. Like the Gordian knot, digital locks can be hacked. And, not unlike the

---

6 W. Russell Neuman, Lee McKnight, & Richard Jay Solomon, *The Gordian Knot: Political Gridlock on the Information Highway* (Cambridge: The MIT Press, 1997) at ix.

7 The gestalt shift refers to an abrupt, involuntary shift in perception that enables an observer to see something in a different manner. The object of the shift is unaltered; the only change is in the viewer's perception of the object. The German word "gestalt" means "shape" or "form" in English. The sudden refocusing is said to take place suddenly and *in toto*. Celebrated examples include an image of a duck that can also be seen as a rabbit or an image of two women in profile facing one another that can also represent a vase. The shift from one to another takes place instantaneously and encompasses the totality of the image — it is not a matter of degrees. See Robert Wade, "Gestalt Shift: From 'Miracle' to 'Cronyism' in the Asian Crisis" (February 2002), London School of Economics and Political Science Development Studies Institute, www2.lse.ac.uk/internationalDevelopment/pdf/WP25.pdf. See also Robert Angelo, "Gestalt Shift," www.roangelo.net/logwitt/gestalt-shift.html.

oracle of Telmissus, some digital lock-makers have even tendered challenges to would-be hackers to try to crack their codes, proffering rewards in exchange for details about how the lock might be defeated.[8] Recognizing that all locks can be broken, many of those who employ digital locks have sought the further protection of law, lobbying lawmakers to make it illegal to circumvent digital locks.[9]

---

8 The Secure Digital Music Initiative (SDMI) was a project designed to prevent digital music sharing through the implementation of anti-piracy measures such as watermarking. To assist in the creation of a robust security system and aid in identifying possible holes in four potential technologies, SDMI issued a public challenge to researchers in the field. Over the course of three weeks in September 2000, researchers were invited to download the watermarked music files and attempt to remove the watermarks. A team of researchers from Princeton and Rice Universities, headed by computer scientist and security expert Edward Felten, successfully met the challenge, removing all four different watermarks without degrading the quality of the music files. They opted against signing a confidentiality agreement that would have made them eligible for the cash prize. Instead, the team wrote a paper detailing their findings, which they planned to present at a 2001 conference. The Recording Industry Association of America (RIAA) and SDMI threatened legal action under the *Digital Millennium Copyright Act* for circumventing an owner's copyright protections (despite having been previously invited to do exactly that), if the findings were made publicly available. Felten chose not to publish under this threat, instead initiating his own lawsuit against SDMI under freedom of expression. The lawsuit was later dismissed by the United States District Court of New Jersey for lack of standing, but it remains a key example to highlight differences in security policies. Felten's paper was not intended to be a "how-to" guide for the layperson, using technical language that would have been unintelligible to everyone but those who intimately understood the technology. From a full disclosure perspective, disclosing the weaknesses of a security system will aid its creators in identifying any loopholes and strengthening protection measures as quickly as possible. In contrast, a security from obscurity viewpoint, seemingly preferred by the RIAA and SDMI in this case, would favour keeping information about system weaknesses secret, hoping that no one will identify them. Felten commented on this issue in particular, stating that the weaknesses in the technology were clear and that interested parties would overcome them, regardless of whether or not his paper was published. See Electronic Frontier Foundation, "*Felten, et. al. v. RIAA, et. al.*" http://w2.eff.org/IP/DMCA/Felten_v_RIAA. See also Electronic Frontier Foundation, "Final Hearing Transcript, *Felten v. RIAA* (Nov. 28, 2001)" http://w2.eff.org/IP/DMCA/Felten_v_RIAA/20011128_hearing_transcript.html. See also Scarlet Pruitt, "Silenced Professor Sues SDMI, RIAA" *PCWorld* (6 June 2001), www.pcworld.com/article/52006/silenced_professor_sues_sdmi_riaa.html.

9 This letter from the US Motion Picture and Television Industry and Labour Organizations to USTR Ambassador Ron Kirk regarding ACTA Negotiations showcases the vested interests of entertainment industries in robust legislative copyright protections. Letter from Motion Picture Association of America *et al.* to Ambassasor Ron Kirk (22 September 2009), www.mpaa.org/resources/ace3793e-cfaf-4749-96ae-385f38506268.pdf.

In this chapter, I investigate various potential uses of digital locks and the social consequences of creating laws that would make it illegal to circumvent them. I suggest that laws protecting an unimpeded use of digital locks — such as the one recently tabled in Canada[10] — are Gordian in the sense of the oracle's prophecy. That is, these laws will ultimately cause digital locks to become better known for what they permit than for what they preclude. This, I claim, is because digital locks are the key technology underlying a relatively new and extremely powerful form of social control: *the automation of permissions*.[11]

While the policy debate about digital locks has to date focused almost exclusively on their narrow role in copyright reform,[12] I will argue that

---

In the Canadian context, while a new Conservative cabinet was being sworn in on 6 February 2006, a lobbyist for the Canadian Recording Industry Association named David Dyer emailed the Director General of Canadian Heritage's Copyright Policy Branch recommending organizing an event about copyright reform. See Michael Geist, "CRIA's Lobby Effort: The Untold Story" (11 June 2006), www.michaelgeist.ca/index.php?option=com_content&task=view&id=1293.

10 Bill C-32 is the third bill designed to amend Canada's *Copyright Act* in recent years. Its predecessors, Bill C-60 and Bill C-61, both died on the order paper due to dissolution of Parliament. Bill C-32, *An Act to amend the Copyright Act*, 3d Sess., 40th Parl., 2010, www2.parl.gc.ca/HousePublications/Publication.aspx?Docid=4580265&file=4 [Bill C-32]. Bill C-61, *An Act to amend the Copyright Act*, 2d Sess., 39th Parl., 2008, www2.parl.gc.ca/HousePublications/redirector.aspx?RefererUrl=Publication.aspx%3fDocid=3570473%26file%3d4. Bill C-60, *An Act to amend the Copyright Act*, 1st Sess., 38th Parl., 2005, www2.parl.gc.ca/HousePublications/redirector.aspx?RefererUrl=Publication.aspx%3fDocid=2334015%26file%3d4.

11 Though not labeled as such, what I am calling the "automation of permissions" is a key strategy in the development of what Professor Lawrence Lessig refers to as a "permission culture"; see Lawrence Lessig, *Free Culture: How Big Media Uses Technology and the Law to Lock Down Culture and Control Creativity* (New York: The Penguin Press, 2004), www.free-culture.cc/freecontent at xiv, 8, 173, 192–93. I will elaborate on both of these concepts below.

12 Andrew A. Adams & Ian Brown, "Keep Looking: The Answer to the Machine is Elsewhere" (2009) 19 Computers & L. 32 http://papers.ssrn.com/sol3/papers.cfm?abstract_id=1329703; Nika Aldrich, "A System of Logo-Based Disclosure of DRM on Download Products" (29 April, 2007), www.ssrn.com/abstract=983551; Stefan Bechtold, "Digital Rights Management in the United States and Europe" (2004) 52 Am. J. Comp. L. 323, http://papers.ssrn.com/sol3/papers.cfm?abstract_id=732825; Dan L. Burk & Tarleton L. Gillespie, "Autonomy and Morality in DRM and Anti-Circumvention Law" (2006) 4 Triple C: Cognition, Communication, Cooperation 239, http://papers.ssrn.com/sol3/papers.cfm?abstract_id=1146448; Lee A. Bygrave, "Digital Rights Management and Privacy — Legal Aspects in the European Union" in Eberhard Beckar *et al.*, eds. *Digital Rights Management: Technological, Economic, Legal and Political Aspects* (New York: Springer, 2003) 418, http://folk.uio.no/lee/publications/DRM_privacy.pdf; Julie E. Cohen, "DRM & Privacy" (2003) 18

digital locks are of even greater social significance when properly understood in light of their role in larger digital rights management (DRM) systems that are employed well beyond the copyright context. I will argue that the broader automation of permissions through DRM is the enabler

---

Berkeley L. & Tech J. 575, www.law.berkeley.edu/journals/btlj/articles/vol18/Cohen.stripped.pdf; Carys J. Craig, "Digital Locks and the Fate of Fair Dealing in Canada: In Pursuit of "Prescriptive Parallelism" (2010) 13 J. World Intellectual Property 503, http://papers.ssrn.com/sol3/papers.cfm?abstract_id=1599610; Jeremy F. DeBeer, "Locks & Levies" (2006) 84 Denv U.L. Rev. 143, http://papers.ssrn.com/sol3/papers.cfm?abstract_id=952128 ; Peter Drahos, *A Philosophy of Intellectual Property* (Sudbury MA: Dartmouth Publishing Group, 1996), http://epublications.bond.edu.au/blr/vol8/iss2/7/; Edward Felten, "A Skeptical View of DRM and Fair Use" (2003) 46 Communications of the ACM 4 at 57–59, http://cacm.acm.org/magazines/2003/4/6849-a-skeptical-view-of-drm-and-fair-use/fulltext; Daniel J. Gervais, "The Purpose of Copyright Law in Canada" (2006) 2 UOLTJ 2 at 315, http://works.bepress.com/daniel_gervais/10; Kamiel J. Koelman, "The Levitation of Copyright: An Economic View of Digital Home Copying, Levies and DRM" (2005) 4 Ent. L. Rev. 75, http://papers.ssrn.com/sol3/papers.cfm?abstract_id=682163; Niva Elkin-Koren, "Making Room for Consumers Under the DMCA" (2007) 22 Berkeley Tech. L.J. 1119, http://papers.ssrn.com/sol3/papers.cfm?abstract_id=1024566; Michael Geist, "Anti-Circumvention Legislation and Competition Policy: Defining a Canadian Way?" in Michael Geist, ed., *In The Public Interest: The Future of Canadian Copyright Law* (Toronto: Irwin Law, 2005) 211, www.irwinlaw.com/pages/content-commons/anti-circumvention-legislation-and-competition-policy--defining-a-canadian-way----michael-geist; Tarleton L. Gillespie, "Designed to 'Effectively Frustrate': Copyright, Technology, and the Agency of Users" (2006) 8 New Media & Society 651, http://nms.sagepub.com/content/8/4/651.abstract; Graham Greenleaf, "Unlocking IP to Stimulate Australian Innovation: An Issues Paper" (2008) 44 University of New South Wales Faculty of Law Research Series, http://papers.ssrn.com/sol3/papers.cfm?abstract_id=1398604; Lawrence Lessig, *Code: Version 2.0* (New York: Basic Books, 2006), http://codev2.cc/; Mark Perry, "Rights Management Information" in Michael Geist, ed., *In The Public Interest: The Future of Canadian Copyright Law* (Toronto: Irwin Law, 2005) 251, www.irwinlaw.com/pages/content-commons/rights-management-information---mark-perry; Matthew Rimmer, *Digital Copyright and the Consumer Revolution: Hands off my iPod* (Cheltenham: Edward Elgar Publishing, 2007), http://works.bepress.com/matthew_rimmer/1; Pamela Samuelson & Jason Schultz, "Regulating Digital Rights Management Technologies: Should Copyright Owners Have to Give Notice About DRM Restrictions?" (2007) J. Telecomm. & High Tech. L. http://people.ischool.berkeley.edu/~pam/papers/notice%20of%20DRM-701.pdf; Pamela Samuelson, "Digital Rights Management {and, or, vs.} the Law" (2003) 46 Communications of the AC 4, http://portal.acm.org/citation.cfm?id=641205.641229 at 41; Kimberlee G. Weatherall, "On Technology Locks and the Proper Scope of Digital Copyright Laws — Sony in the High Court" (2004) 26 Sydney L. Rev. 613 http://works.bepress.com/kimweatherall/2; Peter K. Yu, "Anticircumvention and Anti-anticircumvention" (2006) 84 Denv. U.L. Rev. 13 http://papers.ssrn.com/sol3/papers.cfm?abstract_id=931899.

and catalyst of a potentially debilitating world, in which technology can be used to shift social defaults from inclusion to exclusion by disabling human action across a wide range of activities for all those who do not have prior permission from those controlling the DRM. While a well-established body of literature has very thoughtfully and carefully investigated the risks that excessive legal protection of digital locks can pose to access to information,[13] freedom of expression,[14] privacy,[15] encryption research,[16]

---

13 Bernt Hugenholtz, "Copyright, Contract and Code: What Will Remain of the Public Domain," (2000) 26 Brook. J. Int'l L. 77; Michael Geist, "Canada Rejects One-Sided Approach to Copyright Reform" *The Toronto Star* (28 March 2005), www.michaelgeist.ca/resc/html_bkup/mar282005.html.

14 Ian R. Kerr & Jane Bailey, "The Implications of Digital Rights Management for Privacy and Freedom of Expression" (2004) 2 Info. Comm. & Ethics in Society 87; Mark Perry and Casey Chisick, "Copyright and Anti-circumvention: Growing Pains in a Digital Millennium," (2000) New Zealand Int. Prop. J. 261, http://papers.ssrn.com/sol3/papers.cfm?abstract_id=1622851; Kamiel J. Koelman, "The protection of technological measures vs. the copyright limitations," ALAI Congress 2001, www.ivir.nl/publications/koelman/alaiNY.html; David Nimmer, "A Riff on Fair Use in the *Digital Millennium Copyright Act*," (2000) 148 U. Pa.L.Rev. 673.

15 Julie E. Cohen, "DRM & Privacy" (2003) 18 Berkeley L. & Tech J. 575, www.law.berkeley.edu/journals/btlj/articles/vol18/Cohen.stripped.pdf; Lee A. Bygrave, "The Technologisation of Copyright: Implications for Privacy and Related Interests" (2002) 24 European Intellectual Property Review 2 at 51; Ian Goldberg, "Privacy-enhancing technologies for the Internet, II: Five Years Later" (2002) Workshop on Privacy Enhancing Technologies, www.cypherpunks.ca/~iang/pubs/pet2.pdf at 1–2; Daniel J. Solove, *The Digital Person: Technology and Privacy in the Information Age* (New York: New York University Press, 2004).

16 See *Amicus Curiae* Brief in Support of Appellants, *Universal v. Reimerdes* (26 Jan 2001), www.2600.com/dvd/docs/2001/0126-crypto-amicus.txt. ("The *amici curiae* are cryptographers, individuals whose work or hobby involves research, design, analysis, and testing of encryption technologies. *Amici* are concerned that Section 1201 of the *Digital Millennium Copyright Act* ("DMCA"), as construed by the District Court . . . would deprive cryptographers of the most effective language in which to communicate their research and its results, with the effect of weakening security systems and technological protection of data for the public."); Severine Dusollier, "Electrifying the Fence: The Legal Protection of Technological Protection Measures for Protecting Copyright" (1999) 21 Eur. Int. Prop. R. 285, www.crid.be/pdf/public/4138.pdf; Yochai Benkler, "Free as the Air to Common Use: First Amendment Constraints on Enclosure of the Public Domain" (1999) 74 N.Y.U. L. Rev. 354 at 419; Lawrence Lessig, *Code: Version 2.0* (New York: Basic Books, 2006), http://codev2.cc/; Edward Felten *et al.*, "Lest We Remember: Cold-Boot Attacks on Encryption Keys" (2009) 52 Communications of the ACM 5 at 91, http://citp.princeton.edu/pub/coldboot.pdf.

freedom to tinker,[17] education,[18] and copyright's delicate balance between owner and user rights,[19] my aim in this chapter is to make a more fundamental — perhaps foundational — claim.

I argue that a generalized and unimpeded use of digital locks, further protected by the force of law, threatens not merely the above enumerated legal rights and freedoms but also threatens to significantly impair our moral development. In particular, I express deep concern that digital locks

---

17 According to Ed Felten, the freedom to tinker "is your freedom to understand, discuss, repair and modify the technological devices you own." See Ed Felten, "My Experiment with 'Digital Drugs'" *Ed Felten's Blog*, www.freedom-to-tinker.com/blog/felten.

18 Samuel E. Trosow, "The Changing Landscape of Academic Libraries and Copyright Policy: Interlibrary Loans, Electronic Reserves, and Distance Education," in Michael Geist, ed., *In The Public Interest: The Future of Canadian Copyright Law* (Toronto: Irwin Law, 2005) 375, www.irwinlaw.com/pages/content-commons/the-changing-landscape-of-academic-libraries-and-copyright-policy--interlibrary-loans-electronic-reserves-and-distance-learning---samuel-trosow; C. Risher, "Technological protection measures (anti-circumvention devices) and their relation to exceptions to copyright in the Electronic environment" (Paper presented to the IPA Copyright Forum Frankfurt Book Fair, 20 October 2000) [unpublished]; Neil Postman, *The End of Education: Redefining the Value of School* (New York: Alfred A. Knopf, 1996) at 192; Dan L. Burk & Julie E. Cohen, "Fair Use Infrastructure for Copyright Management Systems" (2001) 15 Harv. J.L. & Tech. 41 at 63, www.law.georgetown.edu/Faculty/jec/fairuseinfra.pdf.

19 Abraham Drassinower, "Taking User Rights Seriously" in Michael Geist, ed., *In The Public Interest: The Future of Canadian Copyright Law* (Toronto: Irwin Law, 2005) 479, www.irwinlaw.com/pages/content-commons/taking-user-rights-seriously---abraham-drassinower; Jane Bailey, "Deflating the Michelin Man: Protecting Users' Rights in the Canadian Copyright Reform Process" in Michael Geist, ed., *In The Public Interest: The Future of Canadian Copyright Law* (Toronto: Irwin Law, 2005) 125, www.irwinlaw.com/pages/content-commons/deflating-the-michelin-man--protecting-users-rights-in-the-canadian-copyright-reform-process---jane-bailey; Jeffrey P. Cunard, "Technological Protection of Copyrighted Works and Copyrighted Management Systems: A Brief Survey of the Landscape" *ALAI Congress 2001*, www.alai-usa.org/2001_conference/pres_cunard.doc at 2; Michael Geist, "'TPMs': A perfect storm for consumers" *The Toronto Star* (31 Jan 2005), www.michaelgeist.ca/resc/html_bkup/jan312005.html; Canadian Internet Policy and Public Interest Clinic, Media Release, "CIPPIC Questions Unbalanced Copyright Bill" (20 June 2005), www.cippic.ca/documents/Media_Release_-_Copyright_Bill_-_20_June_05_Final.pdf; Charles Clark, "The Answer to the Machine is in the Machine," in Bernt Hugenholtz, ed., *The Future of Copyright in a Digital Environment: Proceedings of the Royal Academy Colloqium* (The Hague: Kluwer Law International, 1996); Garry L. Founds, "Shrinkwrap and Clickwrap Agreements: 2B or Not 2B?" (1999) 52 Fed. Comm. L.J. 99; Daniel B. Ravicher, "Facilitating Collaborative Software Development: The Enforceability of Mass-Market Public Software Licenses" (2000) 5 Va. J.L. & Tech. 11.

could be used in a systematic attempt to "automate human virtue"—programming people to "do the right thing" by constraining and in some cases altogether eliminating moral behaviour through technology rather than ethics or law. Originally introduced to improve the human condition, digital locks and other automation technologies could, ironically, be used to control our virtual and physical environments in unprecedented ways, to eliminate the possibility for moral deliberation about certain kinds of action otherwise possible in these spaces by disabling the world in a way that ultimately disables the people who populate it. Not by eliminating their choices but by automating them—by removing people from the realm of moral action altogether, thereby impairing their future moral development.

I begin in Section B with a series of historical and cultural vignettes investigating the nature, purpose and symbolic significance of locks. Recognizing that keys are in fact "the key" to a proper understanding of locking systems, I go on in Section C to examine digital locks and the power afforded to keyholders to control others through the automation of permissions, in effect enabling or disabling the world we live in by setting the terms and conditions for its use. Section D is where I illustrate this through a connected series of anecdotes from my own personal experience. Here, I sketch the potential progression of a widespread digital lock strategy through a series of developments in "carting" technologies and indicate what this might mean. In Section E, I ask how all of this might affect us as moral actors who desire to do good things. Examining Aristotle's account of virtue ethics, I demonstrate that a state sanctioned, unimpeded and widespread digital lock strategy would impair our moral development by impeding our ability and desire to cultivate the practical wisdom necessary for the acquisition of morally virtuous dispositions. Finally, in Section F, I briefly investigate Bill C-32, Canada's proposal for sanctioning the use of digital locks and prohibiting their circumvention. Arguing that the flaws in Bill C-32 are symptomatic of the larger digital lock strategy, I conclude that the proposed legislative solution is inelegant—a brute force formula that fails to achieve a balanced copyright framework. I suggest that those who use digital locks might sometimes owe a positive obligation to provide a key whenever someone else has a right to access or use the thing that has been locked-up. I further suggest that the laws protecting digital locks, like the digital and mechanical locks themselves, must be understood as something more than instruments of exclusion since a series of ubiquitous locks designed to keep people honest will in fact impair the development of a deep-seated disposition necessary for honesty.

B. LOCK AND KEY

Prior to the invention of locks, people, like animals, often buried their valuables, or hid them in caves or the trunks of trees.[20] This rather imperfect means of securing their belongings eventually gave way to innovation. As is evident from the legend of the Gordian knot, cords and ropes were initially used to tie things down. The strength and complexity of the Gordian knot, for instance, was used to physically hamper theft of the king's ox-cart by tethering it to a post firmly rooted in the ground. It was not long before it was discovered that knots could be used in other ways. For example, the "thief knot,"[21] was employed not to hamper but to monitor possible intruders by detecting whether property had been tampered with. This early technology was simple but ingenious.[22] The design of the thief knot very closely resembled the popular maritime "reef knot."[23] A sailor using this technique would "secure" his belongings in a ditty bag using the thief knot, often with the ends hidden.[24] If another sailor untied the knot and rifled through the bag — even if he took nothing — it was likely that he would re-tie the bag using the more common reef knot, revealing to the owner that the bag had been tampered with.[25]

While techniques such as these offered some measure of security, it was the advent of mechanical locks that truly changed the game. It is thought that the earliest locks were constructed approximately 4,000 years ago.[26] However, the first archaeological discovery of a wooden lock — now known as the "Egyptian door lock" — dates back to the reign of Sargon II, who is believed to have used this technology to secure his palace in Khorsabad, near Nineveh, where he reigned from 722 to 705 B.C.[27] Its basic mechanism was a large wooden bolt used to secure a door, which had a slot with

---

20 Access Key and Lock, "A Brief History of Locks," (2010) www.keyandlocksupplies.co.uk/80665/info.php?p=15 [Access Lock].

21 Colin Jarman, *Top Knots*, (London: Quintet Publishing, 2001) at 32–33. See also Lindsey Philpott, *Pocket Guide to Knots*, (Singapore: New Holland Publishers Ltd., 2006) at 158–59.

22 The underlying strategy of the thief knot is utilized to this day in modern cryptographic techniques.

23 Jarman, above note 21 at 32; Philpott, above note 21 at 158.

24 Jarman, *ibid.* at 40; Philpott, *ibid.* at 160.

25 This is because the thief knot unties itself if the lines are pulled when the same action would seize a reef knot.

26 The Keyless Lock Store, "Ancient Roman Key Gallery and a Brief History Lesson" (2010), www.nokey.com/ankeymus.html [Keyless Lock Store].

27 "Schlage's History of Locks!" Dafor OY, www.locks.ru/germ/informat/schlagehistory.htm [Schlage].

several holes in its upper surface. The holes were filled with wooden pegs that prevented the bolt from being opened.[28] The design enjoyed significant longevity and is in fact the forerunner to modern pin tumbler locking systems used today.[29]

The remainder of the lengthy but extremely interesting history of locks — from pin tumblers to warded locks to levers and double-acting levers to tubular locks to digital encryption[30] — can for present purposes be understood as a series of innovations spurred to some degree by the monetary incentives of the patent system but, for the most part, by the ever-escalating arms race between lock-makers and lock-breakers.[31] It is probably fair to say that, throughout the centuries, there are really only two basic means of securing mechanical locks. The first is "by means of fixed obstructions to prevent wrong keys from entering or turning in the locks. The other, which is superior, employs one or more movable detainers, which must be arranged in pre-selected positions by the key before the bolt will move."[32]

There is an old Irish proverb that says, "A lock is better than suspicion."[33] Locks offer an ability to exclude others. They seek to prevent others from exercising control over us, and our possessions. As the proverb suggests, locks are a reassuring alternative to the insecurity we can feel when our possessions remain vulnerable to the incursions of others. For this reason,

---

28 *Ibid.*

29 Lock and Key — History, (2010), http://science.jrank.org/pages/3989/Lock-Key-History.html.

30 The following websites provide similar accounts of the timeline of the development of locks: Keyless Lock Store, above note 26; *Schlage*, above note 27; Brian Morland, "The History of Locks Museum" *History of Locks*, www.historyoflocks.com [Lock Timeline].

31 There is a growing competitive movement called "locksport" that involves learning the theory of locks, analyzing the devices and figuring out ways to quickly defeat the systems without destroying them. These lockpickers thrive on the intellectual thrill of beating all sorts of locks, but oppose attempts to use the skill for mischievous purposes. "Competitive Lockpicking Growing in US Popularity" *NPR* (28 July, 2010), www.npr.org/templates/story/story.php?storyId=128815821. To learn more about the history of lock picking, please refer generally to "Secrets of Lock Picking" by Steven Hampton, as a great example of providing accessible information to anyone who is looking to learn how to pick locks. Steven Hampton, *Secrets of Lockpicking* (Boulder: Paladin Press, 1987).

32 Access Lock, above note 20.

33 In Irish Gaelic, the expression is: "*Is fearr glas ná amhras.*" See Island Ireland, "Irish Proverbs with English Translations," http://islandireland.com/Pages/folk/sets/proverbs.html.

locks are historically and culturally understood to be a crucial and indispensable technological development in the protection of private property. Locks have a long and rich history of use in the attempt to prevent theft and destruction.[34] Not surprisingly, the popular understanding of the proper function of a lock is exclusion. Locks keep intruders out. Locks protect private property. Locks prevent wrongdoing.

Then again, there is an even older Yiddish expression that, "A lock is good only for an honest man."[35] In other words, a thief looks at a lock as an inconvenience but not necessarily as a form of prevention. A lock is unlikely to dissuade an unwavering lock-picker who has significant resources, skill, knowledge and time.[36] Especially if s/he believes that there is a legal right to defeat the lock. Locks have *never* been perfect technologies of exclusion. All locks can be defeated. Today, the Internet operates as a force multiplier in this respect by making it easy to share the means of defeating locks *en masse*.[37] Even though there are many custom-made locks, safes and security systems that are in fact quite difficult to defeat, considerations of efficiency, cost and convenience usually undermine the security that locks are meant to provide. As one expert in the field recently put it:

> there is a basic conflict between security and convenience in the lock field. For example, the use of high-security locks has been resisted by American car-makers because of the difficulties drivers would encounter in finding rare blanks and the machines to cut the keys. Most people talk security, but they really want convenience.[38]

Consequently, it is fair to say that our everyday use of mass market locks is part of a broader "security theatre"—the adoption of *apparent* security

---

34 Lock Timeline, above note 30.

35 See Kehillat Israel Reconstructionist Synagogue, "Yiddish Sayings, Proverbs, Phrases, Aphorisms, Curses, and Insults," http://kehillatisrael.net/docs/yiddish/yiddish_pr.htm.

36 Although, even a standard lock can hamper a lesser intruder, and the disturbance generated in circumventing a decent lock (e.g., breaking windows) will deter many would-be thieves, shifting their attacks to weaker targets.

37 One could spend days browsing tens of thousands of techniques on websites ranging from answer.com to YouTube. See, e.g., "Lock Pick Guide, How to Pick a Lock," www.lockpickguide.com; Lock Picking 101, "Lockpicking, Locksmithing, Locksport, Locks and Picks," /www.lockpicking101.com; Howcast, "How to Pick Any Padlock or Combination Lock," www.youtube.com/watch?v=rRcBNJMoFIw.

38 Quote attributed to Richard Berry, product development manager for Sargent Manufacturing Co. in New Haven, Conn. Quoted in Steven Ashley, "Under lock and key," (1993) 115 Mechanical Engineering 62 at 67.

measures in order to provide *the feeling* of improved security while doing considerably less than might be supposed to improve actual security.[39] In this sense, historical and present day use of standard locks can to some extent be understood as a kind of convention or ritual, a leap of faith in which we place unfounded trust in the mysterious mechanism of lock and key. Whether the lock is mechanical or conceptual, digital or analog, "we religiously follow this ritual, often many times each day, [though] few are fully aware of what mechanical forces have been activated, but we have fulfilled a very fundamental psychological need."[40] "Locking-up" allows us to go out into the world and carry out our daily routines with the *belief* that our homes and possessions are safe. In this respect, we are not unlike the ancients, who believed the iron used to make locks was *apotropeic*—counteracting the forces of evil and all malevolent spirits that tried to enter people's homes, churches, and storage areas through keyholes and other openings.[41]

The ritualistic aspect of "locking-up" is illustrated by a 700-year-old ceremony that still takes place every single night[42] in England at the Tower of London:

> Every night, at exactly seven minutes to 10 o'clock, the Chief Yeoman Warder of the Tower emerges from the Byward Tower wearing

---

39 The term security theatre has been used to describe the implementation of security initiatives that are palliative in nature. Such procedures are designed to reassure users that measures have been taken for their protection, often in response to a crisis or tragedy. Bruce Schneier describes security theatre as "countermeasures [that] provide the feeling of security instead of the reality." His examples include placing unarmed guards in airports following the 9/11 terrorist attacks and introducing tamper resistant packaging following the random Tylenol poisonings of 1982. Air travelers were comforted by the presence of guards and consumers were set at ease by the addition of a thin seal. The fact that either measure could be easily overcome was irrelevant; as Schneier explains, "[m]ost people are comforted by action, whether good or bad." See Bruce Schneier, *Beyond Fear: Thinking Sensibly About Security in an Uncertain World* (New York: Copernicus Books, 2003) at 38–40.

40 Lock Timeline, above note 30.

41 "Protective Iron," History of Locks (22 January 2008), www.historicallocks.com/en/site/hl/Articles/Locks-and-keys-in-folklore/Protective-iron .

42 The single exception occurred during WWII during an air raid on London on 16 April 1941. After a number of incendiary bombs fell on the old Victorian guardroom just as the Chief Yeoman Warder came through the Bloody Tower archway, he stood up, dusted himself off and carried on. It is said that The Tower holds a letter from the Officer of the Guard apologizing to King George VI for the delay in the ceremony, along with a reply from the King which says that the Officer is not to be punished as the delay was due to enemy action. See Colonel E.H. Carkeet-James O.B.E., M.C., *His Majesty's Tower of London* (London: Staples Press Limited, 1950) at 48. See also "Ceremony of the Keys," www.trooping-the-colour.co.uk/keys/index.htm.

> his long red coat and Tudor bonnet. He carries in one hand a candle lantern and in the other hand the Queens Keys. With solemn tread he moves along Water Lane, to Traitor's Gate where his escort, provided by one of the duty regiments of Foot Guards, awaits him. He hands the lantern to an escorting soldier and the party moves to the outer gate. On the way, all guards and sentries salute the Queen's Keys. After locking the outer gate the Chief Yeoman Warder and escort retrace their steps. The great oak gates of the Middle and Byward Towers are locked in turn. They now return along Water lane towards Traitor's Gate where, in the shadows of the Bloody Tower archway, a sentry awaits.
>
> "Halt, who comes there?" the sentry barks.
>
> "The Keys!" answers the Chief Yeoman Warder.
>
> "Whose Keys?"
>
> "Queen Elizabeth's Keys"
>
> "Pass Queen Elizabeth's Keys" replies the sentry, "and all's well"
>
> The party then proceeds through the Bloody Tower archway and up towards the broadwalk steps where the main guard is drawn up. The Chief Yeoman Warder and escort halt at the foot of the steps and the officer in charge gives the command to the Guard and Escort to present arms. The Chief Yeoman Warder moves two paces forward, raises his Tudor bonnet high in the air and calls "God preserve Queen Elizabeth." The guard answers "Amen" exactly as the clock chimes ten and 'The Duty Drummer' sounds The Last Post on his bugle. The Chief Yeoman Warder takes the keys to the Queen's House and the guard is dismissed.[43]

Although there are several accounts of the origin of the key ceremony, the one offered on tours at the Tower of London explains that it was initiated by Richard II in response to mob violence during the Peasant Revolt of 1381, reminding us of the kind of devastation that can take place when our homes (and castles) are not adequately locked.[44] Indirectly, it also reminds us of the power afforded to the key-holder. Indeed, lock technolo-

---

43 *His Majesty's Tower of London*, *ibid.* at 48.

44 While several competing origin stories can be found on the Internet, anecdotal experience suggests that this is the origin story favoured by the Yeoman Guards at the Tower of London. See Marilynn Doore, "The Ceremony of the Keys at the Tower" *Suite 101* (28 December 2009), www.suite101.com/content/the-ceremony-of-the-keys-at-the-tower-a156218.

gies are not properly or adequately understood without simultaneously examining the role and significance of keys.

Technically speaking, a key is a piece of metal mechanically fashioned through the shape of its bit to match the pins, wards or levers in the locking apparatus. However, throughout history, keys have been regarded as much more than just a mechanism. Ancient Greek and Roman keys — like well-crafted statues or carvings — were elegant and artistic.[45] Often ornate and cast in bronze, keys were status symbols indicating that their possessor had property worth protecting.[46] In ancient times, the number of keys a person owned was a measure of his importance as the head of a household.[47] Keys were large and cumbersome and slaves were often needed to carry them all. Having several key bearers indicated a person of great wealth and distinction.[48]

Of course, the symbolism of keys transcends wealth and stature. Conceptually, it is crucial to remember that keys not only lock — they unlock. Keys are therefore a "symbol of all forces that open and close, bind and release."[49] From this perspective it is wrongheaded to understand lock technologies merely as instruments of private property. The power of the key includes the power to exclude. But, surely, it is much more than that. *Keys give us the power to open or close, to turn on or turn off, to grant or deny, to allow or forbid.*

These broader social powers are represented across various cultural domains. For example, several classical paintings portray Christ handing Peter the keys to the kingdom of heaven.[50] Catholic teachings have inter-

---

45 World cultures have afforded considerable clout to locks and keys throughout the ages. For example, in China, miniature padlocks were traditionally given to newborn babies as a talisman. Animal-shaped padlocks would be used to convey messages. A fish padlock is always on guard, since fish sleep with their eyes open; an elephant padlock connotes strength. Ceremonial padlocks were also placed around the waists of expectant mothers, with a knotted cord being placed around a pregnant woman, which would remain until another ceremony in the ninth month. See "Ancient Style Padlocks," *History of Locks*, www.historyoflocks.com/padloo2.html#secret.

46 "History of Keys" Historical Locks (23 November 2007), www.historicallocks.com/en/site/hl/Articles/HistoryAboutLocks/History-of-keys.

47 *Schlage*, above note 27. Gender specific language is, unfortunately, intentional.

48 *Ibid.*

49 "Definition of keys," *Historical Locks*, (12 January 2008), www.historicallocks.com/en/site/hl/AboutHistoricalLocks/Definition-of-keys/.

50 This often-used illustration comes from bible verse Matthew 16:18–20: "I tell you that you are Peter, and on this rock I will build my church, and the gates of Hell will not overcome it. I will give you the keys of the kingdom of heaven; whatever

preted this to mean not that St. Peter would act as gatekeeper of heaven, but instead as his clout over the church on Earth. Indeed, the succession of the papacy has been referred to as the "passing of the keys,"[51] as the ruling Pope assumes Peter's authority to serve as interpreter of the word of God, for "whatever Peter 'binds' as a legal obligation on Earth is bound in heaven; whatever he looses in loosed in heaven."[52] The "power of the keys," in this context, has been interpreted to include the very real and highly political power to admit or exclude from church membership, to set church policy and teachings, to render binding interpretations of sacred scripture, and to bind and loose sins.[53]

Heavenly destinations aside, keys to the gates of a city also carried significant symbolic power through until at least the 18th century.[54] By keeping unwanted strangers out, the keys to the city represented its inhabitants' right to security and self-determination.[55] The surrender of a city to an attacking army was historically symbolized by turning over

---

you bind on earth will be bound in heaven, and whatever you loose on earth will be loosed in heaven." Famous depictions include the fresco "Christ Giving the Keys to St. Peter" in the Sistine Chapel by Pietro Perugino and "The Delivery of the Keys to St. Peter" by Bernardo Strozzi. See Peter Perugino, "Frescoes on the side walls of the Sistine Chapel" *Web Gallery of Art*, www.wga.hu/frames-e.html?/html/p/perugino/sistina/index.html; "European: 1600–1800" *Chazen Museum of Art* (2005), http://chazen.wisc.edu/collection/paintings/euro_pt2.htm#.

51 See generally Francis A. Burkle-Young, *Passing the Keys: Modern Cardinals, Conclaves, and the Election of the Next Pope* (Oxford: Madison Books, 1999).

52 Richard P. McBrien, *The HarperCollins Encyclopedia of Catholicism*, (New York: HarperCollins Publishers Inc., 1995) *s.v.* "keys, power of the" at 735.

53 *New Catholic Encyclopedia*, Vol. 8, (Washington: The Catholic University of America, 1967) *s.v.* "Keys, Power Of" at 172.

54 Indeed "key to the city" ceremonies take place to this day as a way of honouring individuals for significant accomplishments. For example, Harry Winkler, better known to television audiences as Arthur "The Fonz" Fonzarelli of television's hit 70s TV show *Happy Days* currently holds the keys to the cities of Dallas, New Orleans, and Winnipeg. According to news reports, Winkler grew up with undiagnosed dyslexia and has since gained recognition as a children's author, a source of inspiration for those with learning disabilities. Winnipeg mayor Sam Katz admits that bestowing this honour upon Winkler was spurred by most young men in the 1970s who wanted to wake up to be as cool as "The Fonz." See "Fonzie gets key to the city" *CBC News Canada* (26 March 2010), www.cbc.ca/canada/manitoba/story/2010/03/26/mb-winkler-fonz-key-winnipeg.html. See also "Actor who played The Fonz on "Happy Days" receives key to Winnipeg city" *CTV Edmonton* (29 March 2010) http://edmonton.ctv.ca/servlet/an/local/CTVNews/20100329/100329_happydays/20100329/?hub=CP24Entertainment.

55 "The Keys to the City" *Historical Locks* (22 January 2008), www.historicallocks.com/en/site/hl/Articles/Locks-and-keys-in-art/The-keys-to-the-city.

its keys to the conquerors. In one classic example, the Bayeux tapestry portrays the Duke Conan ensnared within the tower of the city and despairingly handing over the keys to the castle of Dinan to William the Conqueror.[56] Similarly, the Spanish painter Velázquez's famous portrait of "The Surrender of Breda (1625)" celebrates the Dutch governor of Breda meekly handing over the key to the city to Spanish general Ambrosio de Spinola.[57] Ironically, Spanish culture did not always have a great deal of trust in locks and keys. At a later point in its history, householders would hire a watchman to invigilate their neighbourhood, who would carry at once the keys to all of the dwellings in that neighbourhood. To enter or leave a house, residents would clap to summon the watchman, such that all comings and goings became a matter of public record.[58] In this context, locks enabled personal privacy, while control of the keys by a trusted third party offered accountability.[59]

While this last example suggests that in the broader security context lock and key are flipsides of the same coin, most historical and technological accounts tend to focus on the lock alone. This is potentially problematic when the ultimate goal is to develop law and policies about locks. The narrower focus on locks creates a misperception in most lay people — *including those responsible for drafting the so-called "digital lock" provisions in Canada's copyright reform bill (*Bill C-32*)* — who come to think of locks, narrowly, as mere instruments of exclusion used to protect private property.

While locks can and do perform this function, our brief consideration of the significance of keys suggests a richer understanding of the nature and function of locking technologies. This more robust understanding of locking mechanisms recognizes symbolic and actual power stemming not from the fact that these mechanisms can be locked but, rather, that they

---

56 On plate 26 of the tapestry, the defenders of the castle of Dinan are pictured resisting the invading Norman troops, while the Normans set fire to the castle. Then Conan surrenders, and transfers they keys of the castle from his lance to William's. See Sir Frank Stenton, ed., *The Bayeux Tapestry: A Comprehensive Survey* (London: Phaidon Press, 1957).

57 Pedro Marrades, *Velázquez Y Su Siglo* (Madrid: Espasa-Calpe, S.A., 1953) at 347. See also Robert Harvard, *The Spanish Eye Painters and Poets of Spain* (Woodbridge: Tamesis, 2007) at 33.

58 *Schlage*, above note 27.

59 Not much has changed in the digital realm, where trusted third parties are used in public key infrastructures (PKI) to authenticate transactions through the creation, management, distribution, use, storage, and revocation of digital certificates. See Carlisle Adams & Steve Lloyd, *Understanding PKI: Concepts, Standards, and Deployment Considerations*, 2d ed. (Boston: Pearson Education, Inc., 2003).

can be unlocked. The fact that locks are *made* to be unlocked suggests that, unlike other security barriers, the essence of their design is not simple or systematic exclusion, but something else. From the perspective of the intended key-holder, locks provide an access-control device that is premised on the notion of appropriate or authorized permission.

Although this point is not commonly acknowledged in typical discussions of locks, it is certainly well known by those working in the security field. Here is how security expert, Bruce Schneier, articulates this point in his leading text, *Beyond Fear*:

> The problem with securing assets and their functionality is that, by definition, you don't want to protect them from everybody. It makes no sense to protect assets from their owner, or from other authorized individuals (including the trusted personnel who maintain the security system). In effect, then, all security systems need to allow people in, even as they keep people out. Designing a security system that accurately identifies, authenticates, and authorizes trusted individuals is highly complex and filled with nuance, but critical to security.
>
> It's not sufficient to protect a valuable asset by encasing it in stone or steel, or by sending it to outer space, or by posting armed guards around it. With a very few exceptions, all security barriers need to be penetrated — under authorized circumstances by trusted people. The barrier needs a system that facilitates penetration, and additional systems to determine who is trusted. Buildings and safes have doors and keys or combinations so authorized people can open them. A casino slot machine has a locked door that lets maintenance personnel repair and refill the machine; it also has an opening through which players can collect their winnings — another avenue of penetration, for the user who has been temporarily "authorized" by a winning spin.
>
> The additional security requirements needed to make a barrier conditionally penetrable necessitate an enormous effort of planning, design, and execution: What was once a simple system becomes a complex one. A barrier is designed to keep attackers out; but since we need to allow people in, we must make a barrier that can be penetrated in authorized circumstances and can't be penetrated under any other circumstances. We need to punch a hole in the barrier and then control access to that hole. Our intentionally created holes — windows and doors, for example — are far and away the most frequent avenues for unauthorized entry. The holes we intentionally put in a

> barrier are very often the weakest link, since they make the security of the barrier depend on the security of the hole and its own systems: identifying the trusted people who are allowed in, the circumstances under which they are to be allowed in, and what privileges they are to have once inside. These ancillary systems of identification, authentication, and authorization are far more complex and subtle than they seem. Understanding the security of barriers means understanding the security of these systems.[60]

As Schneier's lengthy passages reveal, locks are as much technologies of permission as they are technologies of exclusion. The best locking systems not only prevent access to interlopers but also grant access to those who have or ought to have permission. This cannot easily be achieved with a typical mechanical lock since it is difficult to ensure that its key-holder always has permission.[61] This is where digital locks are thought to come into play. Whereas the point of a mechanical lock is to guarantee the key-holder automatic entry, the more sophisticated digital locks automate the actual permission with stunning precision. As will be discussed in the section that follows, digital locks can be used in conjunction with automated identification and authentication systems to ensure that the key-holder is, or ought to be, authorized to do whatever the lock would otherwise preclude. But, as we shall also see, digital locks can do much more than that.

C. DIGITAL LOCKS

Not surprisingly, the invention of digital locks coincided with the advent of digital property. Digital locks are Gordian knots for content owners, a digital antidote to Stewart Brand's famous revelation that "information wants to be free":

> Information wants to be free. Information also wants to be expensive. Information wants to be free because it has become so cheap to distribute, copy, and recombine — too cheap to meter. It wants to be expensive because it can be immeasurably valuable to the recipient. That tension will not go away. It leads to endless wrenching debate about price, copyright, "intellectual property," the moral rightness

60 Schneier, above note 39 at 181.

61 Since keys can be taken by force, forged, found or can be shared without permission.

> of casual distribution, because each round of new devices makes the tension worse, not better.[62]

Digital locks are the newest round of devices, and the tension Brand refers to is not only the escalating technological arms race between digital lock-maker and lock-breaker but also the legal clash between those who would seek further protection of digital locks through legislation and those concerned about the broader social consequences of doing so. Disentangling the technological from the legal is difficult and to some extent artificial, especially in light of the World Intellectual Property Organization's (WIPO) global imperative to provide legal protection to digital locks[63] and the new role that digital locks sometimes play in hybrid techno-legal systems discussed below, known as DRM. Because many others[64] and I[65] have

---

62 Stewart Brand, *The Media Lab: Inventing the Future at MIT* (New York: Viking Penguin Inc., 1987) at 202.

63 Both of the 1996 World Intellectual Property Organization (WIPO) treaties, and the forthcoming Anti-Counterfeiting Trade Agreement (ACTA), include provisions that enhance digital locks through guaranteeing legal protections. In particular, conforming to the requirements of the WIPO treaties is often cited as rationale for increasing domestic protection for technological protection measures. The relevant provisions are Article 11 in the *WIPO Copyright Treaty* and Article 18 in the *WIPO Performances and Phonograms Treaty*. See *WIPO Copyright Treaty*, 20 December 1996, (1997) 36 I.L.M. 65 (entered into force 6 March 2002), www.wipo.int/treaties/en/ip/wct/trtdocs_wo033.html, art. 11 [*WCT*]; Article 18, *WIPO Performances and Phonograms Treaty*, 20 December 1996, (1997) 36 I.L.M. 76, (entered into force 20 May 2002), www.wipo.int/treaties/en/ip/wppt/trtdocs_wo034.html, art. 18 [*WPPT*].

64 Above note 12 and accompanying text.

65 Ian Kerr, "If Left To Their Own Devices: How DRM and Anti-circumvention Laws Can Be Used to Hack Privacy" in Michael Geist, ed., *In The Public Interest: The Future of Canadian Copyright Law* (Toronto: Irwin Law, 2005) 167 www.irwinlaw.com/store/product/120/in-the-public-interest--the-future-of-canadian-copyright-law [*If Left To Their Own Devices*]; Ian Kerr & Jane Bailey, "The Implications of Digital Rights Management for Privacy and Freedom of Expression" (2004) 2:1 Information, Communication & Ethics in Society 87; Ian Kerr, Alana Maurushat, & Chris Tacit, "Technical Protection Measures: Tilting at Copyright's Windmill" (2002) 34:7 Ottawa L. Rev. 13; Ian Kerr, Alana Maurushat, & Chris Tacit, "Technological Protection Measures: Part I — Trends in Technical Protection Measures and Circumvention Technologies" (2004) Department of Canadian Heritage, Copyright Policy Branch, http://ssrn.com/abstract=705003 [*Heritage Report Part I*]; Ian Kerr, Alana Maurushat, & Chris Tacit, "Technical Protection Measures: Part II — The Legal Protection of TPMs" (2004) Department of Canadian Heritage, Copyright Policy Branch, http://ssrn.com/abstract=705081 [*Heritage Report Part II*]; Ian Kerr, "To OBSERVE AND PROTECT? How Digital Rights Management Systems Threaten Privacy and What Policy Makers Should Do About It" in Peter Yu, ed., *Intellectual Property and Information Wealth: Copyright and Related Rights*, vol. 1 (Westport: Praeger Publishers, 2007).

already written extensively on these broader subjects, my aim in this section[66] is limited to a brief description of digital locks and DRM, with a particular focus on their role in what I call "the automation of permissions."

Although digital lock technologies offer an imponderable number of powerful applications across various domains,[67] their early and current use has been driven primarily by the copyright industries. In the copyright context, digital locks are often encoded within software, films, music, books, games and other digital media. The "digital lock" metaphor is colloquial and provocative no matter what side of the "copyfight" fence you sit on. Not long after this and other phrases entered the public lexicon, WIPO and other like-minded stakeholders sought a more neutral linguistic terrain. Through their efforts[68] the term "technological protection measure"[69] or, TPM, has been adopted as the global signifier for the technique of locking-up a digital work.

In its simplest form, a TPM is a technical method employed to control access to work subject to copyright, or to control its subsequent use.[70] While at first blush this might seem similar in effect to the proverbial lock on the cupboard, TPMs enable an incredibly nuanced level of access control as well as a fine-grained ability to monitor and manage the way that

66 Portions of this section are adapted from my own previous writing on the subject, including my co-authored studies for the Department of Canadian Heritage: Ian Kerr, Alana Maurushat, & Chris Tacit, "Technological Protection Measures: Part I — Trends in Technical Protection Measures and Circumvention Technologies" (2004) Department of Canadian Heritage, Copyright Policy Branch, http://ssrn.com/abstract=705003; Ian Kerr, Alana Maurushat, & Chris Tacit, "Technical Protection Measures: Part II — The Legal Protection of TPMs" (2004) Department of Canadian Heritage, Copyright Policy Branch, http://ssrn.com/abstract=705081; and a book chapter written for Michael Geist's previous study of copyright reform in Canada: Ian Kerr, "If Left To Their Own Devices: How DRM and Anti-circumvention Laws Can Be Used to Hack Privacy" in Michael Geist, ed., *In The Public Interest: The Future of Canadian Copyright Law* (Toronto: Irwin Law, 2005) 167, www.irwinlaw.com/content/assets/content-commons/120/Two_03_Kerr.pdf .

67 I shall provide some stark examples in the following sections.

68 *WCT* above note 60; *WPPT* above note 60.

69 They are sometimes also referred to as "technical protection measures."

70 This includes: copying, distribution, performance, and display. See Perry, above note 12. Canada's recently proposed Bill C-32 defines a TPM as "any effective technology, device or component that, in the ordinary course of its operation, (a) controls access to a work, to a performer's performance fixed in a sound recording or to a sound recording and whose use is authorized by the copyright owner; or (b) restricts the doing — with respect to a work, to a performer's performance fixed in a sound recording or to a sound recording — of any act referred to in section 3, 15 or 18 and any act for which remuneration is payable under section 19." See Bill C-32, above note 10.

digital property is used. For example, techniques have been developed in the field of cryptography to link encrypted files to devices or players comprised of hardware or software so that an encrypted message can only be decrypted using that particular device or player.[71] This is what allows companies like Apple to control the kinds of applications that can operate on their devices[72] and, to some extent, the kind of content.[73] It also allows digital content to be tethered to a particular device or player for a particular period of time.

Perhaps the best current example of this is the e-book, the increasingly widespread use of which has constituted a so-called "revolution."[74] More and more, consumers are attracted to this modern spin on an age-old pastime. There is something compelling in the advertising campaign for the

---

71 C. Risher, "Technological protection measures (anti-circumvention devices) and their relation to exceptions to copyright in the Electronic environment" (paper presented to the IPA Copyright Forum Frankfurt Book Fair, 20 October 2000) [unpublished].

72 Despite its business model of allowing developers to design and customize applications for the iPhone, Apple retains the ability to remove an application. Jonathan Zittrain has described this practice as "tethering," raising concerns about external control and autonomy. See Jonathan Zittrain, "The iPhone Kill Switch" *The Future of the Internet and How to Stop It*, (14 August 2008), http://futureoftheinternet.org/the-iphone-kill-switch; see also Brad Stone, "Amazon Faces a Fight Over Its E-Books" *The New York Times Online* (26 July 2009), www.nytimes.com/2009/07/27/technology/companies/27amazon.html.

73 For example, Apple CEO Steve Jobs has decreed that Apple products such as the iPad and iPhone will not run Flash-based applications. The official rationale for this decree includes concerns about reliability, prolonging battery life on mobile devices, and most importantly, reliance on cross-platform development tools hindering the creation of Apple-specific products. Another reason for this decision, revealed in an email debate with Gawker.com writer Ryan Tate, is that eliminating Flash offers users "freedom from porn," since most web-based pornographic videos use the Flash platform. For Apple's official stance on Adobe Flash, see Steve Jobs, "Thoughts on Flash" *Apple.com* (April 2010), www.apple.com/hotnews/thoughts-on-flash/. For the origin of the phrase "freedom from porn," see Ryan Tate, "Steve Jobs Offers World Freedom From Porn" *ValleyWag* (15 May 2010), http://gawker.com/5539717/steve-jobs-offers-world-freedom-from-porn.

74 For use of the phrase "eBook revolution," see Mike Elgan, "Here comes the e-book revolution" *Computerworld* (7 February 2009), www.computerworld.com/s/article/9127538/Elgan_Here_comes_the_e_book_revolution. See also John Anderson, "The Ebook Revolution is Irreversible: Digitization is Replacing Physical Publishing" *Suite 101* (24 February 2010), http://bookpublishing.suite101.com/article.cfm/the-ebook-revolution-is-irreversible.

Kindle: "Think of a book and start reading it in 60 seconds."[75] It doesn't hurt that you can also carry around 3,500 e-books all at once. Despite Steve Jobs' (since repressed) assertion that no one reads anymore,[76] e-books have become the format of choice for many and are stretching the boundaries of the written word. Convenience, economic incentives, aggressive online marketing campaigns, and environmental concerns tied to saving paper have all been given as reasons to embrace e-books.[77] Younger consumers who have grown up in the digital age and may have felt disenfranchised by old-fashioned books are embracing this new medium with fervor. And the revolution is not only in form but also in substance. E-books have the potential to change not only the way consumers view their books, but also the content of the books themselves. As electronic formats are adopted, it is likely that books will be adapted to better suit these new formats: shorter, timelier, more culturally relevant.[78] For example, in Japan and South Korea, where cell phone use is ubiquitous, so is the cell phone novella.[79]

With an increasing consumption of literary and artistic works in a digitized form comes the spectre of external control through TPMs. Here, Jonathan Zittrain's description of Apple's products as "tethered appliances" rings true.[80] As we shall see, this raises questions about what it means to say that a consumer has 'purchased' a book, a song or a movie.

Consider the evolving business model for renting movies. Under the older system of going to a store to rent plastic discs, though it would be inconvenient for the average customer to make illegal copies of those disks, the customer was at liberty to play the movie wherever[81] and as often and

---

75 Jeff Bezos, "Amazon Debuts a 3G Kindle, and That's Only Half of Jeff's News," *[e-reads]*, (29 July 2010) http://ereads.com/2010/07/amazon-debuts-gen-3-kindle-and-thats-only-half-of-jeffs-news.html.

76 Well, he said it! This was his first response to the launch of Amazon's Kindle (his second response being the e-book app for his iPad). See John Markoff, "The Passion of Steve Jobs" *The New York Times* (15 January 2008), http://bits.blogs.nytimes.com/2008/01/15/the-passion-of-steve-jobs/; see also Michael Wolf, "iPad Fueling Enhanced E-Book Revolution" *Gigaom* (21 July 2010), http://gigaom.com/2010/07/21/ipad-fueling-enhanced-e-book-revolution/.

77 Mike Elgan, "Here comes the e-book revolution" *Computerworld* (7 February 2009), www.computerworld.com/s/article/9127538/Elgan_Here_comes_the_e_book_revolution.

78 *Ibid.*

79 *Ibid.* See also William Patry, *Moral Panics and the Copyright Wars* (New York: Oxford University Press, 2009) at 195.

80 Zittrain, above note 72.

81 Subject to regional coding. See e.g., "DVD Regions," www.amazon.co.uk/gp/help/customer/display.html?nodeId=502554. See also "DVD Regions" *Home Theatre Info*, www.hometheaterinfo.com/dvd3.htm.

for as long as she or he wishes, subject to late penalties at the store. Customers not only had the freedom to consume the product however they wished during the rental period but also to share it with others. Using TPMs such as the encryption techniques described above, the movie rental, now downloaded from an online v-tailer, can be limited to the machine used for downloading and can also be programmed to be deleted from that machine at a specified time or, in some cases, at the content owner's whim. Unlike the simple binary (open/close) nature of the analog lock on the neighbourhood video store's door, the level of control afforded by the digital lock puts the content owner/provider, rather than the customer, in the driver's seat. Continuing with the above example, if you did not have a chance to watch the movie you rented before its preset expiry date, or if you wished to keep it a day longer to show it to your roommate the next night,[82] you no longer have the option of simply keeping it and paying late fees. The movie is automatically disabled (or deleted) and can no longer be viewed by your player.

What this example reveals is that TPMs are in fact much more than a lock in digital clothing. The metaphor of the lock is not nearly strong enough to convey the full power of TPMs. This is one of the reasons why proposals to give digital locks further legal protection is so controversial. TPMs already afford copyright owners protection beyond that which would have been guaranteed by copyright law alone. As Professor Carys Craig has recently described it:

> Activities such as reading, listening, and viewing have always been perfectly lawful — and of course desirable from a cultural policy perspective — in the analogue world. *Nothing in the law of copyright would prohibit* someone from flipping through a magazine in a doctor's office, borrowing a novel from a friend, listening to a roommate's music collection, or watching a movie on a home video machine.[83]

---

82 But not until she finished her work slavishly formatting footnotes for her professor! I am grateful to Katie Szilagyi and Shea Loewen for sharing their painful experience of this with me, even though good fortune would have it that the movie in question didn't quite live up to the book upon which it was based. (Alas, a different kind of copyright problem . . .)

83 Carys J. Craig, "Digital Locks and the Fate of Fair Dealing in Canada: In Pursuit of Prescriptive Parallelism" (2010) 13 J. World Intellectual Property 503 at 9 [emphasis added].

Professor Craig's point is important to any legitimate attempt at balanced copyright.[84] But what I like most about the above passage is that its subtle phrasing ("nothing in the law of copyright would prohibit. . .") hints at a far more significant point that has not been carefully articulated in the current literature on digital locks. For starters, TPMs — unlike copyright law — would prohibit, in a digital context, activities that we consider commonplace in the analog world, such as "flipping through a magazine in a doctor's office, borrowing a novel from a friend, listening to a roommate's music collection, or watching a movie on a home video machine."[85]

But, here is the crucial point: by prohibiting these things, TPMs have the ability to radically shift copyright's defaults by automating its system of permissions. Prior to the advent of TPMs, the default for intellectual consumption might have been explained to lay persons through the heuristic of an old adage — "sometimes, it is better to beg for forgiveness than to ask for permission." While obviously hyperbolic and totally inaccurate as an actual statement of the law of intellectual property, in terms of copyright's underlying intellectual consumption defaults, the adage does illustrate the fact that citizens, as consumers, are generally at liberty to consume intellectual products as they think is fair, except to the extent that a content owner subsequently asserts that such consumption is in breach of its copyrights. Citizens are not generally required[86] to ask content owners or anyone else for *prior permission* every time that they wish to gain access to, read, share or otherwise use someone else's intellectual work (especially those that they have already purchased). This kind of copyright clearance *en masse* would not only fly in the face of fair-

---

84 As she goes on to say at page 13: "This is the challenge that now presents itself to policy-makers and the Canadian copyright system: how can copyright's delicate balancing act continue to be performed in any meaningful way when the technological environment is increasingly one of absolutes — absolute freedom versus absolute control." *Ibid.*

85 *Ibid.*

86 Although the above is still generally true, there is an expanding resistance by content owners aimed at thwarting a creative process known as "remixing" (the attempt to integrate, change, improve upon or in some other way remake a work that is subject to copyright). According to Professor Lessig, the response by copyright industries seeks to promote what he calls a *permission culture*: "The opposite of a free culture is a "permission culture" — a culture in which creators get to create only with the permission of the powerful, or of creators from the past." Lessig, above at note 11 at xiv. Digital locks, he thinks, help to ensure that "we are less and less a free culture, more and more a permission culture." Lessig, above at note 11 at 8; See also, Lawrence Lessig, *Remix: Making Art and Commerce Thrive In The Hybrid Economy* (New York: The Penguin Press, 2008).

dealing principles and other user rights, it would cripple most systems of distribution currently in place. That said, in cases where people exceed their rights as users and forgiveness is *not* forthcoming, content owners obviously have the right to seek remedies for copyright infringement by way of legal action.

The digital lock strategy effectively seeks to reverse these intellectual consumption defaults through its automation of permissions. In the case of digital locks it is no longer better to ask for forgiveness (or pay the penalty) since there is no longer anything to forgive or to be penalized for. Returning once again to the movie rental example from above, deliberation over a decision (not) to keep the movie for an extra day is no longer an option. With digital locks, your ability to wait until later to watch the movie that you already rented and paid for is only available by *prior permission.*

Recall, now, my argument in the previous section — that locks are as much technologies of permission as they are technologies of exclusion. Shown in their very best light, TPMs can be used to ensure appropriate or authorized permission. However, as the above examples (and others that will follow) suggest, TPMs can go well beyond appropriate or authorized permission. In fact, TPMs can be employed in even more sophisticated DRMs to automate *all* permissions, shutting down any and every possible course of action except for those pre-selected by the party employing the digital lock. While TPMs might be thought of as the building blocks used to restrict access or use, DRMs are designed to manage an entire array of related activities by using various automation and surveillance technologies to identify digital property and those seeking to use it, in order to technologically enforce certain licensing conditions. In so doing, DRM can be used to automate permission systematically.

In the copyright context, these systems can be used to track royalties or run accounting systems that monitor usage and payment. They enable business models that go beyond sales and subscriptions, including licensing arrangements with variable terms and conditions. But the DRM strategy extends well beyond copyright. More generally, DRM can refer to any "technology systems facilitating the trusted and dynamic management of rights in any kind of digital information, throughout its life cycle, irrespective of how and where the digital information is distributed."[87]

---

87 Nic Garnett, "Outline of Presentation of Nic Garnett, representing InterTrust Technologies" (paper presented to the ALAI Congress 2001, June 2001) [unpublished], www.alai-usa.org/2001_conference/pres_garnett.doc at 1. This is a fairly broad definition of DRMs for, as the author notes, "the term DRM has now come to be applied

Typically, a DRM consists of two components. The first component is a set of technologies that could include encryption, authentication, access control, digital watermarking, tamper-resistant hardware and software, and risk management architectures. In the copyright context, such technologies are used to enforce corporate copyright policies and pricing schemes through a registration process that requires purchasers to hand over certain bits of personal information. The second component is a licensing arrangement. This set of legal permissions establishes the terms of use for the digital property by way of contract.[88]

If a TPM is a virtual fence, then a DRM is a virtual surveillance system. The technological components of most full-blown DRMs are linked to a database, which enables the automated collection and exchange of various kinds of information among rights owners and distributors, about the particular people who use their products. This includes users' identities, their habits, and their particular uses of the digital material subject to copyright. The information collected can be employed in a number of ways that go well beyond ensuring access and use that is authorized by copyright laws. As we have seen, DRM-enabled movie players can limit the ability to copy the digital work, restrict its transmission to other users, prevent or limit its transfer to machines other than the one on which it is registered to run, and even set limits on the number of times that the work can be accessed.[89] In the course of its normal operation, a DRM can even be used to track and record the various uses of works. Consequently, and perhaps most importantly, DRM can be used not only to enforce the rights accorded to content owners pursuant to copyright statutes but can also be used to set entirely new ground rules, giving even more rights to property owners in accordance with the rules that they have set for themselves in the terms and conditions of the licensing arrangement accompanying the DRM, usually on a take-it-or-leave-it basis.[90]

---

to a variety of different technologies, most of which relate to the control of access to information or to its copying."

88 Gervais, above note 12. Hugenholtz has defined a DRM similarly as a contract, typically a licensing agreement, coupled with technology, typically a technological protection measure such as encryption. See Hugenholtz, above note 12.

89 For a complete overview of the attributes of DRMs, see Gervais, above note 12.

90 Jeffrey P. Cunard, "Technological Protection of Copyrighted Works and Copyrighted Management Systems: A Brief Survey of the Landscape" (paper presented to the ALAI Congress, June 2001) [unpublished], www.alai-usa.org/2001_conference/pres_cunard.doc at 2.

The ability to change the ground rules in this way affords tremendous power to those in a position to employ DRM. Purchasers of Amazon's e-book reader, the Kindle, experienced this power first hand in the summer of 2009 after many law-abiding readers who had legally purchased from Amazon copies of George Orwell's *1984* and *Animal Farm* had those titles auto-deleted from their devices without their consent. According to news reports, Amazon mistook a "no" for a "yes" regarding a publisher's decision to extend its permission to publish Orwell's works in e-book format. Fearing serious sanction from the copyright owners after already having sold many e-copies, Amazon capitulated. Using the power of DRM to change the ground rules, Amazon was able to enter the private digital libraries of their many Kindle customers, to scan all of the titles on each and every active Kindle, and electronically seize the two Orwell books from all those who possessed them. Ironically, it was a classic Orwellian moment. Without a formal recall and without having to make a plea to customers to delete the book, with just a simple mouse click, "The Ministry of Truth" expunged the offending material without notice or permission, rectifying what it perceived as a mistaken past by replacing it with a perfected present.

Other than the irony of deleting Orwell's books without consent and contrary to the licensing agreement, Amazon's DRM is not unusual. As is true in most DRM-enabled distribution systems, the ongoing exchange of personal usage information between user-owned devices and content owner/provider servers takes place in an invisible "handshake" occurring in the software layer. This allows for the transmission of personal usage information from the devices that we own back to the content owner/provider — something Professor Graham Greenleaf cleverly and famously characterized as "IP phone home."[91] The surveillance features associated with the database are crucial to the technological enforcement of the licensing component of the DRM. It is through the collection and storage of personal usage information that DRMs are able to "authorize use" in accordance with the terms of the licensing agreement thereby "managing copyrights." In the Amazon case, "authorizing use" is presumably what allowed Amazon to mistakenly sell those e-books to its customers for profit. "Managing copyright," on the other hand, seemed to include the powers necessary to rectify that mistake, such as snooping customers' book-

91 Graham Greenleaf, "IP, Phone Home: The Uneasy Relationship between Copyright and Privacy, Illustrated in the Laws of Hong Kong and Australia" (2002) 32 Hong Kong Law Journal 35 http://papers.ssrn.com/sol3/papers.cfm? abstract_id=884329.

shelves and auto-deleting digital property that they legally purchased at the content owner's whim.[92]

Although debacles of this sort rightly tempt critics to focus on DRM's potential for egregious breaches of privacy, access to information, personal autonomy and so forth, my current aim is to demonstrate that there is something much more fundamental at stake. I say this not because the digital locks on DVDs or the Kindle are primitive prototypes of what is likely to come. I say it because these are rather insignificant one-off examples compared to the potential social consequences of a more generalized strategy that uses digital locks to automate permissions writ large. In the next section, I will try to paint a picture of the gradual evolution of a widespread digital lock strategy and what it might mean.

D. CARTING

My concern is not with one kind digital lock technology versus another. Nor is my goal to shock-and-awe by portraying some dystopic digital lockdown. My aim is more straightforward. Through a reflection of my own anecdotal experiences, I want to try to imagine what would happen if we were to generalize copyright's digital lock strategy across other property-based domains. What affect would this have on fundamental legal institutions? And, how might it affect us as moral actors?

In thinking our way through moral problems the great philosopher, Immanuel Kant, famously suggested that we adopt a "categorical imperative" so that we "act only in accordance with that maxim through which you can at the same time will that it become a universal law."[93] In our current context we ask: what would it mean to will a universal adoption of a state sanctioned, unimpeded use of digital locks across all property-based domains? To set the stage for answering this question, I have very purposely chosen a low-tech, fairly simple form of property — the cart. In tracking a mere snapshot if its evolution, the carting example is offered as a heuristic

92 During all of this, Jeff Bezos, CEO of Amazon, groveled to his consumer base, admitting that its actions were "stupid, thoughtless, and painfully out of line with our principles." He promised that Amazon would "use the scar tissue from this painful mistake to help make better decisions going forward." What he didn't promise was to remove the DRM or rewrite its licensing conditions so that the auto-delete functionality is no longer possible. See Ian Kerr, "Robot law is taking over," *The Ottawa Citizen* (15 September 2009) http://iankerr.ca/index.php?view=article&catid=1:latest&id=749:robot-law-is-taking-over&format=pdf.

93 Immanuel Kant, *Foundations of the Metaphysics of Morals*, trans. by Lewis White Beck (Indianapolis: The Bobbs-Merrill Company, Inc., 1969) at 44.

for envisioning a world wherein the digital lock strategy is adopted much more broadly and then pondering its potential social implications.

Recall that it was King Gordius' famous ox-cart that inspired his son Midas to tie the Gordian knot. Other than its significance in terms of the prophecy of the oracle of Telmissus, one imagines this cart to have been fairly typical, a vehicle with wheels designed to transport items too heavy to carry. As described previously, the king's ox-cart was moored to a post within the palace grounds, preventing anyone unwilling or unable to untie it from moving it very far. Although carts are not always as valuable as the things they are meant to transport, the historic desire to control their use carries forward to present day.

Toy wagons aside, my own experience with carts probably began in my early childhood during a family vacation to Disneyland in the 1970s. Not ironically, this theme park, built in the 1950s and located about 45 minutes from Hollywood, was a key feature of Walt Disney's intellectual property strategy. My favorite part of the Magic Kingdom was unquestionably Tomorrowland. To the best of my recollection, I liked Tomorrowland for pretty much the same reasons that Walt was once said to have liked it:

> Tomorrow can be a wonderful age. Our scientists today are opening the doors of the Space Age to achievements that will benefit our children and generations to come. The Tomorrowland attractions have been designed to give you an opportunity to participate in adventures that are a living blueprint of our future.[94]

Tomorowland was Walt Disney's utopia. My favorite of its many attractions was a go-cart ride cleverly named, "Autopia." Although it is difficult now to imagine, Autopia was initially constructed in 1955 during the early days of the developing freeway system in the United States. With little kids riding wee go-carts along miniature cloverleafs, overpasses and multilane straight-aways, Autopia was a hit from the beginning. It represented a time when the concept of free-flowing, limited-access highways remained an unrealized vision.[95] It was Walt's conception of the ideal high-

---

94 Kim Bellotto, Niki Mcneil & Katie Kubush, *In the Hands of a Child: Custom Designed Project Pack -- Disneyland* (Coloma, MI: Hands of a Child, 2007) at 13. See generally Gordon Morris Bakken, *Icons of the American West: From Cowgirls to Silicon Valley* (Santa Barbara: Greenwood Press, 2008).

95 Citizens were fascinated by the abiding dream of the consummate transportation system. At that time, in July 1955, the Santa Ana Freeway was new and legislation to finance the American interstate highway system was still months away from being signed by President Dwight Eisenhower. See Phil Patton, "In Disney's World, a Per-

way — one where the automobile as the icon of personal freedom now survives as a theme park diversion, defying, as one author put it, "the reality of the smog-generating traffic just outside the gates."[96] Autopia remains a testament to the enduring quality of this dream; it is the only ride in all of Disneyland that remains today from the original 1955 plan of the park.

But, to those little kids, Autopia was something else. It was an enormous and amazing ride that wide-eyed seven-year-olds were permitted to go on by themselves, unaccompanied by an adult. This was made possible by virtue of the fact that the go-carts were secured by a railing affixed to the roadway. Although the child could speed up or slow down a little bit, the cart would automatically steer itself along the seemingly endless highway, banking on corners and holding steady down the straight-aways. With the usual magic of Disney, the technological infrastructure that made this possible went completely unnoticed by the kids on the ride; they believed that they were actually driving! Through the illusion of technology, Walt had figured out how to build the literal instantiation of Thoreau's famous observation that, "we do not ride on the railroad; it rides upon us."[97]

I suggest that Disney's Autopia is a much richer conceptual model for understanding the risks posed by digital locks than copy-protected DVDs or e-book readers. Rendered invisible, Autopia's various technological constraints offer the appearance of freedom while in reality disabling the capacity to act through the design of the architecture.[98] Kids can assume the driver's seat, veering a little left or right of centre, but the hidden rail always guides them back into the middle. Unlike training wheels on a bicycle, Autopia's technological infrastructure does not train kids to learn how to drive. In fact it *un-trains* them. Although I had no idea of this as a seven year-old sitting behind the wheel, Autopia's carts are impossible to crash. What I realized, years later, is that Autopia has passengers, not drivers. On Walt Disney's highway, *mistakes are not permitted.*

---

fect Freeway" *The New York Times* (22 August 2005), www.nytimes.com/2005/08/22/automobiles/22CARS.html.

96 *Ibid.*

97 Henry David Thoreau, *The Annotated Walden: Walden; or, Life in the Woods, and Civil Disobedience*, ed. by Philip Van Doren Stern (New York: Clarkson N. Potter, 1970) at 223.

98 As Mark Weiser famously remarked upon coining the term 'ubiquitous computing in 1991': "The most profound technologies are those that disappear. They weave themselves into the fabric of everyday life until they are indistinguishable from it." Mark Weiser, "The Computer for the 21st Century," Scientific American 94, (September 1991) http://wiki.daimi.au.dk/pca/_files/weiser-orig.pdf.

Then again, neither is good driving. Autopia automates essential aspects of the driving experience so as to ensure desirable outcomes for the property owner. In other words, *no* driving is permitted. Just like copyright's digital locks, the answer to the machine is, once again, in the machine[99] — which means that it is the property owner who, once again, sits in the driver's seat. All permissions — whether the rider may go north or south, turn east or west — are pre-programmed by the owner of the machine, automated to ensure no possible wrongdoing.

Autopia can be understood as a metaphor for my concern about a generalized digital lock strategy and the automation of permissions. I am concerned about a widespread use of technological constraints — whether in private or public spaces, whether owned or operated by a corporation, a government or an individual — imposed on citizens by property owners who seek total command of their environments. I am concerned because those environments are also our environments. These spaces are crucial to our well-being. They are the playgrounds of our moral development. Yet, digital locks and related techniques allow property owners to eliminate the possibility for moral deliberation about certain kinds of action otherwise possible in these spaces by disabling the world in a way that morally disables the people who populate it.[100] Not by restricting their choices but by automating them — by creating world-altering contrivances that remove people from the realm of moral action altogether, thereby impairing their future moral development.

Consider a second carting example that I experienced some thirty years later. There I was, shopping for groceries at my local Loblaws store, part of Canada's largest food distributer.[101] The lot at the strip mall was rather busy that day, so I ended up parking further down, in front of another box store called Michael's Crafts.[102] While trundling a rather large haul

99 Charles Clark, "The Answer to the Machine is in the Machine" in P. Bernt Hugenholtz, ed., *The Future of Copyright in a Digital Environment* (The Hague: Kluwer Law International, 1996) 139. See also Andrew A. Adams & Ian Brown, "Keep Looking: The Answer to the Machine is Elsewhere" (2009) 19 Computers & L. 32; Niklas Lundblad, "Is the Answer to the Machine Really in the Machine?" *Proceedings of the IFIP Conference on Towards The Knowledge Society: E-Commerce, E-Business, E-Government* (Deventer, The Netherlands: Kluwer, B.V., 2002) 733, http://citeseerx.ist.psu.edu/viewdoc/download?doi=10.1.1.101.5735&rep=rep1&type=pdf.

100 As I argue below, a widespread digital lock strategy results in something I call "moral disability."

101 Loblaw Companies Limited, "ABOUT US: Company Profile" (2001), www.loblaw.com/en/abt_corprof.html.

102 Michaels (2010) www.michaels.com.

of groceries back to my car one winter's morning, my shopping cart came to a grunting halt. At first I thought it was caused by snow or a piece of ice stuck in the wheel. But when I investigated, I discovered the cart was *intentionally disabled*. One of its wheels contained a locking mechanism that had been triggered by an infrared sensor device detecting that my cart had crossed the store's property line.[103] In order to prevent shopping cart theft and to avoid paying employees to retrieve carts from the four corners of the vast suburban strip mall complex, Loblaws had installed digital locks on their carts to automate the permissions concerning their use. It turns out that my permission to use the Loblaws cart stopped precisely where the property line for Michael's Crafts began. Unfortunately for me, my car was parked a few hundred metres beyond that. There was no one from whom to seek further permission and no one to re-activate the cart. I had to leave the cart on the Loblaws' property, schlep whatever I could carry, and hope that no one stole the rest of the groceries before I could return for a second load.

While novel at the time, this is by now a wholly unremarkable event: something that happens thousands of times a day, everyday, at parking lots across Canada and the US. Except that, the day it happened to me was about one week after Hurricane Katrina rocked New Orleans. Alongside the usual depictions of devastation and ruin, I noticed significant media attention being paid to the imagery of shopping carts, thousands upon thousands of which littered the parking lot and the interior of the New Orleans Convention Center. This should not be surprising. Ever since 1937, when Sylvan Goldman first invented shopping cart technologies as a way to entice people to buy more than they could otherwise carry,[104] uses of the shopping cart have expanded beyond the archetypical shopping experience. Some uses are legal, others illegal. Some are tolerated, others less so. "They have been used as barbecue pits, go-carts, laundry trolleys and shelters. They wind up mostly in apartment complexes, low-income housing and bus stops. Or anywhere else where the person doing the grocery shopping is unlikely to own a car."[105] According to the Food Marketing

---

103 To learn more about what this looks like, see: Carrtronics LLC, "Carrtronics: Partnering Solutions to Curb Losses and Create Profits" (2009) www.carttronics.com/Resources/TechnologyinAction/tabid/68/Default.aspx.

104 See generally Terry P. Wilson, *The Cart That Changed The World: The Career of Sylvan N. Goldman* (Norman: University of Oklahoma Press, 1978).

105 Kelly Wilkinson, "Wheels of Fortune" *Metroactive News* (3 June 1999), www.metroactive.com/papers/metro/06.03.99/shoppingcarts-9922.html.

Institute in Washington, D.C., global losses total more than $800 million annually.[106]

While digital locks therefore make a lot of sense to grocery retailers,[107] those images of New Orleans gave me considerable pause. Would anyone, including grocery retailers, pass moral judgment on Katrina victims for using those carts as they did? It is difficult to imagine. Especially since the very foundation of our legal and moral institutions are clear that in times of necessity, the institution of property must give way to the preservation of life and other core values.[108] But I was further compelled to imagine: what would have happened had there actually been "effective technological measures"[109] on all shopping carts in New Orleans? What further devastation might have occurred for those thousands of unfortunate people using grocery retailers' property out of necessity if it had been technologically disabled?[110]

Remember that the preemptive nature of digital locks leaves no room for forgiveness. Instead, digital locks simply disable the property so that it does not permit of any uses other than its pre-programmed use — which likely would not have contemplated and/or could not otherwise accommodate the range of uses that necessity so often demands. As pre-programmed, preemptive devices meant to automate permissions, digital locks are not law-abiding. To be sure, they can be programmed to comport

106 *Ibid.*

107 The alternative for those retailers would have been to employ shopping cart bounty hunters to "repo" the carts. See Susan Abram, "City Worker is a Wheel Man: Employee Hunts for Abandoned Grocery Carts" *Daily News of Los Angeles* (14 March 2007), www.thefreelibrary.com/CITY+WORKER+IS+A+WHEEL+MAN+EMPLOYEE+HUNTS+FOR+ABANDONED+GROCERY+CARTS. . .-a0160618096.

108 The principle of necessity generally allows a defendant who commits a private wrong in an effort to protect a person or property from imminent harm to be excused from liability that she would otherwise incur. See, e.g., *Sherrin v. Haggerty* (1953), CarswellOnt 391 (Co. Ct.); *Vincent v. Lake Erie Transp. Co.*, 109 Minn. 456, 124 N.W. 221 (1910). The same general principle applies in criminal law. As stated by Dickson J. in *Perka v. R.*, [1984] 2 S.C.R. 232 at para. 11, "[f]rom earliest times it has been maintained that in some situations the force of circumstances makes it unrealistic and unjust to attach criminal liability to actions which, on their face, violate the law." The defence of necessity articulated in that case, "rests on a realistic assessment of human weakness, recognizing that a liberal and humane criminal law cannot hold people to the strict obedience of laws in emergency situations where normal human instincts, whether of self-preservation or of altruism, overwhelmingly impel disobedience" (*Perka* at para. 33).

109 To use the language of the WIPO Copyright Treaties, above at note 63.

110 Which is something we should perhaps also ask ourselves *every time* we see a homeless person with a shopping cart.

with simple legal rules to some extent.[111] And they can be re-programmed if those simple rules are amended. But, generally, these pre-set permissions are unsophisticated and non-negotiable. Lord Denning MR once remarked on this (though he didn't likely know he was talking about "digital locks") in a case involving an automated parking system that only permitted cars to exit the lot upon payment of a fee:

> The customer pays his money and gets a ticket. He cannot refuse it. He cannot get his money back. He may protest at the machine, even swear at it; but it will remain unmoved.[112]

It is one thing to program a digital lock to accord with the terms of a contract.[113] It is quite another to program digital locks that delicately balance public and private interests—which is precisely what both the necessity principle and, for that matter, the law of copyright would require. In the copyright context, none of the Canadian proposed anti-circumvention rules (i.e., rules that would prohibit breaking a digital lock), including those in Bill C-32, have ever contemplated imposing obligations on property owners requiring them to open digital locks in order to permit access that is appropriate or otherwise authorized by law. At best, the anti-circumvention rules permit self-help remedies (i.e., allowing locks to be hacked) for certain non-infringing purposes[114] or as justified by one of the narrow exemptions set out in the legislation.[115] Of course, breaking

---

111 And, even then, only to the extent that the rules are so clear that legal interpretation is unnecessary. In my experience, this is often not the case.

112 *Thornton v. Shoe Lane Parking Ltd.*, [1971] All E.R. 686 at 689, 2 Q.B. 163.

113 Which is the entire purpose of DRM.

114 Shockingly, Bill C-32 does not tie circumvention to an infringing purpose. These new anti-circumvention rules would therefore make it illegal to break a digital lock even in situations where no copyright violation ever occurred. As such, these rules have sometimes been referred to as "paracopyright." See Peter Jaszi, "Intellectual Property Legislative Update: Copyright, Paracopyright, and Pseudo-Copyright" (May 1998), www.arl.org/resources/pubs/mmproceedings/132mmjaszi. See also Ian Kerr, "To Observe and Protect? How Digital Rights Management Systems Threaten Privacy and What Policy Makers Should Do About It," in Peter Yu, ed., *Intellectual Property and Information Wealth: Copyright and Related Rights*, vol. 1 (Westport: Praeger Publishers, 2007).

115 Bill C-32 permits limited circumvention of TPMs for specific purposes: investigations related to the enforcement of laws; activities related to law enforcement and the protection of national security; making computer programs interoperable; encryption research; protection of personal information; access for persons with perceptual disabilities; broadcasting, or telecommunications service on a radio apparatus; and unlocking mobile devices. These provisions, created in s. 47 of the

the lock yourself requires resources and know-how. One can only imagine the further tragedies that would have been reported had Katrina victims been left to their own devices, trying against all odds to re-activate all of those disabled carts.

Consider now a third carting example that I experienced more recently, this time on the golf course. Although I have driven power carts since my dad first showed me how when I was around the age of twelve, I recently experienced "smart carts" while playing for the first time ever on a high-tech golf course. Global positioning systems[116] (GPS) is the key technology, allowing golfers to determine the distance between golf ball and green, understand the layout of the course, track the location of their golf balls and chart their progress on a real-time map. They can also track the play of others, contact the snack cart for a beer or hot dog delivery and satisfy a host of other consumer desires. GPS also allows the club's marshal to know exactly where all players are on the course and how fast or slow they are playing, ensuring an optimal pace of play. The same applications are used by the head greens keeper to monitor employees and valuable golf course assets such as trucks, cars generators, trailers, mowers, sprinklers and the like.[117]

What I learned that day was that smart carts also had digital locks. After a nice approach shot on the second hole, I was driving my cart toward the green when, all of a sudden, the cart was disabled. I had been driving the cart at a decent clip and it just shut right down. And yet, although it would no longer proceed in the forward direction, I was permitted to reverse the cart away from the green and then it turn in any other direction. I later learned that the cart had been deactivated by a GPS tracking system that used geo-fencing technology[118] to immobilize carts that threatened to encroach upon the greens or course boundaries.[119]

While this may seem (virtually) identical to the shopping cart example just offered there is at least one important difference. Unlike shopping

---

amendment, would become ss. 41.11–41.18 in the existing *Canada Copyright Act*. See Bill C-32, above note 10 at cl. 47 [*Anti-Circ*].

116 See generally Ahmed El-Rabbany, *Introduction to GPS: The Global Positioning System*, 2nd ed., (Norwood: Artech House Inc., 2006). See also, Nel Samama, *Global Positioning Technologies and Performance* (Hoboken, NJ: John Wiley & Sons Inc. 2008).

117 For a more detailed descriptions of these features see RavTrack Complete Real-Time Tracking "Golf Course GPS Solutions" 2010, http://ravtrack.com/Golf-Courses.html [Ravtrack].

118 Wikipedia, "Geo-Fence," http://en.wikipedia.org/wiki/Geofence.

119 *Ravtrack*, above note 117.

cart theft, driving toward the green of a golf course or too close to its boundary line is *not* illegal. So it took a while before I grasped the full significance of what had just happened. And, here is how I would describe it. During my previous thirty years of spotty play, golf was regulated by a quaint set of communal norms instilled in newer golfers by those who had truly come to understand and accept the game. "Golf etiquette" was the social instrument for ensuring safety, maintaining the condition of the course, improving the quality of play and showing care and consideration for other players.[120]

To me, etiquette is something to be taken seriously by those who golf. The rules aren't easily learned and their mastery requires significant trial and error. But there is much to be gained from learning how to behave on a golf course. Among other things, it makes one a member of the community of those who play by the rules. Not those who merely conform to the rules but rather those who follow them because they understand their importance and the reasons why those rules were put into place. This requires adopting what Oxford jurist H.L.A. Hart once called "an internal point of view" of the rules. [121] Those who adopt an internal point of view of golf etiquette see themselves as governed by its rules and accept those rules as the reasons guiding their behaviour on the golf course.

This is precisely what was *not* taking place at the high-tech golf course. There, GPS-enabled digital locks automated an array of permissions that included not only when I could buy hot dogs and beer, where I was permitted to drive and how fast, but also whether I was permitted to breach the rule of etiquette about driving power carts too close to the green — one of a series of rules about taking proper care of the golf course. By disabling my ability to drive too close to the green, the property owners were attempting to automate golf's social norms. Just like at Disneyland, I was once again being prevented from making mistakes. No longer would I have to pay careful attention to the rules of etiquette or thoughtfully weigh my actions against what I perceived as appropriate behaviour in light of a particular standard of conduct. Technology took care of all of this by proxy. To the property owners utilizing these machines, I was no longer a golfer; I was no longer a person being called upon to make right or wrong decisions about the appropriate standards of conduct on the golf course.

---

120 See generally Barbara Puett & Jim Apfelbaum, *Golf Etiquette* (New York: St. Martin's Press, 2003).

121 H.L.A. Hart, *The Concept of Law* (Oxford: Oxford University Press, 1961) at 99.

I had become an autonomic extension of the golf machine, robotized by technology in order to ensure optimal efficiency on the golf course.

Consider, finally, a fourth carting example that I have yet to experience, though I may have the opportunity to do so at the end of my driving career. I say this not because the technology I am about to mention is thought to be such a long way off. I say that it will happen at the end of my driving career because the technology I am referring to is called the "driverless car."[122] While this sounds like pure science fiction — didn't George Jetson have one of these? — it is quickly becoming science fact. General Motors' VP of Research and Development, Larry Burns, claims "GM will begin testing driverless cars by 2015 and have them on the road by 2018."[123]

DARPA, the research agency that developed the precursor to the Internet, issued a competition that took place back in 2007 called "the urban challenge."

> This event required teams to build an autonomous vehicle capable of driving in traffic, performing complex maneuvers such as merging, passing, parking and negotiating intersections. This event was truly groundbreaking as the first time autonomous vehicles have interacted with both manned and unmanned vehicle traffic in an urban environment.[124]

More recently, in 2010, a team of Italian engineers launched what has been billed as the longest-ever test drive of driverless vehicles — a 13,000 km, three-month road trip from Italy to China:

> Two ... vehicles, equipped with laser scanners and cameras that work in concert to detect and help avoid obstacles, are to brave the traffic of Moscow, the summer heat of Siberia and the bitter cold of the Gobi desert before the planned arrival in Shanghai at the end of October.[125]

---

122 That is, once this technology is adopted, I am by definition no longer a driver. Walt Disney's Autopia, it seems, was not so far off the mark.

123 Chuck Squatriglia, "GM Says Driverless Cars Could Be on the Road by 2018" *Wired* (7 January 2008), www.wired.com/autopia/2008/01/gm-says-driverl.

124 The winning team, Tartan Racing, was awarded $20 million. See DARPA, "DARPA Urban Challenge," www.darpa.mil/grandchallenge/index.asp.

125 The Associated Press, "Italy To China In Driverless Vehicles: Italian Team Embarks On 8,000-mile Journey To China Using Driverless Vehicles" *CBS News* (20 July 2010), www.cbsnews.com/stories/2010/07/20/tech/main6694854.shtml.

There are literally hundreds of public and privately funded research consortiums seeking to contribute the future of carting. Projects have included: the US Deptartment of Transportation's "National Automated Highway System Consortium" (NAHS)[126] and, more recently, Europe's Intelligent Speed Adaption (ISA) — "a collective name for systems in which the speed of a vehicle is permanently monitored within a certain area. When the vehicle exceeds the speed limit, the speed is automatically adjusted."[127] ISA experiments have expanded to include broad European participation from countries including: Sweden, the Netherlands, Belgium, Denmark, Britain, Finland, Germany, France, Hungary and Spain.[128] "The standard system uses an in-vehicle digital road map onto which speed limits have been coded, combined with a positioning system."[129] Not unlike the smart golf carts discussed above, one variant of ISA research contemplates a GPS enabled system that "intervenes directly with the fuel supply. As a result it is impossible to exceed the speed limit."[130]

From ox-carts to go-carts, shopping carts, and golf carts, to the driverless carts of tomorrow's Tomorrowland, we see that the potential for corporations, governments, and individuals to control behaviour by placing digital locks and related technological constraints on the devices we have so deeply come to rely upon in daily life is increasing in exponential fashion. This control now extends well beyond the electronic consumer goods that are of interest to the copyright industries. Indeed, one could easily offer detailed accounts along the lines of my carting example across numerous unexpected domains. To mention just a couple, there has been interesting scholarly work[131] applying the digital lock concept to agricul-

---

126 National Automated Highway System Consortium, www.path.berkeley.edu/nahsc/pdf/NAHSC-Presentation_Docs.pdf; see also Richard Bishop, "Whatever Happened to Automated Highway Systems (AHS)?," *Traffic Technology International* (August–September 2001), http://faculty.washington.edu/jbs/itrans/bishopahs.htm.

127 The Netherlands, Ministry of Transport Transport Research Centre (AVV), "Intelligent Speed Adaptation (ISA): A Successful Test in the Netherlands" by Alex van Loon & Lies Duynstee, www.fatedu/~fdimc/laboratorijske_vaje/Inteligentni_transportni_sistemi/Teme_za_studente/Loon%20et%20al%20Intelligent%20Speed%20Adaptation.pdf at 2.

128 European Commission, "Intelligent Speed Adaptation," http://ec.europa.eu/transport/road_safety/specialist/knowledge/speed/new_technologies_new_opportunities/intelligent_speed_adaptation_isa.htm.

129 ISA-UK, "Project Summary" at 1, www.its.leeds.ac.uk/projects/isa/in_depth/project_summary2.pdf.

130 van Loon and Duynstee, above note 127 at 2.

131 Dan L. Burk, "DNA Rules: Legal and Conceptual Implications of Biological 'Lock-Out" Systems" (2004) 92 Cal. L. Rev. 1, http://papers.ssrn.com/sol3/papers.cfm?abstract_

tural biology, wherein "terminator seeds" have been used in "genetic use restriction technologies" to purposely cause second-generation seeds to be sterile.[132] Some of my own ongoing research investigates the use of digital locks in human biotechnology, including human-implantable devices such as RFID chips being used to monitor and maintain biological function,[133] and cochlear implants, which now use digital locks to offer a menu of sound filters and hearing choices for hearing-impaired customer/patients.[134] A stunning array of new examples will emerge with increasing interest in artificial organs and, more generally, the merger of humans and machine systems.

The future is but a question mark. Although the looming uses and limits of digital locks across these broad domains remain uncertain, the examples in this section are meant to provoke and inspire deeper thinking about the potential ethical and legal implications of unimpeded and universal adoption of digital locks. Especially given the strategy of preemption adopted by the powerful entities that currently deploy them.

How might all of this affect us as moral actors who desire to do good things?

E. THE AUTOMATION OF VIRTUE

The question mark that punctuates the end of the previous section is meant as an important point of departure from the existing literature on digital locks and their social implications. As Professors Dan Burk and Tarleton Gillespie have correctly noted, "[t]o date the public debate over deployment of DRM, has been almost entirely dominated by utilitarian

---

id=692061; Jeremy DeBeer "Reconciling Property Rights In Plants" (2005) 8 The Journal of World Intellectual Property 5, http://onlinelibrary.wiley.com/doi/10.1111/j.1747-1796.2005.tb00235.x/abstract.

132 Thus ensuring Bill Gates' famous "planned obsolescence" business model not only in our electronic consumer goods but now, also, for agricultural products used for human sustenance, see generally, Giles Slade, *Made to Break: technology and obsolescence in America* (Cambridge: Harvard University Press, 2006).

133 Ian Kerr, "Chapter 19: The Internet of People? Reflections on the Future Regulation of Human-Implantable Radio Frequency Identification" in Ian Kerr, Valerie Steeves, & Carole Lucock, eds., *Lessons From The Identity Trail: Anonymity, Privacy and Identity in a Networked Society* (New York: Oxford University Press, 2009), www.idtrail.org/content/view/799.

134 Ian Kerr, "The Components of Health," www.iankerr.ca/publications-mainmenu-70/press-mainmenu-76/762-the-components-of-health.html.

arguments regarding the social costs and benefits of this technology."[135] Indeed, so far as I know, there is only one published article in the entire literature on digital locks that focuses on autonomy and morality and its authors are Burk and Gillespie. Examining "the moral propriety of laws endorsing and encouraging the deployment of DRM,"[136] their excellent article offers a deontological analysis focusing on the moral autonomy of information users.

Like these notable scholars, I am interested in the moral repercussions of what they call a "state sanctioned deployment of DRM."[137] However, the focus of my inquiry is neither utilitarian nor deontological in nature. I want to know how a state sanctioned, generalized deployment of digital locks (i.e., deployment beyond the copyright sphere) might affect us as moral actors. To this end, I turn instead to the third strand in the holy trinity of ethical theory: virtue ethics.

Ever since Elizabeth Anscombe penned her "complaint"[138] about modern moral philosophy in 1958, there has been renewed academic interest in the study of virtue ethics. Disenchanted by modern moral philosophy's fixation with legalistic accounts of ethics and its reliance on utilitarian and deontological conceptions of rights and duties — Anscombe thought that these things generate an unrealistic and absolutist moral oughtism that is rigid and meaningless in a secular society — she pushed for a revitalization of Greek ethics and its questions about the nature of the good life. Like Anscombe, I am interested in these questions. In particular, I wish to consider whether — or how — moral character, virtue and human flourishing might be affected by a state sanctioned, widespread deployment of digital locks.

Although, to my knowledge, it has never previously been characterized in this way, a layperson might reasonably describe the digital lock strategy as an attempt to promulgate the "automation of virtue." Something like this seems already to be a popular sentiment as is evident in this varia-

---

135 Dan L. Burk & Tarleton L. Gillespie, "Autonomy and Morality in DRM and Anti-Circumvention Law" (2006) 4:2 Triple C: Cognition, Communication, Cooperation 239, http://papers.ssrn.com/sol3/papers.cfm?abstract_id=1146448 at 239.

136 *Ibid.*

137 *Ibid.*

138 Anscombe was correct in characterizing her own work in its final sentence as a "complaint." Consider, for example, the last line in her opening paragraph where she states her third thesis, namely: "that the differences between the well-known English writers on moral philosophy from Sidgwick to the present day are of little importance." G.E.M. Anscombe, "Modern Moral Philosophy" (1958) 33 Philosophy at 1, www.philosophy.uncc.edu/mleldrid/cmt/mmp.html.

tion on the Yiddish proverb cited earlier—"a lock keeps an honest man honest."[139]

If something like this is the goal of the digital lock strategy, then my professional prognosis for its success is: negatory. This is because the very notion of automating virtue is an oxymoron. The preemption of wrongdoing does not a virtuous person make. A basic account of Aristotle's virtue ethics illustrates not only why this is so but also lays the groundwork for demonstrating what is at stake in the attempt to carry out preemption of this sort. In this section, I will argue that a successful, state sanctioned, generalized deployment of digital locks actually impedes the development of moral character by impairing people's ability to develop virtuous dispositions, thereby diminishing our well-being and ultimately undermining human flourishing. It creates something that I shall call a "moral disability."

Virtue, in the Greek sense, stems from the word *arête*, which is perhaps best understood as "excellence." For Aristotle, the achievement of excellences (there are many) is key to human flourishing. Well-being (*eudaimonia*) is something he understood in terms of the unique function of human beings.[140] What sets humans apart from other animals is the possession of reason. So the proper function of human beings is "activity of the soul in accordance with reason."[141] But to be a person of good moral character, one must not simply act in accordance with reason, one must "perform . . . well and finely, and each thing is completed well when it possesses its proper excellence."[142] Thus, "the human good turns out to be activity of soul in accordance with excellence."[143]

---

139 Wolfgang Mieder, Stewart A. Kingsbury, & Kelsie B. Harder, *A Dictionary of American Proverbs* (Oxford: Oxford University Press, 1992). Copyright owners have taken hold of this particular proverb, equating placing a lock on digital content with simply removing the temptation to break the law. In their paper, "Keep Looking, The Answer to the Machine is Elsewhere," Adams and Brown use the example of a 2003 Congressional committee, in which the Motion Picture Association of America described TPMs as "designed to keep honest users honest." Princeton University encryption expert Ed Felten quipped in response: 'Nothing needs to be done to keep honest people honest, just as nothing needs to be done to keep tall people tall." See Adams and Brown, above note 12 at 2.

140 Aristotle, *Nicomachean Ethics*, trans. by Sarah Broadie & Christopher Rowe (Oxford: Oxford University Press, 2002) at 1097b20-25. Note: all subsequent references to Aristotle's *Nicomachean Ethics* will be cited in the classical style, denoted as *Nic. Ethics* followed by the pinpoint (Bekker number).

141 *Nic. Ethics* 1098a5.

142 *Nic. Ethics* 1098a10-15.

143 *Nic. Ethics* 1098a15.

With this we see that each achievement of virtue is an activity. Well-being "consists in the exercise (not the mere possession of) the virtues."[144] That said, the virtuous character consists in a set of dispositions (*hexeis*)[145] deeply entrenched in the psyche. In good Aristotelian fashion, the development of virtuous dispositions requires both knowing and doing. Most famously, the acquisition of a virtuous disposition requires knowing how and then hitting the right mark (the 'golden mean'):

> excellence of character is an intermediate state . . . it is intermediate between two bad states, one relating to excess and the other to deficiency; and that it is such because it is effective at hitting upon the intermediate in affections and in actions[146]

However, it is important to understand that a virtuous act is not determined by its outcome alone. It also depends upon certain facts about the person performing the act. As Professor David Matheson has characterized it, "[t]he particular kind of dispositions of which the virtues consist is brought about by a consideration of their connection to praiseworthy behaviour, which entails not merely doing the right thing but doing it in the right way."[147] Aristotle sets out three conditions for this, stating that a person's actions are virtuous,

> first, if he does them knowingly, secondly if he decides to do them, and decides to do them for themselves, and thirdly if he does them from a firm and unchanging disposition.[148]

As such, "[c]haracter virtue . . . turns out on Aristotle's account to be deep-seated psychological dispositions to do the right thing (in the relevant context), based on a desire to do the right thing because it is known to be, i.e. recognized as, such."[149]

How, then, is all of this achieved? According to Aristotle, the ability to develop virtuous dispositions to do the right thing based in the desire to

---

144 Roger Crisp, "Virtue Ethics" in Roger Crisp and Michael Slote, eds., *Virtue Ethics* (Oxford: Oxford University Press, 1997) at 2, www.hrstud.hr/hrvatskistudiji/skripte/filozofija/tbracanovic/Etika1/Crisp-Virtue-Ethics.pdf.

145 Virtue is seen as a tendency or disposition, induced by our habits, to have appropriate feelings. See *Nic. Ethics* 1105b25-6.

146 *Nic. Ethics* 1109a20-24.

147 David Matheson, "Virtue and the Surveillance Society" (2007) 3 International Journal Technology, Knowledge, & Society 133 at 135.

148 *Nic. Ethics* 1105a22-b12.

149 Matheson, above note 147 at 135.

do the right things *knowingly* requires, as a necessary precondition, the cultivation of practical wisdom (*phronesis*).[150] *Phronesis* is a special kind of skill, which requires not only an ability to decide how to achieve a certain end, but also the ability to reflect upon and determine that end. As Professor Roger Crisp has noted, *phronesis* is the skillful acquisition of "sensitivity to morally salient features of particular situations which goes beyond an ability to apply explicit rules."[151] Practical wisdom is therefore not something easily acquired and is the reason Aristotle insisted that one must be of a certain age before one can undertake the study of ethics and the development of virtuous dispositions.

> Whereas young people become accomplished in geometry and mathematics, and wise within these limits, young people [endowed with practical wisdom] do not seem to be found. The reason is that *phronesis* is concerned with particulars as well as universals, and particulars become known from experience, but a young person lacks experience, since some length of time is needed to produce it.[152]

Thus the moral attainment of virtue relies fundamentally on practicing, or developing, the virtues in real situations over the course of a lifetime. For, as Aristotle says, "the way we learn the things we should do, knowing how to do them, is by doing them. . .We become just by doing just things, moderate by doing moderate things, and courageous by doing courageous things."[153] Grounded in practice, ethical decision-making of this sort insists that each situation be approached as unique, and considered in its completeness. When the virtuous person finds herself in a difficult situation, she will use all relevant knowledge of the virtues (and of human activity in general), according to the salient moral facts of the circumstances as a guide in making her ethical decision.

With even this rudimentary version of Aristotle's model for understanding and acquiring character-virtue, it is not difficult to see how a universal digital lock strategy would undermine the project of achieving moral excellence.

Honesty, for example, is an intermediary state between an excess and a defect, between exaggeration and fraudulence. To fall short of the mark of honesty is to be dishonest; to exceed it is to be tactless. Among other

---

150 *Nic. Ethics* 1144b14-17.

151 Crisp, above note 144 at 6.

152 *Nic. Ethics* 1142a.

153 *Nic. Ethics* 1103a30-31.

things, honesty involves keeping one's promises. In a legal context, this might sometimes mean honouring the terms and conditions of a contract or licensing agreement. As we have seen, DRM is a souped-up contract—i.e., the terms of its licence can be enforced through the operations of digital locks rather than ethical norms. For instance, if the terms of the license accompanying my e-book are such that I undertake to print no more than ten pages of any books that I download from the service, what this really means, practically speaking, is that the device simply will not permit the printing of an eleventh page.[154]

The e-book reader's lock "keeps an honest person honest" only insofar as someone like me, who has neither the inclination or know-how needed to circumvent it, will probably print ten pages or less. No breach of contract, no broken promises. And, yet, there is *nothing* approaching virtue in my conduct. Recall Aristotle's three conditions for virtuous action set out above. First, it requires being honest knowingly. But, I did *not* knowingly keep my promise. To the extent that the promise was unbroken (since it makes no sense to speak of it in this case as fulfilled), this was not because I knowingly omitted to print an excessive number of pages (heck, I probably didn't even read the terms and conditions of the license requiring such conduct). It was either a coincidence or a consequence of the operations of the software.

Second, according to Aristotle, it is only a virtuous act if my decision to limit myself to ten pages was made *because* it was the honest thing to do. In such case it may never be clear whether my conduct was virtuous. After all, I could have decided to print more than ten pages and yet this still would have made no difference to the outcome, since the digital lock would have complied with the licensing terms no matter what my intentions were. In any event, I probably did not limit myself to less than ten pages because it would be dishonest but rather because it would have been inconvenient to figure out how to do otherwise.

Third, the mere fact that the number of pages printed comported with the licence was not the result of my firm and unchanging disposition toward honesty in the face of temptation but rather because the e-book's robotic code made me do it. The answer to the machine was, as they say, in the machine. But this cannot in any meaningful way be understood as an automation of virtue. To the contrary, technologically compelling me to comply with the terms and conditions of the licence, if anything, pre-

154 In the spirit of Professor Lawrence Lessig's *Free Culture*, I will first borrow, and then later remix, his example found at page 151. See Lessig, above note 11.

vented me from acting in accordance with virtue, let alone acting from any deep-seated disposition towards honesty. Perhaps, eventually, I will reach a point where I simply do anything that the machine doesn't preempt me from doing. *Domo arigato, Mr. Roboto.*

This last point is critical. A series of ubiquitous locks designed to keep people honest would impair the development of a *hexis*, a deep-seated disposition for honesty. Recall the important role that practical wisdom plays in the cultivation of virtue. Virtuous conduct is impossible without *phronesis*—the ability to untie moral knots, to determine both what is good and how to achieve it. Practical wisdom, remember, is a special skill requiring special sensitivity to morally salient features of particular situations. Practical wisdom cannot be programmed. It cannot be cut and pasted. It requires exposure to an array of moral episodes and adventures—opportunities to explore the intricacies of moral deliberation.

Ironically, a ubiquitous digital lock strategy meant to "keep honest people honest" is a self-defeating goal since it impairs the development of *phronesis*, stunts moral maturity and thereby disables the cultivation of a deep-seated disposition for honesty. Woven into the fabric of everyday life, digital locks would ensure particular outcomes for property owners but would do so at the expense of the moral project of honesty.[155]

The cultivation of honesty, like the cultivation of *phronesis*, is a skill. Here, I am reminded of the image of the child riding Walt Disney's Autopia. Recall that the ride permits children to assume the driver's seat, veering a little left or right of centre, but the hidden rail always guides them back into the middle. Just as this is no way to the way to learn how to drive, let alone how to drive well, it is also not how a moral actor achieves the golden mean. The technological procurement of right conduct is not the attainment of virtue.[156]

Although his focus was on the concept of a permission culture rather than its affect on the good life and the attainment of moral excellence, Professor Lawrence Lessig hints at how digital locks might impair the development of *phronesis* and the cultivation of moral virtue:

> The control comes instead from the code—from the technology within which the e-book "lives." Though the e-book says that these

---

155 And, I suspect, not *just* honesty. Other moral virtues are also at stake.

156 Professor Matheson adopts a similar position, arguing that a "surveillance society risks undermining the ability of its citizens to develop virtue for the same sorts of reasons that overprotective parenting can impair the character development of children." Matheson, above note 147 at 133.

> are permissions, they are not the sort of "permissions" that most of us deal with. When a teenager gets "permission" to stay out till midnight, she knows (unless she's Cinderella) that she can stay out till 2 A.M., but will suffer a punishment if she's caught. But when the Adobe eBook Reader says I have the permission to make ten copies of the text into the computer's memory, that means that after I've made ten copies, the computer will not make any more. The same with the printing restrictions: After ten pages, the eBook Reader will not print any more pages.[157]

For a moment, let's try to imagine a world where virtue-locks could ensure that the teenager *is* home by midnight. Maybe Cindy's coach doesn't turn into a pumpkin[158] but the evolution of the carting industry spawns the development of her FROG AGV 3.0.[159] Taking the lead from Walt Disney's Tomorrowland, this driverless vehicle, complete, let's imagine, with identification and authentication systems, manages a series of permissions pre-programmed by her over-protective parents, resulting in version 3.0 of the classic line, "I have to go now, my ride is here." Only this time round, a series of technological locks prevent Cindy from doing anything other than coming home.

Though I am uncertain whether this thought experiment is fun, frivolous, or just plain frightening, the intended "moral" of the story is important, and is meant to be taken seriously. Professor Lessig's original example implicitly acknowledges something important in Cindy's moral development that comes with having to learn whether to adhere to the curfew rule. To name only a few, her deliberations (should she have any) might include: (1) an evaluation of the importance of the original curfew rule, (2) whether there are legitimate exceptions to it, (3) whether the likely penalty is worth whatever was to be gained from breaking the rule, and (4) the importance of other moral values in conflict with the curfew rule (e.g., staying late to help a friend in need), etc. Cindy's moral deliberations might be epicurean, Kantian, consequentialist, existentialist, eudaimonic, hedonistic, egoistic, spiritualistic, nihilistic, stoic, or pragmatic but, regardless of which, she will be morally knee-capped if technology is permitted to systematically deny her the ability to act upon those deliberations.

---

157 Lessig, above note 11 at 151.

158 Although I imagine this to be the sort of DRM that Tim Burton might like.

159 AGV is the acronym for "Automated Guided Vehicle" systems, the enabling technology for driverless vehicles. See generally Frog AGV Systems, "Over Frog AGV Systems" (2008) www.frog.nl/About_Frog_AGV_Systems/index.php.

To be clear, the critique here is not about her freedom to do as she pleases. It is about the moral disability that she will suffer from not being able to do so. Reiterating from above, the moral attainment of virtue relies fundamentally on practicing the virtues in real situations over the course of a lifetime. À la Aristotle: "we become honest by doing honest things." If locks of various sorts prevent Cindy from making mistakes, from negotiating with herself about what honesty entails or from deciding what *she* will morally permit *herself* to do, her ability and desire to cultivate practical wisdom and the achievement of moral excellence will be impaired. She will become morally disabled.

F. ALEXANDRIAN SOLUTIONS

On Wednesday, 2 June 2010, in the Montreal office of US video-game software developer Electronic Arts, Heritage Minister, James Moore, and Industry Minister, Tony Clement, announced that the Government of Canada would take its third crack at unraveling the Gordian knot of "balanced copyright."[160] In front of a room filled with puzzlers and lock-makers, Minister Clement drew his sword and, with a single dramatic stroke, proclaimed:

> For those companies that choose to use digital locks as part of their business model, they will have the protection of the law.[161]

To anyone paying attention to copyright reform in Canada over the last decade, it shouldn't take a rocket scientist[162] to realize that the anti-circumvention laws"[163] to which Minister Clement was referring are a kind of legal lock — promised by Bill C-32 to copyright owners to further secure

160 It is an unfortunate coincidence that this phrase has been officially adopted by both the Government of Canada *and* "Balanced Copyright for Canada," an industry-based coalition funded primarily by the Canadian Recording Industry Association: http://balancedcopyrightforcanada.ca.

161 Government of Canada, "Speaking Points — Minister of Industry" *Balanced Copyright* (2 June 2010), www.ic.gc.ca/eic/site/crp-prda.nsf/eng/rp01191.html.

162 Although, at least one did. Marc Garneau, former Canadian astronaut and MP for Westmount-Ville-Marie identified digital locks as "the major issue that stands out in the bill" and went on to say that, "the bill seems to be missing an exception that would allow people to break digital locks if it was for private, non-commercial use, but added that his party will have to study it further." See Peter Nowak, "Copyright bill would ban breaking digital locks" *CBC News: Technology & Science* (3 June 2010), www.cbc.ca/technology/story/2010/06/02/copyright-bill-clement-montreal.html#ixzzowllnKJbl.

163 For details on the anti-circumvention provisions, see *Anti-Circ*, above note 115.

the digital lock strategy that industry stakeholders have been lobbying for. As Minister Moore recently noted at a luncheon on "Intellectual Property, Innovation, Economic Growth, and Jobs" in Toronto:

> Copyright owners told that us that their online and digital business models depend on strong protections for digital locks. And they're right. With Bill C-32, we are proposing protections for digital locks. The Bill gives creators stronger legal tools for protecting technological measures including 'digital locks' and other methods. . .[164]

Indeed it does. With all the brute force of an Alexandrian solution, Bill C-32's approach adds a fourth layer of protection[165] to copyright owners through a series of strongly worded prohibitions against: (1) circumventing TPMs that control access to a work;[166] (2) offering services to the public to circumvent TPMs;[167] and (3) manufacturing, importing, distributing, or selling technologies that can be used to circumvent TPMs.[168]

In my view, there are three fundamental flaws with Bill C-32's Alexandrian solution that, operating in conjunction with one another undermines the very possibility of balanced copyright.

First, Bill C-32's anti-circumvention provisions are not tied to copyright infringement, thereby expanding the law of copyright to include acts that have nothing to do with copying. Second, the few exceptions wherein circumvention is permitted[169] are, by many accounts, deficient in scope. Third, Bill C-32 provides what in this chapter, following Burk and Gillespie, I have been calling an "unimpeded state sanction" of digital locks. The first two flaws have been thoroughly canvassed by others in this book and I will not address them here.[170] Instead, I will focus on the third funda-

---

164 Canadian Heritage, "Minister Moore's Speech at Luncheon on Intellectual Property, Innovation, Economic Growth, and Jobs Toronto, Ontario June 22, 2010," www.pch.gc.ca/pc-ch/minstr/moore/disc-spch/index-eng.cfm?action=doc&DocIDCd=SJM10 0603.

165 Legal protection begins with the law of copyright and its sanctions against infringement. The second layer of protection, used with increasing frequency, is contract law, where the terms of end user licence agreements (EULAs) are used to override existing copyright limitations. As a third layer of protection, many copyright owners have taken it upon themselves to use digital locks.

166 Bill C-32, above note 10 at cl. 47.

167 *Ibid.*

168 *Ibid.*

169 For details on the anti-circumvention provisions, see *Anti-Circ*, above note 115.

170 My view on the first two flaws has been articulated in *Heritage Report Part I*, above note 65; *Heritage Report Part II*, above note 65; *If Left To Their Own Devices*, above note 65.

mental flaw — which is crucial not only to balanced copyright but also to my concerns about the broader use of digital locks set out in this chapter.

In my co-authored two-part study on digital locks commissioned by Canadian Heritage,[171] I enumerated a few observations crucial to the proper scope of protection for digital locks as well as the broader mandate of balanced copyright and then remarked on their policy implications. One such observation was that

> the exercise of any of the exceptions enumerated . . . is premised on the ability to gain access to the work in question.[172]

Consequently, I went on to suggest that any proposed digital lock provisions must therefore

> include a positive obligation on the copyright holder to ensure that alternative means of obtaining access to a work remain available — a *"copy-duty"* . . .[173]

In other words, those who use digital locks might in certain circumstances be obliged to provide a key or at least open the lock whenever someone else has a right to access or use the thing that has been locked-up.

This point is hardly revolutionary. In the ten years since stating it in my second Canadian Heritage study, it has been adopted in one form or other in various countries around the world. For example, the WIPO Standing Committee on Copyright and Related Rights issued a report in June 2010 describing that national laws in at least nineteen Member States provide mechanisms to make sure that prohibition of circumvention of TPMs does not prevent beneficiaries of copyright limitations and exceptions from exercising them.[174] Norway, for example, has established a Ministerial Board, which is empowered to order rightholders to allow access to protected works. Likewise,

> If the rightholder fails to provide access to protected work, many Member States grant beneficiaries of limitations and exceptions a recourse

---

171 To be fair to Minister Moore, these studies where written nearly 10 years ago, back when he was a very junior Member of Parliament and before he was professionally acquainted with copyright reform.

172 *Heritage Report Part II*, above note 65 at 66.

173 *Ibid.* See also Lessig, *Code*: *Version* 2.0 above note 12 at 190.

174 World Intellectual Property Organization, Standing Committee on Copyright and Related Rights, "Report on the Questionnaire on Limitations and Exceptions," SCCR/20/7, Twentieth Session, Geneva, 21–24 June 2010 at 12 www.wipo.int/meetings/en/doc_details.jsp?doc_id=134432.

to some form of judicial review (e.g. Ireland), arbitration (e.g. Finland), mediation (e.g. Greece) or administrative proceedings (e.g. Estonia).[175]

Poland goes even further, "limiting the application of TPMs only to acts which are not covered by any exception or limitation."[176] In other words, Poland recognizes that there are uses of digital locks that should be outright prohibited (in a way that mere exemptions will not do). In sum, by limiting or prohibiting the use of some digital locks altogether, or requiring the rightholder to open the lock, these Member States have recognized that an absolutist über-protection of digital locks thwarts the possibility of balanced copyright[177] and creates even greater risks outside of copyright's vast empire.

Ten years and three copyright bills later, the Government of Canada has once again tabled a bill that exclusively provides "strong protections *for* digital locks." For the third time running, it has done so without imposing appropriate balancing counter-measures for circumstances in which some measure of public interest might require strong protection *from* digital locks. Bill C-32 contains no countervailing provisions that would set limits or impose obligations concerning the use of locks, and certainly no provisions that prohibit particular uses of them or require them to be unlocked. *In other words, Bill C-32's legal locks provide a total lock on locks*. Those who have them can use them however they so choose with total impunity.[178]

---

175 *Ibid.*

176 *Ibid.*

177 Thanks to Michael Geist for useful discussions on this point, including reference to the following excellent article: Urs Gasser and Silke Ernst, *EUCD Best Practice Guide: Implementing the EU Copyright Directive in the Digital Age*, University of St. Gallen Law School: Law and Economics Research Paper Series Working Paper No. 2007-01, http://papers.ssrn.com/sol3/papers.cfm?abstract_id=952561.

178 In fact, if you read the government's speeches, FAQs and talking points, you will notice the language surrounding digital locks is peppered with soundbytes employing "freedom" and "choice" *for the property owner*. The section of the government's 'Balanced Copyright' website identifying key provisions of Bill C-32 includes this quote: "Businesses that choose to use digital locks as part of their business models will have the protection of the law." See Government of Canada, "What the New *Copyright Modernization Act* says about Digital Locks (8 June 2010), www.ic.gc.ca/eic/site/crp-prda.nsf/eng/rp01189.html. Another part of the website articulates what Bill C-32 will mean for copyright owners, artists and creators. With reference to the digital lock protections required by the WIPO Internet Treaties, the following is stated: "Protecting digital locks gives copyright industries the certainty they need to roll out new products and services, such as online subscription services, software and video games, if they choose to use digital locks. Not only will this promote investment and growth in Canada's digital economy, it will also encourage

The reasons for my broader concerns about this unimpeded, state sanctioned digital lock strategy should by now be clear in light of my analysis in Sections B and C of this chapter. The "permission" that Bill C-32 would give to property owners to make unimpeded use of digital locks is premised on a misconception of the function of locks as mere instruments of exclusion used to protect private property. In its bold Alexandrian reaction to digital copyright's Gordian knot, Bill C-32 fails to acknowledge the fact that locks properly understood are access-control devices premised not only on authorized permission by the copyright owner but, also, *permission authorized by the law.*

The fatal flaw is this: Bill C-32 refuses to recognize that foundational legal rules or principles might sometimes require property owners to open digital locks in order to permit justified access or use. As I stated in my second Canadian Heritage study, this is not merely the passing fancy of wishful academics — or, dare I now say, "radical extremists."[179] It has its basis in Canadian constitutional law, and is already supported in principle in the copyright context by the Supreme Court of Canada in the following passage from *Haig v. Canada:*

> . . . a situation may arise in which, in order to make a fundamental freedom meaningful, a posture of restraint would not be enough, and positive governmental action might be required. This might, for example, take the form of legislative intervention aimed at preventing certain conditions which muzzle expression, or ensuring public access to certain kinds of information.[180]

It is absolutely essential to note that a legal duty requiring property owners to open digital locks in order to permit justified access or use is totally separate and distinct from self-help remedies indirectly available through the exceptions contemplated within the anti-circumvention prohibitions. For example, to say that I have a right to circumvent a lock in

---

the introduction of innovative online services that offer access to content." (21 June 2010) www.ic.gc.ca/eic/site/crp-prda.nsf/eng/rp01189.html.

179 While addressing the International Chamber of Commerce in Toronto on Tuesday, 22 June 2010, Minister Moore advanced the claim that any people opposed to the new legislative provisions prescribed by Bill C-32 belonged to two groups of 'radical extremists'. For news reporting on this event, see Peter Nowak, "Copyright debate turns ugly: Heritage minister stirs hornet's nest with 'radical extremist' comments," *CBC News* (24 June 2010), www.cbc.ca/technology/story/2010/06/23/copyright-heritage-minister-moore.html.

180 *Haig* v. *Canada* [1993] 2 S.C.R 995, http://csc.lexum.umontreal.ca/en/1993/1993scr2-995/1993scr2-995.html at para. 79.

order to protect my personal information pursuant to the exceptions set out in Bill C-32 is *certainly not* the same thing as having a law wherein the state requires a party that collects, uses or discloses information about an identifiable individual to open the lock under circumstances where data protection law would demand it. The same argument could be made in the context of copyright laws where user rights might demand something more than the exception set out in Bill C-32. I further suspect that the principle I am articulating here is of general application. As I tried to make clear in my analysis of digital locks in the case of shopping carts, laws that would authorize, justify or excuse the circumvention of a lock — or, for that matter, impose upon the property owner a duty to open it — will often fall outside of the private ordering rules that are created and controlled in their entirety by property owners. Believe it or not, they could also fall outside of the ambit of law of copyright. ;)

While it is hard to imagine a foundational principle like the law of necessity actually creeping into a copyright infringement case, there are a myriad of legal rules and principles that could do so from both inside and outside of copyright law. The *Haig* case, mentioned above, is one such example. The problem with Bill C-32 is that its bold, unimpeded, absolutist Alexandrian protection of digital locks misunderstands the purpose and function of a lock which, at least in the case of more sophisticated access-control systems, not only hinders unauthorized access but also provides a mechanism for situations where the property owner has not contemplated a need for access but one later arises. The best security systems not only prevent access to interlopers but also grant access to those who have or ought to have permission.

The protection afforded to digital locks in Bill C-32 would, in situations such as the ones we are imagining, allow the property owner to trump the public interest for no other reason than being the *de facto* keyholder. Without a legal mechanism that imposes a duty on a property owner to open or remove the lock when the law would otherwise authorize doing so but the property owner would not, private ordering through the use of digital locks will become the rule and property owners the rule-makers. Balanced copyright doesn't stand a chance.

In witnessing this decade long Sisyphean error, I am tempted to understand the Alexandrian solution[181] offered by Ministers Clement and Moore

181 My use of several historical versions of the Alexandrian myth throughout this chapter is offered as a richer illustration of the difference between brute force and elegant solutions. The methodology of using classical mythology as a framework

not in accordance with the popular version of the legend wherein Alexander the Great is the solver of the knot's puzzle and the hero of the prophesy. Perhaps it seems more in line with a less popular account of the legend. In this alternative version,

> an exasperated Alexander is unsuccessful in every legitimate attempt.
>
> his whole body
> drenched in sweat
> while I
> sat nearby
> quietly
> watching
>
> (Ba. 620-2) — Euripides' Bacchae

---

for understanding contemporary problems is well established. For instance, "[t]wo of our oldest metaphors tell us that all life is a battle and that all life is a journey; whether the *Iliad* and the *Odyssey* drew on this knowledge or whether this knowledge was drawn from the *Iliad* and the *Odyssey* is, in the final count, unimportant, since a book and its readers are both mirrors that reflect one another endlessly." See Alberto Manguel, *Homer's The Iliad and The Odyssey: A Biography* (Vancouver: Douglas & McIntyre, 2007) at 2. James Joyce's *Ulysses* also evokes classic Greek literature. In the despair and unrest that was the shattered modern world post-WWI, Joyce uses the familiar journey of Odysseus to inject a sense of order that will resonate with readers. In a famous review of *Ulysses*, T.S. Eliot makes a similar point: "[i]n using the myth, in manipulating a continuous parallel between contemporaneity and antiquity, Mr. Joyce is pursuing a method which others must pursue after him . . . It is simply a way of controlling, of ordering, of giving a shape and a significance to the immense panorama of futility and anarchy which is contemporary history." See Michael Bell, *Literature, modernism and myth: belief and responsibility in the twentieth century* (Cambridge: Cambridge University Press, 1997) at 122. Joyce calls himself only "a shy guest at the feast of the world's culture," but nonetheless succeeds at characterizing modern life through the veil of antiquity. This technique of using myth to understand modern culture has been seen in countless stories. See Gilbert Highet, *The classical tradition: Greek and Roman influences on western literature* (Oxford: Oxford University Press, 1949) at 518. Another popular mythological figure, Hercules, has "embodied or endorsed" a wide range of ideas or opinions. Such an example has broad cultural appeal, due to the various myths emanating from this fascinating figure. As biographer Alastair Blanchard has written "Biography attempts to make the world understandable. It is our response to chaos." By using these tales as a framework, we are empowered to think critically about our own culture through the eyes of an ancient persona. Alastair Blanchard, *Hercules: A heroic life* (London: Granta Books, 2005) at xix.

> Faced with the specter of conspicuous failure, Alexander slashes the knot in two with his sword.[182]

As one biographer described this outcome, "Alexander was a man incapable of shrugging his shoulders and walking away from an unsuccessful effort. If, as a result of several futile attempts, he was frustrated and angry, he might very well have decided that a sudden stroke of the sword would rescue him from public embarrassment."[183]

However, my goal here is not so much to critique Bill C-32 or its proponents as it is to inspire deeper thinking about the potential ethical and legal implications of an unimpeded and universal adoption of digital locks, especially given the strategy of preemption adopted by the powerful entities that current deploy them. In the spirit of doing so, I offer yet a third account of the legend of the Gordian knot, known mostly by historians and scholars in the field of classical studies.

> [Alexander] saw the celebrated chariot which was fastened to its yoke by the bark of the cornel-tree . . . According to most writers the fastenings were so elaborately intertwined and coiled upon one another that their ends were hidden: in consequence Alexander did not know what to do, and in the end loosened the know by cutting through it with his sword, whereupon the many ends sprang into view. *But according to Aristobulus he unfastened it quite easily by removing the pin which secured the yoke to the pole of the chariot, and then pulling out the yoke itself.*[184]

Like our protagonist in Aristobulus' account, I prefer elegance to brute force. And, yet, elegant solutions are not always the stuff of political expedience. I know that there are many senior government lawyers, policy advisors and bureaucrats working on the digital copyright file who understand these arguments as well—better, actually—than the academics seeking to contribute to their improvement. The flaws in Bill C-32 are symptomatic of the larger digital lock strategy upon which they are modeled. As I have suggested in this chapter, the legal locks, just like the digital locks, just like the mechanical locks, must be understood as something more than instruments of exclusion to be used at the whim of those who hold them in their hands. One must remember that the preemptive nature

182 John Maxwell O'Brien, *Alexander the Great: The Invisible Enemy, A biography* (London: Routledge, 1992) at 70–73.

183 *Ibid.*

184 Plutarch, above note 4 at 271 [emphasis added].

of digital locks leave no room for forgiveness. Instead, digital locks simply disable the property so that it does not permit any uses other than its preprogrammed use. Perhaps more significantly, moving to the moral sphere, I have also suggested that a series of ubiquitous locks designed to keep people honest would impair the development of a *hexis*, a deep-seated disposition for honesty, by discouraging or preventing the development of practical wisdom.

My argument in this chapter has been cast through the lens of virtue, the ancient Greek idea that the good life is to be lived through the attainment of moral excellence. From this point of view, practical wisdom cannot be uploaded or downloaded. It requires a broad variety of life experiences — opportunities to navigate the messy, complex world of moral decision-making. It also requires making mistakes. How could we possibly live well, let alone flourish, in environments that increasingly seek to control our behaviour with fine-tuned granularity, by the flick of a switch permitting or forbidding various courses of conduct not proscribed by law but by lock-makers? How are we to cultivate a moral compass, a sense of right and wrong, good and bad, if we are locked on a course that leads us only from here to there with no opportunity for moral journey, deliberation or error? And what, other than some form of robotic habituation, would make us think that those endowed with the power to use digital locks in this way should have a monopoly on right conduct in the first place, or that they are always justified in using the locks as they do?

As Elizabeth Anscombe has noted, the attainment of virtue is foreign to the law's language of rights and duties. Perhaps the unity of these distinct discourses finds expression in the words of the philosopher, Joseph Raz, whose thoughts on the relationship between the morality of freedom and copyright law's concept of authorship are worthy of citation:

> All too often moralists tend to regard a person's moral life as the story of how he proves himself in the face of moral demands imposed on him by chance and circumstance. Crucial as this aspect is, it is but one side of a person's moral history. The other side of the story evolves around the person not as the object of demands imposed from the outside, but as the creator of such demands addressed to himself. We are all to a considerable degree the authors of our moral world.[185]

. . .

185 Joseph Raz, *The Morality of Freedom* (New York: Oxford University Press, 1986) at 86.

> Autonomy requires that self-creation must proceed, in part, through choice among an adequate range of options; that the agent must be aware of his options and of the meaning of his choices; and that he must be independent of coercion and manipulation by others. Personal autonomy is the ideal of free and conscious self-creation.[186]

If we are to remain, to a considerable degree, the *authors* of our *moral world*, we must maintain the ability to access it and make use of it. While the law of copyright affords protection to the creators of original works, a balanced copyright scheme must not, in the process, diminish the very possibility of self-creation. Excessive protection of digital locks places coercive limits on moral actors, preventing them from acquiring access to an adequate range of life's options. What would be the point in developing entire systems to protect creative works or other forms of property if the means by which this is achieved ultimately undermines *moral authorship* and the project of *conscious self-creation*?

---

186 *Ibid* at 390.

CHAPTER TEN

The Protection of Rights Management Information:

Modernization or Cup Half Full?

Mark Perry*

In the SAVOY:

Printed by *Henry Lintot*, Law-Printer to the King's moſt excellent Majeſty; for D. BROWNE at the *Black Swan*; J. WORRALL at the *Dove*, both near *Temple-Bar*; and A. MILLAR at *Buchanan's Head* opposite *Catherine Street* in the *Strand*, 1757**

A. AN INTRODUCTION TO RIGHTS MANAGEMENT INFORMATION

Many papers in this collection discuss the history and development of Bill C-32, *An Act to Amend the Copyright Act,*[1] introduced into the Canadian Par-

* Thanks to Michelle Alton and Ambrese Montague (UWO law class of 2007) and Dan Hynes and David Morrison (law class of 2012) and Thomas Margoni (Post Doctoral Fellow) for their research assistance.

** This "RMI" is from the front of Lord Chief Baron Gilbert, "A treatise of Tenures in Two Parts" 1757. Lintot and Millar were well known publisher/booksellers in London at the time. The same Andrew Millar was party to *Millar v. Taylor* (1769), 4 Burr. 2303, 98 E.R. 201, with the erroneous judgment proclaiming common law copyright. For more on the latter, denying the existence of common law copyright, see Mark Perry, "Acts of Parliament: Privatization, Promulgation and Crown Copyright— Is there a Need for a Royal Royalty?" (1998) 1993:3 N.Z. L. Rev. 493.

1 Bill C-32, *An Act to Amend the Copyright Act*, 3rd Sess., 40th Parl., 2010 (First reading 2 June 2010), www2.parl.gc.ca/HousePublications/Publication.aspx?Docid=4580265&file=4 [Bill C-32].

liament on 2 June 2010, so that analysis will not be duplicated here. Among the failures of copyright reform has been the lack of addressing the required "balancing" of proprietary rights on the one hand, with user rights and the public domain on the other. Rights Management Information (RMI) can aid in this balancing. The RMI of a work[2] is simply data that provide identification of rights related to that work, either directly or indirectly.[3] Although the Bill aims to address the perceived lack of compliance with the World Intellectual Property Organization (WIPO) Treaties,[4] the drafters may not have seen WIPO's own Scoping Study,[5] which recommended:

> Legal means should be found to prevent the recapture of exclusivity in works that have fallen into the public domain, whether through another intellectual property right (trademark or right in databases), property rights, other legal entitlements or technical protection, if such exclusivity is similar in scope or effect to that of copyright or is detrimental to non-rivalrous or concurrent uses of the public domain work.
>
> The 1996 WIPO Treaties should be amended to prohibit a technical impediment to reproduce, publicly communicate or making available a work that has fallen into the public domain. There is no legal basis for the enforcement of technical protection measures applied to the public domain, as public domain status should guarantee the right to make re-use, modification, reproduction and communication. It could also be clarified that only technological measures protecting copyrighted works that form a substantial part of the digital content to which they apply will be protected against circumvention. Technological measures mainly protecting public domain works, with an ancillary and minimal presence of copyrighted works, should not enjoy legal protection. [6]

Bill C-32 addresses Rights Management Information (RMI) specifically.[7] Although digital works are typically the subject of RMI protection, in

---

2 The term "work" is being used here in the sense given by copyright jurisprudence, so as to restrict this discussion to RMI in data that may be appropriate subject matter for copyright.

3 For example, "by Mark Perry" indicates the authorship of this paper, which may lead to assumptions regarding moral rights or economic rights in the absence of other more detailed indications.

4 Below note 29 with discussion in text.

5 From the World Intellectual Property Organization, *Scoping Study on Copyright and Related Rights and The Public Domain by Séverine Dusollier* (30 April 2010), www.wipo.int/ip-development/en/agenda/pdf/scoping_study_cr.pdf [Scoping Study].

6 *Ibid.*, at 68.

7 Bill C-32, above note 2, s. 41.22.

its plain vanilla form RMI predates the digital content era. The breadth of RMI's impact is now much wider than the simple protection given to pre-digital works by moral rights. For example, the removal of a title and copyright information from a novel can be taken as an attempt to remove authorship information. RMI can be seen as a type of meta-data about a work. In the realm of distribution of digital works, it may be seen as akin to the right of attribution within moral rights jurisprudence, or rights of access in permissions on files in a computer operating system such as Unix.[8] Since the beginning of time, or at least since the beginning of the creation of artistic works, authors and owners of works have wished to be identified, and so have put their name with the title on the front cover, as well as the inside of the book, signed their paintings and pottery, and in some markets, used state authorized marks to authenticate source.[9] In recent centuries, such identifications have typically been accompanied by information specifically related to the rights in the works, such as by the insertion of copyright notices, publishers' information, dates, disclaimers, permissions, International Standard Book Numbers, acknowledgements and so forth, which are typically inserted on the verso of the title page inside the work in printed volumes. An early example can be seen above in the *leader* to this paper. Over the last two decades, the growth in the digital market has led to increased variety in the types of RMI accompanying works, and some would even say that RMI only became meaningful in the digital era. Herein is addressed the application of the technologies that are being used to attach RMI to digital works and the implementations of RMI-related treaty obligations in other jurisdictions, as well as examining the parts of Bill C-32 that deal with RMI.

The basic idea behind RMI for digital works is to include meta-data along with the work that provide information on the rights that are attached to the work. For example, if you play a track on your digital music player, it will typically display the title of the track and the performer on its screen. This is minimal RMI.

B. TECHNOLOGIES

RMI is a cornerstone of systems that are aimed at regulating the rights held in digital works. RMI is often used with watermarking and stegano-

8 This Unix example is used in Jonathan Weinberg, "Hardware-Based ID, Rights Management, and Trusted Systems" in Niva Elkin-Karen & Neil Weinstock Netanel, eds., *The Commodification of Information* (New York: Aspen Publishers, 1999) 343.

9 For example, hallmarking of precious metals began in Britain around 1300AD.

graphy techniques, both of which provide information over and above that contained in the primary work. Although used by technological protection measures that attempt to regulate access or replication of digital materials, the term RMI is used to identify the data *about* the content. Watermarking may use information hidden from all but an intended recipient,[10] whereas other RMI is blatant or reasonably easy (for the technically minded) to find in works, such as those in paper (for example, currency notes) or in digital music tracks (the song title and performer displayed by an MP3 player). Regardless of the technique used, information can be embedded in all types of works. Regrettably, the technology to achieve this is yet to be perfected and may involve, in some cases, the introduction of undesirable artifacts upon reproduction in some cases, for example, a reversed pixel in a photograph.[11]

There are many technologies commercially used to embed RMI in today's digital content.[12] It is also a fertile research area, both for those attempting to crack watermarking technologies as well as those developing new ones.[13] There are many types of technologies applied to RMIs, but

---

10 Steganography is not differentiated from watermarking in this paper and watermarking will be used as a generic term for embedded RMI. In practice, steganography is usually used to describe technologies that hide messages intended for particular recipients inside content that is available to anyone. A recent example is that of the Russian spies who put messages in picture on websites; see Caitlin Stier, "Russian spy ring hid secret messages on the web" *New Scientist* (02 July 2010), www.newscientist.com/article/dn19126-russian-spy-ring-hid-secret-messages-on-the-web.html.

11 See Brian Dipert, "Security scheme doesn't hold water (marking)" (21 December 2000) *Electronic Design News* 35, www.edn.com/contents/images/56211.pdf. For a discussion of how must steganalysis (i.e., looking for steganograpy in works) involves searching for artifacts, which give away the presence of a hidden message, see Sathiamoorthy Manoharan, "An Empirical Analysis of RS Steganalysis" in *Proceedings of the 2008 Third International Conference on Internet Monitoring and Protection* 172, (Washington, D.C.: IEEE Computer Society, 2008).

12 Most technologies that are developed by private companies are then put forward to try to get the technique approved as a standard or adopted by a major content supplier. An early standardization attempt, the Secure Digital Music Initiative (SDMI) seemed promising with 200-plus companies and organizations participating to find the answer to the problems posed to music publishers by digital technologies, but environments such as Napster and Gnutella overtook the initiative, as well as inherent weaknesses in the technology. The SDMI website (www.sdmi.org) seems non-functional and the domain name is registered by the Recording Industry Association of America (date last attempted access: 3 July 2010).

13 Over the last three years, there have been around 1,500 research papers on digital watermarking and steganography published by Institute of Electrical and Electronics Engineers and the Association of Computing Machinery.

most rely on embedding the meta-data into the supplied content and apply some level of cryptography to limit access to such information. One such is *FairPlay*. Apple iTunes includes *FairPlay* Digital Rights Management,[14] with songs that customers purchase and download, but also claims that it has "[o]ver 13 million high-quality, DRM-free songs."[15] Even though these songs do not include DRM technologies to directly control replication or playback, they do contain RMI within the file that contains the work. The overt part of such information is simple to see within the iTunes application.[16] The user can see information related to the song file, some of which will be stored locally, such as when the track was last played, the name of the work, album, singer, "(p)" owner (presumably the performer's performance), the fact that the song is a "purchased AAC audiofile,"[17] the size, bit and sample rates (of encoding), the account name, purchaser name, purchase date, date modified, number of plays, when last played, and the encoding complexity. However, it is not made clear to the user how much of this information is attached to the music file itself, what other information has been recorded and how much is kept on the local computer. With a little investigation it can be seen that in addition to the information related to the work directly (i.e., titles, copyrights, etc.), also embedded is the name of the user and the user's account identity. There may also be other encrypted information. Sometimes it is difficult to see what is strictly RMI relating to the work *itself* and what is information *about the user*. Obviously, some user information will be relevant to RMI (for example, to whom a license is granted to playback a track), but if the information is obfuscated it is unclear what is needed for RMI and what is there for the benefit of the provider's marketing efforts, rather than managing the rights in the particular work. It should be noted that *FairPlay* is not strictly a "copy protection scheme," but rather more of a "distribution

---

14 The FairPlay technology is a digital rights management (DRM) technology created by Apple, Inc., based on technology created by the company Veridisc. FairPlay is built into the QuickTime multimedia software and used by the iPhone, iPod, iPad, Apple TV, iTunes, and iTunes Store and the App Store.

15 See "What is iTunes?," Apple Inc., www.apple.com/itunes/what-is. As of 2009, Apple's iTunes had a 26.7% share of the total USA market, double its 2007 share, according to Billboards analysis of market data: Ed Christman, "Digital Divide" (22 May 2010) *Billboard*, www.billboard.biz/bbbiz/content_display/magazine/upfront/e3i12fe2557a9382597671a522cc1cc901.

16 Select a track on your computer from iTunes and "get info."

17 Advanced Audio Coding (AAC) coded was developed as part of the MPEG-4 specification. Details can be found at: "What is MPEG-4?," MPEG Industry Forum, www.m4if.org/mpeg4.

management scheme." For example, even with DRM loaded files, the user can make as many copies of the same work on an individual computer as he or she likes.[18]

The use of *FairPlay* by iTunes is but one common example of the many other RMI systems in place, not only for music, but also for films and video,[19] photographs,[20] software,[21] cloud services[22]—indeed most digital information supplied as content to a user on a commercial basis will carry some kind of RMI.

C. ALTERING OR REMOVING RMI

A range of technologies are used to affix the RMI to the work, from the trivial (such as the author information on this paper's digital file) to the sophisticated (such as Adobe's digital signatures using a certification authority),[23] but there are always those who will attempt to engage in removing or changing RMI. For some electronic works, simply changing the file name or deleting the RMI is an effective evasion strategy.[24] Unless a very sophisticated scheme of RMI locking or embedding is used, digital RMI remains as easy to remove for the technically minded as it is to re-

18 There are other aspects of such schemes which go beyond the scope of this paper, such as that they typically rely on a user contract (terms of service must be accepted before permission is granted to access and download from the system) defining the terms of use of the service. There are also some fairly simple means of circumventing such protection schemes for the computer proficient, and software is available online ready-made for those that are not so proficient. For discussion of usage contracts see Stefan Bechtold, "Digital Rights Management in the United States and Europe" (2004) 52:2 Am. J. Comp. L. 323.

19 This includes the classic Content Scrambling System (CSS) used on film DVDs and the more recent Advanced Access Content System (AACS) for Blu-Ray Discs.

20 Such as PixelSafe and PixelLive, two products offered by Celartem Technology, Inc.

21 For instance, Microsoft Office contains its own RMI entitled Information Rights Management (IRM) which allows individuals to control access to documents, workbooks, and presentations through permissions. This helps prevent sensitive information from being printed, forwarded, or copied by unauthorized people. After a permission to a file has been created using IRM, the access and usage restrictions are enforced no matter where the information is because the permission to a file is stored in the document file itself.

22 Such as Adobe LiveCycle Rights Management.

23 For a good introduction, see "A Primer on Electronic Document Security: Technical Whitepaper," Adobe, www.adobe.com/security.

24 Although it should be noted that some word processors, such as Microsoft Word, keep a lot of information in the file without the knowledge of most users that relate to the authorship and editing of any particular work.

move printed RMI from a book by ripping off the cover and tearing out its copyright notice. As fast as technological measures are developed, new means of circumvention arise and there is a cycle of escalation in the types of technologies used. For example, iTunes, concomitant with its popularity as a music source, has undergone rapid development in response to circumvention of the technological protection measures.[25] Strong encryption techniques can slow down circumvention, however strong encryption has its own drawbacks. RMI, whether for a music file or text, which has been encrypted with strong techniques will typically take more processing time to handle, thus requiring more powerful chips or greater allocation of resources for rapid access than more weakly encrypted versions. Some techniques require authentication from a remote site, which can be inconvenient for users.[26] In other words, there is a balance required between three primary concerns of user digital materials: security, convenience, and performance. There is also a balance that needs to be struck between security and privacy regarding how much information about a user a content provider should require. In addition, although these measures are often touted as being for the protection of publishers and artists from copyright infringement, in many cases they offer publishers much broader commercial opportunities, such as getting users to pay further for use of the material in a different format or for other "added-value" services including market research and advertising. However, it is clear that the removal of (true) RMI should be discouraged: RMI can serve as a means of furthering the provenance of the often multiple and intertwined rights that may subsist in a digital work.

D. WIPO TREATMENT AND JURISDICTIONAL IMPLEMENTATION

In December 1996 two new treaties were adopted under the management of WIPO: the *WIPO Copyright Treaty* (WCT) and the *WIPO Performances*

25 Norwegian programmer Jon Lech Johansen initiated this cycle when he first enabled iTunes songs to be played on a home computer, see: A. Orlowski, "iTunes DRM cracked wide open for GNU/Linux. Seriously," *The Register* (5 January, 2004), www.theregister.co.uk/2004/01/05/itunes_drm_cracked_wide_open. Jon has since become notorious for cracking Fairplay, see: R. Levine, "Unlocking the iPod", *Fortune* (23 October, 2006), http://money.cnn.com/magazines/fortune/fortune_archive/2006/10/30/8391726/index.htm.

26 Such as with Maxis's game "Spore" which uses Sony's SecuROM technologies. This was inconvenient for users, and led to pirating and criticism by users, and was the most pirated game in 2008. At the end of that year Maxis dropped using SecuROM.

and Phonograms Treaty (WPPT).[27] These were the first treaties to address intellectual property rights in the digital network environment. To date there are eighty-eight contracting parties to the WCT, of which nine, including Canada, have signed but not ratified. Similarly, there are currently eighty-six contracting parties to WPPT, of which ten (including Canada) have not ratified.[28] The majority of countries that first adopted these measures were developing countries or countries in transition, however, now many industrialized countries have ratified these treaties.[29] For example, the entire membership of the European Community has signed these agreements and ratified them,[30] along with USA, China, Japan, and Australia. The EU ratified the WCT and the WPPT on 14 December 2009 and both came into effect on 14 March 2010.[31]

Canada has been a signatory of the WCT and WPPT since 1997 and has, for the third time since becoming a signatory, introduced a bill to entrench WCT and WPPT obligations into Canadian legislation.[32] It can be argued that the WCT and WPPT only make small extensions to copyright as prescribed in the *Berne Convention*,[33] which Canada implemented long

---

27 *WIPO Copyright Treaty*, S. Treaty Doc. No. 105-17 (1997) [WCT]; 36 ILM 65 (1997); *WIPO Performances and Phonograms Treaty*, S. Treaty Doc. No. 105-17, 36 ILM 76 (1997) [WPPT].

28 The preceding information about the WCT and WPPT is current as of 1 July 2010. See "Contracting Parties: *WIPO Copyright Treaty*," www.wipo.int/treaties/en/ShowResults.jsp?lang=en&treaty_id=16; "Contracting Parties: *WIPO Performances and Phonograms Treaty*," www.wipo.int/treaties/en/ShowResults.jsp?lang=en&treaty_id=20.

29 *Ibid.*

30 *Council Decision 2000/278/EC of 16 March 2000 on the approval, on behalf of the European Community, of the WIPO Copyright Treaty and the WIPO Performances and Phonograms Treaty*, [2000] O.J.L. 89/6, http://eur-lex.europa.eu/LexUriServ/LexUriServ.do?uri=CELEX:32000D0278:EN:HTML.

31 *Ibid.*

32 Bill C-32, above note 1

33 According to Article 1(1) of the *WIPO Copyright Treaty*, the WCT is a "special agreement within the meaning of Article 20 of the *Berne Convention*"; Article 20 of the *Berne Convention* provides that "[t]he Governments of the countries of the Union reserve the right to enter into special agreements among themselves, in so far as such agreements grant to authors more extensive rights than those granted by the Convention." See *WIPO Copyright Treaty* (20 December 1996), http://www.wipo.int/treaties/en/ip/wct/trtdocs_wo033.html#P87_12240, (1997) 36 I.L.M. 65 (entry into force 6 March 2002) [WCT]; *Berne Convention for the Protection of Literary and Artistic Works* (9 September 1886; last amended 28 September 1979), www.wipo.int/treaties/en/ip/berne/trtdocs_wo001.html, 1161 U.N.T.S. 3. The *Berne Convention for the Protection of Literary and Artistic Works* (9 September 1886; last amended 28 September 1979), http://www.wipo.int/treaties/en/ip/berne/trtdocs_wo001.html, 1161 U.N.T.S. 3. In 1998, Canada acceded to the 1971 version of the *Berne Convention for the Protec-*

ago,[34] and as well as the World Trade Organization Agreement on Trade Related Aspects of Intellectual Property Rights.[35] In other words, Canada is already complying with much of the requirements of WCT and WPPT. However, the Treaties do impose some significant new obligations and extensions to the law of copyright, most notably in connection with distribution rights, RMI, and technological protection measures (TPM) employed to control the use of copyrighted works.[36]

Following the ratifications and the entry into force of the WCT, there have been a number of jurisdictions implementing new legislation, including specific protection of RMI since the WCT defined RMI and the obligations of contracting parties in Article 12:

> **Article 12**
> **Obligations concerning Rights Management Information**
>
> (1) Contracting Parties shall provide adequate and effective legal remedies against any person knowingly performing any of the following acts knowing, or with respect to civil remedies having reasonable grounds to know, that it will induce, enable, facilitate or conceal an infringement of any right covered by this Treaty or the Berne Convention:
>
> (i) to remove or alter any electronic rights management information without authority;
>
> (ii) to distribute, import for distribution, broadcast or communicate to the public, without authority, works or copies of works know-

---

tion of Literary and Artistic Works. The *Berne Convention* was first established in 1886 and has been revised and amended a number of times. The *Berne Convention* sets minimum standards of protection for authors of literary, dramatic, musical and artistic works and defines the scope and duration of protection.

34 See, e.g., Sunny Handa, "A Review of Canada's International Copyright Obligations" (1997) 42 McGill L.J. 961 at 969, where it is noted that "[a]lthough Canada did not become a signatory to the *Berne Convention* in its own right until 10 April 1928, the *Berne Convention* did apply to Canada as a colony of Britain, one of the original signatories." Canada officially ratified the *Berne Convention* with passage of the 1931 amendments to the *Copyright Act*: see *An Act to Amend the Copyright Act*, S.C. 1931, c. 8.

35 *Agreement on Trade-Related Aspects of Intellectual Property Rights* (15 April 1994) in *Agreement Establishing the World Trade Organization, Annex 1C*, www.wto.org/english/docs_e/legal_e/27-trips_01_e.htm, 1869 U.N.T.S. 299, (1993) 33 I.L.M. 81. This was implemented by Canada through the *World Trade Organization Implementation Act*, S.C. 1994, c. 47, http://laws.justice.gc.ca/en/W-11.8/FullText.html.

36 WCT, above note 33, art. 6 (distribution rights), art. 11 (technological measures), and art. 12 (rights management information).

ing that electronic rights management information has been removed or altered without authority.

(2) As used in this Article, "rights management information" means information which identifies the work, the author of the work, the owner of any right in the work, or information about the terms and conditions of use of the work, and any numbers or codes that represent such information, when any of these items of information is attached to a copy of a work or appears in connection with the communication of a work to the public. [37]

The article carries a footnote:[38]

> **Agreed statements concerning Article 12:** It is understood that the reference to "infringement of any right covered by this Treaty or the Berne Convention" includes both exclusive rights and rights of remuneration.
>
> It is further understood that Contracting Parties will not rely on this Article to devise or implement rights management systems that would have the effect of imposing formalities which are not permitted under the Berne Convention or this Treaty, prohibiting the free movement of goods or impeding the enjoyment of rights under this Treaty.[39]

Article 19 of the WPPT is essentially identical and applies to information that identifies "the performer, the performance of the performer, the producer of the phonogram, the phonogram, the owner of any right in the performance or phonogram, or information about the terms and conditions of use of the performance or phonogram."[40] The first notable feature of these Articles in the WCT and WPPT is the knowledge requirement, or "reasonable grounds to know" for civil suits, that the removal of the RMI will be for infringement. The second point is that the treaty definitions do not restrict RMI to electronic information, though the infringement parts of the articles are aimed at electronic RMI. The implementation of RMI protection in various jurisdictions has been varied, and a brief survey is warranted in light of the Canadian proposals discussed later.

---

37 *WCT, above* note 33, art. 12.

38 *Ibid.*

39 *Ibid.* at n. 11.

40 *WIPO Performances and Phonograms Treaty* (20 December 1996), http://www.wipo.int/treaties/en/ip/wppt/trtdocs_wo034.html#P143_21677, (1997) 36 I.L.M. 76 (entry into force 20 May 2002), art. 19.

E. EARLIER CHANGES IN JURISDICTIONS COMPARABLE TO CANADA

Even amongst those countries that have ratified the WCT or intend to shortly, there are significant variations in the approaches to RMI protection provided by "traditional" copyright regimes. A brief examination of the legislation in New Zealand, Japan, the European Union, and the United States highlights some of the diversity, although further discussion is outside of the scope of this overview.[41]

In 2008, New Zealand introduced an Amendment to their *Copyright Act* that received Royal Assent later that same year. This Amendment includes provisions stating that it is an offence to circumvent a TPM and it is not an offence to shift format of a copyrighted work under certain circumstances. The Amendment also provides protection for copyright management information (CMI), the equivalent of RMI.[42] Specifically, at section 226F CMI is defined as:

> . . . copyright management information means information attached to, or embodied in, a copy of a work that—
> (a) identifies the work, and its author or copyright owner; or
> (b) identifies or indicates some or all of the terms and conditions for using the work, or indicates that the use of the work is subject to terms and conditions.[43]

Further to that, at section 226H(1) the amendment specifies that:

> A person (A) must not, in the course of business, make, import, sell, let for hire, offer or expose for sale or hire, or advertise for sale or hire, a copy of a work if any copyright management information attached to, or embodied in, the copy has been removed or modified without the authority of the copyright owner or the exclusive licensee.[44]

And the act of removal of a "CMI" is criminalized in section 226J:

---

41 For a WIPO review of the legal framework in the US, EU, Australia, and Japan see World Intellectual Property Organization Standing Committee on Copyright and Related Rights, *Current Developments in the Field of Digital Rights Management* (4 May 2004), SCCR/10/2, www.wipo.int/edocs/mdocs/copyright/en/sccr_10/sccr_10_2_rev.pdf.

42 *Copyright (New Technologies) Amendment Act 2008* (N.Z.), 2008/27, www.legislation.govt.nz/act/public/2008/0027/latest/whole.html#DLM1122767.

43 *Copyright Act 1994* (N.Z.), 1994/143, http://legislation.govt.nz/act/public/1994/0143/latest/whole.html?search=ts_act_copyright+act_resel&p=1#dlm345634 , s. 226F.

44 *Ibid.*, s. 226H(1).

> (1) A person (A) who contravenes section 226H commits an offence if—
> (a) A knows that the copyright management information has been removed or modified without the authority of the copyright owner or exclusive licensee; and
> (b) A knows that dealing in the work will induce, enable, facilitate, or conceal an infringement of the copyright in the work.
>
> (2) A person who commits an offence under subsection (1) is liable on conviction on indictment to a fine not exceeding $150,000 or a term of imprisonment not exceeding 5 years or both. [45]

For the New Zealand approach, it is notable that there is no distinction between digital and analogue content.

Japan was an early adopter of the attempt to address digital issues and ratified the WCT before the treaty came into force; thus it became bound by the treaties on 6 March 2002, along with the other nations that had ratified by that time. The Japanese definition of RMI generally follows the WIPO Treaties, however, there exists some specificity that is not found in other international agreements. For example, Article 2 of the Japanese Copyright Law provides:[46]

> (xxi) "rights management information" means information concerning moral rights or copyright mentioned in Article 17, paragraph (1) or rights mentioned in Article 89, paragraphs (1) to (4) (hereinafter in this item referred to as "copyright, etc.") which falls within any of the following (a), (b) and (c) and which is recorded in a memory or transmitted by electromagnetic means together with works, performances, phonograms, or sounds or images of broadcasts or wire diffusions, excluding such information as not used for knowing how works, etc. are exploited, for conducting business relating to the authorization to exploit works, etc. and for other management of copyright, etc. by computer:
> (a) information which specifies works, etc., owners of copyright, etc. and other matters specified by Cabinet Order;
> (b) information relating to manners and conditions of the exploitation in case where the exploitation of works, etc. is authorized;

---

45 *Ibid.*, s. 226J.

46 Copyright Law of Japan, as Amended (19 June 2009) at Article 2, From the Copyright Research and Information Center (CRIC) website, June 2010. Translated by Yukifusa Oyama *et al.*, www.cric.or.jp/cric_e/clj/clj.html.

(c) information which enables to specify matters mentioned in (a) or (b) above in comparison with other information. [47]

The Japanese definition of RMI restricts it to electronic versions. The intentional alteration or removal of RMI, or distribution of copies of works knowing there has been unlawful addition or removal of RMI, is deemed by Article 113[48] to be an infringement of "moral rights of authors, copyright, moral rights of performers or neighboring rights relating to rights management information." Excepting private use, Article 119[49] makes such actions punishable by imprisonment for up to ten years or fines up to ten million yen.[50] Notable in the Japanese legislation is the reference to moral rights and copyright, specifically linking them to RMI.

The EU adopted a Directive on "the harmonization of certain aspects of copyright and related rights in the information society."[51] In addition to EU wide harmonization, the Directive was aimed at gaining compliance with the terms of the WCT and WPPT.[52] The Directive addresses RMI in Article 7:

Obligations concerning rights-management information

1. Member States shall provide for adequate legal protection against any person knowingly performing without authority any of the following acts:

(a) the removal or alteration of any electronic rights-management information;

(b) the distribution, importation for distribution, broadcasting, communication or making available to the public of works or other subject-matter protected under this Directive or under Chapter III of Directive 96/9/EC from which electronic rights-management information has been removed or altered without authority, if such person knows, or has reasonable grounds to know, that by so doing he is inducing, enabling, facilitating or

47 Copyright Law of Japan 19 June, 2009, Law No. 48 (1970), art. 2. This translation is from the CRIC website, translated by Yukifusa Oyama *et al.*, www.cric.or.jp/cric_e/clj/clj.html.

48 *Ibid.*, art. 113.

49 *Ibid.*, art. 119.

50 Around CAN$121,000 as of 3 July 2010.

51 *Directive 2001/29/EC of the European Parliament and of the Council of 22 May 2001 on the Harmonisation of Certain Aspects of Copyright and Related Rights in the Information Society* (EU), O.J.L. 167/10, http://eur-lex.europa.eu/smartapi/cgi/sga_doc?smartapi!celexapi!prod!CELEXnumdoc&lg=en&numdoc=32001L0029&model=guichett.

52 *Ibid.* preamble para. 15.

> concealing an infringement of any copyright or any rights related to copyright as provided by law, or of the sui generis right provided for in Chapter III of Directive 96/9/EC.
>
> 2. For the purposes of this Directive, the expression "rights-management information" means any information provided by right holders which identifies the work or other subject-matter referred to in this Directive or covered by the sui generis right provided for in Chapter III of Directive 96/9/EC, the author or any other right holder, or information about the terms and conditions of use of the work or other subject-matter, and any numbers or codes that represent such information.[53]

The adoption of this Directive meant that Member States agreed to implement it before 22nd December 2002, but only Greece and Denmark met that deadline.[54] It is interesting in that it shows the need, in the mind of the drafters of the Directive, for knowledge by the person who removes RMI and is by this act inducing, enabling, facilitating or concealing copyright infringement. Secondly it is limited to "electronic" RMI. By December 2009 the EU and its member States ratified the treaties, with the usual fanfare, but reaffirming the political preconceptions of the continuing benefits of the WIPO Treaties:

> Internal Market Commissioner Charlie McCreevy commented on the WIPO ratifications: "Today is an important day for the European Union and its Member States and WIPO. We, as a group have shown our attachment to the international system of protection of copyright and related rights. These two treaties brought protection up to speed with modern technologies. As the technological evolution ac-

---

53 *Ibid.* art. 7.

54 In a European Commission press release it is noted, "By adopting the Directive in the Council, Member States agreed to implement it before 22 December 2002. The European Court has already ruled against Belgium, Finland, Sweden and the UK — for the territory of Gibraltar — for their failure to implement the Directive. The Commission has now decided to start infringement proceedings against Belgium, Finland Sweden for non-compliance with the Court's rulings. In the case of the United Kingdom, the Commission has postponed its decision to start infringement proceedings as the UK authorities have informed the Commission that implementation in the territory of Gibraltar is imminent." See European Commission, News Release, IP/05/347 (21 March 2005), http://europa.eu/rapid/pressReleasesAction.do?reference=IP/05/347&format=HTML&aged=1&language=EN&guiLanguage=en.

celerates, protecting creators and creative industries is more urgent than ever."[55]

A common measuring stick for the implementation of WCT and WPPT provisions can be found in the United States where the early adoption of the *Digital Millennium Copyright Act* (DMCA) and case law shows both the potential and the pitfalls of such legislation. The DMCA contains provisions regulating RMI that it refers to as copyright management information.[56] The definition of CMI combines the definitions of RMI in the WCT and WPPT:

> DEFINITION—As used in this section, the term "copyright management information" means any of the following information conveyed in connection with copies or phonorecords of a work or performances or displays of a work, including in digital form, except that such term does not include any personally identifying information about a user of a work or of a copy, phonorecord, performance, or display of a work. . .[57]

The DMCA has two levels of knowledge requirements in this regard. Section 1202 makes it illegal (as in criminally actionable) to knowingly remove or distribute works that are known to have had their CMI removed, "knowing, or, with respect to civil remedies under section 1203, having reasonable grounds to know, that it will induce, enable, facilitate, or conceal an infringement of any right under this title."[58] Thus, only those who have knowledge of the tampering with the CMI and also that the alteration is for infringing purposes, are liable. However, the alteration of a CMI to facilitate a prohibited circumvention would clearly satisfy this requirement. There is also a prohibition on the provision of false CMI for infringement purposes. There are a few particularly interesting facets of section 1202. This section specifically excludes user information in the definition; thus, the alteration of the user information that is included in the Advanced Audio Encoding information in iTunes downloaded files would not be protected by this section. Superficially this may seem surprising and even a weakness in the DMCA as RMI may require user information as noted

55 European Commission, News Release, IP/09/1916 (14 December 2009), http://europa.eu/rapid/pressReleasesAction.do?reference=IP/09/1916&format=HTML&aged=0&language=EN&guiLanguage=en.

56 The New Zealand legislation uses the same taxonomy—see above note 43 at s. 226F.

57 *Digital Millennium Copyright Act*, Pub. L. No. 105-304, § 1202 (c), 112 Stat. 2860 at 2873 (1998), http://frwebgate.access.gpo.gov/cgi-bin/getdoc.cgi?dbname=105_cong_public_laws&docid=f:publ304.105.

58 *Ibid.* at §1202(b)(3).

above, but given the way that the technology now typically binds the RMI (CMI in US parlance) with other Digital Rights Management (DRM) encoding, it could be argued that the user information so bound with DRM is covered under the other anti-circumvention provisions of the DMCA. For example, software that is tied to use on a particular computer or set of computers would probably include user information in its security paradigm (or at least machine information). The types of RMI in the definition of CMI includes the usual suspects: title of work, name of author, copyright owner, other identifying information, conditions for use, identifying symbols, and, with the exception of public performance by radio and television stations, the identification of performer, writer, director, and performer's performance. Section 1202 also includes a number of exceptions for broadcast and cable transmissions and for adoption of standards in the broadcast and cable realm. The civil remedies provided within the DMCA are found in section 1203 while the criminal offenses and penalties are found in section 1204. Both of these sections apply to circumventions outlined in the provisions of sections 1201 and 1202.[59] The DMCA definition of RMI is not restricted to electronic versions.

An early illustration of problems with the DMCA arose in 2000. It was suggested by a group of computer scientists that one of the watermarking technologies being considered in the Secure Digital Music Initiative (SDMI) had some weaknesses. In September 2000, the SDMI called on members of the public to attempt to crack several security technologies that SDMI was contemplating for use with the digital distribution of music. Contestants needed to click through a series of screens and "I Agree" buttons in order to take part in the contest in which SDMI offered a reward of up to $10,000 for each successful attack. However, in order to collect the money the contestants needed to enter into a separate agreement assigning all intellectual property rights in the effort to SDMI and promising not to disclose any details of the attack. A group of researchers was successful in attacking one of the technologies, but subsequently refused to accept the $10,000 as they wished to present their efforts in a scientific paper. After being warned by the SDMI, they decided not to present the paper and instead commenced an action against the constitutionality of the DMCA.[60] This case illustrates one of the problems common to all

---

59 17 U.S.C. §§1201–1204

60 "Computer Scientists Challenge Constitutionality of DMCA", Case Comment on *Felten et al. v. Recording Industry Association of America Inc. et al.*, (2001) 7:24 Andrews Intell. Prop. Litig. Rep. 5. Although this challenge failed, Felten and other researchers in this project were not pursued under the DMCA.

areas of anti-circumvention legislation, namely the dampening effect on research into the area. Although the work described here was directed at developing a means of circumventing an RMI technology, other less targeted research could also fall foul of this "catch-all" legislation.[61]

F. THE CANADIAN APPROACH

In the Copyright Reform Statement there is the suggestion that a simple following of the WCT and WPPT articles is sufficient to achieve the desired effect of modernizing copyright to meet the needs of the digital age:

> In conformity with the WCT and WPPT, the alteration or removal of rights management information (RMI) embedded in copyright material, when done to further or conceal infringement, would itself constitute an infringement of copyright. Copyright would also be infringed by persons who, for infringing purposes, enable or facilitate alteration or removal or who, without authorization, distribute copyright material from which RMI has been altered or removed. [62]

Given the evolution and growing maturity of the digital content market, a simple codification of the minimal requirements of the Treaties is unsatisfactory to meet the needs of today, let alone the future. Unfortunately, this is the approach that the Canadian federal government took when it introduced Bill C-32, its latest attempt to "modernize" the *Copyright Act*.[63] This Bill has been brought in with the explicit purpose of amending the *Copyright Act* to make it compliant with the WCT and WPPT, including prohibitions on the circumvention of technological protection measures and prohibiting tampering of RMI. This is the third such government attempt to reform the *Copyright Act* for these purposes since 2005.[64] There has been very little variation in the sections dealing with RMI over the five year period.

---

61 For example, downloading and testing software that removes user identities from RMI, or even using simple tools to uncover the content of RMI information as used for this paper, could fall foul of a broadly drafted section.

62 "Government Statement on Proposals for Copyright Reform", Government of Canada, http://strategis.ic.gc.ca/eic/site/crp-prda.nsf/eng/rp01142.html. The Bill to amend the *Copyright Act*, Bill C-32 was introduced 2 June 2010.

63 Bill C-32, above note 1.

64 Bill C-60, *An Act to amend the Copyright Act*, 1st Sess., 37th Parl., 2005, 1st session, 37th Parliament, First Reading 20 June 2005; Bill C-61, *An Act to amend the Copyright Act*, 2nd Sess., 39th Parl., 2008 First Reading 12 June 2008.

The Bill modifies the *Copyright Act* with a Canadian version of the RMI definition:

> **Definition of "rights management information"**
>
> 41.22 (4) In this section, "rights management information" means information that
>
> (a) is attached to or embodied in a copy of a work, a performer's performance fixed in a sound recording or a sound recording, or appears in connection with its communication to the public by telecommunication; and
>
> (b) identifies or permits the identification of the work or its author, the performance or its performer, the sound recording or its maker or the holder of any rights in the work, the performance or the sound recording, or concerns the terms or conditions of the work's performance's or sound recording's use.[65]

This definition is broad and not limited to electronic or digital RMI, nor to electronic or digital content — the two could be combined. For example a book could have a radio frequency identity device inserted into the cover that included RMI. Many products have such devices, primarily for asset management and market tracking.[66]

Bill C-32 aims to amend the *Copyright Act* in relation to RMI by adding the following prohibitions:

> **Prohibition — rights management information**
>
> 41.22 (1) No person shall knowingly remove or alter any rights management information in electronic form without the consent of the owner of the copyright in the work, the performer's performance or the sound recording, if the person knows or should have known that the removal or alteration will facilitate or conceal any infringement of the owner's copyright or adversely affect the owner's right to remuneration under section 19.
>
> **Removal or alteration of rights management information**
>
> (2) The owner of the copyright in a work, a performer's performance fixed in a sound recording or a sound recording is, subject to

65 *Ibid.*, s. 41.22(4).

66 Indeed, RFID devices are even being used in hospitals to track patients. Jill Fisher and Torin Monahan "Tracking the social dimensions of RFID systems in hospitals" International Journal of Medical Informatics (March 2008) 77/3: "Radio frequency identification (RFID) is an emerging technology that is rapidly becoming the standard for hospitals to track inventory, identify patients, and manage personnel . . . ."

this Act, entitled to all remedies — by way of injunction, damages, accounts, delivery up and otherwise — that are or may be conferred by law for the infringement of copyright against a person who contravenes subsection (1).

Subsequent acts

(3) The copyright owner referred to in subsection (2) has the same remedies against a person who, without the owner's consent, knowingly does any of the following acts with respect to any material form of the work, the performer's performance fixed in a sound recording or the sound recording and knows or should have known that the rights management information has been removed or altered in a way that would give rise to a remedy under that subsection:

(a) sells it or rents it out;
(b) distributes it to an extent that the copyright owner is prejudicially affected;
(c) by way of trade, distributes it, exposes or offers it for sale or rental or exhibits it in public;
(d) imports it into Canada for the purpose of doing anything referred to in any of paragraphs (a) to (c); or
(e) communicates it to the public by telecommunication.[67]

The Canadian approach, thus far, is closely tied to the terms in the treaties and does not limit the definition of RMI to the digital environment, unlike its Japanese counterpart,[68] but it does restrict RMI in the infringement section, unlike the New Zealand Act[69]. The other point is that the removal or alteration of the RMI should be with knowledge that the change would be to further or conceal copyright infringement, as is common in the DMCA as well as in the New Zealand and Japanese legislation as well as the European Directive. However, the interpretation of the intent required varies between nations. Most legislation to date, with the possible exception of the proposed changes in India that are not reviewed here,[70] has taken the WCT and WPPT templates and implemented with little change.

---

67 *Ibid.*, ss.41.22(1)–(3).

68 Discussed above note 47.

69 Discussed above note 43.

70 This is discussed in Mark Perry, "Towards Legal Protection for Digital Rights Management in India: Necessity or Burden?" (draft of 23 July 2010), http://ssrn.com/abstract=1647582.

G. IS THERE A BETTER WAY?

By combining access, copying, and RMI technologies into a complete DRM environment, a content provider is able to exercise much greater control over the ways in which content can be used by consumers. Such control measures range from limiting access to particular start and end dates, the number of times a product can be used, whether it can be copied and/or the type of device on which a file can be played or transferred. RMI in itself is fairly innocuous as in its naïve form it merely states what every consumer may like to know (i.e., the provenance of the work, what can be done with the work, and when the work may be freely reproduced). Problems for the user of a work can arise when RMI is melded with user information, creating an individualized RMI for the individual user that contains information that is not available to the user. This then becomes a tool that can be used as a quasi-secret tracking device of user behaviour that may be inseparable from the total DRM system applied to the work in question. RMI in digital works offers users a possible benefit that is often overlooked: namely, that the content of the work can be discriminated at a level of granularity unseen in physical works or analogue recordings. There are potential benefits to users in that they can choose to 'buy' just one track of an album, or view a film once, without the need for the larger purchase of the whole album or cinematograph.

The WCT and WPPT, although determined to address new technologies, are arguably already technologically outdated.[71] Rather than continue to pursue piecemeal and fragmented regulatory solutions, a new, more comprehensive approach to the control of distribution of digital works could be formulated. There is an opportunity for Canada to be ahead of the curve in legislation concerning RMI, providing a unique opportunity to benefit all parties from end to end in the digital content stream. The following features introduced in legislation would provide benefits to all:

1. *Transparent*: All RMI attached or embedded in a work should be fully readable by all users;
2. *Complete* and *balanced*: RMI should identify limits on the rights claimed, e.g., parts of works that are not protected by copyright should be clear (e.g., parts in the public domain);

---

71 For example, there was not a commercial product that would allow a content creator to "trace" works over the internet at the time the treaties were developed. Digimarc advises that users of "Mywatermarc" technology are able to "Track your covertly watermarked photos on millions of pages across the public Internet." http://digimarc.com

3. *Private*: User information collected by suppliers of content should be identified, limited, disclosed (to the user) and protected;
4. *Fresh*: The information should be current.

There are technological solutions for these stated objectives, which at first sight may seem burdensome for the provider of content, or even challenging to the purposes for which RMI are employed. For example, *transparency* does not mean that the RMI should not be embedded in the work and encrypted (and thus hard to remove), rather that access to the authorized user could be provided, or the embedded content replicated as stand alone. To provide *complete* and *balanced* RMI would create a burden in the sense that content not protected by copyright would need to be identified and disclosed by the provider, but given that the provider is charging for (access to) such content, this seems a reasonable request. Aspects of securing *privacy* of user-related RMI will also create work and cost for content providers, but even without legislative changes in copyright law, this is likely to be necessary under privacy legislation. Perhaps the idea of keeping RMI *fresh* may seem daunting to some. Indeed, this may seem like a heavy transaction burden to place on the suppliers of content, as noted in an earlier Canadian study:

> Some commentators have noted that certain information currently included as "rights management information" in accordance with the definitions provided in the WCT and WPPT may change often during the lifetime of the copyright. In particular, the rights owner may often change, though the author will not, or in the case of a particular sound recording, the performer will not. Similarly, terms and conditions may not only change, but have uncertain legal validity in Canada. This may cause confusion among users and detract from a rights management regime rather than promote it. [72]

However, as we become increasingly networked, with data flowing back and forth between suppliers on a regular basis, even this doesn't seem too much to ask of a new content-provider industry. It is clear that the old relationships between distributor–publisher–rights-holders–author–consumer as determined under the "traditional" content dissemination

72 Industry Canada Intellectual Property Directorate & Canadian Heritage Copyright Policy Branch, *Consultation Paper on Digital Copyright Issues* (22 June 2001), http://strategis.ic.gc.ca/eic/site/crp-prda.nsf/vwapj/digital.pdf/$FILE/digital.pdf at 28.

framework is crumbling, and likely to need reformation within the next decade anyway.[73]

The use of RMI could move the provision of digital content into the twenty-first century; it can provide information to users *in addition to* the freedoms that they enjoy under the law. This aspect of providing the limitations on the rights of copyright holders and content suppliers is typically ignored, although it would go a long way towards balancing the legislation. This should be mandated in any reform of the Canadian copyright legislation. There is always the potential danger of confusing consumers by giving them information, but this is hardly an argument for keeping them in the dark. A framework can be developed, with the appropriate resources and timeframe, that will support informed digital work use in a fair market environment. The benefits to content publishers of RMI usage, particularly in a digital environment that uses sophisticated DRM, is clear and the evolving business models depend on them. However, this cannot be a one-sided advancement into a digital era with all the benefits accruing to business; instead, balance must be brought to all sides of the digital market. All stakeholders in creative works — creators, copyright holders and users — should be given the protection of transparency, completeness, privacy and freshness that must underpin all RMI related policy initiatives.

The Canadian initiative, Bill C-32, fails to address these issues. It has merely adopted a minimal compliance with the WCT and WPPT, an inadequate solution to the problems facing creators and users in the digital arena. This Bill is clearly an attempt to comply with the WIPO Treaties and respond to the demands of the USA to reform Canadian copyright legislation. Unfortunately, in its current form, legislators have missed an opportunity to amend the legislation to achieve a *new balance* that can address the issues of publishers with unauthorized replication of materials and the issues of consumers and users with avoiding undue impact on their (constantly eroded) privacy, ensuring the maintenance of their rights to materials in the public domain.[74]

Obviously there are many perspectives on the reform of copyright. Those that benefit in the short term from increased profit margins are likely to agree with the perspective of CRIA President Graham Henderson: "Nielsen's figures [falling album sales for 2006–2007] validate an unfortu-

---

73 This overview of Bill C-32 is not the place to discuss such developments in depth, but it would be wise for government instigated reform to at least consider the longer term evolution of the digital content environment.

74 As recognised by Séverine Dusollier in Scoping Study above note 5.

nate truth—that unabated illegal Internet music file-sharing continues to harm artists and the organizations and people behind them. They also underscore the need for updated copyright laws, mirroring those of our major trading partners, to help bring unauthorized downloading under control in Canada."[75] However, the Nielsen Company and Billboard's 2009 Canadian Industry Report shows a small decline in total album sales (2.2 percent) and a large increase in digital album sales (over 40 percent).[76] It is unwise to base long-term copyright policy on fluctuations in the market over such short terms, and clearly futile to attempt to second guess the effect of RMI policy on Canadian society as a whole by looking at a sector's market figures in isolation. If this current Bill C-32 is to meaningfully amend the *Copyright Act*, and thus affect future developments in all facets of creative endeavors aided or restrained by copyright policies, a deep and thorough review also needs to be built into the legislation. Intellectual property reform is not usually very high on the priority list of governments, despite active lobbying by self-interested parties, and it is only through embedding review into reform that the matter is likely to be considered again in the near future.

Rights Management Information is the key to giving creators, users, conducers and all other players in the content driven world, the opportunity to *know* about the works that they are involved with over and above the obvious. This is where the proposed legislation fails.[77]

---

75 Canadian Recording Industry Association, News Release, "Neilsen SoundScan Figures Confirm Canada's Weak Digital Music Market and the Sharp, Ongoing Decline in Overall Recorded Music Sales" (4 January 2008), www.cria.ca/news/08-01-08_n.php.

76 Scoop Marketing, "The Nielsen Company and Billboard's 2009 Canadian Industry Report" (4 February 2009), www.billboard.biz/billboardbiz/photos/covers/2009/Nielsen_Canada_2009.pdf at p. 1.

77 This paper is a criticism of the Bill, but the author refutes any suggestion that criticism of draft legislation implies extremism, but rather a hope for a better Canadian legislative structure on copyright.

CHAPTER ELEVEN

How Virtue Ethics Might Help Erase C-32's Conceptual Incoherence

David Lametti*

The proposed changes to the Canadian *Copyright Act*[1] set out in Bill C-32[2] illuminate the conceptual incoherence of what has come to be commonly known as "copyright plus" or "paracopyright." In terms of copyright reform, the new provisions in C-32 seek to strike a balance between the interests of right-holders and the interests of users. A number of the proposed changes are welcome, and reflect the legitimate — or at least what ought to be the legitimate — expectations of copyright-holders and users. The non-copyright aspects of the Bill — the protection of digital locks, for example — have their grounding in other normative paradigms and are more problematic when juxtaposed against the traditional copyright provisions contained in the Bill and in the rest of the *Copyright Act*. They represent a serious conceptual flaw or incoherence in the Bill. This central conceptual flaw could overwhelm the copyright balances struck in the

* I would like to thank Magda Woszczyk and Carrie Finlay for their assistance in the preparation of this text, and André Saumier and André Lametti for conversations on specific points. I wish to thank Allen Mendelsohn, Michael Geist and an anonymous reviewer for astute comments; some of the more philosophical challenges posed by the reviewer to the virtue ethics approach to copyright will need to be addressed anon, in a forthcoming longer text. I also wish to thank the Faculty of Law, McGill University and the SSHRC for research support.

1 *Copyright Act*, R.S.C. 1985, c. C-42, http://laws.justice.gc.ca/en/C-42 [*Copyright Act*].

2 Bill C-32, *An Act to amend the Copyright Act*, 3d Sess., 40th Parl., 2010, www2.parl.gc.ca/Sites/LOP/LEGISINFO/index.asp?Language=E&query=7026&Session=23&List=toc [C-32].

other parts of C-32, in Canadian jurisprudence, and in copyright theory and history generally.

Others have and will detail these problems more carefully in this collection and elsewhere; I need not do that in this essay. Rather, I will argue how the proposed changes might be able to function, notwithstanding the flagrant, fundamental flaw. This potential operability, or, more accurately, cohabitation, depends not on the following of the explicit text of a revised Act, but rather on the reasonableness and fairness on the part of copyright users and right-holders in the particular context of the protected work that they are dealing with (i.e., the nature of the rights and the nature of the object of copyright). This position might be labeled a "virtue thics" approach to C-32. I am not unrealistic, however. If right-holders in particular are not reasonable about the exercise of their rights under C-32, any promise that C-32 might have for achieving a sense of normative balance will be overwhelmed.[3] The only hope for C-32 — short of legislative amendment — is that an informal normativity based on virtue might somehow emerge to harmonize the incoherence left in place by the formal normativity of C-32.

A. COPYRIGHT'S BALANCES VERSUS PARACOPYRIGHT'S FENCES

The quest to "modernize" copyright in the digital world seems to have been overtaken by lobbyists and power-brokers, especially for the side of large corporate copyright interests.[4] This discussion has taken place in a context of Lockean rights discourse with the seemingly unobjectionable starting point that some act of "creation" automatically leads to full-blooded[5]

---

3 Note that I am not unrealistic about the ability of a formal legal system to function in harmony with open-ended, and often contextual, informal and specifically ethical normative concepts: the civil law tradition generally, and Quebec Civil Law in particular, has long functioned successfully with overarching ethical concepts such as *abus de droit*, good faith, *equité* and *ordre public*. See, e.g., *Civil Code of Quebec*, S.Q. 1991, c.64, arts. 6–7, www2.publicationsduquebec.gouv.qc.ca/dynamicSearch/telecharge.php?type=2&file=/CCQ/CCQ_A.html. Rather, I am troubled by some of the excessive rhetoric of the current debate, and especially that of many right-holders and their proxies.

4 See, e.g., Jessica Litman, *Digital Copyright* (Amherst: Prometheus Books, 2001); William Patry, *Moral Panics and the Copyright Wars* (New York: Oxford University Press, 2009). For the most complete account of lobbying efforts in Canada, see Michael Geist, www.michaelgeist.ca.

5 The term is from James W. Harris, *Property and Justice* (Oxford: Oxford University Press, 1996) at 29–32.

and absolute ownership rights in the "intellectual" object that is created. Of course this Lockean picture—which isn't really even consistent with Locke's writing—is false. While I have no objection to calling copyright a species of property right,[6] there is nothing in that act of creating that somehow implies that a property right is automatically granted[7] or, indeed, that such a right is absolute, as Locke himself well understood.[8] In practice, many property rights known to both the common and civil law traditions are less than the full package or bundle of rights, and, yet, are still held, "owned," or are otherwise, in some sense, "property."[9] These rights are not absolute rights either, but rather are understood in the context—often physical—in which the ensuing rights, limits and obligations are exercised and understood. Moreover, as a number of writers have pointed out,[10]

---

6 See David Lametti, "The Concept and Conceptions of Intellectual Property as seen through the lens of Property" in Giovanni Comandé & Giulio Ponzanelli, eds., *Scienza e Diritto nel Prisma del Diritto Comparato* (Torino: Giappichelli, 2004) 269; David Lametti, "The (Virtue) Ethics of Private Property: A Framework and Implications" in Alastair Hudson, ed., *New Perspectives on Property Law, Obligations and Restitution* (London: Cavendish Press, 2004) 39.

7 Jim Harris has pointed this out rather convincingly in *Property and Justice*, above note 5.

8 While there is debate on the scope of the Lockean provisos, it is clear that Locke understood that all property rights were limited. The "labour" involved in intellectual property creation necessarily relies on the works of previous authors, and so an absolute and unfettered right to the whole cannot be justified. It is ironic that Lockean property theorists have long debated the limits of Locke, but some IP rhetoric—at the very least at the outset—de-emphasized the generally-accepted notion of limits. Thankfully, IP scholarship was quick to correct this idea of unlimied rights. See, e.g., Wendy J. Gordon, "A Property Right in Self-Expression: Equality and Individualism in the Natural Law of Intellectual Property" (1993) Yale L.J. 1533; Seana Valentine Shiffrin, "Lockean Arguments for Private Intellectual Property" in Stephen R. Munzer, ed., *New Essays in the Legal and Political Theory of Property* (Cambridge: Cambridge University Press, 2001) 138, www.law.ucla.edu/docs/lockean_arguments_for_private_intellectual_property.pdf; and Daniel Attas, "Lockean Justifications of Intellectual Property" in A. Gosseries *et al.*, eds., *Intellectual Property and Theories of Justice* (London: Palgrave Macmillan, 2008) 29. The most notable Canadian exception is, of course, Carys Craig: see Carys J. Craig, "Locke, Labour and Limiting the Author's Right: A Warning against a Lockean Approach to Copyright Law" (2002) 28 Queen's L.J. 1, www.forumonpublicdomain.ca/locke-labour-and-limiting-the-author's-right-a-warning-against-a-lockean-approach-to-copyright-law. I have applied a balanced view of Locke; David Lametti, "Publish and Profit: Justifying the Ownership of Copyright in the Academic Setting" (2001) 26 Queen's L.J. 497 at 520–60.

9 David Lametti, "The Concept of Property: Relations *through* Objects of Social Wealth" (2003) 53 U.T.L.J. 325 ["Concept of Property"].

10 See Jessica Litman, "The Public Domain" (1990) 39 Emory L.J. 965 at 969 (on adaptation as better metaphor), https://childedlaw.org/pd/papers/litman_background.pdf;

the metaphor of "creation" is too strong as it downplays the notion that all ideas evolve from the previous base of work in both the public and private domains. Perhaps "adaptation" or "evolution" is a more accurate description. According sweeping rights undermines the public domain and its ongoing role as a source for future creation.

It is rather ironic that at a time when leading Anglo-American property theorists are increasingly beginning to come to terms with "context" in their understanding of traditional property norms[11] and, thus, dealing with the ensuing notions of social obligations and stewardship, the quest to modernize copyright has taken such an outdated and erroneous concept such as "absolute rights" as its rallying cry.

Copyright, particularly in the Anglo-Canadian tradition, was never about absolute rights over every aspect of a work: not even in 1557 England, when literary works fell within the domain of the Stationers, was every aspect of the work under control. Rather, copyright's focus is the power to make copies for the purposes of economic profit (or the prohibition against removing such profits from the copyright-holder). Copyright has never been, historically or conceptually, about total power over the object created. This point is articulated in the oft-cited maxim that copyright is a statutory right that confers only the rights granted in the *Copyright Act*.[12]

James Boyle, *The Public Domain: Enclosing the Commons of the Mind* (London: Yale University Press, 2008) at 179, http://thepublicdomain.org/thepublicdomain1.pdf (on the intellectual commons as a source for creative work); and Abraham Drassinower, "Taking User Rights Seriously," in Michael Geist, ed., *In the Public Interest: The Future of Canadian Copyright Law* (Toronto: Irwin Law, 2005) 462, http://papers.ssrn.com/sol3/Delivery.cfm/SSRN_ID839988_code603.pdf?abstractid=839988&mirid=1 (on the inter-textuality of creation).

11 See, e.g., Gregory S. Alexander, *et al.*"A Statement of Progressive Property" (2009) 94 Cornell L. Rev. 743,www.lawschool.cornell.edu/research/cornell-law-review/upload/A-Statement-of-Progressive-Property.pdf; Gregory S. Alexander, "The Social-Obligation Norm in American Property Law" (2009) 94 Cornell L. Rev. 745, /www.lawschool.cornell.edu/research/cornell-law-review/upload/94-4-Alexander-Article.pdf; Eduardo M. Peñalver, "Land Virtues" (2009) 94 Cornell L. Rev. 821, http://www.lawschool.cornell.edu/research/cornell-law-review/upload/94-4-Penalver-Article.pdf; articles that follow at 889–1071; and Gregory S. Alexander & Eduardo. Peñalver, eds., *Property and Community* (New York: Oxford University Press, 2010). See also "Concept of Property," above note 9.

12 *Compo Co. Ltd. v. Blue Crest Music*, [1980] 1 S.C.R. 357, http://csc.lexum.umontreal.ca/en/1979/1980scr1-357/1980scr1-357.html, 105 D.L.R. (3d) 249 [*Blue Crest Music*]; *Bishop v. Stevens*, [1990] 2 S.C.R. 467, http://csc.lexum.umontreal.ca/en/1990/1990scr2-467/1990scr2-467.html , 72 D.L.R. (4th) 97; and more recently in *Théberge v. Galerie d'Art du Petit Champlain inc.*, 2002 SCC 34, http://www.lexum.umontreal.ca/cscscc/en/pub/2002/vol2/html/2002scr2_0336.html, [2002] 2 S.C.R. 336 [*Théberge* cited to

However, the central point is grounded much more deeply than the idea that copyright is simply a creature of statute.[13] The concept of copyright in any tradition, including the Continental author's rights tradition where some would point to a more absolutist picture of ownership generally, is far from absolute. An author has a certain number of rights in her work—and these rights, within this institutional scope, might be quite powerful—but she nevertheless does not have a claim to critical parts of the whole work: there is no entitlement to the larger ideas expressed in her work, nor to any elements in her work that do not originate from her, but rather came from the public domain. Moreover, specific user rights in a work in any given jurisdiction, such as fair use or dealing, or the right to make personal copies, also limit the core of a copyright-holder's powers, especially when, like fair use, they are open-ended.[14] Even when specific rights are absolute, as for example moral rights in the Continental tradition, the substantive scope of these rights is narrowly defined. And in all cases, the ultimate goal of promoting the progress of the art in question has always been the central organizing idea for the contours of protection.[15]

A key justification for these limitations is users' rights in the works of others. Perhaps, most importantly for the purposes of current Canadian discussions, an author does not have the right, once published, to control access to the work. All are entitled to read the book, listen to the song, look at the painting; what the author can prohibit is the making of unauthorized copies, as per section 3 of the *Copyright Act*. And even here, not all copying is prohibited. The Canadian *Copyright Act*, and the common law tradition, says a substantial amount must be taken to constitute infringement, and hence "insubstantial" takings in terms of quality and quantity have always been permitted. And then, there is the concept of fair dealing, which legitimates specific kinds of copying. In short, the doctrine of fair dealing or fair use has allowed users to deal with copyright-protected

---

S.C.R.]; *CCH Canadian Ltd. v. Law Society of Upper Canada*, 2004 SCC 13, http://www.canlii.org/en/ca/scc/doc/2004/2004scc13/2004scc13.html , [2004] 1 S.C.R. 339 [*CCH Canadian* cited to S.C.R.].

13 In Estey J.'s well-known terms: Copyright is a "creature of statute." See *Blue Crest Music, ibid.* at 373.

14 Samuel Trosow, "The Illusive Search for Justificatory Theories: Copyright, Commodification and Capital" (2003) 16 Can. J.L. & Jur. 217 (where these limits are seen as "safety valves").

15 In the US framework, in fact, the power to grant copyright protection is embedded in the provision in the Constitution which grants Congress the power to enact legislations that "promotes the Progress of Science and useful Arts." U.S. Const. art. I, § 8, cl. 8.

works in ways that do not go to the detriment, especially economic, of the right-holder and which allow significant scope for context in the determination of what is fair.

Copyright's evolving normative structure has tried, through specific norms, to account for both the rights of authors and the rights of users: this is the so-called copyright balance. The parameters of copyright protection have been modified over time by both statute and jurisprudence with the scope of protection (length of protection, types of works covered, scope of fair dealing, etc.) changing in order to address the balance sought at the time. While one can argue for or against some of these shifts,[16] the general overall pattern remained true to the idea that copyright was a limited series of rights in a work, perhaps even a species of property right, with attention paid to both authors and users in the context of promoting future works, future creation, and future creativity. The structure of copyright has always loathed economic monopolies under the guise of copyright, limiting protection to the expression itself and resisting the idea of merger except under very limited circumstances. The balance of copyright has also been particularly vigilant in not allowing rights over ideas and facts. And, for the most part, the balance has maintained sensitivity to the intellectual objects created and the specific nature of the appropriate balance for those objects. If legislative normativity was lacking or lagging, courts stepped in to interpret, often adding to or softening the scope of legislative norms.[17]

Of equal importance is the informal; here I refer to the cultural practices that have existed at the fringes of formal normativity under the radar of copyright and often in contravention of some of the formal aspects of

---

16 As indeed I have done regarding duration of copyright protection: see David Lametti, "Coming to Terms with Copyright" in Michael Geist ed., *In the Public Interest: The Future of Canadian Copyright Law* (Toronto: Irwin Law, 2005) 480 www.irwinlaw.com/pages/content-commons/coming-to-terms-with-copyright---david-lametti.

17 Numerous cases could serve as examples across various jurisdictions: In Canada, the obvious example of gap-filling on fair dealing is the *CCH Canadian* decision, which elaborated a fair dealing test. In the US, a good example regarding reaction to a new technology is *Sony Corp. of America v. Universal City Studios, Inc.*, 464 U.S. 417 (1984) ,www.law.cornell.edu/copyright/cases/464_US_417.htm [*Sony* cited to U.S.]; even the *Grokster* decision does not try to explicitly contradict *Sony*: *MGM Studios v. Grokster, Ltd.*, 545 U.S. 913 (2005), http://www.law.cornell.edu/supct/pdf/04-480P.ZS [*Grokster* cited to U.S.]. Perhaps the best example is in the area of computer software, where courts softened the scope of copyright protection by limiting what was protected in the expression of computer software to only what was truly innovative: *Computer Associates International, Inc. v. Altai*, Inc., 982 F.2d 693 (2d Cir. 1992), www.bitlaw.com/source/cases/copyright/altai.html [*Altai* cited to F.2d].

copyright law that over time have been tolerated, ignored or have been deemed to be otherwise unenforceable. A certain "leakage" or "lag" in formal copyright norms has thus always been an important part of the picture leading to progress. The development of a number of different technologies — file-sharing software, and perhaps even the Internet — could have been stifled had copyright norms been applied too early or too rigorously.[18] Parts of copyrighted works, even when these are the original, protectable parts of a work, have always inspired other works. Confusing Gandalf and Dumbledore, Harry Potter and Percy Jackson, Mozart and Haydn, or trying to write like Joyce, or Proust, or Faulkner, is nothing new or surprising; being inspired by the form or substance of another work, even to the extent of some artistic "borrowing," has always existed and made the artistic whole all the better. With perhaps the exception of Shakespeare or Picasso, the product of creativity largely rests "on the shoulders of giants" who have come before.[19] What is more, it can be argued that "piracy" — a term much bandied about these days — had always been part of the creative forces behind artistic and scientific progress.[20] Until very recently, digital fences did not exist; absolute control over a work was never possible simply because originals once published always existed in a material format that could always be reproduced (by hand or mechanically) and, hence, the imperfection of the system actually helped reinforce the creative cycle. I would go so far as to argue that leakage was a necessary part of the system, especially in terms of learning the arts in question.

The copyright-inspired portions of C-32, laudably in my view, *do* follow in this grand tradition of copyright balancing: personal use exemptions which mirror current use practices such as time and format shifting, allowing for mash-ups that represent one of the newest forms of intellectual creativity, adding education to the definition of "fair dealing," and "no-

---

18 The argument has been advanced by Fred von Lohmann of the Electronic Frontier Foundation, using examples from various points in the history of copyright; see Fred von Lohmann, "Fair Use as Innovation Policy", (2008) 23 Berkeley Tech. Law Journal 829, www.eff.org/files/Fair%20Use%20as%20Innov%20Policy%20Final%20 Galley.pdf . See also Paul Goldstein, *Copyright's Highway: From Gutenberg to the Celestial Jukebox* (New York: Hill & Wang, 1996).

19 Lloyd Weinrib, "Copyright for Functional Expression" (1998) 111 Harv. L. Rev. 1150 at 1224.

20 Adrian Johns, *Piracy: The Intellectual Property Wars from Gutenberg to Gates* (Chicago: University of Chicago Press, 2009). A similar argument has been made in the larger context of property reform: Eduardo M. Peñalver & Sonia K. Katyal, *Property Outlaws: How Squatters, Pirates and Protesters Improve the Law of Ownership* (New Haven: Yale University Press, 2010).

tice-and-notice" as the standard for ISPs, as a way to protect the rights of copyright-holders on the internet while not trenching on the potentially legitimate rights of users. While these changes do not go as far as I would like as regards fair dealing (where an explicit, purposive and open-ended test as articulated in *CCH Canadian* or in the US *Copyright Act*[21] would be preferable in light of the theoretical framework that I have elaborated), one must see the proposed changes as a positive step.

Other provisions in C-32 are not inspired at all by the copyright tradition, but rather by the provisions in the WIPO Treaties[22] and the US *Digital Millennium Copyright Act*.[23] Unlike copyright, these paracopyright rules are grounded in a different normative paradigm and a different realm of emerging technical possibilities. By the latter I mean that absolute control over a work is now technologically possible; technological protection measures allow for certain types of works to be "fenced in," accessible only upon permission, or traced. This in turn, changes the normative paradigm of such measures from copyright and its central metaphor of balance to something more akin to trade secret protected by a wall of contract. The dominant metaphors here are monopoly, fencing and walls; absolute protection is possible. Others have noted this phenomenon, and even questioned its constitutionality.[24]

Obviously, paracopyright falls within another paradigm of the governance for intellectual goods or objects of social wealth, perhaps in the same manner that trade secret presents an option for the holder of the secret instead of patent protection. However, in conceptual terms, the co-existence between paracopyright and copyright is more problematic. First, unlike patent and trade secret, there is no "either-or" choice between regimes: you either apply for a patent and take the trade-off of a twenty-year monopoly in exchange for publishing the "recipe" or the "teaching," obtaining

---

21 U.S. *Copyright Act*, 1976, 90 Stat. 2541; 17 U.S.C., s. 107.

22 WIPO-Administered Treaties, World Intellectual Property Organization www.wipo.int/treaties/en.

23 *Digital Millennium Copyright Act*, Pub. L. No. 105-304 112 Stat. 2860 (1998) (codified as amended at 17 U.S.C. § 1201 (1998)), www.copyright.gov/legislation/pl105-304.pdf [DMCA].

24 The argument here is that while copyright falls explicitly under an enumerated federal head of power, as paracopyright is in its essence contractual, then it would fall under Property and Civil Rights and would thus be under provincial jurisdiction in Canada: see Jeremy F. deBeer, "Constitutional Jurisdiction over Paracopyright Laws" in Michael Geist, ed., *In the Public Interest: The Future of Canadian Copyright Law* (Toronto: Irwin Law, 2005) 89, http://papers.ssrn.com/sol3/Delivery.cfm/SSRN_ID814074_code395605.pdf?abstractid=814074&mirid=1.

the state's authority in protecting your monopoly or you keep the secret yourself, using contracts and licenses to protect your secret or confidential information and resort to private law doctrines as your basis for remedy. If your secret gets out, it is up to you to enforce it; you can, with some legal doing,[25] get the cat partly back in the bag. Finally, trade secret does not posit a monopoly: others can reverse engineer or use trial and error, to get to the same result. Hence, this kind of governance system can co-exist rather peacefully with the patent bargain and monopoly, as the parameters of each being different enough to offer a choice to inventors.

The problem with paracopyright is that copyright-holders want the added option to put up fences around their copyrighted work *in addition to* having base copyright protection; there is no "either-or." A copyright-holder is afforded the automatic protection of copyright (with no registration requirements, unlike patent, and for a much longer period of time) without, in effect, having to "publish" the work in the sense of making the work available to be read or heard or seen. The digital fences can prevent this kind of access at the outset. Or, by restricting access at the outset, they can prevent certain other kinds of legitimate methods of fair dealing, as C-32 will now enable copyright-holders to do. And unlike the trade secret paradigm, if the fence is by-passed, then the right-holder gets to claim a *copyright* violation, even though the right-holder unilaterally altered the copyright bargain.[26] Finally, if the fence is transgressed, the original work is still protected by copyright as against copying, unlike a trade secret that is no longer a secret. This is, as my civil law colleagues would say, *cumul* and not *option*.

The reverse-engineering provisions in C-32 provide a neat example of conceptual confusion. Reverse-engineering can only really be convincingly criticized on some of the grounds that are analogous to copyright infringement; by reverse-engineering one is, in effect, copying the substance of the work (say, for example, a software program). Otherwise, if something is a secret — for instance, the recipe for Coke — then reverse-engineering

---

25 Using trade secret and confidential information as treated by the common law, there is some ability to flag information that is meant to be treated as confidential, thus putting the general reader on guard. The warnings that follow professional email are the best example. There is also, of course, the web of contracts that are often put into place to bind persons more specifically. The same kind of result could be had using the civil law.

26 Unless, as will be discussed, it is by-passed for those exceptions in c. 41.11. 41.12, 41.13, etc. — such as reverse-engineering for some cases; but this proves the confusion, as will be argued; C-32, above note 2 at c.41.11–41.18.

is allowed; if you can make your own version independently, that is fine.[27] A provision protecting against tampering of the digital locks protecting a secret should not be able to be used as an excuse to outlaw reverse-engineering, as this kind of power (i.e., a digital lock over a trade secret) is not within the copyright paradigm.[28] Bill C-32, in its digital locks provisions, is thus confused in conceptual terms from the outset.

Yet, as a part of the provisions on digital locks, there are exceptions permitting the picking of digital locks for the reverse-engineering of computer programs as it pertains to interoperability purposes, reverse-engineering for encryption research, and for network security vulnerability testing purposes. As regards the two latter examples, encryption research and vulnerability testing, one might say that such an exception is evidence of reasonableness on the part of the legislator in recognizing that reverse-engineering has a role to play in protecting certain kinds of software hacking. However, the justification for restricting reverse-engineering in the first place is grounded on the underlying copyright protection of the work and not on the mere power to place a digital lock. If the digital barrier was erected to prevent access to the work, then the justification for the digital lock is parasitic on the justification for copyright protection. Hence, the exceptions set out in C-32 show the opposite of what they were intended to show: instead of being reasonable limitations on digital locks, they help justify the placing of digital locks on confidential information and secrets, implicitly relying on the notion that these are also copyright-protected works, and thus remove the ability to reverse engineer except in exceptional cases.[29] Yet these works are inaccessible, and thus in some sense, contrary to the spirit of being "published."

27 Of course, trademark law and passing off means you have to call it something else!

28 There is an argument to be made that a moral right (or even copyright) would protect the rights of an author as it allows her to prevent a work from being published, thus effectively keep it a secret. This means that some "secrets" fall within the domain of copyright. However, in my view, these unpublished works are not used as the basis for economic activity, or are not an economic resource, in the way that trade secrets are meant to be, thus putting them out of the realm of moral rights and copyright.

29 Copyright scholar, lecturer, lawyer and former computer programmer Sunny Handa had previously insisted that a reverse-engineering right *for any purpose* be added to copyright's *limits*, as part of copyright's balance: "Narrowing the exception creates conceptual difficulties in applying limits to reverse-engineering. Allowing a broad exception would avoid these difficulties while continuing to provide copyright-holders with protection if, after the reverse-engineering process is concluded, their protectable expression is used within another's software product." While Handa's argument is in effect pre-paracopyright, the sentiment expressed is in many ways

It is for this reason — that paracopyright is not really copyright at all — that a number of copyright scholars have found these paracopyright provisions and, in particular, those provisions that protect and legitimate access-denying digital locks to be so problematic. The conceptual metaphor of copyright, entrenched over time, has been one of balance. We can quibble about the balance point, but authors and users co-exist with limited rights in the service of fostering creation and creating. The paracopyright paradigm is one of no-access or limited access, with no implicit or explicit counter-balance: the structure favours the right-holder to the exclusion of all other users, to the exclusion of any notion of enriching the public domain, and with a rather impoverished view of creation. It does not subject the right-holder to the usual responsibilities and limitations traditional to which copyright-holders are subject, while giving the traditional copyright rights and different, new rights of absolute control to the copyright holder. So, for example, fair dealing will become an utterly meaningless concept if one has to pay to get access for an otherwise legitimate use. Ditto for time- and format-shifting. The goals of paracopyright in such cases can only be to reward copyright-holders (financially) without the usual copyright *quid pro quo* of paying attention to the care of the public domain, to the legitimate rights of users or to the overall idea that even protected works have a role in fostering other works simply by being accessible.

Another way to frame the same point is to say that while copyright rights have always been much less than absolute (for good teleological reasons), we have enshrined a type of protection for the same works in the *Copyright Act* that is predicated on absoluteness. Such a paradigm actually guts the balance made by copyright doctrine, legislation and, I suppose, history[30] and ignores the justificatory discourse of copyright that in no way supports the according and protecting of such absolute rights.

---

similar: if we wish this activity to be covered by copyright, then we should discuss the copyright balance directly, as Handa had done. The paracopyright solution merely gives double protection. I thank Carrie Finlay for helping me to elaborate this specific point. See Sunny Handa, *Reverse Engineering Computer Programs Under Canadian Copyright Law* (LL.M. Thesis McGill University Institute of Comparative Law, 1994), (Ottawa: National Library of Canada, 1994), eScholarship@McGill, http://digitool.Library.McGill.CA:80/R/-?func=dbin-jump-full&object_id=22693¤t_base=GEN01. The exception for interoperability might be a different nature: here reverse-engineering is not an exercise with regard to the lock itself, but rather relates to the possible uses to be made of the copyrighted work: i.e., one tampers with the lock precisely to achieve interoperability. I thank the anonymous reviewer for pointing out this distinction.

30 See e.g., Daniel J. Gervais, "The Purpose of Copyright Law in Canada" 2 (2005) O.U.L.T.J. 315, www.uoltj.ca/articles/vol2.2/2005.2.2.uoltj.Gervais.315-356.pdf.

Of course, the state can do whatever it wants in its formal copyright statute. If the duly-elected representatives of the people wish to create these "super-rights" that cumulate other rights on top of copyright rights then they may do so. But the fact that the two are conceptually different paradigms remains quite obvious and, as such, C-32 is mired in fundamental conceptual incoherence.

One solution might be to force holders to choose between copyright protection and paracopyright protection in the same way one chooses between trade secret and patent. Given the current state of domestic and international copyright law, this solution, as intellectually coherent as it might otherwise be and with an obvious intellectual property (IP) parallel to patent/trade secret trade-off, is a non-starter. One might subject the paracopyright to the copyright scheme: this would appear to be just and sound, but it would require attention at the level of architecture in order to (a) not be overly cumbersome and (b) be enforceable. Some have suggested this and it is an indeed valuable and potentially viable solution.[31] Scrapping the digital locks protection would be better, in my view, but the current government is not there.

B. VIRTUE AND COPYRIGHT: SAVING C-32

Short of a legislative solution, how might we go about saving C-32 from this rather problematic juxtaposition of balances and fences? Can we?

One possibility lies in the realm of informal normativity inspired by the school of "virtue ethics." Virtue ethics is the label given to what might be called a rediscovered emphasis on ethical action in particular situations. These situations challenge us to act and, in doing so, force us to effectively define ourselves and better ourselves.

Inspired by the writing of Aristotle (and to a lesser extent Aquinas) and re-formulated by a new generation of scholars,[32] virtue ethics purports to provide the guidelines or the right questions to ask in a situation of

31 Michael Geist, "Fixing Bill C-32: Proposed Amendments to the Digital Lock Provisions" (15 June 2010), www.michaelgeist.ca/component/option,com_docman/task,doc_download/gid,33.

32 The best introductory work is Stan van Hooft, *Understanding Virtue Ethics* (Acumen: Stocksfield, UK, 2006). See also Rosalind Hursthouse, *On Virtue Ethics* (Oxford: Oxford University Press, 1999); Daniel Statman, ed., *Virtue Ethics: A Critical Reader* (Edinburgh: Edinburgh University Press, 1997); and Roger Crisp & Michael Slote, eds., *Virtue Ethics* (Oxford: Oxford University Press, 1997). See also Onora O'Neill, *Towards Justice and Virtue* (Cambridge: Cambridge University Press, 1996) and Charles Taylor, *The Sources of the Self* (Cambridge: Harvard University Press, 1989).

ethical decision-making. Such decisions, following Aristotle's concept of practical reasonableness and attention to context, makes the "positionality" of the ethical decision-maker central to deciding how to act in any given circumstance.[33] That is to say, all norms are culture-relative and supported by intuitions that are grounded by community traditions; these norms are understood and inculcated in the members of a community over time. The hermeneutic tradition that supports this understanding of normativity and the transmission of norms will not necessarily tell agents — us — what the right answer is in all cases, but rather will help us to find the right answer for ourselves. Although set rules form part of the basis for what it means to act virtuously, rules are often less-than-clear, limited, contradictory, and opaque; hence, rule-following is incomplete as an ethical stance, outlook, or way of life. Put simply, we need to do more than follow rules in order to do what is right. Indeed, there is a sense in which one can even disregard, in principle, certain rules while remaining faithful to law.

The beauty of virtue ethics is that it helps individuals circumnavigate the seas of ethical grey in which we sail, whether in life or in copyright. What is required is individual judgment or self-reflection in service of the balanced decision-making that Aristotelians and neo-Aristotelians have favoured in their ethics. The fact that these virtues and values are widely shared in a society, deeply understood, and intrinsically appreciated means that such an ethic is not merely a breed of moral relativism, and positionality, while situated, is not simply a species of situation ethics.[34]

In other terms that might be familiar along Lon Fuller's lines, I am arguing for an "ethics of aspiration"[35] in which we aim (as individuals, or

---

33 The best discussion of "positionality", in my view, is contained in Katherine Bartlett, "Feminist Legal Methods" (1990) 103 Harv. L. Rev. 829, http://scholarship.law.duke.edu/cgi/viewcontent.cgi?article=1119&context=faculty_scholarship. While that article predates the use of the term "virtue ethics" the Aristotelian and neo-Aristotelian sources and substance indicate that Bartlett's positionality narrative fits well within the description of virtue ethics.

34 This suffices for now, though I appreciate that these claims will always be contested. A good analysis, containing a defense of virtue ethics against the charge of moral relativism and differentiating virtue ethics from a duty-based ethics is contained in van Hooft, above note 31 at 7.

35 Lon L. Fuller, *The Morality of Law* (New Haven: Yale University Press, 1969), www.ebook3000.com/Lon-L--Fuller---The-Morality-of-Law--Revised-Edition_81102.html. Happily, I have been "accused" of falling into this camp already: see David Lametti, "The Morality of James Harris's Theory of Property" in T. Endicott, J. Getzler & E. Peel, eds., *The Properties of Law: Essays in Honour of James Harris* (Oxford: Oxford University Press, 2006) 138 at 164, n. 44.

with the law) to aspire to the best sorts of actions or norms. This kind of ethics goes beyond formal norms: it is not mere rule-following. This ethic might serve as the basis for a specific duty, such as a duty to aspire to a certain standard of behavior,[36] but it does not always conform to rules and it goes beyond an ethic of duty to strictly follow rules. Rules are, however, a part of the ethical mix and ought to be followed generally as exclusionary reasons for action.[37] Good ethical reasons, based on positionality, might allow us to look beyond exclusionary reasons in some circumstances in service of some value or virtue. Moreover, the fact that such informal, ethical standards are so widely understood helps to lower the potential so-called information costs of relying on contextual standards as opposed to fixed rules.

I argue elsewhere that virtue ethics is useful in intellectual property and especially in copyright circles, because it helps to identify the boundaries and substance of terms like "fair," "just," and "balanced," which are critical for understanding concepts like fair dealing.[38] (Likewise, the same is true for traditional property.[39]) It also, in the case of C-32, helps the individual actors in the copyright context to resolve the conceptual incoherence of the copyright and paracopyright elements that are forced to co-habit in the *Act*.

As I have argued above, the copyright tradition — comprised of statutes, norms and doctrine — is best characterized by the notion of balance. While the *Copyright Act* remains the ultimate basis for action, decided cases such as *CCH Canadian*, *Théberge*, *Nichols*,[40] and the fundamental underlying principles enunciated therein, also form part of the underlying

36 To adopt the language of clear "rules" and open-ended "standards": for a recent discussion in a property context, see Amnon Lehavi, *The Dynamic Law of Property: Theorizing the Role of Legal Standards* [unpublished, on file with author].

37 A concept elaborated by Joseph Raz; Joseph Raz, *The Authority of Law: Essays on Law and Morality*, 2d ed. (Oxford: Oxford University Press, 2009) at 22*ff*. An exclusionary reason, such as a law, gives a person a reason for acting without forcing or requiring the person to provide any other reason or seek any other justification for acting. A stop sign gives a person an exclusionary reason for stopping; it does not mean, however, that in an emergency a person would not be ethically prohibited from safely running that same stop sign (my example).

38 David Lametti, "The Virtuous P(eer)" in Annabelle Lever, ed., *New Frontiers in the Philosophy of Intellectual Property* (forthcoming) (Cambridge: Cambridge University Press, 2011).

39 See David Lametti, "The Objects of Virtue" in Gregory S. Alexander & Eduardo Peñalver, eds., *Property and Community* (New York: Oxford University Press, 2010) 1.

40 *Nichols v. Universal Pictures Corporation et al.*, 45 F.2d 119 (2d Cir. 1930), www.coolcopyright.com/cases/fulltext/nicholsuniversaltext.htm [*Nichols*].

normativity of copyright. It is also true that ideas such as the goals that copyright is meant to serve, like the promotion of the arts, learning, and literature and creativity generally enshrined in seminal copyright documents like the *Statute of Anne* and the US Constitution and often applied directly and indirectly forming part of the hermeneutics of copyright, also play a large role in our understanding of copyright's normativity. Equally true and emanating from all of the above is that ideas of fairness—to authors and users—also form part of copyright's context. Transcendent values such as the promotion of knowledge are part of copyright's core. Sharing and friendship, longstanding virtues in ethics, are increasingly seen to be important from current internet practices, as is evident in social networking and the wiki as cultural phenomena. The Aristotelean concept of practical reasonableness, as both a value itself as well as a method of determining other values, is also part of the normative structure and is linked to the idea of positionality. While much of this normativity is informal—i.e., not legislative—it simply cannot be ignored as it informs much of our understanding of what we must do as individual agents seeking to come to terms with the formal normativity of the *Copyright Act* with the addition of C-32.

How much might a virtue ethics stance help to illuminate what users and rights-holders ought to do in the face of C-32? We can begin with users. Even the most ardent defenders of the internet and the free-flow of information thereupon must admit that the behaviour of some internet users has been less than virtuous with regards to the works of others. Indiscriminate downloading has negatively affected the income stream of numerous artists and specific industries. Indeed, the so-called piracy of music and films and gaming software has been decried by these various entertainment sectors. However, even these groups would admit that, as noted above, some amount of unauthorized copying has always existed for certain kinds of works and, indeed, that such copying was either unenforced and tolerated, unenforceable, or even encouraged. The question then becomes when is uploading, downloading, or otherwise sharing by "making available" ethical or unethical, "piracy," or something less? The law here is, has been, and will always be incomplete or underdetermined; the resort to informal normativity will be as necessary under the newly revised *Act* as it was under its predecessor.

In all cases, a virtue ethics approach would eschew unequivocal answers and would focus on context. Where the copying forms part of the educational process, one could usually classify it as fair dealing. Certainly the primary norms of the *Copyright Act*, the *CCH Canadian* decision and the C-32 proposals reinforce this idea of educational fair dealing. But even this is not conclusive: as an educator, I might photocopy a handout to distribute to my students[41] or upload a scholarly article to a closed, password-protected class website. There is, I am certain, no serious question of this not being fair dealing. But I might not be acting ethically or dealing fairly—even if the C-32 additions are taken into account—if I were to photocopy, in whole or in large part, a text on copyright that was designed precisely for the educational market and that was readily available at a student price. In that case, I would not be acting ethically or dealing fairly, even if C-32 affords me a stronger case for grounding my activity in the *Act*. The context here is that the author prepared the book for an educational audience and pedagogy and I and my students are part of that target market audience in a way that even ordinary scholarly articles might not be.[42] Here, a number of contextual factors have guided the ethical deliberations by individuals: the copyright statute, a copyright licensing scheme, university practice, respect for the writing of scholars in those sorts of texts, old and new copyright doctrine,[43] the nature of the work in question, the price of the original, etc.

The ethical actor has to do some weighing of these factors and decide how to act. Admittedly, an actor might make a mistake in judgment, but over time—as in all other types of ethical situations—such errors can be corrected. Colleagues, friends, or parents might weigh in to say one should not do that, copyright-holders might weigh in to say how their rights are being affected, etc., and, yes, formal legal claims might be brought to bear

41 I appreciate that making photocopies is currently part of a licensed regime that universities have entered into by contract with Access Copyright, www.accesscopyright.ca, or Copibec, www1.copibec.qc.ca/?action=pr_accueil, and have thus bound their professors. One might argue that the new C-32 provision for fair dealing in education could effectively be used to question aspects of the current licensing regime, in the same way that *CCH Canadian* might have. At the very least, it should alter the bargaining process, augmenting the bargaining power that universities and other educational institutions possess.

42 I doubt that most authors of scholarly articles expect that they will be remunerated for their publications; rather, they are contributing to a scholarly discourse. On the other hand, text-book writers do write for the student market, while other book authors might expect some remuneration from sales.

43 *CCH Canadian* (on what is a contextual approach to fair dealing), *Jennings v. Stephens*, [1936] 1 All E.R. 409 (C.A.) at 418*ff* per Greene LJ (a contextual approach to determining "in public" is centred around the inquiry of who is the author's "public", thus in effect involving the determination of who is the author's market for the economic value of the work).

in some cases. As I am learning with my children, one should never underestimate the power of informal normativity, especially peer pressure.

The same kinds of consideration might be brought to music: the copying and the downloading of recorded music files. Certain types of copying of recorded music have always existed. Most people have always format-shifted their own purchased music and thankfully C-32 will enshrine the practice and protect it. The recording industry effectively accepted the practice of taping and recording when levies were introduced on blank media in Canada: first cassette tapes[44] and later CDs. Technological protection measures, especially the technological incompatibility of certain types of formats, have impeded this practice and were met with resistance by consumers.[45]

Can one say that all other forms of copying of recorded music are either absolute piracy or absolute justifiable? Again the answer is probably not in either case. Working from a law and economics perspective, as well as justice-based reasoning, Geert Demuijnck has questioned whether the sharing of MP3 files is an objectional form of free riding. His conclusion is negative.[46] One of the central points of his argument is contextual. Demuijnck argues that many of the adolescents who share such music files were never in the market anyway, and never have been. While to some extent children and adolescents have bought some music, few have ever paid for all of it. Indeed, this seems to be another variant of the target market audience argument that copyright is quite familiar with: does the copying by adolescents affect the market for the original? At the very least we can admit that while copying necessarily must reduce the potential market for the original, by how much it reduces is unclear as is the question of whether that potential market (from the point of view of the copyright-holder) is so large to include every piece of music ever obtained by an adolescent. I would argue that this latter market has always been purely hypothetical,

---

44 Ironically, perhaps, this too was a Bill C-32, and its amendments came into force in 1998.

45 These include technological locks on CDs: see Jeremy F. deBeer, "How Restrictive Terms and Technologies Backfired on Sony BMG" (2005–2006) 6 I.E.C.L.C. 93, http://papers.ssrn.com/sol3/papers.cfm?abstract_id=901305. Even Steve Jobs, whose iTunes model was constructed on technological incompatibility with other MP3 players, is moving iTunes away from this restrictive strategy.

46 Geert Demuijnck,"Is P2P Sharing of MP3 Files an Objectionable Form of Free-riding?" in A. Gosseries *et al.*, eds., *Intellectual Property and Theories of Justice* (London: Palgrave Macmillan, 2008) 141.

though some artists have managed to tap into it better than others, as is currently being done by Lady Gaga and Justin Bieber.[47]

Indeed, the recorded music market was dependent on a less-than-perfect anti-copying and performance regime for free publicity. I doubt the DJs at my college pubs and dances in the 80s and 90s paid for all their recorded music or paid any sort of licensing fee for what they played, but I heard and bought a whole lot of (sometimes life-changing) recorded music based on what they played. Ditto for recorded tapes and burned CDs from friends, later from nieces and nephews, and finally from students. Back then there was still conventional radio for new music, where a tariff is indeed paid, but these forms of dissemination have been overtaken by sharing on the web, through MySpace and other social networking sites, YouTube, etc. Without some forms of sharing and "leakage," everyone loses out financially. This has simply always been the case.

Other arguments can be brought to bear in the service of other virtues: for example, one might point to the transmission of knowledge and culture through music, the social function of music,[48] or even its social-neurological dimension.[49] One might point to the kinds of virtues that human action attempts to foster through sharing: friendship, sociality, and socialization. But perhaps the strongest ethical arguments in favour of some forms of sharing music are those that point to the way in which listening to music helps to inspire new forms of music. In some cases, blatant copying is part of the picture: think of the digital sampling and re-mixing that leads to new musical creations. New works are made, with or without audible recognition of the sampled original. At bottom, this process is really no different than the way in which music was borrowed, was copied, or provided inspiration in the past, except that one can now take exact samples and need not replay the music on new instruments; in effect, the computer is the instrument.[50] Any changes can be brought to the sample at any point. The fact of the matter is that much new music is created here, and ethic-

---

47 I thank Magda Woszczyk for challenging me on this point.

48 See generally Alan P. Merriam, *The Anthropology of Music* (Evanston, Il: Northwestern University Press, 1964), partially available online, http://books.google.ca/books?id=4bUAFf8CWosC&lpg=PP1&dq=alan%20merriam&pg=PP1#v=onepage&q&f=false.

49 Daniel J. Levitin has written that our brains are hard-wired for music, and part of its impact is social, on its link to dancing, for example; Daniel J. Levitin, *This is Your Brain on Music: The Science of a Human Obsession* (New York, New York: Dutton, 2006).

50 For example, Girltalk; Brett Gaylor, *RiP! A Remix Manifesto* (Canada: National Film Board, 2008), www.nfb.ca/film/rip_a_remix_manifesto/.

ally, one can argue that one has not really done anything different than in the past when one borrowed a riff or a chord structure — often note for note — from another group. Indeed, the reality of what has changed is not the borrowing, but rather the ability of the original group to trace its music and demand a fee with a greater chance of success. How much poorer we would be had this been the case when classical composers borrowed from each other, or much later when rock and roll borrowed from gospel, hillbilly, and blues music. The copyright standard tests — quality of what was taken, and to some extent quantity — are perfectly serviceable standards in this regard, as they go to the ethics of what was done. The mere fact that digital copying makes exact copying possible should not lead to an absolute result of infringement or violation.

Of course, none of the above means that all kinds of copying should be allowed. Obviously, if one takes a substantial part of a song or most of it, especially when taken for economic purposes — whether using analogue or digital technology, or simply re-playing the music — one should have to pay a licensing fee to the copyright-holder. And we should consider downloading for non-creative purposes: the adolescent who is a serial uploader and downloader, but never pays a cent for music and merely uploads to make it available to strangers and downloads at will. To some extent, some of the virtue arguments apply (sharing knowledge, friendship, creating, inspiring, etc.), as do the (no-)market arguments (would not have bought anyway). But it is equally true that some of this music was also bought and paid for in the past, so the free downloading is by some measure unfair. Aristotelian ethics allows one to criticize or condemn this person and offer up a better contextual understanding of the ethics of the act of copying. These correctives will be offered to change behaviour. (As a parent, this is what I try to do all the time.) It may even be so over-the-top that legal action is warranted, although my experience is that the informal pressure and normativity will work a whole lot more effectively and efficiently.

It is important to note the role that the normativity of copyright — formal and informal — plays in allowing us the ethical stance from which to judge fairness or condemn the unethical. In the Aristotelian structure, some will be less than ethical and will never "get it." Education, the example of the virtuous, legal norms and rules, standards, and possibly even threat of legal action all continue to play a role in helping individuals understand their ethical choices.[51]

---

51 I thank Madga Woszczyk for pressing me on this point.

Moreover, in light of the changing remuneration model in the music industry, I believe that there is an ethical duty (based on the aspiration to be fair) to explore, consider, and support other models for artists. The old industry business model for recorded music — a small group of record labels with artists signed to them, giving exclusive rights to the label, and allowing the label to market for them — is drawing to an end. It has lasted around fifty years[52] with its banner years from the sixties to the nineties and especially this last decade when many customers re-purchased works in digital form on CD at a price point much higher than production cost. As with other industrial revolutions, a series of technologies brought the old model to its knees. Artists are already beginning to use social networking and other distribution models for the dissemination of and remuneration for their works.[53] This decline is as much a cause for celebration — many artists were not, to put it euphemistically, well dealt-with under the old model — as it is a cause for mourning. Yet, there is no doubt that some artists and people previously employed in the industry are suffering. Virtue ethics address this situation as well. In my view, it is simply unethical for consumers to not seriously consider and perhaps even actively support some form of remuneration model, such as a tax or tariff on Internet Service Providers (ISPs) or hardware, that puts money back into the hands of artists and value-adding persons in the recorded music industry. (Indeed, here is one case where technological measures that allow tracing of downloads might be positively put to use in determining proportional remuneration via a tariff scheme.)

So, in the end, the ethic of virtue means that, as a user, you ought to deal with all musical works "fairly" using the various copyright norms as your guide — not only the works in which you are claiming a fair dealing right, but in all works. As a result, if you are in the habit of sampling music in order

---

52 See Jonathan Sterne, "Is Music a Thing?" in *MP3: The Meaning of a Format* (Durham: Duke University Press, 2012) (forthcoming).

53 Of course, the now standard example is Radiohead's initial sale of *In Rainbows* directly over the internet — if memory serves, I paid £7 — but there are numerous other examples from a variety of sources: see, e.g., Sasha Frere-Jones, "The Dotted Line: What do record labels do now?" *The New Yorker* (16 & 23 August 2010) at 92 (discussing bands Arcade Fire and Vampire Weekend and their respective independent labels Merge Records and XL Recordings that have used alternative business models from the outset, including social networking and grass-roots marketing). At McGill, the Faculties of Law, Management and Music have, over the past three years, mounted a course focused precisely on developing new business models for remunerating artists, many of which have been focused on educating consumers and social networking.

to decide what music you will later purchase, that practice is ethically justifiable, as one might have done with a cassette in the past; but, in my view, you have to purchase enough music to justify your sampling. In the same vein, if you are sampling to create then you have to create and, in turn, be willing to share what you have created to some extent.[54] If you do purchase you should be able to expect, whatever the license agreement[55], that you can make a copy for your kids, your brother, and your best friend in a format that is compatible to your hardware.[56] This, in my view, is the way that it has always been. Digital locks should not be able to prevent that. Clearly, there are no bright-line answers to questions such as what constitutes "enough music," how you "create," or who is a "best friend," but context should help determine appropriate answers in any given circumstance.

One could extend this type of analysis to other works and media such as film, video games, and books. Each brings different contextual considerations to the table pertaining to both the exercise of rights and the objects or works upon which they are exercised. Software is an area where paradigms of protection — copyright and increasingly patent — compete with paradigms of non-protection and sharing. Here, there is a strong argument that certain forms of software — operating systems, browsers, and search engines — are the motors of knowledge generation. I mean by this that these vehicles help to generate (i.e., disseminate, create and organize) learning and knowledge (in the most ample meaning of *connaissances*), either by organizing, disseminating, or making accessible the information of others (in the case of browsers and search engines) or by making computers themselves functional or organizing one's own information (in the case of operating systems).[57] As such, at least some aspects of even pro-

---

54 C-32 incorporates a non-commercial, user-generated content exception, reinforcing formally what informally is virtuous or ethical.

55 In my view, in ethical terms, purchasing a copy of a work and thus remunerating the creator/right-holder, might give the owner of the purchased copy additional moral weight in making ethical decisions to make copies, or do other acts with the copied work: lend it to a friend, make a back-up, alter the material support, etc. This is evidenced by the first-sale doctrine in Canadian copyright, and is perhaps yet another reason to support the majority in *Théberge*. A license, on the other hand, being more limited, might ground less extensive rights, although making a back-up copy of software purchased by license seems to me to be completely ethical. Again, I suppose context is determinative: is the work normally purchased or licensed?

56 Indeed, another set of practices that C-32 will attempt on copyright's virtuous balancing, to formalize. Whether the digital locks provisions will undermine this, may depend on the ethical behavior of copyright-holders: see below.

57 I thank Allen Mendelsohn for helping me to formulate this point.

tected software must be either in the public domain or not absolutely protectable. In this domain user expectations coupled with a doctrine such as *Altai* will effectively make certain features of any software an "unoriginal," common, or *expected* feature akin to a *scène-à-faire* in a relatively short period of time. An ethics approach might hold that users — or competing programmers — would have to respect the original feature of a protected program until such time as the feature loses its artistic or creative nature and becomes rudimentary, unless perhaps the feature was truly fundamental to advancing the field of knowledge, in which case it might not really be protectable at all.

Gaming software presents an interesting case example. At first glance, this kind of software ought to be highly protectable, at least for the period when it is marketable and being marketed. Unlike an operating system, gaming software does not have as direct a vocation in generating knowledge. As a specific type of digital work it does not have the same kind of vocation as art, literature or music, although I am sensitive to the argument that video games are in themselves an art form,[58] as well as to the social function of gaming (both in-person socializing and online socializing). In such situations, the kinds of public domain/*scène-à-faire* arguments will be less convincing in my view, as we are talking about software products whose vocation is more purely a rather precise form of entertainment and whose paradigm is quite market-oriented. It is harder to find a public justification for users to justify sharing. At the very least, the pace at which unique features become user expectations might be slower than for operating systems and such. It may also be possible to say that, in context, gaming has not evolved in the same way as music, as people expect to pay higher sums for the hardware and software and, therefore, it is no problem ethically to maintain those expectations with digital fences. Even still, people are playing more and more online, where they pay access fees. In sum, the gaming world has developed completely behind a cost wall and there seems intrinsically no need to share freely.[59] Hence, some fences seem to be consistent with this kind of work and are thus ethical. User

58 For a humourous fictional account of gamers and their creative spark, see Douglas Coupland, *JPod* (Toronto: Random House Canada, 2006), partially available online http://books.google.ca/books?id=vl7Xuw4gjGoC&lpg=PP1&dq=JPod&pg=PP1#v=onepage&q&f=false. What tips the balance in this case is that the art form is highly commercialized, the games are generally used to make profit in a market setting, and the highly temporary nature of the "art" form: the technology is outmoded rather quickly as technology and the games evolve.

59 I thank Magda Woszczyk for suggesting these two arguments.

copying seems, to me at least, much more unethical. That being said, the industry argument that digital locks are needed to protect people from cheating in the games seems to me to be spurious: if I buy a book, the author has been remunerated and I can skip a few pages, not read it, or even use it as a doorstop; if I buy a videogame, the creators have been remunerated — why should they care if I download a few cheats? Even with regard to multi-user online games, where cheating goes to ruining the enjoyment of the game for non-cheaters, using digital locks to guard against cheating seems to be using a sledge hammer when a screwdriver would do (and indeed where ethical behavior is already part of the answer).[60]

Film shares some of the public and vocational aspects of music while also sharing aspects of more private, fenced-in ordering models. There has always been a "fence" around traditional movie distribution in the sense that one had to pay to see the movie in the cinema. Once seen, one could borrow ideas, even scenes — the brilliant baby carriage scene in *The Untouchables* taken from Sergei Eisenstein's "Odessa Steps" scene in *The Battleship Potemkin* — but one did not have a copy of the film. With the advent of videocassettes and later DVDs, other monies could be made from sales and rental regimes. Now one had a physical copy of the film. Coupled with the rise of the internet and digital technologies, the possibilities for copying — straight up counterfeiting to personal copying, time and format-shifting — all became increasingly easier. So, here the question of copyright and paracopyright is trickier. Given that the context of the original business model had begun with an effective fence — the ticket booth — there might be a particular sympathy here for allowing more fences. Unlike with music, a person who "samples" a whole movie[61] intuitively seems less likely to buy it afterwards or to legally download a second copy. Given the duration and cost of producing a film or television episode as compared to a single song, it becomes increasingly clear that a person who knowingly takes once will take, with respect to that work, the "virtueless" path for eternity (or until they are stopped by the authorities). Still, the additional income gained from the rental and sales of DVDs must have certainly helped the industry, as have sales to television stations for redistribution and as has internet distribution of certain films. Similarly,

60 As an adolescent, I went through a long phase where I played a lot of cards with the same three friends; euchre, to be precise. We all got pretty good, and we all became excellent at stacking a deck. At a certain point, the games became so unmanageable because of the cheating that we all simply agreed to stop. It was much more fun after that.

61 This applies at least in the case where the copy is of a high quality, I suppose.

taking or sampling analog or digital film — through home taping and now burning — has become easier and sampling pieces for the creation of new works (mash-ups) is a now recognized, legitimate art-form, even in C-32.

My intuition here is that certain fences are acceptable in the distribution of films to cinema, sales, and rental, as they are with CDs and MP3s, but some scope needs to be maintained to allow the arts to progress in the same way that homage could be paid to Eisenstein. Film studies schools need to be able to operate without bumping into digital locks. A virtue ethics approach does not yield a hard-and-fast result, but rather says users should expect to pay to see films and that certain liberties would be allowed to a user after purchasing a legitimate copy and even after simply paying to see the film, especially for private re-copying or re-creating, or sharing with family and best friends, and certainly sampling for the purposes of creating other, derivative works.[62]

And, of course, there are books which are at least part of, if not totally, the lynch pin of knowledge acquisition and transmission, as well as a central point for the progress of the arts. Books need to be read and users need to be able to read them. They are passed on over generations, to friends, and made available in libraries. From an ethical viewpoint, sharing is good and encouraged. Free access to books, if no copying is to be done, is to be protected at all costs1a point that seems to have been lost on certain copyright collectives. And copies made through fair dealing, especially for students and educational institutions — another point lost to copyright collectives — must be protected. Users have a great deal of rights here, and the diminishing of users' rights in this context has a serious potential impact on the transmission of knowledge and access to education in our society.

As book reproduction technology moves from the printed word to iPads and Kindles, we must ascertain that, in some way shape or form, the ability to access and read books (conveniently and for free, by borrowing, shar-

62 One must also note there is something to be said about the social aspect of film-viewing. People do still go to movie theatres, and it is still in some sense special. Going to a movie theater and watching a film with many others is a powerful, shared experience: people are there at the same time, laughing at the same jokes, sighing at the same scenes, and screaming at the same horrifying moments. This is a much different experience than the solipsistic experience of downloading a movie for free and watching it alone on a laptop. The social nature of movie-going acts as an additional, informal protection measure for the film industry — something that doesn't seem to be disappearing anytime soon — and should be considered by the industry before turning to digital locks. I thank Carrie Finlay for reminding me of this point.

ing and library lending) must be maintained. This does not mean that, at present, anyone who currently buys into Kindle and its digital locks is morally inferior. Rather, it means that we all have an ongoing duty to ensure that books continue to be "readable" in accessible forms, whether traditional or electronic. Thus, the producers and consumers of this hardware have an ethical responsibility to work with copyright-holders to ensure that all printed works remain accessible and any printed works that have a digital form have some manner of being read without being copied or being able to be copied and without the reading being restricted by the locked hardware.[63] Users are entitled to a high expectation of access with regard to books.[64]

Finally, regarding books, Cory Doctorow notes a certain reticence with respect to reading on screens.[65] Notwithstanding free ebooks and such online, most people still prefer the traditional format and, at this stage, a major role of online works according to Doctorow is to entice the reader to purchase the hard copy version. While this preference may change over time, especially with technologies such as iPad and Kindle, for the foreseeable future the love of the traditional book format affords a certain protection for authors and publishers.

At bottom, in order for users to make ethical claims on right-holders that are in some sense informal and supererogatory on the part of copyright-holders, users too will have to act ethically. Not every act of copying is fair, just, or justified. Sticking to those acts that are just will help create a context in which one can ask for similar virtuous behaviour from copyright-holders.

Next, we should turn to copyright-holders. Indeed, given the fundamental incoherence identified above in the C-32, copyright-holders will hold the key to determining whether such an Act, unmodified, can actually continue the copyright tradition of balance or succumb to the fence paradigm of digital locks.

---

63 Of course, one might try to distinguish books used directly in the educational process from books with a mass market audience and value. I suppose there is a stronger claim to be able to fair deal with respect to educational books than mass market books. This argument cuts both ways however, and for historical and practical reasons it is easier to keep books together and treat them all alike.

64 This is why the Google books project (http://books.google.com/books) has angered many: not because of the copying of out-of-print books, but rather the access fee.

65 Cory Doctorow, "You DO like reading off a computer screen" in Cory Doctorow, ed., *©ontent: Selected Essays on Technology, Creativity, Copyright and the Future of the Future* (San Francisco: Tachyon, 2008) 51, http://craphound.com/content/download. That I bought the book, all of which is available free online, proves his point.

The first point, as regards right-holders, is that it is in some sense fair that copyright-holders must choose, where appropriate to the context, the benefits of copyright protection (and accepting its limits) *or* the benefits of digital fences/confidential information (and accepting its limits). Fences should only be able to be chosen where impeding access to a work will not have a significant impact on the development of the area chosen or on social virtue; certain objects should be the subject of digital locks that bar access. Similarly, one should never choose a digital lock where fair dealing needs to be considered, without at least allowing for fair dealing to take place. If copyright protection is sufficient, why ever use a digital lock? As we have seen above, putting digital locks around books must be avoided as a matter of ethical duty by copyright-holders and hardware providers.

In both cases, admitting that the certain applications of the digital locks paradigm — those which bar access to content — are really part of the confidential information governance paradigm is instructive. If one has confidential information (such as the recipe for Coke or a client list or other database) and one creates a network of contracts and licensing around the secret in order to protect it, then one cannot protect competitors from doing likewise (developing another cola, assembling a competing client list, or a competing database). Their efficacy is lessened even if there is some inspiration, or reverse-engineering, to the extent that one duplicates the former and to the extent that trade secrets and confidential information will entail some leakage, even some copying. If there has been no leak in this paradigm, you cannot sue a competitor for having "copied." So, if one chooses this paradigm, one should in principle have to forego the benefits of copyright protection. Of course, this is unrealistic as copyright protection is now automatic. Rather, we should take care when we allow the non-copyright protection to cumulate. As C-32 has failed to fully account for this tension between paradigms, then copyright-holders who choose paracopyright digital locks have more control over access than traditional copyright protection would ever afford for similar information. Thus, they should *ethically* forego suing in copyright (the traditional flexible text of substantive copying) where their own chosen method of protection — fences — has fallen short. If you choose an absolute fence and cannot keep out similar works, then you should not ethically be able to fall back on balance. Certainly, a copyright act cannot justify giving a form of super-protection to digital locks; violations should be in contract and not copyright. This is perhaps the most bizarre element of the new paracopyright norms: making the circumvention of digital locks a copyright infringement, when what is being protected is a secret or information that is not even protected by copyright. In sum, paracopyright could work, but not in the copyright regime and certainly not under C-32 if every right is taken to its textual limit.

Put another way, if passed, C-32 becomes part of the normative order and becomes a set of exclusionary reasons or reason for action in and of itself without further need of ethical justification. But given that C-32 contains fundamental internal contradictions, as well as contradictions with the current and historical concept of copyright, following some of its principal rules to the limit will cause inevitable conflicts with other central provisions in the same bill, as well as other entrenched principles of copyright. Put simply, the *only* way paracopyright can co-exist with copyright is if everyone acts with restraint, *i.e.*, ethically.

Of course, not all forms of technological protection measures bar access to content. Rather, they restrict specific uses of content which are accessible in principle. That is, some types of digital locks lock functions or impede functionality without directly obstructing access to content. Ethically, these locks are less problematic, though perhaps bothersome, provided the function is not central to accessing the work or exercising fair dealing rights. A virtue ethics approach is neutral in this regard.

Given the effectively temporary nature of digital fences (all locks can be picked, all fences can be breached) and the persistence of hacking,[66] one wonders if this inevitability would cause anyone to ever opt for a fence, incurring development costs and occasionally the scorn of its customer base. Certain elements of the music industry have begun to understand this[67] and have tried to work around the digital age by developing new business models. A number of these models are based on sharing, user interaction, or both. Some artists simply want their music to be heard, tolerating and even encouraging sharing. Profit can be found in other aspects of the business, even including some sale of recorded music. This seems to me to be a virtuous approach. It may also end up being profitable, especially for artists.

Trade secrets also illuminate where digital fences are appropriate or inappropriate as a governance paradigm in the larger context. Trade secrets and confidential information are used in heavily marketized contexts

---

66 See Cory Doctorow, "Microsoft Research DRM Talk" in Cory Doctorow, *ibid.* at 3.

67 Such is the case especially after the Sony "Rootkit fiasco," where many consumers and artists reacted quite strongly against such measures: see "Sony's Rootkit Fiasco" *CNET News* (November 2005), http://news.cnet.com/Sonys-rootkit-fiasco/2009-1029_3-5961248.html; and Jeremy F. deBeer, "How Restrictive Terms and Technologies Backfired on Sony BMG", above note 45.

where society does not have a real stake in knowing the recipe for Coke or a client list, provided that competition laws are not impeded. These kinds of objects do not, *en soi,* help to enrich the public domain in the same way as a book, a painting, a song, or a movie. So, ethically, a copyright holder ought to consider the object of protection: is it helping to directly advance science or the state of learning or the arts and does it enrich the public domain and inspire others to create in turn? Is it the foundation for a kind of learning or knowledge, etc.? Does it serve to develop some other social virtue? Can others be reasonably expected to want to deal fairly in order to study, learn, re-create (and not simply to get the market secret?). Does the development of the object owe its origins to adaptation from the public domain or the pool of creative knowledge? If so, then others should be able to be inspired in turn as a matter of ethical duty to the creative process (or, for Litman, the "adaptive process"[68]). If the answer to the question of whether the work is important to the knowledge or creative base is affirmative, then my strong ethical intuition is that one should *never* put up a digital fence, whatever the law might allow, but rather trust the traditional balances of copyright to balance the interest of the right-holder and users or society.

Here the analogy to concepts such as the American doctrine of copyright misuse[69] or the concept of *abus de droit* in Quebec Civil law[70] is appropriately drawn. One's right does not allow a person to exercise that right in any conceivable fashion. In all such cases the exercise of the right must be undertaken to foster the overall purposes or teleology of the statute, in the case of copyright misuse, or of both a civil law norm and the larger normative order, in the case of civil law. Misuse or abuse undermines the very principles upon which the right-holder's rights are grounded. Hence, all are to exercise their rights in good faith. Moreover, these doctrines focus on action, target standards of behaviour, and are contextual in terms of their specific substantive understanding and application within a given set of circumstances. And, in a very real sense, none of these doctrines or the principles underlying them is foreign to Canadian copyright law: the civil

---

68 Jessica Litman, "The Public Domain", above note 10.

69 See generally Kathryn Judge, "Rethinking Copyright Misuse", (2004) 57 Stan. L. Rev. 901: in her view any attempt by a copyright holder to effectively expand the purview of copyright protection to gain control over an idea or deter fair use constitutes misuse. See also Dan L. Burk, "Anti-Circumvention Misuse" (2003) 50 UCLA L. Rev. 1095, http://papers.ssrn.com/sol3/papers.cfm?abstract_id=320961. I thank Michael Geist for reminding me of this doctrine.

70 *Civil Code of Quebec*, S.Q. 1991, c.64, art. 6.

law is part of our *copyright* tradition and we are closely linked to our American cousins in terms of Anglo-American copyright doctrine and practice (as proponents of incorporating digital lock protections and other DMCA-like revisions in Canadian copyright law like to remind us). In short, there is no good reason to hermetically seal Canadian copyright from principles that are already familiar and that focus on virtuous behavior.

The beauty of an object-focused, contextualized virtue ethics approach to such questions, as opposed to a formal statute, is that it allows us to draw meaningful distinctions from the question of appropriate governance tools and their parameters in a way that a formal statute cannot. There is a much weaker case for a digital lock on basic operating software or an internet browser, as these are necessary for learning and functioning in our digital world, than there is on a highly market driven, digital FPS video game, where the different features are more about marketing the game against competitors than about the state of knowledge. My own view is that the holder of the operating system is obligated to forego the digital lock, allow interoperability for similar kinds of "knowledge" applications, and maybe even support non-proprietary software, while the game-developer can generally choose a digital lock.

The same advantage holds for understanding databases and information. If the information is wholly market-oriented — client lists, customer databases, etc. — a digital lock is perfectly fine on a virtue-based approach, as the context is competition and the trade secret model is appropriate. But databases that are fundamental to advancing knowledge — space data for example[71] — are subject to an ethical duty not to attach a digital lock at the very least, if not eschew copyright protection altogether. What of the non-original database?[72] The state of copyright law is that some exercise of skill or judgment is required to attract the protection of traditional copyright in terms of originality.[73] This would, as a relatively attainable standard, cover most cases.[74]

---

71 C. Doldirina, *The Challenge of Making Remote Sensing Data More Accessible: The Common Good as a Remedy* (D.C.L. Thesis, McGill University, 2011) (forthcoming; text on file with the author) [unpublished]. This is especially true where public bodies have assisted in gathering, organizing or maintaining the data.

72 Thanks to the anonymous reviewer for asking this question.

73 As set out in *CCH Canadian*, above note 12.

74 However, there could be certain databases that would not meet even this standard, and would thus not be protectable using copyright. While few in number, they present an interesting case: a generic white pages phone book is an obvious example. In effect, the data is known, or is public, available from other sources (though additional sweat is required), and is not organized in any protectable manner, such

Ethical rules of thumb regarding certain objects are also instructive for copyright-holders: don't exercise the locks to impede access, fair dealing, etc. Do nothing to impede the progress of the art (developing computer software, or impeding appropriation art or musical forms). Do not use a digital lock to hinder education or learning. Or, rather, use digital locks to protect works *and values* protected by the copyright tradition. Experience with the DMCA and rumours about the Anti-Counterfeiting Trade Agreement[75] teach us that, thus far, copyright-holders aren't yet thinking in this ethical mode.

C. CONCLUSION

As it tries to straddle two different governance paradigms, C-32 is seriously flawed. At present, should rights-holders in particular opt for the fence paradigm of digital locks, the goals of traditional copyright will be overwhelmed and possibly undermined, particularly where the pegs of digital locks rest on top of a base level of copyright protection.

Bill C-32 might be "saved"[76] in some sense in practice if copyright-holders are reasonable or, as I have argued, ethical in their use of digital locks. As suggested, this could be done by voluntarily opting not to use digital locks with respect to objects or in areas that undermine the traditional values of copyright: promotion of the art in question, development of knowledge, development of the public domain, and users' rights related to all of these. Digital locks should be restricted to areas where the protected resource is more akin to a simple trade secret, is a marketing advantage, and is not a building block to other kinds of development of the art, or state of knowledge.

---

that it cannot be owned. In principle, one might argue that the *Copyright Act*, and hence C-32, would not apply at all; neither its protections nor its restrictions would apply. Nevertheless, the data is possessed in a sense, and thus it remains open as to whether a digital lock might be legally applied to the database. It is also open as to whether a user might be able to challenge or circumvent that lock, and finally whether an "owner" successfully sue for anti-circumvention relief.

75 The official public working version was recently released after a series of high-profile leaks: http://trade.ec.europa.eu/doclib/docs/2010/april/tradoc_146029.pdf. The leaks, as well as the reactions, are too numerous to cite. Wikipedia remains a useful point of entry to this history and this debate: http://en.wikipedia.org/wiki/Anti-Counterfeiting_Trade_Agreement.

76 Or, at least, we might be saved from the eternal reform processes, legislative debates and lobbying that would come as a result of the failure of this project.

If the copyright industry claims it is being reasonable, this might be an opportunity to prove it. Indeed, given the current configuration of C-32, in my view, copyright-holders have much more to lose in not being virtuous. Users, consumers, and governments have, to some extent, heard their pleas and allowed some scope for the use of digital locks. But if digital locks crop up everywhere, even in music where they have been eschewed more recently, then the sympathy may well dry up. At that point, as a society, we may find that it will then be appropriate to remove protection for digital locks from the statute or seek to limit or ban them altogether. Virtue has its burdens.

In turn, users should exercise some restraint in their sharing of protected works where they do not have a good (here, ethical) reason to not pay for their copies. Traditional doctrines of creation and fair dealing already serve as guides. It is only by acting ethically, in good faith, and trying to be fair that users can expect copyright-holders to do likewise.

Of course, one can criticize the aspirational nature of these reflections. One may easily accuse me of being unrealistic. Both sides in the debate can point to abuses by the other side: the serial downloading by many in the world of file sharing versus the fanatical attempts to control access by many large, corporate copyright-holders. But virtuous behaviour and analysis have always been a part of our copyright traditions — witness the substance of doctrines such as fair dealing, of promoting the arts and literature, of judgmental and contextual doctrines for determining infringement, copyright misuse, etc. — not to mention *abus de droit* and good faith in one of our major Canadian private law systems. One will realize that in some quarters this kind of ethical behaviour has been elaborated, valued, understood, and even occasionally required all along. It may not be so idealistic after all: Bill C-32, flawed as it is, can serve as the reminder that a good normative order requires good actors.

Perhaps our expectations of the formal legal copyright order, at each successive attempt at copyright reform, are simply too high. The DMCA created more problems than it solved and its author Bruce Lehman exhorted Canada to do differently.[77] It may simply be that, given the complexity of the technology, the change of pace, and the spirit and rapid pace of human inventiveness, formal normativity in such an area will always

---

77 Bruce Lehman, "Digital Rights Management Dilemma" (Speaker at Musical Myopia, Digital Dystopia: New Media and Copyright Reform Conference, McGill University, March 2007), http://video.google.com/videoplay?docid=4162208056624464666&hl=en# at 12:58. The webcast of the conference is also available at http://www.cipp.mcgill.ca/en/events/past/.

fall short or will always be a step behind. The copyright tradition has *always* relied on informal norms and notions of fairness and ethics to settle claims about the scope of protection and competing claims as between holders and copiers. Our sense of ethics evolves much more slowly than technology[78] and somewhat more slowly than formal normativity. It thus makes good sense to focus first on the virtues and our ethics, as this in and of itself will help us cope with rapid changes. Both the ability to copy and the power to protect more absolutely have been made easier by rapid changes in digital technology. The fundamental idea of resorting to fairness and ethics in the interpretation of acts related to copyright ought to remain the same and, indeed, continue to guide us forward.

78 Though, of course, technological changes will help to shape ethical possibilities and then standards.

PART THREE

Creativity

CHAPTER TWELVE

"Modernizing" ISP Copyright Liability

Gregory R. Hagen*

A. INTRODUCTION

In the intense battle for the spoils generated by the online information ecosystem, it has been a contentious question as to whether Internet intermediaries — especially those who carry, host and index others' information — should be liable for copyright infringement in relation to content provided by third parties. Internet intermediaries include Internet access providers, web hosting providers, Internet payment systems, search engines, portals, e-commerce intermediaries, blogs, video sites, and social networking platforms.[1] Currently, under the *Copyright Act*,[2] those who provide the means necessary for others to communicate works and other subject matter on the Internet (Internet Service Providers or ISPs) will not be liable for copyright infringement if they *merely* provide such means.[3] Under the *Copyright Act*, there are no mandatory notice and takedown (NTD) provisions requiring ISPs to prevent infringement by taking down

---

* I gratefully acknowledge the financial support of Borden Ladner Gervais, the research assistance of Kimberly Howe, and the helpful comments from an anonymous reviewer, Michael Geist, Sam Witherspoon and Maria Lavelle.

1 More generally, Internet intermediaries bring together or facilitate transactions between third parties on the Internet. *See* Organization for Economic Co-Operation and Development, "The Economic and Social Role of Internet Intermediaries" (April 2010), www.oecd.org/dataoecd/49/4/44949023.pdf.

2 *Copyright Act*, R.S.C. 1985, c. C-42, http://laws.justice.gc.ca/en/C-42 [*Copyright Act*].

3 *Ibid*., ss. 2.4(1)(b).

allegedly infringing subject matter when an allegation is received from a copyright owner. Nor is there a notice and notice (NN) system which requires ISPs to forward a notice from a copyright owner of alleged infringement by its customer, in relation to the use of the ISP's facilities, to the allegedly infringing customer. Nonetheless, it has been common practice for a number of years for major ISPs to voluntarily forward a notice of alleged infringement to their customers.[4]

Bill C-32, the *Copyright Modernization Act*,[5] clarifies the liability of Internet intermediaries by adding new immunity provisions for ISPs and search engines. "ISPs and search engines are exempt from liability when they act strictly as intermediaries in communication, caching and hosting activities."[6] By implication, the immunity under Bill C-32 will apply to access providers, hosts, bloggers, video sites, social networking sites and others who communicate third party content and merely act as ISPs. Search engines are treated differently and can enjoy immunity from liability for damages, but are subject to injunctions.[7] Further, the Bill introduces a new form of secondary liability for Internet Intermediaries who know or ought to know that their services are designed primarily to enable copyright infringement.[8] The possibility that ISPs might be found liable for infringement as *authorizers* of infringing activity by others remains.

Further, the Government of Canada comments that "ISPs are in a unique position to facilitate the enforcement of copyright on the Internet."[9] In particular, they are the only parties that can identify and notify subscribers accused of infringing copyright by using the ISPs services.[10] Bill C-32, therefore, mandates a NN system under which an ISP (excepting search engines) must, without delay, forward notices of alleged infringement to

4 Bell, Rogers, Shaw and Telus, "Submission of Bell, Rogers, Shaw and Telus," www.ic.gc.ca/eic/site/008.nsf/eng/02634.html ["Submission of Bell, Rogers, Shaw and Telus"].

5 Bill C-32, *Copyright Modernization Act*, 3d Sess., 40th Parl., 2010, www2.parl.gc.ca/HousePublications/Publication.aspx?Docid=4580265&file=4 [Bill C-32].

6 Canada, Balanced Copyright, "Copyright Modernization Act — Backgrounder" (June 2010), http://www.ic.gc.ca/eic/site/crp-prda.nsf/eng/h_rp01151.html ["Copyright Modernization Act — Backgrounder"].

7 Bill C-32, above note 5, s. 47. Note, however, the limitations to this partial immunity discussed later in this paper.

8 Bill C-32, above note 5, s. 18. (See proposed s. 27(2.3)).

9 Canada, Balanced Copyright, "What the New Copyright Modernization Act Means for Internet Service Providers, Search Engines and Broadcasters" (June 2010), http://www.ic.gc.ca/eic/site/crp-prda.nsf/eng/rp01188.html ["Balanced Copyright"].

10 *Ibid.*

the customers they concern,[11] but ISPs will not be required to take down allegedly infringing content. Nor will ISPs be required to limit or terminate access when they are notified of allegedly infringing conduct of their subscribers under a graduated response system (GR). ISPs will also be required to preserve evidence of the identity of alleged infringers for a period of up to six months, or one year if the content creator commences an action.[12] If an ISP fails to follow the notice procedures, it risks being held liable for an award of damages.[13]

Most striking is the fact that the new secondary liability provision will be ineffective against highly decentralized, peer to peer file sharing networks, such as those using the bitTorrent protocol, because there is no central, coordinating entity that can be found liable. Instead, the primary means of enforcing copyright against peer to peer file sharing networks under the Bill is to control the information itself rather than its distribution through ISPs. This approach, which is suggested by the World Intellectual Property Organization (WIPO) Internet Treaties, builds upon the ability of copyright owners to use technological measures or "digital locks" to control access to their works and other subject matter.[14] Since infringers can also use tools to circumvent such measures, the Bill prohibits the circumvention of digital locks that control access to works and other subject matter.[15] Given a generative Internet,[16] though, one in which individuals are able to quickly respond and adapt to digital locks, it will be a challenge, if indeed it is possible, for private interests to succeed in controlling access to information while serving copyright's goals and maintaining privacy, free expression, fair procedures and the rule of law. That is a topic for a different paper, however.

---

11 Bill C-32, above note 5, s. 47. (See proposed s. 41.26.)

12 *Ibid.* (See proposed s. 41.26(1)(b).)

13 *Ibid.* (See proposed s. 41.26(3).)

14 *WIPO Copyright Treaty*, 20 December 1996, www.wipo.int/treaties/en/ip/wct/trtdocs_wo033.html, 36 I.L.M. 65 at Art. 8; *WIPO Performances and Phonograms Treaty*, 20 December 1996, www.wipo.int/treaties/en/ip/wppt/trtdocs_wo034.html, 36 I.L.M. 76, Art. 16(2).

15 Bill C-32, above note 5, s. 47. (See proposed s. 41.1(1).)

16 "Generativity denotes a technology's overall capacity to produce unprompted change driven by large, varied, and uncoordinated audiences." See Jonathan Zittrain, "The Generative Internet" (2006) 119 Harv. L. Rev. 1974–2040, www.harvardlawreview.org/issues/119/may06/zittrain.shtml at 1980.

B. BACKGROUND

The Internet is an engine of dissemination of information that can benefit the public. As the Supreme Court of Canada said in the *SOCAN* decision, "The capacity of the Internet to disseminate "works of the arts and intellect" is one of the great innovations of the information age. Its use should be facilitated rather than discouraged."[17] However, as the world transitions to a global, digitally-networked information economy, the winners from the old economy are striving to ensure that the benefits from the new economy will accrue to them.[18] Rather than focus on the Internet as a remarkable disseminator of information, many copyright owners are concerned that the Internet has displaced their traditional dominance as distributors of content, diminishing their ability to maximize their revenues.

Copyright owners, therefore, emphasize the Supreme Court's important proviso to its statement above that the dissemination of works "should not be done unfairly at the expense of those who created the works of arts and intellect in the first place."[19] Associations, such as the International Chamber of Commerce, urge that "[i]ntellectual property (IP) theft is a huge and growing global challenge."[20] Canada in particular has been singled out by the International Chamber of Commerce as a "major source of the world's piracy problem."[21] The United States 2010 Special 301 Watch List refers to "the continuing challenges of Internet piracy in countries such as Canada."[22] Canada's copyright laws are often (unjustly) touted to be weak[23] and its failure to ratify the 1996 WIPO Internet Treaties is often

17 *Society of Composers, Authors and Music Publishers of Canada v. Canadian Assn. of Internet Providers*, 2004 SCC 45, http://csc.lexum.umontreal.ca/en/2004/2004scc45/2004scc45.html, [2004] 2 S.C.R. 427 at para. 40 [*SOCAN* cited to S.C.R.].

18 See Yochai Benkler, "The Battle Over the Institutional Ecosystem in the Digital Environment" (2001) 44 Communications of the ACM 84–90, www.benkler.org/CACM.pdf.

19 *SOCAN*, above note 17 at para. 40.

20 International Chamber of Commerce, "International Chamber of Commerce Urges G8/G20 Action on Counterfeiting and Piracy" (22 June 2010), http://smr.newswire.ca/en/international-chamber-of-commerce-and-canadian-intellectual/international-chamber-of-commerce-urges-g8g20-action.

21 International Federation of the Phonographic Industry, "IFPI reacts to publication of draft Canadian Copyright Amendment Bill," (June 2010), www.ifpi.org/content/section_news/20100607.html. For a useful counterpoint, see Michael Geist, "Piracy Haven Label Case of Rhetoric Over Reality" (10 May 2010), www.michaelgeist.ca/content/view/5020/159.

22 United States, United States Trade Representative, *2010 Special 301 Report* (April 2010) at 1, www.ustr.gov/webfm_send/1906.

23 Barry Sookman, "Copyright Reform for Canada: What Should We Do?" www.ic.gc.ca/eic/site/008.nsf/eng/02934.html [Sookman, "What Should We Do?"]. For a useful

criticized.[24]Some politicians have even argued (wrongly) that ratifying the WIPO Internet Treaties is required by international law.[25]

Given the Internet, the ability of copyright owners to maintain control of the distribution of their copyrighted subject matter depends upon their control of Internet communications. However, the ability to control the communication and reproduction of works and other subject matter via the Internet is limited because, unlike conventional telecommunications systems, the Internet was designed without a central point of control.[26] Early Internet theorists believed that the distributed architecture of the Internet rendered it impossible to regulate.[27] Others emphasized that the Internet's architecture — its code — could be changed, making it regulable.[28] Still others countered that Internet intermediaries were natural points of control that could be used to regulate their customers and potentially could be found liable for acts of copyright infringement.[29]

Copyright owners have used various arguments to justify regaining control over the communication of information over the Internet. Access to information, including copyrighted content, on the Internet is a powerful inducement for people to sign up with an access provider,[30] an inducement from which ISPs profit. Copyright owners have claimed that ISPs authorize infringing activity and, therefore, should be considered liable

---

rebuttal, see Howard Knopf, "The Annual 301 Show — USTR Call for Comments — 21 Reasons Why Canadian Copyright Law is Already Stronger than USAs" (February 2010), http://excesscopyright.blogspot.com/2010/02/annual-301-parade-ustr-calls-for.html.

24 *Ibid.*

25 See Gregory R. Hagen, "A Note on Integrity in Treaty-Making & Copyright Law" (11 March, 2008), http://ablawg.ca/2008/03/11/a-note-on-integrity-in-treaty-making-copyright-law/#more-81.

26 Keenan Mayo & Peter Newcomb, "How the Web Was Won" *Vanity Fair* (July 2008), www.vanityfair.com/culture/features/2008/07/internet200807.

27 David R. Johnson & David G. Post, "Law and Borders — The Rise of Law in Cyberspace" (1996) 48 Stan. L. Rev. 1367–1402, http://papers.ssrn.com/sol3/papers.cfm?abstract_id=535. See also John Perry Barlow, "A Cyberspace Declaration" (February 1996), http://w2.eff.org/Censorship/Internet_censorship_bills/barlow_0296.declaration.

28 Lawrence Lessig, *Code and Other Laws of Cyberspace* (New York: Basic Books, 1999).

29 Jack Goldsmith & Tim Wu, *Who Controls the Internet: Illusions of a Borderless World* (New York: Oxford University Press, 2006).

30 *SOCAN*, above note 17 at para. 121.

for infringement.[31] More practically, copyright owners argue that access providers are an "efficient engine of collection"[32] of copyright royalties.

The well-known judgment of the Supreme Court of Canada in *SOCAN* suggests that the copyright liability of ISPs who carry, host and cache third party content should be based primarily upon principles of fault. First, since ISPs, as common carriers, merely carry the communications of others, they do not themselves communicate copyrighted subject matter. Second, ISPs are innocent disseminators of information in defamation law, similar to bookstores, libraries, and news vendors who have no actual knowledge of defamation and have not been negligent in failing to detect the defamation.[33] According to the Supreme Court in *SOCAN*: "To the extent they act as innocent disseminators, they are protected."[34] A well-known common law principle applied to copyright would hold that, as between two innocent parties, the copyright owners and ISPs, losses should normally lie where they fall, with the copyright owners.[35] Third, it is impractical, both economically and technically, to monitor the deluge of information transmitted through an intermediary.[36] Finally, immunity from infringement encourages intermediaries to "expand and improve their operations without the threat of copyright infringement."[37] Consequently, disputes between copyright owners and consumers should not be "visited on the heads of the Internet intermediaries" (i.e., ISPs).[38]

In response, copyright owners and their lobbyists have pressed their case for creating a new form of copyright liability against ISPs who facilitate infringement, especially peer to peer file sharing services.[39] One lobbyist for the Canadian Recording Industry Association, has suggested that "secondary infringement doctrines are essential for pursuing pirate

---

31 *Ibid.*

32 *Ibid.* at para. 3.

33 *Ibid.* at para. 95.

34 *Ibid.* at para. 95.

35 Oliver Wendell Holmes, *The Common Law* (Chicago: ABA Publishing, 2009), www.gutenberg.org/etext/2449 at 34.

36 *SOCAN*, above note 17 at para. 101.

37 *Ibid.* at. para. 114.

38 *Ibid.* at para. 131.

39 The US position is that the *Anti-Counterfeiting Trade Agreement* "is not intended to include new intellectual property rights or to enlarge or diminish existing intellectual property rights." See the Office of the US Trade Representative, "Statement of ACTA Negotiating Partners on Recent ACTA Negotiations" (1 July 2010), www.ustr.gov/about-us/press-office/press-releases/2010/june/office-us-trade-representative-releases-statement-act.

online sites and services."[40] At the same time, copyright owners and their lobbyists have also called for a stronger role for ISPs who are merely information conduits in policing infringement by others over their networks. Some lobbyists continue to insist that a formalized NTD regime, in addition to a NN regime, would benefit copyright users.[41] They have also advocated for a series of graduated responses to alleged copyright infringement that could result in limiting or cutting off Internet access.[42]

C. THE *COPYRIGHT MODERNIZATION ACT*

1) General

How does the *Copyright Modernization Act* modernize the role of ISPs? In introducing the *Copyright Modernization Act*, the Government of Canada billed it as a "key pillar" in the Canadian Government's strategy to make Canada a leader in the "global digital economy."[43] In *Improving Canada's Digital Advantage*, copyright is described as "an important marketplace framework law and cultural policy instrument that must give Canadian creators, citizens, and consumers the tools they need to compete in the global digital economy."[44] According to such a market-based approach, copyright creates a private property right as a reward for the investment of intellectual labour.[45] It is "individuals' right to protect their own creations."[46] The role of ISPs in the digital economy is to "disseminate cre-

40 See Sookman, "What Should We Do?" above note 23. While there are no explicit provisions in the *Copyright Act* concerning liability for inducing infringement or materially contributing to copyright infringement, Sookman comments that "[i]t is probable, but uncertain, that Canadian law provides relief for acts that induce or materially contribute to copyright infringement." This is not the case as, under s. 89 of the *Copyright Act*, copyright is limited to the rights provided for under the *Copyright Act* and remedies are provided only for violation of those rights.

41 *Ibid.*

42 Barry Sookman & Dan Glover, "Graduated response and copyright: an idea that is right for the times," *The Lawyers' Weekly* (January 2010), www.barrysookman.com/2010/01/20/graduated-response-and-copyright-an-idea-that-is-right-for-the-times [Sookman and Glover, "Graduated Response and Copyright"].

43 Canada, Balanced Copyright, "Government of Canada Introduces Proposals to Modernize the Copyright Act" (June 2010), www.ic.gc.ca/eic/site/crp-prda.nsf/eng/h_rp01149.html [*Balanced Copyright*].

44 Canada, Digital Economy Consultation, *Improving Canada's Digital Advantage*, http://de-en.gc.ca/wp-content/uploads/2010/05/Consultation_Paper.pdf at 28, emphasis added [*Improving Canada's Digital Advantage*].

45 *Ibid.* at 28.

46 P2Pnet, "James Moore vs. Radical Extremists," www.p2pnet.net/story/41150.

ative content and connect people across Canada and the world."[47] In short, copyright creates products for a digital market and ISPs are the means by which those products are licensed by copyright owners.

At the same time that ISPs enable the marketing of digital products they can enable copyright infringement by others. A "well-functioning marketplace," on the Government's view, would secure copyright owners against the "stealing" of their products.[48] At its extreme, this view entails that all social benefits of a copyright should accrue to its owner. It implies that, even if inexpensive dissemination of art, literature, music, software and films greatly benefitted individuals in society but cost copyright owners a little (or at least failed to benefit them), the dissemination would be unjustified. The implication of such a view for ISP liability, as Nesbitt pointed out years ago, is that "[a]ny statutory limitation on the liability of ISPs would, according to this [natural rights] perspective, represent a degradation of the protected rights of a copyright owner. . . ."[49] Although the Government of Canada may not push its market-based view to its extreme,[50] its aim is that Canadian companies be able to compete in a global digital market in copyrighted products wherein copyright owners largely control the product and its dissemination.

This world view is, in reality, rather antiquated. The idea that copyright is a common law property right that results from the application of intellectual labour was popular in the second half of the eighteenth century but was rejected by the House of Lords in *Donaldsen v. Becket*.[51] More recently the view that copyright is concerned *only* with the prevention of free riding off the intellectual labour of authors was rejected by the Supreme

---

47 *Balanced Copyright*, above note 43.

48 *Improving Canada's Digital Advantage*, above note 44 at 14.

49 Scott Nesbitt, "Rescuing the Balance? An Assessment of Canada's Proposal to Limit ISP Liability for Online Copyright Infringement" (2003) 2 Canadian Journal of Law and Technology 115 at 124, http://cjlt.dal.ca/vol2_no2/pdfarticles/nesbitt.pdf.

50 For instance, under the proposed s. 29 of the Bill, there are several new fair uses for education, parody and satire, non-commercial user-generated content, format shifting, time shift and backup copies.

51 *Donaldson v. Beckett*, 2 Brown's Parl. Cases 129, 1 Eng. Rep. 837; 4 Burr. 2408, 98 Eng. Rep. 257 (1774), www.copyrighthistory.com/donaldson.html.

Court of Canada[52] and by prominent copyright scholars.[53] Finally, the idea that reproduction and communication technologies, such as ISPs, need to be controlled to prevent the dissemination of certain kinds of works is as old as the Stationer's Company and its censorship of heretical books.[54] Ironically, the *modern* idea that copyrighted content should be freely available in return for compensation to owners provided by a levy or from a compulsory license fee is given short shrift.[55]

The Government's view of the role of copyright in a digital economy might explain its desire for liability for peer to peer file sharing services, but it does not explain its particular choice of a secondary liability provision. The Minister of Heritage says that "[t]he best way to fight piracy is by targeting those who knowingly enable online infringement."[56] Why is that? Why did it not include seemingly stronger secondary infringement provisions such as liability for contributory infringement[57] and for induce-

---

52 *Théberge v. Galerie d'Art du Petit Champlain inc.*, 2002 SCC 34, http://csc.lexum.umontreal.ca/en/2002/2002scc34/2002scc34.html, [2002] 2 S.C.R. 336 at para. 30 [*Théberge* cited to S.C.R.]. The Supreme Court remarked at para. 31 that Canada copyright law is a balance between "promoting the public interest in the encouragement and dissemination of works of art and the intellect" and "obtaining a just reward for the creator."

53 Mark Lemley, "Property, Intellectual Property and Free Riding" (2005) 83 Tex. L. Rev. 1031, http://papers.ssrn.com/sol3/papers.cfm?abstract_id=582602. As Lemley has suggested, to obtain the full social value of works and other subject matter is as fair as charging all pedestrians for viewing the roses in one's garden.

54 Lionel Bently and Brad Sherman, *The Making of Modern Intellectual Property Law: The British Experience, 1760–1911* (Cambridge: Cambridge University Press, 1999) at 11–12.

55 The role of free information on the internet has been discussed at length by Lawrence Lessig, *The Future of Ideas: the Fate of the Commons in a Connected World* (Toronto: Random House, 2001). A right to remuneration for music file sharing was proposed by the Songwriters Association of Canada in "Our Proposal: Detailed" (29 March 2009) http://songwriters.ca/proposaldetailed.aspx. See also the specific proposals by Neil Netanel, "Impose a Noncommercial Use Levy to Allow Free Peer-to Peer File Sharing," (2003) 17:1 Harvard Journal of Law & Technology 1, http://jolt.law.harvard.edu/articles/pdf/v17/17HarvJLTech001.pdf; and William W. Fisher III, *Promises to Keep: Technology, Law, and the Future of Entertainment* (Stanford: Stanford University Press, 2004).

56 James Moore, "Minister Moore's Speech at Luncheon on Intellectual Property, Innovation, Economic Growth, and Jobs Toronto, Ontario June 22, 2010," www.pch.gc.ca/pc-ch/minstr/moore/disc-spch/index-eng.cfm?action=doc&DocIDCd=SJM10 0603 ["Moore's Speech"].

57 Liability for contributory infringement exists where a third party with knowledge of the infringing activity, induces, causes or materially contributes to the infringing conduct of another. See *Gershwin Publishing Corp. v Columbia Artists Management, Inc.*, 443 F.2d 1159, 1162 (2d Cir. 1971).

ment to infringe[58] as in the US? If it is merely because that is not a Commonwealth country approach, why not adopt the Australian approach to authorization, one that is more favourable to copyright owners? Perhaps the Government wanted to find only the clearly faulty liable — those whose know or ought to know that their service is designed primarily to enable infringement. But, then the question that remains is whether ISPs can be liable for authorizing the infringing activity of others by failing to prevent that activity (e.g. by taking down files that are hosted) when given notice of it? Why did the Bill not include a NTD system or GR system for ISPs? Perhaps the Government of Canada believes that the forms of secondary liability are practically equivalent and sufficient to effectively diminish online infringement. Perhaps it heeded the criticisms of NTD and GR systems. More likely, though, is that in its vision of the digital marketplace, it is satisfied that copyright owners will be able to control the digital products themselves using digital locks even if not able to control totally the distribution of their products through third parties.

2) TSP Immunity under the *Copyright Act*

a) TSPs Don't Infringe

The *Copyright Modernization Act* supplements, but does not replace, an existing immunity provision in the *Copyright Act*. In order to better understand the new immunity provision, it is useful to briefly describe the existing provision. The *Copyright Act* currently does not explicitly grant an immunity to ISPs but, rather, to those persons "whose *only* act in respect of the communication of a work or other subject-matter to the public consists of providing the means of telecommunication necessary for another person to so communicate the work or other subject-matter."[59] These intermediaries might be termed "Telecommunications Service Providers" or "TSPs." Section 2.4(1)(b) of the *Copyright Act* deems that TSPs do not communicate:[60]

> 2.4 (1) For the purposes of communication to the public by telecommunication,

---

58 Inducement liability exists when one who distributes a device with the object of promoting its use to infringe copyright, as shown by clear expression or other affirmative steps to foster infringement, is liable for the users' resulting acts of infringement. See *Metro-Goldwyn-Mayer Studios Inc. v. Grokster, Inc.* 545 U.S. 913, www.supremecourtus.gov/opinions/04pdf/04-480.pdf, (2005) 125 S.Ct. 2764 [*Grokster*].

59 *Copyright Act*, above note 2, s. 2.4(1)(b) (emphasis added).

60 *Ibid.*

> . . .
>
> (b) a person whose only act in respect of the communication of a work or other subject-matter to the public consists of providing the means of telecommunication necessary for another person to so communicate the work or other subject-matter does not communicate that work or other subject-matter to the public; . . . .

Section 2.4(1)(b) was originally intended to protect TSPs who acted as intermediaries between broadcasters and retransmitters of broadcast signals.[61] One of the main issues in *SOCAN* was whether TSPs included ISPs (who act in a content neutral way). In *Electric Despatch*, the Supreme Court of Canada ruled that the owners of telephone wires cannot be said to transmit a message the meaning of which they were ignorant.[62] Counsel to SOCAN argued before the Federal Court of Appeal, however, that section 2.4(1)(b) of the *Copyright Act* was intended merely to protect traditional common carriers, such as poles, cables and wires, from liability for the content of the communications that they transmitted rather than to the newer Internet intermediaries, such as Rogers, Shaw, Telus and Bell.[63] In *SOCAN*, the Supreme Court of Canada held broadly that "the *Copyright Act* . . . does not impose liability for infringement on intermediaries who supply software and hardware to facilitate use of the Internet."[64] Or, to put it differently, it ruled—in essence—that neutral ISPs are TSPs. In particular, the Court said: [65]

> So long as an Internet intermediary does not itself engage in acts that relate to the content of the communication, i.e., whose participation is content neutral, but confines itself to providing "a conduit" for information communicated by others, then it will fall within s. 2.4(1)(b).

---

61 Canada. House of Commons, Sub-Committee on the Revision of Copyright of the Standing Committee on Communications and Culture, *A Charter of Rights for Creators* (Ottawa: House of Commons, 1985) at 80, cited in *SOCAN*, above note 17 at para. 90.

62 *Electric Despatch Co. of Toronto v. Bell Telephone Co. of Canada* 1891 CanLII 11, (1891), 20 S.C.R. 83 at 91, www.canlii.org/en/ca/scc/doc/1891/1891canlii11/1891canlii11.html.

63 *Society of Composers, Authors and Music Publishers of Canada v. Canadian Assn. of Internet Providers*, 2002 FCA 166, [2002] 4 F.C. 3 at para. 120, www.canlii.org/en/ca/fca/doc/2002/2002fca166/2002fca166.html.

64 *SOCAN*, above note 17 at para. 101.

65 *Ibid.* at para. 92.

The court also held that section 2.4(1)(b) of the *Copyright Act* applies to caching and hosting by ISPs since they are reasonably useful and proper to achieve the benefits of enhanced economy and efficiency, [66] provided that these activities are content neutral.[67]

It is worth emphasizing that the Supreme Court declined to characterize section 2.4(1)(b) of the *Copyright Act* as an immunity from liability for what would otherwise be an infringing *act*.[68] If section 2.4(1)(b) applies, an ISP does not communicate; rather the person who posts a file communicates it.[69] Similarly, the Federal Court of Appeal recently held that "[i]n providing access to "broadcasting," ISPs do not transmit programs."[70] The Federal Court of Appeal referred to section 4(4) of the *Broadcasting Act*, a common carrier provision analogous to section 2.4(1)(b) in support of its view.[71] However, the Court also made the more general point that the finding that content-neutral transmission intermediaries do not transmit in *Electric Despatch* itself implies that ISPs are not broadcasters.[72] The Federal Court of Appeal ruling suggests that whether an ISP reproduces, communicates, broadcasts, distributes or otherwise acts is a matter of fact, not of law. An ISP can be found liable for copyright infringement when it is more than a mere conduit.[73] As the Supreme Court of Canada noted, section 2.4(1)(b) of the Act protects the function of an ISP, not ISPs *per se*.[74] Similarly, an ISP could be found to be broadcasting if its role was no longer content neutral.[75]

b) Limited Exception: Authorization

Under section 27(1) of the *Copyright Act*, it is an infringement of copyright for anyone to do anything that is the sole right of a copyright owner, including

66 *Ibid.* at paras. 104–19.

67 *Ibid.* at para. 92.

68 *Ibid.*, at para. 87.

69 *Ibid.* at para. 111.

70 *Canadian Radio-television and Telecommunications Commission (Re)*, 2010 FCA 178 at para. 59, www.canlii.org/en/ca/fca/doc/2010/2010fca178/2010fca178.html.

71 *Ibid.* at para. 44. A "telecommunications common carrier" is in turn, defined in subsection 2(1) of the *Telecommunications Act* as "a person who owns or operates a transmission facility used by that person or another person to provide telecommunications services to the public for compensation."

72 *Ibid.* at para. 47.

73 *SOCAN*, above note 17 at para. 92.

74 *Ibid.*, at para. 102.

75 *Ibid.* at para. 59.

authorizing the exercise of an owner's rights.[76] Consequently, ISPs may be found liable if they authorize infringing acts of their subscribers. In *SOCAN*, the Supreme Court of Canada dealt with the question of whether ISPs authorize the downloading of musical works and sound recordings by merely providing the infrastructure necessary for communicating them.[77] In order to answer the question, the Court analogized the situation to another that was discussed in an earlier decision, *CCH*, in which the issue was whether the Law Society of Upper Canada library authorized patrons to make a copy of a work by providing a photocopier.[78] It ruled that authorization requires that one "sanction, approve and countenance" the infringing activity.[79] But what kind of acts of an Internet intermediary constitute authorization?

First, the Court decided in *CCH* that a person does not authorize infringement by merely authorizing the use of equipment that *could* be used to infringe copyright. A similar result was reached earlier by the UK House of Lords when it found that a seller of dual cassette recorders did not authorize reproductions of cassettes since the seller had "no control over the use of their models once they are sold."[80] Applying the reasoning from *CCH* in the Internet context, the Supreme Court found in *SOCAN* that when a massive amount of non-copyrighted material is available to the end user, one cannot impute an authorization to download copyrighted material solely based upon the provision of "Internet facilities." [81] This reasoning applies not only to internet access providers but to other ISPs who communicate content from third parties, including the *Globe and Mail*, YouTube, Google, Facebook, Amazon, eBay and others.

Second, the additional fact that someone who provides a service has *knowledge* that someone *might be using* its service to infringe copyright is not sufficient to constitute authorization by the intermediary. Presumably, in *CCH*, the library could have instituted a system whereby a librarian acts as a gatekeeper to prevent infringement, but it did not and no authorization was found.[82] Later, in *SOCAN*, the Supreme Court stated that "[t]he knowledge that someone might be using neutral technology to violate

---

76 *Copyright Act*, above note 2, s. 27(1).

77 *SOCAN*, above note 17 at para. 121.

78 *CCH Canadian Ltd. v. Law Society of Upper Canada*, 2004 SCC 13, http://csc.lexum.umontreal.ca/en/2004/2004scc13/2004scc13.html , [2004] 1 S.C.R. 339 at para. 38 [*CCH* cited to S.C.R.].

79 *Ibid.* at para. 38.

80 *CBS Songs Ltd v Amstrad Consumer Electronics plc*, [1988] 2 All ER 484 (H.L.), at 492–94.

81 *SOCAN*, above note 17 at para. 123.

82 *CCH*, above note 78.

copyright (as with the photocopier in the *CCH* case) is not necessarily sufficient to constitute authorization. . . ."[83] In coming to this conclusion, the Supreme Court explicitly rejected the reasoning of the Australian High Court in *Moorhouse*[84] which had ruled that where a university library knew or had reason to suspect that the photocopiers it provided were likely to be used for purposes of committing an infringement and could have prevented infringement, but failed to do so, the university infringed.[85]

It follows that, under Canadian law, an internet file sharing service that knew that someone *might* be using its services to infringe copyright and could have prevented the infringement by *adding* a component to filter out copyrighted works, but did not, does not thereby authorize infringement. This contrasts, notably, with the *Sharman* decision of the Australian Federal Court of Appeal in which Sharman, which licensed KaZaA file sharing software to end users, was found liable for authorizing infringement by its users where it knew that its users might be infringing copyright, could have prevented it by programming the software to filter out infringing works, but did not do so.[86] In that case, Sharman had no *actual* control over its users' ability to copy particular films, but had *potential* control because it could have programmed its software to filter out particular content from being downloaded.[87]

Third, to conclude from the fact that an ISP who has knowledge that its service *might* be used to infringe copyright, an ability to prevent infringement by others using the service, and a failure to prevent such infringement, that the ISP infringes is unsound because that service could be used for legal purposes. Even if the supply of an Internet service *did* authorize sharing of copyrighted materials, "[c]ourts should presume that a person who authorizes an activity does so only so far as it is in accordance with

83 *SOCAN*, above note 17 at para. 127.

84 *Moorhouse v. University of New South Wales*, [1976] R.P.C. 151.

85 *CCH*, above note 78 at para. 41.

86 *Universal Music Australia Pty Ltd. v. Sharman License Holdings Ltd.* (with Corrigendum dated 22 September 2005), [2005] FCA 1242 (5 September 2005) [*Sharman*]. The *Copyright Act 1968* (Australia), section 101(A), requires that in determining whether a person has authorized infringement, the following must be considered: (a) the extent (if any) of the person's power to prevent the doing of the act concerned; (b) the nature of any relationship existing between the person and the person who did the act concerned; (c) whether the person took any other reasonable steps to prevent or avoid the doing of the act, including whether the person complied with any relevant industry codes of practice.

87 *Ibid* at para. 414.

the law."[88] Such legal purposes include downloading public domain or licensed works or downloading for the purposes of fair dealing and for uses that fall under the private copying provision of the *Copyright Act*.[89]

Fourth, according to the Supreme Court, in *CCH*, "[t]his presumption may be rebutted if it is shown that a certain relationship or degree of control existed between the alleged authorizer and the persons who committed the copyright infringement."[90] Of central import, of course, are the sources and the degree of control necessary for rebuttal. Elsewhere in the judgment, the Court points to additional sources of possible control: control over which works a user may copy and control over the purposes of copying.[91] It follows that, when an ISP has specific knowledge that it hosts infringing content and the ability to take it down, failure to take it down *might* result in infringement. The Supreme Court stated that "notice of infringing content, and a failure to respond by "taking it down" may in some circumstances lead to a finding of "authorization."" [92] The Court elsewhere said more bluntly that "[i]f the host server provider does not comply with the notice, it may be held to have authorized communication of the copyright material."[93] From the context, a finding of infringement requires actual control over the actions of infringers, rather than merely potential control as in *Sharman*.[94] When the requirements of specific knowledge of infringement and actual control over the acts of infringers are present, there exists a *de facto* NTD system.[95]

---

88 *CCH*, above note 78 at para. 38.

89 For example, one could download the dot torrent file for Canada's Next Great Prime Minister at www.cbc.ca/nextprimeminister/blog/2008/03/download_canadas_next_great_pr.html.

90 *CCH*, above note 78 at para. 38.

91 *Ibid.* at para. 45.

92 *SOCAN*, above note 17 at para. 127.

93 *Ibid.* at para. 110.

94 *Sharman*, above note 86.

95 "Sookman, What Should We Do?" above note 23, and the Entertainment Software Association of Canada, both construe the existing system as a *de facto* NTD system. See Entertainment Software Association of Canada, "Submission to the 2009 Canadian Copyright Consultation by the Entertainment Software Association of Canada," (13 September 2009), www.ic.gc.ca/eic/site/008.nsf/eng/02705.html#p8.3, ["Entertainment Software Submission,"]. By contrast, Sheryl Hamilton considers Canada's system to be one where ISPs are totally immune. See Sheryl N. Hamilton, "Made in Canada: A Unique Approach to Internet Service Provider Liability and Copyright Infringement" in Michael Geist ed., *In the Public Interest* (Irwin Law: Toronto, 2005) 285, www.irwinlaw.com/pages/content-commons/made-in-canada-

A general principle that, given that an ISP has particular knowledge of infringement by its customers in using its services and control over its customers' actions, the failure of the ISP to take action to prevent infringement implies authorization has important limitations. First of all, it may conflict with the legal obligations of ISPs to their customers to provide access and hosting services.[96] Second, a practice of sending unfounded, often automated, notices would undermine the effectiveness of such notices as reliable indicators of infringement.[97] Third, combined with a large number of notices received by Canadian ISPs, it is difficult for ISPs to determine which notices are valid.[98] ISPs would be left only with the knowledge that there might be an infringing use of its services. Left with poor evidence of infringement, ISPs would not have the requisite knowledge of infringement to justify taking down content and risk a breach of contract or, at least, damage to its relationship with its customer. However, the risk remains that if a court judges a notice of alleged infringement to be a reliable indicator of infringement, then failure to take down the content could result in a finding of infringement. ISPs should not be left in this uncomfortable legal limbo.

Finally, it is difficult to define the kind and degree of control that would be necessary to constitute authorization in the context of peer to peer file sharing. Sharman was found liable for authorizing infringement in part because it failed to implement filtering technology in its software.[99] But even under the Australian approach, in some cases it would be too difficult for Internet access providers to control which content is made available through their services to their subscribers. In *iiNet*, for instance, the Australian Federal Court of Appeal held that iiNet, an Internet access provider who knew that its users might infringe copyright by using bitTorrent file sharing clients, did *not* thereby provide the means to infringe.[100] By pro-

---

-a-unique-approach-to-Internet-service-provider-liability-and-copyright-infringement---sheryl-n-hamilton.

96 *SOCAN*, above note 17 at para. 127.

97 Jennifer M. Urban & Laura Quilter, "Efficient Process or "Chilling Effects"? Take down Notices Under Section 512 of the *Digital Millennium Copyright Act*" (22 December 2008) at 15, http://static.chillingeffects.org/Urban-Quilter-512-summary.pdf.

98 "Submission of Bell, Rogers, Shaw and Telus," above note 4.

99 *Sharman*, above note 86 at para. 414.

100 In *Roadshow Films Pty Ltd v iiNet Limited (No. 3)*, 2010 FCA 24 [*iiNet*], the Australian Federal Court of Appeal held that iiNet, who provided access to the Internet, did not thereby provide the means to copy the works in issue. For discussion, see Julian Gyngell, "Hollywood, the hungry Chinaman, and the ISP" (2010) 5 Journal of Intellectual Property Law & Practice 302.

viding access, it said, iiNet merely provided a *precondition* to the means, which was a bitTorrent file sharing network.[101] In Canada, it would be unlikely that an ISP would be liable for merely providing access to a bit-Torrent network for the additional reason that it does not have sufficient degree of control over the content that is carried over its network.

3) Internet Service Provider Immunity "Modernized"

a) The Nature and Scope of Immunity

Section 35 of the Bill introduces an additional immunity for ISPs that is formulated as follows:[102]

> 31.1(1) A person who, in providing services related to the operation of the Internet or another digital network, provides any means for the telecommunication or the reproduction of a work or other subject-matter through the Internet or that other network does not, solely by reason of providing those means, infringe copyright in that work or other subject-matter.

The immunity is not conditioned on the ISP satisfying a NN, NTD or GR regime. The immunity applies more broadly than to just ISPs, as it applies to a service provider utilizing any digital network. Presumably this includes private networks that are not part of the Internet as well as overlay networks on the Internet, including virtual private networks and peer to peer file sharing networks.[103] Finally, it applies to anyone who supplies "any means" for telecommunication rather than to someone who supplies "the means" necessary for telecommunication under section 2.4(1)(b).[104]

The immunity applies to all acts—including reproduction, communication and distribution—that could result in infringement. It is best interpreted as providing an explicitly broader common carrier exemption than does section 2.4(1)(b) of the *Copyright Act*.[105] In other words, on such an interpretation, the provision does not provide an exception from finding that an act infringes, rather, it deems that neutral ISPs *do not engage in any act* above and beyond supplying a means of communication—and so do not infringe copyright.

---

101 *Ibid.* at para 414.

102 Bill C-32, above note 5, s. 35. (See proposed s. 31.1(1).)

103 For simplicity, the remaining discussion will refer to "ISPs" though the context may indicate that it applies to any network service provider.

104 *Copyright Act*, above note 2, s. 2.4(1)(b).

105 *Ibid.*

ISPs are also immune for acts that are *incidental* to providing access. Consequently, the proposed section 31.1(3) provides a similar immunity for an ISP who caches the work or other subject-matter, or who does any similar act in relation to it, to make the telecommunication more efficient does not, by virtue of that act alone, infringe copyright in the work or other subject-matter.[106] The caching immunity is conditioned on caching being a neutral activity.[107] Section 31.1(5) provides immunity for hosts — ISPs do not infringe copyright merely by virtue of hosting.[108] However, this immunity will not apply when a host knows of a decision of a court of competent jurisdiction that the content provider infringes copyright by posting the subject matter or by the way in which the content provider uses that content.[109]

Although Bill C-32 has separate immunity clauses for ISPs and their ancillary services, caching and hosting, in *SOCAN*, the Supreme Court interpreted "the means" of telecommunication referred to in section 2.4(1)(b) of the Act to include "all software connection equipment, connectivity services, hosting and other facilities and services."[110] Caching was also considered to be a necessary means under section 2.4(1)(b) because it is a means that is content neutral and necessary to maximize the economy and cost effectiveness of the Internet conduit.[111] By implication, the new immunity for ISPs should, by implication, apply to their ancillary services.

The Bill contains a distinct form of immunity for Internet search engine providers. Bill C-32 calls search engines "information location tools" and defines them as "any tool that makes it possible to locate information that is available through the Internet or another digital network."[112] Unlike other ISPs, search engines enjoy only a partial immunity contained in section 41.27(1):[113]

> In any proceedings for infringement of copyright, the owner of the copyright in a work or other subject-matter is not entitled to any remedy other than an injunction against a provider of an information

106 Bill C-32, above note 5, s. 35. (See proposed s. 31.1(3).)

107 *Ibid.* (See proposed s. 31.1(4).) Under proposed s. 31.1(4), the immunity does not apply in respect of the work or other subject matter if the ISP modifies it, except for technical reasons; does not comply with executable, automated caching instructions made by the person who made the work or other subject matter available; or interferes with the lawful use of technology to obtain data on its use.

108 *Ibid.* (See proposed s. 31.1(5).)

109 *Ibid.* (See proposed s. 31.1(6).)

110 *SOCAN*, above note 17 at para. 92.

111 *Ibid.*, at para. 115.

112 Bill C-32, above note 5, s. 47. (See proposed s. 41.27(5).)

113 *Ibid.* (See proposed s. 41.27(1).)

> location tool that is found to have infringed copyright by making a reproduction of the work or other subject-matter or by communicating that reproduction to the public by telecommunication.

This immunity differs substantially from the others as it, *prima facie*, merely disentitles the copyright owner from an award of damages. This provision will be discussed in greater detail later.

b) Exception for Services that are Designed Primarily to Enable Infringement

The Bill provides an exception to the immunity that ISPs enjoy. According to the Canadian Government, "[t]he proposed legislation will ensure that those who enable infringement will not benefit from the liability limitations afforded to ISPs and search engines."[114] This is implemented as follows in the *Copyright Modernization Act*:[115]

> 31.1(2) Subsection (1) does not apply in respect of a service provided by the person if the provision of that service constitutes an infringement of copyright under subsection 27(2.3).

Section 27(2.3) creates a new form of secondary liability for services that are primarily designed to enable copyright infringement. This provision will be described and discussed more fully below. A similar exception applies to the immunity for search engine providers.[116]

c) No Exception for Distributing Circumvention Tools

Bill C-32 prohibits the distribution of tools that are used to circumvent technological protection measures or "digital locks."[117] Digital locks control the access to works and other subject matter and restrict the exercise of copyrights and rights of remuneration under the *Copyright Act*.[118] ISPs have complained that section 2.4(1)(b) of the Act, the common carrier exemption, contains no explicit ISP exemption for the distribution of circumvention tools.[119] The proposed common carrier principle, section 31.1(1) of the Bill, does not explicitly exempt ISP from liability for the *distribution* of circumvention tools either.[120] While it is arguable that such a broad common

114 "Copyright Modernization Act — Backgrounder," above note 6.
115 Bill C-32, above note 5, s. 35. (See proposed ss. 31.1(2).)
116 *Ibid.* s. 47. (See proposed s. 41.27(4).)
117 *Ibid.* s. 47. (See proposed s. 41.1.)
118 Bill C-32, above note 5, s. 47. (See proposed s. 41).
119 "Submission of Bell, Rogers, Shaw and Telus," above note 4.
120 Bill C-32, above note 5, s. 35. (See proposed s. 31.1(1).)

carrier principle implies that an ISP neither communicates nor *distributes* circumvention tools, it would be preferable if it were made explicit.

4) Secondary Infringement

a) Services Primarily Designed to Infringe

Section 35 of the Bill amends the *Copyright Act* by providing that the immunity under proposed section 31.1(1) of the Bill does *not* apply when someone infringes under proposed section 27(2.3).[121] Section 27(2.3) introduces a new form of secondary liability as follows:[122]

> It is an infringement of copyright for a person to provide, by means of the Internet or another digital network, a service that the person knows or should have known is designed primarily to enable acts of copyright infringement if an actual infringement of copyright occurs by means of the Internet or another digital network as a result of the use of that service.

This is a new form of secondary infringement by enablement where the (secondary) infringement of one party is based upon the primary (or "actual") infringement by another party. Infringement by enablement is not necessarily co-extensive with infringement by authorizing another to infringe. It may be possible to infringe by providing a service which has been designed primarily to infringe without authorizing anyone to engage in infringing acts.[123]

Second, section 27(2.3) of the Bill does not apply to "offline" tools such as personal video recorders, digital cameras, photocopiers, but only to network services.[124] This distinguishes it from US third party infringement doctrines, such as contributory infringement or inducement to infringe, which can occur whether it is online or offline infringement.[125]

Third, this new form of secondary liability is intended to apply to *services* that enable infringement rather than *products*. In other words, while

121 Bill C-32, above note 5, s. 35. (See proposed s. 31.1(2).)

122 Bill C-32, above note 5, s. 18. (See proposed s. 27(2.3).)

123 For example, it may be possible to provide a search engine that is designed primarily to enable infringement by locating dot torrent files that, arguably, enables one to download bitTorrent movie files. At the same time, the service may fall short of authorizing others to infringe because the service cannot control which works its users search for or download. See Gregory R. Hagen, "Are bitTorrent Search Engines Liable for Copyright Infringement?" Intellectual Property Review (forthcoming).

124 Bill C-32, above note 5, s. 18. (See proposed s. 27(2.3).)

125 Above, notes 57 & 58.

the provision would catch peer to peer services similar to Grokster, it would not apply to the software which runs on such services. This distinction inherits the wisdom of the US peer to peer filing decisions which have resulted in liability for secondary infringement for some who provide services that facilitate infringement by means of the Internet or another digital network but not for those who provide products which have substantially non-infringing uses.[126]

Fourth, section 27(2.3) operates as an exception to the immunity from liability that ISPs enjoy under section 31.1(1) of the Bill.[127] Unfortunately, Bill C-32 is not explicit that caching and hosting are no longer immune from liability when they are part of a service that is designed primarily to enable infringing conduct. This could lead to the inference that hosts are immune from liability even if they are part of such an enabling system. However, "any means" under the new section 31.1(1) would include hosting and caching.[128] Consequently, the exception to immunity under section 31.1(2) could arguably also apply to caching under section 31.1(3) and hosting under section 31.1(5).[129] This issue needs to be clarified in the Bill.

Finally, although stopping infringement over peer to peer file sharing networks is the object of the provision, [130] it cannot succeed against highly distributed file sharing services, such as those operating in accordance with the bitTorrent protocol.[131] If Napster or Grokster were designed primarily to infringe copyright, the provision may have succeeded against them because they utilized a centralized servers to index content or dis-

---

126 Jonathan Zittrain, "A History of Online Gatekeeping" (2006) 19:2 Harvard Journal of Law and Technology 253, http://jolt.law.harvard.edu/articles/pdf/v19/19HarvJLTech253.pdf.

127 Bill C-32, above note 5, s. 35. (See proposed s. 31.1(2).)

128 *Ibid.* s. 35. (See proposed s. 31.1(1).)

129 *Ibid.* (See proposed ss. 31.1(2), 31.1(3), and 31.1(5).)

130 See James Moore, "Moore's Speech," above note 56 describes the object as fighting "piracy." Barry Sookman, in "Some thoughts on Bill-C-32: An Act to Modernize Canada's copyright laws," www.barrysookman.com/2010/06/03/some-thoughts-on-bill-c-32-an-act-to-modernize-canada%E2%80%99s-copyright-laws, describes the Bill as "intended to target pirate services such as illegal peer-to-peer file sharing sites." Michael Geist, "Digital Economy Strategy Consultation Submission" www.michaelgeist.ca/content/view/5193/125 , characterizes the new form of secondary liability as "new liability for BitTorrent search services" at 11.

131 For an introduction to the bitTorrent protocol, see "A Beginners Guide to bitTorrent" www.bittorrent.com/btusers/guides/beginners-guide. For additional difficulties of enforcing copyright against highly distributed file sharing networks, see Gregory R. Hagen and Nyall Engfield, "Canadian Copyright Reform: P2P Sharing, Making Available and the Three-Step Test," (2006) 3:2 UOLTJ 477.

tribute software. Yet, while bitTorrent users may create their individual overlay networks with the intent of enabling infringement by others, and be individually liable for secondary infringement, there is no necessity for a centralized server operator that can be targeted in a bitTorrent network. While some specialized search engines, such as isoHunt, might be caught by this provision, it will not apply to generalized search engines, such as Google, which also can search and find dot torrent files, enabling one to download bitTorrent content files, such as movie files. Nor will it apply to dot torrent search engines which have been designed primarily to find any bitTorrent file, not just Hollywood movie files.[132]

b) Liability Factors

This new form of infringement requires proof that a service is "designed primarily to enable acts of copyright infringement." In other words, the section requires proof that the designer intended the service to primarily enable infringement. Bill C-32 specifies non-exhaustive factors which a court may consider in determining whether a person has infringed copyright under section 27(2.3):[133]

> 27(2.4) In determining whether a person has infringed copyright under subsection (2.3), the court may consider
>
> (a) whether the person expressly or implicitly marketed or promoted the service as one that could be used to enable acts of copyright infringement;
>
> (b) whether the person had knowledge that the service was used to enable a significant number of acts of copyright infringement;
>
> (c) whether the service has significant uses other than to enable acts of copyright infringement;
>
> (d) the person's ability, as part of providing the service, to limit acts of copyright infringement, and any action taken by the person to do so;
>
> (e) any benefits the person received as a result of enabling the acts of copyright infringement; and
>
> (f) the economic viability of the provision of the service if it were not used to enable acts of copyright infringement.

---

132 For a discussion of secondary infringement in the context of peer to peer file sharing see Bob Clark, "Illegal Downloads: Sharing Out Online Liability: Sharing Files, Sharing Risks" (2007) 2 Journal of Intellectual Property Law & Practice 402.

133 Bill C-32, above note 5, s. 18. (See proposed s. 27(2.4).)

These factors appear to be culled from various foreign decisions regarding forms of secondary liability, some of which are distinct from those currently existing under the *Copyright Act* or proposed under the Bill.[134] For example, the factor cited in section 27(2.4)(a) is reminiscent of the test for liability for inducement to infringe established under *Grokster*.[135] As another example, the factor cited in section 27(2.4)(d) is similar to a provision in section 101(A) of the Australian *Copyright Act* according to which "the extent (if any) of the person's power to prevent the doing of the act concerned"[136] must be considered, notwithstanding that the Australian interpretation of authorization was rejected by the Supreme Court of Canada in *SOCAN*.[137] In this respect, the approach of Bill C-32 reflects a trend existing outside of Canada for courts to apply a common set of factors to determine whether a third party is sufficiently connected to an infringing act to be deemed culpable, regardless of the particular form of secondary liability (e.g., inducement to infringe, contributory infringement or authorization).[138] Since secondary infringement by enablement is distinct from extant forms of secondary liability, some of the factors may not be very relevant to showing that a service was designed primarily to enable infringement. Courts will, therefore, need to exercise great care in applying these factors in determining whether a person knows or ought to know that their service is designed primarily to infringe. Specific evidence of intent through, for example, documentary evidence would be of much greater relevance than the application of these factors.

5) Service Provider Regulation: Notice and What?

a) Notice and Take Down and Its Problems

In Canada, there is no legislated, extra-judicial NTD regime requiring that those who host content take it down when provided with a notice alleging copyright infringement. Nor does Bill C-32 propose a NTD system. Any obligation to take down content would arise solely from a remedy imposed by a court to take down such materials. Therefore, a take down notice in

---

134 For a survey of relevant cases, see Allen D. Nixon, "Liability of Users and Third Parties for Copyright Infringements on the Internet: Overview of International Developments" in Alain Strowell, ed., *Peer to Peer File Sharing & Secondary Liability in Copyright Law* (Cheltenham, UK: Edward Elgar, 2009) at 12–42.

135 *Grokster*, above note 58.

136 *Copyright Act* (Australia) 1986, section 101(A).

137 *CCH*, above note 78 at para. 41.

138 See Nixon, above, note 134 at 37.

Canada generally takes, and will continue to take, the form of a lawyer's demand to take down alleged infringing material, the failure of which could result in the commencement of a copyright infringement suit. [139]

It is worth pointing out that, even though there is no legislated NTD system in Canada, failure to take down content once an allegation has been made can trigger infringement by the ISP in some circumstances. As the Supreme Court of Canada said in *SOCAN*, "notice of infringing content, and a failure to respond by 'taking it down' may in some circumstances lead to a finding of 'authorization.'"[140] Whether ISPs have the *obligation* to take down content is tricky, however, as taking down content may conflict with contractual obligations to customers.[141] As a result, the Court suggested in *obiter dicta,* that enacting a legislated NTD procedure similar to that of the United States and the European Community may be a more effective remedy than litigating the issue of authorization. [142] Many in the copyright industry are in favour of a NTD system on the basis that it is effective and fairer than the existing (arguably) *de facto* NTD system[143] and that it is the only expeditious means of removing or disabling access to infringing content hosted on the Internet.[144]

One major limitation of a NTD system, however, is that it is primarily suited to a server-client architecture where the client posts content to the intermediary's server. It is not effective for dealing with highly distributed peer to peer systems, such as those using the bitTorrent protocol, in which content is *not* hosted by a central server, but by multiple individual computers distributed across the Internet. [145] Even the centralized dot torrent search engines can be eliminated by using bitTorrent clients, such as Tribler, [146] that provide their own keyword searching or by simply using a generalized search engine, such as Google. A similar point can be made regarding "cloud computing" architecture. Under this architecture, an ISP

---

139 For an interesting example of a Canadian demand letter, see "Affidavit of Gary Fung. No. 1" http://isohunt.com/img/legal/Affidavit%20of%20Gary%20Fung%20No.1.pdf at 35–55.

140 *SOCAN*, above note 17, at para. 127.

141 *Ibid.* at para. 127.

142 *Ibid.* at para. 127.

143 "Entertainment Software Submission" above note 95 and Sookman, "What Should We Do?" above note 23.

144 International Intellectual Property Alliance, "2010 Special 301 Report" www.iipa.com/2010_SPEC301_TOC.htm

145 BitTorrent, Inc., "FAQ — BitTorrent Concepts" (2010), www.bittorrent.com/btusers/help/faq/bittorrent-concepts#4n5.

146 See "What is Tribler?" www.tribler.org/trac/wiki/whatIsTribler .

may be legally the host, but may not have any knowledge or control over the physical location of data that is hosted.[147]

The most serious issue that has been pointed out, however, is that the NTD system can be abused. For one thing, it has been used to chill legitimate free expression, including fair dealing and fair use, as well as resulted in disproportionate remedies. [148] A study of the NTD system in the US found that the process provides "a simple and expedient process available to victims and abusers alike, encouraging complainants to shoehorn a variety of ill-fitting claims into copyright."[149] Once a notice is sent, the fear of potential liability can result in the taking down of content solely to minimize the risk of liability rather than on its merits. According to Wendy Seltzer, in the US "the copyright notice-and-takedown regime operates in the shadow of the law, doing through private intermediaries what government could not to silence speech."[150] In the US, these notices are being sent not only to prevent infringement, but to create leverage in a competitive marketplace, to protect rights not given by copyright, such as trade-mark infringement, unfair competition or privacy intrusion, and to stifle criticism, commentary and fair use.[151] There is little reason to think the Canadian experience would be significantly different under a NTD system.[152]

b) The Rejection of Graduated Response

Bill C-32 rejects a GR system, but the Government of Canada does not say why. The impetus for a GR system came when, in 2008, the Recording Industry Association of American said that it would stop suing individuals who infringe on the internet and, since then, has requested that ISPs institute a GR system to respond to allegations of infringement. [153] Such a

---

147 Eric Knorr & Galen Gruman, "What cloud computing really means" *InfoWorld*, www.infoworld.com/d/cloud-computing/what-cloud-computing-really-means-031.

148 For a discussion of disproportionality, see Hamilton, above note 95.

149 Jennifer M. Urban & Laura Quilter, above note 97 at 15.

150 Wendy Seltzer, "Free Speech Unmoored in Copyright's Safe Harbor: Chilling Effects of the DMCA on the First Amendment" forthcoming, (2010) 23:2 Harvard Journal of Law and Technology, http://papers.ssrn.com/sol3/papers.cfm?abstract_id=1577785.

151 *Ibid.* at 14–15.

152 Barry Sookman, "What Should We Do?" above note 23, has argued in favour of a Canadian NTD and that abuse can be minimized by sending notices under penalty of perjury and that one must consider in good faith defences to infringement prior to sending the notice.

153 Sarah McBride and Ethan Smith, "Music Industry to Abandon Mass Suits" *Wall Street Journal* (19 December 2008), http://online.wsj.com/article/SB122966038836021137.html.

system would mandate that ISPs enforce a series of gradually escalating responses to alleged copyright infringement that could include educational notices, bandwidth capping, connection speed capping, protocol blocking, website blocking, and the termination of access.[154] Copyright lobbyists have touted the GR system as an effective and proportionate response to online infringement.[155] Versions of a GR system have been legislated in Taiwan, South Korea, France, New Zealand and the UK, though not all are in force to date.[156] However, the GR approach has been rejected by Hong Kong, Germany, Spain, Sweden as well as the European Parliament.[157]

Graduated response furthers an idea that is implicit in NTD systems: once an ISP is faced with specific knowledge of infringement and the actual power to prevent it, it has a duty to prevent further related infringements. Although graduated response systems may vary from country to country, according to Barry Sookman, the key characteristics of a graduated response system are:[158]

> (1) rights holders monitor P2P networks for illegal downloading activities; (2) rights holders provide ISPs with convincing proof of infringements being committed by an individual at a given IP address; (3) educational notices are sent through an ISP to the account holder informing him or her of the infringements and of the consequences of continued infringement and informing the user that content can be lawfully acquired online; and (4) if the account holder repeatedly ignores the notices, a tribunal may take deterrent action, with the most severe sanctions reserved for a court.

Despite the advantages to copyright owners,[159] several drawbacks have been pointed out. Most importantly, the GR system may interfere with the right to access the internet, which is a central means to exercise one's right

---

154 Sookman and Glover, "Graduated Response and Copyright," above note 42.

155 *Ibid.* According to Sookman, "In the United Kingdom, a test of the graduated response system showed that 70% of customers stopped infringing in the six month period after receiving the first notice, with a further 16% stopping after the second notice."

156 Johnny Ryan and Caitriona Heinl, "Internet access controls: Three Strikes 'graduated response' initiatives," http://cambridge.academia.edu/JohnnyRyan/Papers.

157 Peter K. Yu, "Graduated Response" forthcoming, (2010) 62 Florida Law Review at 3–4, http://papers.ssrn.com/sol3/papers.cfm?abstract_id=1579782 [Yu, "Graduated Response].

158 Sookman and Glover, "Graduated Response and Copyright," above note 42.

159 For discussion, see Yu, "Graduated Response," above note 157 and Sookman and Glover, "Graduated Response and Copyright," *ibid.*

to free expression.[160] Second, like an NTD system, to the extent that GR measures are applied extra-judicially, a GR system may be subject to similar abuses that have occurred in the NTD system.[161] On the other hand, if the complaints are subject to review by an administrative panel, there is a risk that the panels could be systemically biased, as occurred with the ICANN Uniform Dispute Resolution Policy.[162] Third, such a system would substantially raise the costs of policing and data retention that ISPs must undertake.[163] Fourth, a GR system could require ISPs to monitor user behaviour which could necessitate the use of deep packet inspection that is privacy invasive.[164] Fifth, a GR system serves to reinforce existing business methods of copyright owners rather than new methods of dissemination, such as compulsory licenses for peer to peer file sharing.[165] Finally, a GR can be disproportionate in its response, cutting off access to essential services provided by the Internet, such as e-mail, banking and VOIP.[166]

c) ISP Notice and Notice

i) *The Existing Voluntary NN System*

In 2000, the Canadian Association of Internet Service Providers, the Canadian Cable Television Association and the Canadian Recording Industry Association agreed to implement a voluntary notice and notice regime to handle online copyright infringement claims.[167] The success of the NN system is indicated by the fact that copyright owners have rarely, if ever, gone to the next step and enforced their statutory rights in Canadian courts against file sharers.[168] Moreover, in a recent study, seventy percent of file sharers report they would stop if they received a warning note from their

---

160 Yu, "Graduated Response," above note 157 at 15–17.

161 William Patry, *Moral Panics and the Copyright Wars* (Oxford: Oxford University Press, 2009) at 14.

162 See Michael Geist, "Fair.com?: An Examination of the Allegations of Systemic Unfairness in the ICANN UDRP," http://aix1.uottawa.ca/~geist/geistudrp.pdf.

163 Yu, "Graduated Response," above note 157 at 13-15.

164 Office of the Privacy Commissioner of Canada. "Review of the Internet traffic management practices of Internet service providers," (18 February 2009) http://dpi.priv.gc.ca/index.php/essays/review-of-the-internet-traffic-management-practices-of-internet-service-providers/.

165 Patry, above note 161 at 12 and Yu, "Graduated Response," above note 157 at 18.

166 Yu, "Graduated Response," above note 157 at 18.

167 Canadian Cable Television Association, "Comments on the Consultation Paper on Digital Copyright Issues" (14 September 2001), http://strategis.ic.gc.ca/eic/site/crp-prda.nsf/fra/rp00336.html.

168 "Submission of Bell, Rogers, Shaw and Telus," above note 4.

ISP.[169] However, since the NN is voluntary, there is a risk that it is not universally followed.

ii) Bill C-32

Bill C-32 rejects both a NTD system and a GR system in favour of a NN system. According to the proposed section 41.25(1), an owner of the copyright in a work or other subject-matter may send a notice alleging infringement to the person who provides the means of telecommunication or is the host.[170] A notice of claimed infringement must be in writing and must identify the individual; identify the allegedly infringing subject matter; state the claimant's interest or right with respect to the copyright in the work or other subject matter; specify the electronic location of the subject matter; specify the infringement that is claimed; specify the date and time of the claimed infringement; and provide any other information that may be prescribed by regulation.[171]

Once received, the recipient would be required to send on the notice to the alleged infringer, if possible. The proposed requirement reads:[172]

> 41.26 (1) A person described in paragraph 41.25(1)(a) [person who provides the means of telecommunication] or (b) [the person who provides the digital memory] who receives a notice of claimed infringement that complies with section 41.25(2) shall, on being paid any fee that the person has lawfully charged for doing so,
>
> (a) without delay forward the notice electronically to the person that the electronic location identified by the location data specified in the notice belongs to and inform the claimant of its forwarding or, if applicable, of the reason why it was not possible to forward it;. . . .

There is no requirement under Bill C-32 to disclose subscriber information upon receiving a notice of alleged infringement as that would be to privacy intrusive.[173] The subscriber is given a chance to remedy the alleged

---

169 *Ibid.*

170 Bill C-32, above note 5, s. 47. (See proposed s. 41.25(1).)

171 *Ibid.* (See proposed s. 41.25(2).)

172 *Ibid.* (See proposed s. 41.26 (1).)

173 In *Irwin Toy Ltd. v. Doe*, [2000] O.J. No. 3318 (S.C.J.), the court said at para. 11 that "some degree of privacy or confidentiality with respect to the identity of the Internet protocol address of the originator of a message has significant safety value and is in keeping with what should be perceived as being good public policy."

infringement. If that does not happen, the copyright owner is free to commence an action in court.

In *BMG*, the issue of whether a defendant ISP must disclose subscriber names of those who used particular IP addresses is raised. [174] The court adopted the *Norwich Pharmacal*[175] approach to interpreting its own rules of civil procedure authorizing pre-action discovery.[176] On that approach, a person who gets mixed up in wrongdoing, even innocently, is obliged to assist the injured part by providing vital information such as the identity of other persons.[177] The Court held that while privacy concerns must be considered, "they must yield to public concerns for the protection of intellectual property rights."[178] However, in court proceedings, subscriber information can only be disclosed to the plaintiff when there is a proven *bona fide* claim of infringement.[179]

The new provision includes a record preservation requirement. Pursuant to section 41.26 (1)(b), when a valid notice is received and the requisite fee paid, the access provider or host shall retain identity records of the person to whom the electronic location belongs.[180] They are required to hold the records for *six months* beginning on the day on which the notice of claimed infringement is received or, if the claimant commences proceedings relating to the claimed infringement and so notifies the person before the end of those six months, for *one year* after the day on which the person receives the notice of claimed infringement.[181]

Such a retention period has been criticized as privacy invasive.[182] Moreover, in *BMG*, the court refused to order the disclosure of identity information when there had been a delay of approximately six months between the copyright owners' investigation and the filing of the application in court. [183] Such a delay, the court held, gave rise to a risk that the iden-

---

174 *BMG Canada Inc. v. John Doe*, 2005 FCA 193, http://decisions.fca-caf.gc.ca/en/2005/2005fca193/2005fca193.html, [2005] 4 F.C.R. 81 [*BMG*].

175 *Norwich Pharmacal Co. v. Customs and Excise Comrs.*, [1974] A.C. 133 (H.L.), [1975] All E.R. 943 at 954 [*Norwich Pharmacal*].

176 *BMG*, above note 174.

177 *Norwich Pharmacal*, above note 175.

178 *BMG* above note 174 at para. 41.

179 *Ibid.*

180 Bill C-32, above note 5, s. 47. (See proposed s. 41.26 (1)(b).)

181 *Ibid.* (See proposed s. 41.26 (1)(b).)

182 Canada's Privacy Community, "Submission of Canada's Privacy Community" (13 Sept. 2009), www.ic.gc.ca/eic/site/008.nsf/eng/02670.html#footnote14 .

183 *BMG*, above note 174. This follows the approach of the UK House of Lords in *Norwich Pharmacal*, above note 175.

tity information could be inaccurate.[184] Since the use of inaccurate records could result in unjustified proceedings against innocent persons and an invasion of their privacy, failure to avoid delay could result in a court's refusal to order the release of identity information.[185]

A claimant may seek statutory damages for the failure of an ISP to fulfill its obligations under section 41.26(1) with respect to forwarding notices and retaining information in an amount that the court considers just in an amount not less than $5,000 and not more than $10,000.[186]

The NN provisions correct the most blatant problems associated with a NTD system. First, rather than force ISPs to make a (possibly inexpert) decision about copyright liability, the decision is left to the courts. As such, risk adverse ISPs might be less likely to err on the side of taking down allegedly infringing material at the expense of its customers and therefore reduce some of the detrimental effects from unfounded notices. Second, leaving the decision to take down content in the hands of the courts is consistent with the approach to hate propaganda and child pornography under the *Criminal Code*.[187] Third, by not requiring the automatic take down of content, the provision offers a less drastic response to a mere allegation of infringement, rather than a take down remedy which, with nothing more, is equivalent to a remedy for infringement. Finally, it does not presume that infringement problems always involve an intermediary host in a server-client relationship, leaving the door open for NN to apply more broadly to situations where ISP customers might be infringing using highly distributed peer to peer file sharing software.[188]

Bill C-32 does not, however, provide compensation from copyright owners to intermediaries for either their capital or operating expenditures resulting from the mandatory NN scheme which is, after all, for the benefit of copyright owners.[189] Furthermore, while the intent of Bill C-32 is to implement a NN system, it does not explicitly exempt an ISP from being found to have *authorized* infringement by failing to take down content once an allegation has been made. This differs from the United

---

184 *Ibid.* at para. 43.

185 *Ibid.* For discussion, see "Critical Privacy Issues in Canadian Copyright Reform" *IntellectualPrivacy.ca* (17 May 2006), www.cippic.ca/uploads/copyright-law-reform/Backgrouner-Copyright_and_Privacy.pdf.

186 Bill C-32, above note 5, s. 47. (See proposed s. 41.26(3).)

187 Sheryl Hamilton, above note 95, at 295-6.

188 "Entertainment Software Submission," above note 95.

189 "Submission of Bell, Rogers, Shaw and Telus," above note 4.

States *Digital Millennium Copyright Act* safe harbour approach[190] and may differ from the intent of Bill C-32. Under the safe harbour approach, once the conditions for a safe harbour are satisfied, including taking down allegedly infringing content, the safe harbour protects the service provider from copyright infringement liability.[191]

The difficulty can be explained by considering the immunity provision for hosts in the Bill. With respect to hosting, the new immunity is worded as follows:[192]

> 31.1(5) Subject to section (6), a person who, for the purpose of allowing the telecommunication of a work or other subject-matter through the Internet or another digital network, provides digital memory in which another person stores the work or other subject-matter does not, by virtue of that act alone, infringe copyright in the work or other subject-matter.

According to this provision, *hosting alone* does not infringe copyright in the hosted content. The difficulty is, however, that it does not make clear the legal effect of *a failure to take down* content that the host knows is infringing. Under proposed section 31.1(6) of the Bill, if the host knows of a court decision where the person who posted the work or other subject matter infringed copyright by posting it or by using the posted information, then the immunity under section 31.1(5) does not apply.[193] However, what if a copyright owner merely provides a notice (in the required form and content) alleging copyright infringement in relation to hosted information? Does the host authorize infringement by *omitting* to take down the content? Does the failure to take down in light of knowledge of infringing activity negate the host's status as a mere conduit? The immunity provision of the Bill should be clarified to ensure that, where a notice of alleged infringement has been received by an ISP in relation to some

---

190 *US Digital Millennium Copyright Act*, Pub. L. No. 10534, 112 Stat. 2860 (1998), http://frwebgate.access.gpo.gov/cgi-bin/getdoc.cgi?dbname=105_cong_bills&docid=f:h2281enr.txt.pdf [DMCA], s. 512.

191 Thus, in *Viacom International Inc. v. Youtube, Inc., Google, Inc. et al*, (USDC, Southern District of NY), 2010 (07 Civ. 2103 (LLS)), http://beckermanlegal.com/Documents/viacom_youtube_080702DecisionDiscoveryRulings.pdf , the court held, at 23, that when Youtube was given notices of infringement, it removed the material, protecting it from liability for contributory, vicarious and direct infringement.

192 Bill C-32, above note 5, s. 35. (See proposed s. 31.1(5).)

193 *Ibid*. (See proposed s. 31.1(6).)

subject matter, it is not liable for failure to prevent future infringement in relation to that subject matter.

d) Information Location Tools: Notice and Take Down?

Under the proposed section 41.25(1)(c) of the *Copyright Modernization Act*, search engine providers can receive notices of infringement from copyright owners in reference to works that they have cached.[194] Once a notice is received, search engines will be required to retain records in order to identify the alleged infringer.[195] Remedies for failure to comply with the retention requirements are the same as for other ISPs, namely, an award of damages between $5,000 and $10,000.[196] Under the proposed section 41.27(1),[197] Bill C-32 limits remedies against search engine providers who have been found to infringe by caching or communicating a cached copy to the public by telecommunication to injunctions, provided that the search provider has remained content neutral,[198] and provided that the search engine does not secondarily infringe under proposed section 27(2.3).[199]

The immunity from damages is limited under section 41.27(3) and this limitation provision appears to introduce a *de facto* notice and take down regime for search engines in cases where the infringing content has been taken down by its host.[200] Suppose, for instance, that a search engine has cached a copy of an infringing work from the Internet and that, as a result of receiving a notice, the infringing work has been taken down by its host. After that, the search engine provider is sent a notice (with the correct form and content) complaining of infringement by the search engine for reproduction of the work and for communicating the work to the public by telecommunication.

The validity of this complaint would be questionable, since under section 2.4(1)(b) of the *Copyright Act*, search engines do not communicate works to the public, at least not prior to the notice, so the notice would appear to be unfounded.[201] Further, on a broad interpretation of the common carrier principle, search engines do not make reproductions either. However, a number of counterarguments might be made at this point. First, it

194 Bill C-32, above note 5, s. 47. (See proposed s. 41.25(1)(c).)
195 *Ibid*. (See proposed s. 41.26(1)(b).)
196 *Ibid*. s. 48. (See proposed s. 41.26(3).)
197 *Ibid*. s. 47. (See proposed s. 41.27(1).)
198 *Ibid*. (See proposed s. 41.27(2).)
199 *Ibid*. (See proposed s. 41.27(4).)
200 *Ibid*. (See proposed s. 41.27(3).)
201 *Copyright Act*, above note 2, s. 2.4(1)(b).

might be argued that section 2.4(1)(b) of the *Copyright Act* does not apply to caching by search engines but only to caching by Internet access providers.[202] Second, it might be argued that, after a notice has been received by the search engine provider, it is no longer a neutral service and so it *is* communicating a work to the public by telecommunication and reproducing it. Third, it might be argued that, given the search engine's knowledge of a cached infringing reproduction and the ability to remove it, failure to remove it would be tantamount to authorizing communication and reproduction of it by others. The Bill needs to clarify these issues.

Under section 41.27(3), the immunity applies, in respect of reproductions made from the electronic location specified in the notice, *only* to infringements that occurred before the thirtieth day after the search engine provider receives the notice ("limitation day").[203] In other words, after the limitation day, a finding of infringement against the search engine provider for caching the infringing work or communicating to the public could result in an award of damages. In short, the search engine has 30 days to take down its cached work or risk infringement proceedings resulting in damages. This limitation provision introduces an unwarranted distinction between a NN system for hosts and a *de facto* NTD system for search engine providers since they are both generally automated and content neutral. It also bases the NTD system on the take down of content by a host for reasons that may be independent of the merit of an infringement claim, such as to obtain the protection of the safe harbour under section 512 of the *DMCA*.[204]

D. CONCLUSION

The intent of Bill C-32 is to modernize copyright law in light of new communications technology. Unfortunately, although the Bill resulted from a recent public consultation on copyright, the Government of Canada produced no comprehensive response paper explaining the rationale for its specific amendments. The Government's discussion in its *Improving Canada's Digital Advantage* and elsewhere suggests that its policy is rooted in a digital market philosophy in which copyright is a property right given as a reward for intellectual labour; that it is to primarily benefit copyright owners and, therefore, its dissemination by ISPs must be controlled for

202 *Ibid.*

203 Bill C-32, above note 5, s. 47. (See proposed s. 41.27(3).) Regulation may alter the limitation day.

204 *DMCA*, above note 190.

the benefit of copyright owners. In reality, this approach is rather antiquated in contrast to recent proposals to enable the free availability of copyrighted subject matter while compensating copyright owners through levies or compulsory licenses.

While the Government's discussion suggests that it aims to prevent online infringement by controlling the dissemination of copyrighted subject matter by ISPs, nevertheless, it introduces a strong immunity for innocent ISPs, rejects a GR system, and adds a form of secondary liability targeting those who intend to enable infringement that will be ineffective against peer to peer file sharing networks which have no centralized server. These choices might be explained by the fact that the Bill also seeks to target online infringement by *controlling the subject matter* itself. But, if the control of the subject matter through digital locks becomes widespread, it would be otiose and counterproductive to also control its dissemination. In the end, whether the control of subject matter is possible while also respecting the goals of copyright, privacy, free expression, and the rule of law remains to be seen.

CHAPTER THIRTEEN

Towards a Right to Engage in the Fair Transformative Use of Copyright-Protected Expression

Graham Reynolds*

A. INTRODUCTION

Networked digital technologies have given Canadians the opportunity to engage with culture in a way that has never before been possible. Empowered and inspired, individuals from Prince George to the Georgian Bay to George Street are rejecting their former role as passive consumers of culture in order to participate in a continuing process of cultural (re)creation, production, and dialogue.[1] One way in which they are doing so is by engaging in the transformative use of existing expression, a type of creative activity in which previously existing expression is reworked for a new purpose, with new interpretations or with a new meaning.[2]

---

* The author would like to thank the Foundation for Legal Research for their financial assistance in the preparation of this chapter.

1 See Henry Jenkins, *Convergence Culture* (New York: NYU Press, 2006); Henry Jenkins, *Fans, Bloggers, and Gamers* (New York: NYU Press, 2006).

2 See Andrew Gowers, *Gowers Review of Intellectual Property* (London: HM Treasury, 2006) at 66, where it is noted that the purpose of the transformative works exception is to "enable creators to rework material for a new purpose of with a new meaning." Many commentators take the position that the starting point for the introduction of the term "transformative use" is Judge Pierre's Leval's article, "Toward a Fair Use Standard" (1990) 103 Harv. L. Rev. 1105 at 1111. Judge Leval defines the term "transformative use" as follows: "The use must be productive and must employ the quoted matter in a different manner or for a different purpose from the original. A quotation of copyrighted material that merely repackages or republishes the original is unlikely to pass the test; in Justice Story's words, it would merely "supersede the objects" of the

This type of creative activity did not originate with networked digital technologies. Individuals have been engaging in the transformative use of existing expression for millennia. J. Harold Ellens has suggested that the Book of Genesis is a rewrite of an "ancient Mesopotamian fertility story of sex and seduction."[3] Chaucer rewrote Ovid.[4] Pope rewrote Chaucer.[5] Alexander Lindey states that Shakespeare "commandeered everything that suited his purpose—Greek biography, Roman history, the tales of the Middle Ages, long familiar anecdotes, old farces, the plays of his predecessors—and cast them into forms popular in his day."[6] Contemporary Canadian artists Gordon Duggan, Brian Jungen, and Diana Thorneycroft, working in the genre of appropriation art, transform existing expression into new works.

Transformative creativity, however, although it did not originate with networked digital technologies, has been "democratized" through their use.[7] Anyone with access to a computer, easily obtainable software, and the internet can now create, distribute, and enjoy transformative works such as mashups (songs made up of the combination of two or more pre-existing sound recordings),[8] machinima (films made within video

---

original. If, on the other hand, the secondary use adds value to the original — if the quoted matter is used as raw material, transformed in the creation of new information, new aesthetics, new insights and understandings — this is the very type of activity that the fair use doctrine intends to protect for the enrichment of society. Transformative uses may include criticizing the quoted work, exposing the character of the original author, proving a fact, or summarizing an idea argued in the original in order to defend or rebut it. They also may include parody, symbolism, aesthetic declarations, and innumerable other uses." In *Campbell v. Acuff-Rose Music, Inc.* 510 U.S. 569, 579 (1994), the Supreme Court of the United States stated that a use is transformative if it "adds something new, with a further purpose or different character, altering the first [work] with new expression, meaning, or message."

3 J. Harold Ellens, *Sex in the Bible* (Westport: Praeger Publishers, 2006) at 55.

4 Michael A. Calabrese, *Chaucer's Ovidian Arts of Love* (Gainesville: University Press of Florida, 1994) at 23.

5 Hayden Carruth, foreword in Stephen Berg, *With Akhmatova at the black gates* (Champaign: University of Illinois Press, 2002) at ix.

6 Alexander Lindey, *Plagiarism and Originality* (Westport: Greenwood Press, 1952) at 74.

7 See Yochai Benkler, "From Consumers to Users: Shifting the Deeper Structures of Regulation Toward Sustainable Commons and User Access" (1999-2000) 52 Fed. Comm. L.J. 561 at 562: "Technology now makes possible the attainment of decentralization and democratization by enabling small groups of constituents and individuals to become *users* — participants in the production of their information environment — rather than by lightly regulating concentrated commercial mass media to make them better serve individuals conceived as passive consumers."

8 See Graham Reynolds, "A Stroke of Genius or Copyright Infringement? Mashups and Copyright in Canada", (2009) 6:3 SCRIPTed 534.

games),[9] digital collage (artistic works made up of the combination of pieces of two or more works), remixes (works which take existing expression and combine it with other expression), and fan fiction (literary works which incorporate a character, setting, or plot from a pre-existing work).[10]

Acts relating to the transformative use of existing expression provide significant benefits to Canadian society. Perhaps most notably, they promote the values underlying the constitutionally protected right to freedom of expression.[11] Under the current *Copyright Act*, however, many such acts would likely be found to prima facie infringe copyright.[12] The application of fair dealing, a user's right contained within the *Copyright Act* which gives individuals the right to use a substantial amount of copyright-protected expression for certain purposes provided the use is done "fairly," will result in various acts relating to the transformative use of copyright-protected expression being deemed non-infringing. However, many acts will not be protected by fair dealing as it is currently written and interpreted.

This chapter argues that the *Copyright Act* needs to be revised to address the conflict between the rights of copyright owners and the public interest with respect to transformative works.[13] Certain amendments proposed

---

9 See Graham Reynolds, "All the Game's A Stage: Machinima and Copyright in Canada", (2010) J.W.I.P. (forthcoming).

10 See Graham Reynolds, "The Impact of Canadian Copyright Laws on the Voices of Marginalised Groups: Towards a Right to Rewrite", (2010) Alb. L.R. (forthcoming); Grace Westcott, "Friction Over Fan Fiction" (2008) Literary Review of Canada, http://reviewcanada.ca/essays/2008/07/01/friction-over-fan-fiction/; Rebecca Tushnet, "Legal Fictions: Copyright, Fan Fiction, and a New Common Law" (1997) 17 Loy. L.A. Ent. L.J. 651.

11 See *RJR Macdonald, Inc. v. Canada (Attorney General)*, [1995] 3 S.C.R. 199 (*RJR Macdonald*). The issue of the intersection of copyright and freedom of expression merits discussion. This discussion, however, is beyond the scope of this paper to address. See David Fewer, "Constitutionalizing Copyright: Freedom of Expression and the Limits of Copyright in Canada" (1997) 55 University of Toronto L.R. 175; Graham Reynolds, "A Step in the Wrong Direction: The Impact of the Legislative Protection of Technological Protection Measures on Fair Dealing and Freedom of Expression" (2006) Volume 5, No. 3 Canadian Journal of Law and Technology.

12 The *Copyright Act*, R.S.C. 1985, c. C-42 [*Copyright Act*] gives copyright owners various rights with respect to works. One such right is the right to reproduce either the entire work or a substantial part of the work. Individuals who reproduce a substantial portion of a copyright-protected work without the permission of the copyright owner prima facie infringe copyright, regardless of whether the work has been altered, transformed, or used in a different context than the original work.

13 Another issue which merits attention is whether the *Copyright Act* needs to be revised to address the conflict between moral rights and the public interest with

in Bill C-32, Canada's most recent attempt at copyright reform — namely, the expansion of the fair dealing defence to include categories of parody, satire, and education; and the introduction of a right to create non commercial user-generated content - will result in more acts relating to the transformative use of copyright-protected expression being deemed non-infringing.[14] These positive developments, however, are undermined by restrictive anti-circumvention provisions, also contained within Bill C-32, which make it an offence to circumvent an access control technological protection measure (TPM) for any purpose save those expressly exempted. Fair dealing is not included in the list of exemptions. If Bill C-32 is passed in its current form it will be an offence to circumvent an access control TPM in order to engage in the transformative use of expression.

This chapter takes the position that acts relating to the transformative use of copyright-protected expression benefit Canadian society and should not be seen as offences under the *Copyright Act*. To this end, it offers two recommendations for copyright reform. First, the fair dealing defence should be amended to incorporate a right to engage in transformative use of copyright-protected expression. Such an amendment would give individuals the right to use a substantial amount of copyright-protected expression for the purpose of engaging in transformative use, provided certain attribution requirements are satisfied and that the copyright-protected work is dealt with fairly. Second, the provisions of Bill C-32 which relate to the legal protection of TPMs should be modified to state that

---

respect to transformative works. While copyright protects the author's commercial interests, moral rights protect the author's non-commercial interests. In Canada, various moral rights are protected under the *Copyright Act*, namely the right to the integrity of the work and the right to attribution. The latter right encompasses "the right, where reasonable in the circumstances, to be associated with a work as its author by name or under a pseudonym and the right to remain anonymous" (s. 14.1(1), *Copyright Act*)).The right to integrity of the work is infringed if the work is, "to the prejudice of the honour or reputation of the author, (a) distorted, mutilated or otherwise modified; or (b) used in association with a product, service, cause or institution" (s. 28.2(1), *Copyright Act*). If, in the process of engaging in the transformative use of copyright-protected expression, an individual modifies, mutilates or distorts a work, the right to integrity, held by the author of the original work, may be infringed. As well, if the transformative work fails to reference the author of the original work, the author's right to attribution may also be infringed. Further research and analysis must be done to determine whether modifications should be made to Canada's moral rights laws in order to ensure that they do not chill the creation and dissemination of transformative works. This topic is beyond the scope of this paper to address.

14 Bill C-32, *An Act to amend the Copyright Act*, 3d Sess., 40th Parl., 2010.

individuals are not committing an offence by circumventing a TPM in order to do something which is otherwise permitted by law. The adoption of such an approach would be consistent with the two 1996 World Intellectual Property Organization (WIPO) internet treaties which Canada has signed but not yet ratified.[15] As well, it would give copyright holders an additional tool to combat copyright infringement while ensuring that individuals are not deterred from engaging in the transformative use of copyright-protected expression through the imposition of an additional legal barrier.

B. DO ACTS RELATING TO THE TRANSFORMATIVE USE OF COPYRIGHT-PROTECTED EXPRESSION BENEFIT CANADIANS?

The Supreme Court of Canada (SCC), in *RJR Macdonald, Inc. v. Canada (Attorney General),* stated that the values underlying the constitutionally protected right to freedom of expression include "the search for political, artistic and scientific truth, the protection of individual autonomy and self-development, and the promotion of public participation in the democratic process."[16] Acts relating to the transformative use of copyright-protected expression promote these values.

Transformative works can assist individuals in the search for political and artistic truth. Some transformative works critique individual politicians, policy positions, and political parties. A search for "Stephen Harper remix," "Jack Layton remix," or "Michael Ignatieff remix" on YouTube, for instance, returns various examples of critical transformative works. In the American context, Richard L. Edwards and Chuck Tryon, in an article entitled "Political video mashups as allegories of citizen empowerment," note that:

> high-profile mashups during the 2008 elections included hip-hop star will.i.am's "Yes We Can" video (a remix of Obama's New Hampshire primary concession speech in February 2008), the eponymous Obama Girl's "Crush on Obama" video, satirist Paul Shanklin's "Barack the Magic Negro" song (a remix of an *Los Angeles Times* column and the

---

15 *World Intellectual Property Organization Copyright Treaty* (adopted 20 December 1996, entered into force 6 March 2002) 36 ILM 65 [WCT], *World Intellectual Property Organization Performances and Phonograms Treaty* (adopted 20 December 1996, entered into force 20 May 2002) 36 ILM 76 [WPPT].

16 *RJR Macdonald,* above note 11 at para. 72.

> song "Puff the Magic Dragon") and Comedy Central's late night host Stephen Colbert's "John McCain's Green Screen Challenge" (a mashup contest centering around a speech given by Republican presidential candidate John McCain). Each of these mashups in turn encouraged or stimulated other users to create their own video mashups, such as the numerous user-generated videos on BarelyPolitical.com that remix video footage of Obama Girl, or users who submitted their own mashup creations into Colbert's remix challenge.[17]

Edwards and Tryon state that "[j]ust as in the case of a video camera in the hands of a video activist at a street rally, engaged online users can produce mashups as a means for political advocacy (tool), political protest (weapon), and political observation (witness)."[18]

Transformative works can also assist in the search for artistic truth. Transformative works that are critical of certain genres of art, artists, individual works, or art movements may help individuals re-examine their own views on art and culture. Some mashups may be created for the purpose of critiquing a specific artist. An individual may wish, for instance, to draw attention to and subvert the macho image of a certain band by creating a mashup which combines their aggressive vocals with a light, playful musical accompaniment. Other individuals use transformative works to critique certain genres of art. Peggy Ahwesh's machinima, *She Puppet*, for instance, created within the video game *Tomb Raider*, provides a feminist critique of both *Tomb Raider* and the "male dominated world of gaming."[19] Non-critical transformative works may also aid in the search for artistic truth. By emphasizing an artist's admirable characteristics, for instance, a transformative work may inspire individuals to look more deeply at that artist's body of work. Examples abound of individuals creating and distributing transformative works which act as homages or tributes to certain artists, art forms, or genres.[20]

Transformative works help protect individual autonomy and self-development. In creating transformative works, individuals take existing expression and rework it, altering its meaning and purpose. The act of re-

---

17 L. Edwards and Chuck Tryon, "Political video mashups as allegories of citizen empowerment" (2009) 14 First Monday 10, http://firstmonday.org/htbin/cgiwrap/bin/ojs/index.php/fm/article/view/2617/2305#p4

18 Edwards and Tryon, above note 17.

19 Peggy Ahwesh, (2001) *She Puppet;* Elijah Horwatt, "New Media Resistance: Machinima and the Avant-Garde" (2008) 73/74 *Cineaction* 8 at 11.

20 See, for example, www.youtube.com/watch?v=eco8IdnHjEQ for a Shania Twain tribute; www.youtube.com/watch?v=7L1HYCV9ScA for a Nickelback tribute.

working existing expression is an empowering experience. Rather than acting as a passive consumer of expression, individuals, through the creation of transformative works, actively engage with it. Through machinima, they can use a video game's characters to tell a story which they want to tell, rather than experiencing the game exclusively in the manner outlined by its creators. Through mashups, individuals can imagine what might occur should their two favourite bands play together on the same stage. Through fan fiction, individuals can write themselves, their friends, their family, and their life into works which they find personally significant or which are culturally significant.[21] In reworking and remaking a text, individuals can assert themselves against it and express their agreement with it. They can mold it to their own experiences and worldview. They are developing alongside (and within) the texts.

Transformative use of copyright-protected expression does not just benefit individuals. It also allows marginalised or oppressed groups to achieve autonomy from more empowered cultures by writing themselves into central roles in culturally significant texts. [22] One noteworthy example of a work in which this occurs is the *Wind Done Gone*, Alice Randall's rewrite of the Margaret Mitchell work *Gone with the Wind*.[23] As Neil Netanel states, Randall's rewrite "upend[s] Mitchell's idealized portrait [of the "antebellum South during and after the Civil War"[24]] by deploying its very story lines, scenes, and characters to reimagine them from the viewpoint of a slave."[25]

Transformative works may also promote public participation in the democratic process. One facet of the democratic process is political participation. Certain transformative works may inspire individuals to become involved in the political process as a candidate, a volunteer for a political campaign, or as a more informed (or first time) voter. Democracy, however, can be seen as something broader than political participation. Jack Balkin states that:

> A democratic culture is more than representative institutions of democracy, and it is more than deliberation about public issues. Rather, a

---

21 See Anupam Chander & Madhavi Sunder, "Everyone's a Superhero: A Cultural Theory of 'Mary Sue' Fan Fiction as Fair Use" (2007) 95 Calif. L. Rev. 597.

22 Jeannie Suk, "Originality" (2002) 115 Harv. L. Rev. 1988 at 1992–93.

23 Alice Randall, *The Wind Done Gone* (New York: Houghton Mifflin Company, 2001); Margaret Mitchell, *Gone with the Wind* (New York: Macmillan, 1975).

24 *Suntrust v. Houghton Mifflin Co.*, 268 F.3d 1257 (11th Cir. 2001).

25 Neil Netanel, *Copyright's Paradox* (New York: Oxford University Press, 2008) at 159.

> democratic culture is a culture in which individuals have a fair opportunity to participate in the forms of meaning making that constitute them as individuals. Democratic culture is about individual liberty as well as collective self-governance; it is about each individual's ability to participate in the production and distribution of culture.[26]

By giving individuals the ability to participate in culture "through building on what they find in culture and innovating with it, modifying it, and turning it to their purposes," in a way that was not previously possible on such a scale, transformative use of existing expression, facilitated by digital networked technologies, promotes public participation in the democratic process.[27]

This part of the chapter has argued that acts relating to transformative use of copyright-protected expression are beneficial for Canadian society. Specifically, it has suggested that these acts further the values underlying freedom of expression, as articulated by the SCC. These acts, however, may also infringe copyright.

C. DO ACTS RELATING TO THE TRANSFORMATIVE USE OF COPYRIGHT-PROTECTED EXPRESSION INFRINGE COPYRIGHT?

Anyone can rework or remake expression which is no longer (or has never been) protected by copyright. However, although some individuals who engage in transformative use rework expression which is no longer protected by copyright,[28] many individuals remake works that are still protected by copyright.[29] In so doing, they may be infringing the exclusive rights of the copyright owner with respect to the works in question. These rights, set out

---

26 Balkin, Jack M. 'Digital Speech and Democratic Culture: A Theory of Freedom of Expression for the Information Society' (2004) 79 N.Y.U. Law Rev. 1 at 3–4.

27 Balkin, above note 26 at 5.

28 Canadians Anthony Del Col and Conor McCreery recently created the "fantasy-adventure" comic-book series Kill Shakespeare, which has been described as the *Globe and Mail* as "a mash-up of heroes and villains from a dozen plays flung together in a new, supernatural adventure." (John Barber, "THWACK! Two Canadians want to kill Shakespeare" *The Globe and Mail* (17 April, 2010), www.theglobeandmail.com/books/thwack-two-canadians-want-to-kill-shakespeare/article1536890/.

29 This is potentially due to two reasons. First, the period of copyright in works extends for approximately the life of the author plus fifty years. Thus, many of the works which are currently available for transformative re-use are protected by copyright. Second, many individuals may wish to engage with recently created content that is currently culturally relevant.

in section 3 of the *Copyright Act*, include the right to, with respect to either an entire work or a substantial part of a work, reproduce it, communicate it to the public by telecommunication, and perform it in public.[30]

Thus, if a transformative work reproduces a substantial amount of copyright-protected expression without the permission of the copyright owner, the creator of the transformative work will have prima facie infringed the copyright owner's right to reproduce the work. The distribution of such a work over the internet will prima facie infringe the copyright owner's right to communicate the work to the public by telecommunication. And the act of downloading such a work will, again, prima facie infringe the copyright owner's right to reproduce the work.

The question of whether a substantial amount of expression has been taken from the copyright-protected work "must be assessed from both a quantitative and qualitative perspective."[31] Even a small taking can be deemed substantial if analysed from a qualitative perspective. As well, the question of whether a taking is substantial depends on the type of work involved. With respect to musical works, for instance, it appears that the amount taken will be considered to be a substantial part of the copyright-protected work if it renders the copyright-protected work recognizable or identifiable within the allegedly infringing work.[32] In *Hager v. ECW Press Ltd.* a case which addressed substantial taking in the context of a literary work, Reed J. found that the defendants had committed copyright infringement by reproducing one-third of a nine page chapter on Shania Twain in a longer work on the Canadian country music icon.[33] As noted by Reed J.:

> the conclusion I draw from the facts is that in terms of quantity, a substantial amount of her work was taken. In addition, the parts of her book that are most valuable to her were taken: the direct quotes from Shania Twain. I conclude that qualitatively a very valuable and significant part of her work was taken.[34]

It is likely that many transformative works could be seen as having reproduced a substantial amount of copyright-protected expression. Many machinima, for instance, feature characters, background scenery, and objects

---

30 *Copyright Act*, above note 12 at s. 3

31 *Hager v. ECW Press Ltd.*, [1999] 2 F.C. 287 at para. 15 [*Hager*].

32 See *Canadian Performing Right Society Ltd. v. Canadian National Exhibition Association*, [1934] 4 D.L.R. 154 (Ont. H.C.J.) [*CPRS*]; *Grignon v Roussel* (1991), 44 F.T.R. 121 (F.C.T.D.) [*Grignon*].

33 *Hager*, above note 31.

34 *Ibid.* at para.16.

from the underlying video game. In writing fan fiction, authors frequently retain elements of the plot, characters, or setting from the original stories. In creating mashups, mashup artists often attempt to ensure that the underlying songs are recognisable. As Gregg Gillis (Girl Talk) has noted, "I like to use [samples] in a way that everything is recognizable. That's a part of the fun where you recognize the sample and you hear how it can be manipulated."[35] In reproducing a "substantial" amount of copyright-protected expression, these works prima facie infringe the exclusive rights of the copyright owner.

Various defences to copyright infringement, described by the SCC as users' rights, are contained within the *Copyright Act*.[36] The user right which may prove most useful with respect to acts relating to the transformative use of copyright-protected expression is fair dealing. The fair dealing defence is set out in sections 29–29.2 of the *Copyright Act* and reads as follows:

> 29. Fair dealing for the purpose of research or private study does not infringe copyright.
>
> 29.1 Fair dealing for the purpose of criticism or review does not infringe copyright if the following are mentioned:
> (*a*) the source; and
> (*b*) if given in the source, the name of the
> (i) author, in the case of a work,
> (ii) performer, in the case of a performer's performance,
> (iii) maker, in the case of a sound recording, or
> (iv) broadcaster, in the case of a communication signal.
>
> 29.2 Fair dealing for the purpose of news reporting does not infringe copyright if the following are mentioned:
> (*a*) the source; and
> (*b*) if given in the source, the name of the
> (i) author, in the case of a work,
> (ii) performer, in the case of a performer's performance,
> (iii) maker, in the case of a sound recording, or
> (iv) broadcaster, in the case of a communication signal.[37]

---

35 Douglas Wolk, "Barely Legal" *The Village Voice* (5 February 2002), www.villagevoice.com/2002-02-05/music/barely-legal.

36 *CCH Canadian et al. v. Law Society of Upper Canada*, 2004 SCC 13 at para. 58 [*CCH*].

37 *Copyright Act*, above note 12 at ss. 29–29.2.

The fair dealing analysis proceeds in three steps. First, in order for an act to be covered by fair dealing, it must have been done for one of the listed fair dealing purposes (namely research, private study, criticism, review, and news reporting). Second, if the act is done for the purpose of criticism, review, or news reporting, certain criteria with respect to attribution must be satisfied. Third, the copyright-protected work must have been dealt with fairly.

It is likely that a large number of the acts relating to transformative works were done for the purpose of one of the listed fair dealing categories. The SCC, in *CCH Canadian et al. v. Law Society of Upper Canada* has indicated that these categories "must be given a large and liberal interpretation in order to ensure that users' rights are not unduly constrained."[38] The category of research has been interpreted broadly. The SCC further noted that research, for the purposes of fair dealing, need not be private and can be for profit.[39] Both "for-profit" research conducted by law firms and thirty-second previews of musical works have been found to fall within the category of research.[40] Transformative works created or used for the purpose of research, such as those created or acquired by researchers studying the history or sociology of user-generated content, for instance, would likely fall within this category.

Transformative works created or used in private may be seen as having been created for the purpose of private study. However, many transformative works, although they may be created in private, are then shared with the world through peer to peer file sharing programs or websites. Reed J., in the leading case to address the scope of the "private study" category, *Hager v. ECW Press Ltd.*, has stated that "the use contemplated by private study . . . is not one in which the copied work is communicated to the public."[41] Thus, the act of making transformative works public would likely remove these dealings from the ambit of the fair dealing category of private study.

Some transformative works may have been created or used for the purpose of news reporting. News reports discussing the topic of user-generated creativity, for instance, may feature clips or photos from mashups or machinima. Some transformative works, as well, may be seen as having been created for the purpose of review. The leading Canadian case to inter-

38 *CCH* above note 36.

39 *Ibid.*

40 *Ibid*; *Society of Composers, Authors and Music Publishers of Canada v. Bell Canada*, 2010 FCA 123.

41 *Hager*, above note 31.

pret the category of review, *Canada v. James Lorimer & Co.* (*Lorimer*), states that fair dealing for the purpose of review "requires as a minimum some dealing with the work other than simply condensing it into an abridged version and reproducing it under the author's name."[42] As transformative works rework existing expression for a new purpose or new meaning, it is likely that they would be seen as surpassing the minimum standard suggested for the category of review in *Lorimer.*

Many transformative works are critical. Whether the fair dealing category of criticism encompasses these types of criticism, however, is an open question. The exact bounds of the fair dealing category of criticism are yet to be determined. A prominent Canadian case interpreting the fair dealing category of criticism, *Cie Générale des Établissements Michelin-Michelin & Cie v. C.A.W.-Canada et al.* (*Michelin*),[43] interpreted criticism narrowly. Specifically, it indicated that the fair dealing category of criticism does not encompass parody. *Michelin,* however, was decided seven years before the SCC, in *CCH* indicated that courts were to interpret the fair dealing categories broadly. It remains to be seen how broadly criticism will be interpreted post-*CCH*

As indicated above, a large number of acts relating to transformative works will likely be seen as having been done for the purpose of one of the listed fair dealing categories. However, many acts relating to transformative works will likely not be seen as having been done for these purposes. For instance, many acts relating to transformative works which are made public and which are not critical will likely not fall within any of the existing categories.[44] These types of dealings include transformative works which are created or distributed as homages, expressions of appreciation, and tributes. One example of such a work is Danger Mouse's *Grey Album,* a mashup of Jay-Z's *Black Album* and the Beatles' *White Album* which has been described as a "sincere, sophisticated homage to two acclaimed works and the musical celebrities who created them."[45] Other types of transformative works which will not be protected by the fair dealing defence as it is currently written and interpreted are transformative works which use copyright-protected expression as the building blocks,

---

42 *Canada v James Lorimer and Co.* (1984), 77 C.P.R. (2d) 262.

43 *Cie Générale des Établissements Michelin-Michelin and Cie v. C.A.W.-Canada et al* (1996), 71 C.P.R. (3d) 348.

44 This conclusion suggests that fair dealing, as it is currently constructed, favours critics over fans.

45 Johanna Blakley, "The *Grey Album,* Celebrity Homage and Transformative Appropriation" (2005) www.learcenter.org/images/event_uploads/DemersNotes.pdf.

or raw material, for new expression, without commenting on or critiquing the expression itself. Acts relating to these types of works will likely not be seen as having been done for any of the listed fair dealing purposes. As they are not protected by fair dealing, these acts can be enjoined by the copyright owner and the individuals who engage in these acts can be exposed to significant financial penalties.[46] As a large number of transformative works will satisfy the first step in the fair dealing analysis, however, this chapter will proceed by discussing the second and third steps.[47]

The second step in the fair dealing analysis only applies to acts done for the purpose of criticism, review and news reporting. Acts done for these purposes, provided they are deemed fair, will not infringe copyright if certain attribution requirements are satisfied. With respect to a work, for instance, both the source of the work and the author (if given) must be mentioned. This requirement will not provide a significant impediment to individuals who wish to create, distribute, or enjoy transformative works. Attribution can be given, for instance, in the end credits of a machinima, in a file name in a mashup, or in the title page of fan fiction.

The third step in the fair dealing analysis requires a court to determine whether the copyright-protected work in question has been dealt with fairly. The term fair is not defined in the *Copyright Act*. Whether something is fair "is a question of fact and depends on the facts of each case."[48] The SCC, in *CCH* (the leading Canadian decision on fair dealing), set out a list of factors which should be considered in determining whether a dealing has been fair. These factors include: the purpose of the dealing, the character of the dealing, the amount of the dealing, alternatives to the dealing, the nature of the work, and the effect of the dealing on the work.[49]

The first factor, the purpose of the dealing, will tend to fairness if acts relating to the transformative use of copyright-protected expression are done for one of the fair dealing purposes. Acts which are not done for one of the fair dealing purposes will not pass the first step in the fair dealing analysis. As noted above, although a large number of acts relating to the transformative use of copyright-protected expression will likely be seen as having been done for one of the fair dealing purposes, many will not.

The second factor, the character of the dealing, looks at how the works which were allegedly infringed were dealt with. The SCC notes that while

46 *Copyright Act*, above note 12 at ss. 35, 38.1.

47 As discussed above, the first step of the fair dealing analysis involves determining whether an act was done for one of the fair dealing purposes.

48 *CCH* above note 36 at para. 52.

49 *Ibid.* at para. 53.

a "single copy of a work . . . used for a specific legitimate purpose" may tend to fairness, "multiple copies of works . . . being widely distributed . . . will tend to be unfair."[50] Many transformative works are distributed widely.[51] In some situations, they may be distributed far more widely than the original work.[52] Whether this factor tends to fairness or unfairness will depend, in large part, on how the transformative work was distributed.

The third factor, the amount of the dealing, looks at the amount of the original, copyright-protected work that is included in the transformative work. The extent to which this factor tends to fairness in any individual case will depend on the quantity of work taken, the importance of the work whose copyright was allegedly infringed, and the purpose of the dealing.[53] The fact that some transformative works may incorporate large portions of the allegedly infringed work will not preclude the application of the fair dealing defence. As noted by Sedgwick J. in *Allen v. Toronto Star Newspapers Ltd.*, it is possible to deal fairly with an entire work.[54]

The fourth factor, alternatives to the dealing, looks at whether there is a "non-copyrighted equivalent of the work that could have been used instead of the copyrighted work."[55] In determining whether this factor tends to fairness, the SCC has stated that it is "useful for courts to attempt to determine whether the dealing was reasonably necessary to achieve the ultimate purpose."[56] If the purpose of the dealing is to critique one song by combining it with another in the form of a mashup, for instance, it is difficult to argue that such a criticism would be equally effective if it didn't "actually reproduce the copyrighted work it was criticizing."[57] If the purpose of the dealing is to critique an elected politician's actions, however, it could be argued that such a criticism could be equally effective in a form other than through a parody of a popular song directed at that politician.

The fifth factor, the nature of the work, looks at whether the work has been published or whether it was confidential. While dealing with confidential works may tend to unfairness, in some circumstances, increas-

---

50 *CCH* above note 36 at para. 55.

51 Over a million tracks have been downloaded from DJ Danger Mouse's *Grey Album*, a mashup of the Beatles' *White Album* and Jay-Z's *Black Album*. Matthew Rimmer, "*The Grey Album*: Copyright Law and Digital Sampling" (2005) 114 Media International Australia incorporating Culture and Policy 40 at 40.

52 See *Rogers v. Koons*, 960 F.2d 301 (2d Cir. 1992).

53 *CCH* above note 36 at para. 56.

54 *Allen v. Toronto Star Newspapers Ltd.* (1995), 36 O.R. (3d) 201 (*Allen*).

55 *CCH* above note 36 at para. 57.

56 *Ibid.*

57 *Ibid.*

ing circulation of an unpublished work could tend to fairness as it "could lead to wider public dissemination of the work—one of the goals of copyright law."[58] It is likely, however, that many of the works which are remade through transformative use are works which have been published. If this is the case, this factor may not play a large role in the fairness analysis.

The sixth factor examines the effect of the dealing on the work. The main question analyzed with respect to this factor is whether the "reproduced work is likely to compete with the market of the original work."[59] If it is, the dealing may tend to unfairness. It is likely, however, that very few transformative works will compete, at all, with the market for the original work. Individuals looking to buy one of the games in the Halo series to play will not, instead, purchase DVDs of machinima set in the Halo world. Someone who wants to read the original Harry Potter books will not be satisfied with one of the myriad Harry Potter fan fiction creations.

Based on the above analysis and, in particular, the factor which looks at the effect of the dealing on the work, this chapter suggests that it is likely that most, if not all, of the acts relating to the transformative use of copyright-protected expression which have been done for fair dealing purposes would be considered fair. However, as discussed above, many acts relating to transformative works will likely not be seen as having been created for fair dealing purposes. Particularly, many acts with respect to transformative works which are made public and are not critical, such as acts with respect to works which use existing culture as the raw material for new expression, without critiquing or commenting on the copyright-protected expression itself, will likely be seen as infringing copyright. Many of these acts further the values underlying the constitutionally protected right to freedom of expression. However, as they cannot be considered to have been created for any fair dealing purpose, they will be excluded from the ambit of fair dealing.

D. TOWARDS A RIGHT TO ENGAGE IN TRANSFORMATIVE USE OF COPYRIGHT-PROTECTED EXPRESSION

1) Bill C-32

Bill C-32, introduced by the Government of Canada on 2 June 2010, provides additional protection for acts relating to the creation, distribution,

---

58 *Ibid.* at para. 58.

59 *Ibid.* at para. 59.

and enjoyment of transformative works.[60] It does so in two main ways: through the expansion of the fair dealing defence and through the addition of a right to create non-commercial user-generated content (provided that certain conditions are satisfied).

First, Bill C-32 proposes to expand fair dealing through the addition of three new fair dealing categories: parody, satire and education.[61] Should Bill C-32 be passed, individuals would have the right to use a substantial amount of copyright-protected expression without the authorization of the copyright-owner for the purposes of parody, satire, and education (in addition to the existing fair dealing categories of research, private study, criticism, review, and news reporting), provided they do so fairly. This amendment would render non-infringing many acts relating to the transformative use of copyright-protected expression which are, under the current *Copyright Act*, likely to be deemed infringing. It would do so by making it easier for acts which would otherwise be seen as fair to pass the first step of the fair dealing analysis — namely, the step in which it is determined whether the act was done for one of the listed fair dealing purposes. The extent to which this proposed expansion to fair dealing increases protection for acts relating to the transformative use of copyright-protected expression depends in large part on how broadly the categories of parody, satire, and education are interpreted.

Parody is an ancient concept which has been defined in many different ways through its long history.[62] The "popular conception of parody and the standard dictionary definition" conceives of parody as a "specific work of humorous or mocking intent, which imitates the work of an individual author or artist, genre or style, so as to make it appear ridiculous."[63] Other conceptions of parody, however, permit the parodist to use the work being

---

60 Bill C-32, above note 14.

61 *Ibid.* at cl. 21.

62 Margaret A. Rose, *Parody: Ancient, Modern, and Post-Modern* (New York: Cambridge University Press, 1993), at 5. See also Graham Reynolds, "Necessarily Critical? The Adoption of a Parody Defence to Copyright Infringement in Canada" (2010) Man. L.J. (forthcoming); Emir Aly Crowne-Mohammed, "Parody as fair dealing in Canada: a guide for lawyers and judges" (2009) 4 Journal of Intellectual Property Law & Practice 468; Giuseppina D'Agostino, "Healing Fair Dealing? A Comparative Copyright Analysis of Canada's Fair Dealing to U.K Fair Dealing and U.S. Fair Use" (2008) 53 McGill L.J. 309; James Zegers, "Parody and Fair Use in Canada After *Campbell v. Acuff-Rose*" (1994) 11 C.I.P.R. 205.

63 Ellen Gredley & Spyros Maniatis, "Parody: A Fatal Attraction? Part 1: The Nature of Parody and its Treatment in Copyright" (1997) 19 Eur. I.P. Rev. 339 at 341.

parodied in order to critique something other than the work itself.[64] These types of parody have been referred to as "weapon" parodies,[65] and can also be seen as satire.[66] Finally, some conceptions of parody do not insist upon criticism at all. Canadian literary theorist Linda Hutcheon, for instance, defines parody as a "form of imitation . . . characterized by ironic inversion, not always at the expense of the parodied text."[67] This definition of parody encompasses works which are characterized by "admiration and reverence,"[68] and, if adopted by Canadian courts, would likely encompass acts relating to the transformative use of copyright-protected expression which can be characterized as homages, tributes, or shows of appreciation for the parodied text. Transformative works which use existing expression solely as the raw material for future expression, however, without commenting upon or critiquing either the existing expression itself or something other than the existing expression, would likely fail to be encompassed by both the satire and parody categories of fair dealing, even if a broad conception of both categories is adopted by Canadian courts.[69]

---

64 See Linda Hutcheon, *A Theory of Parody: The Teachings of Twentieth-Century Art Forms* (London: Methuen, Inc., 1985) at 6; Michael Spence, "Intellectual Property and the Problem of Parody" (1998) 114 Law Q. Rev. 594 at 594.

65 Spence, above note 64 at 594.

66 The Supreme Court of the United States, in *Campbell*, above note 2, noted the following two definitions of satire: "a work 'in which prevalent follies or vices are assailed with ridicule,' 14 *Oxford English Dictionary*, [247 (2d ed. 1989)] at 500, or are 'attacked through irony, derision, or wit,' *American Heritage Dictionary*, [1317 (3d ed. 1992)] at 1604."

67 Hutcheon, above note 64 at 6.

68 Gredley & Maniatis, above note 63 at 340.

69 The Supreme Court of the United States, in *Campbell*, above note 2, stated that "[p]arody needs to mimic an original to make its point, and so has some claim to use the creation of its victim's (or collective victims') imagination, whereas satire can stand on its own two feet and so requires justification for the very act of borrowing" (580–81). Various commentators have noted that in the United States of America, satire generally receives less fair use protection than parody. Adriana Collado, for instance, notes that "[c]ourts have reasoned that, because copyright owners are not inclined to grant parodists permission to use their copyrighted work in a manner that holds the work up to ridicule or criticism, fair use is necessary to advance the goals of copyright law and to prevent censorship. Courts, however, deem that copyright owners are likelier to allow use of their works in satire because satires do not target the copyrighted works directly. Thus, courts have reasoned satires do not need fair use protection in the same way as parodies." Adriana Collado, "Unfair Use: The Lack of Fair use Protection for Satire Under § 107 of the *Copyright Act*" 9 J.Tech. L. & Pol'y 65 at 67–68, http://grove.ufl.edu/~techlaw/vol9/issue1/collado.html.

The proposed addition of the education category of fair dealing could also impact the extent to which acts relating to the transformative use of copyright-protected expression infringe copyright in Canada. Although one way to interpret "education" is to restrict the term to activities taking place in a formal educational institution, the SCC's statement, in *CCH* that fair dealing categories "must be given a large and liberal interpretation," would likely require the term to be interpreted more broadly.[70] For instance, under a large and liberal interpretation, acts could be seen as being encompassed by the fair dealing category of education if they are done for the purpose of educating oneself or others, whether in an institutional educational setting or in a less formal environment.

Though the existing fair dealing categories already encompass many acts relating to education, it is likely that the creation of this new fair dealing category will result in various additional acts passing the first step of the fair dealing analysis, such as non-critical acts performed for others which cannot be considered to be part of any research process but which serve a broad, educative function. Acts relating to the transformative use of copyright-protected expression which are done for the purpose of education, such as the act of creating and disseminating a transformative work in order to bring its content to the attention of a broad audience for their edification or instruction may, for instance, be encompassed by this category.

Bill C-32, by expanding the list of allowable fair dealing categories, will lead to more acts relating to the transformative use of copyright-protected content passing the first step of the fair dealing analysis. It is important to emphasize, however, that fair dealing is a process with multiple steps. The fact that a work may have been done for a fair dealing purpose does not mean that the fair dealing defence will automatically apply, resulting in the act being deemed non-infringing. In order for fair dealing to apply, the copyright-protected work must also have been dealt with fairly. As noted by Trudel J.A. of the Federal Court of Appeal, in a decision which dealt with the question of whether "the photocopying of excerpts from textbooks for use in classroom instruction for students in kindergarten to grade 12"[71] was fair dealing:

> I am also aware that Bill C-32, *An Act to amend the Copyright Act*, 3rd Session, 40th Parliament, 59 Elizabeth II, 2010, section 21 would amend section 29 to state that "Fair dealing for the purpose of research, private

---

70 *CCH* above note 36.

71 2010 FCA 198, para 2.

study, education, parody or satire does not infringe copyright (changes underlined). However, this amendment serves only to create additional allowable purposes; it does not affect the fairness analysis.[72]

The second way in which Bill C-32 provides additional protection for acts relating to the transformative use of copyright-protected expression is through the creation of a defence relating to non-commercial user-generated content, dubbed by some as the "YouTube defence." This provision reads:

> 29.21 (1) It is not an infringement of copyright for an individual to use an existing work or other subject-matter or copy of one, which has been published or otherwise made available to the public, in the creation of a new work or other subject-matter in which copyright subsists and for the individual — or, with the individual's authorization, a member of their household — to use the new work or other subject-matter or to authorize an intermediary to disseminate it, if
>
> (a) the use of, or the authorization to disseminate, the new work or other subject-matter is done solely for non-commercial purposes;
>
> (b) the source — and, if given in the source, the name of the author, performer, maker or broadcaster — of the existing work or other subject-matter or copy of it are mentioned, if it is reasonable in the circumstances to do so;
>
> (c) the individual had reasonable grounds to believe that the existing work or other subject-matter or copy of it, as the case may be, was not infringing copyright; and
>
> (d) the use of, or the authorization to disseminate, the new work or other subject-matter does not have a substantial adverse effect, financial or otherwise, on the exploitation or potential exploitation of the existing work or other subject-matter — or copy of it — or on an existing or potential market for it, including that the new work or other subject-matter is not a substitute for the existing one.
>
> (2) The following definitions apply in subsection (1).
>
> "intermediary" means a person or entity who regularly provides space or means for works or other subject-matter to be enjoyed by the public
>
> "use" means to do anything that by this Act the owner of the copyright has the sole right to do, other than the right to authorize anything.[73]

---

72 *Ibid.*, para. 21.

73 Bill C-32, above note 14 at cl. 22.

This defence would protect many acts relating to the transformative use of copyright-protected expression from being deemed infringing. For instance, it likely would render lawful most non-commercial mashups, sampling, machinima, digital collage, fan fiction, and remix, among other types of non-commercial transformative works. All of these types of expression "use an existing work . . . in the creation of a new work."[74] Certain acts relating to the transformative use of copyright-protected expression, however, would not be able to benefit from this defence. For instance, acts done for commercial purposes are excluded from the ambit of this defence. As a result, creators of transformative works who wish to benefit financially from their creations would not be protected by the proposed section 29.21 defence.[75]

Furthermore, the non-commercial user-generated content defence only applies in situations where "the use of, or the authorization to disseminate, the new work or other subject matter does not have a substantial adverse effect, financial or otherwise, on the exploitation or potential exploitation of the existing work or other subject-matter — or copy of it — or on an existing or potential market for it, including that the new work or other subject-matter is not a substitute for the existing one."[76] The terms "substantial," "adverse,", "effect," and "potential exploitation" are not defined in Bill C-32. It is therefore possible, notwithstanding the statement of the SCC that defences to copyright infringement are users' rights that should not be unduly restricted, that these terms could be interpreted in such a way that significantly narrows the ambit of the defence.[77] Even given these restrictions, however, these two provisions significantly expand the ability of individuals to engage in transformative use of copyright-protected expression without infringing copyright.

Both new and existing users' rights, however, are threatened by those provisions of Bill C-32 that grant legal protection to TPMs. TPMs, sometimes referred to as "digital locks," are technological measures that allow

---

74 *Ibid.* It would also protect acts which are not transformative but which use an existing work in the creation of a new work.

75 Creators of transformative works who wish to benefit financially from their creations would have to rely on the application of the fair dealing defence in order to avoid being found to have infringed copyright. The fact that an individual profits from their exercise of fair dealing is not a bar to the defence. See *CCH* above note 35, where the acts of lawyers conducting the business of law for profit were found to be encompassed by fair dealing.

76 Bill C-32, above note 14 at cl. 22.

77 *CCH* above note 36 at para. 54.

copyright owners to restrict access to and/or use of copyright-protected expression. Bill C-32 makes it an offence to circumvent a TPM which controls access to a work, a performer's performance fixed in a sound recording, or a sound recording for all purposes save those expressly exempted. It also makes it an offence to offer or provide services or devices to the public that are "primarily for the purposes of circumventing a technological protection measure" (provided that certain other criteria are satisfied).[78]

Certain narrowly-circumscribed exemptions to these offences are built into Bill C-32. It is not an offence, for instance, to circumvent a TPM for the purposes of: an investigation related to the enforcement of an Act of Parliament or an Act of a legislature; activities related to the protection of national security; ensuring computer interoperability; encryption research; verifying and preventing the collection or communication of personal information; assessing or correcting computer security; making works, performances, and sound recordings perceptible to a person with a perceptual disability; making an ephemeral reproduction of a work for a broadcasting undertaking; or gaining access to a telecommunications service by means of a radio apparatus (provided, in every case, that certain other criteria are satisfied).[79]

In many instances, however, an individual could commit an offence by circumventing a TPM in order to do something that the individual has the right to do under the *Copyright Act*. For instance, there is no exemption that permits an individual to circumvent an access control TPM in order to exercise their right to fair dealing. As a result, individuals who circumvent an access control TPM for the purpose of research, private study, criticism, review, and news reporting will be committing an offence.

Bill C-32 also makes it an offence to offer or provide services or devices to the public that are "primarily for the purposes of circumventing a technological measure" when the service or device is offered knowingly and for commercial purposes.[80] Committing this offence results in exposure to significant penalties which may chill the creation and distribution of tools used to circumvent TPMs.[81] Although one consequence flowing from the enactment of these provisions may be a reduction of instances of copyright infringement, these provisions may also prevent individuals from exercising their user rights. A paucity of tools to circumvent TPMs

78 Bill C-32, above note 14 at cl. 47.

79 *Ibid*. at cl. 47.

80 *Ibid*. at cl. 47.

81 *Ibid*. at cl. 48.

may render individuals unable to circumvent TPMs, even where the act of circumvention itself is not an offence. Thus, although Bill C-32 contains two provisions which provide additional protection for acts relating to the transformative use of copyright-protected expression, this additional protection is undermined by the manner in which Bill C-32 grants legal protection to TPMs. As a result, Bill C-32 may have the effect of limiting the creation and distribution of transformative works to a greater degree than is the case under the current *Copyright Act*.

2) Reforming Bill C-32

In the attempt to achieve broader protection for acts relating to the transformative use of copyright-protected expression, this chapter offers two recommendations for reform of Bill C-32. First, the fair dealing defence should be expanded to incorporate a right to engage in the transformative use of copyright-protected expression. Second, the provisions relating to the legal protection of TPMs should be modified to ensure that it is not an offence to circumvent a TPM for a lawful purpose (such as to engage in fair dealing).

a) Adopting a Right to Engage in Transformative Use of Copyright-Protected Expression

The adoption of a right to engage in the transformative use of copyright-protected expression will open up space within which individuals can, in a lawful manner, create and disseminate transformative works. Its impact would extend across the spectrum of transformative works, and would benefit both amateur transformative creators and professional transformative creators.

One objection to the creation of such a right could be that it has the potential to be overbroad. As a result, in order to balance this new user right with the rights of copyright owners, this chapter suggests that it should be incorporated within fair dealing as another acceptable fair dealing category. Thus, the mere fact that the use is transformative would not be sufficient to have it declared non-infringing. The use would also have to be "fair." If this proposal is accepted, individuals in Canada would have the right, under fair dealing, to use a substantial amount of copyright-protected expression without the permission of the copyright owner for the purpose of engaging in the transformative use of copyright-protected expression, provided they do so in a fair manner. As is the case with the current list of fair dealing categories, fairness would be determined through an analysis of various factors, including: the purpose of the dealing, the character of the dealing, the amount of the dealing, the alternatives to the dealing, the nature of the work, and the effect of the dealing on the work.[82]

A second objection to the creation of such a right could be that it is unnecessary to add an additional category to fair dealing in order to protect acts relating to the transformative use of copyright-protected expression, as most, if not all acts relating to transformative works could be encompassed by the existing (and proposed) fair dealing categories of research, private study, parody, satire, education, criticism, review, and news reporting. The above analysis has demonstrated that many transformative uses will likely be encompassed by the existing and proposed fair dealing categories. It is possible, however, that courts could interpret the scope of new and existing fair dealing categories in a manner which would result in certain transformative uses of copyright-protected not being encompassed by any of the fair dealing categories. These uses would then infringe copyright, regardless of whether they are "fair" and regardless of the social benefits which arise from their creation and dissemination. The creation of a separate fair dealing category for transformative use would ensure that all fair transformative uses of copyright-protected expression do not infringe copyright. It would also demonstrate a recognition, on the part of the government, of the benefits which flow to both individuals and Canadian society from engaging in acts relating to the transformative use of copyright-protected expression.

Canada would not be the first country to provide protection for acts relating to the transformative use of copyright-protected expression. The question of whether a new work is transformative is a key consideration in the United States of America's fair use analysis.[83] As well, in 2006, the Gowers Review of Intellectual Property, commissioned by then-Chancellor of the Exchequer Gordon Brown and "charged with examining all the elements of the IP [intellectual property] system, to ensure that it delivers incentives while minimising inefficiency,"[84] recommended that the government of the United Kingdom take steps to create a copyright exemption for transformative use.[85]

---

82 In creating this new fair dealing category, care would have to be taken in the drafting process to ensure that courts do not make "transformative use" a mandatory element of every claim of fair dealing.

83 *Campbell*, above note 2. Fair use is the analogous American provision to Canada's fair dealing defence.

84 Gowers, above note 2 at 1.

85 *Ibid.* at 3. It could be argued that the creation of such a right is not necessary, as individuals who wish to engage in the transformative use of copyright-protected

b) Clarifying that It Is Not an Offence to Circumvent a TPM for Lawful Purposes

Achieving broader protection for acts relating to transformative works will also require the modification of the Bill C-32 provisions which grant legal protection to TPMs. As noted above, Bill C-32 makes it an offence to circumvent an access control TPM for any purpose save those expressly exempted. Although various exemptions are set out in the Bill, there is no exemption for fair dealing or other user rights. As a result, a user who circumvents an access control TPM in order to exercise their right to fair dealing will have committed an offence, resulting in the copyright owner being able to pursue various remedies.[86]

In order to ensure that legal protection for TPMs will not prevent users from exercising their rights under the *Copyright Act*, this chapter suggests that the provisions relating to the legal protection of TPMs should be modified to clarify that it is not an offence to circumvent a TPM for lawful purposes. This approach was adopted in Bill C-60, the Liberal Government's failed 2005 attempt to reform the *Copyright Act*. Clause 27 of Bill C-60 states that:

> [a]n owner of copyright in a work . . . [is] . . . entitled to all remedies . . . that are or may be conferred by law for the infringement of a right against a person who, without the consent of the copyright owner . . . circumvents, removes or in any way renders ineffective a techno-

---

expression can simply secure a licence from the copyright owner allowing them to use the copyright-protected expression in the creation of a transformative work. For various reasons, however, licensing is not a suitable alternative. First, the process of determining who owns the copyright in a certain work may be both time consuming and difficult. Second, the process of negotiating a licensing fee can be similarly time consuming and expensive. Third, the licensing fee itself may be unaffordable for certain users. Fourth, some copyright owners may only be willing to licence certain uses of their copyright-protected content. If an individual proposes to use the copyright-protected expression in a manner that conflicts with the copyright owner's list of acceptable uses, the licence may be refused. Fifth, some copyright owners may refuse all requests for licences. Although some of these hurdles can potentially be overcome by the creator or of a transformative work intended for commercial distribution, they are likely to be more difficult for amateur creators to overcome, and may have the effect of chilling the creation and distribution of amateur transformative works.

86 These remedies include an injunction, damages, accounts, and delivery up. Clause 47 of Bill C-32 (specifically, 41.1(3)) indicates that copyright owners "may not elect . . . to recover statutory damages from an individual who [circumvented a TPM] only for his or her private purposes."

logical measure protecting any material form of the work . . . for the purpose of an act that is an infringement of the copyright in it. [87]

Michael Geist and Keith Rose have outlined a variety of ways in which Bill C-32 could be revised to adopt such an approach. One possible revision suggested by Geist and Rose is to "link the prohibition of circumvention to infringement."[88] To give effect to this proposed revision, they suggest revising the definition of "circumvent" set out in section 41 of Bill C-32 to read:

"circumvent" means,

(a) in respect of a technological protection measure within the meaning of paragraph (a) of the definition "technological protection measure", to descramble a scrambled work or decrypt an encrypted work or to otherwise avoid, bypass, remove, deactivate or impair the technological protection measure, for any infringing purpose, unless it is done with the authority of the copyright owner; and

(b) in respect of a technological protection measure within the meaning of paragraph (b) of the definition "technological protection measure," to avoid, bypass, remove, deactivate or impair the technological protection measure for any infringing purpose.[89]

A second possible revision to Bill C-32 which would permit circumvention for lawful purposes is the addition of an explicit exemption for circumvention for lawful purposes.[90] To do so, Geist and Rose suggest adding subsection 41.1(5) and (6) to Bill C-32 as follows:

Lawful purpose

(5) Paragraph (1)(a) does not apply if a technological protection measure is circumvented for any lawful purpose.

(6) Paragraphs (1)(b) and (c) do not apply to a person who supplies a service to a person referred to in paragraph (5) or who manufactures, imports or provides a technology, device or component, for the purposes of enabling anyone to circumvent a technological protection measure in accordance with this Act.[91]

---

87 Bill C-60, *An Act to amend the Copyright Act*, 1st Sess., 38th Parl., 2004–2005 at cl. 27.

88 Michael Geist and Keith Rose, "Fixing Bill C-32: Proposed Amendments to the Digital Lock Provisions" (2010), :www.michaelgeist.ca/content/view/5117/125/.

89 Geist and Rose, above note 88.

90 *Ibid.*

91 *Ibid.*

These proposed approaches to the legal protection of TPMs are consistent with the two 1996 WIPO internet treaties that Canada has signed but not yet ratified: the *WIPO Copyright Treaty* (WCT) and the *WIPO Performances and Phonograms Treaty* (WPPT). Article 11 of the WCT addresses TPMs.[92] It requires Contracting Parties to provide:

> adequate legal protection and effective legal remedies against the circumvention of effective technological measures that are used by authors in connection with the exercise of their rights. . .and that restrict acts, in respect of their works, which are not authorized by the authors concerned or permitted by law.[93]

It does not, however, require Contracting Parties to provide legal protection and legal remedies against the circumvention of TPMs that are used to restrict acts which are permitted by law, such as acts protected by fair dealing. In making it an offence to circumvent an access control TPM for any purpose save those expressly exempted, a list which does not include fair dealing or other user rights, Bill C-32 provides protection beyond what is required by the WCT and the WPPT. It does so at the expense of users' rights, and at the expense of the balance between copyright owners and the public interest mandated by the SCC.[94]

E. CONCLUSION

Acts relating to the transformative use of copyright-protected expression benefit Canadian society. Through the creation, distribution, and enjoyment of transformative works, individuals can question their own political views. They can express their disapproval or support of artists and their works. They can interact with texts, engaging with the works and cultural symbols that pervade the lives of Canadians. They can become more active members of a robust Canadian democracy, both through political participation and participation in the cultural life of the nation. As this chapter has set out, however, many acts relating to the transformative use of copyright-protected expression prima facie infringe copyright and cannot be saved by the fair dealing defence as it is currently written and interpreted. As a result, this chapter has argued that the *Copyright Act*

---

92 The analogous provision in the WPPT, above note 15, is contained in Article 18.

93 WCT, above note 15 at Article 11.

94 See *CCH* above note 36 at para. 48; *Théberge v Galerie d'Art du Petit Champlain Inc.*, [2002] 2 S.C.R. 336, 2002 SCC 34 at paras. 30–31; *Society of Composers, Authors and Music Publishers of Canada v Canadian Ass. Of Internet Providers*, 2004 SCC 45.

should be reformed to grant protection to acts relating to the fair transformative use of copyright-protected expression.

Bill C-32 is the most recent attempt to reform the *Copyright Act*. Although it contains two provisions which expand protection for acts relating to the transformative use of copyright-protected expression, this additional protection is undermined by Bill C-32's approach to the legal protection of TPMs. Under Bill C-32, it would be an offence to circumvent an access control TPM in order to engage in the transformative use of existing expression, even if the act of engaging in transformative use itself is otherwise lawful.

In order to ensure that the social benefits which flow from the creation, distribution, and enjoyment of transformative works are not lost due to restrictive copyright legislation, this chapter has proposed two reforms to Bill C-32: the expansion of the fair dealing defence to include a right to engage in transformative use of copyright-protected expression, and the modification of the provisions granting legal protection to TPMs to clarify that it is not an offence to circumvent a TPM for lawful purposes.

These proposals, which are consistent with the two WIPO treaties (the WCT and WPPT) which Canada has signed but not yet ratified, benefit both copyright owners and users. The ability of copyright owners to take action against copyright infringement is strengthened. If an individual circumvents an access control TPM in order to infringe copyright, they can be sued for both the infringing act and the act of circumvention. In this way, the decision of copyright owners to apply a TPM to prevent unauthorized access to copyright-protected material will receive some protection at law. This protection, however, should not permit copyright owners to sue individuals for circumventing TPMs in order to exercise their user rights. The amendments suggested in the final part of this chapter would clarify that it is not an offence to circumvent a TPM for a lawful purpose.

If these two proposals were incorporated into the *Copyright Act*, individuals would have the right to engage in the fair transformative use of copyright-protected expression, regardless of whether this expression is locked behind a TPM; and regardless of whether this use fits within the existing (and proposed) fair dealing categories of research, private study, criticism, review, news reporting, parody, satire, or education. Copyright owners would not be able to prevent the reworking of existing expression through the application of a technological measure. Private ordering through technological means would not trump user rights.[95] And Can-

95 Another issue which merits attention is the extent to which private ordering, through

adians from sea to sea to sea would be able to continue to use networked digital technologies to mashup, remix, remake, appropriate, and incorporate existing expression into new expression in a transformative manner, helping build both a stronger Canadian democracy and a more vibrant Canadian culture.

---

contracts, should be permitted to trump user rights. TPMs are frequently used in conjunction with contractual arrangements. This topic, however, is beyond the scope of this paper to address.

CHAPTER FOURTEEN

An "Independent" View of Bill C-32's Copyright Reform

Tina Piper*

"Q: ARE YOU IN MYSPACE? DID YOU FACEBOOK? YOU SHOULD DO THAT THINGS! IT IS TERRIFIC EXPOSURE. NOW IS A NEW PARADIGM! WHAT IS A PARADIGM?"
— Silver Mount Zion FAQ[1]

"[Copyright reform] maybe works for Nickelback and Sarah McLachlan, but has nothing to do with us." — Interview Respondent

A. INTRODUCTION

The act of legislating copyright assumes that there is a consensus over what copyright is: that those participating in the dialogue of law-creation use words similarly; that implicated parties have definable interests and use their rights in specific ways; that those uses of copyright are held by owners as property-like rights and entitlements. Reform of that legislation presumes an essence of what copyright does: that rights holders (creators or owners) seek to maximize the strength of their right and sell more products; that the public benefits from increased access; that copyright provides access; that a copyright may be regarded as a reward that incentivizes creative production and artistic labour, and other such assumptions. This notion of consensus is highlighted by the fact that when closely analyzed, the

* My thanks go to the participants in the 23–24 April 2010 *Intellectual Property and the Making and Marketing of Music in the Digital Age* workshop at Princeton University for their helpful comments and insight, particularly Eric Lewis and Charity Chan. I would also like to thank an anonymous reviewer, Becky Lentz, Lucinda Tang, and Michael Geist for their comments. Please note that where the terms "interview respondent" or "interviewee" have been used, the person interviewed has asked to remain anonymous.

1 Silver Mount Zion FAQ at www.tra-la-la-band.com/f-a-q

words used to define copyright are ambiguous: terms like "public," "interest," "creator," "user," and "owner" are notably indeterminate.[2] These words are used as metaphors,[3] metonymies, analogies or projections and among some group of people (or interests) these terms have a shared meaning that allows conversation about copyright to proceed.

What are the contours of that consensus, what I call for the purposes of this study the "copyright culture," that allows legislative reform to proceed with some certainty about basic terms and governing propositions? Like any culture, copyright culture is historical, referential to a time and place, path-determined and contingent; meaning is produced and disseminated through various practices, beliefs, artifacts and institutions.[4] In this introductory section I sketch some of these features.

The members of the copyright culture presumably include courts, legislators and those creators, owners and users who can fit their activities within the shared belief system that allows the business of copyright law to proceed. Copyright law is primarily about the business of artistic commodities. As Gervais has noted, "copyright is 'a professional right': a right used by professionals against other professionals" (or was considered this way up until the 1990s)[5] "because of the need to organize the market for copyright works and the related financial flows among all the professionals involved."[6]

Several elements of this so-called copyright culture can be discerned. First, it subscribes to an individual rights discourse rooted in "liberal and neo-liberal assumptions," governed by notions of individualism, desert, exclusion, and action out of rational self-interest.[7] Within that framework,

---

2 T. Scassa, "Interests in the Balance" in M. Geist, ed., *In the Public Interest — The Future of Canadian Copyright Law* (Toronto: Irwin Law, 2005) at 41, www.irwinlaw.com/pages/content-commons/interests-in-the-balance.

3 On intellectual property metaphors see the "Myths & Metaphors of Private Law and Intellectual Property" series held at McGill University's Faculty of Law in 2009–2010, http://m-m.mcgill.ca/home_en.html; C.J. Craig, "The Canadian Public Domain: What, Where, and to What End?" (2010) 7 Can J L & Technology 221 at 221, http://ssrn.com/abstract=1567711; W. Patry, *Moral Panic and the Copyright Wars* (New York: OUP, 2009).

4 C. Rojek, *Cultural Studies* (Cambridge: Polity, 2007).

5 D. Gervais, "Use of Copyright Content on the Internet: Considerations on Excludability and Collective Licensing" in M. Geist, ed., *In the Public Interest — The Future of Canadian Copyright Law* (Toronto: Irwin Law, 2005) at 519, www.irwinlaw.com/pages/content-commons/use-of-copyright-content-on-the-internet--considerations-on-exludability-and-collective-licensing---daniel-gervais.

6 *Ibid.* at 525.

7 C.J. Craig, "Reconstructing the Author-Self: Some Feminist Lessons for Copyright Law" (2006–2007) 15 Am U J Gender Soc Pol'y & L 207 at 208. I leave open the question of whether the "copyright culture" tends to a particular gender, race, religious

community interest, inclusion, altruism and action out of a non-monetary interest play little role, as evidenced by Bill C-32's focus on digital locks, and its language of "providing rights-holders with recognition, remuneration and the ability to assert their rights."[8] Second, the sources of authority for the Canadian copyright culture are in statute and case law,[9] but written and unwritten industry practice and convention may help define these rules.[10] Third, Canada's copyright culture primarily protects economic rights rather than other types of rights that might inhere in works such as the *droit d'auteur* or moral rights of the continent.[11] Fourth, these individuated economic rights commodify the author's work and are separable from the author, preparing the work to be traded on a market in its entirety or in parts through licences and other agreements. Thus works may have many owners who can do different things with the work. Fifth, Canadian copyright legislation has always been preoccupied with managing the trade of copyright works from other countries across its borders[12] particularly given the size, cultural richness and shared language of the USA and Great Britain. This focus on goods moving across borders rather than within the country continues to the present particularly given the globalization of the culture industries.[13] It manifests itself in the principle that copyright should be as similar to its international counterparts as possible,[14] a fast-food (rather than, say, *terroir*) ethic of copyright law neat-

---

or socio-economic perspective: see, e.g., L. Murray, "Review of RiP: A Remix Manifesto, by Brett Gaylor" *Culture Machine* (June 2009), www.culturemachine.net/index.php/cm/article/view/372.

8 Bill C-32, *An Act to Amend the Copyright Act*, 3d Sess., 40th Parl., 2010, www2.parl.gc.ca/content/hoc/Bills/403/Government/C-32/C-32_1/C-32_1.PDF.

9 It is a truism that copyright is "a creature of statute": *Compo Co. v. Blue Crest Music Inc.*, [1980] 1 S.C.R. 357, at 373; *R. v. Stewart*, [1988] 1 S.C.R. 963; *Théberge v. Galerie d'Art du Petit Champlain Inc.*, 2002 SCC 34, LexUM at 5.

10 *CCH Canadian Ltd. v. Law Society of Upper Canada*, [2004] 1 S.C.R. 339 at 55; *Sillitoe v. McGraw-Hill Book Co. (UK)*, [1983] F.S.R. 545.

11 The Supreme Court of Canada confirms that "Canadian copyright law has traditionally been more concerned with economic than moral rights." This difficulty is attributed to the fact that "[u]nfortunately, the present text of the *Copyright Act* does little to help the promotion of the fusion of moral rights with the economic prerogatives of the law, since there is no comprehensive definition of copyright that embodies both": *Théberge*, above note 7 at 12. See also Y. Gendreau, "Moral Rights" in G.F. Henderson, ed., *Copyright and Confidential Information Law of Canada* (Scarborough: Carswell, 1994) at 171.

12 G.L. Parker, *The Beginnings of the Book Trade in Canada* (Toronto: UTP, 1985).

13 Rojek, above note 4 at 55.

14 "It is desirable, within the limits permitted by our own legislation, to harmonize our interpretation of copyright protection with other like-minded jurisdictions":

ly embodied by the preamble to Bill C-32 which states: "Whereas in the current digital era copyright protection is enhanced when countries adopt coordinated approaches, based on internationally recognized norms."[15] Those international norms are expressed in World Intellectual Property Organization treaty "norms." As a result, Canadian copyright law explicitly prioritizes international harmonization and trade over local texture.

Sixth, the "copyright culture" subscribes to the idea that copyright *does* something beyond merely give an author a copyright in a work, although what that something might be is unclear. According to courts and judges, copyright "balance[s] between promoting the public interest in the encouragement and dissemination of works of the arts and intellect and obtaining a just reward for the creator";[16] its role is "to encourage disclosure of works for the 'advancement of learning'";[17] and finally, copyright addresses the concern that "[e]xcessive control by holders of copyrights and other forms of intellectual property may unduly limit the ability of the public domain to incorporate and embellish creative innovation in the long-term interests of society as a whole."[18] As a mechanism to regulate behavior copyright is a blunt instrument; the benefits touted by lawmakers often fall flat.[19] Researchers have doubted that copyright provides a coherent incentive or reward to produce works[20] and have suggested that instead it restricts (rather than aids) the dissemination of works.[21] Regardless, the copyright culture subscribes to the idea that copyright in fact does something and what it does is sufficiently important to warrant sustaining and reforming copyright.

Théberge above note 9 at 6.

15 Bill C-32 above note 8.

16 *Théberge*, above note 9 at 30. See also *SOCAN v. CAIP*, 2004 SCC 45 CanLII at 132.

17 *Apple Computer, Inc. v. Mackintosh Computers Ltd.*, [1987] 1 F.C. 173 at 200 (T.D.).

18 *Theberge*, above note 9 at 32.

19 But then the idea that a statute could be a "mind-altering substance" is a particularly modern preoccupation: D. Manderson, "Fission and Fusion: From Improvisation to Formalism in Law and Music" (2010) 6(1) Critical Studies in Improvisation, http://journal.lib.uoguelph.ca/index.php/csieci/article/view/1167.

20 See works cited in Scassa above note 2 at 52–54. See also R. Towse, C. Handke, & P. Stepan, "The Economics of Copyright Law: A Stocktake of the Literature" (2008) 5(1) Review of Economic Research on Copyright Issues 22; W.M. Landes & R.A. Posner, *The Economic Structure of Intellectual Property Law* (Cambridge, Mass: Belknap Press, 2003) reflecting similar ideas.

21 R. Ku, J. Sun, & Y. Fan, "Does Copyright Law Promote Creativity? An Empirical Analysis of Copyright's Bounty" (2009) 62 Vanderbilt LR 1669. I am unable to locate equivalent empirical research on Canadian copyright law either supporting or refuting this hypothesis.

Understanding who, what and why the "copyright culture" represents makes it easier to put that notion of copyright in its place[22] as a limited representation of activities involving authorship and creative works in Canada. Bill C-32's proposed preamble[23] which refers to copyright law as both "a marketplace framework law and cultural policy instrument"[24] with goals of "promot[ing] culture and innovation, competition and investment in the Canadian economy"[25] supports a certain kind of creative production and omits activity that does not fit. Since the *Copyright Act* is not particularly adept at representing even major traditional Canadian cultures (French and various First Nations come to mind), it is clear that the Act does not represent more particular cultures and their notions and practices of copyright and artistic production, for example, folk musicians in Winnipeg, improvising playwrights in Toronto and independent documentary filmmakers in Halifax.[26]

This paper considers how a particular culture of artistic production interacts with the culture of copyright by examining, through observation and interview, an example of the former: Montreal's (principally Anglophone) independent music labels. This choice of methodology consciously avoids a strictly functionalist approach that considers how copyright's rules are translated or replicated through corollary informal norms, enforcement, penalties and sanctions in a particular occupational or group setting.[27] It allows for the possibility that there may be no corollary or functional equivalence between the two cultures[28] while attempting to avoid dualities or stereotypes that frequently arise like independent vs. major, local vs. international, authenticity vs. consumption. This study builds on the insights of earlier interviews of Canadian artists by Laura

---

22 Inspired by the title of a SSHRC Collaborative Standard Research Grant recently awarded to Laura Murray, Kirsty Robertson, and Tina Piper: "Putting Intellectual Property in its Place: Rights Discourses, Creative Labour, and the Everyday."

23 Bill C-32 above note 8. Note the current *Copyright Act* does not have a preamble.

24 *Ibid.*, preamble.

25 *Ibid.*

26 L. Murray & S. Trosow, *Canadian Copyright: A Citizen's Guide* (Toronto: Between the Lines, 2007).

27 See, for example, E. Fauchart & E.A. Von Hippel, "Norms-Based Intellectual Property Systems: The Case of French Chefs" (January 1, 2006) MIT Sloan Research Paper No. 4576-06, http://ssrn.com/abstract=881781; K. Raustiala and C.J. Sprigman, "The Piracy Paradox: Innovation and Intellectual Property in Fashion Design" (2006) 92 Virginia LR 1687, http://ssrn.com/abstract=878401.

28 In this case the copyright culture and the indie culture.

Murray and Kirsty Robertson,[29] and Michael Geist,[30] and is influenced by work in contemporary ethnomusicology.[31]

Montreal's independent music has been framed by Straw, Stahl, and others as a "cultural scene"[32] or "bohemia"[33] drawing on Bourdieu's ideas of *habitus*.[34] "Indie" has been held to refer to "a philosophy based on a proactive approach to one's career; retaining complete artistic control to maintain the integrity of one's art, regardless of record label affiliation."[35] It embraces a range of sounds (pop, post-pop, jazz, dance, punk, etc.) traditionally characterized by an oppositional taste culture. The indie ethos celebrates self-reliance, "DIY," creative autonomy from commercial restraint, innovation, geographic localism, increasing access to and participation in music-making, fostering strong music communities, operating on a small, local scale, and encouraging more "shared collaborative and diverse sonic cultures."[36] The indie scene is self-defining, thus when interviewing a label I would ask for recommendations of other labels within their scene and interview them. Interviewees ranged across the label spectrum, from artisanal labels like Fixture to professional, high-profile labels like Last Gang, all conducting business principally in Montreal. Most of the labels were run by musicians and former musicians, and as the study progressed, my definition of what constituted an indie label evolved to include some functions performed by festivals and venues.[37] I interviewed labels as opposed to artists or bands because labels are business-like en-

---

29 Discussed in L. Murray, "Copyright" in M. Raboy & J. Shtern, eds., *Media Divides: Communication Rights and the Right to Communicate in Canada* (Toronto: UBC Press, 2010) and L. Murray above note 26.

30 M. Geist, "Why Copyright: Canadian Voices on Copyright," www.michaelgeist.ca/content/view/3547/406.

31 For example, Wayne Marshall, "Routes, rap, reggae: Hearing the histories of hip-hop and reggae together," Ph.D. Thesis, University of Wisconsin, http://gradworks.umi.com/32/61/3261509.html.

32 W. Straw, "Cultural Scenes" (2004) 27(2) Society and Leisure 411; W. Straw, "In and around Canadian music" (2000) 35 J Canadian Studies 173.

33 G. Stahl, "Tracing Out an Anglo-bohemia: Musicmaking and Myth in Montreal" (2001) Public 20/21 99.

34 P. Bourdieu & L. Wacquant, *An Invitation to Reflexive Sociology* (Chicago: University of Chicago Press, 1992).

35 D. Cool, "What Is Indie?: A Look into the World of Independent Musicians" NFB (Canada 2006).

36 D. Hesmondhalgh, "Indie: The institutional politics and aesthetics of a popular music genre" (1999) 13 Cultural Studies 34.

37 At the time of this article's publication I have interviewed twenty people representing thirteen labels and two festivals and the study is ongoing.

terprises that manage the creative works of artists and thus have a direct interest in copyright-like type rights. Thus I envisioned that they would be "brokers on the boundary"[38] or translators, like technology transfer offices to the tech sector, and versed in indie and copyright culture respectively. My analysis is also framed by my own experience as a Board Member of PopMontreal, Montreal's indie music festival, since 2007.

The independent music sector is one of Canada's most vibrant cultural scenes, both creatively and financially. The Canadian Independent Record Production Association (CIRPA) estimates the market share of Canadian independent labels at approximately 14 percent of Canada's $800 million music industry.[39] According to the Nielsen Music 2009 Year End Music Industry Report for Canada, record companies other than the four major record multinationals[40] and their sub-distributed companies occupied a total market share of 17.93 percent for current and catalogue albums, representing a growth of 0.50 percent since 2008 and the third largest market share after Universal and Sony.[41] Tied with Sony and second only to Universal, independent record labels occupied a market share of 19.33 percent for current albums. While all majors save Universal occupied a greater market share for catalogue albums than current albums, independent companies' market share for catalogue albums was 4.20 percent less than its share for current albums. Independent labels also occupied the second largest market share for digital albums in 2009 at 20.93 percent and for digital tracks at 21.40 percent. Montreal-based independent record labels exist in a milieu where 95 percent of albums released by Québécois artists are produced locally (up from 10 percent in the 1980s).[42] Artists with roots in independent labels or music scenes have a strong presence in Canada's

---

38 D. Fisher & J. Atkinson-Grosjean, "Brokers on the boundary: Academy-industry liaison in Canadian universities" (October 2002) 44(3-4) Higher Education 449. See also M.J. Madison, "Notes on a Geography of Knowledge" (2009) 77 Fordham LR 2039, http://ssrn.com/abstract=1371701.

39 CIRPA, *Music Business Canada*, v. 2009 (2006).

40 EMI Music, Universal Music, Sony BMG Music, and Warner Music.

41 In contrast, all major record companies save Sony suffered diminishing market shares in 2009: *The Nielsen Company and Billboard's 2009 Canadian Industry Report* (2010), http://ca.nielsen.com/content/nielsen/en_ca/news/news_releases/2010/The_Nielsen_Company_and_Billboard_s_2009_Canadian_Industry_Report.html.

42 L'Association québécoise de l'industrie du disque, *Mémoire de l'Association québécoise de l'industrie du disque, du spectacle et de la vidéo (ADISQ) soumis au ministère des Finances dans le cadre des consultations prébudgétaires effectuées par le ministère des Finances en vue de la préparation du budget 2004–2005*, (2004) at 40.

major music awards such as the Junos[43] and the Polaris Prize,[44] and have gained a strong international reputation for the quality of music produced in Montreal.[45] These facts and numbers don't even begin to account for the impact of local music festivals either specializing in, or including, independent artists (in Montreal these include PopMontreal, Osheaga, Mutek, Suoni per il popolo, and JazzFest) that contribute millions of dollars to the local economy.

The Silver Mount Zion[46] quotation that starts this paper highlights how even starting a conversation between the copyright culture and labels in the independent music scene proved challenging. During my interviews many respondents strenuously avoided using terms such as "copyright," "products," "business models" or "branding" by opposing, avoiding, or redefining the terms. For example, the terms "label" or "business model" were replaced with "art project," the term "branding" replaced with "curation." To reflect this, I represent the labels' understanding that copyright (in its informal and formal instantiations) lives in narratives of threat, rumor, conversation, distance, foreignness, gossip, memory, curiosity or materiality and I proceed by considering the ways that copyright is known and observed "in reflection" rather than directly used or opposed. Well in view of legislation and legal rules that attempt to create a sense of certainty about what copyright is, I take as my starting point for reporting on the interviews that there is no such thing as "copyright." Rather a series of interactions define and constitute what copyright is in dialogue over particular practices, artifacts or preoccupations of the indie scene.

I did not identify an overall approach to or perspective on copyright rooted in a common philosophy other than a broad commitment to indie values. The nature of that commitment varies from label to label and is, in most cases, inchoate. In the context of broader social movements, protest against globalization is less compelling to the labels than it was in the 1990s and the rise in importance of the physical medium makes a

43 Including K'naan (Winner: Artist of the Year); Metric (Winner: Group of the Year); Joel Plaskett, Emily Haines, and James Shaw (Nominees: Songwriter of the Year); Bell Orchestre (Winner: Instrumental Album of the Year); Amy Millan and Patrick Watson (Nominees: Recording Package of the Year); and the categories Adult Alternative Album of the Year and Alternative Album of the Year.

44 An annual Canadian music award based on artistic merit regardless of genre, sales or record label: www.polaris.ca.

45 R. Perez, "The Next Big Scene: Montréal" *Spin* (February 2005).

46 A post-rock band in Montreal's independent music scene.

commitment to environmentalism challenging.[47] While many of the indie labels interviewed adopted an outsider ethos, except for Archipel this philosophy was not deliberately law-breaking or anti-authority. In selecting which artists to sign and support, labels tended to sign either those whose sound they loved or who were friends. Labels recounted supporting each other since each was viewed as creating a brand, sound or aesthetic that was distinct and not in direct competition with another. For most labels, pursuing that unique sound was critical to avoid diluting the quality of the label and remaining true to indie values.[48]

B. COPYRIGHT AS A MEMORY

The word "copyright" plays a supporting role in the operations of independent music labels in Montreal. A number of labels retain the publishing rights of their artists, most adopt a fifty-fifty split royalty sharing agreement, and a few do not express what they do in terms of "copyright," "rights," "royalty-sharing" or otherwise. The overwhelming sense from interviewees is that exploiting copyright is something separate and "legal" that labels do to create a diversified, low-maintenance income stream to

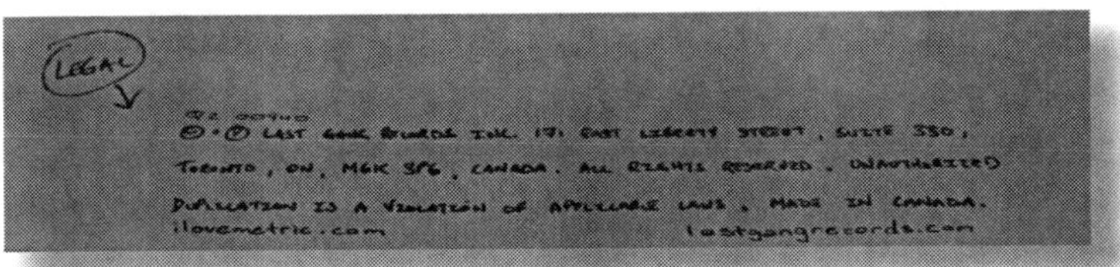

FIGURE 1: *A visual representation from Metric's (2007) "Grow Up and Blow Away" CD case of the interviewees' responses to discussions of copyright.*

provide a financial buffer and a back catalogue of publishing rights, a type of memory of past cultural production by the label (figure 1). Only one label (Archipel) signalled any interest in copyright policy reform: "I think Harper was trying to pass a bill about copyright or something . . . it really scared me . . ." and one interviewee outright rejected the value of copyright reform.[49] None expressed a view that copyright played any role in determining the kind of music the labels promoted or developed. The Canadian Independent Music Association (CIMA, formerly CIRPA)

---

47 Although value the physical object (e.g., a record or album art) could be seen as a reaffirmation of the importance of objects in a disposable consumer society

48 Interview respondent, 18 February 2010.

49 See second quotation that opens this paper.

refers to itself as "the collective voice of the English language, Canadian-owned independent sector of the Canadian sound recording industry."[50] It regards "effective efficient, relevant modern and updated copyright legislation as vital to the rights of its members" and the "slow pace" of copyright reform as a cause of the "decline in our businesses and the lack of progress in digital distribution."[51] CIMA represents a scene whose ethos oftentimes runs counter to the notion of an industry association. Only three interviewees were members of CIMA, none mentioned CIMA during the interviews or reflected its views on copyright reform. Perhaps some of the labels interviewed are too indie for an indie association to have much relevance to their activities.

C. COPYRIGHT AS GOSSIP, RUMOUR

Since anyone can automatically get copyright in a work, copyright embodies a sense of democratic access. The ability, however, to actually profit from that copyright (and the underlying work) is less certain and depends on the skill and industry of the creator in navigating the copyright system. In the independent music scene, a key mechanism for compensating artists for use of their copyrights is regarded with a great deal of skepticism: SOCAN, the Society of Composers, Authors and Music Publishers of Canada.[52] Here, copyright acts as gossip or unsubstantiated rumor of potential reward.

Artists can apply to SOCAN to collect fees for the public performance or broadcast of their work, without assigning the copyright in their work. SOCAN requires venues and anyone performing licensed music, either live or recorded, to purchase a SOCAN licence.[53] Most interviewees voiced strong objections to SOCAN, in particular due to a sense that SOCAN's procedures for determining how artists are rewarded by number of "plays" favour large, commercial artists and that independent artists rarely see any benefit.

Community radio and small venues, many of whom engage in avoidance or obstruction strategies, are seen as particular targets. Their strat-

50 Canadian Independent Music Association: www.cimamusic.ca.

51 Comments on Copyright Reform Submitted by the Canadian Independent Record Production Association (CIRPA), 13 September 2009, www.ic.gc.ca/eic/site/008.nsf/eng/02665.html.

52 SOCAN: www.socan.ca.

53 Those licences vary in price depending on the nature of the venue and the rates are set by the Copyright Board: www.socan.ca/jsp/en/pub/music_users/tariffs.jsp.

egies include listing friends' names repeatedly in playlists, refusing to pay for licences, and misrepresenting the nature of the venue or event to subvert SOCAN's system and avoid paying fees that they deem excessive and irrelevant. As one interviewee stated: ". . . I would say in defense of the establishments, they shouldn't be paying . . . . [A] bar would be paying for Céline Dion, Nickelback to get money, whereas out of principle, they know the people who we would support are not seeing a dime of it. So it's a tax." Because of the intimate, local nature of the indie music scene, the plight of venues affects labels that similarly see themselves as providing spaces for fostering and curating novel sonic experiences. SOCAN is seen to represent an industry-based copyright culture to which musicians in the independent music scene do not belong; Bill C-32's provisions to strengthen performer's rights are likely of limited interest given a regulatory regime that limits the remunerability of those rights.[54]

D. COPYRIGHT AS A DISTANT RELATIVE

Bill C-32's preamble states that the *Copyright Act* is a "cultural policy instrument." Grants are also regarded as a critical component of Canada's cultural policy framework.[55] In this respect Canada differs from the US where labels and their artists have survived largely without any grant support, or public healthcare (which is regarded by some as a form of arts subsidy).[56] In part, Canada has had to adopt a robust granting scheme because of its proximity to the US and "its vast, low-priced cultural output," as well as because of its small population, large territory, two major linguistic groups and "the tension between economic and cultural imperatives."[57] While a detailed comparison of US and Canadian cultural subsidy is beyond the scope of this paper, copyright in Canada probably means something different in relation to independent music works than it does in the US (and other nations with varied forms of cultural subsidy) because of the important role played by grants. More pointedly, this study suggests that the grants regime may play a more prominent role

54 See, in particular, s. 17.

55 J. Jackson & R. Lemieux, "The Arts and Canada's Cultural Policy," www2.parl.gc.ca/Content/LOP/ResearchPublications/933-e.htm#4.%20Department-t.

56 M. Hogan, "What's the Matter with Sweden?" *Pitchfork*, http://pitchfork.com/features/articles/7776-whats-the-matter-with-sweden/. This article is the most recent and comprehensive comparison of Canada's grants system for independent music to other jurisdictions.

57 Jackson & Lemieux, above note 55; *ibid*.

than copyright in shaping the business models and creative decisions of independent music labels in Canada.

In contrast to responses about copyright, label interviewees believed that grants from federal, provincial and private agencies were a significant predictor of or influence on the creative and business choices of the labels. There was a prevailing sense amongst the interviewees that the real potential for income is provided by grants (and the sale of tangible products, to be discussed later). I identified three principle types of relationship between grantor and grantee, with overlaps between them. First, the relationship between grantor and grantee was, in some cases, seen as reciprocal as opposed to unidirectional, a type of partnership between the granting agencies and the label where label success promoted the funding agency. In other cases, the relationship was regarded as one of dependence, a relationship from which labels could ideally gain independence at any stage, emphasizing values of self-reliance.[58] Finally, a third type of relationship regarded grants as cementing a type of gift exchange or network of patronage or support.[59] From a less positive perspective, grants can be perceived as "mysterious" with obscure criteria, "[s]o right now, the best support I've seen is just VISA and MasterCard, they've been doing wonders for me."[60] The relationship between grantor and grantee was often personal and interviewees frequently spoke of their dealings with individuals at granting agencies. Grant-getting is also a way to maintain the divide between commercial production (or sponsorship) and creative production.[61] Some interviewees distinguished grants that were arts-based (e.g., Canada Council), from those that were more industry-based (e.g., FACTOR), and agencies somewhere in-between (e.g., SODEC).[62] There was a perception that grants were growing on "the industry side. And there's less and less on the arts side."[63]

---

58 "Because it doesn't make sense to survive off the back of something else. You're still a business. If we wanted to be a not-for-profit organization we could be, but we're not" (interview respondent, 2 November 2009).

59 "[I]t is like a mentoring aspect . . . you can kind of share the money in your community" (Fixture interview, 5 April 2010).

60 Archipel interview, 1 April 2010.

61 Burton interview, 26 May 2010.

62 *Ibid.*

63 Burton interview 26 May 2010.

© & ℗ 2009 Metric Productions Inc., Under exclusive license to Last Gang Records - 171, Eas
All rights reserved. Unauthorized duplication is a violation of applicable laws. Made in Canada.
We acknowledge the financial support of the Government of Canada through the Department o
and of Canada's Radio Broadcasters. Canada FACTOR

FIGURE 2: *Grants and copyright, side by side on Metric's (2009) "Fantasies" CD case.*

The types of choices influenced by grants included the nationality of artists to sign, the time when albums are released, where to set up residency, international partnerships,[64] how to structure the business, whether the label makes a profit, continues or survives, what type and how much promotion to pursue,[65] what types of sales targets to pursue and where to focus energy (on grant writing), what one interviewee referred to as jumping through the "flaming hoops." The significance of grants is represented visually on the CD cases produced by the labels where in addition to a sign asserting the label's copyright, equivalent physical space is given to reflecting the contributions of various granting agencies (figure 2). Like the copyright system, there was a sense that grants could be "gamed" and that in fact entire corporate structures had been established in a particular form to take advantage of granting schemes.[66] The grants-system, like copyright, generates its own rent-seeking behaviour. The interviews suggested that a grant culture privileges skills like post-secondary education, planning, managerialism and adeptness at grant writing, as well as networking particularly if there is a process of peer review. Copyright seems to be a distant relative to the personal, repeated and sometimes collaborative relationships of labels with granting agencies. More broadly, considering the relationship between the copyright and indie cultures suggests a renewed role for a cultural economics that incorporates grants into a copyright *terroir*.[67]

---

64 You see it internationally as well, we've had people in various countries around the world saying, 'Look, is there a way we could set something up together?' . . . so we could take advantage of the grants" (Secret City interview, 2 November 2009).

65 "We probably wouldn't have spent any of that money if it wasn't for the grants . . . That's the neat thing about it, it really does mitigate your risk . . ." (interview respondent, 2 November 2009).

66 "You also find other types of guys who are just really good at getting government money. We probably got the best track record of grabbing money of any company." (Interview respondent.)

67 Ruth Towse has noted the absence of a discussion about copyright in the context of cultural economics or subsidy and the important role each plays in relation to

E. COPYRIGHT AS A FOREIGN LANGUAGE

An important tool of copyright culture is the licence. A licence or contract is the legal instrument that allows the copyright-holder (generally the creator of the work) to assign or permit others to reproduce or otherwise use copyrighted works in ways that might not be permitted by copyright. Licences have traditionally been used to limit the downstream rights of licence-holders (for example, through shrink-wrap licences) but they have also been developed by the open source software community to enable uses of copyrighted works through "open" licensing.

Licences are key to business practices in the new music industry; artists and/or labels may individually or collectively licence music to third parties for use in movies, compilations, public performances, recordings, video games, ringtones and numerous other uses. Artists may also licence or assign all or particular rights in their works to labels; the "old" music industry major label model was to sign an exclusive recording contract with an artist who would receive royalties and an advance that would generally have to be paid back. The label would manage the recording, marketing and rights of the artist who would generally assign all their rights in a recording and the underlying composition to the label.

The use of contracts and licences between artists and independent music labels, however, has a storied history. Famous US and UK indie labels Rough Trade, Mute, Factory, Touch and Go and others pioneered the "handshake" deal, signing artists on a release by release basis, licensing for limited uses with rights reverting to the artist, pursuing fifty-fifty royalty splits (as opposed to percentage royalties, resulting in greater profits for artists) and eschewing the written contract in favour of musician-centered verbal agreements.[68]

The labels I interviewed subscribed to this indie philosophy, either intentionally or inadvertently reflecting the values of earlier US and UK indie labels. These labels adopted a range of approaches: they did not use formal written agreements, had only recently created these kinds of agreements as a result of receiving funding from a granting agency, or relied on email chains of correspondence. Sharing contractual templates was common.[69]

---

the other: R. Towse, "Why has cultural economics ignored copyright?" (2008) 32 J Cultural Economics 243.

68 R. Strachan, "Do-It-Yourself: Industry, Ideology, Aesthetics and Micro Independent Record Labels in the UK" (2003), PhD thesis, University of Liverpool at 11.

69 Only one label saw drafting particular contracts as important to their self-identity as a label: "Let's develop our own . . . contract from the ground up, and constantly

In the words of one smaller label, Fixture, a contract would "feel like too much. It'd feel like an overkill . . . . We could, but what would it say? What would we put on a contract?"[70] Agreements tended to be entered into on an *ad hoc* basis, with arrangements facilitated by one's reputation in the indie scene and relationships of trust based on friendship or shared musical interest.[71] A recurring theme throughout the interviews was articulated well by one interviewee who said "we've never, through contractual powers, forced an artist to do something that they don't want to do. We don't ever operate on those terms. That's definitely not part of our philosophy." As a result, according to Don Wilkie from Constellation, "[p]robably more importantly, not having a legal document meant that you actually had to work with people in ways that developed trust, that created relationships where the door was always open to have whatever conversations were necessary to resolve whatever might come up, and that you would actually get to know people and develop relationships that legal documents probably very often stand in the way of, because [then] everybody just falls back to what they understand to be the structure of the relationship."[72]

The interviews suggest that a commitment to the relationship between the artist and the label rather than a contractual agreement frames the encounter; in fact, the sense was that a contractual agreement would release the parties from engaging and listening to one another and that this would be detrimental to the artistic direction of the artist, the label and the scene or community within which they are embedded. The unwillingness to sign contracts highlights how the copyright culture's assumptions about contracting labour to produce works contrasts with the indie culture's ways of creating music. As brokers on the boundary, the indie label interviewees basically understood (to varying degrees) the notion of a work as a commodifiable product, rights to which can be further sub-divided and licensed exclusively or non-exclusively to third parties. But they also understood that using a contract to deal with artists, for many of whom licensing works is like a foreign language, was not a useful approach.

---

have them evolve, and hopefully in a couple years' time we'll have these things that really reflect what we do and what we want." (Interview respondent, 2 November 2009).

70 Fixture interview, 5 April 2010.

71 Similar observations have been made by Strachan, above note 68 at 116.

72 Constellation interview, 17 November 2009.

F. COPYRIGHT AS A CURIOSITY

Licensing regimes like Creative Commons (CC)[73] introduce creators to managing their works through CC licences, a written contract between a user and the licensor. CC generates a legal document to allow copyright-holders to permit uses of their works that would not be otherwise permitted by adhering to the strict terms of the *Copyright Act*. An interesting feature of the CC licence is the so-called Share-Alike (SA) provision which, if the licensor stipulates, requires that any person who creates a work derived from the author's work has to licence it under the same conditions. This "viral" copy-left provision embodies an aspiration to create a community of creators who adhere to the CC licence. SA, and the CC organization generally, have fostered the creation of specialized communities of digital remix artists,[74] photographers,[75] and others. Thus the CC licence mediates between a culture of creative work and the copyright culture, encoding and representing the activity of the licensor in legal form to others who might want to use the work in some other social or cultural setting.[76]

As a co-Project Lead for Creative Commons Canada, I had observed low uptake of CC licences amongst Canadian creator communities[77] and particularly low uptake of the licences in the indie scene. This surprised me as indie artists expressed great interest in CC and the values expressed by CC overlap with those I identified in interviewing independent music labels: a commitment to sharing creative works on open terms, the importance of informal social bonds, collaboration, attribution, group reputation and credibility validated by a group of fellow practitioners, and support for amateur art that thrives on exposure when expectations of financial profit are limited. Despite all this there was limited familiarity with and no uptake of CC amongst the labels that I interviewed except for one label, Archipel, which produces electronic music, and has based its business model largely on CC licences. The other independent labels interviewed had either not heard of CC or if they had heard of it, had decided not to further investigate using the licences. As one respondent put it:

---

73 See www.creativecommons.org.

74 ccMixter: www.ccmixter.org.

75 Flickr: www.flickr.com.

76 Madison above note 38 at 2048.

77 In June 2009, a Google search yielded 5,020 users of the Canadian BY 2.5 licence, 2150 users of the BY-SA licence, and 891 users of the BY-NC-SA. The search was performed on the following terms: http://creativecommons.org/licenses/by/2.5/ca; http://creativecommons.org/licenses/by-sa/2.5/ca; http://creativecommons.org/licenses/by-nc-sa/2.5/ca.

> Q: [D]o people talk about Creative Commons in your business?
>
> R: Almost never [do people talk about CC in our business]. There was one point where someone from Creative Commons . . . had approached us to ask if we would be open to putting some stuff out under a Creative Commons licence, but he was never able to even express why it would in our interest to do so.

There are two reasons why CC licences may not be compelling to an indie label. First, given that many of the labels (as discussed previously) do not use formal written agreements or contracts to structure their relationships with artists, it is reasonable to expect that those parties might not think to use a licence to structure their relationships with interested strangers, particularly fans. These labels, however, are unconcerned about licensing synch or publishing rights to third parties. Thus relationships between various parties in this ecosystem could be regarded alternately as sacred (between some labels, the artist and the fan) and profane (with commercial third parties). As discussed previously, the "sacred" relationships avoid using written contracts unless required to do so by a grant.

Second, CC licences do not mediate between the label (or artist) and the community. In the case of small labels the circle of people who might listen to an album is either geographically or relationally confined such that the label interviewees expected that most of the music they release will be listened to by friends and the occasional stranger buying music off a digital download service after going to a show. Thus the dissemination of music from these labels largely depends on a physical link made through performance, friendship or physical community perceived of as inextricably linked to the quality of the music and the values of indie music-making, as opposed to through an Internet community regulated in a "legal" way with liberal copyright terms as the governing parameter of the relationship. When parties barely understand or engage with copyright, using that right as the basis of structuring collaborations seems unlikely. In this context a CC licence is not seen as a useful means of signalling appropriate behaviour or a desire to form community through collaborations.[78]

These observations cohere with those who have studied the characteristics of the CC community. While not addressing Canadian licensees, Kim's 2007 study suggested that the community of CC users is closely related to

78 Much of this analysis applies in the case of larger indie labels where the picture is further complicated by the normative parameters of a robust culture of 'free' (discussed in the next section).

the computer and Internet use. Her study found that the most common occupations of CC licensors were computer professionals (28.6 percent of the survey participants), students (18.2 percent), artists (13.6 percent), and educators (9.3 percent), a high proportion of which were those involved professionally or occupationally with computers.[79] Further, Kim highlighted how on a scale of one to five, where five means "very experienced," the average CC licensor rated their computer ability as 4.74. I doubt that similar results would be found in the indie music community, whether amongst fans, artists or labels. Meanwhile, in a separate study, Todosichuck found that the top five reasons users on the music site Jamendo.com claimed to use CC licences on their musical works, in order of significance, were to share ("music is culture and should be free and non-commercial"); to facilitate distribution and exposure; to manage and protect music with copyright; to make a political statement ("against major labels and/or for CC"); and because CC licences are popular, easy to access and use.[80] While these responses have notable limitations[81] they do suggest that using CC licences is both self-focused (three of the five reasons are about managing copyright and a personal career) and altruistic.

In contrast with the bulk of indie labels, Archipel, which bases its business model on CC perceived itself as rooted primarily in an Internet community and was devoted exclusively to electronic music. Consistent with Kim's results, CC licences make sense for Archipel because fans primarily engage with music on the internet with a high degree of computer literacy—in contrast to the traditional indie scene. It became clear that Archipel does not use CC licences so much as a legal document but as a brand. The label's president had no specific understanding of how the licences operate legally. In his words: "I always felt [CC] was esoteric—even after ten years I'm not too sure how it works exactly." But the licences are valuable for their signaling function to fans, many of whom adopt an anti-corporate stance towards music and its commercialization. CC licences also allow Archipel to participate in a "huge community of people that will

79 M. Kim, "The Creative Commons and copyright protection in the digital era: Uses of Creative Commons licenses" (2007) 13(1) Journal of Computer-Mediated Communication article 10, http://jcmc.indiana.edu/vol13/issue1/kim.html.

80 M. Todosichuk, "Understanding Musical Artists' Motivation to Share Creative Commons Licensed Musical Works: Applying Social Capital and Social Cognitive Theory" (2009) Master's Thesis, http://etdncku.lib.ncku.edu.tw/ETD-db/ETD-search/view_etd?URN=etd-0719109-173414, at 42. At page 45 he discusses the strengths and weaknesses of his conclusions.

81 *Ibid* at 45.

be supporting and helping," referring to CC advocates.[82] Otherwise, the label did not use formal written contracts: "in 95 percent of releases, we just casually talk about what we need, what we want, what would be good for both of us" regarding the need for such contracts as a sign of mistrust, dishonesty or sharp practice.[83]

Archipel is one example that demonstrates that a label does not have to use contracts in its business practices to use CC licences with its fans. Perhaps a label that does not believe in using written contracts will be more likely to use CC licences as branding; more research would be required to demonstrate this. Archipel also saw the CC licences as playing a distinct role in constituting a community. The label was named Archipel because "[t]hat's how we felt: islands in the middle of the sea, not attached to anything. My goal with the label when I started . . . was: just prove we can reach people in other ways, and create a community of people that feel a bit isolated." Thus Archipel's motives for using CC licences reflect the hybrid motivations suggested by Todosichuk's study.

To conclude, for CC licences to be useful ideally they need to mediate between a licensor and others with whom the primary relationship is a virtual one over the Internet. Musicians and labels in the Montreal indie scene do want to connect with strangers but they are a certain kind of stranger — one who can acquire the music commodity online, but who is more richly drawn in by the accoutrements of the entire enterprise: the artful package, the notification by poster, the role-playing of fans in appropriate costume, the performance in a controversial, quirky or historic space where a nuanced type of sharing and free exchange occurs. It remains to be seen whether Bill C-32's expansion of fair dealing to include education, parody and satire will play much of a role in a culture where referencing to others within the scene is part of the definition of the scene.[84] The premise on which a movement like CC is built, that "the default copyright laws of most countries, with their 'lock up the silverware' approach, do not reflect the reality of a 'cut and paste' culture that relies on the ability to manipulate existing material for creation and whose principle measure of success is hits counted" is premised on the idea of an a-local, a-physical online community (even if the licences are ported to national jurisdictions).[85]

---

82 Archipel interview, 1 April 2010.

83 *Ibid.*

84 Section 29.

85 J. Coates, "Creative Commons — The Next Generation: Creative Commons licence use five years on" (March 2007) 4(1) Script-ed 73, http://www.law.ed.ac.uk/ahrc/script-ed/vol4-1/coates.pdf.

CC borrows the assumptions of the "copyright culture": that an MP3 can be divorced from its context and transported across boundaries, which in fact it can, but only for a subset of fans within the indie scene. Indie music is ideally experienced as real, present and tangible, thus the idea of licensing to create an online community is largely unhelpful and the use of copyright as a relationship builder, curious.

G. COPYRIGHT AS A CURRENCY

Despite limited interest in CC, Canadian indie labels exist within a robust culture of "free."[86] As Ian Ilavsky from Constellation put it, free has been good to independent labels:

> [I]ndie labels [were] by [and] large just laughing, maybe not all the way to the bank, but we understood there were hundreds of thousands of music fans who were becoming way more musically literate as a result of the massive expansion of their ability to hear stuff for free. It was only helping drive an awareness of all these micro-producers, and this massive diversity of music. It was also informing the way the musicians themselves were making stuff, because they had so many more reference points.

He noted subsequently, however, that "I think [free downloading is] absolutely, clearly hindering the record label business now, whether you're small or large."[87]

Without exception, all of the labels we spoke to engaged in practices like giving away a popular track for free and providing promotional copies of CDs or vinyl (demonstrated as well by the considerable collection of CDs and vinyl I have accumulated during the study). As one respondent put it, "[t]here's always some type of giveaway at one point" and free tracks are used as a "promotional vehicle." Smaller labels tended even more towards free, gifting much of their music since they appreciated that it had lower market value and viewed P2P networks as important complements to their business. Conor Prendergast from Fixture even expressed difficulty at asking people to pay for CDs or music as expressed in this description: "Even at shows, I think, I just tend to be like, well, I might be able to sell this person a CD, but they just told me they liked the show, so I mean — I'll

86 Mostly in the sense of free beer not just freedom.

87 Ian Ilavsky, Constellation interview, 17 November 2009.

just give them a CD."[88] The interviews suggested that the physical artifact or performance will continue to be an important aspect of the independent music experience and that the MP3 exists as an adjunct to (rather than replacement for) this experience.

The interviewees were realistic about the fact that fans downloaded music for free and expected that their music would be exchanged for free, with some potential benefits, for example "[w]e just realized that our first album had been ripped and put on somewhere recently, which I was pretty flattered by."[89] Benefits of "free" included getting good press, blog attention, radio play and whetting fans' appetite for a new album, provided the track is appropriately labelled with the Canadian label's name. As one interviewee described:

> At one time, there's gonna be a leak and the music's gonna get out there . . . At one point in time it's going to leak; even if you're not the source and you've watermarked, it's almost inevitably going to happen. I look at it . . . as, a certain amount of leakage will ultimately be used to propel or drive your marketing . . . But I guess I look at that in a glass half full kind of way, and say that, "Well, people are sharing it—which is a good thing, because it breathes this real organic driver or it fuels this organic genuine love for the music, that's it's getting out there. This kind of person-to-person feel is really a legit and sometimes creative way to establish a certain profile or get it a certain amount of exposure.

No interviewee suggested curtailing free access to music, even if it is cutting into their profits, and those who spoke of them thought that digital locks were ineffective to pursue, raising serious practical objections to the Canadian government's efforts through Bill C-32 to protect digital locks.

Another aspect of the culture of free was that those who worked for labels were barely remunerated for the work that they performed, which for most is a labour of love. "We're doing a pile of stuff for free."[90] As a result, other aspects of interpersonal relationships increased in importance, particularly the importance of open collaboration and communication. "Since . . . everything is pretty much based around things being free, where people put importance is in communication. So if a label doesn't communicate, doesn't inform what's going on, doesn't follow up with things, then

88 Connor Prendergast, Fixture interview, 5 April 2010.

89 *Ibid.*

90 Don Wilkie, Constellation interview, 17 November 2009.

people get bored, and they get to feel uncomfortable."[91] As Tessa Smith from Fixture described, "[i]n order to bring someone into what we're doing, we need to become friends with them and build a certain amount of trust, or professional trust, with them. We can't really work with someone who's like a stranger. Or they very quickly become not a stranger when we're working with them."[92] As the labels reported, in many cases their most valuable currency is trust and communication.

H. COPYRIGHT AS OBJECT

Underpinning this study is the theme that intangible music plays a limited role in an indie scene that privileges the tangible, a topic that I will address briefly in concluding this paper. In this scene, intangibles become tangible as soon as possible, whether through records, posters, shows, t-shirts, artwork, events in venues or relationships. Interviewees generally veered toward talking about copyright as a material object (the physical object that fixes the work), another conversation entirely from the copyright culture's discussion of the legal interest in an MP3, digital downloads, and revenue streams.[93] This focus is justified by their bottom-line: physical sales form the bulk of revenues of many of the interviewees' labels, although it is unclear whether physical sales are so significant because they cohere with community values or because labels have fostered physical objects which generate more revenue. As Ilavsky from Constellation remarks, "[t]here for sure is a subset of the music consuming public that maybe, at least for now, is a little bit tired of the ephemeral nature of downloading music and not having an object." Without exception, the labels interviewed had issued CDs with artistic (often hand-crafted) cover art or package design and many predict that this aspect of their business will grow, outpacing—if it hasn't already—digital music sales. Some labels explicitly experiment with format, issuing music on cassettes and other historic formats that preserve sonic quality.

A recent debate over postering in Montreal has cemented the links between the intangible and the physical, suggesting that posters play a critical role in "connect[ing] communities, bring[ing] ideas and images to

91 Archipel interview, 1 April 2010.

92 Fixture interview, 5 April 2010.

93 Madison, above note 38 at 2071. He argues that the "property" in copyright exists on three levels: the legal interest (the copyright), the intellectual property work (the song), and the physical object that fixes it to a physical entity (the MP3, CD).

light."[94] Many institutions of the independent music scene in Montreal (labels, venues, festivals, independent artists) have recently received steep fines for postering. For one, typically indie, coalition[95] these have totaled over $40,000. Postering is a critical communication medium; given that their audience is generally local to a neighbourhood, many of these groups deliberately sit outside a MySpace Internet world. For some, up to 50 percent of their attendees arrive because of posters they've seen in their neighbourhood; postering also promises vast advertising potential.[96] To borrow from copyright culture talk, posters mediate between the creative work and the public's interest in accessing it by providing information that it exists in the first place. In a scene where culture is cheap and personal, the goal is often to create a relationship with an audience rather than an income stream. That mediation happens through a claim to attention in a physical space rather than a property right in an object that's exchanged. As a result, strategies resisting postering fines have focused on claims to freedom of expression under section 2 of the *Charter*.

I. CONCLUSION

This study has related the copyright culture embodied by Bill C-32 to the culture of Montreal's independent music scene to investigate how copyright is engaged with by one of Canada's most vibrant creative communities. The study has explored how copyright is an interest that may support the label in the future, a rumor rather than a reality through compensation by SOCAN, a distant relation compared to labels' familiarity with granting agencies, a language unfamiliar in certain relationships, a currency of exchange foreign to a community embedded in networks of free and sharing and is juxtaposed against the indie community's commitment to the physical. It would be worth continuing to examine the role that copyright plays within and beyond the indie scene. Further in-depth examination of other Canadian cultural scenes could provide useful comparisons, trends or data to understand the roles that copyright plays outside the "copyright culture"

---

94 K. Muir on the C.O.L.L.E. website, http://collemontreal.org/wp-content/uploads/2010/05/COLLE-quotes.pdf

95 The groups are Drawn & Quarterly, Semprini Records, the Fringe Festival, PopMontreal, and Casa del Popolo. The group has estimated that in one month, they post almost 6,000 posters.

96 As Hilary Leftick, Executive Producer of PopMontreal Music Festival argues: "If I poster on Yonge Street in Toronto, it's possible that 60,000 people will learn about my show."

consensus that fills the discourse of law reform. So long as copyright reform focuses primarily on individualistic, exclusive rights shaped by translating and harmonizing domestic law to international rules its claims to support "creativity and innovation" or provide a "cultural policy instrument"[97] will remain overbroad and a limited representation of cultural life.

97 Bill C-32, above note 8.

CHAPTER FIFTEEN

User-Generated Content and Music File-Sharing:

A Look at Some of the More Interesting Aspects of Bill C-32

Daniel Gervais*

This chapter is not intended as an update, but rather as an addendum to my chapter in Professor Geist's previous book on Canadian copyright reform.[1] In that chapter,[2] I suggested that the upcoming reform should focus on excludability of Internet-based uses, that is the exercise of exclusive copyright to prevent online uses of copyright material. I also suggested that this excludability was technologically problematic. Users empowered by social norms and ever-changing technological tools going well beyond peer-to-peer software,[3] and even relying on the old

* The author gratefully acknowledges the comments and insights from the editor, Professor Michael Geist, the anonymous peer-reviewer, Mr. Mario Bouchard, and Ms Tanya Woods.

1 See Michael Geist, ed., *In the Public Interest* (Toronto: Irwin Law, 2005), www.irwinlaw.com/store/product/120/in-the-public-interest — the-future-of-canadian-copyright-law.

2 Daniel Gervais, "Rethinking Excludability: Use of Internet-Based Content," in *ibid.* at 517, www.irwinlaw.com/pages/content-commons/use-of-copyright-content-on-the-internet--considerations-on-exludability-and-collective-licensing---daniel-gervais.

3 See Richard Abbott "The Reality Of Modern File Sharing" (2009) 13:5 J. Internet L. 3. This technology-focused analysis concludes as follows:

> Do not listen to anyone pitching a product, service, or legal strategy purporting to eliminate file sharing. The sharing of files via hosting services is far more complex than peer-to-peer networking, and both evolve constantly. The next steps are already being taken. Proxy schemes are working protect uploaders,

USENET,[4] circumvent technological protection measures (TPMs), and ultimately access millions of MP3s. Proxies and anonymous clients make the activity increasingly hard to detect and track.[5] Finding more intrusive ways to track Internet usage is not just a technological challenge; it also pits copyright against other rights, including users' privacy rights and interests. It made sense in the context of that chapter to suggest that more online uses should be permitted (and licensed), where appropriate using a collective model providing licensed access to a repertory of works or other protected subject matter.[6] In this chapter I return to the issue of music file-sharing to see how much progress we have made.

Another aspect of online use that deserves special attention is reuse, especially to create so-called user-generated content.[7] On this front, Bill C-32 would impose a transformative use exemption (already dubbed the "YouTube" exception). Whether an exemption or a license is a better solution depends on whether one thinks that sites such as YouTube (or its owner, Google, Inc.) should pay right holders for use, of their content, or whether it should be free. The current focus of right holders is on removal of the content pursuant to a notification to the host site. As a normative matter, it makes sense to allow this aspect of the Internet to flourish by using *ex post* control (such as the proposed notice and notice[8]) and providing safe harbours, rather than ban the activity completely. Canadians want their children to be fully computer and web-literate and participate in the "remix culture." They do not want them to be creative only by proxy.

> encryption protocols are masking files from inspection, and the dark market of anonymous payment schemes allow sharers to avoid leaving paper trails."

Ibid. at 8.

4 Sascha Segan, "R.I.P Usenet: 1980–2008" *PCMag* (31 June 2008), www.pcmag.com/article2/0,2817,2326849,00.asp.

5 See *ibid.* and mIRC, www.mirc.com; Mark H. Wittow & Daniel J. Buller, "Cloud Computing: Emerging Legal Issues for Access to Data, Anywhere, Anytime" (2010), 14:1 J. Internet L. 1. According a recent IFPI (International Federation of the Phonographic Industry) report, "Although P2P file-sharing remains the most damaging form of piracy due to the volume of files shared by users, the last two years have seen a sharp rise in non-P2P piracy . . . ." IFPI, *Digital Music Report 2010: Music how, when, where you want it*, http://www.ifpi.org/content/library/DMR2010.pdf at 19 [*IFPI Report*]. Unless indicated otherwise, all hyperlinks in this chapter were last accessed on 10 July 2010.

6 The *Copyright Act* protects musical, dramatic, artistic and literary works, but also protects two other "subject matters", namely musical performances and sound recordings. *Copyright Act*, R.S.C. 1985, c. C-42 [*Copyright Act*].

7 I suggest a definition at the beginning of Part B below.

8 Bill C-32, *Copyright Modernization Act*, 3d Sess., 40th Parl., 2010, cl. 47 (ss. 41.25, 41.26).

The proposed "transformative work" exemption should achieve this purpose.

In the following pages, I take an in-depth look at the flawed approach in the Bill to the file-sharing problem, and at possible issues with the UGC exception.

A. FILE-SHARING

1) The File-sharing Phenomenon

In terms of realistic technological options, it seems difficult to "stop the Internet," a network using packet switching technology and designed by the United States Department of Defense's Advanced Research Projects Agency (ARPA) to be virtually unstoppable. From a business standpoint, maximizing access also makes sense in terms of generating revenue for creators and copyright industries.[9] Indeed, despite harsh penalties available against file sharers in the United States since the entry into force of the *Digital Millennium Copyright Act* in 1998, implementing the 1996 *WIPO Copyright Treaty* (WCT) and the *WIPO Performances and Phonograms Treaty* (WPPT), music file-sharing has not stopped, far from it.[10] Even in markets where dramatic action made a significant dent in unauthorized file-sharing, numbers are creeping back up. Paid single downloads are not enough to make up for the drop in revenues.[11] Meanwhile, the size of the record-

---

9 Presumably, money is made by maximizing authorized uses, not minimizing unauthorized uses.

10 There is still hope, however, that the lawsuits will eventually deter file-sharing. Professor Henslee notes for instance that "[w]hile the RIAA suits have not dramatically curtailed illegal downloading, more stories about the large damages accessed Jammie Thomas will begin to deter illegal downloading." William Henslee, "Money For Nothing And Music For Free? Why The RIAA Should Continue To Sue Illegal File-Sharers" (2009), 9 J. Marshall Rev. Intell. Prop. L. 1.

11 See Ethan Smith, "Sales of Music, Long in Decline, Plunge Sharply" *Wall Street Journal* (21 March 2007), http://online.wsj.com/article_email/SB117444575607043728-lMyQjAxMDE3NzIoMTQyNDE1Wj.html.This article notes that "[t]he sharp slide in sales of CDs, which still account for more than 85 percent of music sold, has far eclipsed the growth in sales of digital downloads, which were supposed to have been the industry's salvation."

The *IFPI Report* notes that for instance that "Research by GfK in June 2009 found that 60 per cent of infringing file-sharers had stopped or reduced their activity as a result of the introduction of the IPRED law. However, piracy levels in Sweden are believed to have risen again since then, underlining the need for sustained enforcement and ISP cooperation." *IFPI Report*, above note 5 at 27.

ing industry has been reduced by almost half.[12] In Canada, the industry reported an overall drop of 9 percent from 2007 to 2008, with a 14 percent decline in CD sales obviously not compensated by a 65 percent increase in paid downloads.[13]

The recording industry, used to a model predicated mostly on the sale of physical objects (CDs) or other "units"[14] with *supporting* income streams from live performances (concerts), broadcasting, merchandising revenue, and even private copying levies now finds itself with only those "supporting "income streams, as CD sales are dwindling. The new stream of individual digital downloads probably will never compensate for lost carrier sales.

Looking at this empirical picture, if the purpose of copyright law is to help organize markets to allow those who create and disseminate new music (subject to market forces) to make a living, then it has failed. Put differently, if even successful songwriters and performers (measured by the number of people who listen to their music) cannot live from their work, then I suggest that the system is broken. It also has profound implications for Canadian culture, as only creators successful in much larger markets (such as the United States) will survive, and it is their music that Canadians will be able to download.

As most readers know quite well, the transfer of music files, often in unprotected MP3 format, among Internet users began with the centralized system called Napster, the first generation of file-transfer software designed essentially for musical files. The collapse of Napster was facilitated, to a great extent, by its easily localizable and controllable character.[15]

---

12 From $38.6 billion in 1999 to $27.5 billion in 2008, according to IFPI, as reported at http://en.wikipedia.org/wiki/Music_industry. A 2009 report shows global trade revenues (a subset of total revenues) down 7.2 percent to US$17 billion. Physical sales fell by 12.7 percent globally while digital music sales rose by 9.2 percent to US$4.3 billion. In the US, digital sales account for nearly half—43 percent—of the recorded music market. Adjusted for inflation, the drop is dramatic. Will iTunes compensate? The 2009 number (US$4.3 billion, up 12 percent in 2009 over 2008, is only approximately 10 percent of global 1999 revenues. See *IFPI Report*, above note 5 at 10 and www.ifpi.org/content/section_news/20100428.html.

13 See "Statistics," The Canadian Recording Industry Association, www.cria.ca/stats.php.

14 The best evidence of this is perhaps the way in which the success of an album or song (gold, platinum etc.) was calculated, namely on the sale of individual copies. Still today the industry statistics report "unit" sales even for the digital market. See http://76.74.24.142/A200B8A7-6BBF-EF15-3038-582014919F78.pdf.

15 See Gregory Hagen & Nyall Engfield, "Canadian Copyright Reform: P2P Sharing, Making Available and the Three-Step Test" (2006) 3:2 U. Ottawa L. & Tech. J. 477 at 503, www.uoltj.ca/articles/vol3.2/2006.3.2.uoltj.Hagen.477-516.pdf [Hagen & Engfield].

After all, it consisted of just a few servers and it proved easy to target their owners and operators and make them cease their activities. However, sharing of music files continued, and the events that followed the injunctions levelled against Napster in 2001 raised the question of whether the music industry had underestimated the strength of demand for and role of file-sharing.[16] Now many are asking whether that is in fact desirable, including songwriters themselves:

> File sharing is both a revolution in music distribution and a very positive phenomenon. The volunteer efforts of millions of music fans creates a much greater choice of repertoire for consumers, allowing songs — both new and old, well known and obscure — to be heard. All that's needed to fulfill this revolution in distribution is a way for Creators and rights holders to be paid.[17]

Is it possible that what some perceived as simple theft,[18] which must be fought in the same way as, say, shoplifting, could also be described as a new form of social interaction? Empirically, it seems that there has never been a time in history when more people have listened to more music. Music is everywhere, on every device. People email, blog and text about their favourite artists, but business models lag behind. Indeed, in line with its vision of the traditional world based on ownership and the distribution of discrete carriers such as compact discs, a model in which it controls the manufacturing and use of each copy (as would happen for a car or a house), the recording industry thought that it could implement TPMs in order to limit, control or at least impede copying. But copying is how millions of users access music.

One commentator drew an interesting analogy with traffic regulation:

> The real problem has been poor consumer treatment prior to and in reaction to [P2P] technology. Imagine a city where the traffic lights are notoriously poorly timed. Over time, motorists discover that a trip that ought to take 10 to 15 minutes, takes 25 to 35 minutes as they hit every red light regardless of traffic. Motorists soon discover that if they speed slightly or drive slowly between certain lights, they will hit fewer red lights. Upon discovering this behaviour, the city, rather

16 See Genan Zilkh, "The RIAA's Troubling Solution To File-Sharing" (2010), 20 Fordham Intell. Prop. Media & Ent. L.J. 667, 669–75.

17 Songwriters Association of Canada, "Our Proposal: Detailed (Updated March 2009)" www.songwriters.ca/proposaldetailed.aspx.

18 *IFPI Report*, above note 5 at 3.

> than address the root of the problem by improving the light system, installs cameras throughout the city to catch those speeding. Despite fewer tickets being issued after the initial installation, speeding has not decreased, but has simply changed. Now, rather than speeding slightly between lights, motorists have adjusted their behaviour by memorizing the locations of the cameras, and now speed excessively between them, and hit the brakes immediately before the cameras . . . . Here, we have clear issues of invasion of privacy, criminal tampering, and unauthorised installations by the entertainment industry all in the name of protecting their bottom line.[19]

The industry added "click-wrap" contracts (which are accepted by a mouse click) in order to eliminate legal exceptions or limitations, including fair dealing in some cases, thus combining the legal protection of the contracts with the technical locking mechanisms. This made it illegal and almost impossible to bypass them. This supplementary anti-bypass protection exists in the United States, Europe, and many other countries, and it is now foreseeable in Bill C-32 that it will be applied in Canada. The problem is that, while it may work to bring recalcitrant users back in the mainstream, the measures have been used — in vain it seems — to fight the mainstream itself.[20]

As might be expected, technologists reacted by creating a new technological model that we now call "peer-to-peer," which enabled informal file-sharing networks without a central file servers to make music and other files from millions of personal computers available to the entire world. [21] Moreover, Internet users, who are told they are part of the "problem" that the industry is targeting, may feel the urge to resist.

The guilty parties are now individuals, whom the recording industry tried to identify by taking various Internet service providers (ISPs) to court It is now trying to make ISPs police the Internet via the Anti-counterfeiting Trade Agreement (ACTA).[22] In parallel, Internet users are turning to proxy-based and secure USENET connections, which ISPs can-

---

19 Scott Monkman, "Corporate Erosion of Fair Use: Global Copyright Law Regarding File Sharing" 6 Asper Rev. Int'l Bus. & Trade L. 265, 282–83.

20 *Ibid.* at 285.

21 See Andrea Slane, "Democracy, Social Space, and the Internet", (2007) 57 U. Toronto L.J. 81 at 99–100, http://muse.jhu.edu/journals/university_of_toronto_law_journal/v057/57.1slane.pdf.

22 According to a communiqué endorsed by a number of academics and non-governmental organizations published in 23 June 2010, ACTA, a trade agreement to which Canada would become party, would:

not easily track, to access their music. There is no way for users who might want to, to pay to do what they want to do. The continuing message is that listening to music in the way that an entire generation is taking for granted is wrong and should be stopped, as opposed to being an activity that could be the largest revenue source for the industry in its history.[23]

The "war" against file-sharing is costing the industry billions of dollars (to acquire and use the technology aimed at countering the phenomenon, to pay lawyers and to absorb losses of sales). It has caused enormous frustration and cynicism among consumers, thus probably exacerbating the drop in sales. Trying to make up for lost revenue, the majors have been increasingly relying on contracts, such as "360" deals, which give them control over all sources of income generated by a performer, including merchandising sales.[24] They have also signed agreements, such as the much touted deal with Spotify, that have brought vast amounts in the coffers of record companies, but that have apparently not generated quite the same degree of enthusiasm on the part of creators and performers.[25]

- Encourage internet service providers to police the activities of internet users by holding internet providers responsible for the actions of subscribers, conditioning safe harbors on adopting policing policies, and by requiring parties to encourage cooperation between service providers and rights holders;
- Encourage this surveillance, and the potential for punitive disconnections by private actors, without adequate court oversight or due process.

See American University Washington College of Law, "International Experts Find that Pending Anti-Counterfeiting Trade Agreement Threatens Public Interests" (23 June 2010), www.wcl.american.edu/pijip/go/acta-communique.

This interpretation was denied by a number of participating governments.

23 Even numbers as low as $5/month per broadband user for a file-sharing license could generate total revenues similar to those the industry made in its heyday. See "Peter Jenner Admits That Stopping File Sharing Is Impossible" *TechDirt* (14 July 2010), http://www.techdirt.com/articles/20100714/16215410220.shtml; and Daniel Gervais, "The Price of Social Norms: Towards a Liability Regime for File-Sharing" (2004), 12 J. Intell. Prop. L. 39–74, http://papers.ssrn.com/sol3/papers.cfm?abstract_id=525083.

24 See Susan Abramovitch & Shelagh Carnegie, "'360 deals' offer new options for artists in recording industry" *Lawyers' Weekly* 26:45 (6 April 2007) 12. Officially known as "multiple-rights agreements" they vary enormously in scope and "fairness" towards the artist. Madonna, U2, Shakira, Jay-Z can negotiate 360 contracts that they consider beneficial. New artists may not have the necessary clout, yet a "360" may be all that is on offer. See Edward Pierson, "Negotiating A 360 Deal: Considerations on the Promises and Perils of a New Music Business Model" (2010) 27:4 Entertainment and Sports Lawyer 1, http://new.abanet.org/Forums/entsports/PublicDocuments/winter10.pdf.

25 According to Sony BMG, "Spotify earns us more than iTunes." This is according to a Swedish article quoted in Barry Sookman, "Copyright Reform for Canada: What

This cynicism and even disrespect for the rule of law, and the cat-and-mouse technological game it has induced, may have repercussions in other areas. For example, highly encrypted anonymous peer-to-peer clients developed to thwart the music industry's efforts may be used to transfer child pornography.[26] When music users are encouraged to increase their anonymity, everyone loses.

2) The Impact of P2P

Not all published studies support the assumption that file-sharing is the leading cause for the drop in music sales. This is notably the case with the May 2007 report prepared for Industry Canada.[27] To be clear, it is not the drop in sales of CDs (an average drop of 26 percent in units sold, and of 37 percent in receipts between 1995 and 2005[28]) that is in question, but rather the cause-and-effect link. File-sharing is *a* cause for this drop, but how much? Although file-sharing whether on P2P networks, on torrents or using other, increasingly undetectable technologies,[29] is likely the cause

---

Should We Do? A Submission to the Copyright Consultation" (2009) 22 I.P.J. 1 at n. 43. However, see Dan Martin, "Spotify slammed by songwriters: A songwriters' association has criticised the Spotify streaming service over 'tiny' payments to musicians" *The Guardian*, (13 April 2010), www.guardian.co.uk/music/2010/apr/13/spotify-songwriters (who notes that the British Songwriters Association believes that "there is no clear trail that can be established so that the songwriter can trace back what they ought to have got. These things are behind a blanket of secrecy, and that is extremely worrying." Unlike revenues funnelled through a copyright collective, there is no obvious way for songwriters to obtain data on use of their works.)

26 For example, USENET, which can accessed via a secure connection, is now essentially used for file-sharing and porn. See above note 4. The most extraordinary aspect of USENET is that millions of users pay on average $20 per month to get access (via an encrypted SSL connection to USENT), a multiple of the $5/month file-sharing licensing models discussed in a number of studies. For a pricing example, see http://www.usenet.net. On the monthly fee, see, e.g., Daniel Gervais, note 23 above.

27 Industry Canada, *The Impact of Music Downloads and P2P File-Sharing on the Purchase of Music: A Study for Industry Canada* by Birgitte Andersen & Marion Frenz (2007), www.ic.gc.ca/eic/site/ippd-dppi.nsf/vwapj/IndustryCanadaPaperMay4_2007_en.pdf/$FILE/IndustryCanadaPaperMay4_2007_en.pdf [*Industry Canada Study*].

28 According to the OECD report, the drop in sales of records (units) between 1998 and 2003 was 31.4 percent in Canada, versus 20.1 percent in the United States and a world average of 14 percent.

29 See above note 3 and Ernesto, "Filesharing Report Shows Explosive Growth for uTorrent" http://torrentfreak.com/p2p-statistics-080426, which notes that "[f]rom December 2006 to December 2007 LimeWire lost approximately 25 percent of its user base. By the end of 2007, 17 percent of all PCs in the United States had LimeWire installed, compared to 23.3 percent last year. . . . The uTorrent user base on the other

for a substantial proportion of the drop in sales of CDs, from an empirical point of view the industry's strategy of "counterattack" does not seem to be working very well.[30]

The Industry Canada Study shows that 77.2 percent of Canadians over fifteen years of age have purchased compact discs. However, 29 percent of Canadians have downloaded music through peer-to-peer networks, 20 percent have copied files from friends, and 41.7 percent have downloaded music from promotional, personal, or free sites. At the same time, only 13.6 percent of Canadians had paid to download music. [31] In 2003, 24.3 percent of all Canadian households (compared to 7.8 percent in 1999) obtained music on the Internet and saved it.[32] More important, the proportion of Canadians who have downloaded music from peer-to-peer sites had grown to 35.1 percent for those aged nineteen to twenty-four years, and to 40.7 percent for those aged twenty-five to thirty-four years, while paid downloads by these groups represent 15 percent and 19 percent, respectively.[33] In other words, the largest consumers in the sector download twice as much from peer-to-peer sites than from pay Web sites, and acquire three times as much music from free sites and friends as from pay download sites.

At the aggregate level, the report published by the OECD in 2005 shows that Canada accounted for 8 percent of peer-to-peer users in the OECD

---

hand is rapidly growing. uTorrent installs more than doubled in nearly every part of the world in the last 12 months. The BitTorrent client is most popular in Europe (11.6 percent)." The data reported in this article shows an increase in uTorrent installs in Canada up from 4.1 percent of PCs to 9.3 percent from 2007 to 2008.

30 A already dated OECD report noted, that

> [T]he use of all monitored networks (fast-track plus all other networks) has been on the rise until the peak in April 2004 with almost 10 million users and month-on-month growth (seasonal effects seem to reduce P2P usage in the summer month [sic]). The rather flat trend of the fast-track networks since November 2003 and the parallel rise of simultaneous use of other networks may hint at a migration of P2P users to networks that attract less attention from the music industry and thus fewer lawsuits. This result is confirmed by more recent analysis. Some studies also contest the existence of an impact of the lawsuits on file-sharing; with P2P users recognising the low probability that they will be targeted by a lawsuit.

OECD Working Party on the Information Economy, *Digital Broadband Content: Music*, DSTI/ICCP/IE(2004)12/FINAL (13 December 2005), www.oecd.org/dataoecd/13/2/34995041.pdf at 101 [*OECD Report*].

31 Industry Canada Study, at 17.

32 *OECD Report*, above note 30 at 74.

33 *Industry Canada Study*, above note 31 at 47-28.

countries, while its population represents only 1.2 percent of the total population of these countries.[34] Canada represents about 2 percent of music sales in the world.[35] The conclusions of the Industry Canada Study, which are controversial, discussed the causal link between peer-to-peer and the drop in CD sales. The authors summarize their conclusions as follows:

> In the aggregate, we are unable to discover any direct relationship between P2P file-sharing and CD purchases in Canada. The analysis of the entire Canadian population does not uncover either a positive or negative relationship between the number of files downloaded from P2P networks and CDs purchased. . . .
>
> We also find that both the P2P file-sharing group and the entire population show a positive and statistically significant association between ripping CDs and CD purchases. For the entire population, there is also a positive and significant effect on CD purchasing from individuals downloading via private web sites. . . . However, people who also own an MP3 player appear to be less likely to purchase CD albums. . . .
>
> However, our analysis of the Canadian P2P file-sharing subpopulation suggests that there is a strong positive relationship between P2P file-sharing and CD purchasing.[36]

A well-known commentator, Stan Liebowitz, felt that these results were untenable for a number of reasons, notably the conclusion that the number of music files exchanged would lead to an increase in sales of CDs, which has not been the case.[37] To be fair, the study did *not* state that peer-to-peer has led to an increase in sales of CDs, but that there was a correlation between sales and the intensity of file transfers.[38] Correlation and causality are two different notions. Still, many of the lessons that intuitively apply

34 *OECD Report*, at 106.

35 *Ibid.*, at 21.

36 *Industry Canada Study*. Above note 31 at 26-27 and 33

37 See the substance of and the response to his critique at Birgitte Andersen, "The Impact of Music Downloads and P2P File-Sharing on the Purchase of Music" *Dynamics of Institutions & Markets in Europe* (16 November 2007), www.dime-eu.org/node/477.

38 See also Mark Hefflinger, "Report: Top Songs at Retail Also Most Popular on P2P" *Digital Media Wire* (14 May 2009), www.dmwmedia.com/news/2009/05/14/report percent3A-top-songs-retail-also-most-popular-p2p. Yet even here is the wave of file-sharing all lost sales, or would some of it function as unpaid advertising, as when a someone sends a song to a friend thinking she might like it. If the recipient discovers a new artists that way, sales may increase. Yet for new blockbusters, P2P undoubtedly replaces many a licensed download.

to piracy of carriers do not map well onto the online environment. I return to this in the next section.

Whether the Industry Canada Study properly reflects the behaviour of Canadian consumers or not, the results raise a certain number of complementary questions. For example, if users who have downloaded music from peer-to-peer sites are less likely to pay for their downloads, is it because TPMs make files from paid downloads less friendly than their free versions? Based on a significant experiment in France, TPM-free files sell better than those with a TPM on the same download sites.[39] Record companies must have access to comparable data since they are beginning to adopt formats without a digital rights management system (DRM).

Putting aside the eventuality of a system of remuneration for file transfers, would legal downloading compensate for the drop in sales of CDs? The OECD study observed:

> [T]he online music market was initiated somewhat later than in the United States, with agreement in October 2003 of the Canadian Musical Reproduction Agency and the Canadian Recording Industry Association to issue licenses to Internet music distributors (agreement on standard terms and conditions). Napster, MusicNet and Puretracks (a Canadian-owned service) were the first services to sign framework agreements with the associations. Apple announced an online music store ITunes coming to Canada in November 2004. According to PwC (2004), total digital spending is expected to grow from USD 3 million in 2004 (0.4 percent of total music sales) to USD 102 million in 2008 (14 percent of total music sales).[40]

Even if the growth in sales of single downloads were sustained, it seems highly improbable that the OECD objectives would be reached.[41]

---

39 Denis Rouvre. "La FNAC vend des MP3 sans DRM" *PrésencePC* (17 January 2007). Solveig Emerard-Jammes, "Franck Leprou : Les DRM ont constitué des freins à l'achat de musique sur les sites de téléchargement légal," *Le Journal du Net* (25 October 2006). In general, the "majors" have given up "heavy" TPMs. "Napster moves to MP3-only music download format," *CNET News* (6 January 2008); "Sony BMG to drop copy protection for downloads," *CNET News* (7 January 2008).

40 *OECD Report*, above note 30 at 33.

41 See above notes 10 and 11.

3) Film v. Music

The film industry has fared much better in the Internet era than its music cousin.[42] Why? First of all, the consumption patterns are vastly different. Music is everywhere, and users typically want "their music" on all their devices. Films are generally "consumed" once or a few times at most. Second, file size is an issue, as users cannot easily store 50,000 films on a computer, which they can easily do with songs. This also means that downloading a movie takes much more time and bandwidth. Third, and more importantly, whether a song is downloaded from LimeWire for free or from iTunes, the quality is essentially the same, if one excepts the possibility of spoofs, spyware and viruses when using file-sharing networks. By contrast, a film is not "the same" if the file quality is low, and the experience of watching a movie on a computer does not equal watching it in a theatre. [43] Consequently, quantitatively, there is much less file-sharing of movies than music, and the product resulting from a download is qualitatively different. As such, it is an irritant, but not an existential threat to the industry. Fourth and finally, a common source of piracy for new films, before they are released on DVDs, is camcording in a theatre[44]. This form of piracy is much easier to prevent than file-sharing, because it is not digital. Fighting it means enforcing a ban on the use of a physical device (the camera) in theatres.[45]

---

42 The most recent industry report available notes that "[w]orldwide box office for all films reached $29.9 billion in 2009, up 7.6 percent over 2008's total. International box office ($19.3 billion) made up 64 percent of the worldwide total, while U.S. and Canada ($10.6 billion) made up 36 percent, a proportion consistent with the last several years. U.S./Canada box office and international box office in U.S. dollars are both up significantly over five years ago" (figures in US dollars). See Motion Picture Association, Theatrical Market Statistics 2009, http://mpaa.org/Resources/091af5d6-faf7-4f58-9a8e-405466c1c5e5.pdf. The same may not be true of television. See Rory Cellan-Jones, "File-sharers' TV tastes revealed" *BBC News* (28 August 2009),. http://news.bbc.co.uk/2/hi/8224869.stm.

43 The loss of income is undoubtedly significant, but it does not equal the number of people who appropriate or watch a copy without paying, because not all of them would pay to see it in a theatre. As such "official" estimates of losses due to piracy must be considered with some caution.

44 There were, however, several reports a few years ago suggesting that studio personnel were a major source of bootlegs. See, e.g., John Schwartz "Hollywood Faces Online Piracy, but It Looks Like an Inside Job" *New York Times* (15 September 2003), www.nytimes.com/2003/09/15/technology/15MOVI.html.

45 Bill C-59, which received Royal Assent on 22 June 2007, amended the *Criminal Code* to prohibit the unauthorized recording of a movie in a movie theatre (camcording). See Bill C-59, *An Act to amend the Criminal Code (unauthorized recording of a*

The evidence for the above is there: the film industry has just had its best years ever in terms of global revenues. It loses some revenue to online file-sharing of course, but the issue is manageable. The film industry has also been able to use the Internet to generate additional sales, such as Netflix and advertising, thereby compensating for some and perhaps all of the revenues that may be lost to file-sharing.[46]

4) Bill C-32 and File-Sharing

Bill C-32 has taken on board many of the ideas suggested to the government and Parliament concerning online uses. Unfortunately, as far as the main form of online use is concerned, it only follows the WCT and WPPT.[47] Lest I misguide the reader, I am not opposed to TPMs, but when millions of Canadians are file-sharing — it is now the main mode of access to music, at a ratio approaching forty unauthorized downloads for each one that is paid[48] — the way in which this interdiction will allow Canadian songwriters and performers to make a decent living remains rather obscure.

In jurisdictions which have adopted this property-based view in which each copy must be controlled by the right holder (generally not the creator or performer, but the record company), the situation is not markedly different from the current Canadian picture.[49] Enforcing a ban on circumven-

---

movie), 1st Sess., 39th Parl., 2007, www2.parl.gc.ca/HousePublications/Publication.aspx?Docid=3297657&file=4.

46 Readers in Canada and elsewhere outside the United States may not yet be familiar with NetFlix, a monthly subscription of approximately US$10 offering unlimited access to watch a large database of films online, and DVDs by mail. The service should soon be available to Canadians. See www.theglobeandmail.com/news/technology/netflix-will-cross-border-to-canada-this-year/article1644548/

47 See Carys Craig, "Locking out Lawful Users: Fair Dealing and Anti-Circumvention in Bill C-32" and Michael Geist, "The Case for WIPO Internet Treaty Flexibility" in this volume.

48 Some even put the number at 49:1. See www.songwriters.ca/proposaldetailed.aspx.

49 Somewhat illogically it seems, the industry is comfortable with streaming services and YouTube, now a main source of access to music and often licensed, yet without any direct control over use. Add the widely available technologies that transform YouTube videos into MP3 files, and the industry's virulent opposition to licensing at least some forms of file-sharing may become even harder to justify in the eyes of the average music user. Even YouTube videos promote this application. See, e.g., www.youtube.com/watch?v=tE9ITkjFpZg.

It is true of course that to make an MP3 from a YouTube video, one must watch or at least play the video. See Michael Driscoll, "Will YouTube Sail Into The DMCA's Safe Harbor Or Sink For Internet Piracy?" (2007) 6 J. Marshall Rev. Intell. Prop. L. 550, n. 133.

tion of TPMs may work on a small scale, that is, vis-à-vis a small number of deviant users (probably easier to identify if they stand out in a crowd of compliant users). By definition, a majority of Canadians cannot be deviant. I am also concerned that pushing younger Canadians into illegality (not allowing them to access the music the way they want legally) may actually drive them to become less law-abiding generally.[50] The Bill has thus far missed a golden opportunity to discuss how the online music market is broken, and how it could be fixed.

5) The International Legal Context

Any solution to the problem of online music transfers with neither payment nor control will have to be compatible with Canada's international obligations that result from the treaties to which it is a party. There are five such agreements, four of which are administered by the World Intellectual Property Organization (WIPO) and one by the World Trade Organization (WTO).[51] The WTO administers the Agreement on Trade-Related Aspects of Intellectual Property Rights (TRIPs).[52] Any infringement on Canada's obligations flowing from the TRIPs Agreement may lead to application of the WTO's dispute-settlement procedure. This is not a theoretical recourse. An American exception concerning the performance or public execution of music was successfully contested in 2000, and one year later Canada modified its Patent Act after a WTO special dispute-settlement group concluded that an exception provided in the Act infringed on the three-step test.[53]

---

50 "Morality: Rose-coloured spectacles? Cheats may or may not prosper, but they despise themselves for cheating" *The Economist* (24 June 2010), www.economist.com/node/16422414/print. The article noted that, "The moral, then, is that people's sense of right and wrong influences the way they feel and behave. Even when it is someone else who has made them behave badly, it can affect their subsequent behaviour." This correlates with Eric Posner's finding on tax law compliance. See Eric A. Posner, "Law and Social Norms: The Case of Tax Compliance" (2000), 86 Va. L. Rev. 1781.

51 See World Intellectual Property Organization, www.wipo.int and World Trade Organization, www.wto.org, respectively.

52 *Agreement on Trade-Related Aspects of Intellectual Property Rights* (15 April 1994) in *Agreement Establishing the World Trade Organization, Annex 1C*, www.wto.org/english/docs_e/legal_e/27-trips_01_e.htm, 1869 U.N.T.S. 299, (1993) 33 I.L.M. 81.

53 See *Patent Protection for Pharmaceutical Products in Canada — Chronology of Significant Events*, 6 October 2008, www2.parl.gc.ca/content/LOP/ResearchPublications/prb9946-e.htm; and Daniel Gervais, *The TRIPs Agreement: Drafting History and Analysis*, 3d ed. (London: Sweet & Maxwell, 2008), at 382–83.

The TRIPs Agreement was adopted in April 1994. It integrates most of the provisions in two previous treaties administered by WIPO: the 1971 Act (or version) of the *Berne Convention for the Protection of Literary and Artistic Works* (the *Berne Convention*) and the 1961 *Rome Convention for the Protection of Performers, Producers of Phonograms and Broadcasting Organizations* (the *Rome Convention*).[54]

After the adoption of the TRIPs Agreement, WIPO concluded negotiations on two new treaties in 1996, the WCT and the WPPT. Today, Canada is bound by the TRIPs Agreement, the *Berne Convention*, and the *Rome Convention*. As a consequence, aside from the risk of a trade dispute in the case of a violation of the TRIPs Agreement, it is highly improbable that the Canadian government would support a solution that is not compatible with these instruments.

The TRIPs Agreement is part of the "chain" of trade measures negotiated during the Multilateral Trade Negotiations of the Uruguay Round (1986–94), at the end of which the WTO was established. The agreement does not reinvent the wheel with regard to copyright. It integrates all of the rights and other substantial provisions in the Berne Convention, except for moral rights (which were not considered "trade-related"[55]). This means that all rights (including the rights to reproduction and communication to the public) are covered in the TRIPs Agreement, as are the limitations and exceptions set out in the Berne Convention. However, there is one important difference: a three-step test is used in the TRIPs Agreement to authorize all limitations and exceptions applicable to all of the rights.

The test set out in Article 13 of the TRIPs Agreement authorizes limitations on and exceptions to the right of reproduction:

- In certain special cases
- That do not infringe on normal exploitation of the work
- That do not cause an unjustified prejudice to the legitimate interests of the creator

Very briefly,[56] all exceptions to copyright must satisfy each of these three conditions. The WTO has interpreted the first condition as meaning that an exception or limitation must have a limited field of application or an exceptional scope.[57] The second condition means that an exception will not

---

54 See Daniel Gervais, *ibid.*, at 213–14.

55 See *ibid.* at 214–15.

56 For a more detailed explanation, see *ibid.* at 237–48.

57 *Ibid.*

be allowed if it bears on a type of exploitation that has or would probably have considerable importance.[58] In other words, an exception that is used to limit a significant existing or reasonably predictable potential market and/or to enter into competition with the copyright holder is prohibited. Finally, under the third condition, a prejudice is caused to the interests of rights holders and rises to an unjustified level if an exception or limitation engenders an unjustified lost business opportunity for the copyright holder that is not compensated by, for example, a copyright levy.[59] In sum, it is all about money—which is exactly surprising for a trade agreement.[60]

6) The Way Forward

Clearly, file-sharing reveals a fundamental change in the way in which we consume music. *Music consumption has grown greatly in the last five years*. It is the *financial flows* that have not.

Empirical and theoretical analyses support a few assumptions about future business models. First, many consumers seem ready to pay, even if the question of the price remains an obvious matter for discussion. In fact, consumers do pay for some music and for ring tones for their cell phones. Second, consumers are not attracted to the subscription model; it remains to be determined whether there is a problem with the price or whether subscription simply does not respond to consumer demand. It requires a behaviour modification the outcome of which is less freedom than unpaid access, and with a payment to boot.

Given that consumers pay for other formats, it is conceivable that price is not the main issue. However, paid, authorized music should be as user-friendly as "free music." Business models will develop over licensed "file-sharing," for example by designing unobtrusive clients that can inform a user that an artist whose music she downloaded is coming to her area, etc. To make this possible, however, users must be *allowed* to pay to enjoy the music the way they want and for many of them, the only way, that they know.

---

58 *Ibid.* This is reflected at least indirectly in the transformative use exception discussed in connection with UGC in Part B below.

59 *Ibid.*

60 Daniel J. Gervais, "Intellectual Property, Trade & Development: The State Of Play" (2005), 74 Fordham L. Rev 505, 505–6.

In spite of the music industry's far from brilliant and probably counter-productive efforts to stem the tide of file-sharing,[61] there may be a simple way to re-establish contact with the "moral fibre" of consumers, many of whom I would argue understand that creators and others in the industry must be paid for their work. After all, music consumption has grown and users recognize the value of the music that they love and listen to on their iPods and MP3 players all the time, all over the world. They don't want to be told that they do not have the right to do what they are doing or have the reasons for this ban explained to them. They want to be told *how* they can do it.

A compulsory licence instituting a system of remuneration for unlimited online music file-sharing would be prohibited by international law. The way to make such a system compatible is to make it voluntary, although it can be an opt-out regime, as proposed by the Songwriters Association of Canada (SAC), as opposed to the more traditional opt-in (sign up) model.[62] The simplest system would be based on the payment of a monthly fee by users via their ISP. Absent an agreement, and partly because there is no obvious advocate for all Internet users to make such an agreement, a tariff should be set by the Copyright Board, which could also, as with private copying and other tariffs, set the split among the various categories of right holders.

The idea that providing legal access may work better online than trying to stop use is not exactly new. In a 1998 paper prepared for the World Intellectual Property Organization (WIPO),[63] I had suggested that licensing was a better option. Robert Kasunic similarly observed in 2004 that:

> Copyright owners often want too much control. The public often wants too much for free — something for nothing. All too often, neither side seems capable of empathy. Yet finding a common ground or the proper balance between these conflicting interests is the essence of copyright. The controversy over P2P is an excellent case in point for

---

61 See Thomas Mennecke, "P2P Population Remains Steady" *Slyck* (20 October 2006), www.slyck.com/story1314_P2P_Population_Remains_Steady.

62 See above note 17. The proposal was amended in part to allay concerns expressed by record labels about the compatibility of the initial version with Canada's treaty obligations. See Barry Sookman, "The SAC Proposal for the Monetization of the File Sharing of Music in Canada: Does It Comply with Canada's International Treaty Obligations Related to Copyright?" (2008) 21 I.P.J. 159.

63 Electronic Rights Management and Digital Identifier Systems, 23 Nov. 1998, WIPO Document ACMC/1/1, www.wipo.int/edocs/mdocs/enforcement/en/acmc_1/acmc_1_1-main1.pdf.

> this seeming lack of empathy, both for copyright owners' attempts to control the technology and the public's willingness to abuse it.[64]

And in one of the best copyright essays ever written, Benjamin Kaplan famously wrote, back in 1967:

> [C]opyright or the larger part of its controls will appear unneeded, merely obstructive, as applied to certain sectors of production . . . here copyright law will lapse into disuse and may disappear. . . . [L]arge repertories of works will be made available . . . and charges and remittances figured on rough-and-ready bases, all with liberal application of some principle of "clearance at the source" to prevent undue bother down the line to the final consumer.[65]

The participation of ISPs in a future licensing model may presume that receipts would be shared with them to compensate for their role as fee collectors. Bill C-32 proposes a vast safe-harbour for them. Their agreement to collect a fee could be seen as a reasonable trade-off, given that many users pay for high-speed internet at least in part to access music files. Additionally, the system could allow them to store heavily traded files on their own server legally, thereby reducing their operating costs. It would also allow for better tracking of files that are traded via the type of technology used by BigChampagne,[66] and thus allow for quick and fair distribution by copyright collectives. Alternatively, the Canadian Radio-television and Tele-communications Commission (CRTC) could set as a condition to operate as an ISP a contribution to compensate for file-sharing,[67] but (a) it is imperative that the contribution be at a sufficient level to truly compensate creators and the industry, and (b) it is hard to

---

64 Rob Kasunic, "Solving the P2P 'Problem'—An Innovative Marketplace Solution" March 2004, http://fairuse.stanford.edu/commentary_and_analysis/2004_03_kasunic.html.

65 Benjamin Kaplan, *An Unhurried View of Copyright*, (New York: Columbia University Press, 1967) at 121–23.

66 See BigChampagne Media Measurement, www.bigchampagne.com. Interestingly, their service is also used by large music labels. See Mark Hefflinger, "Universal Music Taps BigChampagne for Online Metrics" *Digital Media Wire* (18 August 2009) www.dmwmedia.com/news/2009/08/18/universal-music-taps-bigchampagne-online-metrics.

67 Although that is debatable under the current Telecommunications Act (1993, c. 38), and the *Broadcasting Act*, (S.C. 1991, c. 11) as interpreted in *In The Matter Of The Broadcasting Act, S.C. 1991, C. 11*, 2010 FCA 178, http://decisions.fca-caf.gc.ca/en/2010/2010fca178/2010fca178.html.

imagine, contrary to proposals made by certain Quebec commentators,[68] to see how an ISP should be asked to pay for file-sharing by their subscribers while maintaining that all file-sharing should remain fully illegal. *On a rien pour rien.*

B. USER-GENERATED CONTENT

1) An Exception for User-Generated Content?

First, let us define our area of enquiry. I propose to define user-generated content (UGC) as content that is created using tools specific to the online environment and/or disseminated using such tools. Bill C-32 contains a transformative use exception ostensibly designed for the online *re*use environment.[69] The proposed solution would remove the most visible irritants for millions of Canadians who neither understand nor accept restrictions they consider obsolete, unjustified, or both. It would ensure buy-in in what has become a participatory democratic environment. It reflects concerns expressed widely in popular deliberations ("listening to the City"), in what is referred to in policy analysis literature as communicative reauthorization.[70] Clearly, the shift from a one-to-many entertainment and information infrastructure to a many-to-many infrastructure has deep consequences on several levels. It has made possible mass fan fiction, mashups, music remixes, cloud computing, collages, etc. Blogs have transformed the access to, and arguably the nature of, information.[71]

The proposed exception is not a license to freely copy anything or to upload it to any social site.[72] It requires transformation. It is a *limited* right to reuse existing works to create new works, in cases where a licensing transaction is not reasonable and there is no demonstrable impact on the market for existing works.

The contours of the exception are unclear and will need to be defined by courts. Three important points in that connection are as follows:

---

68 See "L'AGAMM rights holders demand their fair share" *CNW* (15 June 2010), www.newswire.ca/en/releases/archive/June2010/15/c5205.html.

69 Above note 8, cl. 22 (s. 29.21).

70 Archon Fung, "Democratizing the Policy Process," in Michael Moran, Martin Rein & Robert E. Goodin, eds., *The Oxford Handbook of Public Policy* (Oxford: Oxford University Press, 2006) 669 at 676–78.

71 See above note 21 at 81–83.

72 In any event, the three-step test would not allow this type of exception. It would seem to fail on all three steps. See the discussion in section A(6)).

- If the exception allows "the creation of a *new work or* other subject-matter in which copyright subsists," does this mean that if what is created is in the nature of a copyright work, as opposed to a sound recording or performance, then that work must itself meet the requirements for protection, and most notably originality,[73] to be covered by the exception?
- The "solely for non-commercial purposes"[74] condition must apply *to the user.* If applied to a site like YouTube or even most blog services providers, the exception would seem fleeting at best;
- Then of course the importation into the Act of a three-step test inspired criterion, namely that the "use of, or the authorization to disseminate, the new work or other subject-matter does not have a substantial adverse effect, financial or otherwise, on the exploitation or potential exploitation of the existing work or other subject-matter — or copy of it — or on an existing or potential market for it, including that the new work or other subject-matter is not a substitute for the existing one"[75] will allow Canadian courts to consider previous interpretations of the three-step test, including by the World Trade Organization, and perhaps inform future interpretations of the test. In doing so, courts should bear in mind of course that the exception, as proposed in Bill C-32, differs from the TRIPs test, but that Canada is also bound by TRIPs and that statutes should, wherever possible, be interpreted consistently with Canada's international obligations. My sense is that the impact of this condition will depend in large part on the burden of proof. If users are required to prove a negative (that is, the absence of a "substantial adverse effect") then the exception will shrink into obsolescence. However, with time, even if the primary burden is on the user, categories may develop that are presumptively non-adverse.

---

73 See Elizabeth F. Judge & Daniel Gervais, "Of Silos and Constellations: Comparing Notions of Originality in Copyright Law" (2009), 27 Cardozo Arts & Ent. L.J. 375 http://papers.ssrn.com/sol3/papers.cfm?abstract_id=1545986. The authors note (at 376) that originality "is the sieve that determines which "productions of the human spirit" are protected by copyright and acquire the status of 'work'." The counterargument is that the Act protects "original works" then arguably, there is such a thing as an unprotected, "unoriginal work" that is still a work.

74 This term is used in several proposed amendments to the Act. It will no doubt be the subject of much litigation, to determine whether it has the same meaning throughout (compare this proposed exception to statutory damages), to what extent intentionality of the user governs vs. the right holder perspective, which might be that everything is potentially commercial.

75 Bill C-32, above note 8, cl. 22 (s. 29.21(1)(d)).

2) Amateur Reuse

To answer the questions above, it seems useful to contextualize UGC. This may illuminate the underpinnings of the proposed exception.

UGC discussions typically focus on *amateur* creation and reuse. Is this what the noncommercial condition aims to accomplish? Is the fact that UGC is amateur content a new normative vector to consider? [76] After all, reuse is not a major source of doctrinal tension. Most copyright theories support reuse. If I may be allowed a few analytical shortcuts, one could say that natural rights theory supports reuse. John Locke based his property right on transformative labor. Locke was talking about what one takes from "nature," of course, not other authors.[77] Still, the analogy between transforming nature and creating literary or artistic works holds — admittedly though only up to a point 1 because of the investment of skilled labor. Most authors do not "take from nature" (perhaps an artist does when painting a natural scene?); authors take *from each other* and all those who created before them and made their work available for others to enjoy. Humanity, as Blaise Pascal once said, is but one Person who continually grows.[78] Utilitarianism also supports reuse, at least once a proper return has been made possible by a limited exclusive right. Looking at UGC using an instrumentalist lens, shouldn't one seek the optimal point between protection that induces the creation and dissemination of new works and allowing the creativity of others to flourish?

Yet, in spite of apparent theoretical support and familiarity with reuse, copyright law is undeniably struggling to cope with UGC for many reasons. Some are qualitative (e.g., amateur vs. professional users), but one

---

76 The proposed exemption for parody and satire provides an interesting contrast *Copyright Act*, above note 6, s. 28.2(1)(b). Cultural progress depends on ability to make reasonable use of pre-existing material. In cases where the user cannot reasonably be expected to obtain a license and where societal value will be derived from allowing the use, an exception should apply. But satire is fundamentally different. While parody and pastiche are used to make fun of a copyright work, and possibly its creator, satire uses someone else's copyright work to convey an unrelated political or other message. Moreover, while use of a work for parody is necessary (to identify the work that is parodied), such is not the case for satire. Satire also risks a moral right violation by associating a work with a cause that the author does not support. Yet, some forms of satire would fit in the user-generated content exception.

77 See Samuel E. Trosow, "The Illusive Search for Justificatory Theories: Copyright, Commodification and Capital" (2003), 16 Can. J.L. & Juris. 217 at 224.

78 Quoted in translation in Daniel Gervais, "The Tangled Web of UGC: Making Copyright Sense of User-Generated Content" (2009), 11 Vand. J. Ent. & Tech. L. 841 at 845, http://papers.ssrn.com/sol3/papers.cfm?abstract_id=1444513.

is simply quantitative. Hundreds of millions of Internet users are downloading, altering, mixing, uploading and/or making available audio, video and text content. They are new to the copyright world.

For approximately 290 of its 300 year history (since the 1710 Statute of Anne), the "copy-right" was traded among professionals, including authors, publishers, producers, broadcasters, etc. It was occasionally used against *professional* pirates. Only in the past ten years has it also been used routinely against individual consumers and end-users.[79] This is, I suggest, the source of much of the tension in the copyright system; it also greatly increased the level of attention paid to copyright law and policy. Put differently, while the law has not changed, its target and purpose has.[80] This was possible because formally the copy-right is formulated in terms of technical restricted acts, such as reproduction, public performance, etc. There is little if any focus in copyright legislation on the nature or category of users, except for a few targeted exceptions.[81]

The transition is not an easy one. Trading copyright between and among professionals or enforcing it against those same professionals (or professional pirates) assumed that the users were identifiable (that is, known quantities) and that normal licensing transactions were possible. In other words, the market functioned because copyright owners would contractually grant authorizations to (professional) users. In cases where a large number of users used a large repertory of works owned by a plurality of owners, collective systems were put in place to allow the licensing of hundreds, sometimes thousands of users.[82] Those systems are sometimes supported by compulsory licenses.[83]

---

79 Although in January 2008 the US recording industry announced it would no longer be filing massive amounts of lawsuits against individual end-users. See Sarah McBride & Ethan Smith, "Music Industry to Abandon Mass Suits" *Wall Street Journal* (29 December 2008), http://online.wsj.com/article/SB122966038836021137.html.

80 This also explains the emergence of para-copyright norms such as anti-circumvention of TPMs.

81 For example ss. 30.1–30.5 of the *Copyright Act*, which provide various exceptions for libraries and other institutions. *Copyright Act*, R.S.C. 1985, c. C-42 [*Copyright Act*].

82 See Daniel Gervais, "Collective Management of Copyright: Theory and Practice in the Digital Age" in Daniel Gervais, ed., *Collective Management of Copyright and Related Rights*, 2d ed., (Alphen aan den Rijn: Kluwer Law International, 2010).

83 See, e.g., the compulsory license for cable retransmission in section 31(2) of the Act, above note 6, s. 31(2). Bill C-32 could patch a number of issues in this context. Why, one might ask, is s. 38.1(4) only applicable to certain collectives (i.e., it excludes the "general regime" collectives? Should we not decide who should administer the rights in ss. 17 and 19(2)(b)? Is s. 70.16, which was never used to my knowledge, still relevant? Among the proposals in the Bill, is it optimal to delete the collective man-

Typically, however, collective licenses are for *non-altering uses* and/or integral copying, such as reproduction of sound recordings or public performance. Collectives do not routinely license the right to prepare derivative works, at least not on the basis of pre-existing tariffs.[84] Nor have they licensed individual end-users, other than exceptionally.[85] But now individual Internet users have become "content providers," intermediaries of sorts, even though they are not professionals. Consequently, rights holders have analogized them to (professional) content providers and other intermediaries, and had no hesitation to apply copyright, a hitherto purely professional right, to those individual users.[86] Licensing mechanisms have thus far been unable to follow. In fact, some might say that one reason why end-users were traditionally left out of the equation was the fact the system could not license/integrate them. Digital technology may be changing this and could remove this obstacle.[87] There are other reasons, including privacy, to leave end-users out of the transactional licensing equation, however.

3) Privacy

The fact that copyright was not initially designed to be routinely used in the private sphere of users is evidenced by the fact that exceptions and

---

agement exception to the exception in s. 30.9 while maintaining the obligation to destroy the copy after 30 days? Finally, was it the intention of the drafters of proposed s. 30.03(2)(b) to imply/confirm that tariffs set by the Board may be retroactive?

84 A tariff may be defined for these purposes as a set of licensing conditions, including a price which may be set on various bases (units produced, user revenue, etc.), that any qualified user (normally, any person to whom the tariff applies) may invoke and use a work contained in the repertory of works covered by the tariff according to the conditions contained therein. Competition (antitrust) law often prevents collectives from refusing to issue a license based on such a tariff to a qualified user. For example, if a tariff allows a broadcaster to broadcast a repertory of musical works for a given period of time in exchange for the payment of a percentage of the broadcaster's advertising revenues, then any broadcaster (who qualifies—this may be determined under other (e.g., broadcasting) statutes) would be entitled to the license. In the United States, this is "regulated" by consent decrees negotiated between ASCAP and BMI, on the one hand, and the Department of Justice, on the other.

85 Copyright Clearance Center, Inc. (CCC) grants individual users reproduction licenses. See Copyright Clearance Center, www.copyright.com. However, collectives have not been in the business of granting micro-licenses.

86 And now proposing to use criminal sanctions and ISPs to police their behaviour, having apparently come to the conclusion that individual licenses do not work as well. See above notes 22, 80.

87 One should not belittle the scope of the challenge ahead in that case: millions of users who do not fit existing user profiles, and a system not equipped to grant them licenses.

limitations to copyright were written with the professional user in mind. This explains why in several national laws, the main exceptions can be grouped into two categories: first, private use, which governments previously regarded as "unregulatable" as a practical and/or normative matter,[88] and where copyright law thus abdicated its authority; second, specific uses by professional intermediaries: libraries (and archives) and certain public institutions, including schools, courts and sometimes the government itself. Regarding the former, there are still today several very broad exceptions for "private use."[89] End-users always enjoyed both "room to move" because of exceptions such as fair use and rights stemming from their ownership of a physical copy.

Entering the private sphere also means that copyright must now fight a new, formidable opponent: the right to privacy, which is anchored, *inter alia*, in Article 8 of the *European Convention for the Protection of Human Rights and Fundamental Freedoms*;[90] and in Articles 17 and 19 of the *International Covenant on Civil and Political Rights*.[91] If privacy-invasive tools are used to distribute and/or monitor end-users, privacy will be(come) a major issue. If, however, systems that decouple usage data from individual identities early on (upstream) are used, then the issue may vanish from major policy radars.

Owing to this perceived inadequacy of copyright licensing and normative concerns about privacy and/or ownership of copies, social norms have emerged according to which some uses or reuses of digital content are acceptable. Those norms have not responded well to the traditional prohibitions against reproduction, the preparation of derivative works and communicating/publicly performing protected content. In fact, com-

---

88 Daniel Gervais, "The Purpose of Copyright Law in Canada", (2005) 2:2 Univ. Ottawa L. & Tech. J. 315, n. 47, www.uoltj.ca/articles/vol2.2/2005.2.2.uoltj.Gervais.315-356.pdf. Professor Alain Strowel considers the defence of the private sphere as one of the three main justifications for exceptions to copyright, the other two being circulation of information, and cultural and scientific development. See Alain Strowel, "Droit d'auteur et accès à l'information: de quelques malentendus et vrais problèmes a travers l'histoire et les développements récents" (1999), 12 Cahiers de propriété intellectuelle 185 at 198.

89 The regime designed to protect privacy is expressed as a combination of chattel rights of the owner of the copy and exceptions to copyright, in particular fair dealing.

90 *Convention for the Protection of Human Rights and Fundamental Freedoms*, 4 November 1950, 213 U.N.T.S. 221 (entered into force 3 September 1953, as amended by Protocols No. 11 and No. 14), http://conventions.coe.int/treaty/en/Treaties/Html/005.htm.

91 16 December 1966, 999 U.N.T.S. 171 (entered into force 23 March 1976).

bined with ineffective enforcement,[92] copyright has barely made a dent in the massive reuse of protected content.[93] Those social norms are arguably supported by a rather vague notion of fair or *de minimis* use, buttressed by perceived social value in letting users create freely and, at least for some, making content "more available." There is undeniably a meme, with a strong built-in feedback loop, that many forms of UGC are "acceptable," though within mostly undefined parameters.

4) Applying "Old" Copyright to UGC

Copyright's ineffectual response to the social norms that underpin UGC is multifactorial: Application of a regulatory system not designed for mass reuse (but rather for mass consumptive use); inability and/or unwillingness to license both because of the type of use (reproduction/creation of derivatives) and because of the type of user; normative battles with the rights of end-users, including privacy and consumer protection;[94] and a marked lack of understanding, at least until very recently, of network effects and the use of the Internet to create/join virtual groups of friends or people with similar interests and who, acting gregariously (and, thus, naturally) want to "share" the pictures, shows, books or music they like, but that in most cases they have not authored.[95]

This poses the question how far does the private sphere extend? Does it explode when a digital use inside the sphere is made available to others online? The social norms at play do not seem to reflect the traditional distinction between private (tolerated) and public (unauthorized) use. Those have been the norms for decades and they are reflected in the traditional views expressed by large rights holders. For example, the Recording Industry Association of America condones limited copying for private use, but does not approve of the making available of copyrighted content online.[96]

---

92 At least if measured in terms of overall decrease in unauthorized use. See above note 10.

93 See Brett Lunceford, "Meh. The Irrelevance of Copyright in the Public Mind" (2008), 7 Nw. J. Tech. & Intell. Prop. 33, www.law.northwestern.edu/journals/njtip/v7/n1/3/.

94 See Jeremy Stanley, "Managing Digital Rights Management: Effectively Protecting Intellectual Property and Consumer Rights in the Wake Of The Sony CD Copy Protection Scandal" (2008) J. L. & Pol'y for Info. Soc'y 157.

95 *See* Daniel Gervais, "The Price of Social Norms," above note 23.

96 See "Piracy: Online and On the Street", Recording Industry Association of America, www.riaa.com/physicalpiracy.php?content_selector=piracy_online_the_law

> . . . burning a copy of CD onto a CD-R, or transferring a copy onto your computer hard drive or your portable music player, won't usually raise concerns so long as:

Technologically, however, it is often the same copy that is legal to make (for personal use) but whose use then becomes illegal, again according to the traditional view, if made available to others. On a technical level, making it available would then be an infringement under one of several possible theories, based on each national legal system. In Canada, it could be considered the authorization of a communication to the public.[97] The social norm/legal norm disconnect seems to lie in the blurring of that private/public distinction.

Traditionally there were thus two distinctions made, one between private and public use and another between professional and amateur uses. The technological environment until approximately 2000 meant that those two "Venn diagrams" were almost perfectly superposed. Amateur meant private (and vice versa) and non-commercial and professional meant public and commercial. The shift from one-to-many to many-to-many dissemination modes destabilized this system and amateur no longer meant private.

Normatively, the question is this: should amateur prevail over public when the two Venn diagrams are separated? Some have argued for an amateur "exemption" to allow remix.[98] If, however, the amateur becomes a "player" by leaving her private sphere,[99] then normatively the question is no longer a confrontation of privacy and copyright, but one of amateur intermediary/provider vs. professional. While historically the latter was the (only) focus of copyright law, if the absence of the amateur was not driven by normative considerations but rather practical ones, then those amateurs should probably learn to use exemptions such as fair use or safe harbors. Then again, a valid case can be made that at least "small" everyday usage need not be in copyright's sights, and should focus only on what Paul Ohm calls "superusers."[100] As a practical matter, this rings true if

---

- The copy is made from an authorized original CD that you legitimately own
- The copy is just for your personal use.

97 See *Society of Composers, Authors & Music Publishers of Canada v. Canadian Assn. of Internet Providers*, [2004] 2 S.C.R. 427, http://csc.lexum.umontreal.ca/en/2004/2004scc45/2004scc45.html; Daniel Gervais, "The Purpose of Copyright Law in Canada" (2006), 2:2 Univ. Ottawa. J. L. & Tech. 315 at 323–25, www.uoltj.ca/articles/vol2.2/2005.2.2.uoltj.Gervais.315-356.pdf.

98 See Lawrence Lessig, *Remix: Making Art and Commerce Thrive in the Hybrid Economy* (New York: Penguin Press, 2008).

99 Deciding in which cases this happens would require a different paper, and the answer is likely to be different in each legal system.

100 See Paul Ohm, "The Myth of the Superuser: Fear, Risk, and Harm Online" (2008), 41 U.C. Davis L. Rev. 1327.

transactional licensing (for one-off uses) is envisaged — though blanket licenses for some uses may also be used.

5) Bill C-32's Test

By selecting commerciality as the filtering criterion, Bill C-32 navigates the shoals of amateur vs. professional with some difficulty. An amateur may upload content not with the direct purpose of making money, but in order to gain her 15 minutes of fame. Others might use YouTube, Facebook and other sites simply to disseminate content among friends and family. An expansive definition of commerciality might cover the former, and an exception reduced to the latter type of use would likely fail to achieve any significant adjustment of the current regime.

The three-step test again offers a possible solution, and courts will have to make a fundamental decision early on, namely whether to link up the analysis of commerciality in section 29.21(1)(1) with the condition set forth in section 29.21(1)(d).[101]

If the perceived commercial nature of the upload is looked at ontologically as it were, as a threshold condition *before* turning to impact on the market, it will be necessary to articulate clear standards for both. Parliament could of course amend the Bill to make the link (or absence thereof) clearer. My own sense is that commerciality enunciates the purpose and the adverse effect test enunciates the method by which the protection of right holders should be gauged. In other words, we should protect against unauthorized commercial reuse (except, for example, in parody cases) pre-

---

101 Canadian courts may look at the test also when examining the compatibility of the educational exceptions with the three-step test. The approach taken in proposed section 30.04 is to remove non-TPM protected material and material that includes a "clearly visible notice," a term which may be defined at a later date by regulations. This seems to follow the logic of an implied license or a novel form of estoppel. In equitable terminology, failure to take steps to limit reuse (by using a TPM and/or notice) after making material available online amounts to a waiver of one's right to enforce copyright against educational establishments. This license and/or equity analysis may work for material made available with the authorization of the right holder. A harder case would involve material that is there without such authorization but which does not meet the actual or constructive knowledge test of illegality contained in proposed section 30.04(5).

On the application of international norms by Canadian courts, see Daniel Gervais, "The Role of International Treaties in the Interpretation of Canadian Intellectual Property Statutes" in O. Fitzgerald, ed., *The Globalized Rule of Law: Relationships between International and Domestic Law* (Toronto: Irwin Law, 2006) 549–72.

cisely because it negatively affects an existing or reasonably predictable market for the copyright work.

In spite of those significant areas in need of further clarification, the Bill drafters had the right idea when they decided to add specific exceptions instead of an open-ended "such as" or similar wording in the chapeau of existing section 29. While that option is intellectually appealing due to its apparent unlimited flexibility, the Bill's approach is superior for at least three reasons. First, adding "such as" would not *demonstrably* solve anything; it would merely postpone the issue in hopes of favourable court decisions. There is no guarantee that courts would "add" the purposes Canada needs, those that the policy review leading to the tabling of the Bill, has identified. It thus represents a policy gamble. Second, it would generate uncertainty and associated costs, until and unless we hear from appellate courts on a variety of new fair dealing purposes.[102] Third, in the wake of *CCH*,[103] Canada already has a fair degree of flexibility on the fairness *criteria*.

Adding open flexibility on *purpose* of the use would potentially reach well beyond US fair use, itself already at risk of a three-step test violation. Put differently, Canada limits fair dealing purposes, while the United States codified a historical rule of reason (four factors) that now looks like a rather rigid "formula" to determine fairness.[104] However, in both countries one of the two parts of the exception is constrained (purpose OR fairness), which at least the first step of the three-step test seems to require. Removing all constraints by adding "such as," while acknowledging the flexibility on fairness criteria enunciated in *CCH*, may thus clash with the three-step test.[105] It also transfers policy-making responsibility to courts, thus adding uncertainty to an already complex copyright regulatory scheme,[106] and not addressing the known problems with the current structure of exceptions in the Act.

---

102 Bill C-32 should harmonize the "source identification" component of fair dealing, basing it on the moral right to claim authorship and requiring that the author and original work be identified unless impracticable. Compare, e.g., ss. 29.21(1)(a) and 30.04(2). Then, how will new fair dealing purposes interface with, specific exceptions? See, e.g., s. 30.2(4).

103 *CCH Canadian Ltd. v. Law Society of Upper Canada*, [2004] 1 S.C.R. 339, http://csc.lexum.umontreal.ca/en/2004/2004scc13/2004scc13.html [*CCH*].

104 17 U.S.C. § 107.

105 See above note 53.

106 See Mistrale Goudreau, "Réforme de droit d'auteur et interprétation judiciaire" in this volume.

C. CONCLUSION

Bill C-32 proposes the implementation of several interesting ideas to modernize the *Copyright Act*. Among the most interesting aspects are the proposed exceptions for user-generated content, parody and education. In this chapter, I considered the normative arguments in support of the UGC exception, and questions concerning the proposed wording. I am concerned that superimposing the commerciality and "adverse effect" criteria may create confusion and suggested an approach to reconcile what seem to be a statement of purpose and the applicable test.

However, the Bill has a major flaw. It does not provide a solution to the unpaid file-sharing of music, a solution that Canadian songwriters and performers desperately need The Bill would implement the 1996 WIPO treaties but sings the same tired song that more enforcement will somehow do in Canada what it has failed to do in the choir of countries that have tried it for over ten years. More enforcement may work to target marginal, recalcitrant users and it does seem useful for the film industry, which has been impacted by the Internet very differently from the music industry. While the music industry has shrunk by almost half and record companies are making survival deals that do not seem favourable for creators, Canadian songwriters and performers — other than a very small group of the very successful ones — are suffering. A world in which extremely talented Canadian music creators must abandon their craft for financial reasons at a time in history when people listen to more music than ever before but are simply unable to use it and pay for it the way they want would be a major tragedy, one that is entirely avoidable.

CHAPTER SIXTEEN

Culture Matters:

Why Canada's Proposed Amendments to its Copyright Law Should Revisit Moral Rights

Mira T. Sundara Rajan*

A. INTRODUCTION

Copyright law has not entirely lost its ability to surprise. Canada's latest round of proposed copyright reforms, the third "new" bill in five years, reminds us of one area in which international copyright rules have taken an unexpected twist: performers' rights.[1]

Since 2002, performers have enjoyed more rights than ever before in the history of copyright law. In that year, a Copyright Treaty and a Performances and Phonograms Treaty, prepared by the World Intellectual Property Organization (WIPO) and known collectively as the WIPO Internet Treaties, entered into force.[2] Of the two, the *WIPO Performances and*

* For a comprehensive treatment of moral rights, on which this article is based, see Mira T. Sundara Rajan, *Moral Rights: Principles, Practice and New Technology*, Oxford University Press (New York) 2010. The author would like to thank Tom Horacek, JD (UBC, 2009) for his assistance with citations. This research was supported by the Social Sciences and Humanities Research Council of Canada.

1 The current Bill C-32 was tabled by the government on 2 June 2010. Bill C-32, *An Act to Amend the Copyright Act*, 3d Sess., 40th Parl., 2010, www2.parl.gc.ca/HousePublications/Publication.aspx?DocId=4580265&Language=e&Mode=1. Bill C-60 was introduced in 2005, and Bill C-61 appeared in 2008: www2.parl.gc.ca/HousePublications/Publication.aspx?Docid=3570473&file=4. A commentary on Bill C-60 is available at /www2.parl.gc.ca/Sites/LOP/LegislativeSummaries/Bills_ls.asp?lang=e&source=library_prb&Parl=38&Ses=1&ls=C60.

2 *WIPO Copyright Treaty*, 20 December 1996, www.wipo.int/treaties/en/ip/wct/trtdocs_wo033.html, 36 I.L.M. 65 [WCT]; *WIPO Performances and Phonograms Treaty*, 20

Phonograms Treaty (WPPT) introduced various specific improvements to the international status of performers. Among its innovations, the WPPT counts a new "moral right" that seeks to protect the non-commercial interests of performing artists in their work. In doing so, it focuses on two aspects of the performer's art. First, every performer is entitled to have his or her performance attributed to him or her by name.[3] Second, the integrity of the performance is to be protected by prohibiting distortion, mutilation, or damaging alteration of the work.[4]

In a world where discussion of copyright issues seems fixated on the money to be made, the performer's moral right is a curious stab at altruism — a throwback, perhaps, to a nineteenth-century view of art as a vitally important activity carried on by gifted people. Moral rights such as these, whether for authors or performers, have been strongly opposed by the United States. In particular, an eminently practical copyright lobby in Hollywood apparently sees moral rights as an idea beyond redemption.[5] Among other concerns, the Hollywood film industry views the potential loss of commercial control over the substantial economic investment in films as a disastrous turn for the US film industry.

In response to these concerns, the moral rights of performers mandated by the WPPT do not apply to any situation where a performance is used in the context of a film.[6] But this restriction, though significant, is still a relatively minor one. A much larger issue may be why, and how, moral rights found their way into the international copyright regime at all.

There are at least two interesting ways of responding to this question. The first is to note the preoccupation of the music industry with the expansion of copyright to cover new media activities, such as the downloading of music files from the Internet. The music industry may see any increase of rights as potentially beneficial to copyright-holders — even though performers' moral rights must always remain vested in individual human beings, and, with the limited exception of Japan, can never be exercised anywhere by a corporation.[7] Apart from a few commentators who have

---

December 1996, www.wipo.int/treaties/en/ip/wppt, 36 I.L.M. 76 [WPPT].

3 WPPT, above note 2, Art. 5(1).

4 WPPT, above note 2, Art. 5(1).

5 See, for example, David Nimmer's discussion of this issue: David Nimmer, "Conventional Copyright: A Morality Play" (1992) 3 Entertainment Law Review 94 at 95–97.

6 Note the definition of "phonogram" in Article 2(b) of the WPPT, above note 2.

7 This peculiarity of Japanese law is accomplished by including corporations within the Japanese definition of authorship. See *Japanese Copyright Act*, available in English translation on the website of the Copyright Research and Information Center

laboured to bring moral rights to greater prominence in the US,[8] moral rights remain rather poorly understood. As a result, the music industry may harbour hopes for how moral rights could be used to support their goals. Those hopes may or may not be supported by the theory behind the law, but they could help to explain a favourable perspective on moral rights for performers at the United States Trade Representative's office.

The second response is exponentially more interesting than the first. It is to consider the possibility that moral rights for performers respond, in some way, to a cultural shift — in particular, to the new culture of music that is developing through the use of digital media. Truly, "[p]erformances are not what they used to be."[9] The moral rights of performers in the WPPT reflect the new status of performers in a society where the performing arts are important in a new way. Without performances, and novelty value aside, digital music media would be fundamentally uninteresting to the public. It may be fair to say that modern musical culture is focused on performance in preference to every other kind of musical experience — including composition — and performers have accordingly graduated to the full spectrum of rights enjoyed by authors since moral rights were introduced into the *Berne Convention*, the world's first and pre-eminent international copyright agreement, in 1928.[10]

These international happenings may seem esoteric at first glance. But nothing could be further from the truth. In fact, virtually every aspect of copyright law in Canada, as in most other countries, is driven by international developments.[11] It is worth noting that this basic reality actual-

---

www.cric.or.jp/cric_e/clj/clj.html accessed 28 April 2010 [*Japanese Copyright Act*], Chapter II, Section 2, Arts 14–16. Japanese moral rights receive a detailed treatment in Mira T. Sundara Rajan, *Moral Rights: Principles, Practice & New Technology* (New York: Oxford University Press, 2010) (forthcoming) at c. III.

8 For example, see Roberta Rosenthal Kwall, *The Soul of Creativity: Forging a Moral Rights Law for the United States* (Stanford: Stanford Law Books, 2009).

9 See Mira T. Sundara Rajan, "The 'New Listener' and the Virtual Performer: The Need for a New Approach to Performers' Rights," in Michael Geist, ed., *In the Public Interest: The Future of Canadian Copyright Law* (Toronto: Irwin Law, 2005) 309, www.irwinlaw.com/pages/content-commons/the--new-listener--and-virtual-perfomances--the-need-for-a-new-approach-to-performers-rights---mira-sundara-rajan.

10 A comprehensive history of the *Berne Convention* is available in Sam Ricketson's now-classic treatise: Sam Ricketson, *The Berne Convention for the Protection of Literary and Artistic Works: 1886-1986* (London: Centre for Commercial Law Studies, Queen Mary College, Kluwer, 1987).

11 Notably, the desire for membership in the World Trade Organization (WTO) has been the primary drive behind intellectual property reform in less-developed jurisdictions: noteworthy examples of countries involved in copyright reform based

ly involves two dynamics, one political and one legal, although they are closely intertwined.

From a political perspective, Canada's membership in international treaties places it under an obligation to enact suitable reforms to domestic law that will allow it to fulfill its international obligations. In relation to the WIPO Internet Treaties, Canada has been a signatory to these international documents since 1997. But it has yet to enact reforms to its outdated copyright law that will allow it to meet its obligations at WIPO. Implementation delays have been strongly criticized by the American government, with the US Trade Representative's office going so far as to place Canada on its list of countries that are deficient in intellectual property standards, the Special 301 Watch List.[12] Where moral rights are concerned, the US position is more than gently tinged with irony. In twenty-one years since the United States joined the *Berne Convention*, the country has done little to introduce moral rights for authors in its copyright law—moral rights in works of visual art are a limited exception, created by the *Visual Artists Rights Act* of 1990[13]—and it seems unlikely that the United States will conform to the WPPT's requirement of moral rights for performers in the visible future.[14]

In legal terms, the content of international copyright laws largely determines the shape and substance of Canadian law. Canadian copyright norms must reflect the requirements of the WIPO Treaties. But this statement is more nuanced than it might seem at first glance. There is certainly room for Canadian leadership on copyright issues, but exercising leadership depends on the Canadian government's ability to do three things. It must show expertise in its implementation of international rules; en-

---

on the requirements of the Agreement on Trade-Related Aspects of Intellectual Property Rights of the WTO include Russia, China, and India. See Agreement on Trade-Related Aspects of Intellectual Property Rights, 15 April 1994, 1869 U.N.T.S. 299 (being Annex 1C of the Marrakesh Agreement Establishing the World Trade Organization, 1867 U.N.T.S. 3), www.wto.org/english/docs_e/legal_e/27-trips_01_e.htm.

12 Canada's pharmaceutical patent regime has been another well-known reason for US complaints, although the current report emphasizes copyright enforcement issues. See the summary of the US position towards Canada in the 2010 watch list, www.ustr.gov/webfm_send/1906.

13 *Visual Artists Rights Act of 1990*, Pub. L. No. 101-650, 104 Stat. 5128 (codified at 17 U.S.C. § 106A), www.law.cornell.edu/uscode/17/usc_sec_17_00000106---A000-.html [*VARA*].

14 The USA joined the *Berne Convention* in 1988, with effect from 1 March 1989: see www.wipo.int/treaties/en/notifications/berne/treaty_berne_121.html.

courage compromise in the international dialogue on copyright issues at WIPO and beyond; and demonstrate policy directions within Canada that are clear, and clearly legitimate — that is to say, democratically informed. Given these criteria, how successful is Canada's new bill in meeting its legal obligations at WIPO for the protection of performers' moral rights?

B. MORAL RIGHTS HOLLYWOOD-STYLE: THE WPPT

Moral rights, an awkward translation of the French *droit moral*, bring a new dimension to copyright law. The term refers to rights which seek to protect the non-economic interests of authors in their work. As such, they have little to do with the economic benefits generally derived from copyright.[15]

Through the *Berne Convention*, it has become a standard expectation that moral rights will be included in the package of rights accorded to authors by copyright laws. Notably, in Article 6*bis* of Berne, an author's right to the *attribution* of his own work, and his right to protest actions that violate the *integrity* of his work — for example, by modifying it in a way that is "prejudicial to his honor or reputation" — have been included in the bundle of rights available to authors under international copyright agreements since 1928.[16]

But moral rights have always generated controversy at the international level. This is partly due to their origins. The ancestry of an international moral right for authors lies in the civil law systems of Continental Europe. In contrast, moral rights have long been treated as a foreign import by common-law countries, and viewed with a degree of suspicion by them. It is therefore not surprising that the Berne provisions, over some four

---

15 This does not mean, however, that the impact of moral rights is "non-economic"; indeed, their economic impact, in the form of lost sales revenues, investments, and rights, may be substantial. Though not emphasized in copyright debates, their economic dimension is probably among the most important reasons why the rights remain so controversial. For an interesting economic approach to moral rights, see Henry Hansmann & Marina Santilli, "Authors' and Artists' Moral Rights: A Comparative Legal and Economic Analysis" (1997) 26 Journal of Legal Studies 95, http://cyber.law.harvard.edu/propertyoo/respect/hansmann.html.

16 Art 6*bis* of the on moral rights, was adopted in the 1928 Rome revision conference: see the *Berne Convention for the Protection of Literary and Artistic Works*, 9 September 1886, as last revised in Paris 24 July 1971, and amended 28 September 1979, 828 U.N.T.S. 221, www.wipo.int/treaties/en/ip/berne/trtdocs_wo001.html, 25 U.S.T. 1341 [*Berne Convention*]. For details of the proposals, see Ricketson, above note 10 at paras. 3.28 and 8.96–8.99.

decades of evolution, have come to make some important concessions to common-law attitudes.

Notably, subsection 2 of Article 6*bis*, adopted in the *Stockholm Act* of 1967, makes allowances for countries to protect moral rights through either statutory or non-statutory means, and also, to limit the protection of moral rights to the lifetime of the author.[17] This provision was designed to accommodate the legal traditions of the common-law world, effectively allowing the protection of moral rights through common-law torts as a method of satisfying the requirements of Article 6*bis*. For most of the twentieth century, the United Kingdom relied on it to justify the absence of moral rights from its legislative regime, a position that was affirmed by a British government report of the 1950s.[18] Interestingly, a later review of the British copyright law by the Whitford Committee led to an assessment that, in fact, the UK did not meet Berne requirements in this regard. The Whitford Committee Report of 1986 helped to pave the way for the historic provisions on moral rights adopted in the *Copyright, Designs, and Patents Act* of 1988, the first in British copyright history.[19]

In its provisions on performers' moral rights, the WPPT follows an identical formula to that set out in Berne. Article 5 of the Treaty provides for the "Moral Rights of Performers." Article 5(1) grants to a performer the right to be "identified as the performer of his performances," and "to object to any distortion, mutilation or other modification of his performances that would be prejudicial to his reputation." In doing so, the Article provides for the rights of attribution and integrity granted in the *Berne Convention* to be extended to performers; like Article 6*bis*, it also limits the performer's right to make an integrity-based claim to situations where changes to the work can be shown to have a negative impact on the performer's reputation.[20] Similarly, Article 5(2) parallels Article 6*bis*(2) of the *Berne Convention*

---

17 See *Berne Convention, ibid.*

18 Report of the Copyright Committee, 1952 (UK) Cmnd 8662, paras 219–26, www.bopcris.ac.uk/bopall/ref9312.html (Abstract) [Report of the Gregory Committee] accessed 30 April 2010.

19 *Copyright, Designs, and Patents Act, 1988* (UK), 1988, c. 48, www.opsi.gov.uk/acts/acts1988/Ukpga_19880048_en_1.htm [*CDPA*] accessed 30 April 2010. White Paper on Intellectual Property and Innovation, 1952 (UK) Cmnd 9712, [*Report of the Whitford Committee*]. Moral rights were, however, known to the common law: see the seminal early case of *Millar v. Taylor* (1769), 4 Burr. 2303, 98 E. R. 201 (K.B.).

20 Not every country in the world limits the moral right of integrity in this way, but some consider any change to work that is carried out without the author's consent and approval to be a *prima facie* violation of the integrity right. For example, see

in allowing common-law countries, at least in relation to some part of the rights, to substitute tort protections for statutory moral rights.[21]

In recent years, the United States has become the chief opponent of recognizing authors' moral rights, bringing a somewhat schizophrenic quality to its quest for leadership in the drive to realize dramatic improvements of copyright standards at the international level.[22] While the American position on moral rights is far from settled, it is possible to make at least two noteworthy observations about the American influence on the shape of performers' rights in the WPPT. First, performers' moral rights do not apply to all types of performances: in the words of the Treaty, they apply only to 'live aural' performances. Clearly, this terminology excludes at least one major category of performances, that of performances reproduced in audiovisual works — film. As noted above, the exclusion of performers' moral rights from film responds to the concerns of America's powerful film industry, voiced by the Hollywood lobby at the time of the United States' accession to the *Berne Convention* in 1988.[23]

Second, the perception of US industry about the significance of performers' moral rights in the WPPT is not entirely clear. In particular, the Recording Industry Association of America (RIAA) is definitely interested in expanding the rights of copyright-holders in sound recordings as far as possible. It may perceive the adoption of moral rights for performers as being advantageous, sensing a new opportunity to expand copyright protection. Performers might choose to co-operate with the RIAA; or, very controversially, record labels might potentially seek to assert moral rights on their behalf.

The latter interpretation of moral rights would only be possible through a misunderstanding of the law. Legal theory dictates that moral rights must always be personally linked to the author and, therefore, may only be exercised directly by him. Japanese law presents a controversial and virtually unique exception to this rule.[24] Only after the author's death may they

---

France's *Code de la propriete intellectuelle*, Art L121.1, www.celog.fr/cpi/lv1_tt2.htm [*CPI*].

21 Ricketson, above note 10 at paras. 3.28, 8.94–8.99.

22 The ambiguous US position is discussed by David Nimmer, above note 5.

23 The role of the American film lobby in the debate surrounding Berne accession is described by Nimmer, above note 5. Stephen Fraser, "Berne, CFTA, NAFTA and GATT: The Implications of Copyright Droit Moral And Cultural Exemptions in International Trade Law" (1996) 18 Hastings Communications and Entertainment Law Journal 287 analyzes in detail the specific issue of moral rights in film.

24 A similar provision may be found in the Korean copyright law, Art 9; an English version, updated to December 1995, may be found in the WIPO Collection of Laws

be asserted by anyone else — in this case, his descendants, or a personally-designated representative. However, copyright theory and practice are in a state of flux, and there is no guarantee that moral rights will continue to be applied in a pure, or even conceptually consistent, manner. Nowhere is this uncertainty greater than in the United States, where the idea of a moral right for authors remains relatively underdeveloped.

C. MORAL RIGHTS FOR CANADIAN PERFORMERS: YET ANOTHER OPPORTUNITY MISSED?

The proposed Canadian bill undertakes the overt step of establishing moral rights for performers in the Canadian *Copyright Act*. The move should be viewed as generally positive, in two senses. First, Canada joins the ranks of countries that are signatories of the WIPO Internet Treaties, and have chosen to enact performers' moral rights as part of their implementation of the international accords. Notably, both the UK and Australia, sister common-law jurisdictions, have created moral rights for performers in their copyright laws. Australian implementation, like its regime for moral rights, more generally, is a model of legislative reform.[25] The UK position, like its overall approach to moral rights, is ambiguous, and has been criticized by commentators.[26] Nevertheless, the simple fact of adopting moral rights for performers means that each country, within its respective limits, has signalled its commitment to the international community — to the belief that obligations assumed in the international arena are to be taken seriously by its members. To whatever extent possible, their position helps to enrich international discussions and support better compromises on international copyright issues. Canada, as a good international citizen,

---

for Electronic Access, www.wipo.int/clea/en/text_pdf.jsp?lang=EN&id=2743. The structure of Korean copyright law closely resembles Japanese law and, through it, German law. For a fascinating discussion of the colonial history between Japan and Korea, and Korea's distinctive cultural affinity with moral rights, see Ilhyung Lee, "Culturally-Based Copyright Systems?: The US and Korea in Conflict" (2001) 79 Washington University Law Quarterly 1103.

25 See Australian *Copyright Act 1968* (Cth), www.austlii.edu.au/au/legis/cth/consol_act/ca1968133; *Copyright Amendment (Moral Rights) Act 2000*, www.comlaw.gov.au/ComLaw/Legislation/Act1.nsf/0/D25408DC39D0C132CA257434001EEDAE/$file/1592000.pdf.

26 For example see Ilanah Simon Fhima, "The Introduction of Moral Rights for Performers," Part 1 [2006] European Intellectual Property Review 552 & Part 2 [2006] European Intellectual Property Review 600.

has done the right thing by respecting the letter of the law where international copyright matters are concerned.

Secondly, moral rights for performers are to be implemented into Canadian law on exactly the same terms governing the protection of authors' moral rights. This aspect of performers' moral rights must be cited as a strength, because it emphasizes the equality of performers with authors under Canadian law. The approach confirms that Canada will be at least as serious about performers' moral rights as it is about the moral rights of authors.

But this last point undoubtedly leads to what must be a serious and fundamental critique of the proposed reforms. The problem of implementing the WIPO Internet Treaties in Canadian law presents a valuable opportunity to reconsider Canadian copyright practice — to examine Canada's approaches to copyright problems, and perhaps, improve the sophistication of the solutions generated by Canadian law. Unfortunately, where moral rights are concerned, this opportunity appears to have been wasted. Instead, performers' moral rights in Canada are a copy of authors' moral rights; and the flaws and dissatisfactions generated by the treatment of authors are now perpetuated in the new legislative scheme for performers.

Ironically, this problem must have arisen quite naturally. As noted above, a similar approach was followed by the WPPT in its presentation of performers' moral rights: they are closely resemble authors' moral rights as framed in Article 6*bis* of the *Berne Convention*, though they are not identical to the Berne formulation. No doubt, Canadian drafters took their lead from the practices at WIPO, itself. However, the significance of following the Berne approach is rather different — its provisions on authors' moral rights represented a series of compromises established over five decades, and it could be argued that the WPPT had little scope to move beyond the norms established by Berne. On the other hand, the Canadian treatment of moral rights may render them largely unprotected in practice. A consideration of how moral rights have evolved in Canadian law shows that, if the current bill is adopted, persistent difficulties will plague performers' moral interests much as they have afflicted authors' moral rights over the past eighty years.

D. THE MORAL RIGHTS OF AUTHORS IN CANADIAN LAW: WHAT CAN PERFORMERS LEARN?

Canada, legally and otherwise, is a more or less happy combination of French and English traditions. However, the now relatively smooth surface of French-English relations should not obscure the fact that Canadian legal practice is built on the shifting sands of an alliance between two potentially conflicting cultural traditions. In no area of the law could this be more true than in relation to moral rights.

A closer look at the treatment of moral rights in Canadian law reveals the deep divisions on this issue between French- and English-Canadian jurists. The latest ruling of the Supreme Court of Canada, in the case of *Théberge*, resulted in a decision where the court was split precisely along linguistic lines.[27] What is the status and authority of a majority ruling in a case such as this? The observation that Canadian law must be more accepting of moral rights because of its French roots is appealing in theory, but a consideration of the facts shows it to be fundamentally untrue.

Rather, Canada's approach to moral rights is one of suspicion. In particular, three features of the Canadian regime illustrate the complex status of moral rights. First, it is true that moral rights enjoy explicit formal protection. However, they are simultaneously subject to onerous requirements of proof, represented both by the language of the statute, and by judicial conventions surrounding the issue. Canadian judges prefer to rely on objective assessments of damage to an author's reputation in order to establish a violation of moral rights.[28] The scope for defending a moral rights claim in Canada is correspondingly liberal.

Second, moral rights may be waived comprehensively. The effect of these provisions is to weaken the bargaining power of authors in contractual negotiations with industry, and has encouraged the development of standard practices which fail to respect moral rights. Where waivers are concerned, Canadian law also includes provisions that effectively allow third parties using a work to benefit from waivers of moral rights that were made in relation to the publisher.[29] Arguably, this provision amounts to an effective alienation of moral rights, violating the essence of legal rights that are meant to be personally vested in the author and, thereby, inalienable. All of these features of authors' moral rights have been mechanically transported to the treatment of performers' moral rights in the proposed reform Bill.

---

27 *Théberge v. Galerie d'Art du Petit Champlain inc.*, 2002 SCC 34, www.canlii.org/en/ca/scc/doc/2002/2002scc34/2002scc34.html, [2002] 2 S.C.R. 336..

28 For example, see *Snow v. The Eaton Centre Ltd.* (1982), 70 C.P.R. (2d) 105 [*Snow v. The Eaton Centre*].

29 For example, see Canadian *Copyright Act*, R.S.C. 1985, c. C-42, s. 14.1(4).

1) A Pioneering Common-Law Country

Canada holds the distinction of being the first common-law country to adopt provisions on moral rights into its copyright law. It did so in 1931, only three years after moral rights were first adopted in the *Berne Convention*.[30] It is equally significant that moral rights became a part of Canadian law a mere seven years after the country's first independent copyright law came into effect, the Canadian *Copyright Act* of 1921.[31] Interestingly, rights akin to moral rights enjoyed formal recognition even before the legislative amendments of 1931, but they were not in the *Copyright Act*. Rather, the Canadian *Criminal Code* provisions of 1915 included recognition for attribution and integrity.[32]

Canada's reasons for enacting moral rights were simple: it had signed the *Berne Convention*, and, Canada being a good international citizen, the Canadian government immediately set about enacting provisions to meet its international obligations. More than a desire to meet copyright obligations *per se*, the Canadian government was probably influenced by two other considerations — its peculiar awareness of cultural issues as a close neighbour of the United States, and a growing commitment to human

30 See David Vaver, "Moral Rights Yesterday, Today and Tomorrow" (1999) 7(3) International Journal of Law and Information Technology 270 at 275–76.

31 *The Copyright Act, 1921*, S.C. 1921, c. 24 (entered into force in 1924). Prior to 1921, copyright in Canada was governed by the British *Imperial Copyright Act of 1842*, which applied to all British dominions. The Canadian government did try to enact a Canadian copyright law at various points, but the idea received serious consideration only after a British reform led to a new UK and imperial copyright act in 1911. The Canadian Copyright Act of 1921 was in part a reaction to taxes imposed on American books by British legislation ; Canadian legislation enacted for this purpose also created a tax on American imports, but it was far less than the tax collected by the British. The reason for taxation of American products was the flourishing US practice of re-printing copyright-protected works from other jurisdictions, an industry norm that was only limited by bilateral conventions on copyright initiated by the US, as the United States was not a party to the *Berne Convention* of 1886.

32 David Vaver, *Copyright Law* (Toronto: Irwin Law, 2000) at 159. Vaver is right to note this landmark: although the provisions were not in the *Copyright Act*, codification in the *Criminal Code* shows that the law had already achieved a significant level of acceptance. Formal recognition in criminal legislation certainly represents something beyond the informal recognition of a tort. Given the current emphasis on criminalizing copyright infringement, it is interesting to note that the idea is not a new one; indeed, other laws of the world have called infringement a criminal offence for even longer; see, for example, the discussion of the Russian copyright law of 1911, in Mira T. Sundara Rajan, *Copyright and Creative Freedom: A Study of Post-Socialist Law Reform* (New York: Routledge, 2006) c. IV at 82–85.

rights.[33] The language of the provision adopted in 1931 exactly mirrored the terms of Article 6*bis* of the *Berne Convention*.[34] However, the adaptation of the Berne provision into Canadian law led to an awkward and ambiguous result — what aspects of attribution were protected?[35] Did the right of integrity require proof of damage to reputation, or not?[36] In comparison, a still subtler ambiguity in the drafting of the integrity right in the 1988 British provisions required judicial clarification of the issue by the High Court. The issue arose in the very first integrity claim under the new rules, the "hip" and sparkling *Confetti Records* case.[37] David Vaver points out

---

33 The instrumental role of Canadian lawyer and professor, John Peters Humphrey, in preparing the initial draft of the *Universal Declaration of Human Rights*, G.A. Res. 217A, U.N. GAOR, 3d Sess., U.N. Doc A/810 (Dec. 12, 1948) [UDHR], must be noted.

34 See David Vaver, "Authors' Moral Rights in Canada" (1983) 14 International Review of Intellectual Property and Competition Law 329 [Vaver, "Authors' Moral Rights in Canada"] at 341.

35 See Vaver's discussion of the aspects of the attribution, or "paternity" right: Vaver, "Authors' Moral Rights in Canada," above note 33 at 352–55.

36 So subtle a change as the removal of a comma from the Berne phrase leads to this doubt. The Canadian section states that the author may restrain "any distortion, mutilation or other modification of the said work that would be prejudicial to his honour or reputation." (Quoted in Vaver, "Authors' Moral Rights in Canada," *ibid.* at 341.) In fact, prior to the latest amendments in 1994, the copyright law of India provided for moral rights in much the same language as the Canadian act, but it divided the phrase in its s 57, into two parts. "'Any modification' could lead to a violation of the right of integrity, but it would depend on the artist's ability to show 'damage to his honour or reputation.'" See Mira T. Sundara Rajan, "Moral Rights and the Protection of Cultural Heritage: *Amar Nath Sehgal v Union of India*" (2001) 10(1) International Journal of Cultural Property 79 at 83–84, and the old section 57 of the *Indian Copyright Act* 1957, Act 14 of 1957, s 57; the act is published by the Government of India, http://copyright.gov.in/Documents/CopyrightRules1957.pdf [Indian *Copyright Act*]. The Indian *Copyright Act* is available in many online versions, some of which are out of date; for example, the pre-1994 section 57 provisions can still be found on the website of the Commonwealth Legal Information Institute, www.commonlii.org/in/legis/num_act/ca1957133. Vaver's criticism of the integrity right focuses on the question of whether personal reputation, as well as literary interpretation, is involved, and he concludes that both are legitimately touched by the integrity right. The critique could apply equally to the *Berne Convention* itself, which has also enshrined the term "honour," of uncertain legal connotations in modern copyright law. Vaver also draws attention to the use of the term "restrain," clearly intended to invoke the court's power to grant an injunction: see Vaver, "Authors' Moral Rights in Canada", *ibid.* at 355–60.

37 *Confetti Records v. Warner Music UK Ltd.*, [2003] EWHC 1274 (Ch.). The case involved hip-hop music, known as "Garage" in the UK.

> the folly of transporting virtually verbatim a provision from an international Convention into a domestic statute, without elaborating the provision in the manner intended by the Convention and without adapting it to the existing structure of domestic laws . . .[38]

Subsequent amendment of the Canadian law waited a half-century and more. Reform in 1988 brought some clarification to the moral rights of authors, and the Canadian government took the additional step of codifying a right of publicity which protects authors from the commercial association of their works with products in advertising.[39] However, the greater precision of the 1988 provisions on moral rights was achieved at a cost. It is true that ambiguities in the earlier enactment were resolved, but the solutions invariably took the form of explicit restrictions on the exercise of moral rights.

Two noteworthy examples of these new limits on moral rights arise in relation to the integrity right, and on the question of waivers. As noted above, the drafting of the integrity right in the 1931 amendments created a degree of ambiguity about whether or not proof of damage to reputation was required to show that the right had been violated. When Canadian copyright law was reviewed by Claude Brunet and A.A. Keyes in 1977, they recommended that proof of reputation should not be required under the new Canadian law.[40] The provision was indeed clarified, but the new version actually added a new requirement of proof of damage to reputation. The right was transformed from, potentially, a pure right of integrity, into a limited right of reputation.[41]

---

38 Vaver, "Authors' Moral Rights in Canada," above note 33 at 330.

39 Section 28.2(1)(b) of the Canadian *Copyright Act*, above note 29. Vaver, "Authors' Moral Rights in Canada," *ibid.* at 331–40 mentions this protection of the conditions in which a work receives public exposure as part of the common law of moral rights in Canada. Accordingly, codification in this case represents a further degree of formalization for a pre-existing right, rather than the creation of a new right at Canadian copyright law.

40 Andrew A. Keyes & Claude Brunet, "Le droit d'auteur au Canada : propositions pour la révision de la loi" (Ottawa: Consommation et Corporations Canada, 1977) [Keyes & Brunet]. The Ministry of Consumer and Corporate Affairs, which then had an Intellectual Property bureau. Responsibility for copyright law in Canada is now shared by 2 ministries, Heritage and Industry Canada. The split leads to bureaucratic inefficiencies, between 2 ministries with fundamentally different portfolios, and has probably been one of the structural obstacles to copyright reform in Canada.

41 Keyes and Brunet made two types of recommendations in relation to Canadian moral rights: the first, a general call for clarification, and the second, specific proposals for the treatment of moral rights in amended legislation. For a quick overview of

In relation to the question of whether moral rights could be waived in Canadian law, the changes of 1988 made waivers fully and comprehensively available to authors.[42] Interestingly, the practical consequence of this provision was to transform waivers into a standard feature of Canadian copyright contracts.[43] The example is an important one: it illustrates one of the ways in which the influence of law is felt far beyond the confines of the courtroom. The language of the law can fundamentally shape the terms on which industries deal with copyright works. Litigation is only the final, narrowest, and most extreme consequence of legal provisions on moral rights.

As for the level of general clarity, an area where improvement was needed, the drafting of specific provisions was clarified, but an overall problem remained.[44] The issue concerned the structure of the Act. Canadian moral rights are dispersed throughout the *Copyright Act*, and it is difficult to piece together the complete jigsaw puzzle of the scheme. The rights are expressed in sections 14 and 28 of the Act, and they are separated from each other by a variety of unrelated provisions. The rationale for doing so may be that section 14 defines the rights, while section 28 defines infringement. The placement of the infringement offense in section 28 may reflect the fact that other parts of the Act dealing with the infringement of copyright may be found in the same area of the Act. But this explanation is not satisfactory. The provisions in section 28 also serve to define the integrity right, and to clarify the other definitions of moral rights which are introduced in the earlier set. The two sections need to be read together to make sense.

---

the proposals, see R.J. Roberts' review of the report, in (1978) 4(2) Canadian Public Policy 264. The tone of the review is somewhat overwrought, but, in fact, the proposals made by Keyes and Brunet reflect common practices in civil law countries — including damages and an accounting of profits among the remedies available for a moral rights infringement, for example. The damages awarded in a moral rights case are highly discretionary, and could be symbolic: the recent Hugo case resulted in damages of €1 to the plaintiff. Roberts is also mistaken when he says that the report would allow authors to "force the copyright owner to withdraw from publication the author's work": the French model underlying this proposal would entail serious economic consequences for the author, and is a severely limited right.

42 Currently, section 14(4) of the Canadian *Copyright Act*, above note 29.

43 The Writers' Union of Canada now advises Canadian authors to refuse to sign publishing contracts that include waivers of moral rights. The warning may be found under "Hot Topics: Danger Clauses, Dubious Practices & Cautions" on the Union website, www.writersunion.ca/ht_clausecautions.asp.

44 Keyes & Brunet, above note 39.

2) The Rights Protected: Attribution, Integrity, and Association

Section 14 of the *Copyright Act* defines two rights: attribution and integrity. The attribution right is comprehensive, and represents an innovative aspect of the Canadian moral rights scheme. It not only affirms the author's right to be "associated with the work . . . by name," but it also protects the author's right to maintain a pseudonym, and to protect any chosen anonymity. With regard to integrity, this section only tells us that "The author of a work has, subject to section 28.2, the right to the integrity of the work." For the substance of the integrity right, it is necessary to refer to the latter provision directly.[45] The definition of integrity in section 28.2 exactly parallels Article 6*bis* of the *Berne Convention*. It states that infringement of the integrity right will occur when the work is "distorted, mutilated or otherwise modified," in such a way as to "prejudice. . .the honor or reputation of the author."[46]

But this provision has a second part. It provides that the author's right of integrity will be infringed if his work is "used in association with a product, service, cause or institution" in such a way as to "prejudice the honour or reputation of the author." This right could be considered an aspect of the integrity right, or a third Canadian moral right, known as a right of association. Given the presence of the right of association within a provision defining integrity, the first view seems more accurate. The framing of the right mirrors a similar provision in the UK *Copyright, Designs and Patents Act* of the same year.[47] In the Canadian context, the unauthorized use of a work for commercial or endorsement purposes is not only a violation of the author's copyright. It may also involve a violation of the moral right of integrity, provided that the author can show that the association has caused damage to his reputation.

3) A Special Case: The Visual Arts

It is striking to note that, in one specific case, Canadian law does not require proof of damage to an author's honour or reputation. This will arise where the author is an artist in the exact sense of the word — the creator

45 It is worth noting that the electronic version of the Act does not correct this inconvenience, by offering the facility of a hyperlink to connect directly between sections 14 and 28: see n. 36, http://laws.justice.gc.ca/eng/C-42/index.html.

46 Canadian *Copyright Act*, above note 29, s 28.2 (1) (a).

47 *CDPA*, above note 19.

of a work of visual art, such as a painting, sculpture, or engraving. Any "distortion, mutilation or other modification" is "deemed" to be prejudicial to the author's reputation; rather than eliminate the need for damage to reputation, the Canadian Act tells us to infer it. In practice, this means that in the case of a work of visual art, any modification is, *prima facie,* an infringement of the artist's right of integrity.[48]

This provision accomplishes the important result of shifting the burden of proof from artist to audience, owner, or user. The formula by which this is done is not as straightforward as it could be. The right of integrity could have been left open-ended, with no mention of reputation. This would allow the artist to protest any modification of his work that he found objectionable — the usual practice in civil-law jurisdictions.[49] Regardless, the moral right of integrity is much stronger for visual artists than for others. The special status of visual artists is reminiscent of the American situation, where the *Visual Artists Rights Act* of 1990 enacted moral rights for this class of artists alone.[50] Why the distinction? It may be justified by the unique nature of an artwork: in contrast to other art forms, there is one, and only one, original work of visual art. In this sense, visual art is quite unlike a book, music, or any other type of copyright work. Damage to an original artwork can never be set right.

But if, in fact, this is the rationale behind the separate regime for visual art, the Canadian law then goes on to impose two unexpected limits.[51] The first of these involves the conditions of display: controversially, the circumstances in which an artwork is exhibited will not give rise to a moral rights claim.[52] Secondly, conservation is addressed: "steps taken in good faith to restore or preserve the work" will also be exempted from an in-

---

48 But note that, in Canadian law, "modification" will have to be read *ejusdem generis,* in the context of a phrase beginning with "distortion . . . [and] mutilation," and it is conceivable that an artist might have to show that the modification is inherently damaging, or likely to cause damage to the work.

49 For example, see the French Intellectual Property Code, Art L121-1: *Loi N° 92-597 du 1er juillet 1992 relative au code de la propriété intellectuelle (partie législative), Journal officiel de la République française du 8 février 1994; Légifrance: Le service public de la diffusion du droit,* www.legifrance.gouv.fr/affichCode.do?cidTexte=LEGITEXT000006069414&dateTexte=20100412 [Intellectual Property Code, CPI, *Code de la Propriété Intellectuelle*].

50 *VARA*, above note 13.

51 Canadian *Copyright Act*, above note 29, s. 28.2(3).

52 The "Explanation" to India's section 57 states: "*Explanation.*—Failure to display a work or to display it to the satisfaction of the author shall not be deemed to be an infringement of the rights conferred by this section." See Indian *Copyright Act*, above note 36.

fringement claim. The purpose of the latter provision is clear: the goal is to avoid discouraging or penalizing valuable conservation work. The rationale for exempting the conditions of display from liability is harder to discover. It seems rather arbitrary — a way to limit the liability of galleries, companies, and perhaps government, for the mistreatment of artworks in their possession.[53]

4) Inalienability and Waiver

If the framing of moral rights by Canadian legislators seems generally more favourable than the UK approach, the treatment of waivers in the *Copyright Act* is a caveat to the success of the endeavour. Canadian law follows the British approach of allowing extensive waivers. Indeed, under Canadian law, the only meaningful restrictions on the scope of waivers would appear to be those found in the common-law principles governing the interpretation of contracts. Short of a finding of unconscionable dealings, or waiver under duress, nothing compels an author to retain his moral rights, or restores them to him once they are waived.

Canadian law includes a most controversial provision on waivers. Article 14.1 (4) provides

> Where a waiver of any moral right is made in favour of an owner or a licensee of copyright, it may be invoked by any person authorized by the owner or licensee to use the work, unless there is an indication to the contrary in the waiver.

In other words, should an author waive his moral rights when he sells or offers to licence his copyright to a publisher, he cannot then claim a violation of moral rights by anyone who is subsequently authorized by the *publisher* to use the work. An example helps to understand the implications of this provision. The author of a book signs a contract with the publisher, waiving his moral rights. The publisher authorizes another publisher to produce a chapter of the book as an article in a volume of essays. The author may object to the division of his work into separately

---

53 A similar issue occurs in Indian law; the reason is, most probably, to protect the Indian government from liability for damage to works of art that it owns. In the context of a developing country, the fear is understandable: government is a major owner, and sponsor, of works. At the same time, the importance of its role in protecting culture should not fail to attract obligations. See the comments of the Delhi High Court in the landmark *Amar Nath Sehgal* case: *Amar Nath Sehgal v Union of India* 2005 (30) PTC 253 (Delhi High Court) [*Sehgal*].

published fragments. However, he cannot object to the republication by a third party as a violation of his moral right of integrity. The practical utility of the provision is clear: it allows the publisher to exploit his own rights without creating any inhibition in the purchaser about the possible consequences of moral rights. In effect, the provision is a kind of negative assignment — an alienation in fact, if not in name. The author agrees to forego his moral rights, but the publisher effectively conveys that protection to any person who acquires the authority to use the work from it. At the same time, Canadian law specifies that authors cannot assign their moral rights; they can only be inherited upon the author's death.[54] In this sense, moral rights are formally 'inalienable'; but, can they truly be considered inalienable when they can be waived in favour of a third party with whom the author has no contract?

5) A Drought in the Courts

Although litigation is but one measure of the effectiveness of moral rights, the paucity of cases on moral rights in Canada is remarkable. In the entire history of Canada's moral rights provisions to 1988, only one successful case was ever brought by an artist.[55] It was the well-known case of sculptor, Michael Snow, whose sculpture of Canada geese decorating Toronto's Eaton Centre, one fine winter day, found itself adorned with festive ribbons for the Christmas season.[56] Snow argued that this was a violation of his integrity right, and a sympathetic court ruled in his favor, issuing an injunction for the immediate removal of the ribbons. The case also established the principal of reliance on expert evidence as a way of proving the requisite damage to reputation in Canada:

> The plaintiff is adamant in his belief that his naturalistic composition has been made to look ridiculous by the addition of ribbons and suggests it is not unlike dangling earrings from the Venus de Milo. While the matter is not undisputed, the plaintiff's opinion was shared by a number of other well-respected artists and people knowledgeable in his field.[57]

---

54 See Canadian *Copyright Act*, above note 29, ss. 14.1(2) and 14.2(2).

55 Section 12(7) of the old Canadian *Copyright Act* (pre-1988).

56 *Snow v. The Eaton Centre*, above note 28.

57 *Ibid.* at para. 6.

6) Proof of Infringement: The Significance of the *Théberge* Ruling

The Canadian *Copyright Act* defines the duration of moral rights as the minimum required by Berne: it protects them for the same duration as the economic rights enjoyed by the author, for his lifetime and fifty years after his death. In this sense, the practice of the Act is in keeping with the 'monist' theory, whereby economic and moral rights are protected for the same duration. The monist theory is additionally in evidence in the Canadian Act, because no formal distinction is made between an infringement of copyright and an infringement of moral rights.

In Canada, however, the relationship between economic and moral rights is problematic in a deeper sense. If moral rights and economic rights are seen as two branches of the same tree, the logical possibility of a potential overlap between the two arises. In other words, depending on the facts, an infringement claim could be made on both economic and moral grounds. In a truly monist system, the same facts could give rise to both moral and economic claims. On this theory, it should matter little to Canadian courts whether a claim is framed in terms of economic rights or moral rights. It may matter to the plaintiff, because the nature of the remedies available in the two cases will be different, moral rights leading to the practical solutions offered by injunctive relief, while economic rights lead to damages. And, again, in a single case, on a single set of facts, a plaintiff may be entitled to both.

This conclusion is of little concern to the French-speaking judges of the Supreme Court, who seem prepared to move seamlessly between the economic and moral dimensions of an author's rights. For the English-speakers, however, the point needs to be resolved. The judges appear to be concerned that a monist approach implies a degree of equality between moral and economic claims which they are unwilling to recognize. In their view, it is not supported by the Act. As a result, in the recent ruling of *Théberge*, a majority of the Supreme Court affirmed that Canadian law is based on a dualist approach, where moral and economic rights are distinct. In particular, under Canadian law, the hierarchy between the two places economic rights above moral rights. Accordingly, facts that appear to contain the potential for a successful claim on both economic and moral grounds may nevertheless fail to generate a viable claim for the infringement of moral rights. A claim that would succeed as an economic rights claim, if approached as a moral rights issue, may fail.

The reason for this duality, as affirmed by the Supreme Court, is that the nature and standard of proof required for a moral rights infringement in Canada is higher than that required for an infringement of economic rights. The Court takes its cue from the legislation. The key phrase is to be found in "damage to honour or reputation," which appears as a prerequisite for moral rights claims in relation to all works except for the visual arts. No such evidence of an effect on reputation is required to show a violation of economic rights. On the contrary, any unauthorized action is, by definition, a violation of the author's economic copyright.

A consideration of the facts of *Théberge* illustrates this point, and shows how precariously balanced is the majority's reasoning. The case involved paintings by a Canadian painter, Claude Théberge, who authorized a company to make posters and art cards of his work for sale to the public. Unexpectedly, an art gallery which purchased the cards decided to make a further reproduction—this time, as a canvas-backed copy of the original image. The technique, on which became the case turned, was to lift the ink from the postcard and superimpose it onto the canvas. The card was left blank, and the ink was transferred to the canvas.

Was this a reproduction of the work? The majority of the Court found that, in fact, no reproduction of Théberge's work had occurred. Rather, there was merely a transfer of ink from one medium to another. There was no increase in the overall number of copies of the work. The element of multiplication, required to constitute a reproduction, was missing.[58] This statement is somewhat reminiscent of the notion of media neutrality in a digital environment articulated by the Supreme Court in the 2006 case of *Robertson*,[59] affirming that the conversion of a piece of writing from print to data—newspaper to CD-ROM—would not qualify as a reproduction of the work.

No unauthorized reproduction under section 3(1) had occurred, but something else was at stake: a potential violation of the artist's moral rights and, in particular, an infringement of the artist's right of integrity under section 28.2(1) of the Act. The artist, himself, had alerted the Court to this fact. In his testimony, Théberge affirmed that the canvas-backed reproductions could be confused with his original works, leading to what

---

58 *Théberge*, above note 27 at paras. 42–50.

59 On the other hand, the re-publication of a work in an online newspaper, subject to a new format and regular updates, would. See *Robertson v. Thomson Corp.*, 2006 SCC 43, http://scc.lexum.umontreal.ca/en/2006/2006scc43/2006scc43.html, [2006] 2 S.C.R. 363.

he considered "a dilution of my work."[60] Owners of Théberge originals might misunderstand the artist's intentions.[61]

However, Justice Binnie, writing for the majority, points out that there is an additional onus of proof that must be satisfied in relation to a moral right.[62] In the case of economic rights, any unauthorized reproduction is a prima facie violation of copyright, and this is clearly indicated in the language of the Act.[63] But this is not the case in relation to moral rights. The Act explicitly requires prejudice to reputation, and Théberge had evidently failed to satisfy the additional requirement of proof. Instead, the artist was asserting an economic right in the guise of a moral right. The right, said Justice Binnie, was a *droit de destination* — a right to control the use of the work, among the moral rights recognized in civilian jurisdictions.[64] A clear distinction is drawn between economic and moral rights, with different standards of proof coming into play in relation to each. This is a dualist theory of copyright — although in Canada, the application of the term "dualist" is slightly jarring. French dualism implies a higher status for moral rights in the legal hierarchy, and leads to protection for moral

---

60 *Théberge*, above note 27 at para. 20.

61 *Ibid.* at paras. 17–21, and, especially, the statements of M. Théberge, himself, reproduced at para. 20.

62 *Ibid.* at para. 17.

63 See Canadian *Copyright Act*, above note 29, s. 3(1).

64 Interestingly, it may be more accurate to characterize the '*droit de destination*' as an economic right: in French law, it is recognized as an aspect of the right of reproduction, and allows an author to exercise some control over the treatment of a work in circulation by a third party who is neither author nor *exploitant*. The reference to a moral rights aspect seems unusual; it could be considered a follow-on to the right of disclosure, by allowing an author some control over the fate of a published work. See Pascal Kamina, *Film Copyright in the European Union, Cambridge Studies in Intellectual Property Rights* (Cambridge: Cambridge University Press, 2002) at para. 1.97; he defines the right as, "an expression of the right of the author to limit uses of copies of his work (droit de destination) . . ." Kamina does not mention the moral aspect of the *droit de destination*, but he makes an interesting comment in relation to Belgian law, reformed to include specific aspects of *destination* within its provisions on economic rights; he says, "that the theory could still be valid to justify a control over the resale of copies of copyright works or other acts of distribution not covered by the rental and lending rights." This could be interpreted as the (continued) existence of moral aspects of *destination* under Belgian law. Online sources also emphasize the economic nature of the right; for example, see www.cabinetaci.com/le-droit-moral-et-patrimonial-de-l-auteur.html. The right is the subject of a thesis by Frédéric Pollaud-Dulian, *Le droit de destination: le sort des exemplaires en droit d'auteur*, ed LGDJ, Bibliothèque de droit privé Tome 205 (ISBN : 978-2-275-00791-5), 1989.

rights beyond the scope of economic rights. In Canada, it is just the reverse. Dualism means that moral rights are restricted in scope.

A brief consideration of the dissent in *Théberge* is instructive. Writing for the minority — all of the Francophone judges of the Court — Justice Gonthier argues that the majority approach is artificial. The claim may well involve a moral interest, but it is also a clear violation of the author's copyright. His observations emphasize the fact that the nature of reproduction in a digital environment must receive due consideration:

> . . . [I]t is clear that multiplication of the number of copies of a work is not an essential element of the act of "reproduc[ing it] . . . in any material form whatever". It does not matter that the process which produces a new materialization eliminates another; all that matters is that a new act of fixation occurs. Therefore, what we must *count* in order to determine whether a work has been reproduced is not the total number of copies of the work in existence after the rematerialization, *but the number of materializations that occurred over time.*[65] (emphasis added)

In an interesting afterword to the case, the 2003 *Desputeaux* decision is the latest ruling from the Supreme Court touching on moral rights. It supports the monist idea in Canadian law. The case involved arbitration proceedings, and the interesting question of whether copyright lies sufficiently within the ambit of personal rights to fall outside the jurisdiction of arbitrators. The Supreme Court states:

> Parliament has indeed declared that moral rights may not be assigned, but it permits the holders of those rights to waive the exercise of them. The Canadian legislation therefore recognizes the overlap between economic rights and moral rights in the definition of copyright.[66]

---

65 *Théberge*, above note 27 at para. 149.

66 *Desputeaux v. Éditions Chouette (1987) inc.*, 2003 SCC 17, http://csc.lexum.umontreal.ca/en/2003/2003scc17/2003scc17.html, [2003] 1 S.C.R. 178 at para. 57 [*Desputeaux*]. The Court goes on to say:

> Parliament has indeed declared that moral rights may not be assigned, but it permits the holders of those rights to waive the exercise of them. The Canadian legislation therefore recognizes the overlap between economic rights and moral rights in the definition of copyright. This Court has in fact stressed the importance placed on the economic aspects of copyright in Canada: the Copyright Act deals with copyright primarily as a system designed to organize the economic management of intellectual property, and regards copyright primarily as a

Ironically, this very paragraph concludes with a reference to Justice Binnie's comments in *Théberge*, while the different theory on which *Théberge* is based, passes unremarked. As he affirms:

> The [Copyright] Act provides the respondent with both economic and "moral" rights to his work. The distinction between the two types of rights and their respective statutory remedies is crucial.[67]

E. CONCLUSION

Canada's Minister of Industry, the Honourable Tony Clement, claims that he wants to make Canada one of the world's leading digital societies.[68] In spite of the difficult political context of Canadian copyright reform, the current opportunity to revise the copyright law should be welcomed.[69] Minister Clement correctly observes that Canada's law has fallen behind technological developments. The vacuum in Canadian law is equally damaging to authors and artists, industry, and the public. Everyone stands to gain from copyright reform in Canada. No doubt, this is the true reason why Canadian revision projects over the past several years have become bitterly controversial, as every interested group attempts to promote its particular agenda.

As it stands, the proposed Bill offers a welcome improvement to the status of performers in Canadian law. However, it should be remembered that reform has two distinct objectives: the satisfaction of international obligations, but, equally important, the responsibility of providing guidance on the development of domestic policies towards Canada's own culture. On this second point, the proposed bill falls short.

The current mandate to include moral rights for performers in Canadian law should be seen as something more than an international de-

---

> mechanism for protecting and transmitting the economic values associated with this type of property and with the use of it.

See *Théberge*, above note 27 at paras. 11–12, Binnie J.

67 *Théberge*, *ibid*. at para. 11.

68 Statement by Industry Minister Tony Clement at the Canadian Copyright Roundtable held in Vancouver, July 2009. The Vancouver session was the first of a series of public sessions, held across Canada, to consult experts and stakeholders on copyright reform. Attendance was, of course, by invitation only.

69 See my short editorial on this theme: Mira T. Sundara Rajan, "Copyright: Let's take ownership Outdated legislation hinders Canada's digital engagement" *Globe & Mail* (31 July 2009), http://www.theglobeandmail.com/news/opinions/copyright-lets-take-ownership/article1238407/.

mand. In fact, the happenstance of WIPO implementation provides two outstanding opportunities that are entirely specific to Canada. First, the Bill provides an opportunity to recognize the contribution of performers to Canadian culture. In order to do so, however, the Canadian government has perhaps chosen a poor model — existing provisions for the protection of authors' moral rights in Canada which have probably done very little to improve the conditions of artists' and authors' working lives in this country during their tenure.

At the same time, the government had little choice. If it attempted to improve performers' moral rights beyond the proposed formula, the outcome would have been awkward: performers would enjoy better protection for their moral rights under Canadian law than authors. The second opportunity presented by law reform, and a real solution to this problem, would be different. Canada needs comprehensive reform of authors' moral rights to ensure the enactment in good faith of international obligations under both the WPPT and the *Berne Convention*, and to establish a more equal bargaining relationship between authors and industries in Canada. The real challenge that the government will face is to balance protection for moral rights with adequate protection from free speech: moral rights should not be allowed to become a new justification for restricting the use of copyright works on behalf of corporate interests. The government should do what is necessary to offer real protection for moral rights in Canadian law, and, in some respects, the proposed Bill C-32 provides a solid foundation for these changes. Notably, the Bill clarifies fair dealing exceptions under copyright law, expressly providing that the creation of new works of parody and satire will not be considered an infringement of copyright, and this provision could easily be expanded to stipulate that parodies will not violate the moral rights of the author.[70]

The project is a grand one, but it represents something more than copyright reform — a chance to prove that, at least in Canada, culture still matters. Will Canadian reform of moral rights rise to the challenge?

70 French law implicitly does so: see Mira T. Sundara Rajan, *Moral Rights: Principles, Practice & New Technology* (New York: Oxford University Press, 2010) (forthcoming) at c. II, n. 109 and accompanying text.

PART FOUR

Education

CHAPTER SEVENTEEN

Copyright, Collectives, and Contracts:

New Math for Educational Institutions and Libraries

Margaret Ann Wilkinson*

A. INTRODUCTION

It is more than a decade since the last reforms to the *Copyright Act*[1] came into force.[2] While the statute has remained static,[3] the "copyright worlds" of institutions involved in the provision of education and library services in Canada have changed dramatically. These changes have come as a result

* The author would like to thank law students Justin Vessair, Dan Hynes and Dave Morrison for assistance in the preparation of this chapter. The author would also like to acknowledge conversations with a number of librarians which helped to inform this chapter and, particularly, Dr. John Tooth, Coordinator/Copyright Consultant, Instructional Resources Unit Manitoba Education. The opinions expressed herein are the author's own. The author's current research is supported by the Law Foundation of Ontario. Finally, the author would like to thank the anonymous reviewers of an earlier draft of this paper for their thoughtful and constructive suggestions.

1 R.S.C. 1985, c. C-42, http://laws.justice.gc.ca/en/C-42

2 *An Act to Amend the Copyright Act*, S.C. 1997, c. 24.

3 This is not for lack of legislative effort. Several Parliaments have attempted copyright reform in the interval. First a Liberal government introduced Bill C-60, *An Act to amend the Copyright Act*, 1st Sess., 37th Parl., 2005, first reading 20 June 2005. Second reading was scheduled for fall 2005, but never occurred due to the dissolution of Parliament on 29 November 2005: www2.parl.gc.ca/Content/LOP/LegislativeSummaries/38/1/c60-e.pdf.

Like Bill C-60 in 2005, Bill C-61, introduced by the Conservatives in 2008, never reached Second Reading: Bill C-61, *An Act to amend the Copyright Act*, 2d Sess., 39th Parl., 2008, First reading 12 June 2008. Parliament was dissolved 7 August 2008, www2.parl.gc.ca/Content/LOP/LegislativeSummaries/39/2/c61-e.pdf.

of the ways in which these institutions provide services. They have also come about as a result of the ways in which the actors in the information environment in Canada have changed their behaviours. Whatever the causes of these changes, institutions involved in education, library services, archival activities or museum practice find themselves in increasingly varied positions with respect to changes in the copyright legislation such as those proposed in the current Bill C-32, *An Act to amend the Copyright Act.*[4] Given these varied positions, it may be difficult to assess just what the impact of the proposed changes will be on this sector. As this chapter will illustrate, the impact that Parliament can have by implementing these changes will be directly affected by the individual managerial decisions of each institutional decision-maker involved in education, library services, archival activity and museum practice in Canada.

The chapter will begin by outlining the current copyright worlds of institutions involved in education and library, archival and museum services in Canada. This outline will include discussion of contracts, collectives, the Copyright Board and the courts. Against this complex tapestry, the chapter will then discuss the provisions of Bill C-32 that particularly would affect this tapestry. Specifically, the chapter will highlight several changes proposed which will affect institutions (and, through them, their users) involved in library, archive and museum services as well as provision of education. These include users' rights in fair dealing and the special provision for certain "educational institutions" and "libraries, archives and museums." It will also point out several matters which Bill C-32 does not address, including expanding those institutions that can avail themselves of the rights given to certain educational institutions and libraries, archives, and museums and clarifying the representative nature of collectives in the Canada. Finally, the chapter will point out that, despite the rhetoric surrounding the importance of copyright reform, whether or not Bill C-32 passes,[5] the copyright environment of Canada is being changed by players other than Parliament.

---

4 Bill C-32, *An Act to amend the Copyright Act*, 3d Sess., 40th Parl., First reading 2 June 2010, www2.parl.gc.ca/HousePublications/Publication.aspx?Docid=4580265&file=4. At the time of writing, Bill C-32 has not entered the committee stage. All references herein, therefore, are to Bill C-32 as it was introduced. Note: for the remainder of this chapter, quotes will be used to denote those "libraries, archives and museums" enjoying special statutory exemptions. If there are no quotation marks, the reader should assume that the institutions are being referred to in general terms and are meant to include both those covered by the statutory exceptions and those not.

5 The recent governments attempting copyright reform have all been minority ones. The current distribution of the House of Commons as of June 2010 is: Conservatives 144, Liberals 77, Bloc Quebecois 48, NDP 36, Independent 2, and 1 vacancy due to the

This chapter will establish that Canadian institutions involved in education and the provision of library services are going to experience the reforms in Bill C-32 in very different ways because there are many different copyright worlds currently surrounding these institutions.

Schools inhabit at least three different copyright worlds: many schools are both "educational institutions" under the *Copyright Act* and would be entitled to the expanded users' rights for such institutions that Bill C-32 would bring but are also "educational institutions" under the current *Access Copyright Elementary and Secondary School Tariff, 2005–2009* and proposed *Access Copyright Elementary and Secondary School Tariff 2010–2012* and will therefore only experience expanded rights under Bill C-32 indirectly in respect of rights marketed by Access Copyright; other schools, private non-profits, lie outside the ambit of the two Tariffs promulgated by Access Copyright but still lie within the sphere of "educational institutions" under the *Copyright Act* and would therefore benefit directly from all expansions of users' rights under Bill C-32; still other schools are purely for profit and private and will neither benefit from the expansion of exceptions for educational institutions under Bill C-32 nor be affected by the tariff proceedings before the Copyright Board which Access Copyright has initiated — these latter schools will, however, have a specific and direct interest in the expansion of the concept of "fair dealing" to encompass "education" as proposed under Bill C-32.

Universities and colleges find themselves the target of tariff proceedings before the Copyright Board launched by Access Copyright, just as public schools have experienced. However, because the governance structures of colleges and universities are different from those of schools, those governing each of Canada's colleges and universities will have to make a series of decisions about the Copyright Board proceeding: some may decide to operate in such a way that their uses, including their libraries' operations, fall within the ambit of the users' rights provided in the *Copyright Act* — these institutions will have a direct interest in the expanded ambit of users' rights set out in Bill C-32; others may plan on extending their abilities to serve students and library patrons by purchasing rights from

---

resignation of the NDP MP Judy Wasylycia-Leis in April 2010: www.parl.gc.ca/information/about/process/house/partystandings/standings-e.htm

The 2005 Liberal minority situation was: Liberals 133, Conservatives 98, Bloc Quebecois 54, NDP 19, Independent 3, and 1 vacancy. The Conservative minority situation when Bill C-61 was introduced was almost the exact reverse (at the top) from the 2005 picture: Conservatives 127, Liberals 95, Bloc Quebecois 48, NDP 30, Independent 4, and 4 vacancies.

Access Copyright but will not decide to actively participate in the Tariff proceedings before the Board, and still others will decide to actively oppose the Tariff and participate in the Board's proceedings (in either of these last two cases, the institutions can decide later whether to actually purchase the blanket licences under the Tariff the Copyright Board decides).

The chapter will describe why, where the Copyright Board is deciding the value of the rights to be made available under a tariff, the institutions to whom the tariff is targeted will experience the implications of any relevant changes that Bill C-32 may make to the *Copyright Act* only indirectly, as part of the considerations of the Copyright Board. Thus changes that Bill C-32 would represent would only be experienced indirectly by the educational institutions and libraries in the copyright worlds which involve the jurisdiction of the Copyright Board. The 'copyright worlds' now inhabited by libraries in public schools and private not-for-profit schools are, from this perspective, similar to those which are becoming inhabited by academic libraries and government libraries.

On the other hand, private, non-profit schools which enjoy the educational institution users' rights under the *Copyright Act* and public libraries and any other library which enjoys the library, archive or museum users' rights under the *Copyright Act*, but is not part of an academic institution or provincial or territorial government, will occupy similar, though not identical, copyright worlds — not least because none of them are included in any current tariff proceeding by Access Copyright before the Copyright Board — and will have similar, though not identical, direct experiences of the expansions of users' rights proposed in Bill C-32.

Finally, the copyright worlds inhabited by private, for profit schools; libraries that are operated by for profit organizations; and libraries operated not for profit but which do not maintain collections of documents or other materials open to the public or researchers are all identical in certain respects:

1) these institutions do not enjoy the benefits of the current educational institution or library, archive or museum exceptions in the *Copyright Act* and will not benefit by the extensions in Bill C-32 to them,
2) these institutions are not affected by tariffs being imposed by the Copyright Board in respect of schools, post-secondary institutions, provincial and territorial governments, and
3) these institutions will benefit directly from the addition of "education" to the definition of fair dealing in Bill C-32.

The chapter will also point out that the choices that individual institutions make about what proportion of their resources is subject to directly negotiated licences with the holders of copyright (where copyright collectives are not relevant) will have an impact on the importance of collective processes and, indeed, legislative reform for that institution and will, thus, create further subdivisions between otherwise "like" institutions. Similarly, the uses to which each institution puts works and other subject matter in order to meet the needs of its institution, its students or its patrons will affect the copyright world in which each institution uniquely finds itself.

Bill C-32, even if it passes, will clearly not be solely determinative of future relationships between copyright holders and institutions providing education and library services in Canada.

In particular, copyright holders and institutional players such as those engaged in education, library, archive and museum activities are shaping their own environments. Even if Bill C-32 passes, its effect on these institutions and players will depend on their own actions.

B. THE CURRENT COPYRIGHT WORLDS OF INSTITUTIONS INVOLVED IN EDUCATION AND PROVISION OF LIBRARY SERVICES

1) Worlds of Collectives and Contracts

In 2010, most institutions involved in education in Canada find themselves being virtually fully engaged by a combination of (1) tariff processes before the Copyright Board of Canada with collectives representing some copyright holders and (2) contracts directly with other copyright holders. Similarly, more and more libraries find themselves in the same situation as these schools, colleges and universities.

This is an environment of rapid change, even in five years. In 2005, it was true that

> [t]he English language Canadian print collective, since its inception in 1988, [has] made steady inroads into the education sector, beginning with its flagship agreement, on August 1, 1991, with the Ontario Ministry of Education, and followed shortly thereafter by a similar agreement with the Manitoba Ministry of Education (December, 1991).[6]

---

6 Margaret Ann Wilkinson, "Filtering the Flow from the Fountains of Knowledge: Access and Copyright in Education and Libraries," in Michael Geist, ed., *In the Public Interest: The Future of Canadian Copyright Law* (Toronto: Irwin Law, 2005), 331–74 at

It was also contemplated in 2005, at least in some circles, that copyright collectives would probably come to play an increasing role in Canada's future.[7] On one model of Canada's future, it was thought

> there would be uses paid to the rightsholder (in most cases, on a transactional basis). A subscription to an online publication or the download of a song or pay-per-view movie are good examples. A second universe would encompass free uses, such as those permitted by exceptions or stemming from ownership rights in a copy. . . But that leaves a universe of uses not covered by exceptions and which cannot be realistically [licensed] transactionally. An annual or similar licence then remains the only possible option to compensate rightsholders (within the scheme of the Act). Such licences can only be efficiently offered by copyright collectives.[8]

The situation in 2010, however, is radically different, in a number of respects, to that experienced even in 2005—and dramatically different from the situation which obtained when the *Copyright Act* was last amended in 1997.

The roots of the new environment are primarily recent: since 1988, when the *Copyright Act* was amended to encourage the proliferation of copyright collectives,[9] collectives have come to represent more rightsholders holding different classes of copyright interests in different kinds of works in Canada.[10] Indeed, in Canada, collectives have come to be able to represent

---

342, www.irwinlaw.com/pages/content-commons/filtering-the-flow-from-the-fountains-of-knowledge--access-and-copyright-in-education-and-libraries--margaret-anne-wilkinson

7 *Ibid.* See also Daniel Gervais, "Use of Copyright Content on the Internet: Considerations on Excludability and Collective Licensing," in Michael Geist, ed., *In the Public Interest, ibid.*, 517–49 at 549, www.irwinlaw.com/content/assets/content-commons/120/Three_04_Gervais.pdf [Gervais (2005)].

8 Gervais (2005), *ibid*, at 541.

9 *An Act to amend the Copyright Act and to amend other Acts in consequence thereof*, R.S.C. 1985, c. 10 (4th Supp.), s.14. There were further amendments to the *Copyright Act* in 1997 which provided additional clarification about the collective administration of copyright in Canada. For example, a definition of a "collective society" was added at that time. See *An Act to amend the Copyright Act*, S.C. 1997, c. 24, s. 1(5).

10 Canada is said to have more copyright collectives than any other major developed country. See Howard P. Knopf, "Canadian Copyright Collectives and the Copyright Board: A snapshot in 2008" (2008) 21 I.P.J. 117,at 122. This proliferation has developed from very narrow roots in the performing rights area. Collecting societies in Canada trace their roots back to 1925 when the first Canadian Performing Rights Society (CPRS) was formed. It was related to the British Performing Rights Society.

a great array of rightsholders rights.[11] Many, but by no means all, of the uses sought by institutions involved in education, library, archive and museum activities in Canada *prima facie* would come within the purview of the rights represented by various collective societies in Canada.

Figure 1 groups the collectives currently active in Canada[12] according to the various copyright holders' rights set out in section 3 of the *Copyright Act*.[13] This analysis is not necessarily comprehensive,[14] given the limita-

---

Eventually, BMI Canada was formed in 1941, related to Broadcast Music, Inc (BMI) which had been formed in the United States in 1939. In 1946, the Composers, Authors and Publishers Association of Canada (CAPAC) formed from CPRS and in 1978, the Performing Rights Organization of Canada (PROCAN) descended from BMI Canada. Ultimately, after the *Copyright Act* reforms of 1988, the two organizations merged in 1990 to form the current Society of Composers, Authors and Music Publishers of Canada (SOCAN).

11 Until the statutory reforms of 1988, no collectives were allowed to exist with respect to any rights other than the performing rights—now see the array in Figure 1. And see also the discussion below describing the increasing range of rights which Access Copyright is becoming able to offer with respect to English language print works in Canada.

12 As identified by the Copyright Board of Canada on its website—http://www.cb-cda.gc.ca/societies-societes/index-e.html (last modified 27 August 2010)—using the descriptions of the collectives provided there.

13 This chart does not include collectives exclusively representing rightsholders in "other subject matter" than "works." Thus collectives representing exclusively rightsholders in sound recordings, performers' performances, or broadcasts are not included. For example, a number of collectives listed on the Copyright Board website would appear to have their origins in s.15 (performer's performance rights) and are therefore not shown on Figure 1. The collective now called Re:Sound, (Re:Sound Music Licensing Company)—formerly the NRCC (the Neighbouring Rights Collective of Canada)—is an "umbrella" music licensing company for performance rights. It represents, in this respect, AFM (American Federation of Musicians of the United States and Canada), ACTRA PRS (ACTRA Performers' Rights Society), Artist I (collective society of the Union des artistes (UDA)), SOPROQ and AVLA from this perspective). The Société de gestion des droits des artistes-musiciens (SOGEDAM) represents Canadian musician performers and performers who are members of foreign societies. Others listed on the Copyright Board site appear to be representing rights which have arisen through s.21 (broadcasters' rights in communication signals). Border Broadcasters Inc. (BBI) represents broadcasters along the Canada/US border with respect to local programming. The Copyright Collective of Canada (CCC) relates to comedy and drama programming. The Direct Response Television Collective (DRTVC) relates to certain television programs including "infomercials."

14 Previous published taxonomies have focused on the genres of works covered or characteristics of the rightsholders rather than on which rights under the *Copyright Act* are being represented, as is being done here. See, for example, the taxonomy by Daniel Gervais (2008), below note 18, at 202–6. See also the select briefer listing of "Some of the Canadian Collectives" in Knopf, above note 10 at 122.

tions of its documentary source data, but may serve to reinforce certain points being made herein.

As Figure 1 indicates, most of the collectives group around the *reproduction rights* to various types of works, the *right to perform works in public*, and the *right to telecommunicate* various works. All three of these uses of works would seem to be germane to the modern functions of institutions engaged in educating and serving user needs through library activities.[15] Other rights, such as translating works, converting dramatic works, adapting works as cinematographic works, and making records, would seem to be activities undertaken less frequently by these institutions. For these latter uses, particular transactional licences, as contemplated in Daniel Gervais's "second universe," above, would seem to be more natural. Renting computer programs and sound recordings is probably very rare, if it occurs at all, in these institutional settings.

15 Conversely, since "private copying" under Part VIII of the *Copyright Act* (ss. 79–88, added by *An Act to Amend the Copyright Act*, S.C. 1997, c. 24) is not a users' right which is available to the institutions being discussed here (in terms of delivering services to students or library patrons), it is therefore not included in this analysis. The Canadian Private Copying Collective (CPCC) arises from this new rights regime since copyright holders are compensated through levies on the sale (s. 82(1)) of "blank audio recording media" as defined in s. 79) for the new users' right to "private use of the person who makes the copy" (s. 80(1)) and this compensation is orchestrated through the Copyright Board (see, in particular, s. 83). CPCC represents, in this respect, CMRRA, SOGEDAM, SODRAC, SOCAN and Re:Sound, all identified in full above. The Producers Audiovisual Collective of Canada identified itself as specifically engaged in matters related to private copy levies as well and is therefore not represented in Figure 1. The Canadian Screenwriters Collection Society (CSCS) similarly identifies itself as being concerned with private copying levies and educational use levies — but it is shown above in Figure 1 because of its self-identification with rental and lending levies. The Directors Rights Collective of Canada (DRCC) in its description on the Copyright Board website is most clearly identified with those whom it represents, film and television directors, rather than the particular rights involved. However, the membership application for joining the Directors Guild of Canada, from which it springs, identifies the collective most clearly with the private copying regime in Canada: see www.dgcodc.ca/pdf/Applics/DGCDirectorsMemAppMay3008.pdf.

Figure 1: Collectives Grouped by Copyright Holder's Rights

Section 3(1) Right	Associated Collective Society
Produce or Reproduce the Work	Access Copyright (writing) AVLA (music: videos and audio) CARCC (visual arts) CCLI (church uses) CMRAA (audio & music) COPIBEC (writing) SODRAC (music)
Perform the Work in Public	ACF (films) Criterion Pictures (films) CVLI (films and audio-visual) ERCC (tv and radio, education only) SOCAN (music) SoQAD (theatre, education only)
Publish the Work	
(a) Translate the Work	
(b) Convert a dramatic work	
(c) Convert a non-dramatic work by performance	
(c) Convert an artistic work into a dramatic work by performance	PGC (theatre) SOCAN (music) SoQAD (theatre, education only)
(d) Sound/cinematography film to mechanically reproduce a literary, dramatic or music work	
(e) Adapt a work as a cinematographic work	
(f) Communicate the work by Telecommunication	CBRA (tv) CRC (TV and film) CRRA (TV) FWS (sports) MLB (sports, baseball) SACD (theatre, film, radio, audio) SCAM SOCAN (music) SOPROQ (audio and video)
(g) Present an Artistic work at a Public Exhibition	
(h) Rent out a Computer Program	
(i) Rent out a Sound Recording	CSCS

ACF (Audio Cine Films); AVLA (Audio-Video Licensing Agency); CARCC (Canadian Artists' Representation Copyright Collective); CBRA (Canadian Broadcasters Rights Agency); CCLI (Christian Copyright Licensing Inc.); CMRRA (Canadian Musical Reproduction Rights Agency); Criterion Pictures); COPIBEC (Société québeciose de gestion collective des droits de reproduction); CRC (Canadian Retransmission Collective); CRRA (Canadian Retransmission Right Association); CSCS (Canadian Screenwriters Collection Society); CVLI (Christian Video Licensing International); ERCC (Education Rights Collective of Canada); FWS (FWS Join Sports Claimants); MLB (Major League Baseball Collective of Canada); PGC (Playwrights Guild of Canada (formerly the Playwrights Union of Canada)); SOCAN (Society of Composers, Authors and Music Publishers of Canada); SACD (Société des auteurs et compositeurs dramatiques); SCAM (Société civile des auteurs multimédias); SODRAC (Society for Reproduction Rights of Authors, Composers and Publishers in Canada); SOPROQ (Société de gestion collective des droits des producteurs de phonogrammes et videogrammes du Quebec); SoQAD (Société québecoise des auteurs dramatiques)

The creation of copyright collectives lies within the sole power of the rightsholders themselves under the Canadian *Copyright Act*,[16] and, certainly, it is demonstrably evident in Figure 1 that holders of Canadian rights in only certain rights have found it useful to form collectives. Conversely, it seems clear that other rights are not sought by users in ways that commend themselves to the rightsholders as appropriate to collective administration.[17]

The reality in 2010, as Bill C-32 is introduced, is very different than it has been in the past: for a very rapidly expanding number of institutions involved in education and library services, there are now coming to be only two types of copyright "universes": one comprising contracts for uses paid to the rightsholders (mostly on an ongoing contracted subscription basis, rather than the transactional basis contemplated by Gervais in 2005) and the other, being relationships with copyright collectives. The "second universe" of "free uses" imagined in 2005 appears to have been subsumed largely into the negotiations attendant upon the other two. Again, understanding why this is becoming the case and how this affects the ways in which these institutions will experience all future reform of the *Copyright Act*, including Bill C-32, may assist in predicting the actual effects of the changes proposed in Bill C-32. But one reason for the decline in importance of the "second universe" may be the way in which the "third universe" is coming to be experienced now: the experience of dealing with collectives is rapidly shifting from one of negotiation to one of appearances before the Copyright Board.

2) Enter the Copyright Board

While, as pointed out, the continuing expansion of copyright collectives in Canada has been an ongoing part of the institutional life of educational

16 That the creation of a collective occurs at the instigation of rightsholders is evident in the statutory definition of "collective society" as one "that carries on the business of collective administration of copyright . . . for the benefit of those who . . . authorize it to act on their behalf in relation to that administration . . ." (*Copyright Act*, above note 1, s. 2).

17 Sometime before the 1988 statutory reforms that encouraged the proliferation of collectives in Canada, Peter Grant identified "When A Copyright Collective Makes Sense" as being when there are a "multitude of copyright users, multitude of transactions (uses), unplanned character of uses, multitude of copyright owners, [and] no physical/electronic nexus between owners and users." Figure 2 in "Copyright Collectives in Canada: Current Regulatory Structures and New Ideas," in *Proceedings of the Colloquium on the Collective Administration of Copyright*, organized by the Canadian Conference of the Arts, The Canadian Literary Arts Association (ALIA Canada), The Copyright Board of Canada and The Faculty of Administrative Studies, Arts & Media Administration Program, York University, Toronto, 31 October 1994, 9-41 at 11.

institutions and libraries in Canada since the 1988 *Copyright Act* reforms occurred, it is the suddenly increasing involvement of the Copyright Board that has radically changed the landscape for institutions involved in education and provision of library services. Despite its increasing importance and activity, the role of the Copyright Board has been relatively little examined in the literature.[18]

Once a collective exists, the Canadian *Copyright Act* gives the collective more leverage in controlling the nature of the relationship between users and collectives than it gives the users. While in many cases a collective and a group of users may choose to negotiate blanket licences,[19] the collective society alone has the option, instead, to apply for a tariff from the Copyright Board:

> A collective society may, for the purpose of setting out by licence the royalties and terms and conditions relating to classes of uses,
> (a) file a proposed tariff with the Board; or
> (b) enter into agreements with users.[20]

---

18 See Knopf, above note 10; Daniel Gervais, " A Uniquely Canadian Institution: The Copyright Board of Canada" in Ysolde Gendreau, ed., *An Emerging Intellectual Property Paradigm: Perspectives from Canada* [Queen Mary Studies in Intellectual Property] (Cheltenham: Edward Elgar, 2008) c. IX; and Mario Bouchard, "Collective Management in Commonwealth Jurisdictions: Comparing Canada with Australia," in Daniel Gervais, ed., *Collective Management of Copyright and Related Rights* (The Netherlands: Kluwer, 2006), 197–223. See also Margaret Ann Wilkinson, "The Copyright Regime and Data Protection Legislation," in Ysolde Gendreau, ed., *Copyright Administrative Institutions: Conference Organized by the Centre de recherche en droit public (CRDP) of the Faculty of Law of the Université de Montréal, 11 & 12 October 2001* (Cowansville, PQ: Les Éditions Yvon Blais Inc., 2001) 77–100. Howard Knopf makes the same comment about collectives, above note 10 at 131, as is here being made about the Copyright Board: "Despite the importance of the collective movement in Canada and the enormous amount of money at stake, there is surprisingly little analytical analysis of collective activity in Canada."

19 There are a number of different schemes governing the collective administration of copyrights embedded in the *Copyright Act*. With respect to certain rights, the collective process is mandatory, not voluntary: the retransmission of distant radio and television signals and reproduction and public performance by educational institutions, except for educational and training purposes, of radio and television signals (contained in Part VII of the *Copyright Act*, "Copyright Board and Collective Administration of Copyright," ss. 66–78 at ss. 71–76) and the special situation of compensation for the private copying of sound recordings (in its own new Part VIII of the Act , since the 1997 amendments to the *Copyright Act*, ss. 79–88). In all other cases, the collective management of rights is voluntary.

20 *Copyright Act*, above note 10, s. 70.12. On the other hand, once negotiating, if a collective and a potential user are unable to agree to license terms, either may apply to the Board (s. 70.2(1)). See note 33 below.

While most schools and school/libraries in the country have found themselves involved with Access Copyright before the Copyright Board already, as will be further described below, increasing numbers of libraries find themselves now in the same position (government libraries and academic libraries, for example). It may be important to note here that, *at the option of Access Copyright*, greater numbers of libraries may find themselves also involved in processes before the Board (for example, public libraries).

Having perhaps become used to the process of *negotiating* with copyright collectives for licences (including blanket licences),[21] institutions will discover that the process that ensues when the collective applies to a quasi-judicial tribunal, the Copyright Board, is fundamentally different. Once a tariff is issued, it will apply to all subsequent transactions between the collective and a class of potential users for the duration of the tariff. As the Federal Court of Appeal has said, under the tariff application system, "The Board . . . [has] to regulate the balance of market power between copyright owners and users."[22]

Many institutions involved in education and provision of library services in Canada now find themselves in a transitional phase from voluntary negotiation to mandatory appearances before the Copyright Board of Canada—just at the same time as Bill C-32 is being proposed by the government. Access Copyright, the print collective for English language rights for reproduction, which was just expanding its network of licences back in 2005,[23] is now, in 2010, engaged in aggressively shifting its focus from the consensual negotiation of licences to the forum of the Copyright Board and the tariff process.

The initial signal of what has become evident as a wholesale change in Access Copyright's strategy was the decision to take all the Ministers of Education (except Quebec)[24] to the Board for a Tariff for public schools

21 Or a "model license" such as Access Copyright created with the Association of Universities and Colleges of Canada some years ago and which Access Copyright then used as the basis for individual contracts entered into between Access Copyright and the various colleges and universities across Canada.

22 *Canadian Association of Broadcasters v. SOCAN* (1994), 58 C.P.R.(3d) 190 at 196.

23 And in 2006, Howard Knopf reports its revenue as over $34 million, with another $12 million for COPIBEC, its French language counterpart (above note 10, at.123, citing to the organization's respective websites).

24 Including the Ministers in all three territories. Access Copyright and its French language counterpart COPIBEC have reciprocal agreements in place—according to the News Release of the Copyright Board of Canada dated 26 June 2009 "Access Copyright administers the rights for all of Canada except Quebec, where the repertoire is administered by *La Société québécoise de gestion collective des droits de reproduction* (COPIBEC)."

right through to grade 12, covering the years 2005-2009.[25] The decision of the Copyright Board on that tariff application was just released in June 26, 2009.[26] The tariff itself was published the next day.[27] It replaced the Pan Canadian Schools/Cancopy Licence Agreement which was negotiated without recourse to the Copyright Board and which governed relationships between the schools and the reprographic collective from 1999 until 2009.[28] Under the original agreement, Cancopy/Access Copyright was paid $2.56 per full time student equivalent (FTE) per year for every educational institution in Canada (except Quebec). Under the new tariff, Access Copyright is to receive $5.16 per FTE student per year.

All those Ministries (and, through them, the school boards everywhere except in Quebec) are now coping with Access Copyright's decision to take the Ministers of Education to the Board for a Tariff for 2010–2012.[29] Under this tariff, Access Copyright is seeking $15.00 per FTE student per year. At least part of the reason for the increase sought is that, in addition to those works covered by the 2005–2009 Tariff, Access Copyright will now include permissions to copy sheet music and to make digital copies of paper works.[30] This expansion of its offerings must mean that its members have given it a greater array of rights in their English language print works than they had heretofore.

One of the additional users' rights which the government intends to give "educational institutions" under Bill C-32 is the right to make digital reproductions of paper forms for any educational institution which has

---

25 "Statement of Proposed Royalties to Be Collected by Access Copyright for the Reprographic Reproduction, in Canada, of Works in its Repertoire in the Years 2005 to 2009 (Provincial and Territorial Governments) (Educational Institutions) Supplement," *Canada Gazette*, Part I, 24 April 2004, www.cb-cda.gc.ca/tariffs-tarifs/proposed-proposes/2004/20040424-r-b.pdf

26 *Ministers of Education v. Access Copyright* (26 June 2009,) /www.cb-cda.gc.ca/decisions/2009/Access-Copyright-2005-2009-Schools.pdf

27 *Access Copyright Elementary and Secondary School Tariff*, 2005–2009, above 29 (see para. 1).

28 Cancopy was the original name under which the organization now known as Access Copyright was known.

29 "Statements of Proposed Royalties to Be Collected by Access Copyright for the Reprographic Reproduction, in Canada, of Works in its Repertoire: Educational Institutions (2010-2012); Provincial and Territorial Governments (2010–2014)" *Supplement to the Canada Gazette* Part 1, 9 May 2009, at 4–12, which is to be known as the *Access Copyright Elementary and Secondary School Tariff*, 2010–2012, http://www.cb-cda.gc.ca/tariffs-tarifs/proposed-proposes/2009/20090509-r-b.pdf

30 See definition of "copy" in s. 21 of *Access Copyright Elementary and Secondary School Tariff*, 2010–2012, *ibid.*

a reprographic reproduction licence for a collective society's repertoire.[31] If Bill C-32 passes, it would surely be incumbent on the Copyright Board, in considering the additional cost ($5.16 to $15 per FTE student per year) of the new Tariff for 2010–2012 sought by Access Copyright, to consider that one of the new "rights" purporting to be sold by Access Copyright appears to have been rendered without value by the government by extending users' rights for educational institutions under licence to include precisely these rights.

In the government sector, Access Copyright has applied to impose a Tariff for 2005–2009, and one for 2010- 2012, for uses by all the provincial and territorial governments. [32] This will affect all library services within those government civil services. The proposed tariff here is $24.00 per FTE civil servant. Since the coverage in this proposed tariff is the same as that being proposed by Access Copyright in the 2010–2012 "school" tariff just described and proposed for schools at $15.00 per FTE student, it must be assumed that Access Copyright believes that the provincial and territorial civil servants have access to fewer users' rights under the *Copyright Act* than do students and their agents.

Meanwhile, all the Universities and colleges in Canada (other than those in Quebec) are affected by the recent decision by Access Copyright to abandon individual negotiations with universities and colleges (or with organizations representing them)[33] and to apply instead for a Tariff before

---

31 Bill C-32, above note 4, s. 27, adding to the *Copyright Act*, above note 1, s. 30.02.

32 These two proposed tariffs are curiously difficult to locate: there is a notice on the Copyright Board website about "Access Copyright - Provincial and Territorial Governments Tariffs (2005–2009 and 2010–2014)" advising that there will be a "Hearing beginning Tuesday, September 13, 2011 at 10:00 a.m., Copyright Board's hearing room" in the matter. See www.cb-cda.gc.ca/home-accueil-e.html. There is also a document of what is to be styled the *Access Copyright Provincial and Territorial Governments Tariff, 2010–2014* which, curiously, appears beginning at page 13 of a document that begins with a proposed tariff entitled *Access Copyright Elementary and Secondary School Tariff*, 2010–2012, just discussed. See "Statements of Proposed Royalties to Be Collected by Access Copyright for the Reprographic Reproduction, in Canada, of Works in its Repertoire: Educational Institutions (2010–2012) Provincial and Territorial Governments; (2010–2014)," *Supplement Canada Gazette*, Part I, 9 May 2009, www.cb-cda.gc.ca/tariffs-tarifs/proposed-proposes/2009/20090509-r-b.pdf.

33 In the winter of 2009–2010, colleges and universities across Canada received individual letters from Access Copyright indicating that the existing individual licenses between each of these institutions and the collective were going to be terminated and negotiations begun for new licenses. The letters mentioned that the new license terms and conditions might be created either by agreement of the parties (this is,

the Board.[34] This is the highest tariff yet proposed by Access Copyright: $45.00 per FTE student.[35] However, under this tariff Access Copyright proposes to give rights in both print and digital works. The difference between this proposed tariff and those proposed for the schools 2010-2012 and the provincial and territorial governments, then, must be, in Access Copyright's eyes, the difference between the value of rights to reproduce print and convert print to digital (under the latter proposed tariffs) and the higher value of the rights to reproduce print, convert print to digital, and work with original digital (in the former proposed tariff).

The Copyright Board, in setting the first Tariff sought by Access Copyright,[36] has described the formula it intends to apply to such matters going forward. This formula can be displayed as shown in Figure 2.

Access Copyright and the university or college to whom the letter was addressed) or by the Copyright Board. It is apparently the case that Access Copyright has shifted the process into the realm of the Copyright Board under the *Copyright Act*, above note 1, s.70.2 which provides that

> Where a collective society and any person [including any organization]. . . are unable to agree on the royalties to be paid for the right to the act [which otherwise than under license only the copyright holder represented by the collective has the right to do]. . . either may, after giving notice to the other, apply to the Board to fix the royalties and their related terms and conditions.

34 "Statement of Proposed Royalties to Be Collected by Access Copyright for the Reprographic Reproduction, in Canada, of Works in its Repertoire: Post-Secondary Educational Institutions (2011–2013)," *Supplement Canada Gazette*, Part I June 12, 2010, to be known as *Access Copyright Post-Secondary Educational Institution Tariff, 2011–2013*. Under this proposed tariff, "educational institution" has been given the following meaning: "an institution located in Canada (except in the Province of Quebec) that provides postsecondary, continuing, professional, or vocational education or training." (www.cb-cda.gc.ca/tariffs-tarifs/proposed-proposes/2010/2009-06-11-1.pdf

35 *Access Copyright Post-Secondary Educational Institution Tariff, 2011–2013*, para. 7

> Royalties: The Educational Institution shall pay an annual royalty to Access Copyright calculated by multiplying the number of its Full-time-equivalent Students by the royalty rate of
> (*a*) $45.00 CAD for Universities; or
> (*b*) $35.00 CAD for all other Educational Institutions.

36 "Reprographic Reproduction 2005–2009: Reasons for the decision certifying Access Copyright tariff for educational institutions" (26 June 2009) (Justice William Vancise, Francine Bertrand-Venne, and Sylvie Charron):www.cb-cda.gc.ca/decisions/2009/Access-Copyright-2005-2009-Schools.pdf [Copyright Board decision].

Figure 2: The Copyright Board's Formula for Setting Tariffs

Take all copying done within the institution
(determined by actual surveying, using statistically robust sampling[1])

Subtract all copies for which the rightsholders should not be compensated

(a) because the materials in question were not "works" or not works in which the rightsholders in the collective have rights (e.g., materials created by schools for themselves, in which they hold copyright)[2] AND

(b) because, although the materials in question are prima facie materials in which the collectives' members have rights, there are users' rights (exceptions) which mean the rightsholders are not exercising their rights for these uses (fair dealing, rights for "educational institutions" or "LAMs")[3]

SUB-TOTAL: NUMBER OF COMPENSABLE COPIES

MULTIPLY by the value of each copy as determined on economic evidence by the Copyright Board[4]

EQUALS THE AMOUNT OF THE TARIFF EACH INSTITUTION IS TO PAY TO THE COLLECTIVE

Notes:

[1] The study for the Tariff 2005–2009 for schools is described by the Board at paras. 29–35.

[2] See, in this connection, the Board's reasons at para.136 and para.139 and Table 2 thereto.

[3] See, in this connection, the Board's reasons at para. 137 and Table 1 thereto.

[4] The Board stated, at para.135, "The parties agree to set the tariff using a three-step methodology. First, they estimate the total number of photocopied pages triggering remuneration in all of the institutions involved. Next, they determine the value of a photocopy, followed by the total value of the photocopies, which is the product of the number of photocopied pages multiplied by the value of each. The tariff itself is obtained by dividing the total value of the photocopied pages in one year by the number of FTE [full-time equivalent] students."

As mentioned, under the previous *negotiated* licence, schools had been paying approximately $2.45 per FTE student per year. Under the Board's tariff, the full rate for 2005-2009 would rise to $5.16 per FTE student per year — but the Board imposed a 10 percent discount on this rate for the first four years, bringing the rate from 2005 to 2008 to $4.64 per FTE student per year, and $5.16 per FTE student only for 2009.

The Copyright Board held that copies made within the categories of exception found in the fair dealing provisions of the Act, but made for instruction or non-private study for a group of students, do *not* fall within the criteria to be considered within the users' rights to fair dealing.[37] In this context, it should be noted that such situations will seldom apply to those working within institutions providing library services.

Indeed, only section 29.4(2) was discussed at any length. The Board articulates clearly the position that the special exemptions for "educational institutions" and "libraries, archives and museums" have statutory condi-

37 Copyright Board decision, above note 36, para.118.

tions which are different from the criteria for falling within users' rights to fair dealing.[38]

Discussing section 29.4(2)with respect to "educational institutions" involved the Copyright Board in analysis of the notion of "commercially available" which is defined in section 2 of the Act, since 1997[39] as meaning:

> in relation to a work or other subject-matter,
> (a) available on the Canadian market within a reasonable time and for a reasonable price and may be located with reasonable effort, or
> (b) for which a licence to reproduce, perform in public or communicate to the public by telecommunication is available from a collective society within a reasonable time and for a reasonable price and may be located with reasonable effort.

The Copyright Board noted that the term "commercially available" was also used both in an exception for "libraries, archives and museums" when making copies of works for preservation[40] and in an exception for any person (individual or organization) making a copy for a perceptually disabled user (individual or organization).[41] However, the Board noted that the meaning ascribed to the term "commercially available" was rendered different on the occasion of its use in connection with the perceptually disabled than in connection with "educational institutions" or "libraries, archives and museums." In the case of the perceptually disabled, the presence or absence of available licences is irrelevant while in the cases of the "educational institutions" and "libraries, archives and museums" it is relevant.[42] Thus the current *Copyright Act* has made it more frequently open to the perceptually disabled to use works because they are not deemed to be commercially available than will be the case for uses for "educational institutions" or "libraries, archives and museums."

Altogether the Board found that there had been about 10.3 billion copies made in schools in 2005–2006, of which roughly 250 million (or, only

---

38 *Ibid.*, para. 128. Although the Supreme Court in *CCH Canadian Ltd. v. Law Society of Upper Canada*, [2004] 1 S.C.R. 339 [*CCH v. Law Society*] held that availability of a license is irrelevant in assessing whether the criteria for fair dealing have been met, the definition of "commercially available" for "educational institutions" and "libraries, archives and museums" statutorily requires that the availability of a license be considered relevant.

39 *An Act to Amend the Copyright Act*, S.C.1997, c. 24, s. 1(5).

40 *Copyright Act*, above note 1, s.30.1

41 *Ibid.*, s.32(1).

42 Copyright Board decision, above note 36, para.127

2 percent) related to uses which triggered remuneration: 98 percent of photocopying in schools was found to be photocopying for which copyright holders were *not* entitled to any compensation.

3) The Loss of the Indemnification from Access Copyright

One of the features of the licences into which organizations have previously entered with Access Copyright has been a clause which has indemnified the user organizations from legal costs and damages associated with any lawsuits brought against the organizations by copyright rightsholders who were not represented by Access Copyright.[43] Apparently the clause has never been invoked.[44] One of the challenges in the current state of Canada's copyright law, which is not addressed by Bill C-32, is that the collectives do not represent those rightsholders who choose not to join them.[45] The Copyright Board has taken the position, in its recent schools tariff decision, that the indemnity clause has no place in the tariff between Access Copyright and the schools.[46] The Copyright Board took this position despite acknowledging both that Access Copyright's argument that it represents more than 99 percent of works reproduced by K-12 educational institutions was without evidence[47] and that the Ministers of Education argued that many rights holders are still not affiliated with Access Copyright.[48]

4) The Copyright Board under Review

Given the dollar value of the tariff announced between Access Copyright and the schools and the fact that this tariff was the first amongst a num-

---

43 Since Access Copyright has no control over the actions of rightsholders who are not its members or affiliated with it in any way, it could not prevent such rightsholders from bringing actions against organizations or individuals with whom it had contracts. Nor could it prevent courts from making orders including injunctions and damages against the organizations that were sued.

44 Information provided by Access Copyright to the Copyright Board, see the Copyright Board decision, above note 36, at para. 181.

45 This shortcoming has been noted by Daniel Gervais (2008), above note 18 at 220. In Europe, the "extended licensing" or "extended repertoire" system has been common for some time. Under it, those who do not wish to be represented by the appropriate collective bear the burden of opting out.

46 *Ibid*, above, para. 183.

47 *Ibid*, para. 179.

48 *Ibid.*, para. 182. The Board also notes that the Ministers of Education believed they would be detrimentally affected because they would be vulnerable to proceedings without the indemnity.

ber of tariffs now being sought by Access Copyright, it was perhaps inevitable that this decision of the Copyright Board would be challenged.

The Copyright Board cannot be appealed, but, as a quasi-judicial administrative body, it is subject to judicial review by the courts, specifically the Federal Court of Appeal.[49] The Ministers of Education applied to have the Copyright Board's decision reviewed in *Alberta v. Access Copyright*.[50] On 27 November 2009, the Canadian Association of University Teachers sought leave to intervene in the action. Leave was granted on 23 December 2009. At this point, a publishers' group comprised of the Canadian Publishers' Council, The Association of Canadian Publishers, and the Canadian Educational Resources Council sought leave to intervene (on 7 January 2010). This leave was also granted (on 18 February 2010).[51] The review application itself was argued in Montreal before Chief Justice Blais, Justice Noël and Justice Trudel on 8 June 2010, just after Bill C-32 was introduced in the House of Commons. The decision was reserved.[52] It was released on 23 July 2010.

In reasons written for the Court by Justice Trudell, the Court upheld the Board's decision on one ground and remitted the Copyright Board's decision back to it on another.[53]

Turning to the first ground on which judicial review was sought by the Ministers of Education, the Court found that the Board had not erred in finding not only that photocopying excerpts from textbooks for use in

---

49 "The Federal Court of Appeal has jurisdiction to hear and determine applications for judicial review made in respect of . . . the Copyright Board established by the *Copyright Act*" *Federal Courts Act*, R.S.C. 1985, c. F-7, s. 28(1)(j).

50 *The Province of Alberta et al v. Canadian Copyright Licensing Agency et al*, 2010 FCA 198, http://decisions.fca-caf.gc.ca/en/2010/2010fca198/2010fca198.html [*Alberta v. Access Copyright*].

51 The presence of intervenors in the Federal Court of Appeal is exceedingly rare in intellectual property cases — indeed, almost without precedent. It appears that since 2000, other than in this present case, there have only been 11 applications involving interventions — none in trademark or industrial design cases. Of the 11, in 9 cases intervention was denied. In the case of *Eli Lily and Co. v. Apotex Inc.* [2005] F.C.J. No.964 the Commissioner of Competition was statutorily entitled to status but was denied the opportunity to file a particular affidavit in the proceedings. Thus, other than in the present case, only in *Apple Canada v. Canadian Private Copying Collective*, [2007] F.C.J. No.1441 was an application to intervene allowed. In that case the Canadian Recording Industry Association was given leave to address the court on 3 major issues relating to digital audio as a medium.

52 This information is all available from the court docket at www.fca-caf.gc.ca/DocketQueries/dq_queries_e.php.

53 See *Alberta v. Access Copyright*, above note 50 at paras. 68–71.

classroom instruction was for an allowable purpose under fair dealing (a position which neither party to the action opposed) but also that the taking was nevertheless *not* fair and thus such copies were compensable. The Federal Court of Appeal found the question of the fairness of the taking to be a purely factual question which presented "no reviewable error" and, therefore, it did not disturb the Copyright Board's decision in this respect.[54]

However, the Ministers of Education also argued that certain copies from textbooks found by the Board to be compensable were actually "work or other subject-matter as required for a test or examination" where the work is not "commercially available in a medium that is appropriate for the purpose" and thus not compensable.[55] The Court found that although the Board considered the commercial availability of the works, it did not consider the availability and appropriateness of the media.[56] This decision does not disturb the formula for calculation set out in Figure 2 above. It does, however, require the Board to re-assess its assessment in this instance of the figure to be subtracted from the total amount of copying done in the institutions: the Court found the Board missed an element in assessing how many copies for which the rightsholders should not be compensated. This, in turn, will require the Board, in this case, to re-calculate the subtotal number of compensable copies (to something less than the 2 percent found compensable in the original decision of the Board). This, in turn, will ultimately reduce the amount of the tariff each school is to pay to the collective Access Copyright. No doubt the final amount will be determined to be something less than the $5.16 per FTE student the Board had established in its original decision.[57]

It is clear that the Federal Court of Appeal approves of the approach, outlined above in Figure 2, that the Board is taking to establishing Tariffs. It is also clear that, whether or not there are court interventions, there is an important shift occurring in relationships between institutions providing education and library services in Canada and Access Copyright: at the instigation of Access Copyright, these relationships are shifting away from negotiation and into the jurisdiction of the Copyright Board.

---

54 *Ibid.*, para.5.

55 *Ibid.*, at para.4.

56 *Ibid.* at paras. 7, 69 & 70.

57 At the time of writing, it is not certain whether or not either of the parties will seek leave to appeal the decision of the Federal Court of Appeal from the Supreme Court. Nor has the Copyright Board had time to consider the matter again as directed by the Federal Court of Appeal.

C. BILL C-32

1) Key Proposals in Bill C-32

a) Enlarging Fair Dealing

The first recital of the Preamble of Bill C-32[58] provides

> Whereas the *Copyright Act* is an important marketplace framework law and cultural policy instrument that, through clear, predictable and fair rules, supports creativity and innovation and affects many sectors of the knowledge economy . . . .

This sounds like the language of Justice Binnie, for the Supreme Court, in *Théberge v. Galerie d'Art du Petit Champlain Inc.*:[59]

> The *Copyright Act* is usually presented as a balance between promoting the public interest in the encouragement and dissemination of works of the arts and intellect and obtaining a just reward for the creator (or, more accurately, to prevent someone other than the creator from appropriating whatever benefits may be generated).

And the sixth recital in Bill C-32[60] acknowledges that "the exclusive rights in the *Copyright Act* provide rights holders with recognition, remuneration and the ability to assert their rights, and [that] some limitations on those rights exist to further enhance users' access to copyright works or other subject-matter."[61] This sounds a great deal like the Chief Justice's view, for the Supreme Court, in *CCH v. Law Society*, that

> [t]he fair dealing exception, like other exceptions in the *Copyright Act*, is a users' right. In order to maintain the proper balance between the rights of a copyright owner and users' interests, it must not be interpreted restrictively.[62]

---

58 Like the earlier Bill C-61, introduced by the previous Conservative minority government in 2008.

59 [2002] 2 .S.C.R. 33 at para. 30, www.canlii.org/en/ca/scc/doc/2002/2002scc34/2002scc34.html

60 Again just as recited in the Preamble to Bill C-61, above note 3.

61 Sixth recital in the Preamble to Bill C-32. The Preamble to Bill C-61 was virtually identical to that of Bill C-32. The only change in Bill C-32 occurs in the third last paragraph where the new Bill C-32 uses the phrase "technological protection measures" whereas Bill C-61 said "technological measures."

62 *CCH v. Law Society*, above note 38, at para. 48.

Although the Conservatives have made the same overtures in previous draft legislation, never before has the government so clearly indicated it acknowledges and respects the position of the Supreme Court that "Canada's *Copyright Act* sets out the rights and obligations of both copyright owners and users,"[63] as it does in Bill C-32. This is most strongly indicated by the fact that Bill C-61 of 2008 ignored the "fair dealing" provisions of the Act, whereas Bill C-32 plans to dramatically extend the scope of fair dealing.[64]

Fair dealing was defined in 1921, in the original version of the current *Copyright Act*, as "[a]ny fair dealing with any work for the purposes of private study, research, criticism, review or newspaper summary."[65]

A Liberal majority government narrowed the scope of fair dealing exceptions in 1997[66] as follows:

> **29** Fair dealing for the purpose of research or private study does not infringe copyright.[67]
>
> **29.1** Fair dealing for the purpose of criticism or review does not infringe copyright if the following are mentioned:
> (*a*) the source; and
> (*b*) if given in the source, the names of the
> (i) author, in the case of a work,
> (ii) performer, in the case of a performer's performance,
> (iii) maker, in the case of a sound recording, or

---

63 *Ibid.*, at para.11.

64 There are other provisions which extend the rights of copyholders. For instance, ss. 10 and 13(2) of the *Copyright Act* which gave idiosyncratic treatment to photographs will be repealed by ss. 6 & 7 of Bill C-32, above note 4, if it passes, which will give photographs exactly the same treatment under the *Copyright Act* as is given to other works. In general, this chapter has focused on provisions of Bill C-32 which themselves will have consequences specific to institutions involved in education and provision of library services. It should also be noted that the Liberal attempt in Bill C-60 in 2005 also failed to make any changes to the fair dealing provisions, but note s. 32 creating a new s. 32.2(1)(f) that will continue special treatment for private or non-commercial use of commissioned photographs.

65 *Copyright Act*, S.C. 1921, c. 24, s. 16(1)(i),www.digital-copyright.ca/static/Copyright 1921.pdf. This provision was actually an exact duplication of s. 2(1)(i) of the *United Kingdom Act, 1911*: Guiseppina D'Agostino, "Healing Fair Dealing? A Comparative Copyright Analysis of Canada's Fair Dealing to U.K. Fair Dealing and U.S. Fair Use" (2008) 53 McGill L.J. 309–63 at para 13.

66 *An Act to amend the Copyright Act*, S.C. 1997, c. 24, s. 18(1). By pure coincidence, this Act was introduced as an earlier Bill C-32! (*That* Bill C-32 was in the 35th Parliament of 17 January 1994 to 27 April 1997.)

67 *Copyright Act*, above note 1, s. 29.

(iv) broadcaster, in the case of a communication signal.[68]

29.2 Fair dealing for the purpose of news reporting does not infringe copyright if the following are mentioned

(*a*) the source; and

(*b*) if given in the source, the names of the

(i) author, in the case of a work,

(ii) performer, in the case of a performer's performance,

(iii) maker, in the case of a sound recording, or

(iv) broadcaster, in the case of a communication signal.[69]

The Supreme Court clearly annunciated a broad vision of "fair dealing" in *CCH v. Law Society*.[70] Nevertheless, it is evident that fair dealing is not infinite.[71] For instance, the Federal Court of Appeal has just clearly stated that "'[p]rivate study' presumably means just that: study by oneself . . . [w]hen students study material with their class as a whole, they engage not in 'private study' but perhaps just 'study.'"[72] This interpretation of the existing fair dealing provisions (together with certain other comments)[73] makes it very important that the government is planning to extend fair dealing explicitly to education.

Now, in a dramatic expansion, Bill C-32 will extend section 29 so that, without any conditions about source or names, fair dealing will encompass uses for the purposes of "research, private study, *education, parody or satire*."[74]

There are other proposed extensions of fair dealing proposed in Bill C-32.[75] One extension permits institutions to create back-up copies of works

---

68 *Ibid.*, s. 29.1.

69 *Ibid.*, s. 29.2.

70 Above note 38.

71 See Wilkinson (2005) above note 6.

72 *Alberta v. Access Copyright*, above note 53 at para. 38.

73 The Court explicitly finds reasonable the Copyright Board's interpretation that "since the students in question did not request the photocopies themselves, given the instructional setting, it is likely that the purpose of the photocopying was for the instruction of the students, not for private study" *and* "the Board was entitled to find that when a student is instructed to read the material, it is likely that the purpose of the copying was for classroom instruction rather than the student's private study." (para.46).

74 Bill C-32, above note 4, s.21.

75 For instance, Bill C-32, s.22, amending the *Copyright Act*, above note 1, by adding s.29.22, permits "an individual" — and thus, presumably, not institutions engaged in education and library services, *per se* — to reproduce works for "private purposes" under certain conditions (including that any technological protection measures

or other subject matter under given conditions.[76] One of them, however, upon closer examination, appears to be better characterized with defences to infringement actions rather than positive extensions to the rights of rightsholders. The new exception for "non-commercial user-generated content"[77] initially looks as though it will not be "an infringement of copyright for an individual to use an existing work or other subject-matter or copy of one, which has been published or otherwise made available to the public, in the creation of a new work or other subject-matter in which copyright subsists"[78] but the creation and use of the new work is only permitted where four conditions apply:

> 1. the use . . . is done solely for non-commercial purposes; and
> 2. the source of the [original] existing work is mentioned, if it is reasonable to do so; and
> 3. the person had reasonable grounds to believe that the [original] existing work was not infringing copyright; and
> 4. the use of the new work does not have a substantial adverse effect, financial or otherwise, on the exploitation or potential exploitation of the [original] existing work or its market.[79]

The language of "reasonable grounds to believe" (in the third condition) is language most frequently reserved in statutes for defences, as is evident in the language of the courts in interpreting it. "Reasonable grounds to believe" has been defined by the Federal Courts as "a *bona fide* belief in a serious possibility based on credible evidence."[80] The definition was adopted by the Supreme Court which then went on to state that "The Federal Court of Appeal has found, and we agree, that the "reasonable grounds to believe" standard requires something more than mere suspicion, but less than the standard applicable in civil matters of proof on the balance

---

in place are not circumvented), and, by adding s.29.23, permits individuals to time shift broadcasts under certain conditions. Query whether libraries would be able to act as agents for their patrons in making use of these new users' rights.

76 Bill C-32, s. 22, amending the *Copyright Act*, above note 4, by adding s. 29.24, which applies to "a person" and thus would include institutions.

77 The label in the margins for the new section to be added by s. 22 of Bill C-32 (amending the *Copyright Act* by adding a new s. 29.21).

78 Bill C-32, s.22, in the wording of the first part of the new s. 29.21(1).

79 Paraphrasing from Bill C-32, s. 22, in the latter half of the new s. 29.2(a)–(d).

80 *Chiau v. Canada (Minister of Citizenship & Immigration)*, [1998] F.C.J. No. 131, [1998] 2 F.C. 642 (T.D.) at para. 60, www.canlii.org/en/ca/fct/doc/1998/1998canlii9042/1998canlii9042.html, aff'd [2000] F.C.J. No. 2043, [2001] 2 F.C. 297 (C.A.), www.canlii.org/en/ca/fca/doc/2000/2000canlii16793/2000canlii16793.html.

of probabilities."[81] Thus, the most important change to fair dealing in Bill C-32 is the addition of parody, satire and education as categories of exception.

The inclusion of parody and satire in fair dealing will no doubt be useful because it will settle an ongoing debate[82] in Canadian copyright law about whether the category of "criticism" in Canada's fair dealing provisions was as wide as the category of "comment" in the American legislation, where the United States Supreme Court settled some time ago that comment includes criticism.[83] It will be an important addition to the statute from the point of view of bringing further certainty into Canadian copyright law, but, depending upon your point of view on the existing debate, it will or will not be extending the scope of Canadian concept of criticism in Canadian fair dealing.

It is the extension of fair dealing to cover uses for the purpose of education that is *the* unprecedented and most important extension to users' rights in Bill C-32.[84]

The term "education" used in the new section 29 is not currently defined by the *Copyright Act*. Nor is there a definition proposed in Bill C-32. This means that fair dealing uses for the purpose of education will not be lim-

---

81 *Mugesera c. Canada (Ministre de la Citoyenneté & de l'Immigration)*, [2005] 2 S.C.R. 100 at 114, approving *Sivakumar v. Canada (Minister of Employment & Immigration)* (1993), [1994] 1 F.C. 433 (C.A.), at 445; *Chiau v. Canada (Minister of Citizenship & Immigration)* (C.A.), *ibid.* at para. 60. The Court in *Mugasera* went on to say, at para. 116, that "the 'reasonable grounds to believe' standard of proof applies only to questions of fact," approving *Moreno v. Canada (Minister of Employment & Immigration)* (1993), [1994] 1 F.C. 298 (C.A.), at 311.

82 In *Compagnie Générale des Établissements Michelin-Michelin & Cie v. National Automobile, Aerospace, Transportation and General Workers Union of Canada (CAW-Canada)*, [1997] 2 F.C. 306, Teitelbaum, J., concluded that since parody does not fall under the category of criticism, it should not considered part of the defence of fair dealing. He felt that Canadian courts should be cautious in adopting the reasoning of American courts with respect to the open-ended American "fair use" when interpreting the fixed categories in the Canadian "fair dealing." More recently, however, the Supreme Court's decision in SCC released the more liberal interpretation of the fair use provisions in *CCH v. Law Society of Upper Canada*, above note 38, which holds that even though the number of enumerated categories in fair dealing is fixed in the Canadian *Copyright Act*, new purposes may exist within each enumerated category.

83 *Campbell v. Acuff-Rose Music, Inc.*, 510 U.S. 569 (1994).

84 Interestingly, Justice Trudel alludes to this extension in Bill C-32 in his recent reasons reviewing the Copyright Board's *Elementary and Secondary Schools Tariff* 2005-2009, above, stating "this amendment [adding education, parody or satire] only serves to create additional allowable purposes, it does not affect the fairness analysis." *Alberta et al v. Access Copyright et al* , above note 53at para.21.

ited to any particular institutions or sector: it will apply to any individual or institution engaged in education. As such, education will have to be given its usual meaning in law.

In *Vancouver Society of Immigrant and Visible Minority Women v, M.N.R.*,[85] Justice Iacobucci, speaking for the majority of the Supreme Court, considered the definition of education in the context of asking whether a society could be considered to be advancing education (in the context of making a determination about a charity) and made the following statements:

> There seems no logical or principled reason why the advancement of education should not be interpreted to include more informal training initiatives, aimed at teaching necessary life skills or providing information toward a practical end, so long as these are truly geared at the training of the mind and not just the promotion of a particular point of view.[86]
>
> . . . there is no good reason why non-traditional activities such as workshops, seminars, self-study, and the like should not be included alongside traditional, classroom-type instruction in a modern definition of "education."[87]
>
> To my mind, the threshold criterion for an educational activity must be some legitimate, targeted attempt at educating others, whether through formal or informal instruction, training, plans of self-study, or otherwise. . . . The law ought to accommodate any legitimate form of education.[88]

Justice Iacobucci's definition of education will give a wide ambit to the proposed extension of fair dealing in the *Copyright Act*. Just as fair dealing has been interpreted by the Supreme Court from the users' point of view in recent copyright decisions, education has been interpreted by the Supreme Court from the point of view of a "legitimate, targeted attempt at educating others," a notion not reserved for particular institutional actors but, rather, for any actor undertaking to educate. It is probable, then, that just as the Great Library of the Law Society of Upper Canada was able to justify all its activities under fair dealing even though there are now particular exceptions in the statute for certain "libraries, archives and mu-

85 [1999] 1 S.C.R. 10, http://csc.lexum.umontreal.ca/en/1999/1999scr1-10/1999scr1-10.html.Note the Federal Court in *McKay v. Canada (AG)*, 2010 FC 856 recently (27 August 2010) interpreted "education" broadly.

86 *Ibid*, at para. 168.

87 *Ibid*, at para. 170.

88 *Ibid*, at para. 171.

seums," schools, colleges and universities will all be able to justify most activities as fair dealing under education, despite the fact that Parliament provides specific exceptions to a certain class of educational institution.

b) Additional Rights for "Educational Institutions" and "Libraries, Archives And Museums"

Since 1997 "educational institutions," as defined in the *Copyright Act*, have certain additional users' rights beyond those given to all by the fair dealing sections of the Act.[89] Since the decision of the Supreme Court in 2004 clarifying the application of the fair dealing provisions and their relationship with this type of institution-specific exception, it is evident that these exceptions are not as important as perhaps might have been thought when they were first introduced.[90] Nonetheless, the government has proposed to extend these rights through Bill C-32.

It is interesting to note that these special exemptions for educational institutions did not appear to play a great part in the tariff-setting by the Copyright Board for schools 2005–2009, as discussed above.[91] On the other hand, as discussed above, it is on just such a "special" exception that the Federal Court of Appeal has remitted the Copyright Board's Decision back to it for reconsideration.

Bill C-32 makes significant amendments to the rights of "educational institutions."[92] For example, Bill C-32, if passed, will allow an "educational institution" to take a work or other subject matter from the Internet and communicate it to a public primarily consisting of students provided the original author and source are referenced[93] unless the educational institution knows or ought to know that the source from which the taking is being done did not have the copyright holder's permission.[94] This user right will be subject to either of two limitations: the copyright holder may protect the subject matter with legally enforceable technological protection

---

89 See Wilkinson (2005), above note 6 at 352–55.

90 *Ibid.*

91 They appear to have only engaged the Board's attention briefly in the reasons, see Copyright Board decision, above note 36, paras. 123–29 and148. A total of 6,995,451 pages were added to the total number of compensable copies (2.8 percent of the total) as a result of analysis of these exceptions and rejection of their applicability to certain copies made (of 246,001,462 pages triggering remuneration, see para. 150).

92 See Bill C-32, above note 4, s. 25, amending the *Copyright Act*, above note 1, s. 29.6; Bill C-32, s.26, amending the *Copyright Act* by removing s. 29.9(1)(a); and Bill C-32, s. 27, adding to the *Copyright Act* after s. 30, ss. 30.01–30.04.

93 Bill C-32, *ibid.*, s. 27, amending the *Copyright Act*, *ibid.*, by adding s. 30.04.

94 Bill C-32, *ibid.*, s. 27, amending the *Copyright Act*, *ibid.*, by adding s. 30.04(5)

measures[95] or the copyright holder may provide explicit notice (beyond just a notice of copyright) that the material should not be used for educational purposes.[96]

Bill C-32 will allow a "library, archive or museum" to make copies for patrons without the need for the institution to satisfy itself that "the person will not use the copy for a purpose other than research or private study,"[97] requiring rather that that institution "informs the person that the copy is to be used solely for research or private study and that any use of the copy for a purpose other than research or private study may require authorization of the copyright owner of the work in question."[98] As was the case with amendments proposed for inter-library loan back in 2005, it is probable that this change for "libraries, archives and museums,"[99] while laudable as a clarification to the drafting of the *Copyright Act*, is really unnecessary in light of the language of the Supreme Court in interpreting the ability of all libraries to act as agents for their patrons in the *CCH v. Law Society* case.[100]

Bill C-32 also codifies, in the case of interlibrary operations involving "libraries, archives and museums,"[101] a principle of agency[102] that would appear to apply to all libraries in any case, pursuant to *CCH v. Law Society*: that one library, acting as agent for another, would be also the agent of the patron for which the first library is acting. It may be helpful to make the clarification, but not if other libraries, not falling within the statutory definition of "libraries, archives and museums" provide less service to patrons because they do not realize they already have the same powers under

---

95 Bill C-32, *ibid.*, s, 27, amending the *Copyright Act*, *ibid.*, by adding s. 30.04(3)

96 Bill C-32, *ibid.*, s, 27, amending the *Copyright Act*, *ibid.*, by adding s.30.04(4)

97 As required under the current s. 30.2(4)(a).

98 Bill C-32, above note 4, s.29, replacing section 30.2(4) of the current Act.

99 The current s. 30.21 applies particularly to "archives" (presumably to all archives and not just those archives included in the statutorily defined term "library, archive or museum") and applies to the copying of unpublished works. Bill C-32 would eliminate the same requirement as under the current s. 30.2(4)(a) and replace it with the requirement that the patron be informed. See Bill C-32, above note 4, s. 30(2).

100 See Wilkinson (2005), above note 6 at 360–62.

101 Bill C-32, above note 4, s.29, replacing s. 30.2(5) of the current Act.

102 Floyd R. Mechem, *Outlines of the Law of Agency*, 4th ed. (Chicago: Callaghan, 1952) at 51.

> By delegation . . . the agent is permitted to use agents of his own in performing the function he is employed to perform for his principal, delegating to them the discretion which normally he would be expected to exercise personally. These agents are known as subagents to indicate that they are the agent's agents and not the agents of the principal. Normally (though of course not necessarily) they are paid by the agent. The agent is liable to the principal for any injury done him by the misbehavior of the agent's subagents.

the authority of the *CCH v. Law Society* case interpreting the fair dealing provisions of the statute. It bears repeating that the Supreme Court has said "a library can always attempt to prove that its dealings with a copyrighted work are fair under section 29 of the *Copyright Act*. It is only if a library were unable to make out the fair dealing exception under section 29 that it would need to turn to the *Copyright Act* to prove that it qualified for the library exemption."[103] Bill C-32 would purport, in this connection, to impose fairly onerous requirements on "libraries, archives and museums" acting as agents for other libraries (i.e., in inter-library loan situations) to establish "measures" to ensure that patrons receiving *digital* copies of works or other subject matter from such institutions make only one copy and so on.[104] It seems probable, that, here again, the government is unnecessarily complicating rights which *all* libraries already hold pursuant to the Supreme Court's interpretation of existing users' fair dealing rights in the *Copyright Act* and libraries' roles as agents of their users.[105]

Bill C-32 does clarify one aspect of a right given to a library, archive or museum under the *Copyright Act* that does not seem to be available in any event and to other "libraries, archives and museums" under the interpretation of fair dealing provided by the Supreme Court: this is with respect to the ability of statutory libraries, archives and museums to transfer materials to new formats not only when technology becomes obsolete, as under the present law, but also when such technology is *becoming* obsolete.[106]

Bill C-32, therefore, if it becomes law, will amend provisions dealing with "libraries, archives and museums" to a limited extent and, even more, extends the statutory exceptions for educational institutions" but it goes far beyond its predecessor bills, as discussed herein, by creating the extension of fair dealing to education.

There is one aspect of Bill C-32 and its application to "libraries, archives and museums" which deserves particular mention. Much will be made in discussion of Bill C-32 of its articulation of proposed enactments concerning "technological protection measures" (TPMs), which Bill C-32 defines as

> any effective technology, device or component that, in the ordinary course of its operation,

103 *CCH v. Law Society*, above note 38, para. 49, quoted in Wilkinson (2005), above note 6, at 357.

104 Bill C-32, above note 4, s.2 9, amending the *Copyright Act*, above note 1, replacing s. 30.2(5), *inter alia*, by adding s. 30.2(5.02).

105 See, in this connection, Wilkinson (2005), above note 6, at 355–57

106 Bill C-32, above note 4, s. 28, amending the *Copyright Act*, above note 1, s. 30.1(1)(c).

(a) controls access to a work, to a performer's performance fixed in a sound recording or to a sound recording and whose use is authorized by the copyright owner; or

(b) restricts the doing — with respect to a work, to a performer's performance fixed in a sound recording or to a sound recording — of any act referred to in section 3, 15, or 18 and any act for which remuneration is payable under s. 19.[107]

The important point to note here for our purposes is the proposed s.41.2 which will provide:

> If a court finds that a defendant that is a library, archive or museum or an educational institution has contravened s.41.1(1) [circumventing a TPM or offering services in relation to those purposes or dealing with making available technology for those purposes] and the defendant satisfies the court that it was not aware, and had no reasonable grounds to be believe, that its actions constituted a contravention of that subsection, the plaintiff is not entitled to any remedy other than an injunction.[108]

This partial defence is only made available to "libraries, archives and museums." It will not apply to other libraries, archives or museums (those which operate for profit or do not maintain appropriate collections). If passed, its existence will become part of the copyright world of some institutions and not others. It appears to be a special acknowledgment on the part of the government of the role which at least non-profit libraries, archives and museums, which maintain the requisite collection, can play in the lives of their patrons. It is, of course, a shame that the role played by other libraries, archives and museums is not equally recognized. It must also be recognized that a court would almost certainly order the library, archive or museum to stop its activities if found liable in such an action — so this is not an exception for libraries, archives or museums.

2) Omissions from Bill C-32

a) The Continuing Problem with "Educational Institution" and "Library, Archive or Museum" Exceptions

One important contribution that Bill C-32's inclusion of "education" in the fair dealing provisions will make is that it can diminish somewhat a

107 Bill C-32, above note 4, s. 47, amending the *Copyright Act*, above, by adding s.41.
108 *Ibid.*

growing problem under the *Copyright Act* which was begun by the Liberal reforms of 1997.[109] This problem was the creation of two special statutory classes of institutions in Canada: "educational institutions" and "libraries, archives and museums."[110]

As commonly understood (and described everywhere except in the current *Copyright Act*), "libraries," "archives," "museums," and "education institutions" describe a class of institutions which can be found in both the public and private sectors and which can be operated either on a for-profit or not-for-profit basis. However, under the *Copyright Act* since 1997 "library, archive or museum" and "education institution" comprise only a limited, defined subset of those institutions we normally understand to be included in those terms. Public sector educational institutions are covered under "educational institution" and private sector, non-profit educational institutions are included in "educational institution"[111] — but private, for-profit educational institutions are not.[112] Meanwhile an even more limited group of libraries, archives and museums fall within the statutory

---

109 *An Act to Amend the Copyright Act*, S.C. 1997, c. 24, s. 1(5), amending s. 2 of the *Copyright Act* to add and define "educational institution" and "library, archive or museum"

110 Although in the singular "library, archive or museum" and "education institution" which is defined in s. 2 of the *Copyright Act* (see below), it has become common to refer to these statutorily defined organizations in the plural in quotes, to distinguish those falling with the *Copyright Act* exceptions from other libraries, archives, museums and educations institutions which are not entitled to the exceptions. Indeed, "libraries, archives and museums" within the exceptions are referred to in common parlance as "LAMs."

111 Note that private, non-profit educational institutions are included in the ambit of these special exceptions to the *Copyright Act*, but are not included in the *Access Copyright Elementary and Secondary School Tariff, 2005–2009* just established before the Copyright Board. On the other hand, public schools both benefit from the statutory exceptions for "educational institutions" and are covered, except in Quebec, by the *Access Copyright Elementary and Secondary School Tariff, 2005–2009*. See "Statement of Royalties to Be Collected by Access Copyright for the Reprographic Reproduction, in Canada, of Works in its Repertoire: Educational Institutions (2005–2009)," *Supplement Canada Gazette*, Part I, 27 June 2009, to be known as "Access Copyright Elementary and Secondary School Tariff, 2005–2009": www.cb-cda.gc.ca/tariffs-tarifs/certified-homologues/2009/20090626-b.pdf

112 *Copyright Act*, s. 2,

"educational institution" means

(a) a non-profit institution licensed or recognized by or under an Act of Parliament or the legislature of a province to provide pre-school, elementary, secondary or post-secondary education. [or]

(b) a non-profit institution that is directed or controlled by a board of education regulated by or under an Act of the legislature or a province and that provides continuing, professional or vocational education or training. [or]

definition than is the case with educational institutions because, to be considered a "library, archive or museum" under the *Copyright Act*, not only do these institutions have to fall strictly within the non-profit sector (whether publicly or privately owned) but they must also, unless specially included by regulation, hold and maintain "a collection of documents and other materials that is open to the public or researchers." [113]

One problem which arose in the case of Bill C-60's then proposed extensions to users' rights in 2005was that the Bill did not speak to general extensions of fair dealing but rather concentrated entirely on extensions to the rights of "libraries, archives and museums" and "educational institutions" as defined in the Act.[114] The problem would also have been exacerbated had the subsequent Bill C-61 in 2008 become law.[115] Amendments of this type can only exacerbate the gaps between types of schools, universities, colleges, archives, museums and libraries in Canada[116]—and drive unnecessary wedges between public and private, for-profit and not-for-profit institutions. This problem continues to be present in the proposed reforms of Bill C-32—but is less prominent because of the proposed general amendments to fair dealing just discussed.

(c) a department or agency of any order of government, or any non-profit body, that controls or supervises education or training referred to in paragraph (a) or (b), or

(d) any other non-profit institution prescribed by the regulations.

113 *Copyright Act*, s. 2 "libraries, archives and museums" means

> an institution, whether or not incorporated, that is not established or conducted for profit or does not form a part of, or is not administered or directly or indirectly controlled by, a body that is established or conducted for profit, in which is held and maintained a collection of documents and other materials that is open to the public or to researchers, or any other non-profit institution prescribed by regulation.

114 Wilkinson (2005), above note 6 at 337–38, 372–73.

115 Bill C-61, above note 3, in 2008 would have amended the "educational institution" exceptions with respect to the following sections of the *Copyright Act*: ss. 30.01(3)–(5), 30.02, 30.03, 30.04, 38.1(3), 41.19, and 41.2(2). It would have amended the "library, archive or museum" exceptions with respect to the following sections: ss. 30.1(1), 30.2(5), and 41.19.

116 It should be noted that the federal government itself has recently re-structured its own Health Canada Library such that it is now closed to "outsiders"—which will result in its falling outside the *Copyright Act* definition of a "library, archive or museum" and, thus, despite being operated not for profit and being part of the public sector, being ineligible for the rights Parliament has given to a "library, archive or museum."

As the Copyright Board has recently stated "all exceptions provided in the Act are now users' rights."[117] Surely, as a policy matter, Parliament should not make user resources dependent upon whether users choose to access those resources through the institutions in the for-profit sector or the non-for-profit sector.[118]

It is indeed ironic that if you as a consumer choose to obtain services from an institution that, in one way or another, is profiting from the services offered and therefore for which people pay, you will be additionally penalized by the federal government by not being able to benefit from copyright rights which you would have enjoyed had you patronized institutions which already are limited to charging only that which does not bring them a profit. And, again, the increasing prevalence of public-private partnerships in the delivery of services to Canadians means that these kinds of distinctions in the availability of user rights in copyright will become unwieldy at best.

b) Clarifying the Representativeness of Collectives in Canada

As discussed above, Bill C-32 does not solve the problem in Canada currently that the collectives do not represent those rightsholders who choose not to join them.[119] This makes the absence from the new tariffs of the previous indemnification clause in blanket licences obtained from Access Copyright particularly of concern to institutions considering their options in the emerging copyright environment (as discussed above). It would appear that the government needs to clarify whether Canada is operating on an "extended repertoire" system, especially given the various extensions of privileges to users who have entered into agreements with collectives that already exist in the statute and that Bill C-32 would extend.[120]

---

117 Copyright Board decision, above note 36 at para. 76.

118 An argument equally made in respect of Bill C-60, see Wilkinson (2005), above note 6 at 172.

119 This shortcoming has been noted by Daniel Gervais (2008), above note 18, at 220. In Europe, the "extended licensing" or "extended repertoire" system has been common for some time. Under it, those who do not wish to be represented by the appropriate collective bear the burden of opting out.

120 See, for example, in Bill C-32, s. 27, which would add to the *Copyright Act* s. 30.02 and create an exception for digital reproduction of works only for an "educational institution that has a reprographic reproduction licence under which the institution is authorized to make reprographic reproductions of works in a collective society's repertoire for an educational or training purpose."

D. INSTITUTIONS INVOLVED IN EDUCATION AND LIBRARY SERVICES AND BILL C-32

How will institutions involved in education and the provision of library services experience the reforms in Bill C-32, given their current copyright worlds?

Bill C-32 does seem to indicate that the current Canadian government is recognizing the necessity of balancing user and creator needs, as discussed above. But will institutions involved in education and the provision of library services in Canada directly experience the new emphasis on balance?

It would seem that this will depend very much on the individual institutions, their governance, their assessments of their users' needs, and their collections.

If an institution primarily providing *library* services looks at the users' rights already extant in the *Copyright Act*, augmented by Bill C-32 if it passes, and decides that, in the light of its users' needs and its collection, it can meet its users' needs without any dealings with collectives, then that institution may very well decide that it can ignore the availability of licences through collectives such as Access Copyright (whether negotiated directly or created through the processes of the Copyright Board). In making this decision, of course, such an institution would consider what proportion of its collection or services was already constrained by individual vendor licences that would be unaffected by any blanket licence obtained by a collective such as Access Copyright. The greater the proportion of the library's "holdings" that are actually regulated under individual licences with the copyright holders (such as vendor subscriptions from online publishers), the less the impact of any blanket licence from a collective such as Access Copyright will be. Another factor that would affect the considerations of such an institution is the fact that, if an institution makes the decision to forgo obtaining a blanket licence from a collective, then the scope of the exceptions to the rights of rightsholders under the *Copyright Act* as extended, if Bill C-32 passes, will form the boundary of the services to patrons which these institutions can offer. An institution making this kind of decision might be guided to some extent by the finding of the Copyright Board, in its deliberations over the *Access Copyright Elementary and Secondary School Tariff, 2005–2009*, that, of all the photocopying done in schools, only 2 percent was compensable. If an institution changed the way it delivers services such that that 2 percent was eliminated, then the need for that type of blanket licence would also be eliminated.

It is interesting to note that the individual licences institutions negotiate directly with rightsholders are also only indirectly affected by changes to the scope of users' rights exceptions in copyright. Such contracts typically involve more than just copyright, virtually always involving access rights to various databases and, often, patent rights with respect to various systems. Changes in copyright legislation enlarging users' rights, then, would only affect the strength of the user institution's negotiating position — not, in any way, the legality of the contract between the institution and the vendor once the parties have signed or otherwise entered into the contract.[121]

Thus, for institutions such as public libraries in Canada, where they are not the target of current tariff proceedings before the Copyright Board, the enlarged scope of users' rights which Bill C-32 would create should provide an enhanced bargaining position from which to negotiate for blanket and individual licences from Access Copyright and other copyright holders. Should any of these libraries decide, in any case, that they do not need to purchase rights to uses from collectives or individual rightsholders because the institution's uses all lie within the users' rights provisions of the *Copyright Act* (either currently or as they would be expanded by Bill C-32), then such institutions might well make decisions not to enter into various licences with respect to works and other subject matter where users' rights are sufficient to their needs. In making those decisions, these institutions would be directly affected by the state of their users' rights under the *Copyright Act* and would directly benefit from the extensions in Bill C-32.

Other libraries, such as academic libraries in post-secondary institutions and government libraries, no longer have options for negotiated blanket licences in respect of rights represented by the Access Copyright collective because Access Copyright has placed their institutions (and, therefore, these libraries) before the Copyright Board. The decisions of these institutions (for themselves and, consequently, for their libraries) are limited to deciding between three current options:

1) keeping their activities within statutory users' rights bounds and not acquiring licences for more uses as offered by Access Copyright,[122] or

---

121 There are no provisions in the *Copyright Act* similar to those, for instance, found in Ontario *Consumer Protection Act*, which specifically provides "The substantive and procedural rights given under this Act apply despite any agreement or waiver to the contrary." (S.O. 2002, c.30, Sched. A, s.7(1)).

122 The proposed Tariff anticipates that post-secondary institutions may decide from time to time whether to avail themselves of the licenses from Access Copyright that

2) while planning to enter into licences with Access Copyright, passively accepting the tariff proposed by Access Copyright (or accepting it as imposed by the Board after others have opposed it and the Board has ruled), or
3) while planning to enter into licences with Access Copyright, actively opposing the tariff as proposed and participating in the processes of the Board.

With respect to schools, it would, of course, be possible for the Ministers of Education to decide, on behalf of public schools, not to deal further with Access Copyright for reproduction or other rights in the future but rather to rely upon schools to manage their affairs so that the services offered to students lie within the exceptions to copyright holder's rights (the users' rights), given in the *Copyright Act* and affirmed by the courts, particularly the Supreme Court, especially including the enlarged scope which passage of Bill C-32 would grant. Such a decision, if ever taken, would inevitably reflect the enlarged scope of the users' rights which Bill C-32 will give if passed.

Currently, however, public schools across Canada find themselves within the umbrella of the two proceedings before the Copyright Board initiated by Access Copyright with respect to the entire education process.[123] These educational institutions do not have the opportunity to make individual judgments about the rights which Access Copyright represents. On the other hand, private schools, whether operated for profit or non for profit, do have this opportunity to make individual judgments with respect to entering into blanket licences with Access Copyright or not.[124]

---

will be governed by the *Access Copyright Post-Secondary Educational Institution Tariff, 2011–2013*, once finalized: s. 5(4) provides, for example, that

> Where the Educational Institution is no longer covered by this tariff, the Educational Institution and all Authorized Persons shall immediately cease to use all Digital Copies of Repertoire Works, delete from their hard drives, servers and networks, and make reasonable efforts to delete from any other device or medium capable of storing Digital Copies, those Digital Copies and upon written request from Access Copyright shall certify that it has done so.

123 In the *Access Copyright Elementary and Secondary School Tariff, 2005–2009*, "educational institution" is defined as "an institution providing primary, elementary or secondary school programming funded by a minister, ministry or school board *and* operated under the authority of a minister, ministry or school board" [emphasis added]. Presumably privately funded schools are therefore not covered by this tariff and must seek their own blanket licenses with Access Copyright, whether operated for profit or not for profit.

124 Access Copyright explicitly recognizes this decision-making process for "Independent and Tutorial Schools" on its website and offers such schools an opportunity to

Thus, for public schools, on the one hand, and for those libraries targeted by Access Copyright's current tariff applications whose institutions decide to avail themselves of the tariffs once ordered by the Board, on the other, the extensions to users' rights represented by Bill C-32 will become only indirectly relevant to many of their operations. For them, the effect of extensions to users' rights will be felt as part of the calculations done by the Copyright Board in establishing the tariffs payable from time to time through decisions of the Board.[125] At this moment, the most active collective focusing on educational institutions at all levels and governments (and thus affecting many libraries) is Access Copyright. However, as indicated in Figure 1 above, many other uses that could affect educational institutions and libraries fall under aegis of collectives which might in future target these same institutions in tariff proceedings before the Copyright Board.

Even where the effect of *Copyright Act* amendments are only felt indirectly by educational institutions and libraries (because proceedings before the Copyright Board or negotiations directly with copyright holders for licences are the primary experience of the institutions), it will still be important for such organizations to make their views known on the amendments to the *Copyright Act* which will be created under Bill C-32: extensions to users' rights will affect the bottom line for these institutions because of their effect on the Copyright Board's formula for tariffs and on their negotiating positions with rightsholders. However, the effect of these changes to the *Copyright Act* will not be direct and may not be easily measured because the Board's tariff determinations reflect factors other than just statutory rights just as direct negotiations with rightsholders often involve complex bargaining positions. Recall, in this connection, that although the Copyright Board found only 2 percent of uses of

---

enter into blanket licenses. However, it is not obvious from the public information provided on its website that Access Copyright, in setting the prices of these blanket licenses, differentiates between those schools which are "educational institutions" within the *Copyright Act* exceptions, although not within the meaning of "educational institution" under the *Access Copyright Elementary School Tariff, 2005–2009* (non-profit schools which are not publicly funded) and those schools who do *not* enjoy the benefits of the "educational institution" exceptions under the *Copyright Act* but are also not covered by the *Access Copyright Elementary School Tariff, 2005–2009* (for-profit private schools). Presumably the former should be asked to pay less for a blanket license than the latter if the breadth of potential uses requiring purchase is the only criterion involved in setting the prices for these licenses. See www.access-copyright.ca/Default.aspx?id=99

125 Recall that the Copyright Board dealt with the existing limits of fair dealing in paras. 57–114 of its decision on the school tariff for 2005–2009, above.

photocopied material to be compensable under the recent *Access Copyright Elementary and Secondary School Tariff, 2005–2009*, given the value ascribed to that 2 percent, the Board set the tariff at double the rate set by the earlier voluntarily negotiated licence fee ($5.16 per FTE student as opposed to $2.56).

The fact that Bill C-32 leaves unchanged the role of the Copyright Board of Canada and the definitions of "educational institution" and "library, archive or museum" under the *Copyright Act* must be seen as indications that the government is satisfied with the separation of copyright worlds which is occurring across various types of institutions providing education and library services in Canada. The government must be relying on these institutions themselves to manage within their own individual 'copyright worlds' to provide maximum educational and library benefits to their students and patrons, despite the growing differences in their copyright worlds. Bill C-32, if it passes in the form in which it was introduced, will make changes to various 'copyright worlds' but differences between the copyright worlds experienced by various institutions have developed largely because of the reforms of 1997 and are not diminished directly by anything in Bill C-32, despite the leveling that the addition of education as an aspect of fair dealing would add. Therefore, the fragmentation of educational institutions and institutions providing library services into those involved under tariffs decided by the Copyright Board and those not, and those affected by "educational institution" or "library, archive, or museum" exceptions under the *Copyright Act* and those not, and those affected by neither and those affected by both, will continue in any event, even if Bill C-32 does not pass. The collection patterns of libraries and the proportion of services offered under contracts made directly with copyright holders, rather than copyright collectives, will vary institution by institution and will likely change according to the offerings made available by copyright holders directly or through collectives. Users' needs evolve constantly and must be evaluated continuously by libraries and educational institutions and these evaluations will affect the uses that these institutions will make of works and other subject matter subject to copyright. Much, therefore, rests in the hands of those who govern our Canadian institutions of education and library services to continually evaluate their environments with respect to copyright (of which Bill C-32, if it passes, will form only one aspect) and take appropriate actions in light of those evaluations.

CHAPTER EIGHTEEN

Bill C-32 and the Educational Sector:

Overcoming Impediments to Fair Dealing

Samuel E. Trosow*

This chapter will focus on some of the copyright issues facing Canadian students, teachers, librarians and researchers, and how they will be affected by the educational provisions of Bill C-32[1] which would amend Canada's *Copyright Act*.[2] The bill proposes to add the word "education" as an enumerated purpose to the act's fair dealing provision,[3] it updates some of the special exemptions for educational institutions that were added in 1997,[4] and it proposes some new special exceptions for educational institutions.[5]

While the overall effect of these amendments would be positive, and the government should be given credit for including some reasonable and balanced provisions in the bill, it is important to place these developments within the overall context of the broader copyright policy environment in Canada's educational sector. In particular, the recurring uncertainty and risk aversion that has inhibited Canadian educational institutions from

* Associate Professor, University of Western Ontario, Faculty of Law and Faculty of Information & Media Studies strosow@uwo.ca. The author would like to thank Michael Geist, Joel Kom, Marie Blosh and the anonymous peer reviewers for their helpful comments and suggestions.

1 Bill C-32, *An Act to amend the Copyright Act*, 3d Sess., 40th Parl., 2010, www2.parl.gc.ca/Sites/LOP/LEGISINFO/index.asp?Language=E&query=7026&Session=23&List=toc, [Bill C-32].

2 *Copyright Act*, R.S.C. 1985, c. C-42, http://laws.justice.gc.ca/en/C-42/ [*Copyright Act*].

3 See section B(1) below.

4 See section B(2), below.

5 See sections B(3), (4), & (5), below.

implementing the broad fair dealing policies set forth in the Supreme Court of Canada's (SCC) historical ruling in *CCH Canadian Ltd. v. Law Society of Upper Canada*[6] needs to be addressed, and the proposed amendments need to be assessed in light of these considerations.

In the increasingly complex web of Canadian educational copyright policy, there remain serious impediments, or counter-factors, to the realization of fair dealing as a substantive users' right, at least insofar as it is formally recognized and incorporated into the reality of everyday practice. These impediments include the risk aversion of educational administrators, the aggressive overreaching of content owners and their representatives; and the general lack of understanding about basic copyright rights and obligations. These three factors reinforce each other, and taken together, they have frustrated the implementation of a unanimous SCC decision for over six years.

In addition to reviewing the provisions of Bill C-32 that have the most direct bearing on the educational sector, this paper seeks to scrutinize and confront these counter-factors. Insofar as copyright laws should be designed to promote teaching, learning and research, they need to be carefully crafted, implemented and assessed so that they do not impede the very purposes they were intended to promote. But the careful scrutiny of Bill C-32 cannot stay within the four corners of the document itself; rather, it must also account for the political, economic and social environment in which the outputs of the legislative process operate.

Before proceeding with a section-by-section analysis of the educational provisions of Bill C-32 in section II then, the first section will assess the current copyright policy environment in Canadian educational institutions.

A. THE STATE OF FAIR DEALING SIX YEARS AFTER *CCH*

In framing the 2009 copyright consultation process, the government asked how copyright law could be changed to withstand the test of time based on Canadian values and interests, and what changes would best foster innovation, creativity, competition and investment.[7] These goals are best served by recognizing Canada as a haven for fair copyright practices, reflecting the balanced approach envisioned by the CCH decision. Practising fair copyright, which may take on different forms in different contexts,

---

6 *CCH Canadian Ltd. v. Law Society of Upper Canada*, 2004 SCC 13, www.canlii.org/en/ca/scc/doc/2004/2004scc13/2004scc13.html, [2004] 1 S.C.R. 339 [*CCH*].

7 Government of Canada, "Copyright Consultations," www.ic.gc.ca/eic/site/008.nsf/eng/home.

should become the hallmark of a Canadian copyright culture reflecting Canadian values and encouraging, rather than impeding, the creative and transformative uses of new information technologies. A necessary, though not sufficient requisite of realizing this practice is that the law be clear, consistent and understandable by those who must follow and apply it.

1) Reconnecting the *Copyright Act* with Reality

A recurring theme raised throughout the consultation process included the need to bring the text of the *Copyright Act* into closer harmony with the practices of modern technology, while at the same time striving for consistency and simplicity. A troubling disconnect had emerged between the static text of the act, which continued to reflect the rigidities of the strict categorical approach of the limited fair dealing defence, and the more recent recognition of fair dealing as a substantive users' right—a right that was identified by the SCC as an integral part of the *Copyright Act* that should not be interpreted restrictively.[8] But there are other social and cultural factors at play here, such as an enlarging fissure between the limited categories of fair dealing and the growing range of commonly accepted uses of information technology and new media. As stated in my consultation submission:

> . . . we have an unfortunate disconnect between the actual state of copyright law as it is construed in the courts, and the actual text of the Act itself. This discrepancy should be harmonized so the Act reflects the case-law as set down by the Supreme Court. Not only is there a discrepancy between the text of the Act and the Supreme Court case-law, but there is a whole set of discrepancies between common ordinary everyday practices of Canadians and the text of the Act. For example, while it is common practice to utilize VCR and other types of recorders in the home, it is not at all clear how such use fits neatly within any of the enumerated categories of research, private study, criticism, review or news reporting. Yet these devices are lawfully sold by Canadian retailers and purchased and used routinely by Canadian consumers. There are many other examples of how typical information usage practices do not neatly fit within the narrow confines of the fair dealing provisions of the Act as it was drafted.[9]

---

8 *CCH*, above note 6 at para. 48.

9 Samuel Trosow. "Copyright Submission" (2009) 2 Osgoode Hall Rev of L and Pol'y 169, 180,.http://ohrlp.ca/index.php/Previous-Journal/Samuel-Trosow-Copyright-Consultations-Submission-2009-Osgoode-Hall-Rev.L.Pol-y-169.html.

Social and cultural factors, such as the popularity of new digital media and the consequent breakdown of the old dichotomies between content producers and end users only magnify the growing fissure between copyright law "on the books" and new social realities in the networked environment. This problem could be rectified by adding the words "such as" to the enumerated fair dealing categories, an approach incorporated into resolution M-506, which was introduced in Parliament by M.P. Charlie Angus in March 2010:

> That, in the opinion of the House, the government should amend section 29 of the *Copyright Act* in such a way as to expand the Fair Dealing provisions of the act, specifically by deleting section 29 and inserting the following: "29. Fair dealing of a copyrighted work for purposes such as research, private study, criticism, news reporting or review, is not an infringement of copyright. 29.1 In determining whether the dealing made of a work in any particular case is fair dealing, the factors to be considered shall include: (a) the purpose of the dealing; (b) the character of the dealing; (c) the amount of the dealing; (d) alternatives to the dealing; (e) the nature of the work; and (f) the effect of the dealing on the work."[10]

But there are other more damaging counter-factors underlying this disconnect between practice in the educational sector and the promise of *CCH*. One such impediment standing in the way of end-users' ability to engage in creative uses is the imposition of technological protection measures (TPMs). Their purpose and effect is to lock digital content, even where users might access and utilize the content in a variety of non-infringing and indeed transformative and beneficial ways. The inclusion in both Bill C-61 and now again in Bill C-32 of a strict version of the United States' *Digital Millennium Copyright Act*'s[11] anti-circumvention measures threatens to override many aspects of users' rights, including fair dealing and other educational exemptions. While this significant counter-factor is treated in greater depth elsewhere in this volume, the important and sometime

10 *House of Commons Notice* Paper, No. 10 (16 March 2010) (Charlie Angus), www2.parl.gc.ca/HousePublications/Publication.aspx?Language=E&Mode=1&Parl=40&Ses=3&DocId=4345800&File=11.

11 *Digital Millennium Copyright Act*, Pub. L. 105-304, 112 Stat. 2860 (1998), www.copyright.gov/title17.

overriding role given to TPMs in the newly proposed special exemptions for educational institutions is a recurring problem.[12]

2) Risk Aversion, Licensing and Rights Accretion

A subtler and less visible problem has been the reluctance of educational institutions to take full advantage of the fair dealing rights that became available as a result of the *CCH* decision in 2004. The Canadian Federation of Students has observed:

> Many in the educational community have argued that, when viewed through the lens of the 2004 ruling, the current definition of fair dealing affords broad rights to those in the educational community. While this view is widely held amongst copyright experts, university and college administrators have not prescribed to it, instead off-loading the fees for using copyrighted materials onto students.[13]

Perhaps the most serious impediment to fair dealing in the educational sector has been the confusion caused by what appears to be the broad and all-encompassing scope of the Access Copyright licence, which aggravates the fears of risk of liability. Some background on the license will help frame the problem.

In January 2004, Access Copyright entered into multi-year licensing agreements with Canadian educational institutions.[14] While the agreements expired in 2007 they were extended for an additional three years through August 2010. During the three-year extension, payments were kept at the 2006–07 rate of $3.38 per Full Time Equivalent (FTE) student plus 10 cents per page for materials in course packs. The FTE rate is assessed across the board as an educational fee, but the per page course pack charges are incurred by the student when purchasing a course pack. Under the license, Access Copyright grants the licensee institution non-exclusive rights to reproduce works in its repertoire[15] and agrees to indemnify the

---

12 See particularly the discussions of proposed sections 30.01, 30.02, and 30.04 in sections B(3), (4), & (5), respectively.

13 Canadian Federation of Students. *Member Advisory (May 2010), Copyright Modernization Act: Bill C-32*, www.cfs-fcee.ca/html/english/campaigns/Mem_Advisory-C_32-CFS.pdf at 2.

14 While the model agreement was negotiated by AUCC, it was signed by individual institutions. The agreement between Access Copyright and the University of Western Ontario is available at www.lib.uwo.ca/copyright/access/access_copyright.shtml [Access Copyright License].

15 *Ibid.* at section 2, www.lib.uwo.ca/copyright/access/access_licences.shtml.

licensee for copies made in accordance with the license.[16] In addition to making payments under the contract, the licensees agree to various reporting and record-keeping.[17] Access Copyright is also given the right to inspect and audit university records in order to verify the accuracy of payments[18] and to conduct an annual sampling survey.[19]

Given the potential value of the indemnification clause from a risk management perspective, it was understandable why universities negotiated and entered into these agreements in the years prior to 2004. While there was an exclusion in the license for uses which constituted fair dealing[20] these were not considered to be significant limitations on the scope of the license prior to the CCH decision in March 2004. Even after CCH, the universities may have felt locked into these license terms which were not to expire until 2007. But despite the significant changes in the copyright landscape, the educational institutions continued to extend the contract through 2010 without renegotiating the rate to reflect reasonable offsets for uses which were now fair dealing under CCH. While reliance on the license had created a comfort zone from a liability-avoidance perspective, it came at a cost. Consider this excerpt from the copyright page maintained by the York University library:

> Can I copy something not covered by Access Copyright?
>
> [I]f you want to make copies of materials not covered by the Access Copyright license and the material is not in the public domain, then permission must be obtained from the copyright owner before copying can be done.[21]

Other examples of unduly cautious copyright advice which emphasize licenses and permissions at the expense of fair dealing include the continued reliance on the Association of Universities and Colleges of Canada (AUCC) 2002 publication *Copying Right*[22] and the Council of Min-

---

16 *Ibid.* at section 23, www.lib.uwo.ca/copyright/access/access_indemnification.shtml.

17 *Ibid.* at section 11, www.lib.uwo.ca/copyright/access/access_recordkeeping.shtml.

18 *Ibid.* at section 20, www.lib.uwo.ca/copyright/access/access_audit.shtml.

19 *Ibid.* at section 22.2.

20 See text accompanying notes 26 and 27, below.

21 York University, *Copyright and You*, www.yorku.ca/univsec/documents/copyright/facultyinfo.htm.

22 Association of Universities and Colleges of Canada, *Copying Right: A guide for Canada's universities for copyright, fair dealing and collective licensing* (August 2002), www.bookstore.uwo.ca/copyrightGuide.pdf. The publication continues to be utilized despite its 2002 release date.

isters of Education, Canada (CMEC) 2005 publication entitled "Copyright Matters!"[23] both of which offer weak accounts of fair dealing.[24] These works over-emphasize the importance of the Access Copyright licence and create the impression that it somehow supersedes other principles of copyright law such as fair dealing.[25] The perception that it trumps those principles overshadows the fact that it does no such thing.

The Access Copyright licence itself does not override fair dealing. Its preamble includes the following recitals:

> AND WHEREAS the Institution desires to continue to secure the right to reproduce copyright works for the purposes of education, research and higher learning which reproductions would be outside the scope of fair dealing under the *Copyright Act* R.S.C. 1985 c.C-42, as amended;
>
> AND WHEREAS the parties do not agree on the scope of the said fair dealing . . .[26]

Section 3 of the license lists the exclusions, which explicitly include fair dealing:

> 3. This Agreement does not cover: . . . (c) any fair dealing with any work for the purposes of private study, research, criticism, review or newspaper summary . . .[27]

---

23 Wanda Noel & Gerald Bureau, "Copyright Matters!: Some Questions and Answers for Teachers" Council of Ministers of Education, Canada, 2d ed., (2005), www.cmec.ca/Publications/Lists/Publications/Attachments/12/copyrightmatters.pdf [Copyright Matters].

24 As Howard Knopf points out, the second edition of Copyright Matters is dated 2005 but does not even mention the 2004 *CCH* decision. See "Excess Caution" (8 February 2006), http://excesscopyright.blogspot.com/2006/02/excess-caution.html.

25 Another oft-cited resource is AUCC's copyright flow chart which, if read literally, would indicate that fair dealing is not available for electronic resources. See: Association of Universities and Colleges of Canada, *Copyright* (August 2002), www.lib.uwaterloo.ca/copyright/copying.html#flow.

26 Western Libraries, *Access Copyright Agreement* (January 2006), www.lib.uwo.ca/copyright/access/access_preamble.shtml [*Access Copyright Agreement*].

27 *Ibid.* at s. 3, www.lib.uwo.ca/copyright/access/access_licences.shtml. In addition, s. 4 reiterated the point in made in the preamble that the parties did not agree on the scope of fair dealing, stating: "By entering into this Agreement neither party is agreeing or representing in any way, either directly or indirectly, that the making of a single copy of all or a portion of a periodical article of a scientific, technical or scholarly nature and a single copy of a portion of any other Published Work, without the permission of the owner of copyright therein, is or is not an infringement of copyright."

In other words, the copying that is permissible under the Access Copyright license is *in addition to*, not *instead of*, the copying that can be done under fair dealing and other users' rights provisions. Put another way, you do not need to resort to the Access Copyright licence where a particular use or series of uses would constitute fair dealing. Yet the impression is unmistakable, as indicated on the University of Waterloo library's website, that: "In order to determine whether what you want to do is permissible, you therefore need to check that you comply *both* with the *Copyright Act* and with any agreements or licences covering . . . the work in question"[28] (emphasis added). The emphasized word *both* is incorrect. If the use in question constitutes fair dealing, the license is inapplicable by its own terms.[29]

In his insightful analysis of risk aversion and rights accretion in intellectual property, James Gibson notes that "[b]ecause liability is difficult to predict and the consequences of infringement are dire, risk-averse intellectual property users often seek a license when none is needed."[30] With respect to copyright, he makes the further point that:

> . . . the decision-makers in the real world of copyright practice are typically risk-averse. New works of creativity often require high up-front investment, with the prospect of profit only after the work is completed. With so much at risk, those who work with copyrighted materials try hard to avoid potential pitfalls, and understandably so. They approach legal issues very conservatively, particularly issues like copyright liability, which have the potential to delay or even destroy the entire project.[31]

But Gibson is writing in the American context where the availability of a licence has been recognized as a relevant factor in fair use analysis.[32] In Canada, where the availability of a license is not relevant for fair dealing analysis, the over-reliance on licensing motivated by risk aversion should be much less of a factor.

---

28 University of Waterloo, *Waterloo Copyright FAQ* (17 November 2009), www.lib.uwaterloo.ca/copyright/index.html#copyright_basics.

29 Even though a careful reading of the entire document would lead one to this conclusion, the careless usage of the word "both" indicates the nature of the problem being addressed.

30 James Gibson, "Risk Aversion and Rights Accretion in Intellectual Property Law" (2007) 116 Yale L.J.882. http://ssrn.com/abstract=918871 at 882.

31 *Ibid.* at 891.

32 See *Princeton University Press v. Michigan Document Services, Inc.*, 99 F.3d 1381 (6th Cir. 1996), cert. denied., 117 S. Ct. 1336 (1997), www.bitlaw.com/source/cases/copyright/pup.html. In this case, the fourth fair use factor, economic effect on the work, favoured the plaintiff because of the potential loss of licensing revenue.

As the Supreme Court stated in *CCH*:

> The availability of a licence is not relevant to deciding whether a dealing has been fair. As discussed, fair dealing is an integral part of the scheme of copyright law in Canada. Any act falling within the fair dealing exception will not infringe copyright. If a copyright owner were allowed to license people to use its work and then point to a person's decision not to obtain a licence as proof that his or her dealings were not fair, this would extend the scope of the owner's monopoly over the use of his or her work in a manner that would not be consistent with the *Copyright Act*'s balance between owner's rights and user's interests.[33]

But while the availability of a license is not a relevant factor in Canadian fair dealing analysis, an institution's past practices can be. The *CCH* court also stated that "[i]t may be relevant to consider the custom or practice in a particular trade or industry to determine whether or not the character of the dealing is fair."[34]

So while a Canadian institution needn't be risk-averse because of the availability of a licence, its adoption of risk-averse practices — instead of relying on fair dealing — could nevertheless lead to serious rights accretion that only becomes more difficult to reverse over time. The resulting failure to incorporate fair dealing into routine practices not only increases the direct financial costs to students, it also discourages the full and proper utilization of existing knowledge resources.

Concerned that the lack of accurate copyright information was contributing to the paralysis of fair dealing in the post-secondary sector, the Canadian Association of University Teachers (CAUT) issued a Fair Dealing Advisory in December 2008 which presents the doctrine in a positive and unequivocal manner:

> Fair Dealing is the right, within limits, to reproduce a substantial amount of a copyrighted work without permission from, or payment to, the copyright owner. Its purpose is to facilitate creativity and free expression by ensuring reasonable access to existing knowledge while at the same time protecting the interests of copyright owners.[35]

---

33 *CCH*, above note 6 at para. 70.

34 *Ibid.* at para. 54.

35 Canadian Association of University Teachers, Fair Dealing. Intellectual Property Advisory. No. 3 (December 2008), http://caut.ca/uploads/IP-Advisory3-en.pdf at 1 [CAUT Fair Dealing Advisory].

Fair dealing is characterized as a "right" because *CCH* indicated it is more than simply a technical defence to an infringement action, but rather an integral part of the Act itself.[36] Yet this right is "within limits" and the interests of the owners are protected because it is always subject to the six-factor fairness analysis approved by the Supreme Court in *CCH*.[37] The reproduction can be "substantial" since section 3 of the Act limits the copyright owner's exclusive reproduction right to "the work or any substantial part thereof."[38] If the reproduction does not meet a threshold level of substantiality, the exclusive reproduction right is not even implicated and there would be no need to resort to fair dealing analysis. The right to fair dealing is also without the requirement of "permission from, or payment to" the owner because under section 27 of the Act infringement requires a lack of consent.[39]

The CAUT Advisory goes on to address the issue of uncertainty in fair dealing, but from a positive perspective:

> Theoretically, fair dealing could have been legislated as a precise formula with crisp boundaries, but this is not the way the law has developed. The limits of the practice are imprecise and will always be subject to dispute. Rather than retreating from this grant of discretion, the education community must fully accept it and define for itself, within the parameters set by Parliament and the courts, what is fair.
>
> This means that academic staff must know their fair dealing rights and exercise them to the fullest extent. It is equally important that

---

36 *CCH* above note 6 at para. 49. (Holding that "[a]s an integral part of the scheme of copyright law, the s. 29 fair dealing exception is always available. Simply put, a library can always attempt to prove that its dealings with a copyrighted work are fair under s. 29 of the *Copyright Act*. It is only if a library were unable to make out the fair dealing exception under s. 29 that it would need to turn to s. 30.2 of the *Copyright Act* to prove that it qualified for the library exemption.")

37 *Ibid.* at para. 53. (Holding that the six factors to be considered are "(1) the purpose of the dealing; (2) the character of the dealing; (3) the amount of the dealing; (4) alternatives to the dealing; (5) the nature of the work; and (6) the effect of the dealing on the work.")

38 *Copyright Act*, above note 2, at s. 3(1), which provides that ". . . 'copyright', in relation to a work, means the sole right to produce or reproduce the work or any substantial part thereof in any material form whatever . . ."

39 *Ibid.* at s. 27, which provides that "[i] is an infringement of copyright for any person to do, without the consent of the owner of the copyright, anything that by this Act only the owner of the copyright has the right to do." In other words, any consent (which may itself be implied from the circumstances) would vitiate the infringement itself and the fair dealing analysis would not even be necessary.

universities and colleges codify robust fair dealing practices in institutional policy. Such guidelines can inform the actions of academic staff and will signal to the courts and Parliament the "custom and practice" of fair dealing at universities and colleges.[40]

In summary, due to a convergence of factors, fair dealing is not operating on an even playing field in our educational institutions. It is subject to powerful counter-factors which erode its meaning and constrain its application. These impediments are not due to factors intrinsic to the Copyright Act, but are often ironically self-imposed.

In evaluating the education provisions in Bill C-32, the question must be asked whether they would mitigate, reinforce or aggravate these constraints if enacted.

B. ANALYSIS OF EDUCATIONAL PROVISIONS IN BILL C-32

Bill C-32 contains several provisions that directly bear on the uses of copyrighted materials in educational settings. This section will analyse these provisions in three categories: (1) the inclusion of education as an expressly enumerated fair dealing category; (2) the revision of several existing special exemptions available to educational institutions; and (3) the addition of new special exemptions for educational institutions.

1) Section 29: Inclusion of Education as Enumerated Fair Dealing Category

First and foremost, Bill C-32 proposes to amend section 29 of the *Copyright Act* to read: "Fair dealing for the purpose of research, private study, education, parody or satire does not infringe copyright."[41] While this amendment does not adopt the inclusive "such as" language, or incorporate the fair dealing factors, it is a positive and significant step in the right direction.[42] The importance of this aspect of the amendment is only

40 CAUT Fair Dealing Advisory, above note 30 at 6. The guidelines are in reference to institutional policies along the lines of the Access to the Law Policy of the Great Library which were endorsed by the Supreme Court in *CCH*, above note 6 at para. 61. The policy described the specific purpose of the library's custom photocopy service and indicated that "[a]ny doubt concerning the legitimacy of the request for these purposes will be referred to the Reference Librarian."

41 Bill C-32, above note 1 at cl. 21.

42 The addition of parody and satire do not appear to be particularly controversial, and the uncertainty regarding parody that plagued the courts in the *Compagnie Générale*

underscored by the vehement opposition it has attracted from the content industry. Access Copyright, for example has stated:

> On behalf of creators and publishers Access Copyright is deeply concerned by the extension of fair dealing to cover education and the introduction of numerous other exceptions in the *Copyright Act* which undermine the ability of creators and publishers to get paid for the use of their works.
>
> "It is discouraging to creators and publishers to see that instead of encouraging the use of collective management the Government has chosen to restrict or remove existing uses from collective management in favour of exceptions that do not provide compensation to creators or copyright owners when their works are used," says Access Copyright's Executive Director, Maureen Cavan.[43]

The Writers' Union of Canada similarly noted:

> Canada's book writers are outraged by the inclusion of a new provision for educational uses in Bill C-32. This new "fair dealing" for the purpose of education is a wholesale expropriation of writers' rights and opens the door for the education sector to copy freely from books and other copyright material without paying writers.[44]

Indeed, this will be one of the key sections to watch carefully as Bill C-32 progresses through its next stages. The lessons learned from the fate of the former Bill C-32 in 1996 are instructive. The first reading version of that bill contained numerous educational and library exceptions that were strongly supported by the library and educational communities. CanCopy (the predecessor of Access Copyright) had been established through the

---

des Établissements Michelin-Michelin & Cie v. National Automobile, Aerospace, Transportation and General Workers Union of Canada (CAW-Canada) (1996), [1997] 2 F.C. 306, www.canlii.org/en/ca/fct/doc/1996/1996canlii3920/1996canlii3920.html and more recently in the Canwest litigation in British Columbia (See *Canwest v. Horizon*, 2008 BCSC 1609, www.canlii.org/en/bc/bcsc/doc/2008/2008bcsc1609/2008bcsc1609.html and *Canwest Mediaworks Publications Inc. v. Murray*, 2009 BCSC 391, www.canlii.org/en/bc/bcsc/doc/2009/2009bcsc391/2009bcsc391.html) should be resolved.

43 Access Copyright, News Release, "Access Copyright is Deeply Concerned by the Government's Lack of Support for the Remuneration of Creators through Collective Licensing" (3 June 2010), www.marketwire.com/press-release/Access-Copyright-Is-Deeply-Concerned-Governments-Lack-Support-Remuneration-Creators-1270887.htm.

44 The Writers' Union of Canada, News Release, "Canada's Writers Demand Change to *Copyright Act*" (6 June 2010), www.writersunion.ca/av_pr060810.asp.

Phase I round of amendments to the Act in 1988, and was aggressively asserting that many of the activities conducted by libraries were infringing. The library and educational communities wanted to establish protections that were certain and reliable. As fair dealing was not yet a viable doctrine under the case law, the emphasis on institution-specific special exemptions was understandable in 1996. But the promise of a user-oriented set of amendments did not materialize, and after a series of amendments effectively weakened the measure, the broad coalition of library and education groups who had initially supported the bill in 1996 withdrew their support. The amendment process was reported in the February 1997 CAUT Bulletin:

> On Dec. 11, 1996, the Canadian public received a holiday package of some 70 amendments to the proposals of April 1996 from the Heritage Committee. On balance, these modifications can only be described as a "defeat" for public educational institutions. Sheila Copps congratulated the Heritage Committee on its work.
>
> The manner in which the amendments were pushed through the committee in just a few hours, many without prior consent from representatives of the jointly-responsible Industry Canada left onlookers aghast . . .[45]

It is clear that the content industry remembers the magnitude of this shift in favour of publishers and licensing collectives and will attempt a repeat of its efforts 14 years later with the current Bill C-32. But even if the addition of education to the enumerated fair dealing categories survives the legislative process, there will still be barriers to overcome in order for it to be properly implemented into practice in Canadian educational settings. Adding the word "education" to section 29 does not in itself solve the problems of lack of information, risk-aversion and rights accretion. But it certainly holds the promise of mitigating and ultimately reversing these impediments if it is taken seriously and implemented in a purposeful manner on our campuses.

45 "Ambushed by the Heritage Committee" *CAUT Bulletin*, Vol. 44, No. 2 (February 1997), www.cautbulletin.ca/default.asp?SectionID=0&SectionName=&VolID=247&VolumeName=No%202&VolumeStartDate=February%201,%201997&EditionID=28&EditionName=Vol%2044&EditionStartDate=January%2001,%201997&ArticleID=0.

2) Section 29.4–29.9: Amending Educational Institutional Exemptions

Less crucial than including education in general fair dealing, but also of positive significance, are a series of proposed amendments to the special educational exemption sections that survived the 1997 Phase II Amendments.[46] While fair dealing is generally available to anyone regardless of their institutional affiliation, the special educational exemptions in sections 29.4 through 30 of the Act are only applicable to certain defined "educational institutions."[47]

a) Section 29.4

Section 29.4 currently provides a limited exception for classroom displays in certain circumstances.[48] It would be amended to read:

> 29.4(1). It is not an infringement of copyright for an educational institution or a person acting under its authority *for the purposes of education or training on its premises to reproduce a work, or do any other necessary act, in order to display it* [emphasized text is added by amendment].

---

46 An *Act to amend the Copyright Act*, Assented to 25 April 1997, www.parl.gc.ca/bills/government/C-32/C-32_4/C-32TOCE.html.

47 Section 2 of the Act defines "educational institution" as

> (a) a non-profit institution licensed or recognized by or under an Act of Parliament or the legislature of a province to provide pre-school, elementary, secondary or post-secondary education,
> (b) a non-profit institution that is directed or controlled by a board of education regulated by or under an Act of the legislature of a province and that provides continuing, professional or vocational education or training,
> (c) a department or agency of any order of government, or any non-profit body, that controls or supervises education or training referred to in paragraph (a) or (b), or
> (d) any other non-profit institution prescribed by regulation.

48 Section 29.4(1) currently provides:

> It is not an infringement of copyright for an educational institution or a person acting under its authority
> (*a*) to make a manual reproduction of a work onto a dry-erase board, flip chart or other similar surface intended for displaying handwritten material, or
> (*b*) to make a copy of a work to be used to project an image of that copy using an overhead projector or similar device
>
> for the purposes of education or training on the premises of an educational institution.

While deleting the former reference to dry erase boards and flip charts is a positive step, as is substituting more generally purposeful language, the section is still fundamentally flawed because its benefits are still negated where the work is "commercially available."[49] The carve-out for materials that are commercially available appears in a number of sections added in 1997[50] and remains problematic because it gives the content owner the ability to unilaterally negate the exception.

In any event, section 29.4, like the other special institution-specific exemptions, should be viewed as a statutory safe-harbour which supplements, but does not supplant fair dealing. As the *CCH* Court said with respect to the library exemptions, resort to fair dealing is always available,[51] and the same reasoning should apply to the exemptions for educational institutions as well should any of the conditions not be met.

b) Section 29.5

Section 29.5 of the current act allows certain public performances "on the premises of an educational institution for educational or training purpos-

---

49 Bill C-32 would amend section 29.4(3) to read:

> Except in the case of manual reproduction, the exemption from copyright infringement provided by subsections (1) and (2) does not apply if the work or other subject-matter is commercially available, within the meaning of paragraph (a) of the definition "commercially available" in section 2, in a medium that is appropriate for the purposes referred to in those subsections.

See: Bill C-32, above note 1 at cl. 23(2).

Section 2 of the act defines the term:

> "commercially available" means, in relation to a work or other subject-matter,
> (a) available on the Canadian market within a reasonable time and for a reasonable price and may be located with reasonable effort, or
> (b) for which a licence to reproduce, perform in public or communicate to the public by telecommunication is available from a collective society within a reasonable time and for a reasonable price and may be located with reasonable effort . . .

50 The carve-out for materials that are commercially available is also found in s. 30.1(2) (with respect to the management and maintenance of a library, museum or archival collection), and s. 32(3) (with respect to making materials available in alternative formats for persons with perceptual difficulties).

51 *Ibid.* at para. 49. (Holding that "[a]s an integral part of the scheme of copyright law, the s. 29 fair dealing exception is always available. Simply put, a library can always attempt to prove that its dealings with a copyrighted work are fair under s. 29 of the *Copyright Act*. It is only if a library were unable to make out the fair dealing exception under s. 29 that it would need to turn to s. 30.2 of the *Copyright Act* to prove that it qualified for the library exemption.")

es and not for profit, before an audience consisting primarily of students of the educational institution, instructors acting under the authority of the educational institution or any person who is directly responsible for setting a curriculum for the educational institution."[52]

This section is also a statutory safe-harbour separate and apart from fair dealing. Currently, the exception applies to the live performance of a work done primarily by students[53] as well as to the public performance of "a sound recording or of a work or performer's performance that is embodied in a sound recording"[54] Also exempted is "the performance in public of a work or other subject-matter at the time of its communication to the public by telecommunication."[55]

So long as these conditions with respect to participants, audience and place of performance are met, there will be no infringement liability and there would be no need to resort to fair dealing. If, however, one of these conditions is not met, fair dealing would still be available. For example, if the event is held off of the institution's premises, or if the broader public is in the audience, the institution could still invoke fair dealing if a claim were made that the performance was infringing.

Currently, this special exemption does not apply to films. But the proposed amendment would add a new subsection which would apply to "the performance in public of a cinematographic work, as long as the work is not an infringing copy or the person responsible for the performance has no reasonable grounds to believe that it is an infringing copy."[56] Insofar as this section is additive to fair dealing, it can play a useful purpose. The extension of the exception to films is a positive development, as it should assist academic staff in being able to better incorporate film into classroom instruction without having to incur the costs involved with clearing public performance rights.

c) Sections 29.6 and 29.9

There are also some positive changes proposed for sections 29.6 and 29.9 with respect to the classroom use of news broadcasts. Section 29.6 currently permits making a single copy of a news program or news commentary program (but not a documentary) for subsequent classroom use.[57] The

52 *Copyright Act*, above note 3 at s. 29.5.
53 *Ibid.* at s. 29.5(a).
54 *Ibid.* at s. 29.5(b).
55 *Ibid.* at s. 29.5(c).
56 Bill C-32, above note 1 at cl. 24(2).
57 *Copyright Act*, above note 3 at s. 29.6.

exemption only permits the keeping of the copy for a year, at which time royalties must be paid or the copy must be destroyed.[58] Section 29.9 also authorizes the promulgation of further regulations relating to the record-keeping requirement for the news programs copied under the section.[59] The proposed amendment repeals the "pay or destroy" requirement as well as well the authority for record-keeping regulations. While these are positive developments, at least as far as news or news commentary programs are concerned, news documentaries should be treated in a similar manner. Currently, other broadcasts (including documentaries) are covered by section 29.7, which also has a "pay or destroy" requirement.[60]

Rather than differentiate between different genres of programming in the act, it would make more sense to extend the amendment to section 29.7 as well. The choice of what type of broadcast is appropriate for classroom use is best left to the instructor and the act itself should strive for content-neutrality with respect to its special treatment of classroom uses of broadcasts.

d) Overall Assessment of Amendments to Existing Special Exemptions for Educational Institutions

All in all, these are positive amendments, none of which were included in Bill C-61. Their importance does need to be placed in context, as all of these situations could be subsumed into a general fair dealing analysis, especially with the explicit recognition of education as an enumerated category. But given the assumption that these sections provide an alternative mechanism of protection for institutions, in the nature of statutory safe-harbours where certain conditions are met, they continue to serve a useful function.

But unlike this series of amendments, the proposed new sections 30.01 through 30.04 are not so benign.

3) Section 30.01: New Special Exemption for Lessons

This new proposed section is similar to its counterpart in Bill C-61 and exemplifies undue complexity to the point of obfuscation. Throughout its labyrinthine subsections, it is never clear what is to be gained through the provision. The section starts with a self-referential definition:

---

58 *Ibid.* at s. 29.6(2)(a)

59 *Ibid.* at s. 29.9.

60 The pay or destroy requirement applies to other broadcasts 30 days after the copy is made. See: *Ibid.* at s. 29.7(2).

> For the purposes of this section, "lesson" means a lesson, test or examination, or part of one, in which, or during the course of which, an act is done in respect of a work or other subject-matter by an educational institution or a person acting under its authority that would otherwise be an infringement of copyright but is permitted under a limitation or exception under this Act.[61]

If a lesson means "a lesson, test or examination," it remains unclear how the term "lesson" is defined when it is used in ways other than a test or examination. It is the classic case of the circular definition. Whatever it means, its usefulness is quickly eroded by the carve-outs and requirements contained in the subsequent sections.

Subject to a series of conditions in section 30.01(6), section 30.01(3) provides it is not an infringement of copyright to do certain things with a lesson:

> (a) to communicate a lesson to the public by telecommunication for educational or training purposes, if that public consists only of students who are enrolled in a course of which the lesson forms a part or of other persons acting under the authority of the educational institution;
>
> (b) to make a fixation of the lesson for the purpose of the act referred to in paragraph (a); or
>
> (c) to do any other act that is necessary for the purpose of the acts referred to in paragraphs (a) and (b).[62]

The proposed section 30.01(6) imposes a number of conditions on the educational institution (or person acting on its behalf other than a student). First, the institution must "destroy any fixation of the lesson within 30 days after the day on which the students who are enrolled in the course to which the lesson relates have received their final course evaluations."[63] Classroom instructors may wonder why anyone would want to go to the trouble of preparing a "lesson" (however it is defined) only to have to destroy it after the end of the term.

It is not at all clear how this requirement would play out in practice. Is the institution going to advise instructors that they are under an obligation to destroy course materials each term? And if so, how is that mandate going to be enforced?

---

61 Bill C-32, above note 1 at cl. 27.

62 *Ibid.*

63 *Ibid.*

Second, the proposal says the institution must take measures to limit the communication by telecommunication of the lesson to the enrolled students and other authorized persons.[64] Third, measures must also be taken to "prevent the students from fixing, reproducing or communicating the lesson other than as they may do under this section."[65] Both are examples of forcing the implementation of TPMs. What does it mean to "take measures," as it is so vaguely put in these two subsections, and what level of TPMs is mandated through these requirements?

Unfortunately, Bill C-32 leaves these questions unanswered since subsection 30.01(6)(d) provides that the institution must also "take, in relation to a communication by telecommunication in digital form, any measure prescribed by regulation."[66] Given the importance of TPMs in the overall scope of the bill, not to mention their highly contentious nature, delegating this question to the regulatory process only acts to further frustrate the goals of transparency and Parliamentary accountability. Such measures should not be deferred to the less visible regulatory process, as they need to be fully aired as part of the legislative process.

In addition to the burdens imposed on the institution and its staff, a student who wants to reproduce the "lesson" in order to listen to or view it at a more convenient time must "destroy the reproduction within 30 days after the day on which the students who are enrolled in the course to which the lesson relates have received their final course evaluations."[67] This is a particularly onerous provision, and was not even included in Bill C-61. Telling a student they must destroy the materials they worked from during a course of study is simply not an acceptable practice from the point of view of teachers and librarians. And the problem is compounded for students who want to refer back to materials from earlier courses, as noted by the President of Athabasca University:

> Students are expected to somehow accumulate knowledge as they proceed through their studies. The content delivered in one course builds on the knowledge acquired in previous courses. The provision that content from Algebra 1 must be destroyed so that students taking Algebra 2 cannot refer back to it when needed is counter to the principles of education and how people learn. It just does not make sense.[68]

---

64 *Ibid.*

65 *Ibid.*

66 *Ibid.*

67 *Ibid.*

68 Frits Pannekoek. AU President's Letter Concerning Proposed Copyright Changes (18 November 2008), www2.athabascau.ca/aboutau/news/news_item.php?id=423.

In any event, such a draconian and counterintuitive provision is hardly enforceable. Even if one strains to find a beneficial purpose in this section, its carve-outs and special requirements are hardly worth the effort, so the provision should simply be scuttled.

4 Sections 30.02 and 30.03: Digital Licences

Sections 30.02 and 30.03 are exceptionally complex provisions and they must be read together with the provisions in the proposed tariff in order to fully appreciate their meaning and intention.

On 30 March 30 2010, Access Copyright filed a Statement of Proposed Royalties to Be Collected by Access Copyright for the Reprographic Reproduction, in Canada, of Works in its Repertoire for 2011 through 2013 with the Copyright Board, and it was formally published in the *Canada Gazette* on 12 June 2010.[69] Under the proposed tariff the rate will rise from $3.38 per Full Time Equivalent (FTE) to $45 per FTE for universities ($35 per FTE for community colleges) but the 10 cent per page fee for course packs will be discontinued.[70] The scope of what is considered a "copy" will be expanded to include not only reproduction by a mechanical reprography but also scanning, transmission by fax or e-mail, uploading, displaying or projecting an image, and even posting a link to a digital copy.[71] While per page fees are discontinued, the reporting requirements[72] will apply to materials in "course collections" which will include digital copies that are e-mailed, linked to, or posted on a secure network as well as assembled paper copies.[73]

Bill C-32's proposed section 30.02(1) would allow an educational institution to make a digital reproduction of a work[74] and to communicate it by

---

69 Statement of Proposed Royalties to Be Collected by Access Copyright for the Reprographic Reproduction, in Canada, of Works in its Repertoire, C. Gaz. 2010.I.,Vol. 144, No. 24 (12 June 2010), http://canadagazette.gc.ca/rp-pr/p1/2010/2010-06-12/html/sup1-eng.html [Proposed Tariff]. This notice triggered a 60 day comment period in which interested parties can file objections.

70 For a discussion of the terms under the current Access Copyright Licence, see text accompanying notes 14–19, above.

71 Proposed Tariff, above note 68 at s. 2 (definition of "copy").

72 *Ibid*, at s. 6. The reporting requirements will include, in addition to the general bibliographic data, the electronic address where a work is being stored or can be accessed, information pertaining to any direct licence from a publisher/aggregator for the work, data about new works added to the course collection for every reporting month, and records for digital copies emailed by a staff member.

73 *Ibid*. at s. 2 (definition of "course collection").

74 Bill C-32, above note 1 at cl. 27, proposed s. 30.02(1)(a).

telecommunication for an educational or training purpose.[75] In addition, the person to whom the copy is sent may make one copy of the work.[76] However, there are several carve-outs and conditions on this allowance.

First, the exemption is only applicable to an institution that has a reprographic reproduction licence with a collective society that permits the making of reprographic reproductions.[77] Second, the institution is required to pay the royalty for all persons to whom the digital communication was sent that would have been applicable if a print copy was made, and they must also comply with all of the terms of the licence.[78] By writing a requirement that the institution comply with the terms of the license into the act itself, it appears that these terms could supersede users' rights under the act to the extent they are inconstant with the contract. With respect to the reprography license now in effect between the educational institutions and Access Copyright, this provision foreshadows a significant shift in favour of private ordering. As noted in the earlier discussion about the relationship between the license and fair dealing,[79] the current Access Copyright license is additive, not substitutive, for provisions of the act. This new section would appear to reverse that assumption and provide the collectives with a more robust mechanism to utilize terms that derogate from statutory rights.[80]

Third, the institution must also take measures to prevent the recipient from printing more than one copy or otherwise further communicating or reproducing it,[81] and take any additional measure prescribed by regulation.[82] Finally, the owner of the work may opt out of this arrangement by informing the collective that the institution may not make such digital copies.[83]

Section 30.02 was drafted as a provisional measure because the right to make the digital copy under this section is cut off if a subsequently certi-

---

75 *Ibid.* at cl. 27 proposed s. 30.02(1)(b).

76 *Ibid.* at cl. 27 proposed s. 30.02(2).

77 *Ibid.* at cl. 27 proposed s. 30.02(1).

78 *Ibid.* at cl. 27 proposed s. 30.02(3)(a).

79 See text accompanying notes 25–27, above.

80 The fact that the proposed tariff does not contain language similar to the preamble and sections 3 and 4 of the current license which expressly preserves fair dealing only seems to reinforce this concern.

81 *Ibid.* at proposed s. 30.02(3)(c).

82 *Ibid.* at proposed s. 30.02(3)(d). Here is another instance of requiring the implementation of some (yet to be determined) level of technological protection measures.

83 *Ibid.* at proposed s. 30.02(5).

fied tariff is applicable to such digital reproduction, communication and printing.[84]

With respect to the royalties that have been paid under section 30.02, if there is subsequently a digital reproduction agreement between the institution and the collective, or if a tariff becomes applicable to such digital reproductions, then the difference in the royalties paid by the institution and the royalties which would be due under the agreement or tariff must be made up.[85] While this obligation is reciprocal — that is, if the new royalties are less than what was paid then the institution will receive a refund — the obligation to make up the difference implicitly imposes a massive record-keeping requirement on the institution.[86]

These two sections will place institutions at a severe disadvantage because at the outset, they will lock the institution into a licence with a collective. And in essence, the section bestows all of its terms with the same force of law as they would have if they were included in the act. While the opposition to the tariff will proceed on a separate track at the Copyright Board from developments on Bill C-32, it will remain important to keep their interrelationships in mind.

4) Section 30.04: Special Exception for Publicly Available Materials on the Internet

The proposed section 30.04 would create an exception for educational institutions (or persons acting under their authority) to reproduce, publicly perform or communicate to the public by telecommunication materials that are available through the Internet for educational or training purposes.[87] The exception does not apply where the work or other subject matter or the Internet site on which it is posted is protected by a TPM,[88] or where there is a clearly visible notice prohibiting the act.[89]

84 *Ibid.* at proposed s. 30.04(4)(b).

85 *Ibid.* at proposed s. 30.03.

86 In this regard, it is instructive to look at the reporting and record keeping requirements contained in section 6 of the proposed tariff. See note 68, above.

87 *Ibid.* at proposed s. 30.04(1). The performance and communication exceptions are limited to where the public is primarily students or other persons under the institution's authority.

88 *Ibid.* at proposed ss. 30.04(3) (with respect to an access control) and 30.04(4)(a) (with respect to a use control).

89 *Ibid.* at proposed s. 30.04(4)(b). Section 30.04(6) gives the Governor General the authority to make regulations prescribing what constitutes a clearly visible notice.

There are several problems with this provision, both in how it is specifically drafted in Bill C-32 (which is identical to its predecessor in Bill C-61), as well as in its underlying conceptual basis. Whatever benefits the proposed section provides are overridden if TPMs are involved. Permitting the content owner to avoid the operation of a user's right through the imposition of a TPM is a fundamental flaw that runs throughout Bill C-32, but section 30.04(4)(b) extends the problem even further. The owner does not even have to resort to using effective TPMs; they need only give notice that they do not want the section to be operative. This amounts to what is essentially self-help opting out, and the section does not even specify what requirements the notice must satisfy as this detail is left to subsequent regulations. Should this provision be enacted, it will likely encourage owners of content which is now accessible on the Internet to impose additional restrictions either through the use of TPMs or through the giving of notice opting out of the provision. In its submission on Bill C-61, the Canadian Library Association (CLA) objected

> . . . to provisions that allow owners of works to unilaterally opt-out of user's [*sic*] rights either by terms of a contract, posting a notice on a website, installing a technological protection measure, or otherwise . . . [and recommended] sections 30.01 through 30.04 be reviewed in light of our concerns and that these issues be addressed as part of a broad reaching public consultation.[90]

The special educational internet exemption has become controversial within the educational community. Despite its basic flaws, it is still supported by some groups in the educational community including the AUCC,[91] CMEC,[92] and the Canadian Association of Research Libraries (CARL).[93] While the proponents' underlying motivation may have had merit, the justification for the amendment became based on an undue

---

90 Canadian Library Association, *Unlocking the Public Interest: The views of the Canadian Library Association/Association canadienne des bibliothèques on Bill C-61, An Act to Amend the Copyright Act* (September 2008), www.cla.ca/copyright/Unlocking%20the%20public%20interest-Final.pdf at 8.

91 Association of Universities and Colleges of Canada, News Release, "Proposed copyright law amendments: some very good changes but some cause for concern" (13 June 2008), www.aucc.ca/publications/media/2008/copyright_06_13_e.html.

92 In 2008 CMEC issued a series of five Copyright Bulletins supporting the provision. See: *Copyright Bulletins*, www.cmec.ca/Programs/Copyright/bulletin/Pages/default.aspx and text accompanying notes 100–105, below.

93 Brent Roe, Submission to 2009 Copyright Consultations, www.carl-abrc.ca/projects/copyright/pdf/carl_copyright_consultation_submission_2009.pdf at 2.

level of risk aversion and a corresponding unwillingness to rely on fair dealing. For example, a passage from CMEC's 2005 publication "Copyright Matters!"[94] responds to the question "Can Teachers and Students Copy from the Internet?":

> Most material available on the Internet is protected by copyright.
>
> This includes text (e.g., postings to newsgroups, e-mail messages), images, photographs, music, video clips, and computer software.
>
> Under the *Copyright Act*, reproduction and unauthorized use of a protected work are currently infringements. Therefore, reproduction of any work or a substantial part of any work on the Internet would infringe copyright unless you have the permission of the owner.[95]

A 2008 statement from the Canadian Federation of Teachers 2008 also makes the similar point:

> The proposed educational use of the Internet amendment provides clarity in the copyright law. Parliamentary passage of this amendment will avoid litigation to determine how fair dealing and an implied licence may apply to educational uses of Internet materials.
>
> The amendment is also necessary because during the 2002 consultation facilitated by the Department of Canadian Heritage and Industry Canada, some rights holders and collectives took the position that fair dealing and the implied licence theory do not apply to the educational uses of their works.[96]

In January 2008, CMEC issued the first of five Copyright Bulletins, which attempted to justify the continuing need for the amendment:

> . . . schools, teachers, and students need the permission of rights holders — and can be required to pay royalties — for some educational uses of material on the Internet. These rules apply even to "free stuff" on the Internet. "Free stuff" refers to material posted on the Internet by the copyright owner without password protection or other technological restrictions on access or use. "Free stuff" is posted on the Internet with the intention that it be copied and shared by members of the public using the Internet. It is publicly available

94 *Copyright Matters*, above note 23.

95 *Ibid.* at 16.

96 Canadian Federation of Teachers. Educational Issues in Bill C-61 (29 October 2008), www.ctf-fce.ca/publications/Briefs/Education_Issues_Bill_C-61_CTF_29Oct2008_eng.pdf at 3.

> for anyone who wants to use it, but the current copyright law may not protect schools, teachers, or students even when they are making normal educational uses of this "free stuff."[97]

This justification was criticized on several grounds, including its failure to account for the implied consent for reasonable uses that accompanies posting such material on the internet without restriction, and its failure to account for fair dealing even if there was no such implied consent.[98] It was also argued that a special exemption for users in educational institutions would

> directly and adversely impact on public libraries, corporate users, and millions of ordinary Canadians with their Rogers and Sympatico and other ISP accounts. What the student can do with her campus account will now by implication be illegal with her mother's Sympatico or her father's Rogers account.[99]

CMEC responded in a second Copyright Bulletin that the "amendment is necessary to clarify the law so that students and teachers can have the assurance that they will not infringe copyright law when they engage in routine uses of publicly available Internet works for educational purposes,"[100] and in a third why fair dealing was inadequate for the purpose.[101] In the latter, they again took a narrow of view of fair dealing:

---

97 CMEC, Copyright Bulletin #1 "Changes to the Copyright Law Must Include An Amendment to Address Educational Use of the Internet"(31 January 2008), www.cmec.ca/Publications/Lists/Publications/Attachments/106/note-01.en.pdf at 1.

98 See Samuel Trosow, "Educational Use of the Internet Amendment: Is it Necessary?" (31 January 2008), http://samtrosow.ca/content/view/27/43. See also Howard Knopf, "The 'A Contrario' Scenario & CMEC" (31 January 2008), http://excesscopyright.blogspot.com/2008/01/a-contrario-scenario-cmec.html, and "The CMEC Red Herring" (13 March 2008), http://excesscopyright.blogspot.com/2008/03/cmec-red-herring.html.

99 *Ibid*. Howard Knopf refers to this problem as the "A Contrario Scenario."

100 CMEC, Copyright Bulletin #2, "Education Organizations Need Clarity in Canada's New Copyright Law" (7 March 2008), www.cmec.ca/Publications/Lists/Publications/Attachments/109/bulletin-02.en.pdf at 2. In response see Samuel Trosow "Educational Use of the Internet Amendment: Is it Necessary (Part II)" (9 March 2008), http://samtrosow.ca/content/view/37/43.

101 CMEC, Copyright Bulletin #3 "Educational Use of the Internet: "Fair Dealing" Just May Not Be Enough" (14 March 2008), www.cmec.ca/Publications/Lists/Publications/Attachments/110/bulletin-03.en.pdf. In response see Samuel Trosow "Educational Use of the Internet Amendment: Is it Necessary (Part III)" (22 March 2008), http://samtrosow.ca/content/view/41/43.

> The act does not define what is "fair," nor does it define what is included in research, private study, criticism, or review. It is left up to the judgment of a user to decide whether a use is "fair."
>
> This is a difficult exercise for someone who is not knowledgeable about copyright. What one person thinks of as 'fair,' another may not. If a copyright owner disagrees with your judgment, he or she can sue you for copyright infringement.[102]

The measure has been opposed by the Canadian Association of University Teachers (CAUT) on conceptual grounds. With respect to the sectoral approach to special exemptions, they said:

> This sectoral approach continues to be supported by some educational associations that press for specific educational exemptions.
>
> Such an approach is fundamentally flawed. It cannot be sufficiently flexible to meet changing user needs. For example, artists need more explicit rights of parody; teachers need more explicit classroom display and reproduction rights; and computer scientists need more explicit rights to engage in reverse engineering. As well, reliance on specific institution-based exemptions is divisive as it allows an oppressive copyright regime, but then exempts some users but not others. While seeking a range of specialized exemptions was understandable in the mid-1990s given the limited nature of fair dealing, a broader approach based on fair dealing is a preferable alternative in light of *CCH*. Rather than foster competition between many worthy stakeholders for what might be limited legislative exemptions, a generalized solution is more sensible.[103]

---

102 *Ibid.* at 1. In response to the "A Contrario Scenario" argument, CMEC finally acknowledges the *CCH* case and the potential applicability of fair dealing. See CMEC, Copyright Bulletin #4, "Concerning the Educational Use of the Internet: An Education Amendment Does Not Narrow Fair Dealing" (18 March 1 2008), www.cmec.ca/Publications/Lists/Publications/Attachments/111/bulletin-04.en.pdf. In the fifth and final Bulletin, they stress the uncertainty of an implied license and suggest that a court would be more likely to imply a licence for personal use than in an educational setting. Copyright Bulletin #5, "Educational Use of the Internet: Is There an Implied Licence?" (31 March 2008), www.cmec.ca/Publications/Lists/Publications/Attachments/112/bulletin-05.en.pdf. In response see Samuel Trosow "Educational Use of the Internet Amendment: Is it Necessary (Part IV)" (1 April 2008), http://samtrosow.ca/content/view/44/43/.

103 Canadian Association of University Teachers. Copyright and Academic Staff, CAUT Education Review, Vol. 1, No. 10 (February 2008), http://caut.ca/uploads/EducationReviewvol10no1-en.pdf at 4–5.

The Canadian Federation of Students (CFS) has opposed the exception, stating that [s]eeking further special exemptions that are not available to the general public is a fundamentally flawed strategy. The better option is an expanded and open-ended definition in the Act of fair dealing that reflects the principles laid out in the *CCH* judgement."[104]

The Canadian Alliance of Student Associations (CASA) has also opposed the provision, stating that "[t]he federal government should pursue a clarification of users' rights under fair dealing in future legislation, rather than rely on overly complex special exceptions and conditions for educational institutions.[105]

Given the proposed addition of "education" as an explicit fair dealing category, the need for this amendment is even more tenuous and it is unclear why its proponents continue to press for its inclusion, apparently as a priority. In the case of CMEC, their initial statement in support of Bill C-32 suggests that they consider this provision more important than the addition of the word "education" to section 29. They indicated support because the bill ". . . allows students and educators in elementary and secondary schools, colleges, and universities to have fair and reasonable access to publicly available Internet materials in their educational pursuits."[106] While the CMEC release neither mentioned support for the expansion of fair dealing, nor any concerns with the digital locks provisions AUCC's initial statement on Bill C-32 was broader, including support for the expansion of fair dealing and concern about the digital locks provisions as well as support for the special internet exemption.[107]

An additional problem with expanding special educational exemptions is the Act's limited definition of "educational institution."[108] As the differentiation between what goes on inside and outside of formal educational institutions is becoming increasingly tenuous, the disparate effects of the special exemptions are becoming problematic. Nor are the goals of simplicity and understanding the law promoted by having one set of rules at

---

104 Canadian Federation of Students, *Statement on Copyright Reform*, www.cfs-fcee.ca/html/english/research/submissions/copyright2008.pdf, at 3.

105 Canadian Alliance of Student Associations (CASA). Our Path Forward: Strengthening Post-Secondary Access, Research and Learning in Canada. (2009 Advocacy Week Document), www.casa-acae.com/wp-content/uploads/2010/01/CASA-Advocacy-Week-Document-2009.pdf.

106 Communiqués — CMEC Copyright Consortium Pleased with New Federal Copyright Legislation (3 June 2010), www.cmec.ca/Press/2010/Pages/2010-06-03.aspx.

107 *Media Release: AUCC welcomes new copyright bill* (3 June 2010), www.aucc.ca/publications/media/2010/copyright_06_03_e.html.

108 Above note 47.

school and another at home. Instead of seeking additional special exemptions to promote teaching and learning, educators should be adopting their own sets of best practices for determining what does and does not constitute fair-dealing within their own institutions.[109]

An important principal that should help inform the evaluation of particular provisions is to ask whether it states clear and consistent principles that people can adopt and use in their daily lives. Sections 30.01 through 30.04 of Bill C-32 all fail by this yardstick.

C. CONCLUSION

On its face, the educational provisions of Bill C-32 are cause for some optimism on the part of students and educators. But when placed into the context of the educational copyright environment, several of the provisions become problematic. While recognizing education as an enumerated fair dealing category in section 29 is a critical reform, and while the proposed changes to sections 29.4, 29.5 and 29.6 are also beneficial, proposed sections 30.01 through 30.04 would be harmful additions to the Act. Taken together these measures would reinforce the tendency of risk aversion, they would require the utilization of burdensome TPMs by educational institutions, and they would add an unnecessary level of complexity to the law. In the case of section 30.04, it would have the further deleterious effect of encouraging owners of what is now openly available internet content to take measures to impede access to their works. While the addition of education to the fair dealing categories will reduce uncertainty and perhaps alleviate some of the risk aversion that continues to plague educational copyright policy making, many of its benefits could be offset if not neutralized by these new provisions.

This chapter has, hopefully, dispelled any unwarranted complacency and premature celebration. At the same time, the government should be given credit for including some reasonable and balanced provisions in this latest iteration of copyright reform. Whether these beneficial provisions will withstand the incredible lobbying pressure to which they will be subject is another question. An even bigger question is whether they can make any significant changes in the actual day-to-day practices in our educational system, assuming they are enacted, in the face of the serious counter-factors that continue to be present.

---

109 Above note 40.

PART FIVE

Access

CHAPTER NINETEEN

Copyright Reform and Fact-Based Works

Teresa Scassa*

A. INTRODUCTION

Information is a hot commodity in today's economy. In recent years, there has been a dramatic growth in the number of websites, databases, tools and applications that use data from a variety of public and private sources to offer innovative information-based services to a wide range of users. In some cases, the providers of these information tools are traditional disseminators of information. In others, they are established businesses that have developed new information tools and products. In many cases, the innovators are upstarts — small companies or individuals that see opportunities for new and useful applications. The dissemination of information and the development of new information tools are not limited to commercial enterprises. There is much free content from sources ranging from academic to purely amateur.

Property rights are an important element of control and are the foundation for financing, licensing, transacting and other activities within the marketplace. It is not surprising, therefore, that the issue of rights in

* I am grateful to Ariel Katz for his comments and suggestions on a presentation of some of the content of this paper, to Elizabeth Judge for sharing her thoughts on these issues, and to Michael Geist and an anonymous reviewer for their insightful comments. I am also appreciative of the research assistance of Julien Bourgeois. The support of the Canada Research Chairs Program and the GEOIDE Network is gratefully acknowledged.

facts and information is re-emerging within this flourishing information landscape. Copyright law sets relatively clear boundaries with respect to the protection of works that are the vehicles for information. Text-based accounts are literary works, and the reproduction of all or a substantial part of such works is infringing. Videos, photographs and maps that are vehicles for information are likewise also works that fall within the traditional copyright categories. Yet the law remains uncertain when dealing with issues of rights in the facts or information that is represented in these works. Further, the greater the proportion of data in relation to the "work," the greater the uncertainty regarding the scope of protection. Where the work is merely a compilation of data, the copyright protection is, in the words of the United States Supreme Court, "thin."[1]

Bill C-32[2] does little to address the uncertainties surrounding copyright in facts and in fact-based works. This is perhaps not surprising for several reasons. The uncertainty as to scope is widespread. International copyright treaties exhibit ambivalence around the issue. For example, Article 5 of the *WIPO Copyright Treaty* provides:

> Compilations of data or other material, in any form, which by reason of the selection or arrangement of their contents constitute intellectual creations, are protected as such. This protection does not extend to the data or the material itself *and is without prejudice to any copyright subsisting in the data* or material contained in the compilation (emphasis added).[3]

Similar language is used in the *Agreement on Trade-Related Aspects of Intellectual Property Rights* (TRIPs).[4] The language suggests that while copyright in a compilation will only be in the original selection or arrangement of the work, there may still be separate copyrights in the "*data* or material contained in the compilation." In Europe, database protection was achieved through *sui generis* legislation specifically tailored to this type

1 *Feist Publications, Inc. v. Rural Telephone Service Co.*, 499 U.S. 340, http://caselaw.lp.findlaw.com/scripts/getcase.pl?court=US&vol=499&invol=340, 111 S.Ct. 1282 at 349 (1991) [*Feist* cited to U.S.] .

2 Bill C-32, An Act to amend the Copyright Act, 3d Sess., 40th Parl., 2010, www2.parl.gc.ca/Sites/LOP/LEGISINFO/index.asp?Language=E&query=7026&Session=23&List=toc [Bill C-32].

3 *WIPO Copyright Treaty*, 20 December 1996, 36 I.L.M. 65 at Art. 5 (entered into force 6 March 2002), www.wipo.int/treaties/en/ip/wct/trtdocs_wo033.html, [WCT].

4 *Agreement Establishing the World Trade Organization*, Annex 1 C: Agreement on Trade-Related Aspects of Intellectual Property Rights, 15 April 1994, 1869 U.N.T.S. 299 at Art. 10(2), www.wto.org/english/tratop_e/trips_e/t_agmo_e.htm.

of information asset.[5] Although a similar *sui generis* regime has been considered in the US and in Canada, there has been little appetite to legislate in this area.[6] The status quo, therefore, has represented the government approach to protecting data. The status quo, according to the case law, is that there is no copyright protection for facts themselves but copyright protection for original expressions of those facts. In our dynamic and evolving information economy, the *status quo* is showing signs of strain.

Bill C-32 represents a set of copyright reforms in the works since the last major reforms in 1997.[7] Aspects of the Bill are clearly designed to address Canada's international obligations with respect to copyright on the internet,[8] and the preamble to the Bill speaks of the need to foster innovation in a knowledge economy.[9] Indeed, copyright law is seen by the govern-

---

5 *Sui generis* legislation in the EU member states was required by virtue of EC, European Database Directive *96/9/EC of the European Parliament and of the Council of the European Union of 11 March 1996 on the legal protection of databases*, [1996] O.J. L 77/20, http://eur-lex.europa.eu/LexUriServ/LexUriServ.do?uri=CELEX:31996L0009:EN:HTML [European Database Directive].

6 In 1998, the federal government commissioned a study on the protection of facts and information in Canada. See Robert Howell, prepared for Industry Canada and Canadian Heritage, Database Protection and Canadian Laws (Ottawa: Industry Canada, 1998), http://dsp-psd.pwgsc.gc.ca/Collection/C2-370-1998E.pdf. No further steps were taken. In the US bills to create a *sui generis* regime for the protection of databases were introduced around the same time, and failed. See: US, Bill H.R. 3531, *Database Investment and Intellectual Property Antipiracy Act*, 104th Cong., 1996, http://thomas.loc.gov/cgi-bin/query/z?c104:h.r.3531:.and US, Bill H.R. 2652 , *Collection of Information Antipiracy Act*, 105th Cong., 1997, http://thomas.loc.gov/cgi-bin/query/D?c105:2:./temp/~c105oUfJy1::. See also U. Copyright Office, *Report on Legal Protection for Databases* (1997), http://www.copyright.gov/reports/dbase.html.

7 Copyright reform to modernize the *Copyright Act*, R.S.C. 1985, c. C-42, was conceived of as a three-phase process. The first phase was implemented in 1988. Phase II was initiated with the first Bill C-32, introduced in 1997. Reform has been stalled since that time. See: Canada, Heritage Canada, *A Framework for Copyright Reform* (2002), / www.ic.gc.ca/eic/site/crp-prda.nsf/eng/rp01101.html.

8 Canada has signed, but has not yet implemented two key international treaties dealing with copyright and the internet. These are the *WIPO Copyright Treaty*, above note 3, and the *WIPO Performances and Phonograms Treaty*, 20 December 1996, 36 I.L.M. 76 (entered into force 20 May 2002), www.wipo.int/treaties/en/ip/wppt/trtdocs_w0034.html [WPPT].

9 Bill C-32, above note 2, at Preamble. In particular, the Preamble identifies copyright law as "an important marketplace framework law," and acknowledges its impact on "many sectors of the knowledge economy." The Preamble concludes by noting: "Canada's ability to participate in a knowledge economy driven by innovation and network connectivity is fostered by encouraging the use of digital technologies for research and education."

ment as a pillar in Canada's digital economy strategy.[10] Rather than tackle the issue of the growing commercial importance of fact-based works, digital information tools and resources, Bill C-32 is silent in certain key areas. In addition, some measures in the Bill may pose a barrier to access and innovation in relation to fact-based works. In an innovation economy, clarity around the status and use of data in protected works is crucial.[11]

This chapter will provide an overview of the current state of the law in relation to the protection of fact-based works in Canadian copyright law. The analysis begins with a discussion of the current state of the law using contemporary examples. It next considers the fault lines appearing within the established doctrines. As this is a book about the current state of copyright reform in Canada, the broader question will be whether Bill C-32 does anything to change the settled law or expectations in relation to facts and fact-based works, and whether there are missed opportunities to address an issue crucial to the digital economy and information society.

B. THE NEW WORLD OF FACT-BASED WORKS

The landmark decision in *Feist Publications, Inc. v. Rural Telephone Service Company, Inc.*[12] in the United States, and its Canadian counterpart, *Tele-Direct (Publications) Inc. v. American Business Information Inc.*,[13] came at a time when an increase in computing power and declining costs of computer memory had not only made fact-based compilations more commercially versatile and valuable, they were increasingly easy to reproduce and modify. Fast-forward almost twenty years, and computing power is dramatically greater, memory is far less expensive and the tools for reproduction and manipulation of data are more sophisticated. Perhaps the most significant change of all is that computing power, memory and tools are no longer the exclusive preserve of major corporate interests. The Web 2.0 revolution has put the power to harvest, control and manipulate

10 Canada, Industry Canada, *Improving Canada's Digital Advantage: Strategies for Sustainable Prosperity* (Ottawa: Public Works, 2010) at 14, http://de-en.gc.ca/wp-content/uploads/2010/05/Consultation_Paper.pdf.

11 See, for example: Christine Galbraith, "A Panoptic Approach to Information Policy: Utilizing a More Balanced Theory of Property in Order to Ensure the Existence of a Prodigious Public Domain" (2007) 15 J. Intell. Prop. L. 1, http://papers.ssrn.com/sol3/papers.cfm?abstract_id=1607959.

12 *Feist*, above note 1.

13 *Tele-Direct (Publications) Inc. v. American Business Information Inc.* (1996), 74 C.P.R. (3d) 72 (F.C.T.D.), aff'd [1998] 2 F.C. 22, (1997), 76 C.P.R. (3d) 296 (C.A.), leave to appeal to S.C.C. denied, [1998] 1 S.C.R. xv [*Tele-Direct* cited to S.C.R.].

data — and even more importantly, to disseminate it — in the hands of ordinary individuals.[14] The result is an environment that will generate new conflicts over rights in data and in fact-based works.

An added element that is important to appreciating this new context is the shifting role of government with respect to key collections of data. Government has long been the primary generator of certain types of data. These include geospatial data, as well as data about natural and physical resources, aeronautical data, climate data and a vast range of demographic data. In addition, government is a source of vast stores of information about citizens' interactions with government at all levels. Governments around the world, including Canada, have sought to develop policies and infrastructures for managing and disseminating geospatial data, now recognized as a building block for research and innovation within a knowledge society.[15] At the same time, access to information processes are increasingly relied upon to gain access to a wealth of government information. In keeping with the nature of the Web 2.0 revolution, this information can be used and disseminated in a variety of ways by a wide range of actors.[16] Public records are also being mined for the information they contain, and form the basis for a vast array of commercial and non-commercial initiatives.[17] Yet governments are not the only source of data — data are also

---

14 Christopher C. Miller, "A Beast in the Field: The Google Maps Mashup as GIS/2" (2006) 41 Cartographica 187, http://utpjournals.metapress.com/content/jol053012262n779/fulltext.pdf.

15 Canada's spatial data infrastructure (SDI) is spearheaded by Geoconnections: www.geoconnections.org/en/index.html. It includes portals for free access to collections of government geospatial data. See Geobase, www.geobase.ca (providing geospatial data from all levels of government); and GeoGratis, http://geogratis.cgdi.gc.ca (providing free geospatial data from the Earth Sciences Sector of Natural Resources Canada). In the United States, resources are made available through the National Spatial Data Infrastructure, www.fgdc.gov/nsdi/nsdi.html. For a clearinghouse of international governmental geospatial data initiatives, see Global Spatial Data Infrastructure Association, www.gsdi.org/SDILinks.

16 The online version of the *Toronto Star* used to feature a weekly column, "Map of the Week," which plotted a wide variety of information about Toronto onto a map of the city. In many instances, the information came from access to information requests. See "Toronto Star Map of the Week" *Toronto Star* (10 July 2010), http://thestar.blogs.com/maps/.

17 For example, *USA Today* created a map of mortgage foreclosures in the city of Denver using information from public registries. The map allows users to navigate around a Google map of part of the city that shows in red all houses foreclosed upon, and provides the precise address and amount of money owing at the time of foreclosure; see Brad Heath & Ron Coddington, "Denver Foreclosures: One Hard Hit Neighborhood

generated by researchers and private enterprises.[18] Ordinary individuals are the sources of a wealth of sought-after data; personal information has become a major commodity.[19] Individuals can also be the source of other kinds of information. Increasingly, corporations that create information-based products are involving users in the "crowdsourcing" of this information or in its correction, revision and modification.[20]

Within this environment we have also witnessed a significant movement towards the democratization of information. Open source and open access movements seek to guarantee broad, open access to all manner of copyright-protected works.[21] Other movements have sought to decentral-

---

at a Glance" *USA Today* (2010), www.usatoday.com/news/graphics/foreclosure_map/foreclose.htm.

18 A recent dispute between Century 21 and Rogers, Inc. in Canada involves the scraping of real estate information from real estate agents' web sites in order to populate Rogers' Zoocasa house hunting site. The matter has not yet gone to trial. See Gary Marr, "Century 21 Canada does battle with Rogers" *Financial Post* (7 September 2009), www.financialpost.com/story.html?id=1969611.

19 Personal information is widely sought to create increasingly detailed consumer profiles for marketing and other purposes. See, for example, Perri 6, "The personal information economy: trends and prospects for consumers" in Susanne Lace, The Glass Consumer: Life in a Surveillance Society (Bristol: The Policy Press, 2005) at 17. Recently in the US the popular social networking site Facebook used copyright arguments to attempt to stop PowerVentures Inc. from using scraping technology to mine its site for personal information posted by its users. See *Facebook, Inc. v. Power Ventures, Inc.*, 2009 WL 1299698, http://scholar.google.ca/scholar_case?case=1964888935558356568&hl=en&as_sdt=2002&as_vis=1, 91 U.S.P.Q. 2d 1430 (N.D.Cal.) [*Facebook, Inc.*].

20 Crowdsourcing is a term used to describe an open invitation to the public to contribute to the development of a product (including information based-products) or to the solving of a problem. For example, the news network Al Jazeera used crowd-sourced information to create a map titled "War on Gaza." Users are invited to contribute information, photographs and opinions on events in Gaza. See http://labs.aljazeera.net/warongaza. Openstreetmap.org offers a venue for crowd-sourced mapping around the world, openstreetmap.org. Even Google is getting into crowd-sourcing. It now encourages users to edit, update and modify its Google Maps, www.google.com/help/maps/edit.

21 The Creative Commons movement is a leading example. For Creative Commons in Canada, see, http://creativecommons.ca. In the realm of software, see, Open Source Initiative, www.opensource.org. In 2009, the University of Ottawa became the first Canadian university to join the Compact for Open Publishing Equity, when it announced a new open access initiative to make scholarly research freely accessible to a wide audience: University of Ottawa, News Release, "University of Ottawa among North American leaders as it launches open access program" (8 December 2009), www.media.uottawa.ca/mediaroom/news-details_1824.html. See also, Open Access uOttawa, www.oa.uottawa.ca/index.jsp?language=en.

ize the production and dissemination of information.[22] In Canada, the pushback of ordinary Canadians against a hard-line creators' rights approach to copyright law resulted in an unprecedented set of grassroots consultations on copyright law,[23] which ultimately led to the current Bill C-32. It is fair to say that the public tolerance for laws that unduly limit access to content, or constrain uses that have traditionally been permitted or tolerated, is greatly diminished.

It is in this environment, then, that it becomes necessary to reconsider the state of copyright law in relation to facts and fact-based works.

C. THE STATE OF COPYRIGHT LAW IN RELATION TO FACTS

It is a basic principle of copyright law that there is no copyright in facts, only in the original expression of facts.[24] Facts can be expressed in a number of different ways across a range of copyrighted "works." A photograph, for example, may be considered an original expression of the facts visible within it; the photograph itself is an artistic work.[25] Similarly, a map is essentially an original expression of certain geographical "facts," and maps are also artistic works.[26] A biography or an historical account would be examples of literary works that are expressions of fact, and a documentary film can also be an expression of facts in the form of a cinematographic work. In each of these examples, facts are central to the works, but the works themselves involve significant expressive activity. Extracting the bare facts from the expressive content is less troublesome because the core value of the work lies in its expression.

---

22 Wikipedia is a classic example of an attempt to crowd source information on a massive scale: www.wikipedia.org. See also, Cass R. Sunstein, *Infotopia: How Many Minds Produce Knowledge* (Oxford: Oxford University Press, 2006). Of course, Wikipedia is not without its critics. See, e.g., Roger A. Longhorn & Michael Blakemore, *Geographic Information: Value, Pricing, Production, and Consumption* (Boca Raton, FL: CRC Press, 2008) at 86–87.

23 Industry Canada, News Release, "Government of Canada Launches National Consultations on Copyright Modernization" (20 July 2009), /www.ic.gc.ca/eic/site/ic1.nsf/eng/04840.html [*Consultation*]. The vast majority of submissions to this consultation process were made by individuals.

24 Miriam Bitton, "*Feist*, facts and functions: historical perspective", in Robert F. Brauneis, ed., *Intellectual Property Protection of Fact-based Works: Copyright and Its Alternatives* (Cheltenham, U.K.: Edward Elgar, 2009) 3 at 16.

25 *Copyright Act*, R.S.C. 1985, c. C-42, http://laws.justice.gc.ca/en/C-42/index.html, s. 2, definition of "artistic work."

26 *Ibid.*

More challenging issues arise when one is dealing with facts expressed in more basic ways — ways in which the factual content outweighs the expressive activity (and the core value of the work resides in the facts). For example, directories, lists, tables of data and databases are all works in which the factual content outweighs the expression. Such works are compilations of facts, and while compilations are considered to be copyright-protectable works,[27] the expression of a compilation lies essentially in the original selection or arrangement of the contents, and it is only this selection or arrangement that is protected.[28] In a factual compilation, it is the selection of the facts or their arrangement in the work that can be protected, but not the underlying facts.[29]

Not only must there be a selection or arrangement of facts to give rise to copyright protection in a compilation of facts, that selection or arrangement must be "original." In Canada and the US, originality has been defined to mean something other than labour or investment. Thus, following the *Feist* decision in the US, originality is considered to be a "minimal level" or "spark" of creativity.[30] In Canada, the Supreme Court of Canada in *CCH Canadian Ltd. v. Law Society of Upper Canada*[31] ruled that originality results from of an exercise of "skill and judgment."[32] Both courts exclude labour or investment alone as bases for originality. Moreover, telephone directories have been found in both countries to lack originality — in spite of the fact that they are products of significant labour and investment — because

27 *Ibid.* at s. 2, definition of "every original literary, dramatic, musical and artistic work."

28 *Robertson v. Thomson Corp.*, 2006 SCC 43, www.canlii.org/en/ca/scc/doc/2006/2006scc43/2006scc43.html, [2006] 2 S.C.R. 363, at paras. 37–38 [*Robertson* cited to S.C.R.].

29 Per Abella J. *et al.*, dissenting in part in Robertson, *ibid.* at para. 100.; *Tele-Direct*, above note 13.

30 *Feist*, above note 1, at 358–59.

31 *CCH Canadian Ltd. v. Law Society of Upper Canada*, 2004 SCC 13, www.canlii.org/en/ca/scc/doc/2004/2004scc13/2004scc13.html , [2004] 1 S.C.R. 339 [*CCH Canadian* cited to S.C.R.].

32 It has been suggested that the US and Canadian standards of originality are not significantly different. See, e.g., Teresa Scassa, "Recalibrating Copyright Law?: A Comment on the Supreme Court of Canada's Decision in *CCH Canadian Ltd. v. Law Society of Upper Canada*" (2004) 3(2) C.J.L.T. 89, http://cjlt.dal.ca/vol3_no2/pdfarticles/scassa.pdf, and Daniel Gervais, "Canadian Copyright Law Post-*CCH*" (2004) 18 I.P.J. 131. Note as well that the High Court of Australia in *Telstra Corporation Limited v. Phone Directories Company Pty Ltd.*, [2010] FCA 44, www.austlii.edu.au/au/cases/cth/FCA/2010/44.html [*Telstra #2*], uses both the Canadian and US standards to refer to essentially the same threshold (at para. 344).

they are factual compilations which combine a "whole universe" selection (all subscribers who have not specifically asked to be excluded) with an obvious arrangement (alphabetical).[33] Neither the selection nor the arrangement is "original" in the sense required. Since the facts themselves cannot be copyrightable subject matter, and there is no originality in the expression of those facts, the works are not protectable by copyright.

In contrast, telephone directories in Australia were ruled protectable by copyright. The court's decision defined originality to include the expenditure of significant labour or capital.[34] However, in *Telstra Corporation Limited v. Phone Directories Company Pty Ltd*,[35] a more recent case, the High Court of Australia was careful to distinguish the prior decision[36] by noting that in the earlier case the parties had conceded that the phone directories were authored. In their view, it was impossible to find authorship in the electronic telephone directory databases at issue before them.[37] The court ruled that "[a]uthorship and originality are correlatives,"[38] and found that it was necessary first to identify authors and then to assess their contributions to the work. In a highly automated process, it would be difficult to identify any particular "authorial" contribution to the selection or arrangement.

In Australia, as in Canada or the US, the data contained in a compilation of facts are theoretically not capable of protection under copyright law; protection depends upon an original selection or arrangement of the data. Once such an original selection or arrangement is found (and the threshold may not be particularly high),[39] then the work is protected by copyright. This means that the reproduction of the work as a whole or a

---

33 *Feist*, above note 1; Tele-Direct, above note 13.

34 *Telstra Corporation Ltd. v. Desktop Marketing Systems Pty Ltd.* [2001] FCA 612, www.austlii.edu.au/cgi-bin/sinodisp/au/cases/cth/FCA/2001/612.html [*Telstra #1*].

35 *Telstra #2*, above, note 32.

36 *Ibid.* at paras. 52, 134, 157.

37 *Ibid.* at paras. 90-91, 333.

38 *Ibid.* at para. 344.

39 For example, in *Key Publications, Inc. v. Chinatown Today Publishing Enterprises, Inc.*, 945 F.2d 509 (2d Cir. 1991), http://openjurist.org/945/f2d/509/key-publications-inc-v-chinatown-today-publishing-enterprises-inc, the court found sufficient originality in the selection and arrangement of entries in a yellow pages directory of Chinese-American businesses. See generally, David E. Shipley, "Thin But Not Anorexic: Copyright Protection for Compilations and Other Fact Works" (2007) 15 J. Intell. Prop. L. 91, http://papers.ssrn.com/sol3/papers.cfm?abstract_id=1076789. But note that in both *IceTV Pty Limited v. Nine Network Australia Pty Limited* [2009] HCA 14 [*IceTV*] and *Telstra #2*, above note 32, two Australian cases in the Web 2.0 era, the High Court found, in one case a lack of originality in the expression of the

substantial part of the work is not permissible without licence. Since the expressive content in a compilation of facts is the selection or arrangement of the data, the substantial reproduction that infringes copyright must be of the expressive content and not the underlying facts. Thus, the question becomes: what amounts to a substantial taking of the selection or arrangement of the facts? One approach is to ask how many facts, or which facts, amount to a substantial reproduction of the selection or arrangement expressed in the compilation. In *IceTV Pty Limited v. Nine Network Australia Pty Limited,*[40] by contrast, the court considered whether there was copying of the original authorial contribution, and since there was no originality in the expression of the facts themselves, there could be no substantial reproduction.[41]

Although the basic principles around copyright and fact-based works are fairly settled, there can be a great deal of divergence in how the principles are applied. Since the decisions in *Feist* in the US and *Tele-Direct* and *CCH Canadian* in Canada, there has been considerable uncertainty as to the scope of protection available for fact-based works in these countries—particularly regarding compilations of fact.[42] For example, in *B & S Publications Inc. v. Max-Contacts Inc.,*[43] the plaintiff complained that the defendant had taken and used the facts in its publication, the *Oil and Gas Index*, for the purposes of producing a competing publication. The plaintiff's index listed explorers and producers in the oil and gas industry in Alberta and supplemented these details with additional factual informa-

---

data and in the other, a lack of authorship and originality in the product of an automated data process.

40 *IceTV*, above, note 39.

41 *Ibid.* at para 42.

42 This uncertainty is evident in *GeoConnections*: Canada, Natural Resources Canada, The Dissemination of Government Geographic Data in Canada: Guide to Best Practices, *Version 2* (Ottawa: Natural Resources Canada, 2008), www.geoconnections.org/publications/Best_practices_guide/Guide_to_Best_Practices_Summer_2008_Final_EN.pdf. At page 58, after acknowledging that there is no copyright in data, the Guide refers to "copyrighted digital data." For a discussion of the difficulties with the licensing of data evidenced in this Guide, see Elizabeth F. Judge & Teresa Scassa, "Intellectual Property and the Licensing of Canadian Government Geospatial Data: An Examination of Geoconnections' Recommendations for Best Practices and Template Licences," (2010) 54:3 *Canadian Geographer*, available at http://papers.ssrn.com/sol3/papers.cfm?abstract_id=1567482. See also William M. Landes & Richard A. Posner, *The Economic Structure of Intellectual Property Law* (Cambridge, MA: Belknap Press, 2003) at 104 (noting difficulty in protecting large electronic databases using the Feist analysis).

43 [2001] A.J. No. 143.

tion. Although Hutchison J. found that the design layout and format of the work was "original and unique," and thus copyrightable, he also held that the defendant's copying of the data violated the plaintiff's copyright — not in the selection and arrangement of the data — but in the data itself. He noted:

> I am of the opinion that the data relating to the exploration and production companies as researched and presented by the plaintiff is capable of and by itself of being copyrighted, owing in part to the criteria used to select the names by the plaintiff, the research done on its currency and accuracy, and its categorization.[44]

The decision suggests that some courts might view facts as protectable where they are considered sufficiently 'original' in their own right. This view admits that a fact might be the product of an exercise of skill and judgment and some facts are more than just representations of the world around us.

The uncertainty in the law around the protection of fact-based works has been met, from time to time, with industry calls for *sui generis* legislation, similar to what exists in the EU.[45] This would give separate protection for databases, since they in particular are most vulnerable under this approach.[46] In a realm of virtually unlimited computing power, whole universe sets of relevant data are very attractive but display little original selection. As it is the searcher who uses a search engine to extract the data relevant to them, it is also difficult to identify any original arrangement

---

44 *Ibid.* at para. 44. The case was decided prior to *CCH Canadian*, above note 30, and thus prior to the clear exclusion of labour alone as a basis for finding originality. Nevertheless, Hutchison J. does not appear to be basing his reasons on the sheer labour involved in compiling the data. What he describes arguably involves an exercise in skill and judgment in arriving at the data itself.

45 European Database Directive, above note 5.

46 It is by no means clear that sui generis legislation is the preferred approach. For a sample of perspectives on the pros and cons of such an approach, see Amy C. Sullivan, "When the Creative Is the Enemy of the True: Database Protection in the U.S. and Abroad" (2001) 29 A.I.P.L.A.Q.J. 317; Charles C. Huse, "Database Protection in Theory and Practice: Three Recent Cases" (2005) 20 Berkeley Tech. L.J. 23; Jacqueline Lipton, "Balancing Private Rights and Public Policies: Reconceptualizing Property in Databases" (2003) 18 Berkeley Tech. L.J. 773, http://papers.ssrn.com/sol3/papers.cfm?abstract_id=471885; Yijun Tian, "Reform of Existing Database Legislation and Future Database Legislation Strategies: Towards a Better Balance in the Database Law" (2005) 31 Rutgers Computer & Tech. L.J. 347, www.accessmylibrary.com/article-1G1-139431582/reform-existing-database-legislation.html.

within the overall compilation.[47] North American copyright law offers little real protection for these types of databases.[48] In general, the level of protection for compilations of fact is uncertain and unpredictable.[49]

D. WHY FACTS ARE NOT PROTECTED BY COPYRIGHT LAW

The rationale for not protecting facts in copyright law has typically been rooted in the view that facts are not original. As Justice O'Connor stated in *Feist*, facts "do not owe their origin to an act of authorship."[50] She describes census takers, for example, as "copying" facts from the world around them. Since facts are not original, no one can claim authorship in a fact, and any claim to authorship can only reside in the original expression of a fact. Where a fact is only capable of expression in a very limited number of ways, the doctrine of merger may also be relevant to prevent monopolies where the expression of the fact and the fact itself have "merged."[51]

---

47 Landes & Posner, above note 42 at 104. Of course, it can be argued that a searchable database is actually the result of a complex architecture and a great deal of skill and judgment. In *Telstra #2*, above note 32, however, this made it more difficult to establish copyright in the database as it was impossible to disentangle the myriad contributions to the database in order to identify actual authorship (at para 87).

48 In the United States, the "hot news" doctrine that originated in *International News Service v. Associated Press*, 248 U.S. 215, http://supreme.justia.com/us/248/215/case.html, 39 S.Ct. 68 (1918) has proven useful in protecting some fact-based works. The hot news doctrine is not copyright law — it emerges from unfair competition law more generally, and it applies in situations where someone has compiled information at some expenditure of capital, labour or time, and the information has a certain commercial value. A competitor who appropriates this information for commercial gain can be found liable for a species of misappropriation. Because this is a commercial tort and not a property right, the information is only protected for the period of time in which it has commercial value, and the doctrine only applies in the context of unfair competition. A non-commercial user of the information would not be restrained from using the same information. The hot news doctrine has not been precluded in Canada, nor has it been expressly adopted or applied.

49 Ian Masser, *Governments and Geographic Information* (London: Taylor & Francis, 1998) at 82; Shipley, above note 39.

50 *Feist*, above note 1 at 347.

51 The classic "merger" case in the US is *Baker v. Selden*, 101 U.S. 99, http://scholar.google.ca/scholar_case?case=16308210976883953911&hl=en&as_sdt=2&as_vis=1&oi=scholar, 25 L.Ed. 841 (1880). Just as one cannot have a monopoly over a fact or idea, there is no monopoly in the expression of the fact or idea where there is only one way (or a very limited number of ways) to express the fact or idea. In such cases, there is said to be a "merger" between the fact/idea and its expression. In Canada, the merger doctrine has been considered and approved in *Delrina Corp. v. Triolet Systems, Inc.* (2002),

A better argument for not protecting facts is found in more recent Australian case law. In *IceTV*, for example, the High Court expressly indicated that public policy reasons justified not extending copyright protection to facts. The court stated that copyright "does not confer a monopoly on facts or information because to do so would impede the reading public's access to and use of facts and information."[52] This public policy-based rationale dictates a much stricter approach to copyright in fact-based works. In Australia, courts must now consider the extent of human authorship in compilations of fact, and will protect only original authorial expression in the selection or arrangement of the facts.

The problem with a rationale for not protecting facts that is not based on public policy, but that is founded instead on the character of facts as not original, is that it relies on a very particular concept of fact as a form of observable truth. Yet not all facts are equal, and some things considered to be facts may actually not be the result of simple observation, but of a significant exercise of skill and judgment. Thus, one of the fissures in this area of the law is the potential for what can be called "original" facts.[53] A lack of clear articulation of the law in relation to facts can lead to courts finding, as occurred in *B & S Publications*,[54] that certain facts are themselves original.

E. "ORIGINAL" FACTS

An "original fact" is one which itself displays some of the attributes of authorship. Originality in the Canadian context, as noted above, requires an exercise of skill and judgement and that the work itself not be copied. There are many types of facts that might actually qualify as original under

---

58 O.R. (3d) 339,at para. 52, www.canlii.org/en/on/onca/doc/2002/2002canlii11389/2002canlii11389.html, 17 C.P.R. (4th) 289 (C.A.) where the court stated: "The merger notion is a natural corollary of the idea/expression distinction which, as I have said, is fundamental in copyright law in Canada, England and the United States. Clearly, if there is only one or a very limited number of ways to achieve a particular result in a computer program, to hold that that way or ways are protectable by copyright could give the copyright holder a monopoly on the idea or function itself."

52 *IceTV*, above note 39 at para 28.

53 See Teresa Scassa, "Original Facts: Skill, Judgment and the Public Domain" (2006) 51 McGill L.J. 253, http://lawjournal.mcgill.ca/documents/1224868339_Scassa.pdf; Justin Hughes, "Created Facts and the Flawed Ontology of Copyright Law" (2007) 83 Notre Dame L. Rev. 43, http://papers.ssrn.com/sol3/papers.cfm?abstract_id=1012071.

54 Above note 43.

this standard.[55] For example, much scientific fact is not simply copied from the world around us. A scientific fact may begin with a hypothesis. The scientist may develop a methodology to test this hypothesis, and may run many experiments as a result of this methodology. The results of the experiments may be expressed as data, but it is at least arguable that this data, too, is authored, as different tests following different methodologies may produce other results in other labs. The data is in part the product of an original conception and execution. Where tests repeatedly confirm certain outcomes, the hypothesis may be considered proven and may eventually come to represent scientific fact. Latour and Woolgar characterize the resultant scientific facts as "the set of statements considered too costly to modify [that] constitute what is referred to as reality." [56] They go on to describe scientific activity as being "a fierce fight to construct reality."[57] In the same vein, Justin Hughes writes about "social facts" as being facts that arise from "human agreement."[58]

To offer another example, maps have long been considered to represent facts — the map itself is an expression of fact that is clearly protectable under copyright law, and there is much originality in the expression. Indeed, there is so much originality in the expression of the facts in a map that some of these facts bear only a general approximation to reality.[59] The art of mapmaking is not a precise reproduction of geographic reality. As Wood and Fels put it, "The map is not a picture. It is an argument."[60] Notwithstanding this, while courts have treated maps as artistic works as a whole, they nevertheless consider them to be representations of fact. In *R. v. Allen*, for example, the court stated:

---

55 Green describes the idea that facts are not copyrightable because they are not independently created as a "fallacy": Michael Steven Green, "Two fallacies about copyrighting factual compilations" in Robert F. Brauneis, ed., *Intellectual Property Protection of Fact-based Works: Copyright and Its Alternatives* (Cheltenham, UK: Edward Elgar, 2009) 109 at 109–10.

56 Bruno Latour & Steve Woolgar, *Laboratory Life: The Construction of Scientific Facts* (Princeton, N.J.: Princeton University Press, 1986) at 243.

57 *Ibid.*

58 Huse, above note 46 at 59.

59 Mark Monmonier, *How to Lie with Maps*, 2d ed. (Chicago: University of Chicago Press, 1996). Monmonier observes at 1: "To portray meaningful relationships for a complex, three-dimensional world on a flat sheet of paper or a video screen, a map must distort reality."

60 Denis Wood & John Fels, *The Natures of Maps: Cartographic Constructions of the Natural World* (Chicago: University of Chicago Press, 2008) at xvi.

> In the world of map making, roads exist. Drawing a road on paper to show where that road exists in relation to other roads cannot create a subsisting copyright. It is the manner of compiling and the way that information is presented that creates originality and artistry that qualifies as a subsisting copyright.[61]

This statement reflects the general difficulties in negotiating facts and their expression in copyright law.[62] While the roads represented in the map do exist, and their existence or location cannot be the subject matter of copyright, the statement that "[d]rawing a road on paper to show where that road exists in relation to other roads cannot create a subsisting copyright" conflates the existence of the road with its expression in a map. The representation of a road on a map is nothing other than the expression of that "fact," and a different mapmaker might make different choices in expressing its location and details. Thus, while the "fact" may be the road itself, the line on a map is not a fact, but rather an expression of the fact. The longer or more winding the road, the less likely there will be merger between the fact and its expression.

Perhaps the most extreme example of original facts arises in the context of popular culture, where the popularity of certain works leads to products that explore their internal "facts." In *Castle Rock Entertainment v. Carol Publishing Group*,[63] the owners of the rights in the popular television series Seinfeld successfully sued the publisher of *The SAT* (Seinfeld Aptitude Test). *The SAT* consisted of a series of trivia questions based on the characters and events in the *Seinfeld* series. The Second Circuit Court of Appeals agreed with the court below that the creators' copyright was infringed and rejected arguments that the trivia questions merely reproduced facts derived from the series. Citing *Feist*, the Court stated: "Unlike the facts in a phone book, which 'do not owe their origin to an act of authorship' . . . , each 'fact' tested by The SAT is in reality fictitious expression created by *Seinfeld*'s authors."[64] The court went on to distinguish between "true" facts (for example, the identity of the actors who play the characters) and fictionalized facts (those drawn from events in the series).

---

61 *R. v. Allen*, 2006 ABPC 11 at para. 11 5, www.canlii.org/en/ab/abpc/doc/2006/2006abpc115/2006abpc115.html, 399 A.R. 245.

62 See Green, above note 55 at 110–14.

63 *Castle Rock Entertainment, Inc. v. Carol Publishing Group, Inc.*, 150 F.3d 132, www.law.cornell.edu/copyright/cases/150_F3d_132.htm (2d Cir. 1998).

64 *Ibid.* at 139.

In *Warner Bros. Entertainment Inc. v. RDR Books*,[65] a case which followed *Castle Rock*, the court took a similar view of a Lexicon based on the series of Harry Potter novels. The court stated: "Even if expression is or can be used in its 'factual capacity,' it does not follow that expression thereby takes on the status of fact and loses its copyrightability."[66] In these examples, fact becomes a relative term, perhaps more acutely so because of the iconic cultural status of the works in question.

The fictional "fact" cases represent the far end of a spectrum of facts ranging from the wholly observed to the wholly authored. The difficulty in applying copyright doctrines in this area is most acute with respect to those facts that occupy the middle range of the spectrum. Illustrations can be drawn from contemporary disputes around rights in "facts."

F. THE FACTS ABOUT PUBLIC TRANSIT

A flurry of disputes has recently erupted in the United States over public transit data. These disputes raise interesting questions about the nature of "facts" and their protection under copyright law. In some cases, the disputes have arisen in contexts where public transit authorities have contracted with a company called NextBus.[67] NextBus uses proprietary algorithms to crunch data from transit timetables with data harvested from GPS systems installed on buses and that communicate with electronic readers at set points along routes. The result is prediction data — predictions about when the next bus is likely to arrive at any given stop. The information is made available to transit riders, and the goal is to improve their public transit experience. In a number of American cities that have launched NextBus services, entrepreneurial individuals have created iPhone applications which harvest and make the prediction data accessible to iPhone users in a format more convenient to them than the web-based NextBus interface. NextBus claims copyright in its prediction data;[68] the

65 *Warner Bros. Entertainment Inc. v. RDR Books*, 575 F. Supp. 2d 513, http://scholar.google.ca/scholar_case?case=13852164224811081270&hl=en&as_sdt=2&as_vis=1&oi=scholar, (S.D.N.Y. 2008).

66 *Ibid.* at 536.

67 NextBus, www.nextbus.com. NextBus is a subsidiary of Grey Island Systems, Inc., www.interfleet.com/index.asp.

68 The NextBus licence agreement contains the following: "Nextbus predictions and other information are copyrighted. You agree not to resell our service or use your account access to provide data from our service to any other user or to publish the data in any way." NextBus Mobile Terms and Conditions, http://nextbusmobile.com/s/terms.webui.

application developers insist that the information is "fact" and in the public domain.[69] At least one transit company has muddied the waters by asserting rights in the underlying transit timetable data.[70] The disputes that have arisen over the rights in the underlying data offer a good illustration not only of the uncertainties of copyright law in this area, but also of the dynamic and likely contentious area into which we are moving regarding data, innovation and copyright.

There are two main sets of data that are relevant in the transit data disputes. The first is the transit timetable data. In its printed form, it is easy to say that the route, stop and time information arranged into a coherent timetable is a work in which copyright subsists. The situation is less clear if that data is stripped from the schedules offered by the transit company and made available through an iPhone app, as has already occurred in many North American cities. In such circumstances, some transit authorities have responded by asserting rights in the schedule data and issuing takedown notices.[71] A quick glance at licence agreements suggests that some transit authorities assert rights in their data. For example, although the San Francisco Municipal Transportation Agency (SFMTA) has chosen to provide free public access to their transit data, they do so by way

69 Anthony Ha, "Apple kills Routesy app, my iPhone gets less useful" *Social Beat* (27 June 2009), http://social.venturebeat.com/2009/06/27/apple-kills-routesy-app-my-iphone-gets-less-useful; Rafe Needleman, "Who Owns Transit Data" *CNet News* (24 August 2009), http://news.cnet.com/8301-19882_3-10315749-250.html.

70 This was the case in New York City. See Dan Oshiro, "NY Transit Authority Cites Schedules as Copyrighted Material" *ReadWriteWeb* (20 August 2009), www.readwriteweb.com/archives/ny_transportation_authority_cites_schedules_as_cop.php. In Washington DC, the Washington Metropolitan Area Transit Authority (WMATA), in response to strong demand, made its transit data publicly available. See Washington Metropolitan Area Transit Authority, News Release, "Metro Makes Schedule and Route Data Available Via Web Site" (20 March 2009), www.wmata.com/about_metro/news/PressReleaseDetail.cfm?ReleaseID=2506. However, it also commissioned a study to take "a look at intellectual property, such as schedule data to determine whether there are revenue opportunities in the future." *Ibid*.

71 In New York City, for example, a software developer created an iPhone application called StationStops that provided commuters with schedule information for New York's largest commuter rail system. In the summer of 2009, the New York Metro Transportation Authority (NYMTA) contacted the developer claiming ownership of the information in the schedule and demanding payment of a $5000 license fee. When the developer refused to pay, the NYMTA sent a takedown notice to Apple requesting that the application be banned from iPhone. Apple complied with the takedown notice. The dispute has since been resolved. See Bryan Chaffin, "StationStop Gets Ticket to Ride Again" *The MacObserver* (8 October 2009), www.macobserver.com/tmo/article/stationstop_gets_ticket_to_ride_again.

of a licence agreement, which is premised on underlying rights in the data. The licence states that the SFMTA "retains full title and ownership and all rights and interest in the Data."[72] A similar term is present in the Edmonton Transit Licence Agreement. It reads: "Edmonton Transit retains all right, title, and interest in the Data, and any intellectual property rights embodied in the Data, including any copyright."[73] The contract terms are puzzling, since if the data are "facts" they are in the public domain. Yet it can be argued that transit data actually represent not observed fact, but rather authored "fact." If bus #102 is expected to depart stop #5 at 6:05 a.m., this is because the transit authority has developed their schedule accordingly, and they retain the discretion to change or adjust the times and routes. Indeed, the timetable as a whole is like a careful choreography, with buses scheduled so as to provide the necessary levels of service and the desired connections, depending on the peaks and ebbs of demand throughout the day. Bus arrival and departure times are less "facts" than they are points in the choreography.

If it can be argued that transit timetable data are authored facts, what then can be said of prediction data? The prediction data used by NextBus are generated by algorithms that combine timetable data with GPS data to produce arrival time predictions. On the one hand, one could argue that the results are not "facts" and therefore may have a sufficient degree of authorship to be protected by copyright law. Another company writing its own algorithms might arrive at different predictions, and of course, predictions are merely well-informed guesses as to likely outcomes. Yet counter-arguments are also possible. Prediction data of this kind are not dissimilar to some forms of scientific fact. Indeed, one could argue that predictions are closer to observed fact than transit timetable data. While timetable data must originate with the authors of the timetable, prediction data are based on known and observed information. The issue is not resolved.[74]

---

72 SFMTA Transit Data Licence Agreement and Download, updated to December 17, 2009, www.sfmta.com/cms/asite/transitdata.htm.

73 Edmonton Transit's Google Transit Feed Specification Data Terms of Use, www.edmonton.ca/transportation/ets/ets-data-for-developers.aspx. The Edmonton Transit System makes its transit data available under licence from its website to encourage the private sector development of useful applications for transit users. This data is the basic route and arrival time information. The data is licensed at no cost for non-commercial users, but the ETS retains the right to charge a licence fee to the developers of commercial applications.

74 Note that the Weather Network asserts copyright in the "information" available on its site: "Without the expressed written consent of PMI, no information or material

G. FACTS AND INFORMATION: THE ROOT OF THE PROBLEM

It is possible that the root of the copyright problem lies in the distinction between facts and information. This distinction is one that is well-recognized in the geospatial information field. Geospatial data is typically defined as the raw data recording geographical points, such as coordinates represented by longitude and latitude. These data are classic "observed" facts. Information, by contrast, consists of facts placed in some form of context. It is this contextualization of fact that results in *information* and that may consist of the elusive element of authorship. While there may be no copyright in facts, there will be copyright in information if the element of authorship is readily apparent. The authorship in a map or a biography is evident enough. In a collection or compilation of data, it is perhaps more difficult to discern. But data expressed in a compilation is still contextualized in some way — the compilation tells us something about something — and in this sense it is information.

A classic rationale for not protecting facts (i.e., data) in copyright law is that they are not authored. Information as contextualized fact, by contrast, is the result of authorship. Information can therefore, at least theoretically, be protected by copyright law. Yet not all information will be protected. The rationale for not protecting some forms of information is different from the rationale for not protecting facts. Where information — contextualized fact — is not protected, it is most likely because there has been a merger of expression and fact. In other words, the information conveys the underlying facts in such a way that it is difficult or impossible to separate out the fact from its expression.

The challenge of the information society is to recognize the extent to which facts are constantly being transformed into information, to recognize the difficulties in separating the information from the underlying fact, and to decide what to do about recognizing, protecting and rewarding the authorship of information where warranted. This challenge will only become more difficult with time. The disputes in the US over bus timetables and prediction data offer just one illustration of some of the problems and conflicts that can arise in a context where marked technological advances have blurred the distinctions between users and creators,

---

from this Web site may be copied, reproduced, republished, uploaded, posted, transmitted, or distributed in any way whatsoever. . ."; The Weather Network, www.theweathernetwork.com/copyright.

created new—even if tiny and highly specialized—markets for innovative information products, and rapidly expanded the ways in which data can be used and disseminated.

The transit data context offers a neat encapsulation of some of the issues and tensions in this area. Data compiled by a public body are of relevance to innovators in the private sector who are both traditional and non-traditional players. The public has an interest in useful and innovative data-based products, and in an open and competitive marketplace. The public body has certain responsibilities to the public as well as its own needs to recover or reduce costs. At the centre of it all are sets of data and the ability to control or limit access to them through the vehicle of copyright law. The transit data disputes highlight the unanswered questions in copyright law regarding facts and information—questions that are likely to increase in importance over time. The concern is that this level of uncertainty, and the disparity in power between established and upstart innovators or users, may lead to a brake on innovation around fact-based works and applications.

H. BILL C-32 AND FACT-BASED WORKS

Bill C-32 offers nothing that is particularly addressed to the protection or use of fact-based works. This is not entirely surprising, as the copyright reform process had not identified this area as one needing attention. Nevertheless, the legislative choices reflected in Bill C-32 will inevitably have an impact on such works, and this section will consider some of these effects. The most important of these effects have to do with access to and use of factual content. As noted above, facts fall outside the scope of copyright for public policy reasons. In the words of the Australian High Court, copyright grants no monopoly on facts "because to do so would impede the reading public's access to and use of information."[75] To the extent, then, that Bill C-32 limits access to and use of facts and information, it is highly problematic.

Perhaps the most important impact of Bill C-32 on fact-based works may come from the proposed amendments to the *Copyright Act* that would make it actionable to circumvent technological protection measures. It was inevitable that the Bill should address this issue, as one of the driving forces for copyright reform was the need to implement the WIPO treat-

---

75 *IceTV*, above note 39 at para 42.

ies.[76] The WCT requires that anti-circumvention measures be present in the copyright legislation of ratifying states.[77] What was not inevitable was the form that such measures would take. An earlier Canadian copyright bill,[78] which died on the order paper, had made anti-circumvention actionable only when it was done for purposes that would infringe copyright.

Bill C-32 takes a different approach: circumvention of a technological protection measure that controls access to a work is actionable, regardless of the purpose of the circumvention.[79] The only exceptions to this general rule are limited, and include law enforcement and national security,[80] encryption research,[81] the need to make computer programs interoperable,[82] providing access to persons with disabilities,[83] and protecting personal information.[84] These exceptions operate only within limited parameters. Circumvention to gain access to data not protected by copyright — data in the public domain — would not be permissible if that data were expressed in a compilation that was itself a work, even if all that was protectable by copyright law was the original selection or arrangement of the data and not the underlying facts themselves. The "thin" copyright for factual compilations — a protection that is thin for legitimate public policy reasons — is rendered "thick" by the addition of anti-circumvention technology. It has already been pointed out that anti-circumvention measures may prevent legitimate fair dealing with protected works.[85] In the case of fact-based works, the problem is amplified where the underlying data is not itself

---

76 WCT, above note 3; WPPT, above note 8.

77 WCT, *ibid.* at Art. 11.

78 Bill C-60, *An Act to amend the Copyright Act*, 1st Sess., 38th Parl., 2004–2005, s. 34.02, www.parl.gc.ca/PDF/38/1/parlbus/chambus/house/bills/government/C-60_1.pdf. For a discussion of the anti-circumvention features of this bill, see Michael Geist, "Anti-circumvention Legislation and Competition Policy" in M. Geist, ed., *In the Public Interest: The Future of Canadian Copyright Law* (Toronto: Irwin Law, 2005) at 211.

79 Bill C-32, above note 2, s. 41.1.

80 *Ibid.*, s. 41.11.

81 *Ibid.*, s. 41.13.

82 *Ibid.*, s. 41.12.

83 *Ibid.*, s. 41.16.

84 *Ibid.*, s. 41.14.

85 Ian Kerr, Alana Maurushat, & Christian S. Tacit, "Technological Protection Measures: Tilting at the Copyright Windmill" (2002–2003) 34 Ottawa L. Rev. 6, http://papers.ssrn.com/sol3/papers.cfm?abstract_id=793504 at 47–48.

copyrightable. This could serve as a significant brake on innovation and competition,[86] but also on the free exchange of ideas and information.

Although the anti-circumvention provisions in Bill C-32 will have implications for fact-based works, there are other issues that are also important. Crown copyright,[87] which provides for ownership by the Crown of works created under its direction, remains highly problematic. Because some of the most important and useful collections of data about Canada — its territory, resources, and citizens — are created by government departments or agencies, claims to copyright in these collections of data can pose a barrier to access.

Bill C-32 does not address Crown copyright. Indeed, Crown copyright was not on the table, nor was it addressed in previous rounds of copyright reform. This is notwithstanding the fact that Crown copyright was raised as an issue in the submissions of a number of participants in the consultation process.[88] Crown copyright is an area where there seems to be no government appetite for reform — perhaps not surprisingly. Crown copyright serves government both by permitting it to develop revenue streams based on the sale of its works,[89] and by permitting it to exercise control over the dissemination of its works.[90] This element of control is perhaps most significant in the context of access to information. While copyright is not typically a barrier to an access request for documents in the hands of government, Crown copyright can be used to prevent the publication

---

86 See Geist, above note 78 at 235, discussing the impact of a similar provision in the US *Digital Millennium Copyright Act*, Pub. L. No. 105-304, 112 Stat. 2860 (1998), www.copyright.gov/title17/.

87 *Copyright Act*, above note 7, s. 12.

88 Eight organizations representing users of copyright works raised Crown copyright as an issue, as did four non-profit organizations. The issue was also raised in the submissions of numerous individuals. See *Consultation*, above note 23.

89 Stanbury argues that this rationale for Crown copyright is inappropriate as the Crown requires no economic incentive to produce the materials it does: W.T. Stanbury, "Aspects of Public Policy Regarding Crown Copyright in the Digital Age" (1996) 10 I.P.J. 131 at 138, http://www.lexum.com/conf/dac/en/stanbury/stanbury.html. Longhorn & Blakemore, above note 22 at 76–78, offer a critique of government's role in commercializing geographic information.

90 For a detailed discussion of Crown Copyright, see Elizabeth F. Judge, "Crown Copyright and Copyright Reform in Canada", in M. Geist, ed., *In the Public Interest: The Future of Canadian Copyright Law* (Toronto: Irwin Law, 2005) at 551. Although control is sometimes asserted as necessary to ensure quality, it does not necessarily serve this purpose. See, e.g., David Vaver, "Copyright and the State in Canada and the United States" (1996) 10 I.P.J. 187 at 200, www.lexum.com/conf/dac/en/vaver/vaver.html, and Judge & Scassa, above note 42.

and further dissemination of these documents.[91] Even outside the access to information context, there are numerous examples of governments asserting copyright in fact-based works, as well as in the underlying data.[92] The control exercised by government — or the potential for the exercise of this control — might pose a significant threat to the free flow of information and be a barrier to innovation.[93] While the federal government and some provincial governments are moving towards the dissemination of some government data under relatively open licenses, these licences are vulnerable to changes in policy direction.[94] In Bill C-32, Crown copyright remains an unchanged feature of our copyright law; one that is of real significance in the area of fact-based works.

It was inevitable that Bill C-32 would deal with the issue of the liability of internet service providers (ISPs) or providers of information location

91 See Judge, above note 90 at 572; Teresa Scassa, "Table Scraps or a Full Course Meal? The Public Domain in Canadian Copyright Law", in *Intellectual Property at the Edge: New Approaches to IP in a Transsystemic World, Proceedings of the Meredith Lectures*, (Cowansville, Québec: Editions Yvon Blais, 2007) 347 at 369.

92 See Statistics Canada, "Copyright/Permission to Reproduce" (18 January 2010), www.statcan.gc.ca/reference/copyright-droit-auteur-eng.htm; Geoconnections, above note 42.

93 See, for example, Jacques Frémont, "Normative State Information, Democracy and Crown Copyright" (1996) 11 I.P.J. 19 at 31. In the UK, where data is protected under a *sui generis* database protection regime, the Royal Mail recently faced criticism over its refusal to make postal code data freely available. The Royal Mail derives revenues of £1.3 million a year from licensing this data, but the cost of licences is prohibitive for some who would otherwise use the data in a variety of innovative applications. See, for example, the notice of shutdown by JobCentre ProPlus: www.jobcentreproplus.com., and Ernest Marples Blog, "Ordnance Survey to release postcode data?" (10 December 2009), http://ernestmarples.com/blog.; and Open Rights Group, www.openrightsgroup.org/press/press-releases/royal-mail-stop-job-search.

94 For examples of licence templates for unrestricted use of federal government data, see Geoconnections, above note 42. For a municipal government example, consider the City of Toronto's open data initiative, www.toronto.ca/open/index.htm. Licence terms and conditions can be found at: www.toronto.ca/open/terms.htm. For a discussion of the vulnerability of licensed information to a change in government policy, see Teresa Scassa, "The Best Things in Law are Free: Towards Quality Free Public Access to Primary Legal Materials in Canada" (2000) 23 Dal. L.J. 301. Of course, one can argue that control can be used to ensure the quality and reliability of downstream uses of data and can even ensure that the downstream uses are not exclusive or proprietary. For example, the City of Toronto's open data licence requires licensees to acknowledge that they acquire no proprietary interests in the licensed data or data sets. See City of Toronto, "Terms of Use for our Datasets," www.toronto.ca/open/terms.htm#licence. Of course, this does not avoid the problem of the scope or impact of claims to copyright in an original selection or arrangement of the source data.

tools. In the US, a "notice and takedown" approach has been adopted, requiring ISPs to remove postings or files when they are given notice that the material infringes copyright. Notice and takedown has been criticized as posing risks to freedom of expression.[95] It has also raised concerns about eliminating fair use of copyright protected works. If a mere claim of infringement is enough to force the takedown of a posted work, notice and takedown can significantly chill the dissemination of works that are legitimate and non-infringing. With fact-based works, where there are major issues about the subsistence and scope of copyright, notice and takedown can be used to squelch competition and to stifle the dissemination of information. In the context of the transit data example above, notice and takedown measures were relied upon by NextBus or transit authorities to stop the sale of iPhone applications that made use of transit and prediction data, even though the application creators maintained they had taken only facts in the public domain.

Bill C-32 reflects a different approach to the problem of infringing materials on the internet by adopting a "notice and notice"[96] system that will apply to ISPs or providers of information location tools. Under notice and notice, a copyright owner who believes that their rights in a work are being infringed, where those works are posted or communicated over the internet, may give notice of claimed infringement to the relevant ISP or information location tool provider. The notice must be sufficiently detailed to identify the work in question, the identity of the rights holder, and the interest of the rights holder in the work.[97] The notice must also give details of the claimed infringement. An ISP in receipt of such a notice must forward it to the party who has allegedly committed the infringing acts and must then keep records that will permit the identity of the person to whom the relevant IP address belongs to be determined.[98] A rights holder who then decides to take legal action against the alleged infringer will be able to use legal means to discover this identity. While notice and notice is generally preferable to notice and takedown, in the context of fact-based works, it is particularly important as the copyright claims in such works are often uncertain, tenuous or very limited in scope. Notice and notice favours access to fact-based works by ensuring that they cannot so easily

95 Sheryl N. Hamilton, "Made in Canada: A Unique Approach to Internet Service Provider Liability and Copyright Infringement", in M. Geist, ed., *In the Public Interest: The Future of Canadian Copyright Law* (Toronto: Irwin Law, 2005) 285 at 300.

96 *Bill C-32*, above note 2, ss. 41.25-41.27.

97 *Ibid.*, s. 41.25(2).

98 *Ibid.*, s. 41.26.

be forced from circulation by parties asserting uncertain copyrights. By adopting notice and notice, Bill C-32 reflects an important element of balance between rights holders and users/innovators.

The exception for non-commercial user-generated content in Bill C-32 is also important in the context of fact-based works. This is because many users mine fact-based works to create non-commercial works that rework these facts, either on their own, or in a mashup with other facts.[99] If Bill C-32 is passed into law, a new section 29.21 would permit individuals to "use an existing work or other subject-matter . . . which has been published or otherwise made available to the public, in the creation of a new work or other subject-matter in which copyright subsists." The exception would also extend to the dissemination of such a work as long as the dissemination is solely for non-commercial purposes, the source and author of the existing work are mentioned, and where the use of or dissemination of the new work "does not have a substantial adverse effect, financial or otherwise, on the exploitation or potential exploitation of the existing work."[100] This includes circumstances where the new work cannot be a substitute for the existing one.[101]

The exception is not without its limits. If one were to apply this provision to the transit data example, iPhone application developers who used NextBus data in their iPhone apps would be unable to rely on the user-generated content exception for two reasons: their works are commercial (this alone clearly takes the use out of the scope of the exception); and their apps function essentially as a substitute for the NextBus service. Of course, this analysis presumes that any claim to copyright in the data can be substantiated — a matter that is still an open issue. However, the user-generated content exception might be useful if information were extracted from an information-based product or service, and presented in a non-commercial context. Thus, even where copyright is asserted (with or without justification) in compilations of data, the user-generated content exception could provide a level of security to users who mine the data in order to create free, publicly accessible, non-commercial works. The potential benefits to the

---

99 To illustrate, the website "ProgrammableWeb" offers a listing of mashups created using the Google Maps Application Programming Interface (API). Mashups are created by taking the Google Maps interface and combining it with data from other sources. The list of mashups is enormous and represents an extremely wide variety of information. See www.programmableweb.com/api/google-maps/mashups [*Programmable Web*].

100 *Bill C-32*, above note 2, s. 29.21(1)(d).

101 *Ibid.*

public in the area of fact-based works are significant, particularly because there appears to be a fairly active group of individuals willing to compile and disseminate information at no cost to the public.[102] Of course, licence terms and anti-circumvention measures could both significantly limit the scope of the user-generated content exception.[103] In addition, the exception would not apply if the user-generated works are considered to meet the rather open-ended criterion of having "a substantial adverse effect" on the actual or potential exploitation of the source work.

I. CONCLUSION

Although data and fact-based works are surging in importance in the digital economy, and although new issues are raised by the tools now in the hands of creators — large and small — to fashion new information-based applications, the state of copyright law in relation to facts remains stagnant. For some, the uncertainty over the scope of protection for fact-based works may be a barrier to investing in innovation in this area; for others, the uncertainty over potential liability for using facts contained in other compilations or data sets may also be a barrier to innovation. Although the existing copyright principles can be used to resolve cases as they come before the courts, the principles are such that it will be difficult to give real shape to the law in this area. The uncertain distinction between fact and expression (or fact and information), and the fact-specific nature of any inquiry into originality of a selection or arrangement, or substantial taking from this selection or arrangement, give little hope of clear guidance in this area. Bill C-32 offers no solutions to the core issues. Reforms, if they are to come, will have to wait until some future date.

Government is a major producer of data and a prime data source for many private sector and research activities. The same uncertain rules regarding copyright in facts play out where the Crown is the owner of copyright, with the added implications of the Crown being in a position to censor, restrict or otherwise control public data. Crown copyright thus raises public policy issues in relation to ownership and control of data and its impact on innovation, as well as in relation to ownership and control and their impact on democracy, accountability and freedom of expression.

---

102 For examples, see *Programmable Web*, above note 99.

103 Note that Statistics Canada, which asserts copyright in its data, currently uses a licence to create its own non-commercial user-generated content exception: Statistics Canada, above note 92.

Crown copyright remains far from the legislative agenda, even though it was an issue frequently raised in the consultation process.

Although Bill C-32 does not address fact-based works specifically, a number of its provisions will be relevant to the use and exploitation of such works. Anti-circumvention provisions will effectively extend the copyright protection of a selection or arrangement of data to the data themselves when there is a layer of technology around the compilation restricting access and use. While some might view this as a necessary means of protecting investments in valuable sets of data, it is a clumsy and inadequate tool for addressing the necessary balance between exclusive rights and access, between ownership and the public domain. A notice and notice scheme to manage ISP liability is also important. Experiences in the US have shown how notice and takedown can be used to quickly remove data-based works from circulation or sale over the internet. Where the issues about the scope of any copyright protection in fact-based works and about the protectable elements in any compilation of facts are so uncertain, claims to copyright are difficult to verify or assess. When combined with notice and takedown, this would have an unnecessarily chilling effect.

CHAPTER TWENTY

Enabling Access and Reuse of Public Sector Information in Canada:

Crown Commons Licenses, Copyright, and Public Sector Information

Elizabeth F. Judge*

A. INTRODUCTION

Although the proactive disclosure of public sector information has been called a "basic right of citizens"[1] and a "public right,"[2] Canada has not yet implemented a national strategy to support public access to public sector information and enable its reuse. Public sector information, which is information created by government in the course of governing, is essential for transparency, accountability, democratic participation, and citizen engagement. This article examines public sector information and analyzes developments in Canada and other jurisdictions to promote its public access and reuse. It discusses the extent to which public sector information has been integrated into copyright reform efforts and, where public sector information is copyright protected, it discusses the mechanisms available within the copyright framework to facilitate public access and reuse of public sector information, focusing in particular on licensing. In Canada, Crown copyright restrictions and complicated licensing limit access to public sector information. The article recommends that Canada

* I gratefully acknowledge the support of the GEOIDE Network and the Law Foundation of Ontario.

1 "Web Inventor Calls for Government Data Transparency," *BBC News*, http://news.bbc.co.uk/2/hi/technology/8572809.stm, quoting Tim Berners-Lee.

2 American Library Association, "Key Principles of Government Information," www.ala.org/ala/issuesadvocacy/advocacy/federallegislation/govinfo/key.cfm.

establish a centralized portal for open government data (www.data.gov.ca) and implement Crown Commons licenses, which together would advance the objective of open government data by ensuring that public sector information is accessible online in usable formats, easily found, and not encumbered by restrictive Crown copyright licensing conditions.

Increasingly governments are recognizing public sector information as a public resource and "national asset"[3] and acknowledging that government has a responsibility to publish and publicize this information, which has been publicly funded and generated for public purposes. Many open government data initiatives are in place, which can serve as examples to Canada in the design of a national strategy. Within Canada, provinces and municipalities are advancing open data projects, and at the federal level some categories of information, such as geospatial information, have already been made available through open licensing. Further, many countries, including the United Kingdom, Australia, New Zealand, and the United States, have launched open government data consultations and projects, such as open government data portals and licensing innovations, which Canada could study. Canada should develop a framework for the proactive disclosure of open government data, and this article describes two initiatives that are central to this strategy: an open government data portal and Crown Commons licensing.

In "Crown Copyright and Copyright Reform in Canada," I examined the history, policy, and status of Crown copyright and reform efforts in Canada and internationally.[4] Crown copyright applies to material which is produced by the Crown and its employees in the course of their duties. Although seemingly an arcane area of copyright law, Crown copyright is critical to public awareness and engagement with public sector information. Unlike the United States, where a work of the federal government is in the public domain, and unlike other Commonwealth jurisdictions including the United Kingdom, New Zealand, and Australia, which are actively reforming Crown copyright, Canada's Crown copyright reform is latent. In Canada, Crown copyright protects copyrightable public sector information. In addition to Crown copyright restrictions, there are other barriers to the public's access to this information. Although the govern-

3 Barack Obama, Memorandum on Transparency and Open Government, www.whitehouse.gov/the_press_office/Transparency_and_Open_Government.

4 Elizabeth F. Judge, "Crown Copyright and Copyright Reform in Canada," *In the Public Interest*, ed. Michael Geist (Irwin Law, 2005), 550–96, www.irwinlaw.com/pages/content-commons/crown-copyright-and-copyright-reform-in-canada---elizabeth-f-judge.

ment generates a vast amount of information, which is publicly funded, the public often has limited awareness of, and limited access to, this material. There is no central government data portal in Canada, no central catalogue to search for public sector information or the departments and agencies that create and house it, no centralized site to request access to it, and no uniform set of licensing terms for its reuse.

Although the current bill to amend the Canadian *Copyright Act*, Bill C-32, which proposes the *Copyright Modernization Act*,[5] incorporates many positive developments over its predecessors Bill C-60[6] and Bill C-61,[7] such as provisions enabling non-commercial user-generated content, format- and time-shifting, backup copies, and expanded exceptions for distance learning, libraries, and fair dealing for purposes of education, parody, and satire (although these exceptions are significantly qualified by the digital lock conditions), like its predecessors it fails to address Crown copyright reform. Bill C-32 makes many strides that are to be lauded (such as the provisions enabling academic, non-commercial use of copyrighted material). However, Crown copyright is nowhere addressed specifically in the bill. Some of the exceptions in Bill C-32 could be applied to Crown copyright material, including the exceptions for parody and satire, distance learning instruction, libraries, user-generated content, and the internet exception for education, but without an explicit legislative reform of Crown copyright, the public still must navigate a profusion of copyright terms, proliferating licenses, and multiple access points for material protected by Crown copyright. Additionally, because the existing and proposed general exceptions to copyright (classified according to the purpose for the use or the category of user) are typically based on subjective and flexible criteria, the public would not be able to predict with certainty that a given exception could be relied on to make an intended use of public sector information non-infringing, which impedes access.

Assuming that Crown copyright reform or its abolition is unlikely to be prioritized for the copyright reform agenda in the short- (or medium-) term in Canada, Crown Commons licensing should be adopted as an interim, or

5 Bill C-32, *Copyright Modernization Act, An Act to amend the Copyright Act* (first reading 2 June 2010), www2.parl.gc.ca/content/hoc/Bills/403/Government/C-32/C-32_1/C-32_1.PDF.

6 Bill C-60, *An Act to amend the Copyright Act* (first reading 20 June 2005), www.parl.gc.ca/38/1//parlbus/chambus/house/bills/government/C-60/C-60_1/C-60_cover-E.html.

7 Bill C-61, *An Act to amend the Copyright Act* (first reading 12 June 2008), www2.parl.gc.ca/HousePublications/Publication.aspx?Docid=3570473&file=4.

alternative, means to facilitate the access and use of public sector information. If copyright amendments similar to those proposed in Bill C-32 are implemented and no progress is initiated on Crown copyright reform and abolition, significant advances can still be done by working within the current copyright landscape to facilitate access to public sector information. To promote access to public sector information, the Government should implement two important initiatives as part of Canada's digital agenda: creating a central open government data site (along the models of the recent initiatives of the United States, the United Kingdom, New Zealand, India or Australia and the established proactive disclosure policy of Mexico)[8] and adopting Crown Commons licensing.[9] Crown Commons licensing, modeled on the success of the user-friendly, familiar, and simple Creative Commons licenses, would encourage access and use of public sector information by providing clear and consistent licensing that is easy for the public to understand and apply.[10] The gamut of benefits to encouraging public sector information access, use, and, importantly, reuse, include greater government transparency and accountability, greater citizen participation and engagement, and creative and innovative reuse of public sector information, which would, in turn, provide benefits back to the government and the public.

B. PUBLIC SECTOR INFORMATION

Public sector information (also called PSI or "open government data") is simply information that is created by the public sector. According to the OECD's definition, public sector information is "information, including information products and services, generated, created, collected, processed, preserved, maintained, disseminated, or funded by or for the Government or public institution."[11] "Information" in this context is a broad

8 United States, www.data.gov; United Kingdom, www.data.gov.uk; New Zealand, http://data.govt.nz; India, http://india.gov.in/documents.php; Australia, http://data.australia.gov.au; Mexico, www.portaldetransparencia.gob.mx/pot.

9 I adopt the "Crown Commons" licensing term from the recommendations of the United Kingdom's *Power of Information Taskforce Report* for a Crown Commons branded license, described as a licensing scheme that is transparent, highly permissive, easy to use, and easy to understand. *Power of Information Taskforce Report* (2009), available at National Archives (GBR), http://webarchive.nationalarchives.gov.uk/20090315235357/http://poit.cabinetoffice.gov.uk/poit, Recommendations 8 and 12.

10 Creative Commons, www.creativecommons.org.

11 OECD, *Recommendation of the Council for Enhanced Access and More Effective Use of Public Sector Information*, C(2008)36 (30 April 2008), www.oecd.org/dataoecd/41/52/44384673.pdf at 4, note 1 [OECD, *Recommendation on Public Sector Information*].

notion, encompassing documents, databases, compilations of data, as well as audio and visual media. Typically public sector information is defined so as to exclude from its scope information whose release is limited or prohibited under statutes or common law privileges. Under these exclusions, which are consistent with the public interest, public sector information notably does not include: personal information, defined as information about an identifiable person, which is protected by data protection laws, including protections in federal and provincial privacy legislation and access to information laws;[12] information covered by statutory protections for national defence and security;[13] information protected by an evidentiary privilege (such as solicitor-client communications); and information protected by other statutory and common-law protections for confidentiality. The definition of public sector information also excludes material in which the government is not the owner of copyright or is not authorized to exercise the copyright rights.

The definition for public sector information invokes descriptive and prescriptive aspects. In one sense of the term, public sector information is defined as the full scope of all information that is created by the public sector, and then a normative argument is made that such information, as broadly defined, *should be made open* to the fullest extent possible. As used in another sense, public sector information comprises only that information which *has been made open*, in a manner that facilitates use and reuse, typically by unrestricted or minimally restricted access to digital materials online.[14] For this article, I use public sector information in the first broad descriptive sense — information that is generated by the government — and then normatively argue that it should be made open to the fullest extent possible, with appropriate exceptions in the public interest.

Given that public sector information includes information that is produced or commissioned by the Crown, its scope parallels the material covered by Crown copyright under section 12, and, for subject matter that is eligible for copyright protection, copyright is generally held by the

12 See, for example, *Privacy Act*, R.S.C., 1985, c. P-21, http://laws.justice.gc.ca/en/P-21/index.html, s. 3; *Access to Information Act*, R.S.C., 1985, c. A-1, http://laws.justice.gc.ca/en/A-1/index.html, s. 19.

13 See, for example, *Security of Information Act*, R.S., 1985, c. O-5, http://lois.justice.gc.ca/en/O-5/index.html; *Canada Evidence Act*, R.S., 1985, c. C-5, http://laws.justice.gc.ca/en/C-5, s.3 9; *Access to Information Act*, R.S., 1985, c. A-1, http://laws.justice.gc.ca/en/A-1, ss. 15–16; *Personal Information Protection and Electronic Documents Act*, R.S.C. 2000, c. 5, http://laws.justice.gc.ca/en/P-8.6, s. 7(3)(c.1).

14 See, for example, *s.v.* "open government data," www.opengovdata.org.

Crown.[15] The scope of Crown copyright excludes subject matter that is not eligible for copyright (such as raw data), material produced by government employees outside the scope of their responsibilities, and material that the government commissions but for which the author retains copyright. In the latter two cases, the individual authors could hold copyright in the works.[16] Public sector information can thus be contrasted in scope and copyright protections with information covered by access-to-information legislation. Under access-to-information legislation, the scope includes all information "under the control" of the government,[17] and therefore includes information which third parties submit to government (voluntarily or in accordance with a legal mandate) and information created outside of government but held by government institutions. Access to information legislation thus implicates distinct and significant third-party copyright and privacy interests that public sector information does not trigger.

Public access to public sector information is essential for transparency, accountability, civic education, and citizen participation. The wealth of information generated by the public sector, including legal, technical, financial, and administrative information, is critical to decision making within and outside government. Indeed, government is said to be the biggest user of government data. Public sector information is used by government for decisions related to governance and service delivery (for example, census data, geospatial information, registries, electoral boundaries, budget information, and public health and safety information) and is a critical information source for those outside of government. For members of the public, the press, civil society organizations, academics, businesses, and other groups within the private sector, access to public sector information, such as legislative debates, judicial decisions, government activities, reports, and other research promotes government transparency and accountability, improves democratic participation, informs public policy, supports decision making, and is a foundation for research and innovation. Access to public sector

15 Government-generated information could include personally identifiable information, and the discussion for facilitating access and use of PSI assumes that such information, in accordance with governing privacy legislation and access to information legislation, would not be included.

16 *Copyright Act*, R.S.C. 1985, c. C-42, http://laws.justice.gc.ca/en/c-42/38965.html, ss. 3, 13.

17 *Access to Information Act*, above note 12, s. 2 states: "The purpose of this Act is to extend the present laws of Canada to provide right of access to information in records under the control of a government institution in accordance with the principles that government information should be available to the public, that necessary exceptions to the right of access should be limited and specific and that decisions on the disclosure of government information should be reviewed independently of government."

information enables the public to be informed of governmental policy decisions, obligations, and activities and to be knowledgeable about the duties and rights of citizens. As the Open Government Data Working Group writes: "Open data promotes increased civil discourse, improved public welfare, and a more efficient use of public resources."[18]

Although the benefits to access and *use* of public sector information are profound, the advantages that can be harnessed from a *reuse* of public sector information are just starting to be realized. With social media tools and applications for user-generated content, which facilitate interactive and collaborative information sharing, such as mapping tools, blogs, mashups, wikis, and video-sharing sites, individuals can modify and create new information based on public sector information with momentous implications for innovation and creation. As the OECD summarizes in its *Recommendations on Public Sector Information*, countries should adopt a default rule of openness for public sector information in order to:

> increase returns on public investments in public sector information and increase economic and social benefits from better access and wider use and re-use, in particular through more efficient distribution, enhanced innovation and development of new uses; [and. . .] promote more efficient distribution of information and content as well as the development of new information products and services particularly through market-based competition among re-users of information.[19]

C. OBSTACLES TO ACCESS: CROWN COPYRIGHT AND RESTRICTIVE LICENSING

However, access to public sector information is stymied by Crown copyright restrictions, complicated licensing, and access barriers, which contribute both to the perception and reality of limited access. First, public sector information is generally protected by Crown copyright, which prevents unauthorized reproduction of the material. The *Berne Convention for the Protection of Literary and Artistic Works* permits Member States to "determine the protection to be granted to official texts of a legislative, administrative and legal nature, and to official translations of such texts."[20]

---

18 "Open Government Working Group," www.opengovdata.org/home/8principles.

19 OECD, *Recommendation on Public Sector Information*, above note 11.

20 *Berne Convention for the Protection of Literary and Artistic Works*, 9 September 1886, 828 U.N.T.S. 221, as last revised 24 July 1971, WIPO, www.wipo.int/treaties/en/ip/

Most European countries exclude official texts and other public sector information from copyright protection and database rights, and similarly in the United States federal legal texts are in the public domain.[21] In Commonwealth countries, however, these texts have traditionally been protected by Crown copyright.

In Canada, Crown copyright is set out in section 12 of the *Copyright Act*, which provides that copyright belongs to Her Majesty for any work that "is, or has been, prepared or published by or under the direction or control of Her Majesty or any government department . . . subject to any agreement with the author" and shall continue for a period of fifty years from the end of the calendar year in which it was published and the remainder of that year.[22] Section 12 thus covers any works generated by government and its employees within the scope of their duties and works commissioned by government, unless there is an agreement with the author providing otherwise.[23] It is axiomatic that copyright protects original works of authorship[24] and does not protect "ideas, procedures, methods of operation, or mathematical concepts."[25] Originality is defined as the non-mechanical

---

berne/trtdocs_wo001.html, art.2(4) [*Berne Convention*].

21 See, for example, in the Netherlands, art. 11 of the *Copyright Act 1912* (NED), English version available at www.ivir.nl/legislation/nl/copyrightact.html (no copyright in laws, judicial or administrative decisions) and art. 8(1) *Database Act* (NED), English version available at www.ivir.nl/legislation/nl/databaseact.html (no *sui generis* database protection for databases produced by public authorities and containing laws, judgments, administrative orders, and resolutions); *Copyright Act* (USA), 17 *United States Code* ss. 101, 105, www.copyright.gov/title17/92chap1.html (no copyright protection for any "work of the United States Government," defined as "a work prepared by an officer or employee of the United States Government as part of that person's official duties").

22 *Copyright Act*, above note 16, s. 12.

23 Although Canada does not have a separate database right, in countries that do, such as the United Kingdom, database rights for databases generated by the government are also held by the Crown. Many countries with database rights exempt a subset of Crown material, such as legal cases, from the database right. See above note 21. Creative Commons Zero licenses and Open Data Commons licenses are both designed for database owners to waive sui generis database rights (in jurisdictions where those rights apply) and copyright in original selections or arrangement of data compilations.

24 *Copyright Act*, above not 13, s. 2, *s.v.* "every original literary, dramatic, musical and artistic work," and s. 5.

25 See *Agreement Establishing the World Trade Organization, Annex 1C: Agreement on Trade-Related Aspects of Intellectual Property Rights*, 15 April 1994, 1869 U.N.T.S. 299, WTO, www.wto.org/english/docs_e/legal_e/27-trips_01_e.htm, s. 9(2) [TRIPs or *TRIPs Agreement*].

and non-trivial exercise of skill and judgment.[26] To be eligible for Crown copyright protection, there must be original expression in copyrightable subject matter. Literary and artistic works, such as biographies, maps, debates, court judgments, written reports, photographs, and the like are straight forward copyrightable subject matter. With respect to data, Crown copyright does not protect raw data (unprocessed data, such as numbers entered into a database), but it does protect an original expression of the data (for example, an original map is a copyrightable artistic work based on geospatial data) and compilations (including compilations of data), providing that there is an original selection or arrangement of the data (that is, there has been human intervention where skill and judgment has been exercised).

A non-exhaustive list of material covered by Crown copyright is legislation, regulations, court and tribunal reasons for judgment, consultation papers, government forms, press releases by government, committee reports, annual reports, government research documents, as well as any of the following that are prepared or published by or under the direction or control of Her Majesty or a government department and satisfy copyright originality: standards, original selections or arrangements of data (e.g., original selections of census data or crime statistics), value-added material (e.g., headnotes to cases), statistical analyses, maps, official biographies, histories, photographs, illustrations, websites, software, ministerial speeches, and legislative summaries.[27]

Traditionally, Crown copyright has been justified on the grounds of integrity, accuracy, authenticity, and revenue generation.[28] On behalf of maintaining Crown copyright, it is argued that Crown copyright protects the public by identifying and safeguarding the authentic version. Given that the Crown can control reproduction of Crown-copyrighted material, the Crown conceptually has control of both the version and metadata.

---

26 *CCH Canadian Ltd. v. Law Society of Upper Canada*, 2004 SCC 13, [2004] 1 S.C.R. 339, http://csc.lexum.umontreal.ca/en/2004/2004scc13/2004scc13.html. For an analysis of copyright originality standards internationally and the global influence of *CCH*'s standard, see Elizabeth F. Judge and Daniel Gervais, "Of Silos and Constellations: Comparing Notions of Originality in Copyright Law," (2009) 27:2 Cardozo Arts & Entertainment Law Journal 375–408.

27 An extensive list of the types of material that are protected by Crown copyright is provided in Annex A of the United Kingdom's Green Paper on Crown Copyright: *Crown Copyright in the Information Age*, Green Paper (GBR, 1998), www.opsi.gov.uk/advice/crown-copyright/crown-copyright-in-the-information-age.pdf, App. A.

28 See Judge, "Crown Copyright," above note 4, part C.

Crown copyright, it is argued, deters the misuse of official trusted versions, such as through misrepresentations that an inaccurate or incomplete version is official or by inappropriate juxtapositions that give the appearance that the Crown is endorsing those products or services. Supporters observe that Crown copyright enables the Crown to recoup the costs associated with developing the information, which provides funding for other public services, and, they argue, it is appropriate to charge for access to Crown-copyright protected material on at least a cost-recovery basis. This is particularly so, they argue, when user fees are targeted to commercial enterprises who will be engaged in profit-making endeavours by reselling the information because the public should not have to underwrite the costs of material that appeals only to small groups or specialized interests or to support commercial entities seeking to profit from material that has been generated at public expense. One argument for user fees is that they generate revenue, which can then be used to offset the costs of creating and disseminating public sector information and underwrite its future generation. Finally, supporters of Crown copyright reason that, as copyright is generally intended to be an incentive to create, a consequence of abolishing Crown copyright is that the supply and range of material that government produces will be diminished.

Needless to say, it is in the public interest to ensure integrity and accuracy of public sector information, as supporters of Crown copyright have observed, and Crown copyright is not inherently at odds with these objectives. The goal of facilitating access to public sector information of course presumes that it is accurate, complete, up-to-date versions to which the public is given access. The original justifications for Crown copyright were to control the dissemination and reproduction of Crown works to ensure the material's integrity and accuracy and to provide public notice of its authenticity. In that sense, Crown copyright at its inception enabled access and integrity by exercising government control over the reproduction and circulation of government materials. However, although Crown copyright is not inherently in tension with the goal of access, Crown copyright can be exercised to limit practical and effective public access to public sector information, and there is no longer (if ever) a necessary linkage between rigorous Crown-controlled access, on the one hand, and accuracy and integrity, on the other hand. While at one time and particularly with print publications, Crown copyright may have been a reasonable means to ensure that the public had access to accurate and complete versions of public sector information despite the concomitant control over dissemination, newer technologies enable other means to achieve the dual goals of access and integrity. That is, the ends of Crown copyright are commendable but there are better methods of obtaining them.[29]

Indeed, increased access to public sector information in itself supports accuracy and integrity of those materials. The more accessible the official versions are, the greater the opportunities for the public to find and identify accurate and complete public sector information. In conjunction with increased access, other mechanisms, such as official marks, are preferable mechanisms to meet the objectives of accuracy and integrity than Crown copyright. Digital official copies can and should be made available on official government websites and through other official channels, along with the government's official mark. With the repeal of Crown copyright, the public could access and use this material housed on official sources, on condition that the official mark is not used in association with other copies, which would satisfy the objective that the public have access to an authentic trusted copy of the material. It would also spur value-added projects that would enhance the knowledge base as the private sector exploits the social, cultural, political, and economic potential in public sector information.

As a counter to the assertion by Crown copyright supporters that fees should be charged for public sector information, it should be emphatically stressed that public sector information belongs to the public, is already publicly funded, and hence should be publicly accessible. It is true that the revenue from user fees for Crown-copyright protected information can be substantial. A United Kingdom study of departmental revenue in the period 1996–1997 from royalty income, licensing, direct sales income, and data provision charges for Crown copyright material put the total sums received at 200 million pounds.[30] However, in addition to the fact that the public has already paid for the information to be generated and additional fees impose a second payment for the same material, which should properly be considered a public asset, the full transaction costs of access fees should be considered when weighing the revenue. In addition to the costs of collecting, producing, updating, and distributing the information, user fees add the costs of licensing and fee-setting; costs associated with fulfilling individual information requests, such as searching, retrieving, transmitting, and reviewing information; and other administrative costs. These transaction costs reduce the net financial advantages of assessing

29 See Elizabeth F. Judge, "Copyright, Access, and Integrity of Public Information," (2008) 1 Journal of Parliamentary and Political Law 427-441.

30 *Crown Copyright in the Information Age*, above note 27, App. B.

a fee, and hence a true cost-recovery system is difficult to attain without imposing burdensome high fees. Fees require that the government dedicate significant resources to the administrative task of establishing and maintaining collection systems, including the costs of deciding which public sector information is fee-based, what the fee is, and what the price discrimination is between individuals, non-profit, and commercial enterprises. Fees that target particular types of information or particular classes of users have associated administrative burdens of categorizing information, allocating amounts, classifying users, and establishing verification and recordkeeping procedures.

By contrast, *unlocking* government data, which the public has already been paid for and which has already been generated by government in the process of governing, garners economic efficiencies for the public and the government, as individuals create new applications and uses for this data and commercial enterprises add value to the information by repackaging it, with additional benefits for the economy. Focusing only on the revenues received from user fees ignores the benefits that both the public and the public sector gain from the innovative reuse of public sector information. Governments and intergovernmental bodies are increasingly recognizing the economic efficiencies of opening data. As the United Nations' *E-Government Survey 2010* commented, "Open data enhances public sector efficiency by transferring some of the analytical demands of government to third parties such as non-governmental organizations, research institutes and the media, which have been found to combine data from various sources in original and inventive ways."[31] Similarly, British Prime Minister

31 United Nations, *E-Government Survey 2010: Leveraging E-Government at a Time of Financial and Economic Crisis*, www2.unpan.org/egovkb/documents/2010/E_Gov_2010_Complete.pdf at 16. See also Peter Weiss, *Borders in Cyberspace: Conflicting Public Sector Information Policies and Their Economic Impacts*, Summary Report, National Weather Service (2002), www.weather.gov/sp/Borders_report.pdf (concluding, in a study comparing the United States' open data model for weather data to the European cost recovery model, that charging marginal cost for dissemination (which is negligible and effectively free) leads to optimal economic growth in society and "far outweighs the immediate perceived benefits of aggressive cost recovery," and that open government information policies "foster significant, but not easily quantifiable, economic benefits to society" at 17). Other studies posit that an open government data policy increases citizen self-reliance and reduces government regulatory costs. See Ed Mayo and Tom Steinberg, *The Power of Information: An independent review* (June 2007) www.opsi.gov.uk/advice/poi/power-of-information-review.pdf at para. 117 (government collecting and sharing information with its citizens facilitate citizens' "choice" and "voice" and are "practical, often more efficient, alternatives to top-down traditional regulation"); and *Putting the Frontline First,*

David Cameron's letter to government departments on plans to open up government data highlighted economic benefits: "Greater transparency across Government is at the heart of our shared commitment to enable the public to hold politicians and public bodies to account; to reduce the deficit and deliver better value for money in public spending; and to realize significant economic benefits by enabling businesses and non-profit organizations to build innovative applications and websites using public data."[32]

Other negative effects associated with fees further reduce their attractiveness. Most methods of collecting fees would also be likely to entail recordkeeping about the requestor and the requested information, which has attendant privacy risks.[33] In addition to the privacy implications, the mere imposition of fees has a chilling effect, discouraging the public from asking for the information.

As to the notion that repealing Crown copyright would decrease the amount of public sector information, this seems wholly unlikely. In contrast to individual authors, public sector information has numerous other incentives (and obligations) supporting the generation of public sector information, namely: it is publicly funded; it is generated by employees whose duties it is to produce such information; and government itself relies on the information to fulfill its responsibilities and to provide essential services.[34]

In addition to the structural barriers that Crown copyright poses to public access of public sector information, access problems are exacerbated by the public's perceptions (and misperceptions) of Crown copyright, which deter people from trying to use material that is covered by Crown

---

below note 92 at 26 (stating "data can also be used in innovative ways that bring economic benefits to citizens and businesses by releasing untapped enterprise and entrepreneurship" and citing studies predicting significant increase in economic growth if more publicly held data is released for reuse).

32 David Cameron, Letter to Government departments on opening up data (31 May 2010), www.number10.gov.uk/news/statements-and-articles/2010/05/letter-to-government-departments-on-opening-up-data-51204.

33 For example, under the current transaction-based copyright clearance process, personal information is collected on the Application for Crown Copyright Clearance Form and the Government of Canada Publications website notes that personal information "may also be shared with other government departments if your inquiry relates to these departments for review and decision." "Application for Copyright Clearance," Government of Canada Publications, http://publications.gc.ca/site/eng/ccl/copyrightClearance/apply.html.

34 Judge, "Crown Copyright," above note 4, part H(2).

copyright. The United Kingdom's 2009 *Power of Information Taskforce Report* found that Crown copyright was poorly understood by creators and reusers of data, and, although the Taskforce believed Crown copyright was designed to encourage reuse in the majority of cases, it acknowledged that intent was not appreciated by the public; to the contrary, many felt Crown copyright deterred potential reusers.[35] It is fair to infer that there is also public discontent with the range and type of exceptions for Crown-copyright protected information. As with copyright exceptions generally, the statutory language incorporates subjective criteria such that, even where an individual is familiar with the copyright landscape and understands which exceptions could apply, it is difficult to predict with confidence that a given use will fit the exception's scope. Canada's current fair dealing provision in section 29, which provides that "fair dealing" for the purpose of "research or private study" is non-infringing, is a good example of the inherent subjectivity in the principles, which has the benefit of allowing the statutory exception to be applied to a variety of contexts, but which has the drawback of making it hard for members of the public to know if a given activity will come within the scope of the section. If exceptions are structured to be flexible and to fit a variety of factual contexts, it is a necessary consequence that they will lack certainty and predictability. Thus while Bill C-32's exceptions, on the positive side, enlarge the acts and purposes that can be done with copyrighted works and provide more flexibility, it will remain difficult to ascertain precisely what activities will be non-infringing as long as Crown copyright applies.

Moreover, along with the deterrence of Crown copyright's structural barriers and public perceptions of their complexity, complicated licensing structures exacerbate the obstacles that Crown copyright erects to public access to public sector information. For public sector information that is protected by Crown copyright, individuals must either rely on a statutory exception or (if there is no exception or if an individual wants more predictability that a given act will be allowed) permission to reproduce the material must be obtained in advance. Licenses are the legal mechanism for the copyright holder to grant permission to reproduce copyrighted material. The licensing options for the Crown include the following: the Crown can permit certain described activities for certain categories of material in advance, provide uniform licensing, or have individual licenses. Currently, Canada does not have an "all-of-government" licensing model, under which a uniform license template applies to all public sector information.

35 *Power of Information Taskforce Report*, above note 9 at 25.

There are two positive examples of licenses for Canadian Crown copyrighted material which facilitate open access to public sector information. First, the *Reproduction of Federal Law Order* is an example of preemptive licensing, in which the Crown provides blanket permission to any member of the public to reproduce certain Crown copyrighted material provided specified conditions are met. The *Reproduction of Federal Law Order* permits anyone, "without charge or request for permission," to reproduce federal statutes and regulations and reasons for decision of federally constituted courts and administrative tribunals, "provided due diligence is exercised in ensuring the accuracy of the materials reproduced and the reproduction is not represented as an official version."[36] Another example is the template licenses developed by GeoConnections (an organization that is part of Natural Resources Canada), which are designed to provide model terms and a uniform approach to licensing geographical information held by any federal department or agency.[37] However, these two examples of licenses that facilitate access apply only to circumscribed categories of public sector information and are premised on two different approaches to licensing.

Beyond these examples, the process of seeking permission to use Crown copyrighted works is often a difficult one to navigate. Generally, copyright clearance of Government of Canada works is handled by the Crown Copyright and Licensing Section of Public Works and Government Services.[38]

---

36 *Reproduction of Federal Law Order*, PC 1996-1995, SI/97-5, 19 December 1996, http://laws.justice.gc.ca/eng/SI-97-5/page-1.html, vol. 131, no. 1, *Canada Gazette — Part II* 444 (8 January 1997).

37 GeoConnections, *The Dissemination of Government Geographic Data in Canada: Guide to Best Practices*, version 2 (Ottawa: Natural Resources Canada), http://www.geoconnections.org/publications/Best_practices_guide/Guide_to_Best_Practices_Summer_2008_Final_EN.pdf.

38 The Crown Copyright and Licensing Section "can help to facilitate the use of Government of Canada works in all existing formats through the permission-granting process" and has the following responsibilities: providing assistance, advice and support to the public and to Government of Canada departments and agencies with respect to Crown copyright issues; administering and protecting copyright in works authored by Government of Canada departments and agencies; negotiating and issuing licensing agreements for non-commercial and commercial rights associated with works subject to Crown copyright; offering information sessions to author departments; and investigating potential copyright infringement on Government of Canada works. Government of Canada, "Crown Copyright and Licensing," http://publications.gc.ca/helpAndInfo/cc-dac/about-e.html. Orders for printed publications are made through Publishing and Depository Services, Government of Canada Publications, http://www.publications.gc.ca, which has an online catalogue.

The clearance process is a transactional application, requiring that someone interested in accessing the material seek individual permission in advance, and submit detailed information about the requester, the intended use, the copyright rights involved (reproduction, translation, telecommunication, etc.), the format, number of copies, end use, commercial sale price or cost-recovery basis, area of distribution, and any prior approvals for the same material.[39] Notwithstanding the challenges of this clearance process, there may be additional hurdles. For Crown copyright material, it is not always readily apparent where the desired material resides, if it is available electronically, which license pertains, if any copyright pertains, or whom to ask. There is a proliferation of licenses for Crown copyrighted material, the licenses are housed on different sites, license terms vary, the language is not uniform, access fees may be imposed, and the terms are not always in plain language.[40] By corollary, it may be difficult to determine if material is covered by Crown copyright at all, if copyright is held by a third party, if the copyright has expired, or if the material is otherwise in the public domain. The websites of public bodies, for example, may contain copyrighted works from various third-party owners, material in the public domain, and material where the copyright has expired, and various licensing terms may apply, including preemptive permissions for certain works and individual copyright clearances for others.[41]

---

39 See "Application for Copyright Clearance on Government of Canada Works," http://publications.gc.ca/site/eng/ccl/copyrightClearance/application.pdf.

40 See Judge, "Crown Copyright," above note 4 at parts D and E; Judge, "Copyright, Access, and Integrity of Public Information," above note 29 at "Practical Problems for Increasing Access within Crown Copyright."

41 For example, on Library and Archives Canada, the copyright page provides that copyright for material in the collections may be owned by Library and Archives Canada, or a third party, or may be in the public domain. For the website, prior written permission is required to reproduce material, and the reproductions must comply with standard conditions (identifying Library and Archives Canada as the source, exercising due diligence to ensure accuracy, not representing the reproduction as official or as being endorsed by Library and Archives Canada, and not modifying the reproduction). For the collections, some material is covered by use and reproduction restrictions and requires written permission; some material's copyright is owned by Library and Archives Canada and requires written permission from Library and Archives Canada for reproduction; some material's copyright is owned by third parties and requires written permission from the copyright owners, which is obtained through the Copyright Bureau; some material is in the public domain and can be reproduced without permission or payment but must abide by the standard conditions for reproduction described above; and some material has a pre-authorized license permitting users to reproduce the material for certain purposes without obtaining

Building on the copyright restrictions and complicated licensing, the public's relative inexperience with and scanty knowledge of public sector information compounds the lack of access to the data. In Canada, there is no central catalogue or searchable database for public sector information, making it difficult for the public to identify useful material and once identified to locate it. Public sector information is dispersed and fragmented across different databases and controlled by different departments, with different practices for publicizing the information. Although increasingly public sector information is born digital, it often is not made available in an open format[42] through open architecture, it may not have sufficient security protections to prevent unauthorized access (or it may incorrectly block legitimate access), it may lack metadata, and it may not be in an accessible format that is suitable for people with disabilities or who require translations.[43]

Two reform issues are implicated by the intersection of Crown copyright and public sector information: first, whether the material should continue to be covered by Crown copyright and second, how to make the data more "open." With respect to Crown copyright, there is a spectrum of options ranging from full abolition of Crown copyright to retaining the status quo. The policy options include: abolish Crown copyright for all material that originates with the government and place it in the public domain; abolish Crown copyright for particular categories of material; retain Crown copyright but waive it for certain categories of material or for certain defined purposes; waive Crown copyright except for certain categories of material or certain defined purposes where it is enforced; retain Crown copyright but use uniform licensing with common terms; retain Crown copyright

---

copyright permission. "Copyright," Library and Archives Canada, www.collectionscanada.gc.ca/notices/016-200-e.html.

42 Open formats are machine readable, platform neutral, and available to the public without restrictions.

43 Best practice technical recommendations and implementation guidance for publishing public sector information can be found in Tim Berners-Lee, "Putting Government Data Online," (24 June 2009), www.w3.org/DesignIssues/GovData (recommending linked data (which is open, modular, and scalable), persistent web addresses, and open formats); Webcontent.gov (USA), "Provide Appropriate Access to Data," www.usa.gov/webcontent/usability/accessibility/access_to_data.shtml (guidance for United States federal public websites); Joshua Tauberer, "Open Data is Civic Capital: Best Practices for 'Open Government Data,'" v. 1.3 (14 April 2010), http://razor.occams.info/pubdocs/opendataciviccapital.html (recommending globally unique identifiers (GUIDs) and Linked Open Data (LOD; see www.linked-data.org), and other ideas from the Semantic Web.

but bring all licensing and administration under the control of a centralized body; retain Crown copyright and have decentralized control with multiple licenses, with terms, practices, and fees set by the department or agency that generates the information; or retain Crown copyright and individual permissions but provide fast track licensing.[44]

In "Crown Copyright and Copyright Reform in Canada," I argued that the policy objectives that have been claimed for Crown copyright of maintaining the integrity and accuracy of Crown-generated material can be achieved as well or better through other models which promote open access to this material and detailed the case for abolishing Crown copyright.[45] As yet, repealing Crown copyright has little priority in the copyright reform agenda and that option has failed to be implemented in Bill C-32. While the best option is to abolish Crown copyright, in the meantime, much can be done by working within the copyright structure to facilitate access to public sector information.

Until such time as Crown copyright is repealed, other steps can be taken that would make significant advances toward the goal of open data. But what does "open" mean? The definition and understanding of "open" for open data, open access, open government, and open source are contested, and there is no consensus on the important issue of whether material can be copyrighted and nevertheless qualify as "open." Some definitions of open access require that public sector information be free of copyright, while others reason that the goals of transparency, accountability, and reuse can be accomplished with material that is protected by Crown copyright provided that there is permissive licensing.

Several guidelines for open data have been proposed, and these share many of the same principles. According to the Open Knowledge Foundation, "A piece of knowledge is open if you are free to use, reuse, and redistribute it — subject only, at most, to the requirement to attribute and share-alike."[46] The Open Government Working Group, convened in Nov-

---

44 Options such as these have been canvassed in other jurisdictions in Crown copyright public consultation documents. See for example, *Crown Copyright in the Information Age*, above note 27, ch. 5; United Kingdom, Minister for the Cabinet Office, *Future Management of Crown Copyright*, CM 4300 (London: Her Majesty's Stationer's Office, 1999), www.hmso.gov.uk/archives/copyright/future_management_cc.doc; Copyright Law Review Committee (Aus.), *Crown Copyright Report*, Final Report (April 2005), www.ag.gov.au/agd/WWW/clrhome.nsf/Page/RWP3D1B9A992032DBE9CA256FEB00239309.

45 Judge, "Crown Copyright," above note 4.

46 "Open Knowledge Definition," www.opendefinition.org. The Open Knowledge Foundation Working Group on Open Government Data is developing principles for making

ember 2007, developed "Eight Principles of Open Government Data" for governments to become "more effective, transparent, and relevant to our lives."[47] These eight principles, which have garnered significant support, recommend that the data be

1) *complete* (all public data, which is data that is not subject to valid privacy, security, or privilege limitations, is made available);
2) *primary* (published as collected at the source, with the finest possible level of granularity (e.g., preservation-quality high resolution images) and not in aggregate or modified forms (i.e., non-aggregate numeric and tabular data presented according to best practices));
3) *timely* (made available as quickly as necessary to preserve the value of the data, with the reasonableness of time for releasing data, changes, and updates being determined by the nature of the dataset);
4) *accessible* (available to the widest range of users for the widest range of purposes, meaning access through the internet);
5) *machine-processable* (reasonably structured to allow automated processing, and thus images of text will not suffice for the text itself);
6) *non-discriminatory* (available to anyone, with no requirement of registration and allowing data to be accessed anonymously);
7) *non-proprietary formats* (available in a format over which no entity has exclusive control, and in cases where non-proprietary formats may not reach a wide audience the availability of multiple formats may be necessary); and
8) *license-free* (not subject to any copyright, patent, trade-mark, or trade secret regulation, although reasonable privacy, security and privilege restrictions may be allowed as governed by other statutes).

Additionally, compliance must be *reviewable*, with a contact person designated to reply to people trying to access the data and to complaints about violations of the principles, and a tribunal or court should have jurisdiction to review the application of the principles.

As the Working Group's annotations to the principles indicate, these principles are premised on information that is digital (they define data as "electronically stored information or recordings") being made available digitally. Although the principles observe that it is also desirable that non-digital information be made available digitally, they do not mandate

---

official information legally and technically open: http://wiki.okfn.org/wg/government.

47 "8 Principles of Open Government Data," http://www.opengovdata.org/home/8principles.

that step, which acknowledges the large undertaking required to convert information in other formats and media to digital (e.g., scanning paper documents). The Working Group Recommendations for data accessibility elaborate that accessibility for digital information entails online publishing, in compliance with industry protocols and formats and with accessibility standards for persons with disabilities and those who need translation services. The Working Group additionally notes that complying with the principles of accessibility and machine-processable data require that there be a means to extract and import the raw data and that the data be properly encoded. The technical recommendations for machine-processable data (recommendation 5) include persistent identifiers, documented data formats, notifications of data format changes, and RSS feeds. For licensing, the benchmarks recommended by the Working Group to be in accordance with the principles of non-proprietary data formats and license-free data are that the data can be used in free software applications and that individuals are permitted (and able) to redistribute the data without restriction.

Significantly, these principles address *how* to make data open rather than *what* data to make open. The Working Group emphasizes that the principles "specify the conditions public data should meet to be considered 'open,'" but they "do not address what should be public and open." As it notes, "[p]rivacy, security, and other concerns may legally (and rightly) prevent data sets from being shared with the public." Hence, as to copyright, although principle 8 states that government data must be license free and not subject to intellectual property regulation, the Working Group acknowledges in its comments that because "government information is a mix of public records, personal information, copyrighted work, and other non-open data," the objective is for clarity in what data is available, what licensing applies, what the terms of service are, and what legal restrictions apply. Thus, the recommendation rather is that "[d]ata for which no restrictions apply should be marked clearly as being in the public domain," and that "the data to be made 'open' be properly specified."[48]

Comparable principles are endorsed by other organizations.[49] The American Library Association, for example, offers eleven "Key Principles of Government Information," with similar perspectives to the Working Group. The first two principles succinctly encapsulate the open govern-

48 *Open Data Policy Recommendation*, http://wiki.opengovdata.org/index.php?title=OpenDataPolicyRecommendation, annotations.

49 See, for example, Association of Computing Machinery U.S. Public Policy Committee (USACM), *Recommendations on Open Government*, www.acm.org/public-policy/open-government; OECD, *Recommendation on Public Sector Information*, above note 11.

ment position, asserting that "[a]ccess to government information is a public right that must not be restricted by administrative barriers, geography, ability to pay, or format," and "government has a responsibility to collect, maintain, and disseminate information to the public." Unlike the Open Government Working Group's focus on making digital information publicly accessible, the ALA's aim is comprehensive, emphasizing that the information generated by government serves as the official public record of government, and hence government has an obligation to preserve information from all eras of a country's history and regardless of form or format. For copyright, the ALA's principle 11 eschews the application of any "copyright or copyright-like restrictions" on government information, which impedes public access, because the "property rights of government information reside with the people."[50]

Although there are divergences of opinion on whether copyright is consistent with "open" data, it is certainly consistent with these principles and guidelines that advances toward open data can be made even if the copyright landscape retains Crown copyright in public sector information.

D. ACHIEVING OPEN DATA

If Crown copyright is not repealed, access to public sector information can be greatly enhanced and improved by making it more open, specifically through two initiatives: open access to public sector information on a "data.gov.ca" model, and open licenses on a Crown Commons model. Both of these actions must be accomplished to achieve truly open data. If public sector information is free of copyright restrictions but is not published online in usable formats or cannot be found, it is not accessible; likewise, if the data is available online but encumbered by restrictive license conditions, it is not accessible. Thus, in countries that exclude public sector information from copyright, public sector information may still not be accessible if it is not published electronically or if it is not available in open government data portals where it can be easily found. Conversely, in countries where public sector information is protected under a form of government copyright or Crown copyright, it can still be made available through permissive licensing and open government data catalogues and portals.

To achieve open data, public sector information must be available in an open data catalogue and must either be free of copyright restrictions or

---

50 "American Library Association, "Key Principles of Government Information," above note 2.

published under open licensing. Although this article focuses on those initiatives, a truly comprehensive open government data strategy would also look to history and to the future: first, by addressing measures to digitize both printed archival public sector information and historical information in other non-electronic formats and media; and second, by ensuring that the open government data strategy evolves to consider new technologies for disseminating public sector information, while also preserving public accessibility and reuse of the current repertoire of digitalized public sector information when new media and formats are adopted.

To alleviate the restrictions described in Part C on public sector information, the next most desirable option if Crown copyright is retained is to implement uniform licensing on a preemptive permission model. The license should be made available online, and clearly set out the permitted material and activities in advance in familiar recognizable terms, so that the license, the scope of the material, and the range of permitted uses are publicly known. The default should be public access to public sector information, with limited clearly defined exceptions for restricting access only where such restrictions are in the public interest. The least restrictive conditions that are consistent with the purpose of the document should be imposed, with a default to an attribution-only license where possible. For material such as primary legal sources, where the integrity of the text is especially important, minimal conditions, such as those in the *Reproduction to Licence Order*, could be imposed, whereas for other material, an attribution-only condition would suffice.

1) Data.gov.ca

To achieve (more) open data in Canada, public sector information should be available on a data.gov.ca portal, free of subscriptions and passwords. The W3C eGov Interest Group has developed a working draft of technical guidelines for the "logistics and practicalities of opening government data," emphasizing standards and methodologies to encourage the publication of open government data and public use of the data.[51] The OECD's *Recommendation on Public Sector Information* recommends "information asset lists and inventories, preferably published on-line, as well as clear presentation of conditions to access and re-use at access points to the in-

51 W3C [Daniel Bennett & Adam Harvey], "Publishing Open Government Data," Working Draft (8 September 2009), www.w3.org/TR/gov-data. See also, Tim Berners-Lee, "Putting Government Data Online," (24 June 2009), www.w3.org/DesignIssues/GovData.

formation" in order to strengthen awareness of the public sector information available for access and reuse.[52]

Given that public sector information is publicly funded and generated for public purposes, government has an obligation to publish and publicize public sector information, and this mandate should be fulfilled through an open government data portal. There should be a single portal for data.gov.ca, providing a publicly accessible, comprehensive, and centralized database for public sector information, which catalogues the information and provides it in full text free of charge and free of restrictions. The portal should include an online catalogue identifying the datasets, databases, and other information resources available to the public and the department or body submitting them and should incorporate search tools which allow searches by agency, keyword, file type, and data category.[53] Public sector information should provide cross-references for the location of the data in the websites of the relevant department and in the centralized portal. Finally, the data on the portal should be licensed under Crown Commons licenses, described in the following section.

2) Crown Commons Licenses

In addition to a centralized open government data site, there should be Crown Commons licensing, modeled on Creative Commons licenses, providing a uniform approach across government for public sector information. Creative Commons licenses have the potent advantages of brand loyalty and familiarity for online users. Under Creative Commons licenses, authors can choose among four license conditions: attribution, share alike, non-commercial, and no derivative works. There are six main Creative Commons licenses, which, in ascending order from least to most restrictive conditions, are: Attribution (cc by), Attribution Share Alike (cc by-sa), Attribution No Derivatives (cc by-nd), Attribution Non-Commercial (cc by-nc), Attribution Non-Commercial Share Alike (cc by-nc-sa), and Attribution Non-Commercial No Derivatives (cc by-nc-nd). Each license is identified by a logo with the appropriate symbols for the applicable four conditions.[54] Most jurisdictions that have adopted Creative Commons licences for public sector information are using an attribution-only license. In Canada, when Crown copyright material is made available under a permissive license, the

52 OECD, *Recommendation on Public Sector Information*, above note 11.

53 See, for example, the search tools on the US site, www.data.gov.

54 "About Licenses," *Creative Commons*, http://creativecommons.org/about/licenses.

conditions of the license generally mirror the requirements of the *Reproduction of Federal Law Order*, namely attributing the source, exercising due diligence to ensure accuracy, and not representing that the reproduction is an official version of the information reproduced nor as having been made in affiliation with or endorsement of the issuing governmental body.[55] The closest Creative Commons license to these conditions is an Attribution license; the no-derivatives condition goes farther than these requirements, though it does capture some aspects of the concerns for integrity and accuracy that the standard Canadian conditions reflect.

Crown Commons licenses would exploit and build on the many advantages of Creative Commons licenses to create a branded license that recognizes the special traits of Crown copyright, provides uniform standardized licensing for public sector information in the model of Creative Commons, and is a recognizable symbol of open government data for the public. Further, by building on the Creative Commons model while acknowledging the particular context of Crown copyright, Crown Commons licenses would promote sharing and aggregation of national and international public sector information through a model that would be recognizable to users from other countries and be interoperable with Creative Commons licenses. Crown Commons licenses would keep the benefits of Creative Commons licensing and follow their templates but would importantly identify the material as public sector information, which would build awareness of this public resource and identify the material as having the integrity and accuracy of public sector information.

In keeping with the legacy of Creative Commons licenses, Crown Commons licenses should be open, human- and machine-readable, user-friendly licenses, with simple clear terms that provide public assurance that the material can be used and reused without infringing, and employing easily recognized symbols for open government data practices, similar to the

55 See, for example, *Reproduction of Federal Law Order*, above note 36. An example of a permissive license with similarterms to the *Reproduction of Federal Law Order* is the "Permission to Reproduce" statement in *Improving Canada's Digital Advantage: Consultation Paper on a Digital Economy Strategy for Canada* (Canada, 2010), http://de-en.gc.ca/wp-content/uploads/2010/05/Consultation_Paper.pdf, copyright page. Often the copyright page does not have a "permission to reproduce" statement and includes only a copyright notice. See, for example, Office of the Privacy Commissioner of Canada, *Annual Report to Parliament 2009: Report on the Personal Information and Electronic Documents Act*, www.priv.gc.ca/information/ar/200910/2009_pipeda_e.pdf, which identifies copyright in the Minister of Public Works and Government Services Canada 2010. An electronic copy of that document is available to the public through www.priv.gc.ca.

iconic symbols that brand Creative Commons licenses. Rather than merely "allow" public access and use, the license should positively encourage the reuse of public sector information. Across public sector information, the default should be to allow, and encourage, reuse of the material, with only limited exceptions as required for the public interest.

In contrast to the traditional Crown copyright model, which is based in part on revenue generation and is publicly perceived to deter use, a Crown Commons license would promote the innovation and efficiencies created when the public is free to add value. Such benefits include integrating datasets, using the data across multiple databases for new purposes, developing new applications, creating mashups and visualizations to re-present information in a qualitatively different manner, and enabling information to be localized and personalized.[56] The reuse of such publicly funded information through Crown Commons licenses will add to the knowledge base, facilitate research, increase productivity, and enlarge cultural and informational output. Crown Commons licenses promise to be more efficient and more cost effective than the multiple and customized licenses and individual clearance processes that currently govern Crown copyright material, and the reuse of public sector information is itself likewise an efficient, cost-effective, and value-maximizing use of publicly funded datasets.

Although in special cases, some public sector information may require more complicated or customized licensing (perhaps because of exceptional public interest concerns, such as an enhanced need to control versions more tightly for reasons of public safety or health), such instances should be rare, and the norm should be that public sector information is made publicly accessible and is licensed according to Crown Commons templates with minimal conditions.

The concept of a Crown Commons license advocated here would build on the success of Creative Commons and other open licensing models, and on the efforts of other Commonwealth jurisdictions to open access to Crown-copyrighted material. The idea of a Crown Commons branded license was vetted in the United Kingdom *Power of Information Taskforce Report* in 2009.[57] Recommendation 8 states that government should ensure there is a uniform system for releasing and licensing information across all public bodies and individual public bodies should not be permitted to vary those standard terms. Specifically, "the system should create

---

56 See, for example, Patrick Cain's "Map of the Week" series in the *Toronto Star*, http://thestar.blogs.com/maps.

57 *Power of Information Taskforce Report*, above note 9, Recommendation 8.

a 'Crown Commons' style approach, using a highly permissive licensing scheme that is transparent, easy to understand and easy to use, modeled on the 'Click Use' license." Recommendation 12 further recommended that the Office of Public Sector Information (OPSI), which is part of the National Archives, should "begin a communications campaign to re-present and improve understanding of the permissive aspects of Crown Copyright along the lines of creative commons." It also recommended that there should be permission to scrape Crown copyright data and that prosecution under the *Computer Misuse Act* should be removed, and that these initiatives could also fall under the Crown Commons brand.[58]

It should be emphasized that adopting Crown Commons licenses is not tantamount to a waiver or abolition of Crown copyright. The licenses work within the current copyright structure (or as amended under Bill C-32, since the proposed amendments do not change Crown copyright) to facilitate access, use, and reuse of public sector information, but Crown copyright is retained. Until Crown copyright is repealed, such licenses would greatly improve access to public sector information by institutionalizing a culture of least restrictive terms for Crown-copyrighted material to change both the public's and the public sector's perception of the role of Crown copyright. By providing clear and advance notice of permitted activities and conditions of use for Crown-copyrighted material, Crown Commons licenses would encourage the public to access public sector information and stimulate the reuse of public sector information.

However, given that Crown Commons licensing would be implemented within the Crown copyright regime, some caveats need to be highlighted. First, Crown Common licenses are based on copyright residing with the Crown, and premised on those rights the Crown then authorizes public use. The licenses therefore should clearly define the Crown-copyright protected subject matter so that the Crown does not erect further access restrictions by asserting rights in information which is in the public domain or by claiming rights held by third parties. Thus, the licenses should differentiate three categories of material:

1) Crown-copyrighted material;
2) material that is in the public domain (i.e., the subject matter is not eligible for copyright (such as raw data or other information that does not qualify as an "original expression") or copyright has expired); and

58 *Ibid.*, Recommendation 12. The open data initiatives that the UK Government has launched are discussed in part F.

3) third-party material to which the government does not have copyright.

Crown Commons licenses are intended to be applied to public sector information and thus should exclude third-party copyrighted material (which material might be physically held by the government but where third parties retain copyright). In addition to distinguishing between Crown-copyrighted material and third-party copyrighted material, the licenses should also distinguish between non-copyrightable subject matter (such as raw data and whole-of-universe compilations of data), on the one hand, and copyrighted and copyrightable material such as original expressions of data, on the other hand.[59] Government websites are a common context where such distinctions are critical, given the number of rights holders and types of material. The task of identifying copyrights and rights holders of material housed on a government website is admittedly complex but is an important step to ensure that Crown Commons licensing is not applied to public domain material, which needs no permission for reuse, and is not applied to third-party material, where the copyright is not held by the Crown. Disambiguating the copyright ownership would avoid public misperceptions that a daunting permission process involving multiple copyright owners, including the Crown, must be navigated, if the Crown does not in fact have a claim to the information.

Although third-party copyright is by definition not "public sector information" and not suitable for Crown Commons licenses, there are many contexts where both third-party copyright and public sector information will be closely implicated. For example, publications by researchers who are supported by a federal granting agency are typically copyrighted to the individual author. These publications should be deposited in open access databases, published in open access journals, and/or licensed under Creative Commons or similar open licensing models, but they would not fall under the scope of Crown Commons licenses.[60] Similarly, third-party copyrighted material held by federal or provincial museums, libraries, archives, and universities or on government registries or in submissions to

---

59 This aligns with *Open Data Policy Recommendation*, above note 48, Recommendation 8.

60 For open access licensing, open access journals, and self-archiving for scholarly works, see the Science Commons' Scholar's Copyright Project, http://sciencecommons.org/projects/publishing; Directory of Open Access Journals, www.doaj.org (open access journals); and SHERPA/RoMEO, www.sherpa.ac.uk/romeo/ (publisher copyright policies and self-archiving).

government would not come within the scope of Crown Commons licenses, unless an appropriate assignment of rights is made.

In conjunction with the adoption of Crown Commons licenses, therefore, the government should clearly identify which material is protected by Crown copyright and which of that material is under a Crown Common license (and preferably all Crown copyright material should be licensed under Crown Common licenses, except for discrete categories of information where a thoughtful analysis concludes it is in the public interest to exclude them; in those exceptional cases, the least restrictive license that safeguards the public interest should govern). New Zealand, in its "Suggested All-of-government Approach to Licensing" made a similar recommendation that if Creative Commons licensing was adopted for public sector information, then appropriate guidance material should be released which would explain copyright and Crown copyright, the categories of public sector information that are not subject to copyright, and the key differences between the existence of copyright in the material and the licensing of such material.[61] Importantly, non-copyrightable information, such as raw data and third-party copyrighted material, should be as clearly differentiated as possible from Crown-copyright protected material.

It is also important to emphasize that licensing alone does not resolve the lack of access to public sector information and therefore must be done in conjunction with an open government data portal. After all, if the public cannot find public sector information, the fact that it is under a Crown Commons license does not make the information "open." Canada should make public sector information accessible in a centralized searchable open government data portal, and, until Crown copyright is repealed, the portal should be branded with Crown Commons licenses, with generous permissions.

The next sections look at current initiatives for open data in Canada and other jurisdictions, and the final section concludes with recommendations for Canada.

---

61 New Zealand, "A Suggested All-of-government Approach to Licensing of Public Sector Copyright Works: Discussion Paper for Public Service and Non-Public Service Departments," Open Government and Data Re-use Project (2009), www.scribd.com/doc/19092928/Open-Government-Information-and-Data-ReUse-Project-Discussion-Paper at para. 190.

E. CANADA'S OPEN DATA INITIATIVES

Canada lacks a centralized open data portal, but discussions to explore access to public sector information are beginning.[62] The House of Commons' Standing Committee on Access to Information, Privacy and Ethics announced in April 2010 that it would study proactive disclosure, with the Chair noting "this is the way governance is going," and although "we have activity in that regard in Canada, . . . certainly there are other countries that are ahead of us."[63] Canada's Office of the Information Commissioner is actively advocating for a "made in Canada" strategy for proactive disclosure. The Interim Commissioner speaking before the Committee called proactive disclosure, which she described as government making government records available in open standard formats and permitting unlimited use and reuse of the information, an "essential component of the broader concept of open government." The speech laid out five overarching principles for a Canadian strategy, which flagged Crown copyright as an issue. The five principles are commitment to a cultural change for open government through accountability and deliverables, broad public consultations, accessibility for the public to integrated information from a variety of sources to reduce bureaucratic silos, addressing and resolving related issues (privacy, confidentiality, security, Crown copyright, and official languages), and anchoring open government principles in statutory and policy instruments.[64] In March 2010 and May 2010 appearances before the Committee, Commissioner Robert Marleau urged that the "more

---

62 With the lack of a federal Canadian centralized resource for public sector information, some private initiatives for open data directories have been created, including http://openparliament.ca and www.datadotgov.ca. DatadotGov.ca is led by David Eaves, an advocate for open government. But of course, as the creators of these sites would acknowledge, citizen-led sites cannot substitute for a government-run site since control to the supply of public sector information is in the hands of the government and is precisely what necessitates an open government data portal run by the government. Examples from other countries of citizen-run sites publishing available open government data include My Society (www.mysociety.org) in the United Kingdom and Watchdog.net (http://watchdog.net) and GovTrack.us (www.govtrack.us) in the United States.

63 House of Commons, Standing Committee on Access to Information, Privacy and Ethics, Meeting No. 5, 3d Sess., 40th Parl., (1 April 2010), www2.parl.gc.ca/HousePublications/Publication.aspx?DocId=4408693&Language=E&Mode=1&Parl=40&Ses=3, at 1110.

64 Suzanne Legault, "Proactive Disclosure," Address by the Interim Information Commissioner of Canada, Standing Committee on Access to Information, Privacy and Ethics (29 April 2010), www.infocom.gc.ca/eng/pa-ap-appearance-comparution-2010_3.aspx.

proactive disclosure we have . . . the better" and emphasized that user fees are not in keeping with the principle of the right of citizens to have access, where the normal way to get information is simply to ask for it for free, since the taxpayer has already paid for the document that he or she may be looking for."[65] The Commissioner noted that Canada's access to information laws regime lags behind the "next generation of laws," which include "features such as universal access," and make "use of modern technologies to proactively disseminate information."[66]

At the federal level, some individual federal departments have their own open data initiatives. Additionally, discrete public sector information is also released, usually because of statutory mandates for that category of information. For example, the *Public Servants Disclosure Protection Act* mandates that if wrongdoing (such as misuse of public funds or criminal violations) is found, public access to the information describing the wrongdoer and the corrective action must be provided promptly.[67] The Treasury Board mandates proactive disclosure on federal government departments' and agencies' websites of travel and hospitality expenses, contracts over ten thousand dollars, grants and contributions over twenty-five thousand dollars, and position reclassifications.[68]

Perhaps the most exciting federal project for open data and open licensing is GeoConnections' GeoGratis, GeoBase and Discovery Portal databases for geospatial information and template licenses.[69] The open architecture database design reflects extensive consultation on intended user applications, purposes, requirements, and operability, which is further enabled by the open licensing. The GeoConnections templates are a positive example at the federal level of an open data license. In connection with the geospatial databases, GeoConnections published a *Best Practices*

65 Robert Marleau, Information Commissioner of Canada, Evidence, House of Commons, Standing Committee on Access to Information, Privacy and Ethics, 2d Session, 40th Parliament (9 March 2009), www2.parl.gc.ca/HousePublications/Publication.aspx?DocId=3732736&Language=E&Mode=1&Parl=40&Ses=2, at 1615.

66 Robert Marleau, Information Commissioner of Canada, Evidence, House of Commons, Standing Committee on Access to Information, Privacy and Ethics, 2d Session, 40th Parliament (27 May 2009), www2.parl.gc.ca/HousePublications/Publication.aspx?DocId=3924567&Language=E&Mode=1&Parl=40&Ses=2, at 1535.

67 *Public Servants Disclosure Protection Act*, R.S.C. 2005, c. 46, http://laws.justice.gc.ca/en/P-31.9/FullText.html, s. 11(1)(c).

68 Treasury Board of Canada Secretariat, "Proactive Disclosure," www.tbs-sct.gc.ca/pd-dp/index-eng.asp.

69 Geobase, www.geobase.ca/geobase/en/about/faq.html; GeoGratis, http://geogratis.cgdi.gc.ca; GeoConnections Discovery Portal, http://geodiscover.cgdi.ca.

Guide, which explains various distribution models for open government data and contains several template licenses for access, use, and reuse of the geospatial data; all of the licenses provide unrestricted rights for internal use, two have no restrictions on data use, and four permit value-added derived products.[70] The web-wrap license agreement is a no-fee unrestricted license promoting the widest public use and private benefit of the data at no cost to the licensee, and grants unrestricted data use, downstream data distribution (on share-alike license terms), and the right to create and market value-added products.[71] This is a pertinent illustration of how a combination of an open data portal and open licensing together support "open data."[72]

In 2010, Canada launched a national consultation on a digital economy strategy. The consultation paper, *Improving Canada's Digital Advantage*, is organized around five themes: innovation using digital technologies, digital infrastructure, growing the ICT industry, Canada's digital content, and building digital skills. Although open data is within the mandate of digital content, the consultation document lamentably does not include

---

70 For a table with the key distinctions between the licenses, see "Key Characteristics of Model Licence Agreements," table, GeoConnections, *The Dissemination of Government Geographic Data in Canada*, above note 37 at 31–32.

71 GeoConnections, *The Dissemination of Government Geographic Data in Canada*, above note 37 at App. A, s. 3.1, "royalty-free, non-exclusive, world-wide, non-assignable licence to use, reproduce, extract, modify, translate, further develop and distribute the Canada Digital Data, and to manufacture and license Value-Added Products, and to sublicense any or all of such rights."

72 Although the GeoConnections uniform templates, which can apply to any geospatial data held across federal departments and agencies, are a positive development for simplified open licensing, the licenses do not adequately differentiate between Crown-copyrighted material and uncopyrightable raw data. For example, the Agreement defines "data" as any "expression of original data," rather than the copyright standard of an "original expression" of data or an original selection or arrangement of a compilation of data. The license terms could be interpreted to include material that is outside the scope of Crown copyright, and the potential overreaching may also then result in downstream users asserting questionable copyright claims to data products generated from this geographic data. See Elizabeth F. Judge and Teresa Scassa, "Intellectual Property and the Licensing of Canadian Government Geospatial Data: An Examination of Geoconnections' Recommendations for Best Practices and Template Licences," (2010) 54:3 *The Canadian Geographer / Le Géographe canadien* 366–74. These licenses do provide a positive example of open licensing for public sector information being applied at the federal level, and if licenses like GeoConnections' templates were applied to public sector information where the copyrights clearly are held by the Crown, the concern about uncopyrightable raw data potentially being included in the scope of the license would not arise.

a comprehensive open data strategy, and mentions only open access to research that is federally funded.[73] As Michael Geist observed, the consultation document "lacks a clear vision of the principles that would define a Canadian digital strategy," and one "missed opportunity was to shine the spotlight on the principle of 'openness' as a guiding principle."[74] Notably, however, many of the public submissions advocate open data for public sector information, and the most popular idea by public votes in the idea forum for the digital content theme is a passionate call for open government data, indicating the strong interest within the online community for access to public sector information.[75]

Provincially, Quebec is the only province to have established a program for access to public sector information. Quebec's regulation, *Règlement sur la diffusion de l'information et sur la protection des renseignements personnels*, came into force in November 2009 and requires that the province, municipalities, and other public bodies publicly disclose through government websites fifteen categories of information to the public interest, such as documents disclosed in response to access to information requests, research, and statistical reports.[76] The regulation was provided for by a 2006 amendment to the *Loi sur l'accès aux documents des organismes publics et sur la protection des renseignements personnels*.[77] British Columbia has es-

73 *Improving Canada's Digital* Advantage, above note 55. Incidentally, the document's "Permission to Reproduce" statement on the copyright page gives broad permission to reproduce without charge or further permission, provided due diligence is exercised to ensure accuracy, Industry Canada is identified as the source, and that the reproduction is not represented as an official version nor as having been made with the endorsement of Industry Canada.

74 Michael Geist, "Opening Up Canada's Digital Economy Strategy," (16 June 2010), www.michaelgeist.ca/content/view/5122/125.

75 Tracey Lauriault, "Open Access to Canada's Public Sector Information and Data," http://de-en.gc.ca/idea-list/?idea_theme=18&idea_filter=0. This comment is incorporated in *Consensus Submission to the Federal Government Consultation on a Digital Economy Strategy for Canada*, Faculty of Information Identity, Privacy and Security Institute (IPSI), Knowledge Media Design Institute (KMDI), University of Toronto (9 July 2010), s. 4.9, "Open Data."

76 *Règlement sur la diffusion de l'information et sur la protection des renseignements personnels*, L.R.Q., c. A-2.1 (23 April 2008), www.institutions-democratiques.gouv.qc.ca/acces-information/documents/reglement-diffusion.pdf (in force November 2009).

77 Loi sur l'accès aux documents des organismes publics et sur la protection des renseignements personnels, L.R.Q., c. A-2.1, www2.publicationsduquebec.gouv.qc.ca/dynamicSearch/telecharge.php?type=2&file=/A_2_1/A2_1.html, art. 16.1, which provides: "16.1. *Un organisme public, à l'exception du Lieutenant-gouverneur, de l'Assemblée nationale et d'une personne qu'elle désigne pour exercer une fonction en relevant, doit diffuser, dans un site Internet, les documents ou renseignements accessibles en vertu de*

tablished a website for open data (http://data.gov.bc.ca/); however, thus far the site includes only aggregated data from various levels of government on climate change.[78] In several other provinces, consultation processes are in place, with the support of provincial information and privacy commissioners.

Interestingly, the most active Canadian initiatives and experiments for open government data are by municipalities (to which Crown copyright in right of the province applies). Edmonton, Mississauga, Nanaimo, Ottawa, Toronto, and Vancouver all have open data catalogues online, and Calgary passed a motion in March 2010 for a pilot data catalogue.[79] These municipal data catalogues are in early iterations and most post only raw data, although some also include reports and other city documents. Typically, the sites include alphabetical catalogues, multiple formats, and subscriptions for updates through RSS feeds. The open licenses retain Crown copyright and generally grant permission to modify and distribute the datasets in other media and formats, on condition that the reference URL be provided for downstream users, thus encouraging applications development and integration of datasets.

For example, in Vancouver, the city council motion endorsed the principles of open and accessible data (to "freely share with citizens, businesses and other jurisdictions the greatest amount of data possible while respecting privacy and security concerns"), open standards (for "data, documents, maps and other formats of media") and open source software (placing open source software on an "equal footing with commercial systems during procurement cycles").[80] The motion further resolves that Vancouver will identify immediate opportunities to distribute more of its data; index, publish, and syndicate its data to the internet using prevailing open standards, interfaces, and formats; develop plans to digitize and

---

la loi qui sont identifiés par règlement du gouvernement et mettre en oeuvre les mesures favorisant l'accès à l'information édictées par ce règlement."

78 Ministry of Environment, British Columbia, "Climate Change Data Catalogue," http://data.gov.bc.ca.

79 See City of Edmonton, "Open Data Catalogue," http://data.edmonton.ca; Mississauga Data, www.mississauga.ca/data; Nanaimo Data Catalogue, www.nanaimo.ca/datafeeds; Open Data Ottawa, www.ottawa.ca/online_services/opendata/index_en.html; City of Toronto, www.toronto.ca/open; City of Vancouver, "Open Data Catalogue," Beta Version 2, http://data.vancouver.ca; City of Calgary, "Access to City Data and Services," Minutes of the Regular Meeting of Council (22 March 2010), 26–27.

80 "Open Data, Open Standards and Open Source," Motion B2 (mover Councillor Andrea Reimer) (May 2009), http://vancouver.ca/ctyclerk/cclerk/20090519/documents/motionb2.pdf.

distribute archival data to the public; ensure that data supplied to the city by third parties (e.g., developers, contractors, and consultants) be in a prevailing open standard format and not copyrighted unless legal considerations prevent that; and license software application, so that other municipalities, businesses and the public can use them without restriction. The City of Vancouver's Beta Data Catalogue currently provides a panoply of open data, including bikeway paths, recycling schedules, easements, election boundaries, sanitary lines, one-way streets, street lighting, and water mains.[81]

The public access granted so far to federal, provincial, and municipal information has already spawned interesting applications and mashups, including maps of restaurant health inspections,[82] applications to report local potholes and broken street lights to which several municipal governments respond,[83] postal code lookup services to track MP votes,[84] a garbage and recycling collections reminder service for Vancouver residents (where collection dates revolve),[85] an application for finding licensed childcare providers in Toronto,[86] and VisibleGovernment.ca's two initiatives (Expense Visualizer and Disclosed.ca), which scrape and aggregate information whose disclosure is mandated by the Treasury Board directive described above but which are published on over a hundred different government sites in different formats.[87] Expense Visualizer scrapes federal government travel and hospitality data and offers a web visualization tool for users to compare expenses,[88] and Disclosed.ca scrapes information about past contracts across Canadian government department and agencies.[89]

In addition to open licensing, some governments do acknowledge the reciprocal benefits to the government and the public when public reuse of open government data is encouraged, a phenomenon David Eaves characterizes as the "long tail of public policy."[90] As an example of a governmental

---

81 City of Vancouver, Open Data Catalogue, http://data.vancouver.ca/datacatalogue/index.htm.

82 Eatsure.ca, www.eatsure.ca.

83 FixMyStreet.ca, www.fixmystreet.ca.

84 How'd They Vote, http://howdtheyvote.ca.

85 Vantrash, http://vantrash.ca.

86 City of Toronto, Data Catalogue, Licensed Day Care Centres, www.toronto.ca/open/datasets/child-care.

87 "Projects," Visible Government, www.visiblegovernment.ca/projects.

88 Expense Visualizer, www.visiblegovernment.ca/projects/expenses.

89 Disclosed.ca, www.disclosed.ca.

90 David Eaves, "Open Data: An Example of the Long Tail of Public Policy at Work," http://eaves.ca/2010/05/21/open-data-an-example-of-the-long-tail-of-public-policy-at-work.

body recognizing these synergies and explicitly sponsoring public initiatives for open government data reuse, the City of Edmonton is hosting an "Apps4Edmonton" contest for new Edmonton municipal applications for data analysis or visualizations that use the city's open data catalogue or any public data. The City of Edmonton also asks participants to identify additional datasets required to create or enhance applications and the City will prioritize making that data available.[91]

F. INTERNATIONAL OPEN DATA INITIATIVES

Globally there are numerous interesting projects to facilitate public access and use of public sector information through open government data portals and open access licensing. In December 2009, the governments of the United States, United Kingdom, and Australia all launched major open government programs, which included open government data initiatives.[92] Many jurisdictions are considering adopting or have implemented Creative Commons licenses for public sector information, and usually use Creative Commons Attribution 2.5 or 3.0 licenses. Other jurisdictions, such as the United Kingdom, are using or planning to use customized government licenses that are interoperable with Creative Commons. Notably these efforts are going on at all levels of government, from national federal governments, to state and provincial governments, to local and regional governments at the level of cities and counties. Major open government data portals have been established in the United States, United Kingdom, Australia, New Zealand, Mexico, and Norway, which Canada could emulate.[93] Significant projects to open particular categories of public sector information have been implemented in numerous countries.

---

91 Apps4Edmonton, www.edmonton.ca/city_government/open_data/apps4edmonton.aspx.

92 United States, "Open Government Directive" (8 December 2009), www.whitehouse.gov/open/documents/open-government-directive; United Kingdom, *Putting the Frontline First: Smarter Government*, (December 2009), www.hmg.gov.uk/media/52788/smarter-government-final.pdf; Australia, *Engage: Getting on with Government 2.0*, Report of the Government 2.0 Taskforce, (December 2009), www.finance.gov.au/publications/gov20taskforcereport/doc/Government20TaskforceReport.pdf [Australia, *Report of the Government 2.0 Taskforce*].

93 United States, www.data.gov; United Kingdom, www.data.gov.uk; New Zealand, http://data.govt.nz; India, http://india.gov.in/documents.php; Australia, http://data.australia.gov.au; Mexico, www.portaldetransparencia.gob.mx/pot; Norway, http://data.norge.no. See also Estonia's statistical database, http://pub.stat.ee/px-web.2001/Dialog/statfile1.asp.

Moreover, inter-governmental bodies, such as the European Union and the United Nations, and other international bodies have recommended opening access to public sector information and are implementing Creative Commons-compatible licenses for their materials.[94] Globally in other nations and intergovernmental bodies, geospatial information is an early and the most dynamic category of datasets of public sector information to be made available under open licensing and catalogued through open data portals, as geospatial data likewise is for Canada's federal open data initiatives.[95]

In the United States, federal government works are free of copyright restrictions and thus the federal initiatives focus on proactive publishing of public sector information in usable formats.[96] The Obama Administration issued an Open Government Directive in December 2009 directing the heads of Executive branch departments and agencies to take specific actions to implement the three open government principles of transparency, participation, and collaboration, which had been laid out in the President's Memorandum on Transparency and Open Government.[97] Specifically, the Open Government Directive requires that federal departments and agencies expand access to information, by making it available online in open formats, and mandates that each agency publish at least three high-value datasets which have not been previously available online or in a downloadable format and register them on www.data.gov, and create an Open Government webpage with mechanisms for public feedback on the quality

---

94 A wiki with a working list of individual governmental and intergovernmental projects using Creative Commons or other open licensing for public sector information can be referenced at "Government Use of Creative Commons," http://wiki.creativecommons.org/Government_use_of_Creative_Commons. Other bodies are also adopting open data policies: see, for example, the World Bank's Open Data Catalog, http://data.worldbank.org.

95 See, for example, EU, *Directive 2007/2/EC of the European Parliament and of the Council of 14 March 2007 establishing an Infrastructure for Spatial Information in the European Community (INSPIRE)*, *Official Journal* L 108/1 (25 April 2007), http://eur-lex.europa.eu/LexUriServ/LexUriServ.do?uri=OJ:L:2007:108:0001:0014:en:PDF (addressing the sharing, access, and use of interoperable spatial data and spatial data services across levels of public authority and different sectors by establishing an EU-community-wide infrastructure for spatial information based on Member States implementing common rules); Geoscience Australia, www.ga.gov.au (licensed under a Creative Commons 3.0 Attribution Australia license).

96 *Copyright Act* (USA), above note 21, at s. 105.

97 "Open Government Directive," above note 92; Obama, Memorandum on Transparency and Open Government, above note 3.

of published information and priorities for publication.[98] Data accessed through www.data.gov has no restrictions on end uses. For data quality, the submitting agency retains version control of the datasets.[99]

In the European Union, the 2003 Directive on the Reuse of Public Information provides a general framework of minimal conditions for reuse of public sector information, with reuse defined as any purpose other than the initial purpose within the public task for which the documents were produced, but not including documents exchanged between public sector bodies for public sector tasks.[100] Namely, the Directive's conditions mandate that public sector information that Member States make available for reuse should be accessible in all formats and languages and by electronic means where possible, and that Member States have transparent conditions for reuse, avoid discrimination between market players, publish standard licenses online which do not unnecessarily restrict either reuse or competition, and have practical finding tools such as portal sites or lists of information assets.[101]

The Directive states as an objective for institutions at the local, national, and international level that "[m]aking public all generally available documents held by the public sector — concerning not only the political process but also the legal and administrative process — is a fundamental instrument for extending the right to knowledge, which is a basic principle of democracy."[102] However, the Directive does not oblige Member States to allow reuse of all public sector documents or to create or adapt documents for

---

98 Each agency's webpage will be located at www.[agency].gov/open.

99 Data Policy Statement, www.data.gov/datapolicy.

100 European Union, *Directive 2003/98/EC of the European Parliament and the Council on the Re-Use of Public Sector Information* (17 November 2003), http://ec.europa.eu/information_society/policy/psi/docs/pdfs/directive/psi_directive_en.pdf, *Official Journal* L345/90-96 (31 December 2003) [*EU Directive on Re-Use of Public Sector Information*] at ch. 1, art. 2, s. 4.

101 *EU Directive on Re-Use of Public Sector Information*, above note 100. Preceding the Directive, a 1998 green paper, European Commission, *Public Sector Information: A Key Resource for Europe: Green Paper on Public Sector Information in the Information Society*, COM(1998)585 (1998), ftp://ftp.cordis.europa.eu/pub/econtent/docs/gp_en.pdf, considered whether Europe's different conditions for access to public sector information (such as different exemptions, time, format, and quantity) created European-level barriers, discussed whether existing policies in EU institutions for access and dissemination of information were adequate, canvassed issues associated with European-level action (including different copyright and liability regimes, privacy considerations, competition, and the possibility of European meta-data), and highlighted a range of actions that could be initiated at the European level.

102 *EU Directive on Re-Use of Public Sector Information*, above note 100 at para.16.

reuse or to continue to produce certain types of documents for reuse; rather, the Directive builds on existing national access regimes, and its rules apply to those documents that the Member States make accessible.[103] Thus, the Directive's general principle is that "where the re-use of documents held by public sector bodies is allowed, these documents shall be re-usable for commercial or non-commercial purposes in accordance with the conditions set out . . . and shall be made available through electronic means."[104] Further, a Member State can decide "to no longer make available certain documents for re-use or to cease updating these documents," if the decision is made publicly known at the earliest opportunity by electronic means wherever possible.[105] The Directive does not change the existence or ownership of copyright held by public sector bodies or limit its exercise, as long as the Member State is in compliance with the Directive; however, public sector bodies should exercise their copyright so as to facilitate reuse.[106] If Member States license documents for reuse, the Directive mandates that license conditions be fair and transparent and be in a digital format that can be processed electronically and that Member States encourage standard licenses.[107] Additionally, although the Directive helpfully supports making public sector information available for reuse, it does not mandate free access and allows public sector bodies to impose a charge equal to cost recovery plus a reasonable investment, where cost recovery is the "total costs of collecting, producing (which includes the costs of creation, collation, dissemination and user support), reproducing and disseminating documents."[108] Member States can also differentiate charges between commercial and non-commercial reuse.[109] The Directive does not apply to documents which are excluded from access regimes (e.g., to protect national security or commercial confidentiality) nor to documents held by public service broadcasters, educational institutions, research facilities, or cultural establishments (e.g., museums, archives, libraries, and theatres).[110]

---

103 *Ibid.* at para. 9; ch. 3, art. 5, s. 1. "Document" is defined broadly as "any representation of acts, facts or information — and any compilation of such acts, facts or information — whatever its medium (written on paper, or stored in electronic form or as a sound, visual or audiovisual recording), held by public sector bodies" (at para. 11 and ch. 1, art. 2, s. 3.).

104 *Ibid.* at ch. 1, art. 3.

105 *Ibid.* at para.18.

106 *Ibid.* at para. 22.

107 *Ibid.* at para.17 and ch. 3, art. 8.

108 *Ibid.* at para.14.

109 *Ibid.* at para.19.

110 *Ibid.* at ch.1, art. 1.

Many European countries have expanded beyond the Directive's obligations with open public sector initiatives. The European Public Sector Information Platform, which is funded by the European Commission and bills itself as "Europe's One-Stop Shop on Public Sector Information (PSI) Re-use,"[111] reports developments, monitors progress, and circulates best practices on public sector reuse, both in Europe and internationally.

In the United Kingdom, *The Re-use of Public Sector Information Regulations* 2005 implement the EU Directive.[112] Additionally, the Government has launched several open government projects. The Information Asset Register notifies the public of information resources held by the UK Government, focusing on unpublished resources.[113] The United Kingdom's "Smarter Government" initiative presents an action plan for open government. One of the five ways under action one's plan to strengthen the role of citizens and civic society is "radically opening up data and public information to promote transparent and effective government."[114] In *Putting the Frontline First*, which describes the action plan, the government sets out five principles for public data, defined as "government-held non-personal data that are collected or generated in the course of public service delivery." Specifically, public data will be published in reusable, machine-readable form, using open standards following the recommendations of the World Wide Web Consortium; public data will be available and easy to find through a single online access point; published raw data will be represented in linked data form; more public data will be released under open licenses enabling free use (for commercial reuse as well); data underlying the government's own websites will be published in reusable form; and data that is personal, classified, commercially sensitive, or belongs to third parties will be protected.[115] The UK Government also pledged to have the majority of government-published information to be reusable linked data by June 2011 and to establish a common license to reuse data that will be interoperable with the Creative Commons license.[116]

In furtherance of the open government goals, a panel of technical experts, including Tim Berners-Lee, is working on overseeing the creation of a single online point of access for public sector information, selecting and

---

111 European Public Sector Information Platform, www.epsiplatform.eu.

112 United Kingdom, *The Re-use of Public Sector Information Regulations* 2005, No. 1515, www.opsi.gov.uk/si/si2005/20051515.htm (in force 1 July 2005),

113 United Kingdom, OPSI, *Information Asset Register*, www.opsi.gov.uk/iar/index.

114 United Kingdom, *Putting the Frontline First*, above note 92 at 19.

115 *Ibid.* at 26.

116 *Ibid.* at 28.

implementing common standards for the release of public sector information, developing Crown copyright and Crown Commons licenses, and working on standards for public data.[117] Thus far, the United Kingdom has established an open government data portal, as part of the Government's wider transparency program, and is developing customized open licenses for public sector information that will be interoperable with Creative Commons licenses. On data.gov.uk all content is made available for reuse commercially and non-commercially under terms that are designed to be interoperable with the Creative Commons Attribution 3.0 license.[118]

In June 2010, the UK Government announced the "next generation" of its licensing framework to allow reuse and repurposing of a broad range of public sector information. Part of the new framework is a new license, which builds on the licensing experience with data.gov.uk and is intended to be interoperable with Creative Commons licenses. [119] The new common license will be machine-readable, non-transactional (users do not need individual permission for-reuse) and free, and is designed to be more open than the current Click-Use online licenses for the reuse of Crown and Parliamentary copyrights, which are transactional licenses requiring individual application through the HMSO's online licensing system, and which are intended to be replaced by the new license.[120]

Australia's Government 2.0 Taskforce Report makes explicit recommendations on public sector information accessibility, Crown copyright, and licensing, and urges the Government to extend those principles into a national information policy by all levels of government in Australia (federal, state, territory and local). Recommendation 6 of the Report states "[b]y default public sector information should be free, based on open standards, easily discoverable, understandable, machine-readable, freely reusable and transformable, and released as early as practicable and regularly updated to ensure accuracy." Both the Taskforce Report and the Government Response support using a Creative Commons attribution license (CC BY)

---

117 United Kingdom Cabinet Office, Digital Engagement Blog, http://blogs.cabinetoffice.gov.uk/digitalengagement/?tag=/tim+berners-lee (June 2009).

118 "Terms and Conditions," http://data.gov.uk/terms-and-conditions (permitting users to freely copy, distribute and transmit data, adapt data, and exploit data commercially by sub-licensing, combining it with other data, or including it in the users' products or applications).

119 "Development of the UK Licensing Framework," (29 June 2010), http://data.gov.uk/blog/development-uk-government-licensing-framework.

120 National Archives (GBR), "Licences for Re-using Public Sector Information," www.nationalarchives.gov.uk/information-management/our-services/click-use.htm.

as the default standard for licensing public sector information owned by the Commonwealth. Both support amending copyright policy so Crown copyrighted works are automatically licensed under a Creative Commons attribution license when they become available for public access under Australia's *Archives Act 1983*. In addition to licensing and Crown copyright, both also endorse agencies ensuring that the public sector information they release is "discoverable and accessible" on Australia's open government data portal and providing details about the nature and format of the information.[121] Additionally, at the state level, Queensland supports Creative Commons attribution licensing for state public sector information, and Victoria supports open access as the default for public sector information and developing a whole-of-government framework using Creative Commons licenses as a default for public sector information.[122] Australia has established an open government data portal site (data.australia.gov.au) for Australian government public information datasets, though it is still beta.

New Zealand's Open Government Information and Data Re-use Project, part of the State Services Commission, is studying approaches for opening New Zealand's public sector information and encouraging its reuse. In March 2009, the Project released a Discussion Paper calling for an "all-of-government approach to opening up public sector copyright material for re-use."[123] As the Discussion Paper described, the "fragmented approach to licensing of Crown copyright and other copyright material," the "confusion around the concept of Crown copyright and distinctions between copyright and licensing," and the "proliferation of different and inconsistent licenses across government" "can give rise to confusion among users" and "impede rather than motivate the re-use and positive exploita-

---

121 Australia, *Report of the Government 2.0 Taskforce*, above note 92 at Recommendation 6; Australia, *Government Response to the Report of the Government 2.0 Taskforce, Engage: Getting on with Government 2.0* (May 2010) at 10–11.

122 Queensland (Aus.), *Government Information Licensing Framework*, www.gilf.gov.au; Victoria (Aus.), *Report of the Economic Development and Infrastructure Committee on the Inquiry into Improving Access to Victorian Public Sector Information and Data* , Parliamentary Paper No. 198, Session 2006–2009 (June 2009), www.parliament.vic.gov.au/images/stories/committees/edic/access_to_PSI/EDIC_ACCESS_TO_PSI_REPORT_2009.pdf, ch. 6; Victoria (Aus), *Whole of Victorian Government Response to the Final Report of the Economic Development and Infrastructure Committee's Inquiry into Improving Access to Victorian Public Sector Information and Data* (2009), www.diird.vic.gov.au/diird-projects/access-to-public-sector-information at 8.

123 New Zealand, "A Suggested All-of-government Approach," above note 61.

tion of public sector information."[124] The Discussion Paper considered the possibility of adopting Creative Commons licenses for Crown copyright material. Although the project notes that Creative Commons licenses are unlikely in themselves to alleviate public confusion around the intricacies of Crown copyright, their introduction would bring "much greater clarity and consistency of approach to the licensing of Crown copyright material and other public sector copyright material."[125] The Discussion Paper recommended an all-of-government adoption of a suite of open content licenses for copyrighted public sector material that was appropriate to be made available for reuse. It also concluded that Creative Commons licenses were the most obvious candidate of licenses for the government to adopt, possibly in conjunction with more restrictive licenses.

Public sector bodies commenting on the Discussion Paper strongly supported the all-of-government adoption of Creative Commons licenses for public sector information, along with one or more restrictive licenses. The Feedback Summary considered including Creative Commons Zero licenses, in effect waiving Crown copyright, in the suite of applicable Creative Commons licenses for public sector information.[126]

New Zealand has both an open government data portal and a framework of principles for open licensing of Crown copyrighted works.[127] In August 2010, following the release of a draft framework the previous year, New Zealand released its New Zealand Government Open Access and Licensing framework (NZGOAL), which sets out open access and open licensing principles for public sector information, including both non-copyrighted data and copyrighted works.[128] In its principles, NZGOAL's framework usefully distinguishes between non-copyright data and copyrighted works. For non-copyright information and data, NZGOAL supports an "Open Access Principle" of providing online public access and unrestrictive copying and reuse and including a no-known rights statement at the point of release.[129] For Crown-copyrighted works, the Framework supports an "Open Licens-

---

124 *Ibid.* at para. 185.

125 *Ibid.*above note 61 at paras. 186-189.

126 New Zealand, *Suggested All-of-government Approach to Licensing of Public Sector Copyright Works: Discussion Paper for Public Service and Non-Public Service Departments: Summary and analysis of departmental feedback*, Open Government Information and Data Re-use Project (29 May 2009), www.e.govt.nz/library/info-and-data-reuse-feedback-summary-may-2009.pdf.

127 New Zealand Government Datasets, www.data.govt.nz.

128 New Zealand, New Zealand Government Open Access and Licensing framework (NZGOAL) (27 August 2010), www.e.govt.ns/library/NZGOAL.pdf.

129 NZGOAL, above note 128 at para. 29.

ing Principle" to make Crown-copyrighted works available online using the Creative Commons Attribution (cc by) license as the default license in order "to promote the greatest reuse of state services agencies' copyright works and interoperability between the different license types."[130] The framework sets out restrictions where these principles do not apply, and in those contexts, the agency should first consider other Creative Commons licenses, and if they cannot be applied, then consider making the work available under the NZGOAL restrictive license.[131] Although the Feedback Summary vetted the idea of Creative Commons Zero licenses, NZGOAL concluded they were unnecessary and would raise policy and legal issues. While the open government data portal is being populated, New Zealand has already published a list of some of the datasets, databases, and other information resources which are already available online and their location.[132]

G. CONCLUSION

To achieve open public sector information, it must be published, easy to find, in reusable formats, and either free of Crown copyright restrictions or available under open licenses that allow and encourage reuse. Preferentially, Canada's digital copyright strategy should examine reforming Crown copyright and study existing working models of public domain government information. Until Crown copyright repeal is prioritized, however, several initiatives can be developed to advance open public sector information, including establishing an open government data portal and adopting Crown Commons licensing.

The government should establish a single portal for public sector information at data.gc.ca, which should be a comprehensive and cumulative catalogue of public sector information that lists the public sector information, indexes information by the governmental body submitting the dataset and by category, provides search tools, and cross-references data

---

130 *Ibid.* at para. 26, note 6.

131 *Ibid.* at paras. 29–31. The restrictions include instances where open access or open licensing would be contrary to legislation, the agency's own legitimate commercial interests, or the public interest, or that "would . . . threaten the control over and/or integrity of Māori or other traditional knowledge or other culturally sensitive material" or "jeopardize the economic or other potential to Māori or other indigenous groups of Māori or other traditional knowledge or other culturally sensitive material" (at para. 29).

132 New Zealand, "Exposing Non-Personal Government Data in New Ways," http://www.e.govt.nz/policy/information-and-data/exposing-nonpersonal-government-data-in-new-ways.

between the website of the relevant department and the data in the centralized portal. Public sector information in the centralized portal should be licensed under an open Crown Commons license, which should be interoperable with Creative Commons licensing. Through uniform licensing and branded symbols, Crown Commons licenses will enable the public to readily identify material as public sector information and will encourage the public to access and reuse it.

As the American Library Association stated in its principles, "government information is a public resource collected at public expense" and the public should have "knowledge of and access to this resource."[133] Many countries, including the United Kingdom, Australia, New Zealand, and the United States, have recently engaged the public in national consultations on opening up public sector information and have launched significant open government data initiatives. Canada's recent consultation paper on a digital economy strategy disappointingly was a missed opportunity to address open government data. But, there are exciting initiatives already in Canada both for specific categories of open data at the federal level, such as GeoConnections' open licensing and data portal for geospatial information, and at the municipal level, such as Vancouver's open data project, which can help provide a framework for a federal open government data plan that would include both an open government data portal and open licensing of public sector information.

Canada should take steps now to develop a comprehensive open government data strategy with the goals of indexing and publishing digital public sector information online in open formats on a centralized open government data portal under open Crown Commons licensing, digitizing and publishing archival public sector information, and seeking new opportunities to distribute public sector information through new technologies and media as they are developed to ensure public access to this important public resource of public sector information.

---

133 American Library Association, "Key Principles of Government Information," above note 2 at principle 10.

About the Contributors

Sara Bannerman is an SSHRC postdoctoral fellow with the Centre for Governance of Knowledge and Development, a part of the Regulatory Institutions Network (RegNet) at the Australian National University in Canberra. In 2009–2010, Sara was a Fulbright postdoctoral researcher working as a Visiting Scholar at the Elliott School of International Affairs, George Washington University. She has taught at Carleton University and the University of Ottawa in the areas of communications policy, media industries, and intellectual property. She has published in the areas of international copyright and intellectual property and development, and is currently working on a comparative history of international copyright. Her history of Canadian international copyright is forthcoming with UBC Press.

Carys Craig is an Associate Professor at Osgoode Hall Law School, York University, and the Director of Osgoode's Executive LL.M. Program in Intellectual Property Law. She holds a First Class Honours Bachelor of Laws (LL.B.) from the University of Edinburgh, a Master of Laws (LL.M.) from Queen's University in Kingston, and a Doctorate in Law (S.J.D.) from the University of Toronto, where she was a graduate fellow of the Centre for Innovation Law & Policy. She teaches and writes in the areas of domestic, comparative and international intellectual property law and policy, with an emphasis on public interest theory and the public domain. Her recent publications include "The Canadian Public Domain: Where, What, and to What End?" (2010) 7 Canadian Journal of Law & Technology 221, and "Digital Locks and the Fate of Fair Dealing in Canada: In Pursuit of 'Prescriptive Parallelism'" (2010) 13 Journal of World Intellectual Property 503. Her forthcoming book, *Copyright, Communication & Culture: Towards a Relational Theory of Copyright Law* (Edward Elgar Press, 2011), employs critical legal and social theory to examine the theoretical foundations of copyright law and their implications in the digital age.

Abraham Drassinower is Associate Professor and Chair in the Legal, Ethical and Cultural Implications of Technological Innovation at the University of Toronto Faculty of Law. Before joining the Faculty of Law in 1999, he held a Postdoctoral Fellowship in the Department of Political Science at the University of Toronto (1993–1995); lectured principally on political philosophy at York University (1993–1995) and at the University of Toronto (1995–1998); and served as a Law Clerk to Mr. Justice John C. Major of the Supreme Court of Canada (1998–1999). He was Director of the Centre for Innovation Law and Policy from 2006 to 2009. His interests include property, intellectual property, legal and political philosophy, critical theory, and psychoanalysis. He has published in the areas of charitable trusts, unjust enrichment, intellectual property, and psychoanalysis and political theory. He has spoken widely and internationally on copyright law and theory and on intellectual property generally. His current work is focussed on developing a rights-based account of the public domain in copyright law.

Dr· Michael Geist is a law professor at the University of Ottawa where he holds the Canada Research Chair in Internet and E-commerce Law. He has obtained a Bachelor of Laws (LL.B.) degree from Osgoode Hall Law School in Toronto, Master of Laws (LL.M.) degrees from Cambridge University in the UK and Columbia Law School in New York, and a Doctorate in Law (J.S.D.) from Columbia Law School. Dr. Geist is an internationally syndicated columnist on technology law issues with his regular column appearing in the *Toronto Star* and the *Ottawa Citizen*. Dr. Geist is the editor of *In the Public Interest: The Future of Canadian Copyright Law*, published in 2005 by Irwin Law, the editor of several monthly technology law publications, and the author of a popular blog on Internet and intellectual property law issues. Dr. Geist serves on many boards, including the Canarie Board of Directors, the Canadian Legal Information Institute Board of Directors, the Privacy Commissioner of Canada's Expert Advisory Board, the Electronic Frontier Foundation Advisory Board, and on the Information Program Sub-Board of the Open Society Institute. He has received numerous awards for his work including the Kroeger Award for Policy

Leadership and the Public Knowledge IP3 Award in 2010, the Les Fowlie Award for Intellectual Freedom from the Ontario Library Association in 2009, the Electronic Frontier Foundation's Pioneer Award in 2008, Canarie's IWAY Public Leadership Award for his contribution to the development of the Internet in Canada and he was named one of Canada's Top 40 Under 40 in 2003. In 2010, Managing Intellectual Property named him on the 50 most influential people on intellectual property in the world. More information can be obtained at www.michaelgeist.ca.

Daniel J· Gervais is Professor of Law and Co-director of the Technology & Entertainment Law Program at Vanderbilt University Law School. Prior to joining Vanderbilt, he was the Acting Dean, University Research Chair in Intellectual Property at the Faculty of Law of the University of Ottawa (Common Law Section). Before he joined the Academy, Prof. Gervais was successively Legal Officer at the GATT (now WTO); Head of Section at the World Intellectual Property Organization (WIPO); and Vice-President, International of Massachusetts-based Copyright Clearance Center, Inc. (CCC). He also served as consultant to the Organization for Economic Co-operation and Development (OECD) in Paris. He is Editor-in-Chief of the peer- eviewed Journal of World Intellectual Property and the author of several books, book chapters and articles published in six different languages. Dr. Gervais studied computer science and law at McGill University and the University of Montreal, where he also obtained LL.B. and LL.M. degrees, and received several awards. He also received a Diploma summa cum laude from the Institute of Advanced International Studies in Geneva and a doctorate *magna cum laude* from the University of Nantes (France). He was a visiting professor at several universities in Europe and North America and a visiting scholar at Stanford Law School. He is a member of the Law Society of Upper Canada (Ontario) and of the Bar of Quebec and a biography in the Canadian Who's Who.

Mistrale Goudreau holds an LL.L. from the Université de Montréal (Faculté de Droit, Montréal, 1979) and an LL.M. in Commercial Law from the London School of Economics and Political Science, (Department of Law, London, England, 1981). She has been a member of the Quebec Bar since 1981 and is full professor at the Civil Law Section of the University of Ottawa where she teaches since 1982. Her teaching responsibilities deal with intellectual property, law and technology and statutory interpretation. She has been also lecturer and visiting professor at the Faculty of law of the University of Montréal, at the Faculty of Law of the University of Nantes

(France), and at the Canadian Foreign Service Institute (CFSI) in Ottawa, as well as research fellow at the Max-Planck-Institut für ausländisches und internationales Patent-, Urheber- und Wettbewerbsrecht (Munich, Germany). She published numerous articles on copyright, unfair competition, legislative drafting and legal theory. She is the author of *International Encyclopaedia of Laws: Intellectual Property Canada*, (Alphen aan den Rijn (Netherlands): Kluwer Law International, 2009) and she collaborated to the publication of *Le droit de la propriété intellectuelle* (Yvon Blais, 2006).

Gregory Hagen is an Assistant Professor of Law at the University of Calgary where he teaches in the areas of intellectual property, internet, biotechnology, and tort law. He has written on internet intermediary liability, the domain name system, peer to peer file sharing, the foundations of copyright, and the patentability of biotechnology. He is currently a co-investigator on the four year PhytoMetaSyn project, investigating regulatory and ethical issues surrounding the production of plant natural products from recombinant microorganisms. He is a board member of the University of Calgary's Institute for Information Security, Privacy and Information Assurance (ISPIA). Dr. Hagen earned an LL.B from Dalhousie Law School and an LL.M. from the University of Ottawa (with concentration in law and technology). He holds a Ph.D. in the philosophy of science from the University of Western Ontario and a B.A. and M.A. from the University of British Columbia. He has been a visiting professor in the Faculty of Law at the University of Ghana and at Duke University's Asia America Institute in Transnational Law at the University of Hong Kong. He formerly practiced law in Vancouver and is a member of the Law Society of British Columbia.

Blayne Haggart (M.A. Economics, University of Toronto; M.A. International Relations, Carleton University) is a Ph.D. candidate in Political Science at Carleton University in Ottawa. His dissertation analyzes regional integration in North America through the lens of digital-copyright policy in Canada, Mexico and the United States. He has previously worked as a journalist and as an economist with the Parliamentary Information and Research Service of the Library of Parliament, serving as an analyst for various parliamentary committees and associations.

Elizabeth F. Judge is an Associate Professor and member of the Law and Technology group at the University of Ottawa, Faculty of Law, Common Law Section, where she specializes in intellectual property, law and literature, and privacy. She holds an honours Bachelor of Arts from Brown University (English and American Literature; Political Science), a Juris Doctorate from Harvard Law School, a Master of Arts (English) from the University of Toronto, and a Master of Laws and a Doctor of Philosophy in English Literature from Dalhousie University, and she has taught in both law and literature. She is the author of *Intellectual Property: The Law in Canada*, in its second edition, and *Le droit de la propriété intellectuelle*, both with Daniel Gervais, and has published articles in law and literature. Her research focuses on interdisciplinary law and literature scholarship, especially intersections between legal and literary ideas of originality and authorship, and on intellectual property rights, open access, and reuse of public sector information, including geospatial data. She is a founding editor and editor-in-chief and faculty advisor for the University of Ottawa Law & Technology Journal and project leader for Open Access Law Canada. She is a member of the Law Society of Upper Canada and is admitted to the Bars of the State of California, the District of Columbia, and the United States Tax Court. Prior to joining the Faculty of Law, she practised law in Washington, DC, and she served as a law clerk to the Honourable Mr. Justice Ian Binnie at the Supreme Court of Canada.

Ian Kerr holds the Canada Research Chair in Ethics, Law & Technology at the University of Ottawa, Faculty of Law, with cross appointments in Medicine, Philosophy and Information Studies. Dr. Kerr's research lies at the intersection of ethics, law and technology and is currently focused on two broad themes: Privacy and Surveillance, and Human-Machine Mergers. Building on his recent Oxford University Press book, *Lessons from the Identity Trail*, his ongoing privacy work focuses on the interplay between emerging public and private sector surveillance technologies, civil liberties, and human rights. His recent research on robotics and implantable devices examines legal and ethical implications of emerging technologies in the health sector.

Dr. Kerr's research has attracted more than five million dollars in support. His devotion to teaching has earned six awards, including the Bank of Nova Scotia Excellence in Undergraduate Teaching, the UWO Award of Teaching Excellence, and the University of Ottawa's CLSS, Teaching Excellence Award. His innovative, interdisciplinary courses garner international attention, with regular invitations to teach at prestigious institutions across North America, Europe, the Middle East, and Asia. He is co-author of *Managing the Law*, published by Prentice Hall and used by thousands of students each year at universities across Canada.

David Lametti is the Associate Dean (Academic) and Associate Professor of Law, Faculty of Law, McGill University. He is a founding member of the Centre for Intellectual Property Policy (CIPP) at McGill, and currently the Director. He teaches and writes in the areas of Civil and Common law property, intellectual property and property theory. His work to date has attempted to understand the parameters of traditional and intellectual resources in analytic terms, linking them to their underlying justifications and ethical goals. Professor Lametti is conducting research under the auspices of an SSHRC grant entitled "Copyright's Cross-Currents." A recent representative publication is "The Objects of Virtue" in G. Alexander & E. Peñalver, eds., *Property and Community* (New York: Oxford University Press, 2010) 1–37.

Meera Nair received her Ph.D. from the School of Communication at Simon Fraser University in March 2009 and is currently teaching there in a sessional capacity. Her interest in intellectual property law stemmed from a B.Sc. in Mathematics and ten years as a private consultant working on technology transfer projects between academia and industry. Her doctoral dissertation, *From Fair Dealing To Fair Duty: The Necessary Margins Of Canadian Copyright Law*, examines the system of copyright through the writings of Harold Adams Innis (1894–1952). Her recent work includes "Copyright and Ethics: An Innisian Exploration" (Global Media Journal — Canadian Edition, November 2009) and "The *Copyright Act* of 1889 — A Canadian Declaration of Independence" (Canadian Historical Review, March 2009). Informal commentary on copyright can be found at her blog, Fair Duty (http://fairduty.wordpress.com). She also serves on the Board of Directors for the British Columbia Freedom of Information and Privacy Association.

Mark Perry is the Associate Dean of Research, Graduate Studies, and Operations in the faculty of Law at the University of Western Ontario. He is also an Associate Professor in the Faculty of Science. He is a Barrister and Solicitor of the Law Society of Upper Canada, a Faculty Fellow at IBM's Center for Advanced Studies, a member of the International Association for the Advancement of Teaching and Research in Intellectual Property, the Institute of Electrical and Electronics Engineers, the Intellectual Property Institute of Canada, and the Association of Computer Machinery. He is a reviewer for multiple granting societies and professional associations. Professor Perry's research is focused on the nexus of law and science, both digital and biological, and in the area of cloud computing management systems. He holds grants from SSHRC and Genome Canada to pursue his research in both law and science and has supervised numerous graduate and undergraduate theses. He has been invited by law schools in Australia, India, Italy, China, New Zealand, the United Kingdom, the United States, and Canada to speak at research-intensive colloquia and to classes, and he is often interviewed by national media. Further information is available at www.markp.ca. He lives in London with his sweetheart.

Tina Piper is an Assistant Professor of Law at McGill University and a member of McGill's Centre for Intellectual Property Policy. She completed her doctorate at the University of Oxford on the history of medical patenting. She was a co-Project lead of Creative Commons Canada, a Board member of PopMontreal and teaches primarily in the areas of intellectual property law, property law and legal history.

Graham Reynolds was appointed to the faculty of Dalhousie University, Schulich School of Law in 2008. His teaching and research interests include copyright law, property law, intellectual property law and law and technology. Prior to joining the faculty, Professor Reynolds attended graduate school at the University of Oxford on a Rhodes scholarship. He also served as the law clerk to the Honourable Chief Justice Lance Finch of the British Columbia Court of Appeal. Professor Reynolds is a member of the Law and Technology Institute at Dalhousie University and is the Co-Editor-in-Chief of the Canadian Journal of Law and Technology.

Dr. Teresa Scassa is a Canada Research Chair in Information Law at the University of Ottawa, Faculty of Common Law. She holds undergraduate law degrees in civil and common law from McGill University, as well as an LL.M. and an S.J.D. from the University of Michigan. She taught at Dalhousie Law School for fifteen years before joining the Faculty of Law at the University of Ottawa as a full professor in July 2007. She is a former editor of the Canadian Journal of Law and Technology, and is co-author of the book *Electronic Commerce and Internet Law in Canada*, (CCH Canadian, 2004). She is also a member of the External Advisory Committee of the Office of the Privacy Commissioner of Canada and a Member of the Geoconnections Privacy Advisory Group. Her research and scholarship is primarily in the areas of intellectual property law, law and technology, and privacy, and she has written numerous articles in these areas.

Mira Sundara Rajan holds the Canada Research Chair in Intellectual Property Law at the University of British Columbia, Faculty of Law. She is the author of a book, *Copyright and Creative Freedom*, and has been appointed Series Editor for a new Oxford University Press series on Intellectual Property in Central and Eastern Europe. Her current research also includes projects on copyright harmonization in Europe, moral rights, and traditional knowledge, and is supported by the Social Sciences and Humanities Research Council of Canada.

Mira joined the Faculty of Law at UBC in 2004, after five years of research and teaching in the UK. She holds a doctorate specializing in Copyright Law from Oxford University, and has been a law tutor at St Peter's College, Oxford and a Herchel Smith Fellow in Intellectual Property Law at the Queen Mary Intellectual Property Research Institute of the University of London. Mira's teaching experience ranges from tutoring law undergraduates in the Oxford tutorial system to training judges from developing countries in the intricacies of intellectual property rights.

Myra J. Tawfik is a Professor of Law and Co-Director of the Centre for Enterprise and Law at the University of Windsor, a joint initiative between the Faculty of Law and the Odette School of Business. She holds degrees from McGill University (B.A (Hons.) 1981; B.C.L, LL.B 1985) and the University of London (LL.M., Queen Mary College, 1989). Professor Tawfik teaches in the area of intellectual property law including copyright law, trademark law, and the law of confidential information. She is the founding Director of the Intellectual Property Legal Information Network, a student-led community education outreach and clinical program. Her research focus is on intellectual property law, primarily, but not exclusively, in the area of copyright and she has published nationally and internationally on a wide range of intellectual property law issues. Her recent publications include "When Intellectual Property Rights Converge — Tracing the Contours and Mapping the Fault Lines 'Case by Case' and 'Law by Law'" in Y. Gendreau, ed., *A New Intellectual Property Paradigm: The Canadian Experience* (London: Edward Elgar, 2008) and the co-authored inaugural chapter "Internet Law" for the *Canadian Encyclopedic Digest* (Toronto: Carswell, 2008). She is currently completing a book on the historical origins of Canadian copyright law.

Dr· Margaret Ann Wilkinson is a Professor in the Faculty of Law at the University of Western Ontario (UWO) and Director of the Area of Concentration in Intellectual Property, Information and Technology Law. Also a member of the Health Sector faculty at the Richard Ivey School of Business (UWO) and Masters of Information Management (Dalhousie

University), she teaches and writes widely on copyright and moral rights, personal data protection and privacy, and other areas of intellectual property and information law, including those affecting the health sector, as well as on management and professional ethics. Dr. Wilkinson supervises graduate students in both the Faculty of Law and the Faculty of Information and Media Studies, where her doctoral students have won international awards (for fifteen years, until 2007, she was jointly appointed to both faculties). She has held visiting positions at Dalhousie University, University of Toronto, and Newcastle University (UK).